T0314235

HANDBOOK ON THE ECONOMICS AND THEORY OF THE FIRM

Handbook on the Economics and Theory of the Firm

Edited by

Michael Dietrich

Senior Lecturer, Department of Economics, University of Sheffield, UK

Jackie Krafft

Research Professor in Economics, University of Nice Sophia Antipolis and CNRS-GREDEG, France

Edward Elgar
Cheltenham, UK • Northampton, MA, USA

Published by
Edward Elgar Publishing Limited
The Lypiatts
15 Lansdown Road
Cheltenham
Glos GL50 2JA
UK

Edward Elgar Publishing, Inc.
William Pratt House
9 Dewey Court
Northampton
Massachusetts 01060
USA

A catalogue record for this book
is available from the British Library

Library of Congress Control Number: 2012930564

ISBN 978 1 84844 648 9 (cased)

Typeset by Servis Filmsetting Ltd, Stockport, Cheshire
Printed and bound by MPG Books Group, UK

Contents

PART IV   THE MULTINATIONAL FIRM

PART V   DYNAMIC APPROACHES TO THE FIRM

PART VI   MODERN ISSUES

PART VII   FIRM STRATEGIES

Contributors

Zoltan J. Acs, George Mason University, USA

Michel Aglietta, University of Paris 10, France

Cristiano Antonelli, University of Torino and Collegio Carlo Alberto, Italy

Markus C. Becker, University of Southern Denmark, Denmark

Marco Bellandi, University of Florence, Italy

Michael H. Best, University of Massachusetts, USA

Hong Bo, Department of Financial & Management Studies (DeFiMS), SOAS (School of Oriental and African Studies), University of London, UK

Jan Jaap Bouma, Delft University of Technology, the Netherlands

Hugues Bouthinon-Dumas, ESSEC Business School, France

Tobias Buchmann, University of Hohenheim, Germany

Richard Carter, business economist, Brighton, UK

Mark Casson, University of Reading, UK

Cécile Cézanne, University of Paris 13, France

Myriam Cloodt, Eindhoven University of Technology, the Netherlands

Alex Coad, SPRU (Science and Technology Policy Research), University of Sussex, Brighton

Alessandra Colombelli, DIGEP, Polytechnic of Turin, Italy, University of Nice Sophia Antipolis and CNRS-GREDEG (Centre National de la Recherche Scientifique-Groupe de Recherche en Droit, Economic Gestion), France

Aad Correljé, Delft University of Technology, the Netherlands

Lisa De Propris, University of Birmingham, UK

Michael Dietrich, University of Sheffield, UK

Ciaran Driver, Department of Financial & Management Studies (DeFiMS), SOAS, University of London, UK

Stephen P. Dunn, NHS Midlands and East, UK

Peter E. Earl, University of Queensland, Australia

Nicolai J. Foss, Copenhagen Business School, Denmark

Martin Fransman, University of Edinburgh, UK

Jean-Luc Gaffard, SKEMA Business School and OFCE (Observatoire Français des Conjonctures Economiques), France

John Groenewegen, Delft University of Technology, the Netherlands

Sarah Guillou, OFCE, France

John Hagedoorn, University of Maastricht, the Netherlands

Gerhard Hanappi, University of Technology of Vienna, Austria

Geoffrey M. Hodgson, University of Hertfordshire, UK

Werner Hölzl, WIFO (Austrian Institute of Economic Research), Austria

Grazia Ietto-Gillies, London South Bank University and Birkbeck University of London, UK

Albert Jolink, Erasmus University Rotterdam, the Netherlands

Thorbjørn Knudsen, University of Southern Denmark, Denmark

Jackie Krafft, University of Nice Sophia Antipolis and CNRS-GREDEG, France

William Lazonick, University of Massachusetts Lowell, USA

Sébastien Lechevalier, EHESS, France

Brian J. Loasby, University of Stirling, UK

Frédéric Marty, University of Nice Sophia Antipolis and CNRS-GREDEG, France

Lionel Nesta, OFCE, France

Eva Niesten, Utrecht University, the Netherlands

Bart Nooteboom, Emeritus of Tilburg University, the Netherlands

Ugo Pagano, University of Siena, Italy

Pier Paolo Patrucco, Department of Economics, University of Torino and BRICK (Bureau of Research on Innovation, Complexity and Knowledge), Collegio Carlo Alberto, Moncalieri, Italy

Andreas Pyka, University of Hohenheim, Germany

Francesco Quatraro, University of Nice Sophia Antipolis and CNRS-GREDEG, France

Jacques-Laurent Ravix, University of Nice Sophia Antipolis and CNRS-GREDEG, France

Antoine Rebérioux, University of Antilles Guyane and EconomiX (Paris Ouest Nanterre), France

Andreas Reinstaller, Austrian Institute of Economic Research (WIFO), Austria

Evens Salies, OFCE, France

Pier Paolo Saviotti, INRA-GAEL (Institut National de la Recherche Agronomique-Grenoble Applied Economics Laboratory) and CNRS-GREDEG France and ECIS, School of Innovation Sciences, Eindhoven University of Technology, the Netherlands

Nils Stieglitz, University of Southern Denmark, Denmark

Morris Teubal, The Hebrew University, Israel

Steven Toms, University of York, UK

Nigel Wadeson, University of Reading, UK

Olivier Weinstein, University of Paris 13, France

John F. Wilson, University of Liverpool, UK

Preface

The basic idea, or the intellectual driver, behind this volume is that we should create bridges between the economics of the firm and the theory of the firm. The title is intended to convey this bridge-building objective. As discussed in Chapter 1 in some detail, these two aspects to the study of the firm characteristically inhabit different and separate intellectual spheres and traditions. This separation suggests that, at least potentially, a partial analysis is developed. It is argued in Chapter 1 that what is needed is an economic understanding of real firms that are both institutional and technical. The intention, therefore, with the current volume is that the chapters collectively offer a more unified perspective on real firms. Note the qualification 'collectively' here. Not every chapter provides a bridge between the economics of the firm and the theory of the firm, although many do. But taken as a whole the chapters create the linkages required to analyse real firms. The particular rationale for the specific topics involved here is considered in detail in Chapter 1.

As with any volume, the thinking, writing and intellectual energy and enthusiasm are not developed in a vacuum. The editors of this handbook would like to put on record their gratitude and thanks to the authors who have cooperated in this project. We are all very busy people and the fact that everyone involved used some of their scarce time to write a contribution is much appreciated by the editors. We would also like to thank Matthew Pitman and Edward Elgar Publishing for initiating the project and being patient and understanding with the extended gestation period. Both editors are grateful to the other for encouragement and understanding given the obstacles (some of which were perhaps inevitable) encountered while editing this handbook. Last but not least we would like to thank our respective institutions (the University of Sheffield, Université de Nice Sophia Antipolis and the Centre National de la Recherche Scientifique [CNRS]) for providing an environment that allows us to pursue our research. Despite recent changes to the higher education systems in both England and France we have to admit that there are definitely worse ways to earn a living.

Michael Dietrich, Sheffield, UK
Jackie Krafft, Nice, France

PART I

INTRODUCTION

1 The economics and theory of the firm
Michael Dietrich and Jackie Krafft

1.1 INTRODUCTION

The title of this handbook makes reference to the *economics* of the firm and the *theory* of the firm. The economics of the firm characteristically concerns itself with issues of firm internal structure, organization and boundaries. The theory of the firm analyses behaviour and strategies in particular market contexts. Traditionally within economics these are viewed as separate spheres of analysis. What happens inside the firm has long been studied independently of what composes the details of the competitive environment of the firm and, alternatively, market strategies emerge from a firm conceived as a black box. An early statement of this separation is provided, for example, by Penrose (1959): 'we shall not be involved in any quarrel with the theory of the "firm" as part of a theory of price and production, so long as it cultivates its own garden and we cultivate ours (ibid., p. 10). And to reinforce the same point: 'The economist's "main conceptual schema" is designed for the theory of price determination and resource allocation, and it is unnecessary and inappropriate to try to reconcile this theory with "organization theory"' (ibid., p. 14).

In a similar vein, but from a different tradition, Williamson (1985) suggests that *exogenous* technologically separable units exist, which are characterized by some degree of asset specificity. Exchange between these units takes place with resulting transaction costs. The minimization of these costs then results in firm organization and more generally institutional development.

Without wishing to undermine the fundamental contributions of either Edith Penrose or Oliver Williamson, it is argued in this chapter that we must move beyond this separation and, for example, examine how firm behaviour, strategies and competition (a characteristic of the theory of the firm) interact with firm organization. Hence, one guiding principle behind this handbook is that bridges should be created between these two areas of study. Without these bridges potentially partial analysis can result. Two examples, developed in more detail below, will be sufficient to illustrate this potentially partial analysis. First, an industry or technological life-cycle perspective suggests that the nature of competition changes through time. It is argued below that different approaches to the economics of the firm similarly evolve through time in a manner linked to the underlying changes in the competitive environment. Second, it is shown below that when account is taken of strategic interaction in oligopoly contexts this has implications for a basic transaction cost account of the firm. Both examples illustrate the potential importance of creating bridges between traditionally separate areas.

This potential interaction is not, of course, a fundamentally new idea. For example, Casson (1997), Morroni (1992, 2006) and Langlois (2007) have developed work on the firm that can be viewed as analysing this interaction. For example, these authors suggest that organizational characteristics and decisions can be analysed as affecting firm scale economies. For the current authors, interest in this approach to the firm goes back some time. Dietrich (1994) suggested that we can really understand the firm only by taking account of governance structure benefits as well as costs. The 'benefits' encompass what is called here the theory of the firm with a focus on external issues and the 'costs' the economics of the firm with a focus on internal issues. More recently, Dietrich and Krafft (2011) present a framework to analyse firm development, and specifically vertical integration, based on creating links between technical and organizational aspects of the firm. They suggest that it is a truism that real firms are both technical and institutional entities. In reality, the firm is obviously a technical unit, namely a unit that transforms factor inputs into outputs. This is originally where the theory of the firm starts from analysing the impact of production and costs functions with demand on the market. Equally, the firm is also an institutional unit, requiring that one pays attention to its basic definition, its identity, its structure and boundaries, which has become the usual playground of the economics of the firm.

Of course it is always possible to *assume* one aspect exogenous (or in the extreme even ignore it) and analyse the other in isolation. However, the outcome is likely to end up with a partial analysis. For instance, one can focus on the issue of asset specificity, an exogenous technical characteristic supposed to generate motivation problems in a context of bounded rationality and opportunism, and creating the development of institutional solutions. But an obvious complexity here is that asset specificities imply non-contestable economic relationships that can impact on the nature of the competitive environment. In turn the competitive environment may feed back on to motivation problems. Alternatively, one can also focus on a given organizational structure that may constrain the set of productive opportunities, leading to increasing costs in terms of managerial and complementary assets.

1.2   RONALD COASE AND REAL FIRMS

This handbook develops a vision of the economics and theory of the firm that echoes work opened up by Ronald Coase with his notion of realism. In his 1937 article 'The nature of the firm', Coase proposes a research project that revolves around a realistic theory of the firm (Coase, 1937, 1993a):

> it is all the more necessary not only that a clear definition of the word 'firm' should be given but that its difference from a firm in the 'real world', if it exists, should be made clear. Mrs. Robinson has said that 'the two questions to be asked of a set of assumptions in economics are: Are they tractable? and: Do they correspond to the real world?'. Though, as Mrs. Robinson points out, 'more often one set will be manageable and the other realistic', yet there may well be branches of theory where assumptions may be both manageable and realistic. It is hoped to show [. . .] that a definition of a firm may be obtained which is not only realistic in that it corresponds to what is meant by a firm in the real world, but is tractable [. . .] (1937, p. 386)

This idea is reflected throughout his various writings, each time further clarified. In one of his most recent articles, Coase (1998) returns to the notion of realist theory that the new institutional economics can offer. According to Coase this theory is quite different from the institutional economics of Commons and Mitchell, which does not offer any robust theory to organize the vast collection of facts. This theory also differs from traditional analysis, which is a pure theory, highly abstract and little affected by what happens in the real world (ibid., p. 72). Since Adam Smith, economists have mainly focused on the formalization of the invisible hand, that is, on the analysis of extreme decentralization. However, there are other possibilities to develop economic analysis. We may be interested in how supply and demand determine prices, but we may also analyse the factors that determine what goods and services will be traded on markets and are charged a specific price. Coase believes that economists have focused only on the first question, as they focused essentially on the issue of refining the toolbox rather than the object of study:

> In saying this I should not be thought to imply that these analytical tools are not extremely valuable. [. . .]. My point is different. I think we should use these analytical tools to study the economic system. I think economists do have a subject matter: the study of the working of the economic system, a system in which we earn and spend our incomes. (Ibid., p. 73)

The realist theory of the firm should provide answers to questions like: what are the factors that determine the relative costs coordination within a firm or on the market? What factors determine the coordination between a firm and its supplier, client, partner or competitor? How, ultimately, is the coordination of this complex and interconnected structure of the industry, which is also subject to the influence of the laws, of the social system, of technological changes, achieved?

This distinction between pure theory and realistic theory of the firm is also strongly denounced in his speech when he received the Nobel Prize in 1991, when he says that in the pure theory of mainstream analysis (Coase, 1991): 'What is studied is a system which lives in the minds of economists but not on earth. I have called the result "blackboard economics". The firm and the market appear by name but they lack any substance' (ibid., p. 195). However, in his 1993 article entitled 'The nature of the firm: meaning', Coase explains the methodology of his research project. Going back into the reasons that motivated the 1937 article, he explains that the argument has to be based on hypotheses both usable and realistic (Coase, 1993b):

> My article starts by making a methodological point: it is desirable that the assumptions we make should be realistic. Most readers will pass over these opening sentences (Putterman omits them when reprinting my article), and others will excuse what they read as a youthful mistake, believing, as so many modern economists do, that we should choose our theories on the basis of the accuracy of their predictions, the realism of their assumptions being utterly irrelevant. [. . .] In effect what this comes down to is that when economists find that they are unable to analyze what is happening in the real world, they invent an imaginary world which they should be capable of handling. (Ibid., p. 52)

This idea is even further reinforced in a comment on a 1993 article by Posner (Coase, 1993c):

> Posner [. . .] refers to my 'dislike of abstraction'. This is wrong. It is true that I said, in my Warren Nutter lecture, that the assumptions of our theory should be realistic. 'Realism in assumptions forces us to analyse the world that exists, not some imaginary world that does not' (Coase, 1988, p. 65). But I go on to say: 'it is, of course, true that our assumption should not be completely realistic. There are factors we leave out because we do not know how to handle them. There are others we exclude because we do not feel the benefits of a more complete

theory would be worth the costs involved in including them. Their inclusion might, for example, greatly complicate the analysis without giving us greater understanding about what is going on. Again, assumptions about other factors do not need to be realistic because they are completely irrelevant [. . .] There are good reasons why the assumptions of one's theories should not be completely realistic but this does not seem that we should lose touch with reality' (Coase, 1988, pp. 65–66). As this quotation indicates, I do not dislike abstraction. But the right degree of abstraction depends on the problem that is being analysed. What I object to is mindless abstraction or the kind of abstraction which does not help to understand the working of the economic system. My aim is to bring into existence an economic theory which is solidly based. (Coase, 1993c, p. 97)

It is therefore clear that the definition of the firm in the real world and in the analysis is a fundamental issue in Coase's work, leading to possible propositions on what a theory is to understand how economic systems work.

In his article 'Industrial organization: a proposal for research', published in 1972 following a conference in honour of the 50th anniversary of the NBER (National Bureau of Economic Research), Coase stresses that the object of study of the realist theory he developed is the organization of industry, and not just the firm (Coase, 1972):

> We all know what is meant by the organization of industry. It describes the way in which the activities undertaken within the economic system are divided up between firms. As we know, some firms embrace many different activities; while for others, the range is narrowly circumscribed. Some firms are large; others, small. Some are vertically related; others are not. This is the organization of industry or – as it used to be called – the structure of industry. What one would expect to learn from a study of industrial organization would be how industry is organised now, and how it differs from what it was in earlier periods; what forces were operative in bringing about this organization of industry and how these forces have been changing over time; what the effects would be of proposals to change, through legal action of various kinds, the forms of industrial organization. (Ibid, p. 60)

And he adds: 'But if we are to tackle the problem of industrial organization seriously, a theory is needed (ibid, p. 63).

The work he considers as important in guiding a realistic theory of the organization of industry, are those by William Thorp, D.H. Robertson and Alfred Marshall. These references have inspired his 1937 theory on the nature of the firm and fit also with his article of 1972 on the organization of industry:

> The way in which an industry is organized is thus dependent on the relation between the costs of carrying out transactions on the market and the costs of organizing the same operations within that firm which can perform this task at the lowest cost. Furthermore, the costs of organizing an activity within any given firm depends on what other activities it is engaged in. A given set of activities will facilitate the carrying out of some activities, but hinder the performance of others. It is these relationships which determine the actual organization of industry. [. . .] But having said this, how far ahead are we? We know very little about the costs of conducting transactions on the market or what they depend on; we know next to nothing about the effects on costs of different groupings of activities within firms. About all we know is that the working out of these interrelationships leads to a situation in which viable organizations are small in relation to the economic system of which they are part. (Ibid, p. 64)

Although the NBER contributions in this area were very few in 1972, Coase emphasizes in particular three names: Solomon Fabricant (1952), 'The trend of government activity in the United States since 1900'; Ralph Nelson (1959), 'Merger movements in American industry'; and Michael Gort (1962), 'Diversification and integration in American industry' (Coase, 1972):

> This proposal for more research is founded on my belief that it is unlikely that we shall see significant advances in our theory of the organization of industry until we know more about what it is that we must explain. An inspired theoretician might do as well without such an empirical work, but my own feeling is that the inspiration is most likely to come through the stimulus provided by the patterns, puzzles, and anomalies revealed by systematic data-gathering, particularly when the prime need is to break our existing habits of thought (ibid., pp. 70–1).

> Of the three works that I have mentioned, that by Professor Gort comes closest to what I have in mind when I speak of the research on industrial organization that we need today. Professor Gort does deal with the question of a range of activities organized within the firm, and there can be few problems of importance in industrial organization on which he does not touch. However, Professor Gort abandoned the more straightforward methods of earlier investigators, such as William Thorp. He makes the central theme of his book a study of diversification. He measures trends in diversification, and seeks to discover the economic characteristics of diversifying firms, and of the industries entered by diversifying firms. Degrees of diversification are not, however, easy to define or to measure, and the results which Professor Gort presents are difficult to interpret without knowledge of the underlying industrial structure. (Ibid., pp. 72–3).

As we shall see later in this chapter, the reference to Michael Gort by Ronald Coase is of high importance, since his work together with Steven Klepper on industry life cycles are considered today as a central representation of how the drivers of change operate at the level of firms and industries. This is, according to Coase, the premise of a realistic theory of industry organization.

To develop a general approach to the firm in the spirit of Coase's real firms, one has to recognize that any real firm is made of two bases: technical (T) and institutional (I). The T base is the traditional arena of the theory of the firm and the I base is covered by the economics of the firm. To create linkages between T and I factors we can recognize that each can act in one of three ways (Dietrich and Krafft, 2011): they can act as *drivers* of change, they can govern change *processes* and they can act as *attractors* of change. To understand the philosophy behind this handbook each of these can be (briefly) considered in turn.

Analyses of the firm that emphasize T and I drivers of change are characteristically Schumpeterian in nature. Although Schumpeter originally suggested that innovation covers both T and I factors, modern Schumpeterian analyses of the firm tend to prioritize T drivers with I implications following from this in a manner that can be viewed as governing the details of change processes. Although Schumpeter tends to inspire modern discussions of firm change, equally, other early writers on the firm emphasize T and I drivers, for example Smith and Marx. In terms of more modern writing, the competence and cognitive views of the firm emphasize that change drivers are firm-specific and frequently based on tacit and/or system-based knowledge.

The analysis of firm change processes can also be viewed as being governed by T and I factors. For example, the modern analysis of modularity and network effects emphasizes that firm adaptation is an important topic for analysis. I process factors are similarly important to the analysis of the firm. For example, Galbraith's technostructure can be viewed in this light or the way that cognition and knowledge channel firm development.

In addition, Commons's analysis of the firm as an amalgam of rules can be viewed in this light. Finally, exogenous T and I changes can act as attractors to which firms adjust. This is the method characteristically adopted by Austrian views of entrepreneurship in which firm orientation is viewed as adaptation to market and technical change. In addition, transaction cost economics adopts the same abstract logic. With regard to the latter tradition an important implication follows from the attractor logic that is used. As Williamson (1991) himself emphasizes, firm adaptation is viewed as economizing not strategizing. This point is taken up in later discussion in this chapter.

While different approaches to the firm can be analysed in terms of T and I factors that create change drivers, govern change processes and act as attractors, three complexities can be recognized that have influenced the structure and content of this handbook. First, the various elements of the T-I drivers, processes and attractors framework can be combined. Often this combination is logically necessary. For example within transaction cost economics exogenous technical innovation can change asset specificities that lead to institutional development because of the new attractor(s). But also note that certain combinations create logical difficulties. For example, an emphasis on firm processes tends to downgrade the importance of change attractors. In addition, frequently combining the various elements of real firm analysis creates complexities that need to be managed. One approach here is to constrain analysis to concentrate on particular aspects of firm activity as is done in Parts VI and VII of this handbook, which cover what are called 'modern issues' and 'firm strategies'. The second complexity of real firm analysis is that the various possible linkages upon which it is based do not create closed systems. Instead wider institutions and government policies channel the manner in which various linkages can function. This is reflected in this volume by a number of the chapters in Part IV (on the multinational firm) and also in Part VIII on economic policies and the firm.

The final complexity of real firm analysis, is one in which the editors are particularly interested. It involves locating the analysis of the firm in particular market or similar effects. This is the logic for the inclusion of the chapters in Part VI of this handbook that cover various 'modern issues'. Two such specific market effects are useful tools to create bridges between the theory and the economics of the firm: life-cycle theory and oligopoly theory. In the rest of the main body of this chapter, these two approaches to the analysis of firms and markets will be used to explore possible interactions between the economics and theory of the firm. The intention here is that the two approaches provide complementary insights – although we will see that some of these insights are remarkably consistent. The complementarity here is, of course, fundamentally methodological: on the one hand an evolutionary perspective and on the other a comparative static and optimizing approach. The intention is not to provide an exhaustive discussion but instead to provide sufficient evidence that analysis of the firm should create bridges between characteristically separate areas of discussion.

1.3   THE FIRM IN INDUSTRY LIFE CYCLES

The growing body of analysis in the field of industrial dynamics since the 1980s may lead people to think that a new domain of research has emerged. This is, of course, a misperception since some early contributions provided first steps towards the elaboration of such an approach. Schumpeter ([1912] 1934, 1942) did significant work emphasizing the role of the entrepreneur in the development of innovation, as well as the evolution of industry in a context of radical change. Marshall ([1890] 1925, 1920) also proposed many lines of inquiry, such as the fact that the economy is composed of different sectors, the growth and decline of which is unequal and intrinsically dependent on the organization of knowledge. Over the 1980s, however, some authors built on the neglected work of Schumpeter and Marshall, and focused on major changes that have taken place in industry structure, industrial leadership, economic growth and innovation. The research programme initiated by Nelson and Winter (1982), which focused on evolutionary theory and economic change, opened the door to new interpretations. In one of these new interpretations, Gort and Klepper (1982) tried to understand the long-term evolution of innovative industries, and assessed that this long-term evolution is essentially characterized by a life cycle in which industries, like bio-organisms, arise in their birth phase, grow and mature in their development time, and decline in their death phase. The industry life cycle clearly added value to the explanation of a large number of regularities occurring in innovative industries: production increases in the initial stages and declines in the final stages; entry is dominant in the early phases of the life cycle and is progressively dominated by exit (a massive process of exit – a shakeout – occurs in the final stages of the life cycle); market shares are highly volatile in the beginning, and tend to stabilize over time; product innovation tends to be replaced by process innovation; first movers generally have a leadership position that guarantees their long-term viability; product variety disappears over time, as a dominant design emerges.

One of these regularities, that is, the shakeout, progressively became a central regularity to be explored in industrial dynamics. Most of the recent debates attempted to clarify when and why a shakeout occurs. Given the large body of literature it is somewhat surprising that linkages have not been created with the insights offered by the economics of the firm. This is what we intend to do here.

1.3.1 Development of Technology, Development of Knowledge: Possible Sources of Shakeout

In the 1990s, the literature on industrial dynamics focused more and more on the shakeout phenomenon, and attempted to clarify what occurs in pre-shakeout versus post-shakeout periods. This attention is, of course, related to the crucial role of shakeout in the industry life cycle: a cycle cannot be observed without a shakeout in mature stages of the industry. But shakeout is also a key to understanding why a given industry is declining, and why major actors of this industry tend to be superseded by new actors creating a new industry. Behind this, there is the idea that a given technology can create profit opportunities for some time, but that new technologies will recurrently be created and replace older ones. This Schumpeterian vision of the dynamics of an economic system has been explored in recent contributions on the shakeout in industry life cycle, with an emphasis on different determinants from a purely external technological shock to more endogenous arguments related to the development of knowledge at the level of the firm.

For Jovanovic and McDonald (1994), shakeout is generated by an external technological shock, exogenous to the industry. The first technological shock sets in with the development of the new product being launched on the market. Entry is stimulated by the emergence of new profit opportunities related to this new technology/new product, but subsequently there is a progressive reduction in profit margins and the industrial structure stabilizes on a limited number of firms in the industry. At this stage, which corresponds to the maturity of the industry, a new technological trajectory emerges and again stimulates the process of entry, in the meantime, involving an adjustment of incumbent firms. The process of adjustment is driven by a stochastic process and only a few firms survive this external shock. The shakeout thus eliminates firms that failed to adapt themselves to the new technology.

Alternatively, Abernathy and Utterback (1978) and Abernathy and Clark (1985) have developed an analysis of shakeout and dominant design. When a firm launches a new product in the market, it must face a high level of uncertainty affecting both the conditions of demand and supply. On the demand side, uncertainty comes from the fact that the firm does not know the details of customers' preferences. On the supply side, the conditions of production are also highly uncertain and may evolve over time. Over time, uncertainty decreases and selection operates. On the demand side, uncertainty decreases once customers of the new product have tested the alternative characteristics, and acquired experience on what they expect from the new product, which characteristics are more adapted to their personal taste and usage. On the supply side, rival producers learn over time and accumulate experience on what customers prefer. In time they also select a series of production techniques that are adapted to low-cost production. Since uncertainty decreases, the shakeout appears as an endogenous phenomenon. Product innovation diminishes because most of the actors (producers and customers) are naturally oriented towards the production and consumption of a standardized good. The progressive emergence of a dominant design involves higher barriers to entry that correspond with investments by incumbents in process innovation. Entry is thus limited, and less efficient incumbent firms exit the industry.

Finally, Klepper (1996) relates the shakeout to the timing of entry. The reference is, here again, the Schumpeterian hypothesis on the relation between firms' size and R&D capacity. But the novelty is that this hypothesis is discussed on the basis of a finer distinction between firms that can eventually be incumbent, new entrant, or latecomer. Process innovation decreases the average costs of large firms, which are the major actors of this type of innovation. However, some key elements may erode the advantage of larger firms. For instance, large firms have to cover specific costs, such as expansion costs, which limit their growth. The activity of R&D can also exhibit decreasing returns to scale over time. Because of these elements, early entrants can develop process innovations, sometimes much better than incumbents or latecomers. Early entrants can thus enjoy a leadership position in process innovation as, on the one hand, incumbents have to deal with other problems that are related to their large size and, on the other hand, latecomers have to concentrate on product innovation that allows them to grow to a minimum size in order to survive. The timing of entry is thus a major determinant in the formation of a competitive advantage over incumbents, as well as in long-term survival over latecomers. This mechanism provides an alternative explanation of the shakeout.

The idea of a shakeout essentially driven by the evolution of technology over the course of the industry life cycle is thus progressively challenged by a new vision. The development, accumulation, diffusion and usage of competencies are thus key elements that drive the industry life cycle and, as an outcome, involve a sensibly different vision of shakeout that is closer to the Marshallian tradition. Mueller (1990, 1997) shows that the long-term viability of first movers is related in a large number of industries to specific features of demand (such as set-up and switching costs, network externalities of final users, inertia effects due to the customer's uncertainty on quality, inertia effects due to the customer's experience of existing products and services), as well as supply (such as set-up and network externalities of producers, economies of scale, cost-decreasing learning by using). Finally, Van Dijk (1998) shows that increasing returns in R&D is not the major element in the first movers' competitiveness, but that network effects have a rather decisive effect.

Industry life cycle analyses generally focus on industries in which competition and innovation proceed from the interaction between firms (incumbents and entrants) within a given market, delimited by the purchases and sales of a homogeneous product. On some occasions, however, vertical relationships between firms in the industry and their direct suppliers or customers have a strong impact on the evolution of industries. Innovation processes require the accumulation of complementary competencies, as well as an effective coordination between firms that generate these competencies. Since the industry is characterized by strong coordination between suppliers and producers, or producers and retailers, processes of entry and exit become industry-specific. Alternative life-cycle patterns thus appear, eventually with non-shakeout phenomena. In some industries the emergence of specialized suppliers tends to re-dynamize the entry process in the phase of maturity. They develop new production processes, new specialized equipment, new technology at the upstream level and sell it to any downstream potential entrant who can pay the price. They significantly decrease barriers to entry and favour competition (Fransman, 1999; Krafft, 2010). In some cases, an industry was created by an initial inventor or an academic researcher who decided to set up a firm to exploit the commercial opportunities of his or her innovation. Many times, however, the production and distribution of this innovation required the contribution of other actors, usually larger firms. The coordination of competencies related to innovation on the one hand, and complementary competencies related to production and distribution on the other hand, strongly shaped the profile of evolution of the industry, and stimulated new entries (Bresnahan and Raff, 1991; Mitchell, 1995; Klepper, 1997).

The coordination of similar competencies is also an important topic for researchers interested in how innovations occur and their implications for firms and economic change. In some industries there is a somewhat paradoxical phenomenon that both small, specialized firms and large, diversified firms co-exist in the long run. Specific firms may come and go, and there are certainly mergers, alliances and bankruptcies, but the two types of firms seem to an extent mutually dependent. This situation may lead to non-shakeout profiles of evolution, with small firms and large firms surviving over the long run. It seems important to combine such alliances with in-house R&D and competencies, because otherwise the firm has difficulties in evaluating the potential of new ideas and techniques that are developed outside the firm. In many cases, the intrinsic characteristics of knowledge in terms of codification and appropriability requires extended interaction, and explains why collaboration occurs amongst firms with similar competencies in order to stimulate innovation. But in the meantime, ownership and control rights are important to understand who has alliances with whom and are absolutely crucial in the evolution of the industry (McKelvey, 1996; Saviotti, 1998).

Finally, the coherence that firms tend to develop in the coordination of similar and complementary competences tends to appear as a major issue in industrial dynamics. Nearly 20 years ago, Foss (1993) and Teece et al. (1994) claimed that coherence becomes a cognitive concept incorporating elements such as organizational learning within the firm, path-dependency characteristics, the depth and scope of technological opportunities in the neighbourhood of the firm's own technology and R&D activities, and the influence of the selection environment. Today, the notion of coherence tends to get an operational content in the industrial dynamics literature with the development of metrics on relatedness, proximity, similarity and interconnectedness and how they tend to evolve over time (Nooteboom, 2004; Krafft et al., 2011).

1.3.2 Industry Dynamics and the Nature of the Firm

What conclusions can be drawn from this discussion of industry dynamics and life cycles with regard to the nature of the firm? As a preliminary comment, we can first think that technology essentially drives the life cycle of an industry, and is responsible for the shakeout. This calls to mind Schumpeter's vision of creative destruction in industrial dynamics. An entrepreneur sets up a firm to introduce an invention. This firm grows and holds a monopoly position for some time. But in time this firm is imitated by new entrants that eventually outperform the initial firm. This situation can continue until another entrepreneur develops a new project involving the exit of older and larger firms and the entry of new ones.

But we can also think about the shakeout in a different manner. We can consider that knowledge and competencies drive the life cycle of the industry. In that case, closer to Marshall's vision, the growth of knowledge is linked to the ability of firms to ensure coherence between internal economies (organization and direction of the resources of the firm) and external economies (general development of the economy, including the role of firms in the neighborhood). In this perspective, the shakeout affects firms differently, since some firms might have the opportunity to accumulate specific knowledge and competencies, and survive. In some cases non-shakeout patterns may thus emerge.

Beyond these background points about the relevance of earlier analysis to organizational as well as technical factors we can suggest that the diversity of the empirical evidence, and interpretations of this evidence, suggests that no single approach to the firm is relevant in all circumstances. Consider, first, a Schumpeter-inspired analysis that life cycles are technologically driven with a key role played by the management of demand- and supply-side uncertainties. To a large extent this can be mapped into, for example, a transaction cost analysis of the firm. The technological driver is essentially exogenous to organizational adaptation. The key role of uncertainty, and its link with large firm size, is also consistent with this perspective on the firm (Williamson, 1985). But now consider a Marshallian-inspired analysis that emphasizes the creation and management of knowledge. Here we can echo, for example, Barnard (1938) and suggest that the creation of new knowledge is endogenous to firm decisions and in terms of the economics of the firm we must account for change *processes* not just adaptation to exogenous technological changes. In addition, Barnard is useful because he emphasizes that firms are not long-lived. In terms of modern writing we can incorporate competence perspectives on the firm, as suggested above. We are not suggesting here that one approach (Schumpeter or Marshall) is universally relevant, instead we prefer to suggest that the approaches are relevant in different circumstances.

Consider now what might be considered the key insight of empirically based studies of industry dynamic: the role of shakeout. Two key issues would appear to be appropriate here. First, the nature and type of competition changes pre- and post- any shakeout. Pre-shakeout intense competitive pressures result from firm entry and exit. Post-shakeout increased firm size and reduced entry/exit implies the emergence of oligopolistic structures with the complexity of strategic interdependence this implies. Arguably the economic-institutional aspects of this post-shakeout world have been under-analysed. Hence an oligopoly model that incorporates transaction costs is suggested below. The second issue we can take from the earlier shakeout discussion is that we cannot automatically link shakeout with technical progress because of the observed continuation of 'old' technologies is some areas. This continuing relevance of old technologies suggests a non-adaptation to technological attractors because of the dominance of process considerations. In an organizational context, this observation (once again) echoes Barnard's work.

Finally, in this section, we can consider the issue of the boundaries of the firm. If we accept the logic of an organizational life-cycle analysis, firm boundaries can be analysed in terms of the dominance of driver, process or attractor effects, and so (once again) no single approach is likely to be relevant. In early life-cycle stages, with the dominance of technical and organizational drivers we can suggest that firm boundaries are based on the restructuring of institutional and technical knowledge linkages. In this context we can recognize the earlier discussion of the restructuring of vertical relations and hence the relevance of a Richardson- (1972) based analysis of the firm and industry. When process considerations dominate firm activity we can suggest that firm boundaries are based on attempts to establish organizational and institutional rules. This establishment of rules will involve scale and scope effects along the lines suggested by Chandler (1977, 1990) and hence increasing firm size. Using earlier discussion we can suggest that this dominance of process, and the emergence of established rules, requires a shakeout of firm activity and hence limitation on entry and exit. But at the same time we should not over-simplify the emergence of large firms, and expanding firm boundaries, because of the possible complementarity between small and large firms. Hence the established rules that govern organizational processes cover inter-firm as well as intra-firm activity. Finally, when attractors dominate firm development this will be a response to diffusing knowledge and rule stability in a post-shakeout world. In this context firm boundaries can be understood in the context of efficiency-seeking behaviour.

1.4 A FORMAL MODEL OF REAL FIRMS

In the previous sections links have been created between the theory and the economics of the firm. The basic conclusion has been that no approach to the firm is uniquely dominant. In this section a different approach to creating theoretical linkages is developed in terms of a simple model of the firm. The basis of this modelling is the introduction of transaction cost features into an otherwise standard model of the firm. This would appear to be an appropriate mode of analysis for two reasons. First, there is a methodological consistency in the use of comparative statics (Dietrich, 1994). Second, the assumption of economizing on transaction costs is the dual of optimizing behaviour.

1.4.1   A Single Firm

The simplicity of the modelling here is that all basic relationships are assumed linear, a feature that is commented on as the discussion proceeds. The discussion is presented in two stages. In this section a basic model for a single firm is developed. It is shown that predictions apparently consistent with some observations in the life-cycle literature are forthcoming. Following this a Cournot-based duopoly analysis is presented. The objective here is to explore the idea suggested above that transaction cost economics may gain particular relevance in later life-cycle stages that are characterized by relative knowledge stability and strategic interaction. But, once again, linkages are created to the life-cycle and other literatures.

The basic model involves a standard and simple, single product firm but introduces possible transaction cost effects into this. Obviously any firm undertakes many specific organizational tasks that cover the management of output markets, intra-firm activity and input markets. Following standard analysis we can think of these tasks in general terms as managing search, negotiation and policing activities. To simplify technical detail we assume that these various managerial tasks are undertaken in fixed proportions with no substitution between organizational human and non-human inputs being possible. This simplification allows us to create an aggregate measure of transaction costs (C_T) that is simply the sum of the various specific organizational costs. We therefore have a single measure of managerial activity that can be applied in the different contexts. In addition, this measure will be used as an indicator of organization size rather than using real output as a measure of firm size.

In terms of a firm's demand for real output we assume the following linear form:

$$X = (a_0/a_1) - (1/a_1)p + (a_2/a_1)C_T \qquad (1.1a)$$

In (1.1a) X is output sold per period and p is selling price. The role of C_T here involves, for example, greater search and negotiation activity, increasing output sold for any selling price. The linearity assumptions in (1.1a) are clearly not realistic for large changes in the variables but significantly simplify technical detail. It is more useful to re-write (1.1a) as an inverse demand function:

$$p = a_0 - a_1X + a_2C_T \qquad (1.1b)$$

In turn (1.1b) allows us to define a firm's total revenue:

$$TR = pX = a_0X - a_1X^2 + a_2C_T(X) \qquad (1.1c)$$

A firm's average production costs (AC_P) are modelled as follows:

$$AC_P = b_0 - b_1C_T > 0 \qquad (1.2a)$$

With given C_T, formulation (1.2a) defines, of course, constant returns technology. The C_T effect can be thought of as either a more effective management of intra-firm activity affecting productivity and costs and/or more effective search, negotiation and policing in input markets. In (1.2a) it is clearly inappropriate to extrapolate beyond reasonable bounds, hence the requirement that AC_P is positive. This requirement suggests an organizational capacity constraint:

$$C_T < b_0/b_1 \tag{1.2b}$$

Using (1.2a) we can define a firm's total production costs (TC_P):

$$TCP = b_0X - b_1C_T(X) \tag{1.2c}$$

In turn we use (1.2c) to define a firm's total costs (TC):

$$TC = b_0X - b_1C_T(X) + C_T \tag{1.2d}$$

Using (1.1c) and (1.2d) a firm's profit function is:

$$\pi = a_0X - a_1X^2 + a_2C_T(X) - [b_0X - b_1C_T(X) + C_T] \tag{1.3a}$$

We can analyse (1.3a) in terms of short-run and long-run solutions. The short-run solution involves profit maximizing with two choice variables X and C_T. Differentiating (1.3a) with respect to these variables and setting the derivatives equal to zero:

$$\partial\pi/\partial X = a_0 - 2a_1X + (a_2 + b_1)C_T - b_0 = 0 \tag{1.3b}$$

$$\partial\pi/\partial C_T = (a_2 + b_1)X - 1 = 0 \tag{1.3c}$$

Using (1.3b) we can define profit maximizing output in terms of C_T:

$$X = \frac{a_0 - b_0}{2a_1} + \frac{a_2 + b_1}{2a_1}C_T \tag{1.4a}$$

In (1.4a) the first element on the right-hand side is a traditional short-run viability condition for firm activity. In the absence of transaction costs, the maximum price that can be charged (a_0) must be greater than exogenous unit costs (b_0) to generate positive output. But by introducing transaction costs this viability condition is amended. In the short run (but not the long run as considered below) positive output can be generated with $a_0 < b_0$ as long as C_T is sufficiently large, an observation that allows us to create links, suggested below, between this model and life-cycle analysis.

To solve the system defined by (1.3b) and (1.3c) we substitute (1.4a) into (1.3c) and hence define optimal C_T:

$$C_T = \frac{2a_1}{(a_2 + b_1)^2} - \frac{a_0 - b_0}{a_2 + b_1} \tag{1.4b}$$

The system defined by (1.4a) and (1.4b) presents a unique solution. Substituting (1.4b) into (1.4a):

$$X = \frac{1}{a_2 + b_1} \qquad (1.4c)$$

The short-run solution implied by (1.4a) – (1.4c) can be analysed in the context of the life-cycle literature introduced above. Early in a life cycle small firm entry and exit tends to be high. For successful firms profitability is high. Firm success, in terms of the current model, requires large $a_0 - b_0$, that is, a large difference between maximum price and exogenous unit cost. From (1.4b), large $a_0 - b_0$ implies small C_T (ceteris paribus). So, early in a life cycle, when profit opportunities are large, we can expect small organizational size. Another way of interpreting this result is that with $a_0 > b_0$ a firm is viable in the traditional economic sense and this reduces the requirement for organizational effort. But as a life cycle proceeds market growth slows down. In terms of the current model this slowing can be interpreted as falling $a_0 - b_0$. In turn from (1.4b) this maturing life cycle implies larger C_T (ceteris paribus) and so larger organizational size. Furthermore, equation (1.4b) says more than this. Markets that are unviable in the traditional sense, that is, with $a_0 < b_0$, are short-run viable in our model as they generate large organizational effort and size. Short-run non-viability in our model is exogenous and produced by the organizational capacity constraint (1.2b). If the large C_T predicted in (1.4b), because of possibly negative $a_0 - b_0$, is greater than the constraint defined in (1.4b) a firm may experience short-run non-viability. In short the simple model developed here can predict an evolution of organizational size that is apparently consistent with life-cycle analysis.

One peculiarity of this model can be identified. While organizational size (C_T) varies with $a_0 - b_0$ in a way that is understandable, from (1.4c) it is clear that physical output (X) does not vary with $a_0 - b_0$. Actual output is determined by the interaction between C_T and revenue and cost determination, that is, a_2 and b_1, but not directly by C_T. To some extent this is an interesting property of the model: physical output is determined by the interaction terms in the model and so indirectly by transaction cost rather than simply by profit potential. Intuitively, any profit potential requires appropriate organizational effort. But equally, one reason for this result is the linearity of the basic relationships in the model. With increasing organizational effectiveness as C_T increases, or with increasing physical returns to scale, we would not expect this result to hold.

The long-run solution to the model presented here to some extent, but not completely, qualifies the conclusions just drawn. Long-run firm viability requires non-negative profits. Re-writing (1.3a) and imposing this constraint:

$$\pi = (a_0 - b_0)X - a_1 X^2 + [(a_2 + b_1)X - 1]C_T > 0 \qquad (1.3a')$$

Using (1.4c), that is, the condition for profit-maximizing output, it is clear that $[a_2 + b_1]$ X is always unity if we impose profit maximization. Hence the non-negativity of profit in (1.3a') depends on $(a_0 - b_0)X - a_1 X^2$. It follows that long-run firm viability requires $a_0 > b_0$, as we would expect in a non-transaction cost model. An implication here is that in our simple model transaction costs have a short-run but not long-run impact on firm viability

Table 1.1   Impact of changing a_0

a_0	6	5.5	5	4.5	4	3.5	3	2.5
X	5	5	5	5	5	5	5	5
C_T	0	2.5	5	7.5	10	12.5	15	17.5
π	12.5	10	7.5	5	2.5	0	−2.5	−5

Note: Parameter vales: $a_1 = 0.5$, $a_2 = 0.1$, $b_0 = 1$, $b_1 = 0.1$.

and activity. But once non-negative profits are earned the organizational size effects discussed above are relevant.

One final point is appropriate in this discussion. We have interpreted the single firm model in terms of possible life-cycle effects. But an alternative, and perhaps more standard, interpretation is possible. Competitive market analysis suggests that firm entry occurs with positive profitability, in the absence of entry and exit barriers. In this context our model can be viewed as a developed monopolistically competitive firm. Successful firm entry will reduce the market shares of existing firms. In terms of our simple model successful firm entry reduces a_0. Firm entry will therefore eventually impose a non-negative profit constraint as in (1.3a'). The possible effects here are illustrated in Table 1.1, which shows the impact of changing a_0 for particular parameter values.

As we move from left to right across the columns of Table 1.1 we see the impact of declining a_0 interpreted as either a maturing life cycle or greater competition from firm entry. We can see the unchanged physical output, a feature already discussed. More importantly we see increasing organizational size (C_T) and declining profitability. If we interpret changing a_0 as a response to firm entry the change in C_T warrants discussion. With traditional monopolistic competition a movement to long-run equilibrium resulting from firm entry produces excess capacity. The latter, in turn, may introduce an incentive for larger firm size, perhaps via merger, to eliminate the excess capacity. In the model developed here we see larger organizational size emerging with greater competition but this is not because of excess capacity. It is due to the interaction between transaction costs and firm revenue and costs. Intuitively, greater competition generates greater profit-seeking incentives that require larger transaction costs and hence organizational size. In the comparative static model developed here this process has a long-run equilibrium with zero profits being earned. This long-run solution is clear in Table 1.1. This long-run constraint on firm size occurs even though we have exogenous constant returns to scale. Hence the constraint is produced by the interaction between the economics and theory of the firm.

1.4.2   A Duopoly Model of Real Firms

In this section the discussion of the firm just presented is further developed in terms of a Cournot-based duopoly analysis. The objectives here are twofold. First we further explore linkages between the economics and theory of the firm. Second, we develop the idea that transaction cost economics may gain particular relevance in later life-cycle stages that are characterized by relative knowledge stability and strategic interaction.

The basic structure of the analysis is the same as that used above except that we have two firms. The inverse demand functions are:

$$p_1 = a_0 - a_1 X_1 - a_2 X_2 + a_3 C_{T1} \tag{1.5a}$$

$$p_2 = a_0 - a_1 X_2 - a_2 X_1 + a_3 C_{T2} \tag{1.5b}$$

Note the following features here. The two demand functions have identical parameters. In principle this is unnecessary but simplifies technical detail. The two firms have individual prices because of individual organizational efforts (C_{T1} and C_{T2}) and because of potential product differentiation when a_1 and a_2 are not equal. The issue of potential product differentiation is important in this model and will be discussed further below. But even though there are individual prices in (1.5a) and (1.5b), in a Cournot equilibrium prices will be the same because of identical parameters and cost functions (as detailed below). X_2 has an impact on p_1, in turn C_{T2} impacts on X_2, hence there is an indirect effect of C_{T2} on p_1 but in (1.5a) there is no direct effect. Similarly there is an indirect impact of C_{T1} on p_2 but no direct impact. Using (1.5a) and (1.5b) we can define firm total revenues:

$$TR_1 = p_1 X_1 = a_0 X_1 - a_1 X_1^2 - a_2 X_1 X_2 + a_3 C_{T1} X_1 \tag{1.5c}$$

$$TR_2 = p_2 X_2 = a_0 X_2 - a_1 X_2^2 - a_2 X_1 X_2 + a_3 C_{T2} X_2 \tag{1.5d}$$

Firm costs are structured in the same way as in the previous section. Average production costs are:

$$AC_{P1} = b_0 - b_1 C_{T1} > 0 \tag{1.6a}$$

$$AC_{P2} = b_0 - b_1 C_{T2} > 0 \tag{1.6b}$$

There is the same requirement for organizational capacity constraints:

$$C_{T1}, C_{T2} < b_0/b_1 \tag{1.6c}$$

Total costs are:

$$TC_1 = b_0 X_1 - b_1 C_{T1} X_1 + C_{T1} \tag{1.6d}$$

$$TC_2 = b_0 X_2 - b_1 C_{T2} X_2 + C_{T2} \tag{1.6e}$$

Firm profits are:

$$\pi_1 = a_0 X_1 - a_1 X_1^2 - a_2 X_1 X_2 + a_3 C_{T1} X_1 - [b_0 X_1 - b_1 C_{T1} X_1 + C_{T1}] \tag{1.7a}$$

$$\pi_2 = a_0 X_2 - a_1 X_2^2 - a_2 X_1 X_2 + a_3 C_{T2} X_2 - [b_0 X_2 - b_1 C_{T2} X_2 + C_{T2}] \tag{1.7b}$$

As above we have two choice variables for each firm (output and transaction costs) but in addition we have the added complexity of the strategic interaction of the firms. The relevant first-order conditions are:

$$\partial\pi_1/\partial X_1 = a_0 - 2a_1X_1 - a_2X_2 + a_3C_{T1} - b_0 + b_1C_{T1} = 0 \tag{1.8a}$$

$$\partial\pi_1/\partial C_{T1} = (a_3 + b_1)X_1 - 1 = 0 \tag{1.8b}$$

$$\partial\pi_2/\partial X_2 = a_0 - 2a_1X_2 - a_2X_1 + a_3C_{T2} - b_0 + b_1C_{T2} = 0 \tag{1.8c}$$

$$\partial\pi_2/\partial C_{T2} = (a_3 + b_1)X_2 - 1 = 0 \tag{1.8d}$$

(1.8a) − (1.8d) can be solved in an equivalent manner to that used above but the strategic interaction renders the solution more complex. We use [1.8a] and [1.8c] to define profit-maximizing outputs:

$$X_1 = \frac{a_0 - b_0}{2a_1} + \frac{a_3 + b_1}{2a_1}C_{T1} - \frac{a_2}{2a_1}X_2 \tag{1.9a}$$

$$X_2 = \frac{a_0 - b_0}{2a_1} + \frac{a_3 + b_1}{2a_1}C_{T2} - \frac{a_2}{2a_1}X_1 \tag{1.9b}$$

(1.9a) and (1.9b) define output reaction functions for the two firms but with the addition of own firm transaction cost effects on output. Solving (1.9a) and (1.9b) simultaneously defines equilibrium firm outputs in terms of both firm transaction costs:

$$X_1 = \frac{(2a_1 - a_2)(a_0 - b_0)}{(2a_1)^2 - (a_2)^2} + \frac{2a_1(a_3 + b_1)}{(2a_1)^2 - (a_2)^2}C_{T1} - \frac{a_2(a_3 + b_1)}{(2a_1)^2 - (a_2)^2}C_{T2} \tag{1.9c}$$

$$X_2 = \frac{(2a_1 - a_2)(a_0 - b_0)}{(2a_1)^2 - (a_2)^2} + \frac{2a_1(a_3 + b_1)}{(2a_1)^2 - (a_2)^2}C_{T2} - \frac{a_2(a_3 + b_1)}{(2a_1)^2 - (a_2)^2}C_{T1} \tag{1.9d}$$

Substituting (1.9c) into (1.8b) and (1.9d) into (1.8d) defines transaction cost reaction functions for the two firms:

$$C_{T1} = \frac{(2a_1)^2 - (a_2)^2 - (a_3 + b_1)(2a_1 - a_2)(a_0 - b_0)}{2a_1(a_3 + b_1)^2} + \frac{a_2}{2a_1}C_{T2} \tag{1.9e}$$

$$C_{T2} = \frac{(2a_1)^2 - (a_2)^2 - (a_3 + b_1)(2a_1 - a_2)(a_0 - b_0)}{2a_1(a_3 + b_1)^2} + \frac{a_2}{2a_1}C_{T1} \tag{1.9f}$$

Discussion of (1.9e) and (1.9f) is undertaken in the context of Figure 1.1. In both the left and right-hand diagrams RF_1 and RF_2 are the two reaction functions that refer to respectively (1.9e) and (1.9f). The first point to note about the reaction functions is their positive slope defined by $a_2/2a_1$. We will comment shortly on possible implications here. If we assume, for the moment, a follower–follower analysis, equilibrium transaction

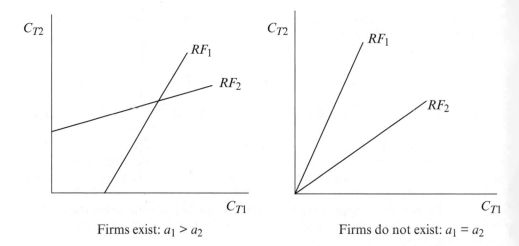

Figure 1.1   Transaction cost reaction functions

costs exist where the reaction functions intersect at some positive transaction costs for both firms. In the left-hand diagram the positive intercept implies that firms can exist. In the right-hand diagram the non-positive intercept implies there is no equilibrium with positive firm size and so the two firms cannot exist.

The difference between the two parts of Figure 1.1 is summarized in terms of the relative sizes of a_1 and a_2. To see the logic here we can observe from (1.9e) and (1.9f) that the denominator of the intercept must be positive. It follows that the intercept difference shown in the two sides of Figure 1.1 depends on the numerator. Using (1.9e) or (1.9f) the left-hand diagram requires:

$$\frac{(2a_1)^2 - (a_2)^2}{2a_1 - a_2} > (a_3 + b_1)(a_0 - b_0) \tag{1.9g}$$

To understand the implications of (1.9g) we can first use earlier discussion and observe that long-run firm viability requires $a_0 > b_0$. We will not reproduce here the discussion of short-run viability with large transaction costs and $a_0 < b_0$ and instead assume long-run non-negative profits. It follows that a necessary condition for the relevance of the left-hand diagram, and hence the possible existence of firms, is that the left-hand side of (1.9g) is positive. This latter condition is only possible with $a_1 > a_2$ as stated in the diagram.

We can offer an intuitive explanation of the existence of firms requiring $a_1 > a_2$ in the following way. Referring back to the demand functions (1.5a) and (1.5b) $a_1 > a_2$ implies that product differentiation exists. With product homogeneity $a_1 = a_2$ hence the left-hand side of (1.9g) is zero with the implication that the existence of firms requires that the right-hand side of (1.9g) is negative. The latter is not possible if we assume non-negative long-run profits. This importance of product differentiation can be explained in the following terms. The benefits of transaction cost expenditures on demand must be realizable as increased profitability. With product homogeneity such expenditures can be viewed as public goods with the benefits accruing to all firms rather than the individual firms undertaking the expenditures.

This reasoning suggests a strategic motive for the existence of firms. It is perhaps relevant to cite earlier discussion of Williamson's view that strategizing is unimportant for the firm. But the discussion here, by linking the economics of the firm and the theory of the firm comes to a somewhat different conclusion. The interpretation offered here of the left-hand side of Figure 1.1 is more consistent with the neo-Austrian dynamic transaction cost literature or the dynamic competence literature. The organizational expenditures required to promote long-run progress must promote long-run profitability. In these literatures the link between expenditures and profits is based on such factors as first-mover advantages, tacit knowledge and so on. Given the formal logic used here an equivalent link requires product differentiation. But a strict equivalence between dynamic approaches to the firm and the strategic perspective offered here cannot be taken too far. There are two obvious differences: (1) a comparative static equilibrium analysis rather than process reasoning and (2) the assumption here of a follower–follower model that is not obviously consistent with entrepreneurship and dynamic firm leadership. Difference (1) is a fundamental characteristic of the methodologies but difference (2) can be accommodated, to some extent, by moving beyond a follower–follower framework as suggested below.

Before considering a transaction cost leader–follower framework a few remaining issues can be taken up. First, as with earlier discussion we can create a link between the analysis presented here and earlier discussion of life-cycle models. Earlier discussion emphasized that as a life cycle matures there is a shift from process to product innovation. This reasoning therefore implies increased product differentiation as life cycles mature. In terms of (1.9e) and (1.9f) and the left-hand side of Figure 1.1, increased product differentiation implies increased intercept and slope of the reaction functions. In turn these changes suggest an increase in equilibrium transaction costs, that is, an increase in firm size. Intuitively, increased product differentiation increases returns to transaction cost expenditures. The resulting change in firm size is also emphasized in life-cycle analysis. Hence the strategic transaction cost model presented here has an important connection with the empirically based life-cycle analysis.

The second issue that can be briefly explored concerns the notion of transaction cost economizing, an important principle of conventional (non-strategic) transaction cost analysis (Williamson, 1985). The problems here can be considered in the context of the left-hand side of Figure 1.1. If, for example, the second firm does not exist that is, $C_{T2} = 0$ we have a single firm analysis as considered earlier. In the diagram setting $C_{T2} = 0$ suggests that profit-maximizing C_{T1} is where RF_1 cuts the horizontal X axis; this is the single firm (non-strategic) solution. The addition of the second firm increases firm and industry transaction costs. In short we cannot assume that competition automatically reduces transaction costs when we take account of the links between the economics of the firm and the theory of the firm.

The third issue concerns the final part of the strategic solution. The details of the algebra are unnecessary here given the nature of the current discussion. But intuitively the solution is straightforward. From the left-hand side of Figure 1.1 profit-maximizing equilibrium transaction costs are defined for both firms where RF_1 and RF_2 intersect. These C_{T1} and C_{T2} can be substituted into (1.9c) and (1.9d) to define firm output levels.

Hence the system can be solved. For illustrative purposes we can use an equivalent parameterization to that used above: $a_0 = 5$, $a_1 = 0.5$, $a_2 = 0.1$, $a_3 = 0.1$, $b_0 = 1$, $b_1 = 0.1$. Given these values we can specify the transaction cost reaction functions. Using (1.9e) and (1.9f):

$$C_{T1} = 6.75 + 0.1C_{T2} \qquad\qquad (1.9e')$$

$$C_{T2} = 6.75 + 0.1C_{T1} \qquad\qquad (1.9f')$$

Solving the simultaneous equations: $C_{T1} = C_{T2} = 7.5$. Using these equilibrium transaction costs in (1.9c) and (1.9d):

$$X_1 = X_2 = 3.636 + 0.202*7.5 - 0.020*7.5 = 5 \qquad\qquad (1.9c')$$

Hence, using (1.7a) and (1.7b), firm profits are: $\pi_1 = \pi_2 = 5$.

This solution can be used as a stepping stone to one final aspect of the discussion. Earlier the strategic perspective suggested here was linked, with qualifications, to competence and entrepreneurial approaches to the firm. One qualification involved the follower–follower framework underlying Figure 1.1. While this framework has facilitated the development of useful insights it is straightforward to extend it to cover the possibility of firm organizational leadership. Intuitively a leader firm can use its transaction cost decisions to influence a follower firm. It is most straightforward to do this using the parameterization just adopted. In addition we will assume firm 1 is the leader. We can solve the leader–follower model in a somewhat standard manner. In terms of abstract theory firm 1 uses firm 2 transaction cost and output reaction functions to predict responses to firm 1 behaviour. This is solved in the standard way by substituting the reaction functions into firm 1's profit function. Using parameter values we can re-write the profit function (1.7a):

$$\pi_1 = 5X_1 - 0.5X_1^2 - 0.1X_1X_2 + 0.1C_{T1}X_1 - [X_1 - 0.1C_{T1}X_1 + C_{T1}] \qquad (1.7a')$$

Using parameter values along with (1.9d) we substitute for X_2 in (1.7a'). In addition we use (1.9f') to substitute for C_{T2}. After simplification the leader's profit function is then:

$$\pi_1 = 3.65X_1 - 0.5X_1^2 + 0.2C_{T1}X_1 - C_{T1} \qquad\qquad (1.7a'')$$

Formulation (1.7a'') is solved as a single firm model using the method discussed above:

$$\frac{\partial \pi_1}{\partial X_1} = 3.65 - X_1 + 0.2C_{T1} = 0 \qquad\qquad (1.10a)$$

$$\frac{\partial \pi_1}{\partial TC_1} = 0.2X_1 - 1 = 0 \qquad\qquad (1.10b)$$

The solution suggests that $C_{T1} = 6.75$ and using firm 2's reaction function (1.9f') $C_{T2} = 7.45$. These transaction cost levels are compared to 7.5 in the follower–follower version

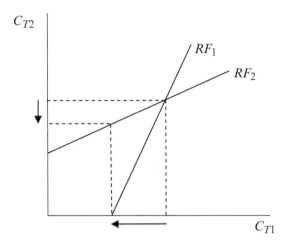

Figure 1.2   Transaction cost leader–follower solution

of the model. Because of the parameterization used here the leader firm sets transaction costs as if it is a monopolist, at a level that would occur if $C_{T2} = 0$: see (1.9e'). This leader–follower solution is depicted in Figure 1.2. Although it is based on a specific parameterization the resulting order of change shown in the diagram is a generalizable result. The strategic leadership involves a *reduction* in transaction costs for both firms but particularly for the leader firm. The leader firm can economize on transaction costs knowing that the follower firm will simply react to this. The leader firm basically exploits the reactions of the follower firm, an aspect of transaction cost economics that is apparently lacking in the literature. The leader–follower analysis suggested here is closer to the internalization transaction cost literature (as surveyed in Chapter 14 and 15 of this volume) used to analyse multinational companies. The internalization decision can be viewed as an act of strategic leadership, to exploit unique firm advantages, that economizes on organizational costs.

Continuing with the leader–follower solution, using the output reaction functions we find that $X_1 = X_2 = 5$. This invariance of firm outputs is based on the characteristics of the model and parameterization used here as discussed earlier. The profit for firm 1 is (using (1.7a'') 5.75, that is, as we would expect strategic leadership increases profits. For the follower firm we use firm 2's profit function with the assumed parameter values and find $\pi_2 = 5$, that is, the follower is no worse off. This latter result is a consequence of the parameterization and the assumed linearity of the model. Hence it is not a generalizable result.

1.5   OUTLINE OF THE VOLUME

The rest of this volume is organized as follows. In Part II there are a number of shorter 'background' essays. The intention here is to present brief surveys of key founding writers on the firm. The writers covered are not intended to present an exhaustive historical survey, as this would involve a handbook in its own right. Instead, the intention is to link the work of founding writers on the firm to modern understanding. The essays in the other six parts are intended to cover longer surveys of important topics on the theory and economics of the firm. Part III considers equilibrium and new institutional theories. Note that the topics covered here are guided by already existing handbooks, or equivalent, published by Edward Elgar. These already existing volumes cover in a comprehensive manner transaction cost and more generally new institutional theory. But in many of the chapters in the current volume the obvious importance of transaction costs is reflected in the discussion in a more applied way. For the same reasons there is no single chapter on entrepreneurship. The essay on agency theory and firm governance (Chapter 11) could have equally appeared in Part VI as a 'modern issue' but the balance of the contents suggested the current position. The same logic applies to Chapter 12 on hybrid governance. While this is usually considered a topic in transaction cost economics, as reflected in the current chapter, it is also a key 'modern issues' topic that reflects the overall emphasis here of bridge-building between the economics and theory of the firm. Finally in Part III, Chapter 13 is included because it reflects a gap in many discussions of the economics of the firm. Consideration of the transaction cost empirical work recognizes the importance of the bridge-building suggested here.

Part IV of the volume includes four essays on the multinational firm. This reflects the importance of this topic as a key modern issue. But the balance of the volume suggests a separate section on this topic rather than an overly long Part VI. In addition to a contextual discussion (Chapter 14) there is a review of internalization theory (Chapter 15) and also consideration of how the institutional contexts of Japan and Europe have affected the firm (Chapters 16 and 17). Part V surveys various topics under the general heading of dynamic approaches to the firm: Edith Penrose and George Richardson (Chapter 18); Nelson and Winter revisited (Chapter 19); modern resource-based theory(ies) (Chapter 20); and the cognitive theory of the firm (Chapter 21). The way in which these chapters are linked into the overall philosophy of this volume should be clear from earlier discussion in this introductory chapter.

Parts VI and VII cover 12 chapters on what are called 'modern issues' and 'firm strategies'. These two parts reflect the earlier suggestion that the potential complexity of real firms, involving the interaction between the economics and theory of the firm, can be rendered tractable by considering particular issues and strategies. In Part VI there are discussions that revisit Chandler (Chapter 22); consider the topic of financialization and the firm (Chapter 23); the analysis of firm growth (Chapter 24); corporate governance again (Chapter 25) but this time in the particular context of innovation and executive pay; innovation platforms and the knowledge-intensive firm (Chapter 26); and small firms (Chapter 27). In Part VII the various firm strategies covered are mergers and acquisitions (Chapter 28); R&D and the firm (Chapter 29); vertical relationships in the context of novelty (Chapter 30); product innovation (Chapter 31); modularity (Chapter 32); and innovation networks (Chapter 33).

The final section of the volume reflects the view suggested above that real firms do not constitute a closed system. The chapters in Part VIII open the analysis of real firms to the topic of economic policy. Here the five essays cover cartel and monopoly policy (Chapter 34); R&D and industrial policy (Chapter 35); entrepreneurship and policy (Chapter 36); regulation and networks (Chapter 37); and venture capitalism (Chapter 38). To reiterate earlier discussion, the various chapters are collectively intended to create bridges between the economics and theory of the firm and so reflect an important development in firm analysis.

REFERENCES

Abernathy, W. and K. Clark (1985), 'Innovation: mapping the winds of creative destruction', *Research Policy*, **14**(1), 3–22.

Abernathy, W. and J. Utterback (1978), 'Patterns of industrial innovation', *Technology Review*, **80**(7), 41–7.

Barnard, C. (1938), *The Functions of the Executive*, Cambridge, MA: Harvard University Press (reprinted 1968).

Bresnahan, T. and D. Raff (1991), 'Intra-industry heterogeneity and the great depression: the American motor vehicles industry, 1929–1935', *Journal of Economic History*, **51**(2), 317–31.

Casson, M. (1997), *Information and Organization: A New Perspective on the Theory of the Firm*, Oxford: Oxford University Press.

Chandler, A.D. (1977), *The Visible Hand: The Managerial Revolution in American Business*, Cambridge, MA: Harvard University Press.

Chandler, A.D. (1990), *Scale and Scope: The Dynamics of Industrial Capitalism*, Cambridge, MA: Belknap Press.

Coase, R. (1937), 'The nature of the firm', *Economica*, **4**(16), 386–405.

Coase, R. (1972), 'Industrial organization: a proposal for research', in V. Fuchs (ed.), *Policy Issues and Research: Opportunities in Industrial Organization*, New York: NBER, pp.59–73, reproduced in O. Williamson and S. Masten (eds), *Transaction Costs: Critical Writings* (1995), Aldershot, UK and Brookfield, VT, USA: Edward Elgar.

Coase, R. (1988), 'How should economists choose?', in *Ideas, their Origins and their Consequences*, Washington: American Enterprise Institute.

Coase, R. (1991), 'The institutional structure of production', Nobel lecture, 9 December 1991, reproduced in O. Williamson and S. Masten (eds), *Transaction Costs: Critical Writings* (1995), Aldershot, UK and Brookfield, VT, USA: Edward Elgar.

Coase, R. (1993a), 'The nature of the firm', in O. Williamson and S. Winter (eds), *The Nature of the Firm: Origins, Evolution and Development*, New York and Oxford: Oxford University Press.

Coase, R. (1993b), 'The nature of the firm: meaning', in O. Williamson and S. Winter (eds), *The Nature of the Firm: Origins, Evolution and Development*, Oxford and New York: Oxford University Press, pp.48–60.

Coase, R. (1993c), 'Coase on Posner on Coase', *Journal of Institutional and Theoretical Economics*, **149**(1), 96–8, reproduced in O. Williamson and S. Masten (eds), *Transaction Costs: Critical Writings* (1995), Aldershot, UK and Brookfield, VT, USA: Edward Elgar.

Coase, R. (1998), 'The new institutional economics', *American Economic Review*, **88**(2), 72–4.

Dietrich, M. (1994), *Transaction Cost Economics and Beyond: Towards a New Economics of the Firm*, London: Routledge.

Dietrich, M. and J. Krafft (2011), 'Firm development as an integrated process: with evidence from the General Motors–Fisher Body case', *Journal of Evolutionary Economics*, **21**(4), 665–86.

Fabricant, S. (1952), *The Trend of Government Activity in the United States Since 1900*, with the assistance of Robert E. Lipsey, New York: National Bureau of Economic Research.

Foss, N. (1993), 'Theories of the firm: contractual and competence perspectives', *Journal of Evolutionary Economics*, **3**(2), 126–44.

Fransman, M. (1999), *Visions of Innovation: The Firm and Japan*, Oxford and New York: Oxford University Press.

Gort, M. (1962), *Diversification and Integration in American Industry*, New York: National Bureau of Economic Research.

Gort, M. and S. Klepper (1982), 'Time paths in the diffusion of product innovations', *Economic Journal*, **92**(367), 630–53.

Jovanovic, B. and G. McDonald (1994), 'The life cycle of a competitive industry', *Journal of Political Economy*, **102**(2), 322–47.

Klepper, S. (1996), 'Entry, exit, growth and innovation over the product life cycle', *American Economic Review*, **86**(3), 562–83.

Klepper, S. (1997), 'Industry life cycles', *Industrial and Corporate Change*, **6**(1), 145–81.

Krafft, J. (2010), 'Favouring entry and limiting exit: how knowledge can shape the evolution of the info-communications industry', *Technological Forecasting and Social Change*, **77**(2), 265–78.

Krafft, J., F. Quatraro and P. Saviotti (2011), 'The knowledge base evolution in biotechnology: a social network analysis', *Economics of Innovation and New Technology*, **20**(5), 1–31.

Langlois, R. (2007), *The Dynamics of Industrial Capitalism: Schumpeter, Chandler and the New Economy*, London: Routledge.

Marshall, A. ([1890] 1925), 'Some aspects of competition', reprinted in A.C. Pigou (ed.), *Memorials of Alfred Marshall*, London: Macmillan.

Marshall, A. (1920), *Principles of Economics*, London: Macmillan.

McKelvey, M. (1996), *Evolutionary Innovations: The Business of Biotechnology*, Oxford and New York: Oxford University Press.

Mitchell, W. (1995), 'Medical diagnostic imaging manufacturers', in G. Carroll and M. Hannan (eds), *Organizations in Industry*, Oxford: Oxford University Press.

Morroni, M. (1992), *Production Process and Technical Change*, Cambridge, UK: Cambridge University Press.

Morroni, M. (2006), *Knowledge, Scale and Transactions in the Theory of the Firm*, Cambridge, UK: Cambridge University Press.

Mueller, D. (1990), *The Dynamics of Company Profits*, Cambridge, UK: Cambridge University Press.

Mueller, D. (1997), 'First-mover advantages and path-dependence', *International Journal of Industrial Organization*, **15**(6), 827–50.

Nelson, R. (1959), *Merger Movements in American Industry*, New York: National Bureau of Economic Research.

Nelson, R. and S. Winter (1982), *An Evolutionary Theory and Economic Change*, Cambridge MA: Harvard University Press.

Nooteboom, B. (2004), 'Governance and competence: how can they be combined?', *Cambridge Journal of Economics*, **28**(4), 505–26.

Penrose, E. (1959), *The Theory of the Growth of the Firm*, Oxford: Basil Blackwell.

Posner, Richard A. (1993), 'The New Institutional Economics Meets Law and Economics', *Journal of Institutional and Theoretical Economics*, **149**(1), 73–87.

Richardson, G. (1972), 'The organization of industry', *Economic Journal*, **82**(327), 883–96.

Saviotti, P. (1998), 'On the dynamics of appropriability of tacit and of codified knowledge', *Research Policy*, **26**(7–8), 843–56.

Schumpeter, J. ([1912] 1934), *The Theory of Economic Development*, Cambridge MA: Harvard University Press.

Schumpeter, J. (1942), *Capitalism, Socialism and Democracy*, New York: Harper.

Teece, D.J., R. Rumelt, G. Dosi and S. Winter (1994), 'Understanding corporate coherence; theory and evidence', *Journal of Economic Behavior & Organization*, **23**(1), 1–30.

Van Dijk, M. (1998), 'Industry life cycles in Dutch manufacturing', Working Paper, Center for Research of Economic Micro-Data (CeReM) of Statistics Netherlands.

Williamson, O. (1985), *The Economic Institutions of Capitalism: Firms, Markets and Relational Contracting*, New York: Free Press.

Williamson O. (1991), 'Strategizing, economizing, and economic organization', *Strategic Management Journal*, **12**(2), 75–94.

PART II

BACKGROUND

2 The obscure firm in the *Wealth of Nations*
Michael H. Best

> For the pattern is more than the sum of the threads;
> it has its own symbolic design of which the threads know nothing.
> (Arthur Koestler, in Faulks, 1996)

2.1 INTRODUCTION

Adam Smith did not elaborate a theory of the firm. He did, however, go inside the work-shop to explore production, which was the starting point of his economic masterpiece *An Inquiry into the Nature and Causes of the Wealth of Nations*.[1] Is there conceptual space within Smith's economic landscape in which a nascent theory of the firm might be discovered? If so, what are its functions and characteristics?

Three core concepts are central to Smith's economic perspective, and so to characterizing a latent concept of the firm in Smith's work. Behind each core concept is a dynamic process. First is the principle of the division of labor, which focuses attention on increasing differentiation of skills, improvement in the 'arts' (contemporary term for technical knowledge), and advances in the 'productive power of labor'. Second is the 'invisible hand', a metaphor for the processes by which overall coordination or organizational order is achieved within a decentralized economic system. Third is capital accumulation. Smith articulated the links and feedback effects between profits and capital in the work-shop and the growth in aggregate capital and national output. The chapter examines each of these with a view to characterizing the otherwise obscure functions and roles of the firm in Smith's economic landscape.

2.2 THE PRINCIPLE OF INCREASING SPECIALIZATION

Adam Smith begins the *Wealth of Nations* (*WN*) with a description of the division of labor in a pin factory. The division of labor is not, in the words of George Stigler, a quaint practice of eighteenth-century pin factories; it is a fundamental principle of economic organization (Stigler, 1951, p. 193). Smith's purpose was to illustrate the leveraged impact on output of organizing a workshop according to the logic of the division of labor.[2]

In the pin factory example, ten persons organized into 'a proper division and combination of. . .[18] different operations' and. . .'educated to this particular business' could make 'upwards of 48,000 pins in a day' or 4800 per person but which 'wrought separately and independently. . .they certainly could not each of them have made twenty, perhaps not one pin in a day' (*WN*, p. 15).

Smith chose the example of pin-making to illustrate the economic significance of the division of labor, not because it was exceptional (in fact it was increasingly widespread) but because it was a clear example of the organizational source of a rich nation's wealth. It is also an early example of *product engineering* before such knowledge was codified and widely deployed.

Smith's account of the pin factory can be read as an implicit five-stage organizational procedure for increasing labor productivity. A product's architecture is first subject to decomposition into constituent parts. Second, each part is subject to methodical examination and decomposition into a sequence of the activities required to convert it from raw material to finished item. Next each separate activity is examined and simplified to economize on time, to characterize the requisite skills, and to identify opportunities for introducing machines to improve performance. The fourth stage is to reorganize and lay out the workshop to achieve economies of speed or time (throughput efficiency in modern parlance) in the conversion of raw material into finished product.[3] Finally, the workforce has to be trained according to the requirements of the diverse, newly defined and highly specialized activities. These stages outline a procedure to apply the logic of the division of labor to virtually all workshops.

Smith stresses the general applicability of the division of labor as a means of increasing the productivity of labor:[4]

> In every other art and manufacture, the effects of the division of labour are similar to what they are in this very trifling one; though, in many of them, the labour can neither be so much subdivided, nor reduced to so great a simplicity of operation. The division of labour, however, so far as it can be introduced, occasions, in every art, a proportionable increase in the productive powers of labour. (*WN*, p. 15)

The performance-enhancing effects of the division of labor was not Adam Smith's discovery. William Petty illustrated the concept with tailoring, watch-making, and Dutch ship-making as well as applying it to the surveying of Ireland in the previous century (Hutchison, 1988; Peaucelle, 2006).[5] For Smith, however, the division of labor was not confined to the workshop.

To explore the division of labor in the greater society, Smith takes the reader inside the product to the embodied physical materials. The examination of the *product architecture* in terms of the constituent materials reveals the interconnectedness of a vast range of specialist labor and activities that are coordinated in the making of even the simplest product.

Smith illustrates with a woolen coat 'the joint produce of a great multitude of labour' (*WN*, p. 22) for which he provides a page and a half of specialized skills. Again, Smith is not claiming novelty here. John Locke, in the previous century, used the example of a loaf of bread to capture the interconnectedness of production:[6]

> Twould be a strange catalogue of things, that industry provided and made use of, about every loaf of bread, before it came to our use, if we could trace them; iron, wood, leather, bark timber, stone, bricks, coals, lime cloth, dyeing, drugs, pitch, tar, masts, ropes, and all the materials made use of in the ship, that brought any of the commodities used by any of the workmen, to any part of the work: all of which it would be almost impossible, at least too long, to reckon up. (*WN*, p. 23)

Smith's contribution was to reveal how the division of labor in the two spheres, inside the workhouse and in the greater economy, are part of a single mutual adjustment process that underlies economic progress. He did not conceptualize the workshop and the 'market' as alternative modes of coordination of economic activities. His focus was on the *interconnectedness*, interplay, and overlap of the divisions of labor within and outside the workhouse in driving technological improvements, increasing knowledge, and organizational change, all of which are driven by competitive pressures to reduce costs from organizationally and technically more advanced other manufactories.

Machine-making, in particular, is a new source of increased specialization that expands the population of interconnected workhouses and, at the same time, contributes to the ongoing innovation processes within workhouses.[7] Smith combines the process of increases in the division of labor with the invention of specialized machinery:[8]

> What takes place among the labourers in a particular workhouse, takes place, for the same reason, among those of a great society. The greater their number, the more they naturally divide themselves into different classes and subdivisions of employment. More heads are occupied in inventing the most proper machinery for executing the work of each, and it is, therefore, more likely to be invented. (*WN*, p. 104)

The process of establishing a machine-making industry enhances a nation's innovation capability, but Smith's incipient theory of industrial innovation has yet another arrow in its quiver: the incorporation of science into the nation's division of labor. And in the process the nation's stock of knowledge increases:

> All the improvements in machinery, however, have by no means been the invention of those who had occasion to use the machines. Many improvements have been made by the ingenuity of the makers of machines, when to make them became the business of a peculiar trade; and some by that of those who are called philosophers or men of speculation, whose trade it is, not to do any thing, but to observe every thing; and who, upon that account, are often capable of combining together the powers of the most distant and dissimilar objects. In the progress of society, philosophy or speculation becomes, like every other employment, the principal and sole trade and occupation of a particular class of citizens. Like every other employment too, it is subdivided into a great number of different branches, each of which affords occupation to a particular tribe or class of philosophers; and this subdivision of employment in philosophy, as well as in every other business improves dexterity, and saves time. Each individual becomes more expert in his own peculiar branch, more work is done upon the whole, and the quantity of science is considerably increased by it. (*WN*, pp. 21–2)

The competitive process amongst producers is the driver of organizational and technical improvements, ever lower prices and economic progress. Increases in demand, given competition and 'improvements of art', generate lower not higher prices in the long run. In Smith's words:

> [T]hough in the beginning it may sometimes raise the price of goods, never fails to lower it in the long run. It encourages production, and thereby increases the competition of the producers, who, in order to undersell one another, *have recourse to new divisions of labor and new improvements of art*, which might never otherwise have been thought of. (*WN*, p. 748, italics added)

It is critical to note that lower prices are not a consequence of increasing returns to scale for an unchanging process of production, but of the *adaptation of process* to meet the *opportunities* of an increase in demand or an expanded market. Long before the arrival of the managerial enterprise, Smith foreshadows a Penrosian iterative dynamic between the emerging market opportunities and cumulatively advancing production capabilities (Penrose, 1959; Loasby, 2002).

2.3   THE COORDINATION CHALLENGE: SPONTANEOUS ORDER

Albert Hirschman reviewed the early arguments for capitalism before Smith's time. The strongest arguments were tied to the hope that the new economic order would prevent tyranny and foster a stable and just political order. Bernard Mandeville was the first to proclaim ([1714] 1924) that the individual's pursuit of private interest was not a vice but a virtue; not contradictory to, but a means of, achieving the public interest. The expansion of commerce was a key ingredient. Passions like 'greed, avarice, or love of lucre' that had been previously condemned could now be 'usefully employed to oppose and bridle such other passions as ambition, lust for power or sexual lust' (Hirschman, 1971, p.41).

The thinkers of the Scottish Enlightenment were early advocates of what is today called emergence, the idea that an 'interconnected system of relatively simple elements self-organizes to form more intelligent, more adaptive, higher-level behavior' (Johnson, 2001a).[9] Order is achieved but not as a consequence of design: Many human institutions are the 'result of human action, but not the execution of human design' in the words of Adam Ferguson, Smith's contemporary Scottish moral philosopher (Ferguson, 1767, p.187).

Herein lies the central concern and defining challenge of the then emerging discipline of economics. Smith proclaims 'Without the assistance and coordination of many thousands, the very meanest person in a civilized country could not be provided, even according to, what we very falsely imagine, the easy and simple manner in which he is commonly accommodated' (*WN*, p.23).

For even the simplest product the 'number of people of whose industry a part. . .has been employed. . .exceeds all *computation*' (*WN*, p.22, my italics). How are production activities coordinated across a large and increasing differentiated division of labor for even the simplest product?

Smith applied the 'private vice and public virtue' theme to a vision of the market economy as a bottom-up, self-regulating system that 'spontaneously' solves the computation problem and thereby extends the division of labor, the source of the progress. The pursuit of avarice is converted from a deadly sin to the driver of economic progress. Chapter II begins with the following paragraph:

> This division of labour, from which so many advantages are derived, is not originally the effect of any human wisdom, which foresees and intends that general opulence to which it gives occasion. It is the necessary, though very slow and gradual, consequence of a certain propensity in human nature which has in view no such extensive utility; the propensity to truck, barter, and exchange one thing for another. (*WN*, p.13)

He adds: 'it is this same trucking disposition which *originally* gives occasion to the division of labour' (*WN*, p.15, my italics).

The price system does the rest as if by 'invisible hand'. Without design or central direction, price adjustments coordinate the activities of millions of individual decision-makers. The Austrian school of economics, led by Carl Menger, Ludwig von Mises, and Friedrich Hayek, would later conceptualize price as information: 'Through it [the price system] not only a division of labor but also a coordinated utilization of resources based on an equally divided knowledge has become possible' (Hayek, 1945, p. 528).

The price system, like language, is an outcome of 'spontaneous order'. Hayek amplifies: 'man has been able to develop that division of labor on which our civilization is based because he happened to stumble upon a method which makes it possible'. He continues: 'The price system is just one of those formations which man has learned to use. . .after he stumbled upon it without understanding it' (ibid.).[10]

Smith's 'invisible hand', Hayek's 'spontaneous order', and emergence theory all involve interconnectedness amongst individuals within a population: birds flock, ants form colonies, and urbanites create neighborhoods. But there is a problem. The unit of analysis and behavior in complexity theory, as in the invisible hand, is the individual, not distributed groups of individuals.

The invisible hand as a decentralized information system is a powerful critique of central planning. It has been less successful as an account of economic systems populated by firms in which economies of scale persist, price competition is limited, and in which strategic behavior has consequences. Unlike individuals, once firms become big enough to influence prices in the market a split between private and public interest is the likely consequence.

Smith was clear that competition amongst producers was necessary to ensure the convergence of private and public interest. Otherwise dealers, a term Smith used for employers, could collude against the public interest: 'To widen the market and to narrow the competition, is always the interest of the dealers. To widen the market may frequently be agreeable enough to the interest of the public; but to narrow the competition must always be against it' (*WN*, p. 267). This conundrum has bedeviled economics and led to constructs of the firm that do not conflict with the price competition requirements of the invisible hand. Marshall's construct of the representative firm became the archetypal approach to economic theories of the firm: a Platonic mode of representing full systems by a single essence or exemplar – and then studying how this entity adjusts to external parameter shifts (Marshall [1890] 1920). The assumptions of competition over price amongst numerous, uniform firms engaged in the same activity meet the requirements of a mathematically 'rigorous' theory of price determination and allocative efficiency and a powerful teaching tool, but at a cost.

The construct of the representative firm is not consistent with the logic of increasing differentiation and specialization amongst firms and, if not, suggests that the concept of spontaneous order may require rethinking (see also Chapter 4 by Jacques-Laurent Ravix in this book). An alternative approach is developed below, one in which the concept of spontaneous order plays a role as a self-organizing, bottom-up information system that does address the computation problem but which does not sacrifice the role of either increasing specialization or heterogeneous firms in both understanding economic progress and fostering macroeconomic order. But we must detour briefly to bring capital accumulation into the economic landscape.

2.4 CAPITAL ACCUMULATION AND ECONOMIC PROGRESS

In the business world observed by Smith, the size of enterprises was limited by stock available to employ labor in advance of product revenue. This was not only an observation about the growth and size of workshops but a link that allowed Smith to integrate a macroeconomic growth story driven by capital accumulation with a dynamic microeconomic story of increasing differentiation and technological change. The extension of the division of labor, for Smith, was limited by availability of stock.

At the level of the nation, growth in stock (capital) and output are related: 'The quantity of industry. . .not only increases in every country with the increase of the stock which employs it, but, in consequence of that increase, the same quantity of industry produces a much greater quantity of work' (*WN*, p. 277). The accumulation of stock precedes and advances with the extensions in the division of labor: 'till some stock be produced there can be no division of labour, and before a division of labour take place there can be very little accumulation of stock: 'As the accumulation of stock must. . .be previous to the division of labour, so labour can be more and more subdivided in proportion only as stock is previously more and more accumulated' (*WN*, pp. 276–7).

The historically progressive role of employers as a class takes shape:[11]

> [E]mployers constitute the third order, that of those who live by profit. It is the stock that is employed for the sake of profit, which puts into motion the greater part of the useful labour of every society. The plans and projects of the employers of stock regulate and direct all the most important operations of labour. (*WN*, p. 266)

The employer is driven by competitive pressure to foster improvements in production:

> As the accumulation of stock is previously necessary for carrying on this great improvement in the productive powers of labour. . . The person who employs his stock in maintaining labour, necessarily wishes to employ it in such a manner. . . He endeavors. . .to furnish [his workmen] with the best machines he can either invent or afford to purchase. His abilities in both these respects are generally in proportion to the extent of his stock, or to the number of people it can employ. (*WN*, p. 277)

Smith did not envision joint stock companies as an organizational advance. In the few comments he makes he describes them as inflexible.[12] In his words:

> The only trades which it seems possible for a joint stock company to carry on successfully, without an exclusive privilege, are those, of which all the operations are capable of being reduced to what it called a Routine, or to such a uniformity of method as admits of little or no variation. (*WN*, p. 756)

Smith's most scathing comments were targeted at the chartered East India Company and its complaints against competition: 'The miserable effects of which the company complained, were the cheapness of consumption and the encouragement given to production, precisely the two effects which it is the great business of political economy to promote' (*WN*, p. 748).

Smith's capital accumulation account of economic growth became the basis of macroeconomic growth theory. However, the lack of empirical support in growth-accounting exercises led Simon Kuznets and Moses Abramowitz to argue that the stock of 'capital' is made up of two asset classes, tangible and intangible. Forms of intangible capital include the 'infrastructure of the economies of scale and scope' such as 'corporate managerial structure' and 'business capability' (Kuznets, 1971, p. 2; Abramowitz, 1993, pp. 229–30).[13] Like Smith, these theorists do not treat technological progress as either exogenous or a 'residual'. Nevertheless the integration of business organization into theories of technological advance and growth remains a challenge.

2.5   ECONOMIC ORDER IN AN ECONOMY WITH FIRMS

What would a theory of the firm involve that is consistent with the three dynamic processes central to Smith's vision of the economy outlined above: increasing differentiation in the division of labor, spontaneous order or emergent properties of a self-organizing coordination system, and capital accumulation in which capital has both material and organizational dimensions?

The invisible hand is not the only form of coordination of economic activities in the *Wealth of Nations*. Smith's concept of production, and with it innovation, describes the division of labor within the workshop. Relations within the workshop are not mediated only by prices in a market. In fact, individuals who begin and end their working life with a single company will only enter into the labor market when joining the company. Yet, they will likely be party to processes that involve both the creation and unique combination of increasingly diverse skills. In this case, the firm mediates between the individual and the population of individuals in the economy.

Smith's description of the division of labor in the pin factory illustrates the potential productivity gains of organization: working 'separately and independently. . .they could not each of them have made twenty, perhaps not one pin in a day; that is, certainly, not the two hundred and fortieth, perhaps not the four thousand eight hundredth part of. . .a proper division and combination of their different operations' (*WN*, p. 15). By forming or joining a production organization an individual can participate in the productivity gains from applications of product engineering, the principle of flow (economies of speed), a *kanban* scheduling system, or the integration of R&D and new product development.[14] To engage in these activities requires cooperation and the enactment of organizational capabilities. Capability development is a function of firms.

The existence of firms, however, does not undermine the validity of the concept of spontaneous order in economic life. It extends it to new domains. The phenomenon of spontaneous order as a decentralized information system by which a complex order emerges from the bottom up can also apply to practices within very large managerial enterprises. The thousands of activities along Henry Ford's Highland Park production line, for example, were not coordinated by a central planner or scheduler. Instead the plant was laid out and continuously improved to meet the rule of equal cycle times for the production of every piece-part required to make a single car (Sorensen, 1957; Ohno [1976] 1988; Best, 2001, pp. 28–35). Organizing production according to the rule of equal cycle times was and is today a simple, locally based, decentralized rule that 'spontaneously' fosters throughput efficiency.[15] The institutional innovations associated with world class manufacturing, such as the *kanban* informational scheduling system were not designed to generate 'spontaneous order'. Initially, they were established to solve local problems. The desirable global outcomes led to such practices becoming operational protocols.

Here the firm is a mid-level aggregator of diverse skills and local information and a generator of new skills operating between, and overlapping with, individuals and the macroeconomy.[16] It is also a means by which organizational capabilities, such as product engineering and technology management become embedded in and transform the economy. But whilst such firms compete in the marketplace, it is not a market populated by isolated individuals driven by the 'propensity to truck, barter and exchange'.

Smith's concept of the interconnectedness of the internal and external divisions of labor in the economy suggests a second extension of the phenomenon of spontaneous order to inter-firm adjustment processes. Firms compete on the basis of distinctive capabilities, a strategy that is enhanced by an 'open-system' business model. This process, of increasing specialization and mutual adjustment amongst a 'networked' group of enterprises suggests the emergence of Marshallian 'industrial districts' of mutually cooperating enterprises. As each firm within the district adopts a strategy or business model of focus on core capability and partner for complementary capabilities, the networked group of companies will develop a collective capability of system integration.[17] Moreover, the population of technologically diverse companies can itself be a resource in the creation of new technologies and 'trades' or new sub-sectors of the economy.

Consequently, the same logic of increasing specialization and differentiation of labor within the workshop can be applied to increasing specialization and differentiation of capabilities amongst workshops or companies. This can be seen more clearly if the example shifts from that of 'trifling manufacturer', which Smith described as pin-making to say furniture-making or the personal computer industry. Here the production activities are sufficiently complex to suggest a potential for 'speciation' in the form of the spinning out of business units that specialize in a subset of activities of the mother company. The advantage of the new specialist firm may be the application of economies of speed, scale or scope not available within the mother company.

As the new workshop undertakes production, offering services to a range of customers, it will undergo the same innovation processes described by Smith's pin-making example. This sets in motion an internal and external dynamic process that both increases the market for the output of individual workshops and the opportunity for innovation amongst the group of companies that are collectively undergoing a process of increasing specialization and differentiation in skills and capabilities.

This bottom-up, self-organizing aspect of 'spontaneous order' is arguably as relevant to today's high-tech cities and in understanding the sustained competitiveness of cities such as Boston as to the early developments in the division of labor conceptualized by Smith.[18] In both cases the division of labor is not designed by anyone or any group.[19] The complex system is not even understood by any single individual. Each individual understands only a small part of the whole system. The function of markets is in aggregating this diverse information. In these accounts of connectedness, each individual operates according to simple rules.

The introduction of a population of firms, or a business system, into the story suggests a new concept of economic order in which firms count. Instead of spontaneous order mediated by prices alone we find a complex order or a multi-level concept of economic order. But this is true to Smith's ambition to combine a theory of increasing differentiation of skills with economic order; later theorists abandoned the economic process of increasing division of labor and conceptualized firms as homogeneous and technological change and innovation as exogenous to the 'laws of supply and demand'.[20]

The logic of increasing specialization and division of labor within and amongst firms suggests more complex and interactive adjustment processes than captured by the firm or market dichotomy in which the two are conceptualized as separate modes of coordination of the same standardized activities. Instead of a theory of the *firm* based on the plan or market dichotomy, we find in Smith the outlines of a theory of *firms* based on an iterative dynamic between the internal and external, inside and outside divisions of labor. Instead of homogeneous firms in a market, we see increasingly differentiated firms within a dynamic population of mutually adjusting companies.

2.6   CONCLUDING COMMENTS

Smith's economic perspective remains surprisingly relevant to understanding modern economies. Part of the reason is that he conceptualized the firm and the market not as alternative means of coordinating economic activities but as complementary institutions in fostering 'new divisions of labour and new improvements of arts' (*WN*, p. 748). Smith did not sacrifice the concepts required for understanding the sources of economic growth to the assumptions required for a market theory of optimal resource allocation.

For example, if capital is conceived not simply as a fungible asset but as a social entity, progress is enriched to encompass organizational capabilities. This suggests an early treatment of an evolutionary theory of firms in the *Wealth of Nations* that resonates with a Penrosian focus on the internal dynamics of growth in knowledge and application of the logic of increasing differentiation to a firm's technological capabilities. But, unlike Penrose, Smith's economic perspective envisioned growth of the individual production unit with adjustment processes in the growth of the economy as a whole; his concern was more an early statement about the sources of growth of a *population of 'networked' firms* than of the individual firm in isolation.

But the contribution of Smith was not simply that he focused attention on the sources of progress at the level of the economy but that his nascent concept of the firm, and therefore of inter-firm dynamics, was anchored in processes of increasing differentiation within the firm. He remains a pioneer in conceptualizing the economy in terms of the interplay between the division of labor inside and outside the firm.[21]

To Smith's credit, he went inside the firm to examine the sources of increased productivity in the organization of production. It is at the workshop level that the 'improvement in the arts' or technological advances are operationalized, complementary skills and capabilities are developed, and new inter-firm networks arise. The progress of nations can be read in terms of advances in and the diffusion of organizational capabilities of production as exemplified by product engineering in the pin factory. I would suggest that the application of the principle of interchangeability that defined the 'American system of manufacturers', the principle of flow as applied by Henry Ford, the concept of just-in-time pioneered at Toyota are consistent with Adam Smith's production-oriented economic perspective. Here the accumulation of capital represents advances in knowledge and technology embedded in and fostered by organizational capabilities.

The organization of production, for Smith, was not an independent, isolated process that took place inside the firm because each workshop was part of a system of interdependent workshops. The division of labor within any single workshop was, to paraphrase Koestler, like a single thread within a pattern about which each thread knows nothing. Or, to use another analogy, just as an individual's capacity for communication depends upon the pre-existence of a language, an individual's productivity in the workplace depends upon the extent of the division of labor and associated production capabilities. Smith's primacy to the division of labor in the *Wealth of Nations* implies the invisible hand was a concept for understanding the complex, self-organizing, bottom-up inter-relations of production and exchange.

From this reading of Smith his legacy may have been as profound in evolutionary biology as in conventional economics. The intellectual idea of the advantages of increasing diversity was driven home by Darwin. Not surprisingly, Darwin used the term division of labor, if in a different context: 'The advantage of diversification in the inhabitants of the same region is, in fact, the same as that of the physiological division of labour in the organs of the same individual body – a subject so well elucidated by Milne Edwards' (Darwin [1859] 1979, p. 158).[22,23]

Darwin's theory of natural selection drew from Thomas Malthus, an early economist (Marshall [1890] 1920, p. 240; Hodgson, 1993, p. 63). Some have claimed that the division of labor triggered Darwin's theory of increasing diversity; this is long debated.[24] But evolutionary biology does highlight the enduring importance of the economic principle of increasing differentiation of skills. It also highlights the critical importance of mutual adjustment processes within a population.

NOTES

1. All references are to Smith, A. ([1776] 1976), *An Inquiry into the Nature and Causes of the Wealth of Nations*, hereafter *WN*, edited by R.H. Campbell, A.S. Skinner and W.B. Todd, 2 Volumes, Oxford: Oxford University Press.
2. Smith's pin factory example was drawn from French sources (Hamowy, 1968; Peaucelle, 2006).
3. Strangely, Smith did not follow his French sources in using measures of time to illustrate the advances in each of the 18 stages of pin manufacturing; he instead used weight. For a definitive account and a possible explanation see Peaucelle (2006). It is worth noting that Alfred Chandler uses economies of speed and throughput, as distinct from economies of scale, to explain the organizational advantages of the 'visible hand' in production (1977) as did Henry Ford (Sorensen, 1957) and Taichi Ohno, creator of the Toyota Production System (1988).
4. 'In consequence of better machinery, of greater dexterity, and of a more division and distribution of work, all of which are the natural effects of improvement, a much smaller quantity of labour becomes requisite for executing any particular piece of work' (*WN*, p. 260).
5. Schumpeter (1954) writes with respect to Petty: 'On division of labour. . .we find all the essentials of what Adam Smith was to say of it, including its dependence upon the size of markets' (1954, p. 214). The idea goes back further: Xenophon's application of the principle of the division of labor to Athenian shoe-makers reads like modern day audits of shoe-making in Third World countries (Peaucelle, 2006, p. 498).
6. Campbell and Skinner offer Mandeville's account as perhaps the most amusing: 'A Man would be laugh'd at, that should discover Luxury in the plain Dress of a poor creature that walks along in a thick Parish Gown and a coarse Shirt underneath it; and yet what a number of People, how many different

Trades, and what a variety of Skill and Tools must be employed to have the most ordinary *Yorkshire* Cloth?' (*The Fable of the Bees*, 1723 edition, cited by Campbell, Skinner and Todd, editors, *WN*, p. 22).

7. A sub-population of machine-making workshops increases the inventive capabilities of the greater population. In a simpler economy, innovation is on a smaller scale. In the words of Smith: 'A great part of the machines made use of in those manufactures in which labour is most subdivided, were originally the inventions of common workmen, who, being each of them employed in some very simple operation, naturally turned their thoughts towards finding out easier and readier methods of performing it' (*WN*, p. 20).

8. 'Many improvements have been made by the ingenuity of the makers of the machines, when to make them became the business of a particular trade' (*WN*, p. 21).

9. 'Emergence is what happens when an interconnected system of relatively simple elements self-organizes to form more intelligent, more adaptive higher-level behavior. . . In. . .these systems, agents residing on one scale start producing behavior that lies a scale above them: ants create colonies, urbanites create neighborhoods' (Johnson, 2001a).

10. Lawrence Summers proclaims Hayek's place in modern economics: 'What's the single most important thing to learn from an economics course today? What I tried to leave my students with is the view that the invisible hand is more powerful than the [un]hidden hand. Things will happen in well-organized efforts without direction, controls, plans. That's the consensus among economists. That's the Hayek legacy' (quoted in Yergin and Stanislaw, 1998, pp. 150–51).

11. Employers are also referred to as 'Merchants and master manufacturers [who] are, in this order, the two classes of people who commonly employ the largest capitals' (*WN*, p. 266).

12. He lists the trades that might be appropriate for joint stock governance as banking, insurance, making and maintaining a canal, water supply.

13. In an oft-cited essay Abramowitz advanced the term social capabilities to explain comparative levels of productivity. These include 'organization and management of large-scale enterprise and with financial institutions' and 'well-established connections of [a nation's] science, technology and industry' (1986, pp. 388, 405).

14. *Kanban* is a visual, direct communication system that coordinates information needed at each work station. In the words of Taiichi Ohno, creator of the just-in-time system: 'A *kanban* ('tag') is a tool for managing and assuring just-in-time production, the first pillar of the Toyota production system' ([1976] 1988, p. 123).

15. The equal cycle time rule for mass production firms is an account of how large firms can achieve Toyota production system performance standards of cost, quality, and time; it is not a rule that meets the test of optimal resource allocation. The latter criterion is met by the equally simple rule that textbook firms follow to maximize profits: they increase output until the point at which marginal revenue equals marginal cost. Under conditions of perfect competition this will be synonymous with price equal to marginal cost. This is the global rule that establishes the optimum allocation of resources and it is spontaneously achieved by the invisible hand under certain conditions including that all firms are price takers.

16. The two populations are inter-related. For example, a company like DEC (Digital Equipment Corporation), which led in the development of a new product and industry (minicomputers) employed tens of thousands of individuals and in the process increased and advanced the diverse skills and technological capabilities within both the company and the region in which it operated. When such a company loses out to competitors, thousands of skilled individuals are thrown onto the labor 'market' where the population of individuals are coordinated via the price system as assumed by the metaphor of the invisible hand. This population of individuals forms a regionally distinctive labor pool to facilitate the formation and growth of new, as well as existing, companies and, in the process, extend the division of labor to yet new products and production techniques. In the process both skills and organizational capabilities are propagated cumulatively and collectively across the population of companies.

17. System integration signals the capability to develop new products and processes to take full advantage of technological change and market opportunities.

18. Referencing Jane Jacobs, Johnson writes that cities such as Boston 'have turned out to be incredibly useful at facilitating the sharing of ideas and information'. Such cities benefit from a critical mass of connections, a network that enables 'a group intelligence, instead of isolated group of smart people' (Johnson, 2001b, p. C6).

19. In the example of Boston, we find inter-regional competition based on distinctive organizations of industry. The idea is that regions can have similar industrial sectors but different extents to which the firms that constitute each regional sector have undergone mutual adjustment processes.

20. Marshall appealed to Smith's division of labor to argue 'The tendency to variation is a chief cause of progress' ([1890] 1920, p. 355).

21. Alfred Marshall drew on Smith's postulate that advances in productivity are a consequence of increasing specialization of labor combined with more 'intimate connections' integrating the increasingly differentiated activities ([1890] 1920, p. 241).
22. Milne-Edwards attributed his concept of 'physiological division of labour' to political economists (Schweber, 1980, p. 197).
23. According to Hodgson (1993, p. 55), Bernard Mandeville invented the term 'division of labor' to express the interconnectedness of this social arrangement. The inspiration was the complex but productive order of the social insects in his *The Fable of the Bees*. Public virtues can spring from private vices and social order and harmony can be derived even from separate individuals pursuing their self-interest. Hodgson adds 'in many respects Darwin is the culmination of a development which Mandeville more than any other man had started' (ibid.).
24. See Schweber (1980); Gordon (1989); Chapter 4, 'Political Economy and the Darwinian Revolution' (Hodgson, 1993); and Finch (2000).

REFERENCES

Abramovitz, M. (1986), 'Catching Up, Forging Ahead, and Falling Behind', *Journal of Economic History*, **46**(2), 385–406.
Abramovitz, M. (1993), 'The Search for Sources of Growth: Areas of Ignorance, Old and New', *The Journal of Economic History*, **53**(2), 217–43.
Best, M. (2001), *The New Competitive Advantage*, Oxford: Oxford University Press.
Chandler, A. (1977), *The Visible Hand*, Cambridge, MA: Harvard University Press.
Darwin, C. ([1859] 1979), *The Origin of Species*, New York: Random House.
Faulks, S. (1996), *The Fatal Englishman*, London: Hutchinson Radius.
Ferguson, A. (1767), *An Essay on the History of Civil Society*, London: Millar and Cadell.
Finch, J. (2000), 'Is post-Marshallian Economics an Evolutionary Research Tradition?' *European Journal History of Economic Thought*, **7**(3), 377–406.
Gordon, S. (1989), 'Darwin and Political Economy: The Connection Reconsidered', *Journal of the History of Biology*, **22**(3), 437–59.
Hamowy, R. (1968), 'Adam Smith, Adam Ferguson, and the Division of Labour', *Economica*, **35**(139), 249–59.
Hayek, F. (1945), 'The Use of Knowledge in Society', *The American Economic Review*, **35**(4), 519–30.
Hirschman, A. (1971), *The Passions and the Interests: Political Arguments for Capitalism Before its Triumph*, Princeton: Princeton University Press.
Hodgson, G. (1993), *Economics and Evolution: Bringing Life Back into Economics*, Ann Arbor: University of Michigan.
Hutchison, T. (1988), 'Petty on Policy, Theory and Method', in *Before Adam Smith: The Emergence of Political Economy 1662–1776*, Oxford: Basil Blackwell.
Johnson, S. (2001a), *Emergence: The Connected Lives of Ants, Brains, Cities, and Software*, New York: Scribner.
Johnson, S. (2001b), quoted in D. Denison, 'Tech Network Gives Local Firms a Competitive Advantage', *Boston Globe*, 3 December, C6.
Kuznets, S. (1971), 'Modern Economic Growth: Findings and Reflections', Nobel Prize Lecture, 11 December.
Loasby, B. (2002), 'The Significance of Penrose's Theory for the Development of Economics', in C. Pitelis (ed.), *The Growth of the Firm: The Legacy of Edith Penrose*, Oxford: Oxford University Press, pp. 45–60.
Mandeville, B. ([1714] 1924), *The Fable of the Bees: or Private Vices, Public Benefits*, edited by F.B. Kaye, Oxford: Clarendon.
Marshall, A. ([1890] 1920), *Principles of Economics*, eighth edition, London and New York: Macmillan.
Ohno, T. ([1976] 1988), *Toyota Production System: Beyond Large-scale Production*, Cambridge, MA: Productivity Press. The original Japanese edition, *Toyota seisan hōshiki*, is published by Diamond, Inc., Tokyo, Japan.
Peaucelle, J. (2006), 'Adam Smith's Use of Multiple References for his Pin Making Example', *European Journal of Economic Thought*, **13**(4), 489–512.
Penrose, E. (1959), *The Theory of the Growth of the Firm*, first edition, Oxford: Basil Blackwell and New York: John Wiley and Sons. Second edition (1980), Oxford: Basil Blackwell and New York: St. Martins. Revised edition (1995), Oxford: Oxford University Press.
Schumpeter, J. (1954), *History of Economic Analysis*, New York: Oxford University Press.
Schweber, S. (1980), 'Darwin and the Political Economists: Divergence of Character', *Journal of the History of Biology*, **13**(2), 195–289.

Smith, A. ([1776] 1976), *An Inquiry into the Nature and Causes of the Wealth of Nations*, eds R.H. Campbell, A.S. Skinner and W.B. Todd, 2 Volumes, Oxford: Oxford University Press.

Sorensen, C.E. (1957), *Forty Years with Ford*, London: Cape.

Stigler, G. (1951), 'The Division of Labor is Limited by the Extent of the Market', *The Journal of Political Economy*, **59**(3), 185–93.

Yergin, D. and J. Stanislaw (1998), *The Commanding Heights: The Battle Between Government and the Marketplace that is Remaking the Modern World*, New York: Simon & Schuster.

3 Marx
Ugo Pagano

3.1 INTRODUCTION

The capitalist firm plays a central role in the Marxian analysis. On the one hand, anticipating Coase and the institutional literature, Marx saw the firm as an organization alternative to the market. Comparison between the anarchy of the market and the deliberate order of the firm induced him to extol the latter and to propose its extension to society as a whole. On the other hand, according to Marx, the firm was the key locus where labour exploitation and alienation were perpetrated and he criticized the detailed division of labour introduced under capitalism. His model of communism, to be realized after single-firm socialism, was meant to overcome the depressing human condition existing in the capitalist firm.

Thus, the Marxian treatment of the firm can be divided under two headings: the firms vs markets issue and the criticism of alienated labour. We will start considering these two points separately. We will later consider the relevance that, in spite of their contradictions and limitations, both points still bear for the modern theory of the firm.

3.2 FIRMS VS MARKETS

Besides being a political proposal, single-firm socialism was, according to Marx, a historical necessity imposed by the development of productive forces. The firm's greater efficiency (relatively to markets) had already been evinced by the growth in firms' size during capitalism, and productive forces exerted strong pressure for their further growth. By eliminating private property, socialism did nothing other than complete an inevitable process of concentration, whose onset was 'scientifically guaranteed' by historical materialism. According to Marx, capitalism was a dual economy in which firm and market coexisted. 'Single-firm socialism' would definitively supersede that dualism and enable the greater development of the productive forces. Market's limitations sprang from the anarchy of production due its nature as an a posteriori coordination mechanism that operated only after decentralized, often inconsistent, decisions had been implemented:

> The *a priori* system on which the division of labor, within the workshop, is regularly carried out, becomes in the division of labor within the society, an *a posteriori*, nature-imposed necessity, controlling the lawless caprice of the producers, and perceptible in the barometrical fluctuations of the market-prices. (Marx, 1967, p. 355)

This negative conception of the market's workings induced Marx to advocate the extension of firm-type of organization to society as a whole:

If one took as a model the division of labour in a modern workshop, in order to apply it to a whole society, the society best organized for the production of wealth would undoubtedly be that which had a single chief employer, distributing tasks to different members of the community according to a previously fixed rule. (Marx, 1955, p. 151)

The extension of the planned organization of production of the capitalist factory would complete a process already ongoing in the historical dynamics of capitalism whereby productive forces tended constantly to increase the size of firms. Socialism was the final outcome of this tendency of the productive forces to shift production relations within the firm. The scientific certainty of the advent of socialism was, for Marx, inherent in the tendency of the productive forces to influence production relations. The extension of the authoritarian world of the capitalist firm to the whole of society was necessary to reap the benefits of a planned coordination made more and more necessary by the increasing interdependence among the production sectors.

3.3 ALIENATED LABOUR

According to Marx, capitalism produced a very detailed and hierarchical division of labour, and he criticized it principally in this regard: the capitalist-owned firm was a structure that involved a massive deskilling of workers and made labour alienated and painfully homogeneous. Indeed, in the early stage of socialism, planning could be made on an objective basis because, according to Marx, capitalism had eliminated the possibility of subjective preferences among repetitive and simple tasks. These conditions suggested, for the first phase of a socialist society, a form of authoritarian planning based on the theory of labour value that ignored the subjective preferences for different kinds of work. Whilst a vision of a future society in which work would entirely match the preferences and development of individuals was constantly present in Marx's critique of capitalism, its implications were postponed to a distant future (Marx, 1978). Still, his criticism of the internal organization of the capitalist firm was forceful and effective. Marx emphasized how intellectual faculties were disembodied from the workers to become private ownership of the employers:

> It is a result of the division of labour in manufactures that the laborer is brought face to face with the intellectual potencies of the material process of production, as the property of another, and as a ruling power. This separation begins in simple co-operation, where the capitalist represents to the single workman, the oneness and the will of the associated labor. It is developed in manufacture which cuts down the laborer into a detail laborer. It is completed in modern industry, which makes science a productive force distinct from labor and presses it into the service of capital. (Marx, 1967, ch. 14, section 5)

In the modern post-TRIPS world, where intellectual property rights have become the most relevant part of the firm's capital, Marx's view of capitalist development sounds like a over-fulfilled prophecy: ideas themselves are faced as intellectual potencies of the material process of production that belong to the employers and cannot be used outside the firm without its permission.

3.4.   NEOCLASSICAL THEORY VS 'NORMATIVE MARXISM'

Unlike most neoclassical economists, Marx's theory did not have the purpose of providing a normative theory spelling out the optimality requirements of a certain system. However, Marx's criticism of alienated labour implies an implicit 'normative Marxism' that offers a powerful critique of the optimality properties of the neoclassical profit-maximizing firm (Pagano, 1985).

In the neoclassical firm, preferences for work are ruled out by assuming that work enters the utility function only as forgone leisure. Given a certain level of leisure, changes in workers' employments do not affect workers' welfare. However, according to Marx, the absence of the preferences for work is not a feature inherent to the subjectivity of workers but a consequence of the organization of the capitalist firm. Marx assumes work preferences to be truly important. No logic of maximum profit can unilaterally suggest efficient forms of work organization that do not take these preferences into account. In principle, less 'efficient' technologies characterized by inferior output levels may lead to superior well-being: free time remaining equal, lower productivity may be off-set by work activities more in keeping with workers' preferences. However, the technologies employed may make it pointless to express preferences among equally alienating forms of work.

More in general, Marx enables us to go beyond a dichotic view of an economy divided into two institutions: the household, where goods and free time are consumed (and nothing is produced); and the firm, where the output from work is the only end (and the job preferences of individuals count for nothing). In general, Marx believes that every work activity is at once consumption and production, and that it is potentially both an end and a means for the individual who performs it. Only on the basis of given technologies and individual preferences can we establish whether some of these activities are only means (that is, nothing but pure 'toil' or labour) or, also, ends in themselves. The importance of job satisfaction, so much emphasized by modern theories of management, finds in Marx an early rigorous and coherent advocate.

3.5   MARX'S DYNAMIC COASIANISM

The firms–market distinction, outlined by Marx, anticipated Coase's view of the firm and his criticisms of the neoclassical theory of the firm that did not consider the multiplicity of the institutions of capitalism. However, unlike Coase, Marx did not perceive that all institutions are costly and that their costs matter in the determination of their complex mix, which characterizes modern economies. In some respects, Marx made a mistake mirroring orthodox economics when he assumed that, while the costs of market coordination were very high, the costs of firm-type coordination were negligible, with the consequence that all the economic transactions could be coordinated at zero costs by centralized planning. However, in spite of these severe analytical deficiencies, which were going to have dramatic consequences in the real-life application of Marxism, Marx gained a remarkable advantage, in comparison to the Coasian approach, by framing the comparative institutional analysis of the firm in a dynamic setting.

The Coasian tradition has highlighted those transaction costs of the market (relative to the firm) that can be observed even when demand and supply are in equilibrium: for example, the costs of discovering relevant prices, and the costs of negotiating and writing contracts. The neo-institutionalist literature inspired by Coase (1937) has evidenced other costs similarly observable in equilibrium: monitoring costs (Alchian and Demsetz, 1972) and possible free-riding by agents, which may be especially damaging when resources are highly specific (Williamson, 1985) (see also Chapter 11 by Hong Bo and Ciaran Driver, and Chapter 13 by Richard Carter in this book).

However, besides these transaction costs, which have always been stressed by the neo-institutionalist literature, there are coordination costs, which Marx carefully analysed. Of course, the diverse costs and benefits of firms and markets cannot be observed and compared in equilibrium situations, where the problem of coordinating decisions has been largely solved. In equilibrium, it is more useful to concentrate on the problem of implementing decisions, and on the costs that this entails. However, the analytical convenience of studying equilibrium situations does not gainsay the fact that the market's principal role consists precisely in coordinating demand and supply. Likewise, one may argue that firms' managers are not merely useful like police officers or judges; for they also match production needs and the resources required to satisfy them. That is to say, just like the market, they balance demand and supply within their firms (Pagano, 1992). In a market economy, imbalances between demand and supply give rise to substantial costs, and their elimination only comes about after a considerable waste of resources. If this were not so, the employment of managers to remedy those imbalances would certainly be a waste. In the Marxian approach, a coordination mechanism is a priori when an attempt is made to eliminate contradictions among decisions before they are implemented. A coordination mechanism is a posteriori when no attempt is made to eliminate such inconsistencies a priori, but agents react by seeking to eliminate them after they have emerged. Firms' managers enable an a priori coordination of decisions that may be more efficient than the a posteriori mechanism operating in the market.

Marx's approach may still be of interest because it does not merely compare forms of authority in situations of demand/supply equilibrium but also examines forms of a posteriori and a priori coordination: in other words, it also analyses what we may call *disequilibrium transaction costs*. In this respect, he shares a common methodology with the Austrian school and, in particular with Hayek, who also carried out the comparative institutional analysis of markets and firms in disequilibrium (Hayet, 1935). A common dynamic setting stands in sharp contrast with their opposite political conclusions.

3.6 TECHNOLOGY AND RIGHTS: BEYOND THE NEOCLASSICAL DUAL NEUTRALITY ASSUMPTION

Neoclassical theory a-critically assumes a dual neutrality (no reciprocal influence) between rights and technology. As a consequence, the theory becomes a-historical in that the historical links between property rights and productive forces are severed. Different firm types are framed in an analytical night in which all the cows are black and no comparative institutional analysis is possible.

A famous dictum by Samuelson (1957, p. 894) states this dual neutrality of the neoclassical theory very clearly: 'In a competitive economy it really doesn't matter who hires whom'. Samuelson thus asserts the irrelevance of firm ownership in so far as it does not matter whether it is the owner of the machines who hires the workers, or whether instead it is the workers who hire the machines. Neutrality thus holds in a twofold sense: whilst the various technologies and productive forces have no influence on the efficiency of the various kinds of ownership, the various kinds of ownership (for example, control of the firm by workers or capitalists) have no influence on the nature of the productive forces and the type of technology used.

The analytical night of orthodox theory stems from the assumption of nil transaction costs and complete and perfectly enforceable contracts. A market characterized by zero transaction costs and complete contracts will protect agents whether or not they have property rights over the means of production. From this point of view, the characteristics of the productive forces are not important: a competitive equilibrium with complete contracts will in any case entail the efficient organization of production, both when the capitalist employs the workers, and when the contract provides for the workers to rent the means of production from the owner. The types of resources and technologies used will have no effect on the efficiency of the controlling actor. It will always be possible to stipulate contracts guaranteeing productive efficiency with other individuals in possession of physical and human capital. The nature of the productive forces does not tend to favour particular property rights, and accordingly are neutral.

In a world of complete contracts, the firm's owners will not be able to alter the nature of the productive forces in their favour. The firm does not really exist and the owners can only formally manage a production process, which in reality is exclusively organized by the constraints imposed by the enforcement of complete contracts. Upon realization that they are completely protected by their contracts, workers who have no rights to the means of production will not invest any less in human capital. For the same reason, the owners of the means of production will feel themselves equally protected if they rent their means of production to others rather than utilize them directly. In other words, the ownership form does not influence the types of resources and the nature of the technologies employed. The ownership structure, therefore, does not tend to favour particular productive forces, and consequently it too is neutral.

The Marxian theory of history contains an implicit ante litteram criticism of this double neutrality assumption: productive forces do influence property rights and property rights do, in turn, have also an important feedback influence on productive forces. Recent contributions of neo-institutional economists vindicate the Marxian view and reject the neoclassical hypothesis that technologies are neutral in regard to the nature of property rights and types of control over firms. According to Williamson (1985), when it is impossible to write complete contracts, the characteristics of the productive forces influence the attribution of control rights. In the presence of contractual incompleteness, those in possession of relatively specific resources (i.e., resources that cannot be put to other uses without losing some of their value) find themselves in a very difficult situation. In the neoclassical world of zero transaction costs and complete contracts it is always possible to protect oneself against opportunism by the counterparties with a complete contract. The specificity of resources becomes a problem if it is not possible to obtain adequate guarantees by means of a sufficiently complete contract. In this case, those with control over the firm have greater guarantees than do other individuals. In these circumstances, because those who invest in specific resources are made vulnerable by the absence of alternative uses, they will seek to obtain such guarantees. Samuelson's proposition no longer holds, because in this situation 'who hires whom' becomes important. When the technologies change, the specificity characteristics of resources change as well, and so do the kinds of property and control rights that are efficient to use. There thus again arises the idea that changes in the productive forces influence production relations and property rights.[1]

3.7 CONCLUSION: MICRO-MARXISM AND THE COMPARATIVE INSTITUTIONAL ANALYSIS OF THE FIRM

The recent new institutional theory has re-launched the Marxian ideas that organization of production typologies must be also explained on the basis of the technologies and the resources employed in them. However, the Marxian theory contains also the opposite direction of causation and offers the possibility of completing the criticism of the second neoclassical neutrality assumption as well as of some unidirectional neo-institutional reasoning. Thus, from Harry Braverman's (1974) contribution, Marx has inspired the idea that also property rights are not neutral and that they shape the nature of technology de-skilling labour and embodying in the capital of the firm an increasing number of capabilities. Indeed, with reference to new institutional theory, if it is true that those who possess resources specific to a firm seek to acquire control over it, the opposite is the case as well: in situations of contractual incompleteness, those with control rights over a firm have relatively fewer inhibitions about developing resources specific to that organization.[2] Because rights influence the specificity characteristics of resources, they also influence the nature of the productive forces employed.

Thus a crucial message of Marx remains that rights and technology can influence each other. This insight of Marx provides an important key to unlock the complexities of the comparative institutional analysis of the organization of production in different countries, following a perspective that Albert Hirschman (1981) has called 'micro-Marxism'. This approach focuses on the analysis of the numerous modes of production that simultaneously exist both in different capitalist societies and within a single society. Thus abandoned are the theoretical claims of a universalist history in which all production systems must follow the same line of development, which involved the wrong prediction of necessary convergence to single-firm socialism. Favoured instead is careful analysis of the multiplicity of forms that organizations may assume and the interlocking complementarities[3] between rights and technologies that characterize the different types of firms.

NOTES

1. The same reasoning applies to information asymmetries. By virtue of the latter, some agents may possess hidden private information, which makes complete contracts impossible to stipulate. Also in this case the monitoring attributes of resources (productive forces) influence property rights (Alchian and Demsetz, 1972). In addition, the direction of causation can be inverted.
2. Initially developed by Marx in the first book of *Capital*, this point has been taken up by numerous 'radical economists' on the lines initiated by Braverman (1974), Marglin (1974) and Rowthorn (1974).

3. The focus on interlocking complementarities is an important characteristic of modern comparative institutional analysis of the organizations of production (Pagano and Rowthorn, 1994; Aoki, 2001; Hall and Soskice, 2001; Pagano, forthcoming).

REFERENCES

Alchian, A. and H. Demsetz (1972), 'Production, Information Costs and Economic Organization', *American Economic Review*, **62**(5), 777–95.
Aoki, M. (2001), *Towards a Comparative Institutional Analysis*, Cambridge, MA: MIT Press.
Braverman, H. (1974), *Labor and Monopoly Capital*, New York: Monthly Review Press.
Coase, R.H. (1937), 'The Nature of the Firm', *Economica*, **4**(16), 386–405.
Hall, P.A. and D. Soskice (2001), *Varieties of Capitalism. The Institutional Foundations of Comparative Advantage*, Oxford: Oxford University Press.
Hayek, F.A. (1935), *Collectivist Economic Planning*, London: Routledge.
Hirschman, A.O. (1981), *Essays in Trespassing. Economics to Politics and Beyond*, Cambridge, UK: Cambridge University Press.
Marglin, S. (1974), 'What Do Bosses Do?', *Review of Radical Political Economy*, **6**(2), 60–112.
Marx, K. (1955), *The Poverty of Philosophy*, Moscow: Progress Publishers.
Marx, K. (1967), *Capital. Vol. I*, New York: International Publishers.
Marx, K. (1978), 'Critique to the Gotha', in T. Borodulina (ed.), *Marx, Engels, Lenin on Communist Society*, Moscow: Progress Publishers.
Pagano, U. (1985), *Work and Welfare in Economic Theory*, Oxford: Basil Blackwell.
Pagano, U. (1992), 'Authority, Co-ordination and Disequilibrium: An Explanation of the Co-existence of Markets and Firms', *Economic Dynamics and Structural Change*, **3**(1), 53–77. Reprinted in G.M. Hodgson (1993), *The Economics of Institutions*, Aldershot, UK and Brookfield, VT, USA: Edward Elgar.
Pagano, U. (forthcoming), 'Technical Assets and Property Rights', in A. Grandori (ed.), *Handbook of Economic Organization: Integrating Economic and Organization Theory*, Cheltenham, UK and Northampton, MA, USA: Edward Elgar.
Pagano, U. and R. Rowthorn (1994), 'Ownership, Technology and Institutional Stability', *Structural Change and Economic Dynamics*, **5**(2), 221–43.
Rowthorn, R. (1974), 'Neo-classicism, Neo-Ricardianism and Marxism', *New Left Review*, **86**, 63–82.
Samuelson, P. (1957), 'Wage and Interest: A Modern Dissection of Marxian Economic Models', *American Economic Review*, **47**(6), 884–912.
Williamson, O.E. (1985), *The Economic Institutions of Capitalism*, New York: The Free Press.

4 Alfred Marshall and the Marshallian theory of the firm

Jacques-Laurent Ravix

4.1 INTRODUCTION

Economists' opinion is divided over the way Alfred Marshall treated the firm in his works, the author being considered either as a precursor of the neoclassical theory or, more appropriately in our sense, as a forerunner of neo-institutionalism and evolutionary economics. As most of the modern interpreters of Marshall rightly argue, an appraisal of Marshall's approach to the firm cannot be separated from his conception of the dynamics of industry. Careful readings of the author's works reveal that his concept of the firm is intertwined with that of industry within an evolutionistic framework mainly based on biological analogies (Raffaelli et al., 2006).

Consider, for instance, the well-known notions and images that characterize Marshall's approach to the firm. The famous metaphor of the 'trees of the forest' and the rather mysterious and sometimes ill-interpreted concept of the 'representative firm', first appear in Book IV of the *Principles*, in conclusion to the chapters dedicated to the study of industrial organization. Conversely, Book V on demand, supply and value, while referring to the representative firm, uses a toned-down notion of the firm and the industry in the ceteris paribus view of partial equilibrium. This version seems to be better adapted to the abstract theory of value and price developed by neoclassical theory and elaborated to avoid 'the incredible banalities of much of the so-called theory of production' (Robbins, 1932, p. 65). Quoting Lionel Robbins again:

> One has only to compare the masterly sweep of Book V of Marshall's *Principles*, which deals with problems which are strictly economics in our sense, with the spineless platitudes. . .of much of Book IV to realise the insidious effect of a procedure which opens the door to the intrusions of amateur technology into discussion which should be purely economic. (Ibid.)

In what follows, we argue that it is quite inappropriate to oppose those two books of the *Principles*. Marshall's vision of firm and industry shows a great homogeneity because it inextricably links two principles: the principle of organization resulting from the division of labour, the analysis of which is developed in Book IV, and the principle of substitution, which is the main methodological tool utilized in Book V. The latter should be regarded as the engine translating empirical evolutionary mechanisms at work in Book IV into value theory, rather than a simple device for marginalist or equilibrium reasoning based on the mechanism of prices and costs. According to Marshall, 'the application of this principle extends over almost every field of economic inquiry' (Marshall, 1920, V, III, 3, p. 284). Later on, the author writes: 'the law of substitution – which is nothing more than a special and limited application of the law of survival of the fittest – tends to make one method of industrial organization supplant another when it offers a direct and immediate service at a lower price' (Marshall, 1920, VI, 7, 1, p. 495).

Thus, evolutionary reasoning is the backbone of the *Principles*. As Marshall's theory of value cannot be separated from his theory of development (Metcalfe, 2007b), So Marshall's view of the firm cannot be but intimately grasped in his conception of industry (Loasby, 1989). In the next section we study the way Marshall integrates industry and the firm under the principle of organization. In section 4.3, we develop Marshall's vision of the firm according to the principle of substitution, expressed through the dynamics of firm differentiation and integration, entry–exit, and the rise and fall of individual businesses. Finally, in section 4.4, we conclude that the modern theory of the firm inspired by Marshall and mainly developed by Ronald Coase and George Richardson is 'Marshallian' because it is a theory combining the concept of the firm and that of industry, a theory in which the 'nature of the firm' cannot be separated from the fact that industry is by nature dynamic and evolving.

4.2   INDUSTRIAL ORGANIZATION AND THE FIRM WITHIN AN EVOLUTIONISTIC FRAMEWORK

Post-Marshallian authors consider Book IV of Marshall's *Principles* as one of the most interesting parts of the author's magnum opus. Contra Robbins's disdainful attitude, Coase insists on the importance of the productive process and institutional forms described in Book IV in the understanding of the nature of the firm (Coase, 1993, pp. 53–4). For Loasby, we find there the central concepts of dynamic economics based on the relation between organization and knowledge (Loasby, 1989). Marshall introduces Book IV with some strong often-quoted phrases: 'Capital consists in a great part of knowledge and organization. . . Knowledge is our most powerful engine of production. . . Organization aids knowledge' (Marshall, 1920, IV, I, 1, p. 115). These sentences make their sense in the chapters dedicated to industrial organization where industry is defined through an evolutionary notion of the division of labour, emerging from a fundamental unity between biological and moral sciences:

> This central unity is set forth in the general rule, to which there are not very many exceptions, that the development of the organism, whether social or physical, involves an increasing subdivision of functions between its separate parts on the one hand, and on the other a more intimate connection between them. (Marshall, 1920, IV, VIII, 1, pp. 200–201)

The increased subdivision of functions is called 'differentiation', and 'manifests itself with regard to industry in such forms as the division of labour, and the development of specialized skills, knowledge and machinery', while 'integration' is 'a growing intimacy and firmness of the connections between the separate parts of the industrial organism' (Marshall, 1920, IV, VIII, 1, p. 201).

Marshall's theory of economic progress, as well as his theory of economic coordination, are based on the relationship between knowledge and organization, the 'twin themes' of Book IV of Marshall's *Principles* being 'the effects of the growth of knowledge on organisation and costs of production, and the effects of the organisation of production on the growth of knowledge' (Loasby, 1989, p. 54). In Marshall's own words, when organization aids knowledge, 'it has many forms, e.g. that of a single business, that of various businesses in the same trade, that of various trades relatively to one another, and that of the State providing security for all and help for many' (Marshall, 1920, IV, I, 1, p. 115). Indeed, this simple description draws a more complete picture of the organization of industry than the usual modern industrial organization literature does. Particularly, the specific nature of cooperation in the organization of industry is put forward in Marshall's work. Large portions of Marshall's *Industry and Trade* (Marshall, 1923), and more specifically Chapter XII, are devoted to the study of 'various forms of cooperation, in which there is some constructive purpose' (Marshall, 1923, p. 599). The ways in which the various forms of organization aid knowledge and knowledge improves organization are not presented in a well-structured fashion in Marshall's five chapters dedicated to 'Industrial Organisation' (*Principles*, Book IV, Chapters VIII to XII). This task has been completed by Brian Loasby who delineated a convincing picture of Marshall's industry as a consequence of both the division of labour and organization (Loasby, 1989, 1990, 1994; see also Chapter 18 by Brian Loasby in this book).

Book IV concludes with the 'trees of the forest' and the 'representative firm' in relation to the dynamic aspects of increasing and diminishing returns (Marshall, 1920, IV, XIII, 1–2, pp. 263–5). These notions clearly constitute the first approximation of the empirical evolutionary world described in Book IV to be transposed, in Book V, into an abstract theory of value based on demand and supply. The parable of the trees of the forest is used to illustrate the life cycles of any businesses along the course of their growth and the rivalry among them:

> Though the taller ones have a better access to light and air than their rivals, they gradually lose vitality; and one after another they give place to others, which, though of less material strength, have on their side the vigour of youth. . . And as with the growth of trees so was it with the growth of businesses as a general rule before the great recent development of vast joint-stock companies, which often stagnate, but do not readily die. (Marshall, 1920, IV, XIII, 1, p. 263)

But, in the end, the joint-stock company is also submitted to the great rule of nature: 'it is likely to have lost so much of its elasticity and progressive force, that the advantages are no longer exclusively on its side in its competition with younger and smaller rivals' (Marshall, 1920, IV, XIII, 1, p. 264).

The trees of the forest play more than a simple metaphoric role in Marshall. This image is the first step of an argument leading to the definition of the representative firm as a general abstraction for production theory. What is important to keep in mind is that the growth of wealth and population leads to 'economies of production', internal as well as external. As for internal economies, 'there is a constant rise and fall of large businesses, at any one moment some firms being in the ascending phase and others in the descending' (ibid.). As for external economies:

> The most important of these result from the growth of correlated branches of industry which mutually assist one another, perhaps being concentrated in the same localities, but anyhow availing themselves of the modern facilities for communication offered by steam transport, by the telegraph and by the printing-press. (Ibid.)

4.3   VALUE, SUBSTITUTION AND FIRM DYNAMICS

The most significant result of Marshall's approach to the firm and industry is certainly the one that relates internal business organization and external trade connections to the processes leading to internal and external economies. According to Loasby, these processes are much more a matter of improvements in knowledge and organization than a matter of standard neoclassical definition in terms of scale economies. See, for instance, Marshall's wording of the law of increasing returns: 'An increase of labour and capital leads generally to improved organization, which increases the efficiency of the work of labour and capital' (Marshall, 1920, IV, XIII, 2, p.265). Later on, Marshall draws attention to 'the length of time that is necessarily occupied by each individual business in extending its internal, and still more its external organization' (Marshall, 1920, V, XV, 4, p.414). As pointed out by Loasby, the term 'external organization' suggests 'the network of social, technical, and commercial arrangements which link a business with its customers, suppliers (who are usually of many kinds), and also its rivals, whose own experiments provide it both incentive and information' (Loasby, 1989, p.57).

Interactions, competition and cooperation among firms, stay at the centre of the concept of the representative firm. This concept is entirely equipped with the elements of theory of production and industrial dynamics that are transposed from Book IV to constitute the basis of the argument of Book V. These dynamic effects will be of great importance for the discussion of the mechanisms that govern the supply price of a commodity, and particularly the 'normal cost of production' relatively to a given aggregate volume of production. This is the reason why Marshall needs to know the expenses of a 'representative firm'. This firm is 'one which has had a fairly long life, and fair success, which is managed with normal ability, and which has normal access to the economies, external and internal, which belong to that aggregate volume of production' (Marshall, 1920, IV, XIII, 2, p.265). Such a representative firm is 'in a sense an average firm' (ibid.), which is not obtained by statistics but 'by selecting, after a broad survey, a firm,. . .that represents, to the best of our judgment, this particular average' (ibid.).

The representative firm is the bridging concept that articulates Book IV and Book V. This looks obvious in the analysis of the equilibrium of normal demand and supply. The role played by the representative firm is quite in accordance with what has been written by Marshall in Book IV in terms of industry dynamics and differential growth of firms. As Metcalfe argues, the concept of the representative firm participates in the notion of industrial dynamics (Metcalfe, 2007a, 2007b). Besides the static role of the marginal firm, the dynamic role of the representative firm is a useful device for value theory:

> We need the marginal firm to distinguish different instantiations of long period order, and we need the representative firm not simply to deal with the messy facts of heterogeneous firms but rather to understand the dynamic consequences of their variation for the transformation of the prevailing order. (Metcalfe, 2007b, p.3)

In Marshall, the market equilibrium is better described by a concept of 'order' in which different variables evolve at different rates. It follows that Marshall's famous periodization scheme is not a static device to distinguish different notions of equilibrium; it is 'a dynamic device to distinguish variables with different velocities' (Metcalfe, 2001, p.575).

The long and short periods do not describe different kinds of equilibria; they define different temporal processes.

Entry–exit of businesses, first illustrated by the trees of the forest, runs across different chapters of the *Principles* (Metcalfe, 2008). The explanation of long-period normal supply price of commodity produced is based on 'the incomes which are expected to be earned' in the business (Marshall, 1920, V, V, 8, p. 315), and the expected profit is the reason of the choice to enter the trade in view. This expected profit is obtained by comparing the earnings with the costs 'to build up and to work a representative firm' (ibid., p. 314). In Marshall, entry–exit appears in different contexts. For instance, economic change leads to the distinction between 'those who open out new and improved methods of business, and those who follow beaten tracks' (Marshall, 1920, VI, VII, 1, p. 496). Another case is related to entry barriers: 'the new man with but a little capital of his own is at a disadvantage in trades which move slowly' but 'in all those industries in which bold and tireless enterprise can reap a kick harvest. . .there the new man is in his element' and 'forces the pace' (Marshall, 1920, VI, VII, 5, pp. 500–501). The principle of substitution as a struggle for survival is everywhere at work. As Metcalfe writes: 'The supporting idea, which makes Marshall's approach explicitly evolutionary, is his principle of substitution in which the multidimensional heterogeneity of firms provides the material on which market framed selection processes can work their adaptive effects' (Metcalfe, 2008, p. 5).

4.4 MARSHALL AND THE NEO-MARSHALLIAN VIEW OF THE FIRM

The evolutionary dimension of Marshall may help explain why, in the modern theory of the firm, the concept of institutional division of labour goes beyond the dichotomy expressed by the 'make-or-buy' problem of transaction cost economics. Transaction costs explain why firms decide to make internally, that is, to use vertical integration, or buy on the market, but transaction costs do not explain more. In order to explain that the industry is structured by such strategic decisions made by firms, it is necessary to put industrial organization back into its dynamic dimension. In that case, the problem is not only a quantitative problem of costs but a qualitative problem of activities and capabilities.

The necessary complements to Coase's (1937) seminal paper are two articles published in the same year: Coase (1972) and Richardson (1972). Both articles are dedicated to the same question: how will we transform industrial organization analysis so as to integrate firms' strategies and firms' interactions into the analytical framework, that is, 'what firms actually do' (Coase, 1972, p. 65) and 'the dense network of co-operation and affiliation by which firms are inter-related' (Richardson, 1972, p. 883). The answer given by both authors is based on the way firms choose their activities and the way they build their competencies. The main result of the neo-Marshallian theory of the firm is that the simple firm–market dichotomy is only a sub-case of the division of labour among different business institutions that involves firm, market and cooperation as alternative and complementary modes of organizing industrial activities. As Richardson writes, '(t)he dichotomy between firm and market, between directed and spontaneous co-ordination, is misleading; it ignores the institutional fact of inter-firm co-operation and assumes away the distinct method of co-ordination that this can provide' (Richardson, 1972, p. 895).

The patronage of Marshall explains why the modern theory of the firm develops through an evolutionary framework in which industrial organization results from division of labour, substitutions and re-combinations among firms and business institutions. Those mechanisms are simultaneously governing the boundaries of the firm as well as entry and exit of firms. Reciprocally, the logic of the neo-Marshallian theory of the firm helps explain the structure of the *Principles*, that is, the links between industrial organization and the institutional structure of production. This explanation of Marshall after the neo-Marshallians contradicts the standard Marshallian *vulgate* based on Robbins's denial of the interest of Book IV and the Pigou/Viner formalistic interpretation of Book V.

REFERENCES

Coase, R.H. (1937), 'The Nature of the Firm', *Economica*, **4**(16), 386–405.
Coase, R.H. (1972), 'Industrial Organization: A Proposal for Research', in V.R. Fuchs (ed.), *Policy Issues and Research Opportunities in Industrial Organization*, New York: NBER, Columbia University Press.
Coase, R.H. (1993), 'The Nature of the Firm: Meaning', in O.E. Williamson and S.G. Winter (eds), *The Nature of the Firm: Origins, Evolution, and Development*, Oxford: Oxford University Press.
Loasby, B.J. (1989), *The Mind and Method of the Economist*, Aldershot, UK and Brookfield, VT, USA: Edward Elgar.
Loasby, B.J. (1990), 'Firms, Markets, and the Principle of Continuity', in J.K. Whitaker (ed.), *Centenary Essays on Alfred Marshall*, Cambridge, UK: Cambridge University Press.
Loasby, B.J. (1994), 'Organisational Capabilities and Interfirm Relations', *Metroeconomica*, **45**(3), 248–65.
Marshall, A. (1920), *Principles of Economics*, 8th edition, London: Macmillan.
Marshall, A. (1923), *Industry and Trade*, London: Macmillan.
Metcalfe, J.S. (2001), 'Institutions and Progress', *Industrial and Corporate Change*, **10**(3), 561–86.
Metcalfe, J.S. (2007a), 'Alfred Marshall and the General Theory of Evolutionary Economics', *History of Economic Ideas*, **15**(1), 81–110.
Metcalfe, J.S. (2007b), 'Alfred Marshall's Mecca: Reconciling the Theories of Value and Development', *The Economic Record*, **83**(Supp.), 1–22.
Metcalfe, J.S. (2008), 'On Marshallian Evolutionary Dynamics, Entry and Exit', Manchester Business School Working Paper, No. 540.
Raffaelli, T., G. Becattini and M. Dardi (eds) (2006), *The Elgar Companion to Alfred Marshall*, Cheltenham, UK and Northampton, MA, USA: Edward Elgar.
Richardson, G.B. (1972), 'The Organisation of Industry', *Economic Journal*, **82**(327), 883–96.
Robbins, L. (1932), *An Essay on the Nature and Significance of Economic Science*, 1st edition, London: Macmillan.

5 Veblen, Commons and the theory of the firm

Geoffrey M. Hodgson

5.1 INTRODUCTION

The original institutional economics was a highly prominent school of economic thought in the United States between World War I and World War II (Rutherford, 1994, 2001; Yonay, 1998; Hodgson, 2004). It was a broad and heterogeneous movement, drawing its inspiration from Thorstein Veblen (1857–1929), John R. Commons (1862–1945) and several others.

Among the myths peddled by critics is the idea that the original institutionalism was 'atheoretical' or 'against theory'. Despite their prevalence, these allegations are relatively easy to refute by citing examples of theoretical developments – including growth accounting and rudiments of Keynesianism – that owe their origins to the original institutionalism (Rutherford, 2001; Hodgson, 2004).

Veblen and Commons made a number of important statements – reviewed below – concerning the nature and behaviour of capitalist firms. Subsequent institutional economists made important contributions to the analysis of large or oligopolistic firms. Highlights include John Maurice Clark's (1923) theory of 'overhead costs'. Institutionalists also influenced Edwin Chamberlin's (1933) theory of monopolistic competition (Cordell, 1972; Peterson, 1979) and Gardiner Means's (1935, 1972) theory of administered prices (Goode, 1994; Lee and Downward, 1999).

But we search in vain for a well-defined 'theory of the firm' within the old institutional economics. Instead we have a number of often overlooked insights. They endure alongside the more recent contribution of the 'new' institutional economics to transaction cost analysis and the theory of the firm.

The contributions of Veblen and Commons emerged a few years after the publication of Marshall's *Principles* in 1890. Marshall's work pervaded economics – including in the United States – until after World War II. Although institutionalists attacked the hedonistic and equilibrium-oriented assumptions of much neoclassical theory, these critiques applied more to less nuanced and static formulations than the work of Marshall himself. Many institutionalists saw their work as complementary to much Marshallian theory, rather than its negation (Burns, 1931). Even Veblen (1892, 1893, 1904, 1905) made use of some elements of Marshallian analysis, including the concepts of supply and demand (Mitchell, 1969, vol. 2, pp. 685–6).

The above caveats should be borne in mind while we consider the contributions of Veblen and Commons below. This chapter concludes with a brief comparison of the approaches of Commons and Oliver Williamson.

5.2   VEBLEN

Many of Veblen's insights on the firm are found in his second book, *The Theory of Business Enterprise* (1904). This book addresses the role of expectations and financial speculation in business cycles and the influence of the machine process on habits of thought. The first theme inspired Veblen's student Wesley Mitchell in an entire career of research. Veblen thus foreshadowed some key ideas on business fluctuations in the economics of John Maynard Keynes (Vining, 1939; Raines and Leathers, 1996).

Veblen also discussed the nature of the modern business corporation. Among several insights, he notes that the capital value of an enterprise is based not only on its material assets but also its earning capacity and 'goodwill'. Veblen (1904, p. 158) also develops his characteristic argument 'that there unavoidably results a discrepancy, not uncommonly a divergence, between the industrial needs of the community and the business needs of the corporations'.

Veblen (ibid., p. 159) observes that the 'ready vendibility of corporate capital has in great measure dissociated the business interest of the directorate from that of the corporation whose affairs they direct and whose business policy they dictate', and 'the management is separated from the ownership of the property, more and more widely as the scope of corporation finance widens'. This pointed to the separation of ownership and control (Means, 1931). In line with this later literature, Veblen observes that in a modern capitalist economy trade in corporate financial assets tends to drive economic development, rather than the direct needs of industry itself or the demands of its managers.

Unlike much of the 'theory of the firm' during the twentieth century, Veblen pays particular attention to legal forms. He underlines the emergence of the corporate legal structure and the important corporate protective device of limited liability. Veblen (ibid., p. 141) argues that 'with the assumption of the corporate form is associated a more modern method of capitalization and a freer use of credit'. Here he briefly foreshadows a modern argument that the legal structure of the corporation helps to explain its nature and dynamism. In particular the corporation has the capacity to attract and 'lock-in' capital, and to shield it from the personal creditors of its owners (Blair, 1999, 2003; Hansmann et al., 2006; Gindis, 2009). Like these modern theorists, Veblen indicated that legal corporate structure of the firm has important economic consequences, and the development of this legal structure helps to explain the Western take-off of capitalism in the nineteenth century.

Veblen (1904, p. 48) also hinted at the concept of transaction costs by noting that 'business consolidation' eliminates 'the pecuniary element from the interstices of the system. . .with the result that there is a saving of work and an avoidance of that systematic mutual hindrance that characterizes the competitive management of industry'. He thus suggested that business integration can reduce costs relative to a disaggregated and market-driven mode of governance (Coase, 1937; Williamson, 1975).

Veblen criticized the view that production is primarily a matter of 'inputs' into some mechanical function. Instead he emphasized knowledge and routines: 'the accumulated, habitual knowledge of the ways and means involved. . .the outcome of long experience and experimentation. . .the product and heritage of the group' (Veblen, 1908a, p. 153). Economic growth is favoured when firm organization facilitates individual learning:

'The possibility of growth lies in the feasibility of accumulating knowledge gained by individual experience and initiative, and therefore it lies in the feasibility of one individual's learning from the experience of another' (Veblen, 1908b, p. 521). As Nicolai Foss (1998) has observed, this recognition of organized knowledge and capabilities means that Veblen's work can be regarded as a forerunner of the modern, competence-based theory of the firm.

Last but not least, Veblen (1898) was the first to use the term 'evolutionary economics' in a prominent academic journal, and he was the first economist to attempt a major recasting of economic principles along Darwinian lines (Hodgson, 2004). Hence Veblen foreshadowed the modern evolutionary theory of the firm, developed by Richard Nelson and Sidney Winter (1982) and others. For a long time this affinity was masked by Nelson and Winter's neglect of Veblen as a forerunner and their failure to acknowledge the Darwinian structure of their evolutionary theory. (Both these defects have since been rectified.) But Curtis Eaton (1984) noted the Veblenian character of Nelson and Winter's theory in an early review.

With his emphasis on the role of groups as repositories of knowledge, his understanding that much knowledge is tacit and ingrained in habits, and his focus on the processes of selection of firms, Veblen prefigures many of the key ingredients of Nelson and Winter's approach. Furthermore, with his insistence that Darwinian principles have to be used to reconstruct economic theory, Veblen points to a road of potentially enriching theoretical development that has yet to be travelled by modern evolutionary economists (Hodgson and Knudsen, 2010). Here and elsewhere, many of Veblen's recommendations have yet to be fully realized.

5.3   COMMONS

Commons was elected president of the American Economic Association in 1917 and became one of the most influential economists of the twentieth century. John Maynard Keynes (1931, pp. 303–4) was attracted by some of his ideas (Skidelsky, 1992, p. 229; Hodgson, 2001, p. 216). The organization theorist Chester Barnard (1938, pp. 202–5) cited Commons in his classic *The Functions of the Executive*. In addition, three Nobel Laureates in economics, Gunnar Myrdal (1978, p. 771), Herbert Simon (1979, p. 499) and Oliver Williamson (1975, pp. 3, 254; 1985, pp. 3–5) have claimed to be influenced by Commons.

In both content and character, Commons's work is very different from that of Veblen. Kenneth Boulding (1957, p. 8) described Commons's contribution as a 'tangled jungle of profound insights, culled by an essentially nontheoretical mind from a life rich with experiences of economic realities'. I have argued elsewhere (Hodgson, 2004) that the philosophical and psychological foundations of Commons's work are less robust and enduring than those of Veblen. But unlike Veblen, Commons (1934, 1950) attempted to build a systematic framework for the development of economic policy. Whether this was successful is a matter of debate.

Like all American institutionalists, Commons was influenced by the German historical school. This influence is clear in his extended discussion of 'ideal types' (Commons, 1934). It is also evident in his focus on the historically specific character of institutions.

Also redolent of the historical school, Commons (1924) saw property and exchange as dependent on the politico-legal structures of the state.

Like Veblen, Commons (1925, p. 682) emphasizes the role of nineteenth-century 'general incorporation laws' in helping to facilitate dynamic innovation and growth. For Commons, these legal institutions simultaneously enabled 'the concentration of capital and the deconcentration of ownership'. Marx had pointed to the concentration of capital but neglected the diffusion of ownership.

Commons's conception of the firm has a strong legal dimension. He regarded law as part of the essential foundation of capitalism. By contrast, Marx (1976, p. 178) not only neglected legal incorporation but generally regarded law as an epiphenomenon or 'mirror' of underlying but ill-specified 'economic relations'. In further contrast to Marx, Commons identified the system of private property, the profit incentive and the countervailing threat of bankruptcy, as the sources of capitalism's dynamism and efficiency.

In examining the legal foundations of the firm, Commons stressed the role of the state as well as the importance of custom. For Commons (1925, p. 687), custom both 'regulates the individual proprietor' and constrains arbitrary action by the state. But he did not follow legal theorists (such as Friedrich Hayek, 1973) that equate custom with law. For Commons, while law has customary foundations, common law as such does not emerge 'until disputes arise'. Furthermore: 'The peculiar common law of the State comes in only when a decision is made by a court which directs the use or the collective physical violence of the community' (Commons, 1925, p. 687). Law is more than custom; it results from disputes that are resolved in the context of courts and the state monopoly of physical force (Diamond, 1935; Seagle, 1941; Samuels, 1971; Hodgson, 2009). Consequently, for Commons, the state plays an essential role in constituting the basic legal mechanisms that underlie production and exchange.

This understanding of the role of law is evident in his discussion of the concept of a transaction. Commons (1932, p. 4) saw 'conflict, mutuality and order' as central to transactions. Commons (1934, p. 59) identifies 'bargaining transactions', which are conducted between 'legal equals'. By contrast, both 'rational' and 'managerial' transactions are conducted between legally 'superior' and 'inferior' parties. 'In the managerial transaction the superior is an individual or a hierarchy of individuals, giving orders which the inferiors must obey, such as the relations of foreman to worker, or sheriff to citizen, or manager to managed'. By contrast, in a rationing transaction a legitimate institutional authority redistributes or reallocates resources.

Oliver Williamson (1981, p. 1543) writes: 'Following Commons (1934), the transaction is made the basic unit of analysis'. But for Commons (1934, p. 55), the transaction is a '*unit of economic activity*' (emphasis in original), and an element of the 'larger unit of economic activity, a Going Concern'. Although there is a superficial resemblance of terminology, Williamson's mode of analysis differs from that of Commons. For Williamson the initial and elemental ontological unit is the given 'opportunistic' individual, whereas at the outset Commons presupposes relational and collective qualities of institutions.

Commons's (1934, p. 56) rationale for describing the transaction as a unit of economic *activity*, is to break from the classical idea that the units in economics should be the '*commodities owned* and the *individuals* who owned the commodities, while the 'energy' was human *labor*' (italics original). Commons criticizes this conception as downplaying 'law or ethics' because of a concentration on 'relations between man and nature, not between man and man'. For Commons (ibid., p. 57) if 'the subject matter of political economy is not only individuals and nature's forces, but is human beings getting their living out of each other by mutual transfers of property rights, then it is to law and ethics that we look for the critical turning points of this human activity'. His analysis of the firm is entwined with both legal and ethical issues.

While Commons stresses the role of the state and law in constituting the firm and other basic institutions of capitalism, in contrast Williamson (1975, 1983, 1985, 2000) treats these institutions as outcomes of 'private ordering' – as emerging through the interactions of individuals without any essential role for the state. Indeed, the transaction could not logically be taken as the first and basic 'unit of analysis' if it itself depended on prior legal forms that do not arise simply as the spontaneous outcome of interactions between individuals. Contrary to Williamson, Commons does not treat law as a purely spontaneous or customary outcome. Overall, despite Williamson's praise for Commons, substantial and fundamental differences between the perspectives of the two institutional economists are still apparent.

5.4   CONCLUSION

For most of the twentieth century, much of the 'theory of the firm' has treated its object of analysis in an ahistorical manner, downplaying the legal and other specific institutions that constitute the modern business corporation. While institutionalists such as Veblen and Commons do not provide us with a systematic alternative theory, they point to the need to root our analysis of the firm in historically specific institutions. In this manner they tie in with modern legal scholarship on the nature of the firm and offer a means to help understand the sources of phenomenal economic growth under capitalism. Veblen also redirects our attention to the foundations of evolutionary theory that may be used to help develop a more dynamic conception.

REFERENCES

Barnard, Chester I. (1938) *The Functions of the Executive* (Cambridge, MA: Harvard University Press).
Blair, Margaret M. (1999) 'Firm-specific Human Capital and Theories of the Firm', in Margaret M. Blair and Mark Roe (eds), *Employees and Corporate Governance* (Washington, DC: Brookings), pp. 58–89.
Blair, Margaret M. (2003) 'Locking in Capital: What Corporate Law Achieved for Business Organizers in the Nineteenth Century', *UCLA Law Review*, 51(2), 387–455.
Boulding, Kenneth E. (1957) 'A New Look at Institutionalism', *American Economic Review (Papers and Proceedings)*, 47(2), May, 1–12.
Burns, Eveline M. (1931) 'Does Institutionalism Complement or Compete with "Orthodox Economics"?', *American Economic Review*, 21(1), March, 80–87.
Chamberlin, Edward H. (1933) *The Theory of Monopolistic Competition: A Re-orientation of the Theory of Value* (Cambridge, MA: Harvard University Press).
Clark, John Maurice (1923) *Studies in the Economics of Overhead Costs* (Chicago: University of Chicago Press).
Coase, Ronald H. (1937) 'The Nature of the Firm', *Economica*, 4(16), November, 386–405.
Commons, John R. (1924) *Legal Foundations of Capitalism* (New York: Macmillan). Reprinted 1968 (Madison: University of Wisconsin Press), 1974 (New York: Augustus Kelley) and 1995 with a new introduction by Jeff E. Biddle and Warren J. Samuels (New Brunswick, NJ: Transaction).

Commons, John R. (1925) 'Marx Today: Capitalism and Socialism', *Atlantic Monthly*, **13**(6), November, 682–93.
Commons, John R. (1932) 'The Problem of Correlating Law, Economics and Ethics', *Wisconsin Law Review*, **8**, 3–26.
Commons, John R. (1934) *Institutional Economics – Its Place in Political Economy* (New York: Macmillan). Reprinted 1990 with a new introduction by M. Rutherford (New Brunswick, NJ: Transaction).
Commons, John R. (1950) *The Economics of Collective Action*, edited by K.H. Parsons (New York: Macmillan).
Cordell, Arthur J. (1972) 'Imperfect and Monopolistic Competition: The Role of the Robinson-Chamberlin Theories in the Demise of Institutionalism', *American Journal of Economics and Sociology*, **31**(1), 41–60.
Diamond, A.S. (1935) *Primitive Law* (London: Watts).
Eaton, B. Curtis (1984), 'Review of *An Evolutionary Theory of Economic Change* by R.R. Nelson and S.G. Winter', *Canadian Journal of Economics*, **17**(4), November, 868–71.
Foss, Nicolai Juul (1998) 'The Competence-based Approach: Veblenian Ideas in the Modern Theory of the Firm', *Cambridge Journal of Economics*, **22**(4), July, 479–95.
Gindis, David (2009) 'From Fictions and Aggregates to Real Entities in the Theory of the Firm', *Journal of Institutional Economics*, **5**(1), April, 25–46.
Goode, Richard (1994) 'Gardiner Means on Administered Prices and Administrative Inflation', *Journal of Economic Issues*, **28**(1), March, 173–86.
Hansmann, Henry, Reinier Kraakman and Richard Squire (2006) 'Law and the Rise of the Firm', *Harvard Law Review*, **119**(5), March, 1333–403.
Hayek, Friedrich A. (1973) *Law, Legislation and Liberty; Volume 1: Rules and Order* (London: Routledge and Kegan Paul).
Hodgson, Geoffrey M. (2001) *How Economics Forgot History: The Problem of Historical Specificity in Social Science* (London and New York: Routledge).
Hodgson, Geoffrey M. (2004) *The Evolution of Institutional Economics: Agency, Structure and Darwinism in American Institutionalism* (London and New York: Routledge).
Hodgson, Geoffrey M. (2009) 'On the Institutional Foundations of Law: The Insufficiency of Custom and Private Ordering', *Journal of Economic Issues*, **43**(1), March, 143–66.
Hodgson, Geoffrey M. and Thorbjørn Knudsen (2010) *Darwin's Conjecture: The Search for General Principles of Social and Economic Evolution* (Chicago: University of Chicago Press).
Keynes, John Maynard (1931) *Essays in Persuasion* (London: Macmillian).
Lee, Frederick S. and Paul Downward (1999) 'Retesting Gardiner Means's Evidence on Administered Prices', *Journal of Economic Issues*, **33**(4), December, 861–86.
Marx, Karl (1976) *Capital*, vol. 1, translated by Ben Fowkes from the 4th German edition of 1890 (Harmondsworth: Pelican).
Means, Gardiner C. (1931) 'The Separation of Ownership and Control in American Industry', *Quarterly Journal of Economics*, **46**(1), December, 68–100.
Means, Gardiner C. (1935) 'Price Inflexibility and the Requirements of a Stabilizing Monetary Policy', *Journal of the American Statistical Association*, **30**(140), June, 401–13.
Means, Gardiner C. (1972) 'The Administered-price Thesis Reconfirmed', *American Economic Review*, **61**(2), June, 292–306.
Mitchell, Wesley C. (1969) *Types of Economic Theory: From Mercantilism to Institutionalism*, 2 vols, edited by Joseph Dorfman (New York: Augustus Kelley).
Myrdal, Gunnar (1978) 'Institutional Economics', *Journal of Economic Issues*, **12**(4), December, 771–84.
Nelson, Richard R. and Sidney G. Winter (1982) *An Evolutionary Theory of Economic Change* (Cambridge, MA: Harvard University Press).
Peterson, R.D. (1979) 'Chamberlin's Monopolistic Competition: Neoclassical or Institutional?', *Journal of Economic Issues*, **13**(3), September, 669–86.
Raines, J. Patrick and Charles G. Leathers (1996) 'Veblenian Stock Markets and the Efficient Markets Hypothesis', *Journal of Post Keynesian Economics*, **19**(1), Fall, 137–51.
Rutherford, Malcolm H. (1994) *Institutions in Economics: The Old and the New Institutionalism* (Cambridge: Cambridge University Press).
Rutherford, Malcolm H. (2001) 'Institutional Economics: Then and Now', *Journal of Economic Perspectives*, **15**(3), Summer, 173–94.
Samuels, Warren J. (1971) 'Interrelations Between Legal and Economic Processes', *Journal of Law & Economics*, **14**(2), 435–50.
Seagle, William (1941) *The Quest for Law* (New York: Knopf).
Simon, Herbert A. (1979) 'Rational Decision Making in Business Organizations', *American Economic Review*, **69**(4), September, 493–513.
Skidelsky, Robert (1992) *John Maynard Keynes: Volume Two: The Economist as Saviour, 1920–1937* (London: Macmillan).

Veblen, Thorstein B. (1892) 'The Price of Wheat Since 1867', *Journal of Political Economy*, **1**(1), December, 68–103.

Veblen, Thorstein B. (1893) 'The Food Supply and the Price of Wheat', *Journal of Political Economy*, **1**(3), June, 365–79.

Veblen, Thorstein B. (1898) 'Why is Economics Not an Evolutionary Science?', *Quarterly Journal of Economics*, **12**(3), July, 373–97.

Veblen, Thorstein B. (1904) *The Theory of Business Enterprise* (New York: Charles Scribners).

Veblen, Thorstein B. (1905) 'Credit and Prices', *Journal of Political Economy*, **13**(3), June, 460–72.

Veblen, Thorstein B. (1908a) 'Professor Clark's Economics', *Quarterly Journal of Economics*, **22**(2), February, 147–95.

Veblen, Thorstein B. (1908b) 'On the Nature of Capital I: The Productivity of Capital Goods', *Quarterly Journal of Economics*, **22**(4), August, 517–42.

Vining, Rutledge (1939) 'Suggestions of Keynes in the Writings of Veblen', *Journal of Political Economy*, **47**(5), October, 692–704.

Williamson, Oliver E. (1975) *Markets and Hierarchies: Analysis and Anti-trust Implications: A Study in the Economics of Internal Organization* (New York: Free Press).

Williamson, Oliver E. (1981) 'The Modern Corporation: Origins, Evolution, Attributes', *Journal of Economic Literature*, **19**(4), 1537–68.

Williamson, Oliver E. (1983) 'Credible Commitments: Using Hostages to Support Exchange', *American Economic Review*, **74**(3), September, 519–40.

Williamson, Oliver E. (1985) *The Economic Institutions of Capitalism: Firms, Markets, Relational Contracting* (London: Macmillan).

Williamson, Oliver E. (2000) 'The New Institutional Economics: Taking Stock, Looking Ahead', *Journal of Economic Literature*, **38**(3), September, 595–613.

Yonay, Yuval P. (1998) *The Struggle Over the Soul of Economics: Institutionalist and Neoclassical Economists in America Between the Wars* (Princeton, NJ: Princeton University Press).

6 Schumpeter
Gerhard Hanappi

6.1 INTRODUCTION

Till today Joseph Alois Schumpeter remains an enfant terrible in the arena of well-respected economists. Despite his often systematic-sounding style he never produced a consistent theory concerning any of the numerous subjects of investigations he set out to describe. At least, this is how many of his contemporaries perceived his contributions. A well-defined theory of the firm thus cannot be found in Schumpeter's oeuvres. What can be found there is a patchwork of interconnected ideas, of reflections and meditations, concerning capitalist firms. And as the reader of Schumpeter's texts tries to discover patterns and main themes in this mosaic it often proves to be more fascinating (and actually reveals more knowledge) than any elegant, self-contained and consistent treatment of the subject possibly could be.

In other words, Schumpeter's theory of the firm is itself evolutionary in the sense that (1) it revolves around a small diversity of theoretical aspects of capitalist firms, (2) selects this set of characteristics as dominant and thus characteristic for an economic epoch, and (3) expresses the transitory status of his suggestions by immediately adding caveats and even contradictions. Instead of arriving at a finally adequate theory of the firm, rather Schumpeter accompanies important features of firms in their historical development, with one eye always on their emergence at a certain point in history and the other eye on their foreseeable redundancy in the future. Three of his favorite topics will be discussed in what follows.

6.2 THE CAPITALIST FIRM AS MOTOR OF TECHNOLOGICAL ADVANCE

When the young Austrian economist Joseph Schumpeter, inspired by his teacher von Wieser, set out to write his first book he gave it the rather megalomaniac title *The Nature and Essence of Theoretical Economics* (Schumpeter [1908] 1970). This choice can easily be explained. The contradictory element so typical for Schumpeter on the one hand made him admire the mathematician Leon Walras, whose pure (market dynamics) theory ignored history and in particular disequilibrating forces on the firm level, while on the other hand he had, all of his life, investigated mainly the blind spots of Walrasian pure theory. In the fierce theoretical confrontation between the German historical school around Gustav Schmoller and the emerging Walrasian camp amongst German speaking economists, the extroverted young Schumpeter firmly took sides with the latter. His book is simply a statement of this attitude.[1]

Nevertheless he must already have felt some shortcomings of the 'pure theory' when he gave a more careful evaluation of the concept of 'social value' in 1909 (Schumpeter,

1909). Arguably he needed his own insistence on the rigid static market model of Walras as background for his own contribution, his second book called *Theory of Economic Development* (Schumpeter [1911] 1997). What motivated Schumpeter to depart from his celebration of equilibrating market forces is a scientific attitude, which he much later considered to have in common with Karl Marx: the final decisive element for scientific truth is the empirical fact, '*Tatsachenbeobachtung*' as Schumpeter writes.[2] And in a world hurtling towards the explosion of World War I, the clash of empires instead of classes, it certainly was counter-intuitive to describe it as an equilibrium process.

As a trained economist and devoted to starting from empirically observed facts Schumpeter identified the major advance in societies since Adam Smith to be the improvements in production technologies and products. But technical progress was explicitly excluded from the system of pure exchange that constituted the core of contemporary 'pure theory'. Every change there would have to be derived from changes in the marginal utilities of individuals, changes that in turn could only be seen as external shock. This was too far from empirical fact for Schumpeter: for him the introduction of novelty – as observed in the past – always came from the suppliers, from the firms. This basic insight, namely that – contrary to the causal structure of the Walrasian school – new production processes and new products are not called into existence by the wants of consumers but rather by proposals for novelty made by firms, remained a recurring element in Schumpeter's work throughout his life.

There are important consequences of this reversal of causal structure. First of all it implies that the goal variables of firms have to be separated from the goals of their customers. The goals of customers (households, public bodies, and other firms) enter a firm's goal function, but only indirectly as a constraint to be met. Firms have to build internal models of their prospective consumers to derive expected effective demand. So Walras's structure of marginal utilities of commodities for each individual is still important, but now it appears as anticipation of such a structure in the internal models built by firms. And each firm will add other elements to this building block of its internal model. (1) '*Effective* demand' already means that it has to be anticipated how much disposable money a prospective customer can spend. Some kind of wage–price system has to be assumed. (2) But since even in local firm environments wages and prices are always vectors assigned to heterogeneous labor processes and commodities the final task of the internal model clearly must be to anticipate the overall global dynamics – a task always too complicated and too costly for a single firm. The art of the firm thus consists in striking the profit-maximizing balance between the cost of additional internal model building and the additional profits made by better anticipation. (3) Schumpeter identifies profit as the central goal variable of firms, and as the classics identify it, as the difference between revenues and cost. Since every new process or new product needs finance, the cost of this finance, that is, capital cost, enters a firm's goal function too. But as Schumpeter already saw, the banking structure of an economy since Adam Smith had developed into a rather complicated system not easily disentangled from political developments. To include some of this, at least very sketchily, in the internal model of the firm would again call for strong assumptions and simplifications.

To sum up: whatever Schumpeter's vision of a firm is, it has to solve a tremendously difficult modeling task. But since it has to come up with decisions in time it will always be forced to be subjected to a trial and error process validating its highly preliminary internal model building. This trial and error process, which weeds out survivors and eliminates losers, evidently is a social process involving all parts of society. The entities trying to anticipate this social process, the firms, are collectively driving it. They are the ones that can be considered the motor of technological advance. As Schumpeter recognized, the impact of capitalist firms on all other parts of society had become so overwhelming that they indeed were becoming the dominating social institutions.

6.3   THE CAPITALIST FIRM AS A SOCIAL INSTITUTION WITHIN A BROADER CONTEXT

It is not without a certain melancholy that the economic historian Schumpeter observes the demise of the old feudal order, which constituted the system of social institutions dominating his youth in the Austrian-Hungarian Empire. The two new types of social institutions – *capitalist firms* and *labor movement institutions* – seemed to inevitably become the major pillars of the twentieth century's societies. Evaluating their successes more than 50 years after Marx, he took a much more skeptical attitude than the latter. The triumphant praise of the labor-productivity-enhancing role of big industry to be found in Marx's manifesto (Marx, 1848) appears in Schumpeter's writings only as a kind of requiem for the golden days of British capitalism in the nineteenth century. And while Marx, instead of forecasting any more detailed features of a future mode of production, used an emphatic belief in the proletariat's political victory as an ideological tool, Schumpeter – again with a vague prediction of socialism's coming dominance – with some regret just foresaw the emergence of large socialized production units rendering the original innovative function of individual entrepreneurs obsolete.

   It is obvious that a social scientist as involved in everyday politics as Schumpeter certainly was, cannot be expected to carry out his scientific work without being influenced by his personal political experiences. To take sides with one of the above-mentioned two pillars of the upcoming socioeconomic system was mandatory for intellectual leaders of the time. And Schumpeter took sides with the bourgeois representatives of capitalist firms. But as his gusto for contradictory choices commanded, he at the same time was prepared to become Minister of Finance in the first socialist-led coalition government of the Austrian Republic: 'It needs a doctor if someone is going to die', he is reported to have commented on his new role. This cynical attitude became characteristic of most of his judgments. Some kind of arrangement with the social institutions of the labor movement, some kind of social partnership, appeared to be inevitable – though he did not like it. The end of the innovative role of individual entrepreneurs, of their historical mission, seemed to be in sight – though he did not like it. The overwhelming importance of crude state power was becoming more and more visible – and he was not sure if he should like it. Evidence of empirically observed trends in the inter-war period ran counter to Schumpeter's own social preferences, but as an adept of '*Tatsachenbeobachtung*', he rather accommodated his theoretical fragments to fit reality.

   When he witnessed the surge of large corporations acting on a more and more global scale he sensed that his original concept of the innovative entrepreneur, the individual leader of the capitalist firm, had to be updated. Certainly, in any future society production units, entities that organize the commodities and services that the population needs will still exist. In which form the creation of novelty, of new combinations, can survive was not clear for Schumpeter. He anticipated the emergence of more large, globally operating corporations with teams sharing a scaled-down innovative punch, embedded in a rather dull socialist political setting. The necessary falling apart of managerial duties and individual incentives of capital owners was already visible for him, which implied a loss of creativity, and after the end of World War II he recognized that the majority of the intellectual elites of advanced countries supported socialist ideas and thus were lost as carriers of the 'entrepreneurial spirit' he considered to be a substantial ingredient of capitalism. Understandably – and despite his correct intuitions – Schumpeter's interest in this new type of firm was somewhat limited. For him the internal organization of this newly dominating type of firm was not a determining element of the course of the global economy any more: direct socialist policy forms, less creative, and less colorful had taken its place. So while Schumpeter from the 1940s onwards was one of the most influential teachers of a new generation of economists in Harvard and even across the USA, his own leitmotif – capitalism as guided by entrepreneurial individuals – was already outdated.

6.4   THE INNER ORGANIZATION OF CAPITALIST FIRMS – THE ENTREPRENEUR

It took almost 40 years until the early 1980s for his core invention, the entrepreneur, to come into fashion again. And it is not too far-fetched to consider this change of focus in mainstream economic theory as having been stimulated by the conservative rollback in politics, which occurred when Thatcher (1979), Reagan (1980), and Kohl (1982) were elected leaders. The ideological underpinnings to fight social-democratic ideas that Schumpeter's concept of the entrepreneur seemed to provide were suddenly highly welcome. But as a closer look at Schumpeter's original concept reveals, to claim relevance of his concept first introduced in Schumpeter ([1911] 1997) to support conservative economic policy in last two decades of the century has been rather inadequate.

When Schumpeter decided to introduce elements in the prevailing economic theory that could explain accelerating disequilibrium in markets, he had to choose either between forces coming from the surge of labor movement institutions or forces represented by capitalist firms. When he worked on his theory of development (probably starting in 1908) membership in unions had risen sharply since the last decade of the nineteenth century, a failed attempt at revolution in Russia had occurred in 1905, and the hitherto stable, feudal political superstructure started to crumble. Schumpeter's contradictory attitude evidently made it impossible for him not to oppose many of his intellectual contemporaries who saw progress in a coincidence of the fall of feudal power and participation of the labor movement in politics. He thus rather preferred to choose the capitalist firm as the driving force of progress, in particular capitalist firms in their heroic, anti-feudalist period – in the early nineteenth century. The methodological setting he introduces by this choice is interesting: he starts with the historical conflict between feudal political superstructure and bourgeois firm-owners and dissolves it into a fight of firms for profits via the introduction of novelty on the one hand, and a retreat from considering the interaction between political levels (here the feudal politics) and economic processes on the other hand. Development is taken care of by equilibrium-disturbing capitalist firms; political evolutions are just epiphenomena.

Add now his early inclination to emphasize methodological individualism[3] – inherited from Menger and von Wieser – and you get Schumpeter's 'entrepreneur'.[4] In the capitalist firm in Britain during the Industrial Revolution the owner of the firm, the one who introduced new techniques, and the one who borrowed the necessary money were indeed one and the same physical person. This was the individual that a theory of development needed to be able to position within the realm of methodological individualism.

But while this happy marriage of a methodological recipe and empirical observations of an (inappropriate) historical epoch solved the immediate problem of introducing development in 1911, it turned out to be difficult to defend as the turbulent first half of the twentieth century continued.

Firms typically financed their innovative activity not by borrowing money from a rich uncle, as seems to have often been the case in nineteenth-century Britain. Schumpeter had to assume an independent banking system, a well-functioning banking system. To divorce banking from general entrepreneurial behavior but to keep the entrepreneur proper as the hero of the economic tale to be told was a heroic step. Schumpeter's contemporary Rudolf Hilferding had published a book, *Das Finanzkapital* (1910), thought to be an update of Marx's *Das Kapital* (1867, 1885, 1894), which saw finance capital taking the center stage in modern capitalism – while Schumpeter treated 'well-functioning' banking only as a necessary side constraint.[5] But this procedure allowed Schumpeter to concentrate on the main characteristic of the entrepreneur, namely to shift the production function upwards, to carry out innovations. It was only straight forward that he insisted that only for this core activity a positive interest rate should be assumed. Capital owners get a part of the interest rate that entrepreneurs earn, and if the latter do not innovate, then the interest rate is zero.

In 1931, during the Great Depression, Schumpeter evaluates this crisis and comes to the conclusion that the main cause could be the coincidence of waves of innovative behavior of different length. This innovation-bound dynamics is the central endogenous cause of the crisis; the many less important exogenous influences (like bad monetary policy) are mentioned too, but only cursorily (Schumpeter, 1931).

In his major work on business cycles (Schumpeter [1939] 1989) a further consequence of this conceptualization of the entrepreneur is drawn. As new products and processes are only new for a rather limited time span, so are the agents that bring them into existence. Firms are timed – actually are equivalent – to their innovations, firms and even their plants come and go as they are able to innovate (ibid., pp. 68–70). In a sense what he describes is a mirror image of the usual product life cycle: in his perspective the vanishing demand for a product is caused by an innovative entrepreneur offering a competing new product. This view on business demography, as it is labeled today, is one of the reasons why he (despite his own assertions) can be considered an evolutionary economist: there is always a heterogeneous set of firms of different sizes and at different stages in their finite life times. While relative innovative power translated via market forces permanently weeds out some of them, there is also incessant birth of new firms trying to survive.[6]

While the entrepreneurial soul of Schumpeter's vision of a capitalist firm has experienced an interesting renaissance in modern evolutionary theory, in particular when it was reformulated in simulation environments, his claim that the growth of multinational corporations undermines their innovative behavior has received more empirically oriented attention. As Schumpeter's nineteenth-century vision of a capitalist firm cannot be easily compared with the complicated internal structures of contemporary firms, it cannot be expected that (apart from some singular issues) a reliable judgment concerning the decreasing innovative power caused by firm growth will ever be possible. So far it seems to be difficult enough to characterize the behavior of large transnational firms at all[7] – even without any evolutionary assumptions on creative innovation.[8] Schumpeter's attempt to isolate innovative behavior and to define it as the core of the definition of a capitalist firm is not helpful when the goal is to describe and to understand contemporary large, transnational corporations.

6.5   CONCLUSION

Despite, or perhaps due to his often cursory and partly contradictory style Schumpeter has inspired more economists than most of his contemporaries. This also holds for topics concerning the theory of the firm. All kinds of supply-side economics, which in last resort have to discuss the behavior of production units, will find valuable – though singular – insights in Schumpeter's texts.

His most well-known theoretical innovation, the notion of the entrepreneur, experienced a more ambivalent fate. Being more of an artificial, even ideologically oriented concept from its very start, it lent itself too often to misuse in superficial economic policy debates. Indeed it has mostly inadequately been used to argue for the privatization of public funds, as justification of involuntary unemployment of people who do not possess enough 'entrepreneurial spirit', and the like. But parallel to this misuse the concept also hinted at the necessity to discuss the internal structure of firms: what really is the role of hierarchy in production units? How can we describe the process of innovation?[9] Based on these questions a wide array of literature has been produced ranging from industrial organization to more intrinsic questions of creativity per se. Schumpeter, the economist who always provoked dialogue, to a considerable extent was responsible for that creative theoretic response.

Finally, he can be charged with playing a similar trick with respect to the embedding of the theory of the firm in a wider social context. By isolating the innovative function in his theoretical vision of the capitalist firm, while engaging himself with empathy in the general political turmoil of the troubled times he lived in, he again was a living example of the tight connection between political attitudes and theoretical, microeconomic constructs. His incessant attempts to come to quits with empirically observed processes while insisting on several ideological visions – necessary visions, as he often said – led him to sometimes contradictory, but always interesting issues. It is this appearance of a synthetic aspiration, the aspiration to understand the overall process[10] within which firm behavior is embedded, that seems to be Schumpeter's most precious legacy today. And in this respect it is definitely an open, evolutionary process.

NOTES

1. In an earlier paper he fiercely defends what he calls the 'exact theory' of Jevons and Walras against the German historical school (Schumpeter [1906] 1952). Though Schumpeter had long admired mathematics, he personally never mastered it – despite lessons he demanded from his desperate assistant Richard Goodwin.
2. Parallels between Schumpeter and Marx do exist, but predominantly in their methodological approach – one is tempted to say in their 'dialectical' style – and their aspirations to explain the laws of motion of a capitalist society. With respect to the content of such an explanation there are, of course, essential differences. See Elliott (1980) and Foster (1983) for a concise treatment of this question.
3. The marginalist approach initiated by Menger, Jevons, and Walras in 1884 had introduced methodological individualism in economic theory mainly to copy the successful formal apparatus of the natural sciences, which needed clear-cut smallest atoms. A single physical individual of homo sapiens seemed to be the ideal starting point for a social theory akin to a physical system. An evident side-effect most welcome to conservative politicians was that the dangerous concept of social classes, so prominent in classical political economy till Marx, could be completely purged.
4. A very concise discussion of Schumpeter's definition of entrepreneurs can be found in Oakley (1990, pp. 110–21).
5. In 1925 he already saw that the tendency towards large public bodies taking central economic decisions also included the (in his view somehow 'exogenous') monetary system: 'This [the last consequences of the new banking policy, G.H.] is no longer management of the monetary system, but management of the whole national economy, without any visible boundaries. It means an actual limitation of the possibilities of private initiative and a marked deviation from the economic principle of private property and free competition. The decision on what is to be produced, and how, would from now on, be in the hands of a central body: the same would apply to the distribution of the proceeds of production amoung the various social classes' (Schumpeter [1925] 1994, p. 113).
6. A nice survey on the empirics of these processes can be found in Coad (2009, pp. 14–38).
7. Compare, for example, Navaretti and Venables (2004).
8. Schumpeter himself just noted: 'Thus, economic progress tends to become depersonalized and automatized. Bureau and committee work tends to replace individual action' (Schumpeter [1942] 2003, p. 133).
9. A more thorough treatment of that issue in a Schumpeterian perspective can be found in Hanappi and Hanappi-Egger (2004).
10. As a consequence every aspect of the highly interconnected overall process can propagate some Shumpeterean impact. For example, Reinert (2009) puts forward a most interesting Schumpeterian trade theory in the area of industrial organization.

REFERENCES

Coad, A. (2009), *The Growth of Firms. A Survey of Theories and Empirical Evidence*, Cheltenham, UK and Northampton, MA, USA: Edward Elgar.
Elliott, J.E. (1980), 'The Political Economy of Joseph Schumpeter: A Theory of Capitalist Development and Decline', *The Quarterly Journal of Economics*, **95**(1), 45–68.
Foster, J.B. (1983), 'Theories of Capitalist Transformation: Critical Notes on the Comparison of Marx and Schumpeter', *The Quarterly Journal of Economics*, **98**(2), 327–31.
Hanappi, H. and E. Hanappi-Egger (2004), 'New Combinations. Taking Schumpeter's Concept Seriously', Proceedings of the ISS Conference 2004, Bocconi University (Milan, Italy).
Marx, K. (1848), *Das Manifest der Kommunistischen Partei*, printed at the Office of the Workers' Educational Society, 46 Liverpool Street, Bishopsgate, London.
Navaretti, G.B. and A.J. Venables (2004), *Multinational Firms in the World Economy*, Princeton, NJ: Princeton University Press.
Oakley, A. (1990), *Schumpeter's Theory of Capitalist Motion. A Critical Exposition & Reassessment*, Aldershot, UK and Brookfield, VT, USA: Edward Elgar.
Reinert, E.S. (2009), 'Emulation versus Comparative Advantage: Competing and Complementary Principles in the History of Economic Policy', in M. Cimoli, G. Dosi and J.E. Stiglitz (eds) (2009), *Industrial Policy and Development. The Political Economy of Capabilities Accumulation*, Oxford: Oxford University Press.
Schumpeter, J.A. ([1906] 1952), 'Die mathematische Methode in der Okonomie', in *Aufsätze zur ökonomischen Theorie*, Tübingen: J.C.B. Mohr, pp. 529–48.

Schumpeter, J.A. ([1908] 1970), *Das Wesen und der Hauptinhalt der theoretischen Nationalökonomie* (The Nature and Essence of Theoretical Economics), Berlin: Duncker & Humblot.

Schumpeter, J.A. (1909), 'On the Concept of Social Value', *Quarterly Journal of Economics*, **23**(2), 213–32.

Schumpeter, J.A. ([1911] 1997), *Theorie der wirtschaftlichen Entwicklung I* (Theory of Economic Development), Berlin: Duncker & Humblot.

Schumpeter, J.A. ([1925] 1994), 'Old and New Banking Policy', in Y. Shionoya and M. Perlman (eds), *Schumpeter in the History of Ideas*, Ann Arbor: University of Michigan Press.

Schumpeter, J.A. (1931), 'The Present World Depression: A Tentative Diagnosis', *American Economic Review*, **21**(1), Supplement, Papers and Proceedings of the Forty-third Annual Meeting of the American Economic Association, 179–82.

Schumpeter, J.A. ([1939] 1989), *Business Cycles. A Theoretical, Historical and Statistical Analysis of the Capitalist Process*, New York/Toronto/London: McGraw-Hill.

Schumpeter, J.A. ([1942] 2003), *Capitalism, Socialism and Democracy*, London: Routledge Publishers.

7   Berle and Means
Cécile Cézanne

7.1   INTRODUCTION

Law professor Adolf Augustus Berle, Jr (1895–1971) and economist Gardiner Coit
Means (1896–1988) coauthored a single and famous book, *The Modern Corporation and
Private Property*, which represents a landmark in the American institutionalist tradition.
Published in 1932, in the context of the American New Deal following the 1929 crisis, this
book describes the mutations of industrial capitalism during the 1920s and early 1930s.
It shows how the traditional personal capitalism regime building on competitive interactions among small firms within industries was challenged by managerial capitalism,
which remained dominant until the 1980s. Berle and Means observed that 'big industry'
was born in most occidental economies as a response to firm restructuring. Firms tended
to integrate both upstream and downstream, which resulted in markets dominated by
powerful enterprises. Big industry coincided with the emergence of the public corporation. The authors emphasize the ubiquity of these types of large companies in the modern
productive process: 'These great companies form the very framework of American
industry' (Berle and Means, 1932, p. 19). The hierarchical structure and organization of
giant companies whose productive activity was based on a large stock of specific physical capital are examined in depth. Thus, Berle and Means's book can be viewed as a first
step toward an analysis of firm boundaries legally delimited by property rights over
tangible assets. It also studies the effects of the way modern business corporations are
owned and controlled, on inter-individual contractual relationships within the firm. In
this perspective, Berle and Means's book is the seminal work on corporate governance.
   This chapter offers an analysis of the two main contributions of *The Modern
Corporation and Private Property* to the economics of the firm. The chapter is organized
as follows. Section 7.2 focuses on the implications of the separation of ownership and
control for the theory of the firm. More precisely, we suggest an original understanding of the impact of the legal structure of corporations on the issue of firm boundaries.
Section 7.3 revisits how the separation of ownership and control raises problems of
power relationships within the firm. In other words, we revisit the emergence of corporate governance as a major field of analysis in the economics of the firm. Section 7.4
concludes the chapter.

7.2   SEPARATION OF OWNERSHIP AND CONTROL AND THE
BOUNDARIES OF THE FIRM

The separation of ownership and control within public companies depends heavily on
the structural, organizational and productive corporate changes that occurred at the
beginning of the twentieth century. In exploring the transition from the entrepreneurial

firm to the managerial corporation, Berle and Means highlight first the role of legal property rights on physical assets in this changing context. This is an indication that the legal boundaries of the firm can be viewed from a broad historical business perspective as described in Berle and Means (1932). During the nineteenth century, the business world was dominated by entrepreneurial firms characterized by founders and owners/managers being the same person. Because of the growth of these small firms, owner-entrepreneurs were faced with the incapacity of financing the development of their firms and forced to go into joint ownership and create corporations. This resulted in the owner-entrepreneurs losing some of their legal power over the firm. And the increasing size of these small firms made it difficult for an owner-entrepreneur to retain overall control. These entrepreneurs were forced to employ specialized professionals and to confer on them some management power. In addition, following the crisis in 1929, owner-entrepreneurs were seen as speculators whose functions were constrained to provision of funds while control of firms was gradually transferred to the managers. Thus, the two basic attributes of an owner-entrepreneur began to be questioned. These attributes were property rights and controlling power.

The result was the emergence of the managerial corporation associated with the division between owner and manager. Berle and Means (1932, pp. 110–11) note that 'In the largest American corporations, a new condition has developed. . . [T]here are no dominant owners, and control is maintained in large measure apart from ownership', a statement that has strong connections with business history-oriented analyses. Dispersed ownership associated with concentration of power in the hands of top management defines the 'managerial revolution' (Chandler, 1977). From an institutional viewpoint, managerial capitalism can be seen as an economic system based on the logic of endless accumulation in which firms are run by the real decision-makers – the managers – and not by the owners of the capital (Galbraith, 1967). The managerial corporation is referred to in Chandler (1977, p. 1) as the 'modern business enterprise'. Chandler argues that the modern multi-unit firm replaced the traditional single-unit firm when administrative coordination by the 'visible hand of management' (ibid.) became more efficient than market coordination based on the system of prices. Berle and Means's work also gave rise to modern economic analyses.

First, the managerial corporation, which was created to exploit scale and scope economies, was traditionally vertically integrated and physical capital intensive. As a major organizational innovation, this kind of large firm quickly began to dominate existing production units and to make profits in the United States, and gradually spread across the world in the mid-twentieth century. The different productive activities, from the processing of raw materials to the distribution of final goods, were built on an important stock of specialized materials and equipment. In the 1920s and 1930s, these tangible and transferable assets were difficult to imitate and it was this characteristic of non-reproducibility that differentiated the corporation. In addition, there was a lack of mobility in human capital, which, in large part, was subordinated to the development of physical assets. Hart (1989) shows that control of physical capital can lead to control of human assets in the form of organizational capital. Therefore, property rights over specific non-human assets were the unique, acknowledged source of power in the corporation. Thus, Berle and Means's representation of the managerial corporation can be examined as a historical business approach within the contractual theory of the firm. The managerial corporation was stable and well defined and its boundaries were clearly delimited to the legal structure of property rights over unique physical capital. The managerial corporation embodies the model of vertical integration (Klein et al., 1978), which describes the administrative mode of coordination of productive activities. More precisely, division of labour is ensured, on the one hand, by hierarchies and, on the other hand, by markets (Coase, 1937; Williamson, 1975). In other words, vertical integration (i.e., the firm) and vertical disintegration (i.e., the market) are the two polar modes of coordinating economic agents. Also, according to this transactional view, the firm is a combination of commonly owned, physical assets. As modelled by the incomplete contracts theory (Grossman and Hart, 1986; Hart and Moore, 1990, Hart, 1995), ownership of physical assets determines a planned coordination by firms, whereas non-ownership corresponds to a spontaneous coordination by markets. In this context, the realm of transactions governed by hierarchical power rather than market prices tended to coincide with the legal boundaries of the corporation (Rajan and Zingales, 2000).

Second, the managerial corporation, on the one hand, is legally owned by widely dispersed shareholders and, on the other hand, is controlled by layers of salaried management. Since property rights on physical assets were delegated to top management by shareholders, power and rents were concentrated in the hands of the few agents at the top of the organizational pyramid in the vertically integrated company. In this context, Berle and Means (1932, p. 46) note that:

> [T]he economic power in the hands of the few persons who control a giant corporation is a tremendous force which can harm or benefit a multitude of individuals, affect whole districts, shift the currents of trade, bring ruin to one community and prosperity to another. The organizations which they control have passed far beyond the realm of private enterprise – they have become more nearly social institutions.

This poses a substantial problem for the modern corporation: how rightfully to distribute the surplus accumulated by top management to dispersed shareholders? This is the fundamental issue in corporate governance.

7.3   SEPARATION OF OWNERSHIP AND CONTROL AND CORPORATE GOVERNANCE

The distinction between ownership and control leads to an opposition between shareholders' and managers' interests:

> Have we any justification for assumption that those in control of a modern corporation will also choose to operate it in the interests of the owners? The answer to this question will depend on the degree to which the self-interest of those in control may run parallel to the interests of ownership and, insofar as they differ, on the checks on the use of power which may be established by political, economic, or social conditions. . . If we are to assume that the desire for personal profit is the prime force motivating control, we must conclude that the interests of control are different from and often radically opposed to those of ownership; that the owners most emphatically will not be served by a profit-seeking controlling group. (Berle and Means, 1932, pp. 113–14)

Because of the dispersion of functions traditionally assumed by a single agent, the owner-entrepreneur, Berle and Means suggest an innovative conception of how to regulate power relationships between owners and managers. They show that the interests of the shareholders need to be protected without detracting from the interests of the managers. In other words, shareholders are not the sole partners involved in the evolution of firm activities. Berle and Means conclude that the modern corporation must take account of the interests of all its stakeholders,[1] and thus can be seen as supporting the stakeholder approach to corporate governance.[2] Paradoxically, their thesis gave rise to measures to uphold the shareholder view of corporate governance, considered in the context of the New Deal programme. During the 1930s, the United States strengthened its stock market regulation: the Securities and Exchange Commission was created in 1933 to protect financial investors and the role of the institutional investors increased in the context of financial liberalization. In sum, the growing importance of financial markets empowered shareholders, and intensified shareholder activism prevented managerial drift and management's exclusive power was severely questioned. Corporate governance emerged to protect external investors by limiting the obstacles that affect their rights of control. Greater transparency, voting rights for all shareholders, shouldering of responsibility by top management, contestability of corporate control, and compensation for management associated with maximization of shareholder value were advocated. Thus, corporate governance was developed in order to regulate managers' behaviour, and to define the rules of management.

Agency theory is based on the separation between a large number of owners of physical assets, and the managers who took over the control of firms, highlighted by Berle and Means (1932), as the basic shareholder view of corporate governance. Agency theory focuses on relationships that involve moral hazard for the principal (the shareholder) who commissions and pays the agent (the manager) within a large public company. The underlying idea is that the separation of ownership and control generates conflicts of interest between shareholders and managers, which can be solved by contractual mechanisms (Jensen and Meckling, 1976; Fama, 1980; Fama and Jensen, 1983). Agency theory stresses that, despite complete contracts, informational asymmetries associated with the personal interests cause inter-individual conflicts between shareholders and managers. The two parties pursue a plurality of differentiated – often contradictory – objectives. On the one hand, shareholders have patrimonial rights and aim to maximize the profitability of their firms. Shareholders own the non-human assets of the firm and provide permanent capital funds; they see that this financial risk justifies exclusive appropriation of the firm's profits. Shareholders can exercise legal rights to the benefits of property owning once all other claimants (lenders, suppliers, employees, etc.) have been satisfied. In other words, shareholders have residual claims on the firm's tangible assets; they have residual rights of control 'that is, the right to decide how these assets should be used, given that a usage has not been specified in an initial contract' (Hart, 1995, p. 680).

On the other hand, managers expect high incomes and personal prestige; managers are interested in their firms growing bigger. As insiders, managers have better information about tasks, based on their organizational positions within firms. They are also the only ones to be aware of their *real* professional skills. Thus, managers may be encouraged to adopt discretionary behaviour that is inconsistent with maximizing the shareholder's utility function. Nevertheless, in accordance with property rights theory (Alchian and Demsetz, 1972), each party is required for a transaction: the shareholder needs the capital incorporated in the manager and, reciprocally, the manager needs the funds invested by the shareholder. As shareholders cannot completely control managers, they need to find appropriate means to incite these insiders to behave according to their expectations. Various market-oriented mechanisms can be used to discipline managers. Managerial incentives in the form of performance-oriented compensation, monitoring by external referees, or the market for corporate control can help to align the interests of top management and shareholders. Therefore, corporate governance has to serve the interests of residual claimants (Tirole, 2001). The main purpose is to maximize shareholder value by minimizing or wiping out the agency costs caused by potential conflicts of interest between owners and controllers. In this way, 'corporate governance [traditionally] deals with the ways in which suppliers of finance to corporations assure themselves of getting a return on their investment' (Shleifer and Vishny, 1997, p. 737).

7.4 CONCLUSION

Despite differences in the pace, timing and nature of change, large firms in the United States, Europe and Japan evolved in the 1920s and 1930s according to a common pattern (Chandler, 1984). These large firms were characterized by what Berle and Means (1932) identified as the separation of ownership and control within modern public companies. Based on historical evidence, Berle and Means (ibid.) approached two major aspects of the economics of the firm: (1) the essential elements required to understand the boundaries of the firm, which were later analysed in the seminal work by Coase (1937); (2) the terms of the modern debate on corporate governance that has taken place only since the 1980s. The primacy in this debate of the shareholder value perspective implies that Berle and Means's seminal analysis is often misinterpreted. However, the debate on corporate governance now tends to be balanced by alternative views, as mainly the stakeholder value perspective.

Finally, Berle and Means's work suggested that it is impossible to have a complete understanding of the general system by which firms are owned and managed without having some notion of what a firm is, and of how its boundaries are established. The characteristics and workings of a firm need to be seen within the context of the relationships between different groups of individuals with different interests. We would suggest that there is a need to restore the link between the nature and governance of the firm – an area that is often overlooked in the literature (Bolton and Scharfstein, 1998). Some attempts have been made to reconcile these two – traditionally separate – fields of analysis (Rajan and Zingales, 2000; Cézanne-Sintès, 2008; Ravix, 2008), and show that the way a firm is governed changes with the way its boundaries are incorporated into the theoretical framework.

NOTES

1. Stakeholders are groups of individuals who have legal rights over and duties in the firm. Stakeholders include shareholders, managers, creditors, employees, customers, suppliers, and so on, and each of these families of economic agents owns critical resources and in return expects that their interests will be satisfied (Freeman, 1984).
2. For a complete survey of stakeholder theory, see Donaldson and Preston (1995).

REFERENCES

Alchian, A.A. and H. Demsetz (1972), 'Production, Information Costs, and Economic Organization', *American Economic Review*, **62**(5), 777–95.
Berle, A.A. and G.C. Means (1932), *The Modern Corporation and Private Property*, New York: Harcourt, Brace and World.
Bolton, P. and D.S. Scharfstein (1998), 'Corporate Finance, the Theory of the Firm, and Organizations', *Journal of Economic Perspectives*, **12**(4), 95–114.
Cézanne-Sintès, C. (2008), 'Modern Corporate Changes: Reinstating the Link between the Nature, Boundaries and Governance of the Firm', *International Review of Applied Economics*, **22**(4), 447–61.
Chandler, A.D. Jr. (1977), *The Visible Hand: The Managerial Revolution in American Business*, Cambridge, MA: The Belknap Press of Harvard University Press.
Chandler, A.D. Jr. (1984), 'The Emergence of Managerial Capitalism', *Business History Review*, **58**(4), 473–503.
Coase, R.H. (1937), 'The Nature of the Firm', *Economica*, **4**(16), 386–405.
Donaldson, T. and L.E. Preston (1995), 'The Stakeholder Theory of the Corporation: Concepts, Evidence and Implications', *Academy of Management Review*, **20**(1), 65–91.
Fama, E.F. (1980), 'Agency Problems and the Theory of the Firm', *Journal of Political Economy*, **88**(21), 288–307.
Fama, E.F. and M.C. Jensen (1983), 'Separation of Ownership and Control', *Journal of Law & Economics*, **26**(2), 301–26.
Freeman, R.E. (1984), *Strategic Management: A Stakeholder Approach*, Boston, Pitman Press.
Galbraith, J.K. (1967), *The New Industrial State*, New York: Mentor.
Grossman, S.J. and O.D. Hart (1986), 'The Costs and Benefits of Ownership: A Theory of Vertical and Lateral Integration', *Journal of Political Economy*, **94**(4), 691–719.
Hart, O.D. (1989), 'An Economist's Perspective on the Theory of the Firm', *Columbia Law Review*, **89**(7), 1757–74.
Hart, O.D. (1995), 'Corporate Governance: Some Theory and Implications', *Economic Journal*, **105**(430), 678–89.
Hart, O.D. and J. Moore (1990), 'Property Rights and the Nature of the Firm', *Journal of Political Economy*, **98**(6), 1119–58.
Jensen, M.C. and W.H. Meckling (1976), 'Theory of the Firm: Managerial Behavior, Agency Costs and Ownership Structure', *Journal of Financial Economics*, **3**(4), 305–60.
Klein, B., R.G. Crawford and A.A. Alchian (1978), 'Vertical Integration, Appropriable Rents, and the Competitive Contracting Process', *Journal of Law & Economics*, **21**(2), 297–326.
Rajan, R.G. and L.G. Zingales (2000), 'The Governance of the New Enterprise', in X. Vives (ed.), *Corporate Governance: Theoretical and Empirical Perspectives*, Cambridge, UK: Cambridge University Press, pp. 201–27.
Ravix, J-L. (2008), 'Nature and Governance of the Firm: In Search of an Integrated Perspective', *International Review of Applied Economics*, **22**(4), 463–78.
Shleifer, A. and R.W. Vishny (1997), 'A Survey of Corporate Governance', *Journal of Finance*, **52**(2), 737–83.
Tirole, J. (2001), 'Corporate Governance', *Econometrica*, **69**(1), 1–35.
Williamson, O.E. (1975), *Markets and Hierarchy: Analysis and Antitrust Implications*, New York, Free Press.

8 John Kenneth Galbraith and the theory of the firm

Stephen P. Dunn

8.1 INTRODUCTION

A large part of John Kenneth Galbraith's professional career was devoted to examining modern industrial society and the large firms that dominate it. The modern corporation occupies a pivotal role in Galbraith's theorizing in general, and *The New Industrial State* ([1967] 1972) in particular. It is thus perhaps surprising that Galbraith's contribution to the theory of the firm has almost disappeared from view. While theorists like Coase (1937), Penrose (1955, 1959), Marris (1964) and Richardson (1959, 1960, 1964, 1972) have seen a resurgence of interest in their respective theories of the firm, Galbraith's contribution is hardly mentioned. Galbraith is without a doubt a neglected theorist of the firm, ignored by economists of all schools.

There are several possible interrelated reasons for this oversight. Perhaps the main reason for this neglect of Galbraith lies in the fact that he has generally been associated with the managerialist theories of the firm that grew out of the recognition by Berle and Means ([1932] 1991) that large firms were no longer controlled and dominated by their owners, but instead run by their managers (see Chandler, 1962, 1977, 1990). A second reason for this neglect of Galbraith is his caustic wit and irreverent populist rhetorical style (Solow, 1967; Gordon, 1968, 1969). Since he eschewed the mathematical presentation of more orthodox treatments by Baumol, Williamson, and Marris, theorists of the firm generally view Galbraith's contribution as a less rigorous, literary expression of the managerialist approach and thus tended to ignore it (cf. Marris, 1968; Demsetz, 1974). The third reason for Galbraith's neglect relates to the widely held perception that, while he was a great synthesizer and an ambitious system builder, he was not wholly original (Solow, 1967; Allen, 1967; Gordon, 1968, 1969; Leathers and Evans, 1974). Economists generally view *The New Industrial State* as an exercise in social philosophy rather than as an original contribution to economics in general, or the theory of the firm specifically (Gordon, 1968, 1969; Friedman, 1977). The cumulative effect of all these factors has been that Galbraith's vision of the modern corporation has not attracted the attention of contemporary theorists of the firm.

This needs redressing. This chapter reconsiders Galbraith's much neglected contribution to the theory of the firm, which occupies a pivotal role within *The New Industrial State*. Galbraith has typically been viewed as a great synthesizer, and system builder, and not as a theorist of the firm. I consider here, his particular view of the firm advanced in *The New Industrial State*, paying particular attention to Galbraith's discussion of how the firm deals with uncertainty, especially with regard to a firm's activities and boundaries. In doing so it will be clear that Galbraith is an original theorist of the firm, who considered many of the key issues raised by Coase, Knight, Schumpeter, and Penrose, among others, as well as advancing a distinct theory of the multinational corporation (Dunn, 2011). Galbraith anticipates much recent research into the theoretical origins of the firm. Galbraith focuses on the significant uncertainties that surround major investments of time and money and serves as a useful starting point for future research into how the relationship between uncertainty and the firm should be viewed.

8.2 PLANNING AND THE TECHNOSTRUCTURE

Today the firms that produce and sell the majority of the goods and services are large powerful bureaucracies, dominated by professional managers (see Table 8.1). Although markets have evolved beyond the mainstream competitive ideal, Galbraith (1952, [1967] 1972) argued that the standard predictions regarding the consequences of this shift – inefficiency and the ruthless exploitation of economic power – have not been supported by the facts. The modern firm has ushered in an era of tremendous affluence. Few customers of large corporations complain of exploitation, anti-trust laws are seldom invoked, and the instances of oligopoly are typically associated with the greatest output and the most robust growth (Galbraith, 1952, [1967] 1972, 1973). For Galbraith this required explanation.

Galbraith highlighted how the rise of the modern corporation facilitates tremendous technological change by insulating itself from, as well as mitigating, a variety of market uncertainties (see Table 8.2). *American Capitalism* introduced the idea that America's large and dominating corporations, though they had power to control their markets, also sustained the modern technological progress fundamental to economic growth (see Galbraith, 1952). The main argument of *American Capitalism* was, however, that new

Table 8.1   The size and distribution of firms in the USA, 2002

	Firms	Establish-ments	Employ-ment	Payroll Annual ($1000)	Sales or Receipts ($1000)
Employer firms	5 697 759	7 200 770	112 400 654	3 943 179 606	22 062 528 196
Less than $100 000	1 291 552	1 292 473	1 945 928	26 447 381	64 040 172
$100 000 to $499 000	2 387 780	2 396 006	8 724 876	167 457 202	596 925 336
$500 000 to $999 000	819 513	835 546	6 869 133	166 589 812	576 474 893
$1m to $4.9m	906 936	1 038 624	17 430 229	519 122 708	1 896 143 798
$5m to $9.9m	138 195	225 217	7 054 818	242 369 521	957 896 121
$10m to $49.9m	122 785	350 320	14 465 046	522 395 899	2 504 242 359
$50m to $99.9m	15 895	104 599	5 430 875	203 490 400	1 095 837 221
$100m to $249.9m	8 732	123 220	6 648 609	259 027 065	1 330 102 972
$250m to $499.9m	2 880	93 491	5 201 186	199 189 814	1 006 886 217
$500m to $999.9m	1 544	107 929	5 380 010	204 735 327	1 078 980 045
$1bn to 2.499bn	1 056	174 666	7 132 953	280 897 627	1 642 368 662
$2.5bn or more	891	458 679	26 116 991	1 151 456 850	9 312 630 400

Source: Statistics of US Businesses, 2002, http://www.census.gov/epcd/www/smallbus.html; accessed 13 January 2012.

Table 8.2   Funds expended on industrial R&D in the USA, 2005

Selected Characteristic	$ Millions
Total industrial R&D performance	200 602
Source of funds	
Company and other non-federal	181 169
Federal	19 433
Size of company (number of employees)	
5–24	6540
25–49	6642
50–99	6337
100–249	9160
250–499	7228
500–999	12 411
1000–4999	31 017
5000–9999	16 117
10 000–24 999	29 770
25 000 or more	75 380

Note: Excludes data for federally funded research and development centers.

Source: National Science Foundation, Division of Science Resources Statistics, Survey of Industrial Research and Development, 2005.

restraints on private economic power emerged on the other side of the market to limit the power of large firms – what Galbraith labeled countervailing power.

In *The New Industrial State* Galbraith ([1967] 1972, pp. 32–5) further identified the key dynamics that underpin the modern business enterprise. At its core his thesis was that advanced technology requires large dedicated commitments of capital, skilled labor, and time. As the firm grows and as production processes become increasingly complex and technologically more sophisticated, there is an increasing need for a team of dedicated bureaucratic specialists to administer the decisions of the modern business firm. Echoing the notion of bounded rationality (Simon, 1955, 1957, 1959; Williamson, 2004; cf. Dunn, 2001b), Galbraith noted that the complexities of modern technology mean that one person can no longer be familiar with all the aspects of engineering, procurement, quality control, labor relations, and marketing, which are necessary for doing business.

As group decision-making and technical expertise become more important, power passes from the individual owner to those people with the requisite knowledge of the production process – the technostructure. The technostructure represents a new class and a new factor of production. It is comprised of the diffuse decision-making structure of the large corporation, and it affects the use and promulgation of modern technology. It encompasses an array of managerial, technical, scientific, legal, engineering, accounting, and advertising expertise. And it underpins the expansion in the scientific and educational elite, which accommodates this need (Galbraith [1967] 1972, p. 364).

Organization is the manner by which the technostructure achieves coordination and makes decisions. Organization exists as a necessary response to the imperatives of complex technology and the diffusion of requisite knowledge that needs to be brought to bear in its realization (cf. Simon, 1972, 1976, 1979). The technostructure selects products and chooses production techniques, including the number and type of workers to employ; they develop marketing and pricing policy; they conduct research and development; and they are responsible for organizing access to finance (internally or externally). Its decision-making conventions and governance structures permit informed, reliable, and coordinated decisions, and it enables the pursuit and alignment of common objectives across a range of specialists. The decisive factor in economic success is no longer the heroic individual, but organized intelligence (Galbraith [1967] 1972, p. 75).

As power passes to the technostructure, the behavior of the modern corporation will increasingly reflect its aims and objectives. The technostructure will choose those goals and strategies that facilitate its survival and reproduction, such as driving growth, controlling and dominating the supply chain, and lobbying governments and regulators – what Galbraith refers to as 'the protective need' – and those that enhance its status and position, such as pursuing technical virtuosity – what Galbraith refers to as 'the affirmative need'. Focusing on growth and survival also directs attention to the various policies pursued by the technostructure to make the market more reliable and predictable. The market and the forces of competition generate considerable uncertainties for the large firm. Inflexibly making large investments over an extended period of time increases the firm's vulnerability to outside threat. As the price of failure is great, it must be avoided at all costs. To thrive, firms seek to control the market rather than being subservient to it. For example, investment in new technology is costly; and firms wish to avoid the prospect that, after expensive investment, there will be little or no demand for the goods they produce. Large investments of time and money must be protected if the costs of technological change are to be recovered and its benefits realized (Galbraith [1967] 1972, p. 41).

8.3   PLANNING AND THE MARKET

Galbraith viewed the firm as an institution that coordinates production and shelters it from the uncertainties that are generated by the market process. If the uncertainties that surround large commitments of time and money are to be mitigated then the firm must either supersede the market or subordinate it to the requirements of planning (Galbraith [1967] 1972, p. 122). The Galbraithian view of the firm is that it emerges in response to the uncertainties that surround major and complex, long-term investments. Rather than viewing the firm as resulting from a purely instrumental choice of economizing on transaction costs between alternative modes of contracting, Galbraith ([1967] 1972), like both Knight (1921) and Schumpeter (1943), saw the firm as an institution for coping with, or getting rid of, market uncertainties (cf. Langlois and Robertson, 1995). Galbraith outlined five main strategies used by the technostructure for dealing with the uncertainties that surround the market process. The firm can either ignore market uncertainty or absorb it via growth, diversification, and agglomeration or it can mitigate the impact of the market, by superseding it, controlling it, or suspending it via a network of contracts (Galbraith [1967] 1972, pp. 44–5). These are strategies that are broader than a simplistic focus on the make or buy decision. And they also include the prospect of control outwith the formal boundaries of the firm.

First if an item is relatively unimportant in terms of the production process then a firm may disregard the market uncertainties that surround its price, availability, and quality. Clearly, General Motors has little need to control the supply of paper clips to its vast organization. In relation to its total activity its expenditure on paper clips is tiny and their importance in the production of cars is peripheral. General Motors can ignore such uncertainties that surround the supply of paper clips to its organization. Another approach to mitigating the impact of market uncertainty is to absorb that uncertainty that cannot be ignored by pursuing growth, or combining size with diversification (Galbraith, 1973, p.119). Similarly, producing for several different unrelated markets allows the uncertainties associated with any one particular market to be spread across several markets (Galbraith [1967] 1972, p.45). Of course producing in several markets and industries, while a strategy for spreading risk, can also increase complexity and generate uncertainty (cf. Balakrishnan and Wernerfelt, 1986; Gatignon and Anderson, 1988). So ultimately the assessment will reflect the interests and capabilities of the relevant technostructure, as well as the conventional wisdoms that pervade the business community (Galbraith, 1973, p.121).

The other strategies for dealing with the uncertainties of the market concern its replacement, control or suspension. For example, the most common strategy for replacing the market relates to what is typically referred to as horizontal and vertical integration (Williamson, 1971). Horizontally integrating allows the firm to reduce the amount of price competition that it is subject to and facilitates detailed planning: 'unless a firm has a substantial share of the market it has no strong incentive to undertake a large expenditure on development' (Galbraith, 1952, p.92). Similarly, placing successive stages of production and distribution under the authoritative determination of one center of control enables the modern corporation to appropriate the profit margin of intermediaries and to secure the sources of supply (Galbraith [1967] 1972, pp.44–5).

The large capital commitments necessitated by modern technology must also be insulated from vagaries of the market and must be protected (cf. Joskow, 1985, 1987):

> Control of the supply of savings is strategic for industrial planning. Capital use is large. No form of market uncertainty is so serious as that involving the terms and conditions on which capital is obtained. Apart from the normal disadvantages of an uncertain price, there is danger that under some circumstances supply will not be forthcoming at an acceptable price. (Galbraith [1967] 1972, p.55)

With the firm less dependent upon the capital markets for funds, its investment activity is likely to be relatively uninfluenced by the market rate of interest. Over the last twenty years the increased availability of credit and capital has reduced this dependence on retained earnings. The consequence has been, however, that this has increased vulnerability and instability of both firms and the wider (global) financial system when the availability of such credit is restricted.

Obtaining the control of markets represents a fourth route for mitigating uncertainty: 'This consists in reducing or eliminating the independence of action of those to whom the planning unit sells or from whom it buys. . . At the same time the outward form of the market, including the process of buying and selling remains formally intact' (ibid., p.46). This involves the large firm controlling and managing smaller firms via subcontracting relationships. This suggests, moreover, that conventional measures of firm size will

Table 8.3   Advertising spend in the USA, 2007

Rank	Industry	Spending ($ billions)	Rank	Corporation	Spending ($ millions)
1	Retail	18.70	1	Procter & Gamble Co.	5230.1
2	Automotive	18.54	2	AT&T	3207.3
3	Telecom	10.91	3	Verizon Communications	3016.1
4	Medicine & Remedies	9.30	4	General Motors Corp.	3010.1
5	Financial Services	9.22	5	Time Warner	2962.1
6	General Services	8.93	6	Ford Motor Co.	2525.2
7	Food, Beverages & Candy	7.46	7	GlaxoSmithKline	2456.9
8	Personal Care	6.31	8	Johnson & Johnson	2408.8
9	Airlines, Hotels, Car Rentals	5.41	9	Walt Disney Co.	2293.3
10	Movies, Recorded Video & Music	5.41	10	Unilever	2245.8

Source: 100 Leading Advertisers: Annual Advertiser Profile Edition, Advertising, www.adage.com, 23 June 2008.

underestimate the power and influence of the large firm (cf. Cowling and Sugden, 1998a, 1998b; Cowling et al., 2000; Cowling and Tomlinson, 2005).

Securing the control of markets may also include the firm attempting to manage the consumption of its products at the prices that it controls – part of what Galbraith ([1967] 1972, pp. 216–23) referred to as 'the revised sequence'. This 'need to manage consumer behavior. . . arises from the circumstances of modern industrial life – sophisticated technology, large commitments of capital, long-term planning in product development and production and, in consequence, large, inflexible and vulnerable organization' (Galbraith, 1971, p. 58). The firm must ensure that what is produced is bought and to this end it must manipulate the desires and wants of the consumer (see Table 8.3). If the large capital outlays on the advanced technologies are to be recouped then the response of the consumer must be managed. This explains the growth in expenditure on advertising: 'The purpose of demand management is to ensure that people buy what is produced – that plans as to the amounts to be sold at the controlled prices are fulfilled in practice' (Galbraith [1967] 1972, p. 208). I elaborate further on the implications of this view in Dunn (2011).

The fifth strategy for coping with uncertainty concerns the use of long-term, money-denominated contracts (cf. Davidson, 1972, 2007). While vertical integration offers the prospect of controlling the price and supply of strategic factors, so too does the contract (Joskow, 1985, 1987, 1988). The firm can enter into large long-term contracts as a strategy for dealing with uncertainty (cf. Davidson, 1972, 2007). Contracts and their enforceability are a major source of stability and security for the modern corporation (Galbraith [1967] 1972, p. 48). The nexus of money-denominated contracts occupies a pivotal role in protecting the prices and costs and safeguarding the sales and supplies at these prices and costs. As production takes time and planning, money-denominated contracts represents a means by which uncertainties about the future may be mitigated (Davidson, 1972, p. 149). A large and extensive web of money-denominated contracts, cascaded hierarchically downward, greatly facilitates the future planning and stability necessitated by advanced technology (Galbraith, 1973, pp. 141–2).

Thus, according to Galbraith the problems of market uncertainty can either be ignored or absorbed via diversification, or the firm can replace, control or suspend it. The strategies of supercession, control, and suspension all 'require that the market be replaced by an authoritative determination of price and the amounts to be sold or bought at these prices' (Galbraith [1967] 1972, p. 45). And it explains how the different strategies available for the mitigation of uncertainty are inextricably bound up with size: 'The large organization can tolerate market uncertainty as a smaller firm cannot. It can contract out of it as the smaller firm cannot. Vertical integration, the control of prices and consumer demand and reciprocal absorption of market uncertainty by contracts between firms all favor the large firm' (ibid., p. 49).

A major shortcoming leveled at Galbraith's discussion, however, is that he did not present a detailed historical analysis of how the technostructure had evolved, adapted, and changed over time. For example, there is no discussion of why the U-form mode of organization was replaced by the M-form mode of organization. While all the elements of the modern new institutional economics appear to be there – complexity, uncertainty, and asset specificity – orthodox theorists are inclined to dismiss Galbraith's thesis, due to the absence of an economizing perspective – which reflects his acknowledgements of the more diffuse objectives of the technostructure. Nevertheless, although Galbraith does not specifically evaluate the reasons for the evolution of certain governance structures his framework and analysis of the motivations of the technostructure does permit such an explanation – organizational changes that enhance or protect the power of the tech-nostructure are pursued (see Galbraith, 1973, pp. 109–25). Galbraith's analysis of the affirmative and protective motivations of the technostructure and its resultant strategies offers an alternative theoretical perspective to the narrow economizing perspective that dominates the conventional wisdom.

Similarly Galbraith is often accused of downplaying the role of competition. Galbraith did not minimize the role of competition, but he did highlight its evolution. Complacent technostructures may be challenged by other emerging and rivalrous tech-nostructures who are seeking to grow. Similarly Galbraith also acknowledged the role and power of shareholders in policing inefficient technostructures: 'if the corporation is failing to make money, stockholders may be aroused – although individual stockhold-ers will usually accept the cheaper option of selling out. Proxy battles in very large firms occur all but exclusively in those that are doing badly'. This is an important point and further highlights Galbraith's focus on the evolving nature of the competitive process, which has moved away from price competition towards other forms of competition such as advertising, mergers, and acquisitions, product innovation, and development (Galbraith, 1973, p. 135).

Accordingly it is mistaken to interpret Galbraith's analysis of the large corporation as implying a durable and permanent immortality insulated from financial markets. Galbraith's analysis of the modern firm is an analysis of the dynamics of firm growth, focusing on the increasing importance of mergers and acquisitions. What is more, Galbraith does acknowledge that stockholders *do* possess the ability to intervene. But they are prompted to act only when earnings or rates of return are less than might other-wise be expected: 'Given some basic level of earnings, stockholders are quiescent. They become aroused, either individually or collectively, only when earnings are poor or there are losses, and dividends are omitted' (ibid., p. 110). This underpins Galbraith's analysis of the dynamics of growth, which focuses on the evolving competitive process of merger and acquisition (ibid.). For Galbraith the process of corporate mergers and acquisitions, in recent times held up as exemplifying the return of the market, is in fact a fundamental feature of the competitive processes that characterizes the new industrial state. But it is a competitive process driven by the various motivations of differently sized firms, rather than the outmoded view of price competition between small, similarly sized, and matched competitors that continues to dominate economic thinking (cf. Schumpeter, 1943, p. 84).

8.4   THE THEORY OF THE FIRM

Nobel Prize winner Ronald Coase (1937) provided the now famous definition of the firm that permitted its nature to be more fully understood. According to Coase, markets and firms are alternative means of coordination. Firms represent the internal supersession of the market mechanism by command. Galbraith ([1967] 1972, p. 140) acknowledged this, noting that the 'most famous definition of an organization' is of a 'system of con-sciously coordinated activities or forces of two or more persons'. As markets and firms are alternative mechanisms for resource allocation, a choice is offered. The allocation of resources by planning or command, as opposed to movements in the structure of relative prices, is conditional on the fact that the use of the price mechanism is costly. In finding what the relevant prices are, undergoing a process of negotiation and in engaging in con-tractual behavior, resources are consumed. Command, with one party obeying the direc-tion of another, reduces the need for costly continual renegotiation and reformulation of contracts. Economic institutions such as the firm economize on, but do not eliminate, contracting costs that arise when using the market. Williamson (1975, 1985, 1996, 2005) labeled such contracting costs as transaction costs.

   For Williamson, transaction costs arise due the complexities associated with asset-specific investment. Indeed Galbraith's discussion of the relationship between technol-ogy and organization clearly pre-dates, and has many parallels with, Williamson's (1975, 1981, 1985) recognition of the importance of asset specificity in the study of organiza-tions. While Williamson uses this notion to derive a transaction cost rationalization of the modern corporation, however, Galbraith argued that asset specificity neces-sitates the need for *planning*. Galbraith's argument is that the imperatives of modern technology and the associated commitments of time, capital, and specialized labor in an uncertain environment entail that planning supersedes the market (cf. Langlois, 1995a, 1995b). Galbraith's is not a Williamsonian argument that 'in the beginning there were markets', but rather one that 'in the beginning there was an absence of a need for extensive planning as technology was not that sophisticated!' Low levels of technology, according to Galbraith, do not require extensive organization or large firms. Similarly Galbraith's focus on the rise of the technostructure and their pursuance of a wider range of goals beyond strict profit maximization is similar to Williamson's stress on bounded rationality and opportunism. That is to say, Galbraith's modern corporation is an organization that plans to mitigate and engage the uncertainties that surround advanced technological development.

There are also parallels with Galbraith's approach and the radical re-evaluation of Coase by Cowling and Sugden (1998a; cf. Foss, 1994a, 1994b). According to Coase, markets and firms are alternative means of coordination. Coase drew attention to the fact that a distinction can be made between coordination through a decentralized price mechanism and coordination by hierarchical centralized decision-making (Coase, 1937, pp. 332–3). Coase's approach, however, can be re-interpreted as emphasizing the coordinating role of planning (Cowling and Sugden, 1998a; see also Dunn, 2001a). This is similar to Galbraith's view of the supersession of the market by conscious, coordinating planning. Conventional interpretations of Coase fail, however, to contemplate the control of markets as a strategy for minimizing uncertainty, as suggested by Galbraith (cf. Dunn, 2001a, 2001c, 2006, 2008). Planning for Galbraith embodies the make, buy *or control* decision. And it is a creative, as well as a coordinating process. Galbraith's discussion of the firm emphasizes the strategic coordinating role of managers, interest groups, and other specialists within the firm, that is, the technostructure and their associated need to plan in an uncertain environment.

Galbraith's approach to the firm should not, therefore, be thought of as a variant of the transaction-cost-type story, such that the firm replaces the market on account of its capacity to minimize the uncertainties and thus the transaction costs that engulf markets. Rather, Galbraith's argument is that firms and markets possess different *capabilities* that cannot be broken down and decomposed into their individual elements (Galbraith [1967] 1972, p. 50). These are themes that were also highlighted by Edith Penrose (1955, 1959). There are also several parallels between Galbraith's view of the modern firm and Frank Knight (1921) and Joseph Schumpeter (1943), who also recognized the impact of technology and uncertainty on the evolution of the firm.

Such theoretical considerations need to be further explored. The salience of Galbraith's approach is that the boundaries of the firm, or multinational firm, should revolve around the delineation of its power. It should incorporate all market and non-market transactions coordinated from one center of strategic decision-making, for example, subcontracting relationships could be viewed as falling within the scope of a single firm depending upon the dependency and contractual conditions binding organizations together. Intra-firm transactions may be conceived as either being composed of market or non-market transactions given that production is coordinated from one center of strategic decision-making. On this view inter-firm transactions represent market transactions although they are different in character to intra-firm market transactions. Inter-firm (market) transactions take place between two centers of strategic decision-makers. Intra-firm (market) transactions originate from one center of strategic decision-making.

The salience of such an approach is that by narrowly focusing on the type of transaction, market or non-market, one may fail to appreciate fully the scope of a firm's production and the subsequent extent of concentration and influence of the multinational enterprise (Cowling and Sugden, 1998b; Cowling and Tomlinson, 2005; cf. Dugger, 1985b; Gatignon and Anderson, 1988; Grant, 1997). Domestic and overseas outsourcing that appear to reduce the scope and influence of the firm are more likely to be consolidating the power of strategic decision-makers. The subcontracting relationships of the large brand-managing firm reflect its global power and reach.

Galbraith's analysis suggests, moreover, that the modern firm or multinational corporation should not be viewed as an optimal outcome from a collective choice process as typified by the conventional wisdom. Strategic decision-makers such as the technostructure, may make decisions that benefit themselves, for example, yielding distributional gains, at the expense of others, reflecting their exercise of power (cf. Peoples and Sugden, 2000; Coffey and Tomlinson, 2006). A key contribution of Galbraith's, as well as Cowling and Sugden's approach, therefore, is that capitalist firms should not necessarily be conceived of as pursuing Pareto-efficient decisions. This assessment underpins Galbraith's argument that the strategic decisions of transnational corporations need not operate in the wider public interest (cf. Cowling and Sugden, 1999; Cowling et al., 2005; Branston et al., 2006). It is also why he directs our attention to improving corporate governance and regulation and monitoring the activities of large transnational firms (Galbraith, 1973).

In his discussion of the technostructure, Galbraith also directs our attention to situations where decisions and power meet, concentrating on the particular processes and structures of decision-making (cf. Dugger, 1980, 1985a, 1988; Cowling and Sudgen, 1998a, 1998b). A much-neglected aspect of Galbraith's contribution is that the locus of power and decision-making is divorced from the formal hierarchy of the firm. And as Tirole (2001, p.17) acknowledges, 'the allocation of formal control. . . cannot be the full story'. This represents an important qualification and contribution by Galbraith and should be disentangled from the managerial thesis that it has come to be associated with. The divorce of ownership from control is clearly distinct, although related, to the divorce of hierarchy from control. Group decision-making, for Galbraith, is not solely related to hierarchy, as we might infer from a Williamsonian-type approach, but to specialized (tacit) knowledge and peer review. This is quite a distinct reformulation of the principal agent problem that has occupied economists over the last 40 years. And it is a principal agent problem that is both under-analyzed and under-appreciated.

8.5   COORDINATION, PLANNING, AND THE PROSPECT

Such a brief review suggests that there is good reason to consider Galbraith's neglected contribution in more detail, not least because of the degree of similarity with many seminal contributions to the theory of the firm. Galbraith offered an approach to the modern firm that links technology, capital, money contracts, power, and planning to the problems of uncertainty. For Galbraith the firm is a relatively enduring institutional structure that depends upon the decisions and governance structure that surround the technostructure. But it is not a permanent structure. It means small firms may seek to grow and evolve into large firms. This might improve the chances of survival. But it does not assure it. This must be acknowledged. Galbraith's corporation, existing in historical time, represents an enduring institutional response to an uncertain future specifically designed to mitigate its impact. Galbraith presented a rich taxonomy that captures the main strategies open to the firm for coping with uncertainty. Moreover, it anticipates many of the more recent theoretical developments in the transaction cost and knowledge-based approaches to the firm. It represents a novel attempt to examine the nexus between the firm and uncertainty and serves as a useful starting point for future research into this relationship.

REFERENCES

Allen, G.C. (1967), *Economic Fact and Fantasy: A Rejoinder to Galbraith's Reith Lectures*, Institute of Economic Affairs Occasional Paper No. 14, London: IEA.

Balakrishnan, S. and B. Wernerfelt (1986), 'Technical Change, Competition and Vertical Integration', *Strategic Management Journal*, **7**(4), 347–59.

Berle, A.A. and G. Means ([1932] 1991), *The Modern Corporation and Private Property*, Somerset, NJ: Transaction Publishers.

Branston, J.R., K. Cowling and R. Sugden (2006), 'Corporate Governance and Public Interest', *International Review of Applied Economics*, **20**(2), 189–212.

Chandler, A.D. (1962), *Strategy and Structure*, Cambridge, MA: MIT Press.

Chandler, A.D. (1977), *The Visible Hand: The Managerial Revolution in American Business*, Cambridge, MA: Harvard University Press.

Chandler, A.D. (1990), *Scale and Scope: The Dynamics of Industrial Capitalism*, Cambridge, MA and London: Harvard University Press.

Coase, R.H. (1937), 'The Nature of the Firm', *Economica*, **4**(16), 386–405. Reprinted in G.J. Stigler and K.E. Boulding (eds) (1953), *Readings in Price Theory: Selected by a Committee of the American Economic Association*, London: George Allen and Unwin Ltd, pp. 331–5.

Coffey, D. and P.R. Tomlinson (2006), 'Multiple Facilities, Strategic Splitting and Vertical Structures: Stability, Growth and Distribution Reconsidered', *The Manchester School*, **74**(5), 558–76.

Cowling, K. and R. Sugden (1998a), 'The Essence of the Modern Corporation: Markets, Strategic Decision-making and the Theory of the Firm', *The Manchester School*, **66**(1), 59–86.

Cowling, K. and R. Sugden (1998b), 'Strategic Trade Policy Reconsidered: National Rivalry vs Free Trade vs International Cooperation', *Kyklos*, **51**(3), 339–57.

Cowling, K. and R. Sugden (1999), 'The Wealth of Localities, Regions and Nations; Developing Multinational Economies', *New Political Economy*, **4**(3), 361–78.

Cowling, K. and P.R. Tomlinson (2005), 'Globalisation and Corporate Power', *Contributions to Political Economy*, **24**(1), 33–54.

Cowling, K., F.M. Yusof and G. Vernon (2000), 'Declining Concentration in UK Manufacturing? A Problem of Measurement', *International Review of Applied Economics*, **14**(1), 45–54.

Cowling, K., S. Sacchetti, R. Sugden and J.R. Wilson (2005), 'The United Nations and Democratic Globalisation', in Marco Di Tommaso and Stefano Giovannelli (eds), *United Nations and Industrial Development*, New York: UN, pp. 142–60.

Davidson, P. (1972), *Money and the Real World*, London: Macmillan.

Davidson, P. (2007), *John Maynard Keynes*, London: Macmillan.

Demsetz, H. (1974), 'Where is the New Industrial State?', *Economic Inquiry*, **12**(1), 1–12.

Dugger, W.M. (1980), 'Corporate Bureaucracy', *Journal of Economic Issues*, **14**(2), 399–409.

Dugger, W.M. (1985a), 'The Continued Evolution of Corporate Power', *Review of Social Economy*, **43**(1), 1–13.

Dugger, W.M. (1985b), 'The Shortcomings of Concentration Ratios in the Conglomerate Age: New Sources and Uses of Corporate Power', *Journal of Economic Issues*, **19**(2), 343–53.

Dugger, W.M. (1988), 'An Institutional Analysis of Corporate Power', *Journal of Economic Issues*, **22**(1), 79–111.

Dunn, S.P. (2001a), 'Uncertainty, Strategic Decision-making and the Essence of the Modern Corporation: Extending Cowling and Sugden', *The Manchester School*, **69**(1), 31–41.

Dunn, S.P. (2001b), 'Bounded Rationality is not Fundamental Uncertainty: A Post Keynesian Perspective', *Journal of Post Keynesian Economics*, **23**(4), 567–88.

Dunn, S.P. (2001c), 'A Post Keynesian Approach to the Theory of the Firm', in S.C. Dow and J. Hillard (eds), *Post Keynesian Econometrics and the Theory of the Firm: Beyond Keynes, Volume One*, Cheltenham, UK and Northampton, MA: USA: Edward Elgar.

Dunn, S.P. (2006), 'Prolegomena to a Post Keynesian Health Economics', *Review of Social Economy*, **64**(3), 273–92.

Dunn, S.P. (2008), *The Uncertain Foundations of Post Keynesian Economics*, London: Routledge.
Dunn, S.P. (2011), *The Economics of John Kenneth Galbraith: Introduction, Persuasion and Rehabilitation*, Cambridge, UK: Cambridge University Press.
Foss, N.J. (1994a), 'The Theory of the Firm: The Austrians as Precursors and Critics of Modern Theory', *Review of Austrian Economics*, **7**(1), 127–44.
Foss, N.J. (1994b), 'The Two Coasian Traditions', *Review of Political Economy*, **6**(1), 35–61.
Friedman, M. (1977), *From Galbraith to Economic Freedom*, London: Institute of Economic Affairs.
Galbraith, J.K. (1952), *American Capitalism: The Concept of Countervailing Power*, London: Hamish Hamilton.
Galbraith, J.K. ([1967] 1972), *The New Industrial State*, 2nd edition, Harmondsworth: Penguin.
Galbraith, J.K. (1971), *Economics, Peace and Laughter: A Contemporary Guide*, Harmondsworth: Penguin.
Galbraith, J.K. (1973), *Economics and the Public Purpose*, Harmondsworth: Penguin.
Gatignon, H. and E. Anderson (1988), 'The Multinational Corporation's Degree of Control over Foreign Subsidiaries: An Empirical Test of a Transaction Cost Explanation', *Journal of Law, Economics, & Organization*, **4**(2), 305–36.
Gordon, S. (1968), 'The Close of the Galbraithian System', *Journal of Political Economy*, **76**(4), 635–44.
Gordon, S. (1969), 'The Galbraithian System: Rejoinder', *Journal of Political Economy*, **77**(6), 953–6.
Grant, R.R. (1997), 'Measuring Corporate Power: Assessing the Options', *Journal of Economic Issues*, **31**(2), 453–60.
Joskow, P.L. (1985), 'Vertical Integration and Long-term Contracts: The Case of Coal-burning Electric Generating Plants', *Journal of Law, Economics, & Organization*, **1**(1), 33–80.
Joskow, P.L. (1987), 'Contract Duration and Relationship-specific Investments: Empirical Evidence from Coal Markets', *American Economic Review*, **77**(1), 168–85.
Joskow, P.L. (1988), 'Asset Specificity and the Structure of Vertical Relationships: Empirical Evidence', *Journal of Law, Economics, & Organization*, **4**(1), 95–117.
Knight, F.H. (1921), *Risk, Uncertainty and Profit*, London: LSE.
Langlois, R.N. (1995a), 'Transaction Costs, Production Costs and the Passage of Time', in S.G. Medema (ed.), *Coasean Economics*, Dordrecht: Kluwer.
Langlois, R.N. (1995b), 'Do Firms Plan?', *Constitutional Political Economy*, **6**(3), 247–61.
Langlois, R.N. and P. Robertson (1995), *Firms, Markets and Economic Change*, London: Routledge.
Leathers, C.G. and J.C. Evans (1974), 'Thorstein Veblen and the New Industrial State', *History of Political Economy*, **5**(2), 420–37.
Marris, R. (1964), *The Economic Theory of Managerial Capitalism*, London: Macmillan.
Marris, R. (1968), 'Review of *The New Industrial State*', *American Economic Review*, **58**(1), 240–47.
Penrose, E.T. (1955), 'Research on the Business Firm: Limits to the Growth and Size of Firms', *American Economic Review*, **45**(2), 531–43.
Penrose, E.T. (1959), *The Theory of the Growth of the Firm*, London: Macmillan.
Peoples, J. and R. Sugden (2000), 'Divide and Rule by Transnational Corporations', in C.N. Pitelis and R. Sugden (eds), *The Nature of the Transnational Firm*, London: Routledge.
Richardson, G.B. (1959), 'Equilibrium, Expectations and Information', *Economic Journal*, **69**(274), 223–37.
Richardson, G.B. (1960), *Information and Investment*, Oxford: Clarendon Press.
Richardson, G.B. (1964), 'The Limits to a Firm's Rate of Growth', *Oxford Economic Papers*, **16**(1), 9–23.
Richardson, G.B. (1972), 'The Organization of Industry', *Economic Journal*, **82**(327), 883–96.
Schumpeter, J.A. (1943), *Capitalism, Socialism and Democracy*, London: Allen and Unwin.
Simon, H. (1955), 'A Behavioral Model of Rational Choice', *Journal of Political Economy*, **69**(1), 99–118.
Simon, H.A. (1957), *Models of Man: Social and Rational*, New York: Wiley.
Simon, H.A. (1959), 'Theories of Decision-making in Economics', *American Economic Review*, **49**(3), 253–83. Reprinted in P.E. Earl (ed.) (1988), *Behavioural Economics: Volume 1*, Aldershot, UK and Brookfield, VT, USA: Edward Elgar.
Simon, H.A. (1972), 'Theories of Bounded Rationality', in C.B. McGuire and R. Radner (eds), *Decision and Organisation*, Amsterdam: North-Holland.
Simon, H.A. (1976), 'From Substantive to Procedural Rationality', in S. Latis (ed.), *Method and Appraisal in Economics*, Cambridge, UK: CUP.
Simon, H.A. (1979), 'Rational Decision Making in Business Organization', *American Economic Review*, **69**(4), 493–513.
Solow, R.M. (1967), 'The New Industrial State, or Son of Affluence?', *The Public Interest*, No. 9.
Tirole, J. (2001), 'Corporate Governance', *Econometrica*, **69**(1), 1–35.
Williamson, O.E. (1971), 'The Vertical Integration of Production: Market Failure Considerations', *American Economic Review*, **61**(2), 112–23.
Williamson, O.E. (1975), *Markets and Hierarchies: Analysis and Anti-trust Implications: A Study in the Economics of Internal Organization*, New York: Free Press.

Williamson, O.E. (1981), 'The Modern Corporation: Origins, Evolution, Attributes', *Journal of Economic Literature*, **19**(4), 1537–68.
Williamson, O.E. (1985), *The Economic Institutions of Capitalism: Firms, Markets, Relational Contracting*, London: Macmillan.
Williamson, O.E. (1996), *The Mechanisms of Governance*, Oxford: OUP.
Williamson, O.E. (2004), 'Herbert Simon and Organization Theory', in M. Augier and J. March (eds), *Models of a Man: Essays in Memory of Herbert A. Simon*, Cambridge, MA: MIT Press, pp. 279–95.
Williamson, O.E. (2005), 'The Economics of Governance', *American Economic Review*, **95**(1), 1–18.

9 Managerial theories: Baumol and Marris

Olivier Weinstein

9.1 INTRODUCTION

It was inevitable that the rise of the modern corporation and corporate capitalism, and the many reflections they have provoked, starting with the seminal work of Berle and Means, should raise fundamental questions for the economic analysis of the firm. Managerial theories constituted the first systematic attempt to rethink the theory of the firm in the light of the transformation of capitalism. The foundations were laid by Baumol, with his work on the theory of oligopoly and the question of the objectives pursued by the firm. Managerial theory was then extended beyond issues of market theory, to propose a theory of the firm per se, and more specifically an overall theory of the 'managerial' corporation, of which Robin Marris was the principal architect. This theory of the managerial corporation represented one of the first attempts by economists to look inside the 'black box' of the firm: it set out to reconsider the behaviour of the firm and its consequences by taking into account the specific characteristics of the large modern firm – the 'corporation'. Thus, one of its primary objects of study is the rise to power of managers and the relationship between managers and shareholders, through the intermediary of the capital markets. It also focuses on the question of the growth of the firm, following the work of Edith Penrose (1959).

9.2 THE HYPOTHESIS OF INCOME MAXIMIZATION AND THE REWORKING OF OLIGOPOLY THEORY

The first works of Baumol (1958, 1959) were a continuation of the great debates of the 1940s about the behaviour of the firm and the theory of profit maximization.[1] Baumol proposed a model of oligopoly to account for the behaviour of big corporations in the United States and to explain certain observations that appear to contradict the neoclassical theory of the firm, particularly as regards pricing policy. This model replaced profit maximization by a hypothesis of sales maximization, under a minimum profit constraint. Baumol took up the ideas that could be found among observers of the firm: salaried managers, who have de facto control of the corporation, attach more importance to size than to profitability. Furthermore, the volume of sales should not be considered as an instrument used in the pursuit of other objectives (notably profit), but 'sales have become an end in and of themselves' (Baumol, 1959, p. 47).

Nevertheless, profit remains an essential variable, and there is conflict between the objective of sales and profit, and hence the need for a compromise that is expressed in the minimum profit constraint. The minimum level of profits is determined by two factors: the need to maintain a certain rate of return on securities over the long term – the condition for obtaining capital – and the need for a level of retained earnings related to the objectives of the firm. This, according to Baumol, is the view that best matches the behaviour observed (at the time he was writing): the aim is to obtain a profit level allowing the long-term financing of the maximization of sales. The rational behaviour of managers leads them to choose at the same time the desired level of profit and a retained earnings ratio: the expression of a compromise between current financing (self-financing) and future financing (dependent of the return on securities).

On this basis, Baumol built a static oligopoly model, remaining within the tradition of oligopoly theory. The fundamental break thus lay in the change of objective function. This accounted more satisfactorily for the behaviour observed, especially pricing policies similar to average cost pricing. At the same time, it conserved the hypothesis of rational behaviour of economic agents and 'the standard apparatus of marginal analysis' (Baumol, 1962, p. 1087).[2] Thus, managerial theories remained largely within the framework of standard analysis based on the hypothesis of rationality and the method of equilibrium. Baumol (1962) developed his analysis further, replacing the hypothesis of sales maximization with the hypothesis of maximization of the rate of growth of sales, in a balanced growth model. For Baumol, this allowed a better understanding of the nature of the profit 'constraint': in fact, from the point of view of growth, profit should no longer be considered as a constraint, but as an instrumental variable, as the means to obtain the capital necessary for the expansion of the firm. The optimal rate of profit is then determined, within the frame of this model, as that which allows the rate of growth to be maximized.

From that point, managerial theories broke with the neoclassical theory of the firm on two points, over and above the question of the objective function: first by emphasizing the growth of the firm, and second by constructing a theory of the firm that was no longer simply a development of oligopoly theory – in other words a theory of the firm subordinate to the analysis of markets – but a theory about the firm as an object in its own right. And this led managerial theory to enter inside the firm, or more specifically the 'corporation', before the development of contractual theories. This was mainly due to Robin Marris, who proposed an overall theory of the firm and managerial capitalism, based on detailed consideration of the characteristics – the 'nature', one might say – of the managerial corporation and the behaviour of managers.

9.3   CHARACTERIZATION OF THE MANAGERIAL FIRM

As his point of departure, Robin Marris adopted what we can consider an institutionalist conception of the firm, an extension of the many reflections on the modern corporation, and in particular the work of Berle and Means.

First, the company must be considered as a distinct entity that exists in its own right: 'The company. . .is a legal institution owning productive assets as if it were an individual' (Marris, 1967, p. 12). One important feature is that 'company law creates concepts of income and corporate capital. . .the existence of corporate income is the essence of managerial capitalism' (ibid., p. 13).[3] Thus, the company is 'a transcendent organisation with a will of its own' (ibid., p. 113), which is, moreover, capable of transforming its environment.

Second, a distinction must be made between shareholders and managers, and it is the managers who run the firm, with a good deal of autonomy. The fact that managers enjoy a certain discretionary power lies at the heart of the analysis of the managerial firm: 'even in a fairly closely-held company, the management has a considerable autonomy through economic influence, because its members represent an organisation capable of operating the assets' (ibid., p. 17).[4] The management's freedom of action derives from its ability to manage not only the structure of the managerial corporation – in which the managerial group 'effectively carries out the functions legally vested in the board' (ibid., p. 15), but also the imperfection of the markets, and of the capital market in particular: 'Most of the relevant markets are imperfect, and in one case, that of the capital market, this is a critical factor in the intra-corporate balance of power' (ibid., p. 46). However, this affirmation of managerial power does not eclipse the shareholders, or the role of the capital market. On the contrary, the 'balance of power between investor and managers' (ibid., p. 20) and the influence of the stock market, particularly through takeovers, lies at the centre of Robin Marris's theoretical construction, as we shall see. Share prices are a key variable in the analysis of the firm and its growth, because they can enter the utility function of managers, but also through their impact on the supply of capital and the risk of takeover. Robin Marris also draws on the theses of Edith Penrose (1959). In addition to the importance of managerial capabilities, he also takes up several of her ideas that break with the conception of the firm prevailing in theorizations based on market analysis:

Third, the firm is not tied to any particular market or industry. It is 'an administrative organization by no means necessarily tied to a particular industry or line of products. At any moment of time it represents a collection of human and physical assets inherited from the developments of the past' (Marris, 1963, p. 191). Hence the importance of diversification for the growth of the firm.[5]

Fourth, the firm, and more precisely the modern capitalist corporation, is an institution with the capacity for continuous growth. It is 'an autonomous organisation capable of growth (subject to rules of the game) at a limited rate in a pliable environment' (Marris, 1967, p. 124). The growth of the firm must be the central subject of the analysis. This results equally from the very nature of the managerial corporation and from the preferences of managers, as we shall see. The key question then arises of what limits the firm's growth (and not what limits the *size* of the firm, as in standard industrial economics).

9.4   THE BEHAVIOUR OF MANAGERS

The study of the behaviour of managers thus moves to the heart of the theory of the firm: it is a matter of identifying the preferences and objectives of managers, together with the constraints that limit their action. For Marris, as for Baumol (and for Williamson, in his first works), this is done within a standard microeconomic framework: a hypothesis of rational, maximizing behaviour.

Before arriving at a formalization of this type, Marris (1967) explored in depth the question of the motivations of managers and the policies that they are likely to pursue. Exploration of the psychological, sociological and economic approaches to behaviour moves the spotlight onto the role of personal ambition, identification with the firm, the 'desire for power, status, wealth and personal security' (ibid., p. 47), the importance of standards of professional competence and pay systems, especially the role of bonus schemes and stock-option plans. This detour gives rise to a synthetic representation of managerial preferences centred on two variables: growth and security.

Growth establishes itself as an objective, insomuch as the different components of managers' utility functions, both pecuniary (their pay) and non-pecuniary (their status and power) are strongly correlated with the size of the company. And also insomuch as growth imposes itself both as a collective and individual objective and as a means to strengthen the manager's integration within the organization. In the managerial firm, 'personal ability also becomes judged by achieved growth' (ibid., p. 102); the manager is evaluated on his or her ability to promote growth, as much if not more than profit. On this point, and in the light of the corporation's evolution at the end of the twentieth century, we can see how the managerial theory of the firm is the theory of a certain form of capitalism.

In Marris's view, the search for security plays an essential role: it introduces the financial dimension into his analysis of the corporation. Alongside income, prestige and power, managers – like other economic agents – seek security. This is not guaranteed by the growth of the firm, and may even conflict with it. What threatens the security of managers above all is the loss of their position, and this can be the result of one of two circumstances: the financial failure of the company, or a successful takeover raid. The risk of bankruptcy may arise from over-risky investments, excessive indebtedness or insufficient liquidity. This may cause conflict between the objective of growth and the objective of security. According to Marris, the risk of takeover raids is more complicated to analyse. It increases essentially when the return on assets is too low, below what a change in management would allow, and when the level of retained earnings is too high, leading to a low share price relative to the value of the company's assets (Marris, 1963, p. 190).[6]

Growth and security do not share the same position: security has decreasing utility and reaches a 'saturation level' (which is not the case for growth), a level that can be considered as a constraint. Whence two possible formalizations of the behaviour of managers: one in which there is growth maximization under the constraint of security, which can lead back to a constraint of minimum profit; and one in which the two variables are present in the utility function, so that there is a constant trade-off between growth and security (or between growth and profit).

9.5   THE GROWTH OF THE MANAGERIAL CORPORATION

Analysis of the determinants of the growth of the firm, in the form of exercises of comparative dynamics, within the framework of balanced growth models,[7] lies at the centre of Marris's theorization of the managerial firm, as it does for Baumol (1962).

As growth is the primary objective of managers, the key question, as we have said, is to find out what limits the growth of the firm. In addition to the constraint of security, two factors play a part: limits to the expansion of managerial competences, since the training and integration of new managers takes time – an aspect studied by Edith Penrose – and external limits linked both to the conditions of the financing of growth – an aspect already present, as we have seen, in Baumol – and to the growth of demand for the firm's products. These constraints are responsible for expansion costs that increase with the rate of growth of the firm.

Marris's modelling thus centres on determining the maximum rate of growth of the firm, and more precisely on the growth of the 'corporate capital'[8] considered as a proxy for managerial power (following Penrose). On this point, Marris differs from Baumol (1962), who focuses on the maximization *of sales*. In a context of balanced growth, however, the two rates are equal. That being the case, this growth is subject to two types of constraint.

The first involves the growth of demand. This is linked, in particular, to diversification.[9] The growth of demand is an increasing function (but at a decreasing rate) of the rate of diversification and the success rate of new products. Overall, the rate of success is a (decreasing) function of the mark-up, inasmuch as a lower mark-up is, ceteris paribus, linked to lower prices and higher spending on advertising and product development (or R&D).

The second involves the supply of finance. The financial policy of the firm is a central dimension of managerial theories, already present in Baumol (1962), and considerably developed by Marris. The growth of the firm is dependent on access to financing, either internal, through self-financing, or external, notably though the capital markets. On an imperfect capital market, the use of external financing is limited. This is expressed by the constraint of financial security (which is also, as we have seen, the condition of managers' security), in the form of a maximum long-term debt ratio (and a minimum long-term liquidity ratio). The level of retained earnings, which provides internal financing, is also limited: 'partly by the normative concern for shareholders, and partly by fear of takeover raids' (Marris, 1963, p. 200).

By formalizing these constraints (in different forms) a rate of growth can be determined for the managerial firm, as a function of the key variables of corporate policy: mark-up, rate of diversification and financial policy (the ratios of indebtedness and liquidity and the retention ratio, that is, the portion of profits retained by the firm). The maximum or 'optimal' rate of growth is obtained by considering the constraints of risk (the limit values of the above ratios), under the assumption – which is central to the managerial approach – that the firm chooses a 'growth-maximizing financial policy' (ibid., p. 203). The mark-up and profit margin are determined endogenously, at the same time as the growth rate.

In some of his writings, Marris also laid great emphasis on the importance of share prices. Thus, in summing up his work, he wrote that: 'the underlying task of a theory. . . was to determine the connection between desired and/or expected growth-rate on the one hand and the likely demand-price for the shares on the other' (Marris, 1971, p. 313). The link is made by assuming that the share price is essentially dependent on two factors: the current dividends distributed and the expected long-term growth. There is therefore a direct – but complex – link between growth and share price. Consideration of a minimum profit constraint can also be seen as an expression of the need to safeguard shareholders' interests, and therefore share prices. In this way, the theory is focused on the relation between managers and shareholders, within an institutional configuration that gives managers the upper hand.

9.6   CONCLUSION: THE MAIN FEATURES OF MANAGERIAL THEORIES

Managerial theories were an important step in the development of the modern theory of the firm, and some of the reflections they proposed remain very relevant today. Three main features can be noted.

First, what they were theorizing was a particular phase of capitalism. In this regard, managerial theories have an essential institutionalist dimension, largely developed in Marris: the aim was to understand the consequences of a certain institutional structure – the managerial corporation and its financial environment – for the behaviour of the company, and eventually beyond that, as Marris suggested (1967), on the overall growth of the economy. This is expressed in the fact that growth becomes the central objective of the managerial corporation, with profit (Baumol, 1962) or broader financial policy (Marris) being no more than instruments at the service of the growth of the firm. By contrast, one could characterize the shareholder-dominated firm, which established itself as the new institutional form in the 1980s, by a reversal of objectives: profit, or more precisely shareholder value, has now – or once again – become the final objective of company management, and growth is no more than an instrument at the service of this objective.

Managerial theories were built within a specific analytic framework, which remained largely neoclassical, from two points of view. First, they kept the neoclassical microeconomic conception of rationality, in which agents are maximizers and, as Baumol stated, marginalist methods of calculation remained valid. Marris certainly mentioned the behaviourist theories and analyses of Herbert Simon, but he did not incorporate them into his own analysis. Second, they also retained the other central aspect of the neoclassical approach: analysis in terms of equilibrium, and more precisely in terms of balanced growth and comparative dynamics, a method that can also be found in the macroeconomic theory of growth of the same period. These choices have a profound influence on the different models proposed. Within this context, one of the major problems of these models is that the results are highly dependent on the precise specification of the constraints limiting the discretionary power of the managers, as Yarrow (1976) showed. In particular, a lot depends on whether the constraints derive from external financing (Baumol, 1962), or rather from the risk of takeover (Marris, 1963, 1967; Williamson, 1966). This highlights the importance of the precise institutional context of the corporation.

There remains one key question raised by the analysis and modelling of the growth of the managerial firm: is there really a conflict of interest between managers and shareholders? Closely related is the question of whether the maximization of growth produces different results, *over the long term*, from the maximization of profit? A priori, the answer is not obvious, but it is most often positive. Williamson (1966), in an article devoted to this very subject, showed precisely how firms' policies depend on the nature of their objectives.[10] And Marris, from a wider perspective, upheld that managers' preference for growth could ultimately have 'the effect of increasing the national rate of technical progress and innovation' (Marris, 1971, p. 317). Here we come to the most interesting and currently relevant questions raised by managerial theories. But the analytic framework of balanced growth models does not allow us to answer them in a satisfactory manner, because it neglects an essential aspect of the analysis of firms' behaviour and the comparison between growth and profit objectives: the choice of decision-making horizon, the trade-off between short- and long-term results, which is now central to study of the transition from managerial capitalism to shareholder-value capitalism and its consequences.

NOTES

1. See Machlup (1967).
2. Baumol (1959, p. 92) also wrote: 'Perhaps never before has the businessman been so much a rational calculator'.
3. Marris added, not without interest for the currently prevailing conception of 'fair value', that 'the value of company assets is not necessarily equal to the market value of corresponding stocks'.
4. The study of this 'discretionary behaviour' of managers was, in particular, the subject of Williamson's early works (1963, 1964).
5. Diversification is central to Marris's model (1963).
6. The risk of takeover may also stem from an excess of liquidity, while insufficient liquidity increases the risk of bankruptcy.
7. Comparison between balanced growth paths with constant rate, where capital, profit, production and income therefore grow at the same rate.
8. More precisely: 'book-value of fixed assets, plus inventory, plus net short-term assets, including costs reserve' in Marris (1963, p. 217).
9. See notably Marris (1963).
10. More precisely, he showed that maximization of sales (of their discounted value) gives a higher level of production than profit or corporate capital growth maximization.

REFERENCES

Baumol, W.J. (1958), 'On the Theory of Oligopoly', *Economica*, **25**(99), 187–98.
Baumol, W.J. (1959), *Business Behavior, Value and Growth*, New York: Macmillan.
Baumol, W.J. (1962), 'On the Theory of Expansion of the Firm', *The American Economic Review*, **52**, 1078–87.
Machlup, F. (1967), 'Theories of the Firm: Marginalist, Behavioral, Managerial', *The American Economic Review*, **57**(1), 1–33.
Marris, R. (1963), 'A Model of the "Managerial" Enterprise', *Quarterly Journal of Economics*, **77**(2) 185–209.
Marris, R. (1967), *The Economic Theory of Managerial Capitalism*, 2nd edition, Glencoe, New York: Free Press.
Marris, R. (1971), 'The Economic Theory of "Managerial" Capitalism', in G.C. Archibald (ed.), *The Theory of the Firm*, Baltimore: Penguin Books.
Penrose, E.T. (1959), *The Theory of the Growth of the Firm*, New York: Wiley.
Williamson O.E. (1963), 'Managerial Discretion and Business Behavior', *The American Economic Review*, **53**(5), 1032–57.
Williamson, O.E. (1964), *The Economics of Discretionary Behavior: Managerial Objectives in a Theory of the Firm*, Englewood Cliffs, NJ: Prentice-Hall.
Williamson, O.E. (1966), 'Profit, Growth and Sales Maximization', *Economica*, **33**(129), 1–16.
Yarrow, G.K. (1976), 'On the Predictions of Managerial Theories of the Firm', *The Journal of Industrial Economics*, **24**(4), 267–79.

10 Behavioural theory
Peter E. Earl

10.1 INTRODUCTION

Proponents of the behavioural approaches to the firm believe it may be unwise to begin theorizing about firms from the comfort of one's armchair with analytically convenient assumptions. Rather, one should first try to acquire knowledge about the behaviour of actual firms and human decision-makers in general. This research strategy has a long history. Over a century ago, Marshall's evolutionary view of the firm reflected his considerable knowledge of actual firms, while early work on mark-up pricing by Hall and Hitch (1939) was based on interview/questionnaire data. However, what emerged as the behavioural theory of the firm during the 1950s and 1960s via the work of Herbert Simon, Richard Cyert and James March and their colleagues at the Carnegie Institute of Technology in Pittsburgh (later Carnegie-Mellon University) reflected not just knowledge about firms but also insights from psychology, sociology and organizational science. The key contribution is Cyert and March's (1963) book *A Behavioral Theory of the Firm*. This not only offered a view of the firm that was radically innovative in analytical terms but it looked unlike any previous economics book since it was replete with complex decision-tree diagrams and masses of computer program code.

Cyert and March's book broke new ground by focusing on the firm as an organization of diverse interest groups trying to cope with the complex challenges arising from external forces and internal politics. It portrays the firm's behaviour as being both driven by expectations and shaped by its past. It is one of the most heavily cited works in the literature on the theory of the firm (Google Scholar lists over 14 000 hits). The publication of a new edition in 1992 (with some of the original's subsidiary chapters by their colleagues removed and a new reflective chapter) and special issues of *Organization Science* (2007) and the *Journal of Economic Behavior & Organization* (2008) devoted to it further testify to the enduring significance of this approach. However, its impact on economics is actually rather limited and its biggest impact has been mainly with organization and management researchers. Although 'behavioural economics' has in the twenty-first century increasingly become part of mainstream economics, the behavioural theory of the firm (hereafter, BTF) initially received a hostile reception from mainstream economists and was then largely ignored by them. The BTF did little to inspire what is now being branded as 'behavioural economics', though both approaches are interested in the significance of cognitive biases (for example, what is now commonly referred to as 'sunk cost bias' can be seen as driving what March and Simon, 1958, label as unwarranted 'persistence').

10.2 DECISION-MAKING PROCESSES AND THE GOALS OF FIRMS

The failure of the BTF to win widespread approval from economists is easy to understand: it clashes with mainstream economics in key areas. Most significantly, it rejects the assumption that all choices should be seen as acts of constrained optimization. Thus while Baumol and Marris rejected profit maximization in favour of sales revenue maximization and growth maximization, respectively, the BTF rejects *any* notion of optimization. Instead, it adopts Simon's (1955, 1959) view that decision-making involves 'satisficing', that is, searching for satisfactory-looking solutions to past or anticipated failures to meet performance targets or aspiration levels. Optimization is problematic in the face of recognized potential for surprising new inventions and creative choices that may be made by rival firms or fickleness in consumer spending. Where the incompleteness of relevant information is exacerbated by the dispersion of information that does exist, relative payoffs to different search strategies cannot be specified in advance. Even if information is freely available, attention is limited. People have limited information-processing capacities that preclude them from dealing with complex problems without making simplifications. Though they may want to take good decisions, they have limited capacities to do so: in Simon's words, they suffer from 'bounded rationality', and they seek to cope with the challenges they face by using simple decision rules, routines or heuristics that they believe will give good enough results.

This is reflected in the view of choice at the heart of the BTF, which is based on 'yes/no' status checks with linked 'if/then' instructions (which in some cases will initiate further status checks, and so on). This is similar to how a thermostat functions: if room temperature exceeds a pre-set level, the thermostat is programmed to switch off the heating system; this allows room temperature to fall until it hits a pre-set 'too cold' level, whereupon the thermostat turns the heating back on. If we know the rules and procedures used in the firm to classify situations and then generate actions, that is, if we know the programs according to which the firm operates, we may be able to predict its behaviour. This is essentially what Cyert and March (1963, Ch. 7) do, with remarkable accuracy, in their study of how a department store set its prices, and when and how far it opted to mark down stock that was moving too slowly. Their 'general model' (ibid., Ch. 8) consists literally of a computer program with aspiration levels for profit, production, inventory and sales, linked by feedback loops.

10.3 SATISFICING AND EFFICIENCY

From the standpoint of conventional economics, firms that use simple decision rules seem to be operating in a naive and sloppy kind of manner and are likely to be wiped out by rivals that employ much more sophisticated processes. Sometimes this is exactly what happens with sleepy, low-achieving firms that do not wake up in time and learn better decision rules. However, Winter (1964) proposed that the reverse can also hold: firms with simple rules and procedures for dealing with changes in their environments or internal difficulties may respond very quickly, whereas firms that gather as much information as possible and then carefully process it may achieve inferior performances since, by the time they have worked out the best response to the original problem, further changes could have taken place.

A further indication that satisficing theory does not necessarily imply lethargic business behaviour comes from the fact that the targets/aspiration levels that decision-makers strive to meet are seen in the BTF as neither static nor purely self-defined. Central to the theory is the idea that aspiration levels tend to follow attainments with something of a lag, that is, decision-makers raise their sights after a run of above-target results and do not cling to targets that they repeatedly fail to meet despite trying to find better ways of meeting them. As well as using their achievements as guides to whether they are setting appropriate aspirations, decision-makers use external reference standards – the performance of rivals or benchmark organizations – as indicators of what they should be hoping to achieve. Given this, the opening up of national markets to external competition could have significant potential to promote productivity growth by forcing domestic firms to make their products 'world class' rather than focusing on local references standards.

The adjustability of aspiration levels in a competitive context can be seen to align the BTF with the non-equilibrium thinking of Schumpeter, whose vision of innovation-driven processes of 'creative destruction' implies that firms have to keep trying harder or thinking smarter in order to stay in business as rivals improve their products and production methods. However, before Winter (1971) pointed this out, the potentially revolutionary impact of the BTF had been diminished by attempts to show that a satisficing perspective was unnecessary since rule-based behaviour could be absorbed into an equilibrium framework: Baumol and Quandt (1964) offered a model of 'optimally imperfect' behaviour using decision rules and Day (1967) portrayed the BTF as ultimately implying that successive iterative adjustments by firms would lead them to converge to a profit-maximizing outcome.

10.4   SEQUENTIAL ATTENTION TO GOALS

The BTF sees firms and other organizations as pursuing multiple aspirations, such as targets for their rate of return, growth of sales, ratios of inventories to sales or production, market share, rate of reduction of unit costs, and so on. This involves a dual clash with mainstream thinking: not only are there multiple goals specified in terms of targets rather than a single profit-maximization objective, but the firm is also seen as giving sequential attention to goals rather than being willing to make trade-offs between them. That is to say, managers are viewed as failing to give attention to the possibility that what they do in trying to achieve the goal on which they are currently focusing will have adverse implications for their ability to meet other performance goals. Instead, they follow a 'we'll cross that bridge when we come to it' policy: they focus on finding a solution to the most important target that is not currently being met and they try to find a means of meeting it, normally by searching locally and/or following particular obsessions (Winter et al., 2007), that is, looking for a solution within their familiar domain rather than by making radical explorations of unfamiliar territory. If their chosen course of action fixes the problem in question but causes other targets not to be met, they shift their attention to the most important of the latter and search for a sufficiently promising way of meeting it, and so on.

Not worrying about spillover effects between different goals greatly simplifies short-run management of the organization but has potential to cause it to 'go round in circles' in the long run, something that is commonly observed. For example, car-makers may oscillate between cost cutting and allowing engineers and stylists a freer rein. Sequential attention to goals may sound inefficient compared with working out an optimal trajectory but it may help the firm survive in the long run if its customers are themselves coping with bounded rationality by setting checklists of targets and ranking their goals in order of priority rather than trying to compute overall values for products they are appraising. If trade-offs are made in directions that reflect some goals being easier to reach than others, the firm will gain more experience in the favoured direction, biasing its choices that way in future – in much the same way that mainstream economists have let their grasp of reality slip whilst pursuing the goal of doing economics formally using their favoured techniques (Augier and March, 2008, pp. 103–4). So long as no goal that is assigned high priority has an unrealistic aspiration level, sequential attention to goals makes it less likely that other goals will fade away since they will receive attention periodically. The firm will thereby maintain some capacity as an all-rounder rather than getting excellent in some areas at the catastrophic cost of failing to meet customer targets in other areas.

10.5   ORGANIZATIONAL CHOICE AND ORGANIZATIONAL SLACK

Though the firm as a whole is seen in the BTF as having a set of goals, the BTF follows Simon (1945) and March and Simon (1958) in seeing organizations as consisting of individuals who are striving to attain their own 'sub-goals'. The firm-level goals serve as a means of focusing the organization on collective, coordinated action and, to some extent, individuals do pick up the values and aspirations of the firms within which they work. All the time, however, the different parties are asking themselves whether what is being proposed for the firm as a whole is going to enable them to meet their own goals. If the answer looks like it will be 'no', then they will try to bargain for alternative policies (for example, bigger budget allocations to their own departments) and if they cannot get satisfactory policies they may leave the organization altogether.

As a collection of individual agents with different aspirations and different things to offer, the firm is best seen as a coalition of different interest groups and sub-groups. This coalition includes not merely managers and line workers (in various different departments) but also shareholders, bankers, supply chain partners and regular customers. They all may have relationships with the firm over a significant period. Their willingness to stay loyal in the face of short-term disappointments while voicing their dissatisfaction about the situation may help the firm survive into the long run as a means of enabling them meet their own goals (Hirschman, 1970). However, they will exit if they cannot meet their 'transfer earnings'/'reservation price', that is, if it looks like their net returns from being part of the coalition are chronically falling short of their targets. As with firm-level goals, individuals' reservation prices may be shaped by their knowledge of returns being achieved in other organizations: their discontent may be aroused by discovering they could do better elsewhere rather than by a decline in what they get from membership of their current firm. They can be persuaded to stay in the coalition by being offered more, which must either come from search within the organization leading to the discovery of how to achieve a Pareto improvement in what it does (for example, a way of producing more output, at lower price, without sacrificing profits and jobs or requiring anyone to work harder), or it must come at the expense of someone else in the coalition.

The concept of organizational slack plays a key role in the BTF in explaining how a firm copes with changes in external competitive pressures and/or increasing demands of its coalition members. The amount of slack available in the firm at any moment is the sum of the difference between the actual returns being achieved by coalition members and their reservation prices. It arises not because of any collective decision that slack should be created to make the firm more resilient but rather as a result of rising attainments being followed by lags in increases in aspiration levels when coalition members bargain over returns. Because bargaining involves asymmetric access to information, coalition members are unsure of each other's reservation prices; they cannot be sure how far they can push their demands without their attempt to extract more backfiring and resulting in a situation where the coalition disintegrates or they are forced to leave it. So long as their returns are not less than their reservation price they moderate their demands, potentially enabling other coalition members to achieve returns above their respective reservation prices. However, when their returns fall below their targets they take the risk of bargaining more aggressively and may extract a bigger slice of the firm's resources if others have been earning above-target returns and are prepared to make concessions rather than risk losing the ability to meet their targets. Under pressure, then, shareholders may tolerate lower dividends, workers may accept more demanding production schedules, bankers may allow delays in repayments of loans, customers may put up with higher prices, suppliers may agree to supply components more cheaply, and so on.

10.6   STRATEGY VERSUS MUDDLING THROUGH

Impressions that the BTF lacks a vision of firms as lean, aggressively competitive and entrepreneurial are reinforced by Cyert and March's emphasis on the tendency of firms to attempt to 'achieve a negotiated environment' (for example, by lobbying politicians for supportive policies) and by 'uncertainty avoidance' (much in line with Galbraith's views of the modern corporation). Certainly, the focus of the BTF has mostly been on everyday administrative choices rather than on major choices about which strategic direction a firm should take. However, the BTF can be employed to understand strategic choices. For example, diversification and vertical integration decisions may be seen (as in Earl, 1984) as responses to perceived problems, with the set of options that are considered and deemed feasible being limited by established ways of thinking – for example, some changes of direction will be 'unthinkable' and some threats impossible to acknowledge (see also Schoenberger, 1997) – and the existing balance of power within the organization.

10.7 LOOKING AHEAD TO LATER CHAPTERS

The behavioural approach is particularly significant in relation to transaction cost theory (see Chapter 13) – whose leading proponent Oliver Williamson was a product of the Carnegie group and employs their 'bounded rationality' assumption (albeit in a less radical way than his mentors: see Augier and March, 2008) – and to the dynamic approaches covered in Part V. Useful bridges to Part V are provided by Winter (1986), who reflects on orthodox critiques of the behavioural approach, and by Pitelis (2007), who compares and contrasts the behavioural theory of the firm with Penrose's theory of the growth of the firm.

REFERENCES

Augier, M. and J.G. March (2008), 'Realism and Comprehension in Economics: A Footnote to an Exchange Between Oliver E. Williamson and Herbert A. Simon', *Journal of Economic Behavior & Organization*, **66**(1), 95–105.

Baumol, W.J. and R.E. Quandt (1964), 'Rules of Thumb and Optimally Imperfect Decisions', *American Economic Review*, **54**(1), 23–46.

Cyert. R.M. and J.G. March (1963), *A Behavioral Theory of the Firm*, Englewood Cliffs, NJ: Prentice-Hall (2nd edition, 1992, Maldon, MA and Oxford: Blackwell).

Day, R.H. (1967), 'Profits, Learning and the Convergence of Satisficing to Marginalism', *Quarterly Journal of Economics*, **81**(2), 302–11.

Earl, P.E. (1984), *The Corporate Imagination: How Big Companies Make Mistakes*, Brighton: Wheatsheaf.

Hall, R.L. and C.J. Hitch (1939), 'Price Theory and Business Behaviour', *Oxford Economic Papers*, **2**(1), 12–45.

Hirschman, A.O. (1970), *Exit, Voice and Loyalty*, Cambridge, MA: Harvard University Press.

March, J.G. and H.A. Simon (1958), *Organizations*, New York: Wiley.

Pitelis, C.N. (2007), 'A Behavioral Resource-based View of the Firm: The Synergy of Cyert and March (1963) and Penrose (1959)', *Organization Science*, **18**(3), 478–90.

Schoenberger, E. (1997), *The Cultural Crisis of the Firm*, Oxford: Blackwell.

Simon, H.A. (1945), *Administrative Behavior: A Study of Decision-making Processes in Organizations*, New York: Macmillan.

Simon, HA. (1955), 'A Behavioral Model of Rational Choice', *Quarterly Journal of Economics*, **69**(1), 99–118.

Simon, H.A. (1959), 'Theories of Decision-making in Economics and Behavioral Sciences', *American Economic Review*, **49**(3), 253–83.

Winter, S.G. (1964), 'Economic "Natural Selection" and the Theory of the Firm', *Yale Economic Essays*, **4**(1), 224–72.

Winter, S.G. (1971), 'Satisficing, Selection, and the Innovating Remnant', *Quarterly Journal of Economics*, **85**(2), 237–61.

Winter, S.G. (1986), 'The Reseach Program of the Behavioral Theory of the Firm: Orthodox Critique and Evolutionary Perspective', in B. Gilad and S. Kaish (eds), *Handbook of Behavioral Economics, Volume A, Behavioral Microeconomics*, Greenwich, CT: JAI Press, pp. 151–88.

Winter, S.G., G. Cattani and A. Dorsch (2007), 'The Value of Moderate Obsession: Insights from a New Model of Organizational Search', *Organization Science*, **18**(3), 403–19.

PART III

EQUILIBRIUM AND NEW INSTITUTIONAL THEORIES

11 Agency theory, corporate governance and finance
Hong Bo and Ciaran Driver

11.1 INTRODUCTION

The Principal–Agent (P–A) relationship operates when a party, the principal, contracts or instructs the other party, the agent, to perform a delegated task. At the centre of the P–A relationship is the assumption that both parties are utility maximizing and agents are extrinsically motivated and opportunist. The assumption on the agent matters because of uncertainties involved in observing the agent's action by the principal. Moral hazard problems (such as low effort) and adverse selection problems (such as taking advantage of information held only by the agent) are likely to arise, and there can be no presumption that the parties will find an arrangement to reach the first best solution that would be possible in the absence of these distortions. Corporate governance is an institutional form that addresses this problem; the costs incurred in setting up these governance mechanisms form part of what are known as agency costs.

The context of the P–A relationship can range from the management of an entrepreneurial firm to regulatory rules for education, policing or care services. Although widely applied, agency theory originated in a consideration of the separation of ownership and control in the modern corporation (Jensen and Meckling, 1976). Shareholders are principals and managers are agents. Shareholders are held to maximize firm value, while managers, if assumed to be self-interested, may have other goals; instead they intend to derive private benefits by managing the firm. How to resolve that issue to the benefit of shareholders has been central to the agency theory agenda. Agency theory has been a key influence on the design of managerial incentives, the form and composition of corporate boards, codes of governance, desirable ownership forms, optimal capital structure and the use of external finance.

Agency concerns are historically specific: they seem not to have arisen for managers or investors in the expansionary years of the 1950s and 1960s (Holmstrom and Kaplan, 2001). In that period, there was more interest in information flows and accountability between divisions and headquarters (Taggart, 1987). Managers in that era simply asserted the control rights of owners, thus providing one solution to the P–A problem (Berle, 1965; Rebérioux, 2007). It is not entirely clear why a concern with opportunism later came to dominate so strongly; many have continued to argue that other corporate issues such as the tasks of managerial coordination and innovation affect value creation as much if not more than agency costs (Demsetz, 1993; Foss et al., 2000; Lazonick, 2007). Rebérioux (2007) links the relatively modern conception of shareholder primacy (that the function of the firm is to add shareholder value) to a philosophy of 'dispossession' that investors in advanced countries experienced under increased global competition. Agency theory legitimates governance rules that protect investors from dispossession.

The P–A model, like much of economic theory is somewhat abstract. Nevertheless, it involves a rudimentary behavioural and institutional approach to the economics of the firm and represents an advance on the impersonal view of market exchange that pre-dated it. The very phrase 'principal–agent' implies an asymmetry that must be justified by some underlying view of what characterizes the principal and agent roles – why 'x employs y' rather than the converse. The answer may be that the parties differ in access to finance (Tirole, 1999a, 2006) or access to intellectual property (Pagano and Rossi, 2009) or in their ability to bear risk (Stiglitz, 1974; Williamson, 1985).

Nevertheless if agency theory opens up a wide array of interesting theoretical questions, the agenda has in practice been circumscribed by assumptions that have proved to be controversial. Especially so is the common indentification of managers with agents (opportunistic) and owners (who pursue value maximization). Much legal and economic writing on governance has challenged that simple dichotomy with the argument that any contracted manager who bears risk also has the characteristics of a principal. The stakeholder perspective arises out of this critique of agency theory in that it questions the conceptual status of the principal (Blair, 1995; Michie and Oughton, 2003; Roberts and van der Steen, 2004).[1] This argument is often ignored in the identification of good governance with a resolution of the P–A problem, an approach that assumes rather than derives much of what is at issue.

In this chapter we focus on agency theory in corporations. We start by taking the standard agenda of agency theory as given and evaluate how managerial incentives can contribute to a resolution of agency concerns. The remainder of the chapter introduces the wider issues of finance and new institutional economics. The structure of this chapter is as follows: in section 11.2 we introduce a classic model that illustrates the role of profit-sharing and discuss the implications this basic P–A model has for related issues such as pay-for-performance. Section 11.3 points to some limitations of incentive pay as a solution to agency problems. Section 11.4 reviews the alternative mechanisms of monitoring and managerial labour markets. Section 11.5 discusses the role of finance in governance; Section 11.6 reviews the contribution of new institutional economics; and Section 11.7 concludes.

11.2   THE P–A MODEL – ILLUSTRATION

The role of governance in facilitating value creation may be illustrated by the classic sharecropping model where the owner leases his or her land to a tenant farmer who chooses a level of risky effort (Stiglitz, 1974; see Olsen, 2006 for a broader treatment). The owner's problem is to design a compensation contract to motivate the tenant to engage in this effort. Direct monitoring is assumed to be infeasible so that effort can only be inferred from realized output. Assume that the expected output is $Y = a + \varepsilon$, where a stands for the tenant's action (effort), and ε is a random factor, for example, weather, which is out of the control of both the owner and the tenant and is distributed $N[0, \sigma^2]$.[2] The expected output of the enterprise depends on two factors: the tenant's effort (a) and the unforeseeable weather condition (ε). Because of the variance in ε, the tenant's effort cannot be inferred with precision from the observed output. Arguably this model is applicable to a wide range of modern firms where management teams are risk-averse and can hide opportunities from top management, thus leaving value on the table (Pitelis, 2004).

Different employee contracts will induce different degrees of effort:

(a)   the fixed wage contract: $Pay = W$;
(b)   the franchise contract: $Pay(Y) = Y - F$;
(c)   the sharecropping contract: $Pay(Y) = sY + B$, where $0 < s < 1$ and B can be zero or positive, for example, where there are side payments such as loans or cost-sharing arrangements; in the case of a mixed model with wage or rental components the sign of B is indeterminate.

Contract (a) provides the tenant with a fixed wage payment; the owner bears all the risk relating to production, while the tenant is wholly insured against risk. In this contract, there is no incentive for the tenant to perform, because the difference between the realized output and the fixed wage payment received by the tenant will be claimed by the owner.

In contract (b), the tenant pays the owner a fixed fee (F) for renting the land. After this fixed payment, the difference between the realized output and the fixed rent accrues to the tenant and constitutes an incentive. However, in this contract, the tenant alone has to bear all the risk and has to be able to finance the franchise.

In contract (c), the risk-neutral principal designs a contract to maximize his or her utility U_P such that when an agent chooses an effort level to maximize utility of the agent U_A for a given cost function, the expected income will exceed the reservation wage. The tenant or agent is assumed to be risk-averse but because of unobserved effort is best given some autonomy and must share some risk. Assuming that the tenant's utility function is exponential so that: $U_A = -e^{r[S-c(a)]}$, where r is the tenant's absolute risk aversion and $c(a)$ is the cost of effort, then the owner may motivate the tenant to incur risk and this may be shown to result in an optimal sharing rate: $s = 1/1 + r\sigma^2 c''$ (e.g., Aggarwal and Samwick, 1999; Murphy, 1999). Not surprisingly, profit sharing is more favoured by the owner the more that the tenant is able to increase effort at low cost in response to incentives (the lower c''). Note also that the model predicts that lower uncertainty and/or less risk-aversion will be associated with a high sharing rule. The results of this model have been used widely to infer appropriate pay structures for employees and managers.

The sharing contract is not a first best solution that would be available under certainty, in part because the risk-averse agent needs to be compensated for increased risk exposure and because the contract does not replicate costless monitoring – the agent cannot be incentivized enough. Alternative forms of contract that include some monitoring and penalties may be superior (Agrawal, 2002). In all cases, however, the basic set-up of external risk and costly monitoring ensures that agency costs will be incurred. Using the terminology of Jensen and Meckling (1976), it is clear that the sharecropping model with monitoring contains residual loss (unavoidable loss from the separation of ownership and control that is minimized but not eliminated by contracts), bonding cost (the cost of compensating the agent – in this case for extra risk) and monitoring costs.

11.3   ROBUSTNESS OF THE PROFIT-SHARING MODEL AS A SOLUTION TO AGENCY PROBLEMS: PAY-FOR-PERFORMANCE

The sharecropping model suggests a profit-sharing arrangement so as to incentivize the agent to take risk. Sharing contracts such as performance-based pay have always been an element of compensation in a minority of firms and in recent decades their use has become ubiquitous in top managerial pay. Here we review some recent trends in executive performance pay and ask whether it helps to resolve the governance problem.

The components of executive compensation include four basic elements: a base salary including benefits, an annual bonus tied to accounting performance, stock options and long-term incentive plans (e.g., restricted stock plans and multi-year accounting-based performance plans). Insofar as compensation is connected to the firm's performance, the components most sensitive are stock options and stock ownership (Murphy, 1999). In the USA, stock option plans constitute the single largest component of CEO pay following profound changes in the level and structure of executive compensation in the last three decades (Murphy, 1999; Jensen and Murphy, 2004). Average total remuneration for CEOs in S&P 500 firms (adjusted for inflation using 2002 constant dollars) increased from about $850000 in 1970 to over $14 million in 2000, falling to $9.4 million in 2002. Over this time period, the average grant date Black-Scholes value of options soared from near zero in 1970 to over $7.0 million in 2000, before falling to $4.4 million in 2002 (Jensen and Murphy, 2004, pp. 24–5). While average worker pay stayed flat from 1990 for the next 15 years, CEO pay increased by nearly 300 per cent, with the proportion of equity-based pay doubling to two-thirds (Clarke, 2007). The practice of CEO pay in countries outside the USA has to some extent mirrored that of the USA, though at lower levels (Abowd and Kaplan, 1999). As documented by Conyon et al. (2009) the difference in CEO pay between the USA and the UK has narrowed over time.

Despite the enormous increase in compensation of top managers in recent years, there is little direct evidence supporting the view that higher pay–performance sensitivities lead to better long-run performance even as measured by market criteria. Nor is it clear how to measure performance in a context where excessive risk is correlated with high-powered incentives.[3]

Criticism of existing practices originates in part from those who argue for more direct shareholder control of corporation. The argument here is that the board of directors is captive to managers who may manipulate accounting indicators, adjust the performance standards, and so on in order to influence compensation committees' decisions concerning the executive pay (Bebchuk and Fried, 2004). On this view the failure of pay-for-performance systems is due merely to their design. Other critics have responded differently, noting the drawbacks of any system of high-powered incentives within the firm. Such incentives are problematic in the presence of 'multi-tasking' so that anything that is not prescribed as a target tends to be neglected (Roberts, 2004).

11.4   ALTERNATIVE GOVERNANCE APPROACHES TO INCENTIVIZING EFFORT

11.4.1   Monitoring

The assumption of many P–A models is that monitoring is either impossible or comes with high cost. The incentive systems that involve performance pay have accordingly featured strongly in the governance practices informed by agency theory. Nevertheless, the efficacy of monitoring cannot be dismissed as a general rule. If it were indeed the case that incentives are the key way of aligning interests, we would find that most use would be made of performance-based pay in less risky situations where the cost of incentivizing managers is less. In terms of the cross-section use of performance-based pay, the prediction of the P–A sharing rule of section 11.2 is that:

> [T]he pay-performance sensitivity will be decreasing in the riskiness or variance of the firm's performance. Executives in firms with more volatile stock prices will have less performance-based compensation. (Aggarwal and Samwick, 1999, p. 67)

Prendergast (2002) tests and rejects this hypothesis: performance-related pay dominates in risky rather than stable business, a result that may be attributed to the fact that monitoring is often an effective alternative to incentives in the latter. This effectiveness probably arises from greater transparency and ease of benchmarking in stable industries. Thus, direct monitoring has its part to play in the resolution of P–A issues, as indeed Alchian and Demsetz (1972) argued in their work on team production. Team production theory applies to co-production in small groups in which both the outcome and the effort of the individual participant are difficult to measure and reward unless there is direct monitoring. Even if there were no exogenous source of uncertainty (as there is in the sharecropping model) it would be difficult to measure the marginal product for any particular individual in the team and thus difficult to provide output-based incentives. This would be the case even if team members were rewarded on the basis of total output because each team member could free-ride on others. Alchian and Demsetz (ibid.) propose instead to set up a specialist monitor who will also act as the residual claimant while all others receive a contractual wage. This is not a full solution to the moral hazard problem since this danger is now displaced onto the owner-monitor who has an incentive to mis-report effort (Holmstrom, 1989). Nevertheless the theory is useful in highlighting that when governance involves direct monitoring (active blockholdings, private equity etc.), there remains a governance problem among the principals themselves. This applies also within the board of directors (Hermalin and Weisbach, 2003).

11.4.2   Competition in Managerial Labour Markets

It has long been argued that the boards of directors of modern corporations are unable to engage in effective monitoring (Fama, 1980). Fama's preferred institutional form – which is said to be behind the success of the large corporation – is the managerial labour market that provides a discipline to contain agency problems without the need for direct monitoring.

Managerial prospects have increasingly been seen as alternatives to explicit incentives.

For example, the likelihood of promotion to CEO is an alternative incentive to pay-for-performance. Some work shows a negative relationship between the two measures, suggesting that implicit incentives of promotion can substitute for explicit ones (Meng and Zhou, 2007).

The managerial labour market (MLM) can be effective in reducing the agency costs of managerial opportunism where benchmarking is possible (Fama, 1980). *Internal* MLM involves competition among different-level managers inside the firm, which works just like a tournament, that is, it relies on relative performance (Lazear and Rosen, 1981). In the tournament models, promotion is the central mechanism that provides incentives. The prize set up in the tournament provides incentives for both the principal and the agents. A larger-sized prize induces more effort and better performance; in addition, the prize is fixed ex ante, which restrains the principal from opportunistic behaviour. However, tournaments may also induce negative incentive effects. For example, cooperation is affected since more able contestants will have no incentives to help less able ones in the tournament. Furthermore, underdogs in the contest will be tempted to take more risky actions, and so forth (Prendergast, 1999).

The *external* MLMs operate mainly through evaluation of the manager's human capital outside the firm. Any deviation of the manager's behaviour (from that contracted) will be detected and used as information to update the evaluation on the manager's future wage whether or not he or she remains in his or her present job. However, the information requirements of the model are formidable and require that the variance of noise in the manager's marginal product is such that imputing the managerial contribution is not too difficult. Given what has been said earlier about team production that assumption is unlikely even where firm outcomes can be benchmarked.

External managerial labour markets also have other disadvantages; they may make managers more risk-averse or cause managers to manipulate short-term results or ignore long-term benefits in order to influence the market assessment of their ability (Palley, 1997). Others worry that high-powered incentives encourage excessive risk-taking and leverage (Coles et al., 2006). Herding among managers is also likely. Managers may imitate the decisions of other managers with whom they are likely to be benchmarked even when their private information suggests a different action (Scharfstein and Stein, 1990; Zwiebel, 1995).

Our conclusion is that use of managerial labour market as a disciplining device is not a clear answer to agency problems and may even raise new ones. Were the reputational labour market to work as effectively as Fama (1980) predicted, it would have been improved further by the thick global markets for corporate talent that emerged subsequently. But the increased global competition of recent years has, if anything, amplified the concern with agency problems.

11.5   AGENCY AND FINANCE

11.5.1   Pledgeable Income

In the sharecropping model, agents are incentivized by a costly risk-based sharing but they provide no finance. Inevitably this raises the question of the willingness of owners o finance all potentially welfare-increasing projects. This is addressed in the pledge-able income model (Tirole, 1999a). If a manager foregoes private benefits B, revenue R s generated with probability p_h and revenue zero with probability $(1 - p_h)$. Similarly, the manager receives formal compensation w in the case of success (probability p_h) and zero for failure. Managers who decide to receive private benefits B, generate R (and receive w) with a lower probability of p_l. Since the manager trades off the loss of private benefit B with the differential probability times w, it must be the case that $w > B/(p_h - p_l)$ to provide incentives for managers. It follows that the maximum amount of available surplus (pledgeable income) is $p_h(R - B/(p_h - p_l))$, which must be greater than the cost of the project less the amount put up by the insiders. This constraint implies that some positive net present value projects may not be funded unless insiders put up enough capital. Direct monitoring may be a solution if available at low cost but a more general solution is the ceding of control rights to the outside providers of finance. We postpone consideration of this to section 11.6.

11.5.2 The Capital Market and Capital Structure

Financial models of the firm show that capital structure – how the firm is financed by a combination of internal funds, equity and debt – may interact with agency concerns. Theoretically and empirically this is a difficult topic due to the multitude of non-nested theories that have arisen to challenge the Modigliani-Miller (MM) hypothesis on the irrelevance of capital structure for a corporation's borrowing cost. Broadly speaking there are two classes of alternatives to MM (Fama and French, 2002). One argues for an equilibrium (sometimes a dynamic equilibrium or target adjustment) trade-off between debt and equity due to the tax advantages of interest finance and the cost of bankruptcy or distress. The second argues for an ordered preference (pecking order) of the use of different forms of funds arising from investors' imperfect information (Myers and Majluf, 1984). Good surveys of recent work may be found in Myers (2003) and Frank and Goyal (2008). We address these problems here only insofar as they touch on agency concerns, a theme that is sometimes seen as a third and separate challenge to MM.

Agency issues in the *trade-off* theory relate to potential conflicts between principals rather than between managers and owners. This arises because the interests of stockholders and debt-holders are not aligned when there is a likelihood of financial distress or bankruptcy. It is the interaction of anticipated financial distress and managerial agency costs that explain why debt is not as attractive as its tax status might imply; high debt represents a temptation to dispossess the debt-holder in ways that damage growth. Specifically, if managers have high debt levels and are incentivized sufficiently to act in stockholders' interests they may be tempted to engage in excessive risk (risk-shifting), increasing debt further or reducing capital investment (since investment benefits debt-holders more at the margin by increasing assets in place). Anticipated financial distress will also lead to cautious commitments by employees and other suppliers. The downside of high debt is held to most damage firms with good growth opportunities who thus have a greater incentive to use equity finance and avoid debt even though they also have more taxable income to shield (Myers, 2003).[4] On balance, however, these firms have higher profitability and thus use less of either source of external finance.

The notion of a financial hierarchy or *pecking order* descending from internal funds through debt to equity is a standard alternative theory to the notion of a trade-off between sources of finance. It arises because managers of a currently under-valued firm (e.g., with good growth prospects) are argued to prefer new debt so as not to share the value correction with new stockholders. Using the logic of information economics, managers seeking to raise equity are signalling that the firm is over-valued so that new equity can only be raised at an information discount less favourable than for debt, which is in turn less attractive than internal finance.[5] Interestingly, the reverse case is rarely argued, for example, that firms hoarding cash to finance growth can credibly signal good prospects.

11.5.3   Empire Benefits, Free Cash Flow and Debt

Debt financing is also argued to work as an independent mechanism to control agency costs of free cash flow, that is, cash flows in excess of that required to finance all projects that have positive net present values (Jensen, 1986). Jensen's basic idea is to use debt interest (a hard constraint) as a substitute for dividend payout. One problem with this view is that it appears to substitute one agency cost (associated with managerial slack) with another (the agency cost of debt detailed in Jensen and Meckling, 1976).[6] In Jensen's view, all free cash flows should be distributed to shareholders as dividends. At best, this one-sided view is likely to be relevant only to mature firms with significant free cash flow (Myers, 2003; Chirinko and Schaller, 2004). However, even in such cases managers may reasonably oppose higher debt because it interferes with dividend stability, because of the effect on confidence, or because it prevents forward planning of strategic investments or internally financed diversification. In relation to the latter, Jensen's definition of free cash flow appears to rule out the existence of growth options (Driver and Temple, 2010). Survey results also fail to confirm the importance of managerial discipline in choice of debt or capital structure; indeed, the general evidence for signalling and agency effects on capital structure is also quite weak (Graham and Harvey, 2001; Brounen et al., 2006).

11.6   THE NEW INSTITUTIONAL ECONOMICS (NIE) APPROACH

The distinctive feature of new institutional economics (NIE) is the added context that is offered by viewing the firm as a combination of formal contracted obligations and informal ones, such as social norms, though the latter also are seen as subject to rationality constraints (Menard and Shirley, 2005). Agency concerns in this framework may be resolved by informal agreements that often amount to shared control. In the remainder of this section, we review how these institutional features of NIE contribute to the resolution of agency concerns within the firm.

11.6.1   Implicit and Relational Contracts

Contacts are said to be incomplete when formal legal agreements are impossible. Arguments for incompleteness include the difficulty of foreseeing future contingencies and the costs of writing or enforcing the contract.[7] Where conditions for incompleteness arise, there may be recourse to implicit or relational contracts. An employment contract for example, in addition to a wage may include non-formal commitments such as job security, stewardship of pension funds or conditional expectations of promotion. Such contracts may also involve unspecified and variable effort contributions from the employee. Such implicit contracts imply a certain level of trust within organizations and are sustained by reputation as are similar contracts between firms and suppliers or those involving inter-firm agreements.

Implicit contracts are sometimes analysed in terms that are distinct from formal economics, where effort is generally assumed to be elicited by extrinsic motivation. It has been noted that this orthodoxy is at variance with empirical evidence that greater involvement in work is accompanied by higher, not lower satisfaction (Pugno and Depedri, 2009).

Frey and Osterloh (2005) challenge the conventional pay-for-performance scheme and propose a so-called 'common pool approach' to executive compensation. Building on the team production theory of the firm (Alchian and Demsetz, 1972), they argue that pay-for-performance not only does not solve the incentive problem in a team but also discourages workers' pro-social intrinsic motivations. In effect, it sends a signal to managers that effort without pecuniary reward is 'socially inappropriate'. Consequently, there is insufficient investment in firm-specific common goods. Frey and Osterloh (2005) also argue that pay-for-performance undermines the neutrality of managers and leads to perceived unfairness by those lower down in the hierarchy that are managed with low-powered incentives. Similar arguments may be found in Michie and Sheehan (2003) and Osterloh and Frey (2000).

However, a culture of intrinsic motivation is unlikely to emerge spontaneously. It would most likely require an environment where certain activities are constrained or an institutional arrangement where it is made difficult to renege on commitments as in a signalling approach. Neither of these solutions is costless. For example, constraints imply that opportunities that might be approved ex post would not even be possible to investigate ex ante. All regulation works like this to some extent; for example, the governance of professions such as opticians involved restrictions on advertising (Matthews, 1991). An alternative approach is to rely on reputation but principals and perhaps agents must be willing to sink capital to achieve this. The value of that capital, however, has to balance the (discounted) gains from reneging (Gibbons, 2001). In general it seems probable that systems of constraints and regulation yield higher social than private returns and so are unlikely to emerge as market solutions (Deakin and Michie, 2003).

There have also been some formal approaches to understanding implicit contracts, generally relying on dynamic game theory but also using information assumptions similar to those in Fama (1980). The models develop a structure to predict the feasibility of agreement under uncertainty and rationality (Bernheim and Whinston, 1998; Levin, 2003). Cooperative behaviour between agent and principal is self-enforced due to each having an outside option but also an interest in the cooperative solution. If either party reneges, the relationship is hurt, which may lead to the end of the partnership. Hence, implicit contracts are most likely to emerge when the context can involve repeated interactions between the principal and the agent and where the value of continuing the relationship is high (Williamson, 1985; Levin, 2003).[8] An extension to these ideas links them to the theory of the firm. If the form of the firm (unitary asset ownership) allows certain implicit contracts that are unavailable with separately owned assets (the firm is a reputation carrier), the boundary of the firm can be determined from the importance of implicit contracts to the creation of surplus (Baker et al., 1997; Gibbons, 2001). Regulation has a role to play in facilitating this (Deakin and Michie, 2003).

In the context of implicit contracts, the principal–agent problem also becomes an agent–principal problem in that the agent cannot trust the principal to always deliver on implicit contracts. The problem for the principal then becomes one of incentivizing the agent to invest resources beyond what is fully contracted for. That may be an issue where the agent is being asked to bear risk or where the agent is expected to commit resources, for example, skill training, that are specialized to the firm and that have little outside value (Blair, 1995; Hart, 1995).

Property rights theory argues that incentives may be preserved by the allocation of control rights to defend the non-contractable investments that otherwise would lack incentives. A variant of this approach considers shared decision rights under uncertain returns. We explore these ideas in the next two sub-sections.

11.6.2 Property Rights Theory: Human Effort and Finance Inputs

Where inputs are sunk either in the form of specialized labour or assets in place, control rights may be important in persuading investors in these assets to invest (Blair, 1995; Hart, 1995). Consider the case where a firm's insiders have to provide effort (e.g., R&D inputs) for a project that will pay off randomly in a later period. As long as the firm is closely held with concentrated ownership, monitoring by investors ensures that the full (expected) value of the efforts will be available. However, such close ownership will not be consistent with insider effort due to the risk of expropriation. A solution is for the firm to be floated with dispersed ownership (weak oversight), thus providing a basis for delayed reward for the initially under-rewarded effort (Myers, 2000).

The Myers model has some similar features to that of Tirole reviewed earlier. An interesting elaboration to that model (Tirole, 1999a) allows managers to take profit-enhancing actions that increases the probability of project success by a flat increment τ for both the low-probability regime and the high-probability regime so that the differential $(p_h - p_l)$ is unaffected. Assume that the profit-enhancing action (e.g., firing workers) is indeed welfare *reducing* with the private cost for the entrepreneur/other insiders higher than the gain in profits. If the entrepreneur retains control, the profit-enhancing action is not taken and the pledgeable income remains constant at $p_h(R - B/(p_h - p_l))$. With relinquished control, the new pledgeable income is now $(p_h + \tau)(R - B/(p_h - p_l))$, which is bigger than before. This provides a potential argument for control rights to rest with the provider of finance, even though the result of the action is welfare reducing. Indeed, Tirole writes that this reasoning 'provides us with a first argument in favour of shareholder value' (p. 16). Unlike the model in Myers (2000), Tirole (1999a) does not consider the need to motivate non-contractual inputs from managers or knowledge workers, though such questions are examined in an earlier contribution (Aghion and Tirole, 1997) reviewed below. Governance of knowledge-intensive firms probably requires a consideration of shared control rights.

Property rights theory assumes that re-contracting is always possible after sunk investments have been made. The subsequent bargaining reflects a game structure whose solution is determined by the threat points created by the previous irreversible investments of the parties and thus has implications for the willingness to invest in the first place (Hart, 1995). Property rights theory has had mixed success possibly due to the difficulty of testing it, given the restrictive assumptions. However, it has underpinned much of the modern arguments for stakeholding in corporate governance. The idea here is that employees' commitment in a knowledge-based context is not fully subject to a reward-based contract and that investment in specific skills is best assured through granting some form of control rights in the form of stakeholding (Blair, 1995; Roberts and van der Steen, 2004).[9]

11.6.3   Power and Information

Transaction cost theory (Williamson, 1985) is concerned with hierarchy, arguably to the neglect of the corresponding topic of power (Chassagnon, 2009). There is now increasing interest in how power is exercised in hierarchies (Hart and Moore, 1990; Rajan and Zingales, 1998; Ortega, 2003). Rajan and Zingales (1998) argue that it is the 'access' to both physical and human capital assets rather than the ownership of physical assets that matters in reducing agency costs.[10] They define 'access' as 'the ability to use, or work with, a critical resource'. According to this theory, the agent who is given access to the resource will be motivated to invest in specialized human capital that is needed to benefit from the access. This obviates the need for property rights. However, while seemingly distinct from property rights theory, the notion of access can be equated with ownership of some specific intangible asset.

A related approach to ensuring non-contractable investments was pursued by Aghion and Tirole (1997). These authors go beyond the property rights framework in introducing uncertainty and information. Ceding autonomy and power to agents is in the interests of principals who seek to encourage search activity by agents. Autonomous agents may, of course, tend to select projects that are aligned with their private benefits. There is thus a trade-off between these private agency costs and the costs of search. More fundamentally this poses the question of when monitoring and intervention to avoid opportunism becomes excessive and discourages creative actions by managers.[11]

11.7   CONCLUSIONS

In this chapter we have provided an overview of agency theory in the firm by focusing mainly on agency conflicts between shareholders and managers. We evaluated some conventional mechanisms that are used to contain agency problems, in particular compensation schemes, monitoring, managerial reputation and capital structure. We have also discussed agency in a broader context where finance is provided by outside investors. In particular we have assessed the implications of incomplete contracts and discussed solutions based on intrinsic motivation, property rights and shared control. At present no unified theory exists or is in prospect for the issues covered in this chapter but the richness of the specific models goes a long way to make up for this.

NOTES

1.   This is a distinct argument from the 'stewardship theory' of corporate governance in which managers are not self-interested; their objective is aligned with the firm so that managers should be given sufficient autonomy to control.
2.   The assumption of a normal distribution guarantees that the solution to the optimization problem, that is, the optimal contract relating wages to the observed signals, is linear, which makes comparative statistics simple to illustrate (see Holmstrom and Milgrom, 1987; Prendergast, 1999).
3.   Conyon et al. (2010) point out that the widely accepted CEO pay scheme has two fundamental problems: first, the pay–performance relation is asymmetric, that is, it provides rewards for success without penalties for failure. Second, the performance measurement is often based on quantity rather than quality. This problem can be seen in the performance measure for bankers, that is, bankers' performance is evaluated based on the quantity of loans but not the riskiness of loans. Conyon et al. (ibid.) claim that these two problems promote risk-taking behaviour, which contributed to the 2008–09 financial crisis.
4.   A somewhat broader treatment of the trade-off based on transaction cost was discussed in Williamson (1996). He sees debt as preferred to equity because of transaction cost features of the latter – the set-up is less rule-bound than debt. Furthermore, capital structure needs to be related to asset specificity because the collateral value is lower with specific assets. Finally although the cost of all forms of external finance increase in uncertainty Williamson suggests that this is more so for debt given that rule-bound systems are placed under greater 'stress' when outcomes are volatile. These issues are further developed in more recent literature, for example, the discussion of international differences in the structure of financing in Carlin and Mayer (2003). Frank and Goyal (2008) suggest that transactions cost may explain the greater use of equity than debt for small public firms.
5.   The pecking order theory is sometimes represented as an agency theory where the firm is owner-managed so that private benefits are internalized and thus new outside equity is costly as it bears the cost of private benefits as a tax (Jensen and Meckling, 1976).
6.   Jensen's view is normative but it may be better to regard leverage as determined within an agency perspective that is, influenced by managers who may be motivated to press for a capital structure that adjusts to the risk features of their compensation (Coles et al., 2006). More generally, it is difficult to interpret econometric evidence on capital structure without taking account of the specific historical context. The use of debt as a disciplinary device does not really arise from a theoretical model (Hart, 2001) but it became popular after the publication of Jensen (1986); the resulting bankruptcies at the end of that decade modified laws and behaviour once again.
7.   See Tirole (1999b) for a consideration of the validity of incompleteness.
8.   In models of implicit contracts such as Levin (2003), there is no ex post negotiation and no 'hold-up' problem so that they do not deal with the appropriability concerns of sunk investment costs.
9.   Criticism has come from a number of sources. Williamson (2005) dismisses the approach on account of its reliance on assumed knowledge of pay-offs and cost-less bargaining. O'Sullivan (2005) is concerned that an unbalanced focus on incentives does not allow enough consideration of the managerial resource building that is needed to ensure innovation inputs.
10.   Here but not always subsequently Rajan and Zingales (1998) suggest that ownership of the resources needs to be allocated to a third party to ensure incentives.
11.   See Myers (2000) and Burkart et al. (2001).

REFERENCES

Abowd, J.W. and D.S. Kaplan (1999) Executive Compensation: Six Questions That Need Answering, *Journal of Economic Perspectives*, **13**(4), 145–68.

Aggarwal, R. and A. Samwick (1999) The Other Side of the Trade-off: the Impact of Risk on Executive Compensation, *Journal of Political Economy*, **107**(1), 65–105.

Aghion, P. and J. Tirole (1997) Formal and Real Authority in Organizations, *Journal of Political Economy*, **105**(1), 1–29.

Agrawal, P. (2002) Incentives, Risk, and Agency Costs in the Choice of Contractual Arrangements in Agriculture, *Review of Development Economics*, **6**(3), 460–77.

Alchian, A.A. and H. Demsetz (1972) Production, Information Costs, and Economic Organization, *American Economic Review*, **62**(5), 777–95.

Baker, G., R. Gibbons and K.J. Murphy (1997) Implicit Contracts and the Theory of the Firm, NBER WP No. 6177.

Bebchuk, L.A. and J.M. Fried (2004) *Pay Without Performance: The Unfullfilled Promise of Executive Compensation*, Cambridge, MA and London: Harvard University Press.

Berle, A. (1965) The Impact of the Corporation on Classical Economic Theory, *Quarterly Journal of Economics*, **79**(1), 25–40, reprinted in T. Clark (ed.), *Theories of Corporate Governance: The Philosophical Foundations of Corporate Governance*, London: Routledge, 2004.

Bernheim, B.D. and M.D. Whinston (1998) Incomplete Contracts and Strategic Ambiguity, *American Economic Review*, **88**(4), 902–32.

Blair, M. (1995) *Ownership and Control: Rethinking Corporate Governance for the Twenty-first Century*, Washington, DC: Brookings Institute Press.

Brounen, D., A. De Jong and K. Koedijk (2006) Capital Structure Policies in Europe: Survey Evidence, *Journal of Banking & Finance*, **30**(5), 1409–42.

Burkart, M., D. Gromb and F. Panunzi (2001) Large Shareholders and the Value of the Firm, *Quarterly Journal of Economics*, **112**(3), 693–728.

Carlin, W. and C. Mayer (2003) Finance, Investment, and Growth, *Journal of Financial Economics*, **69**(1), 191–226.

Chassagnon, V. (2009) The Theory of the Firm Revisited From a Power Perspective, ENEF Conference Paris 14 September.

Chirinko, R.S. and H. Schaller (2004) A Revealed Preference Approach to Understanding Corporate Governance Problems: Evidence from Canada, *Journal of Financial Economics*, **74**(1), 181–206.

Clarke, T, (2007), *International Corporate Governance: A Comparative Approach*, London: Routledge.

Coles, J.L., N.D. Daniel and L. Naveen (2006) Executive Compensation and Managerial Risktaking, *Journal of Financial Economics*, **79**(2), 431–68.

Conyon, M.J., J.E. Core and W.R. Guay (2009) Are US CEOs Paid More than UK CEOS? Inferences from Risk-adjusted Pay, available at: papers.ssrn.com/so13/papers.cfm?abstract_id=907469; accessed 16 January 2012.

Conyon, M.J., N. Fernandes, M.A. Ferreira and K.J. Murphy (2010) The Executive Compensation Controversy: A Transatlantic Analysis, available at: digitalcommons.ilr.cornell.edu/ics/5; accessed 16 January 2012.

Deakin, S. and J. Michie (2003) The Theory and Practice of Contracting, introductory chapter in S. Deakin and J. Michie (eds), *Contract, Cooperation and Competition*, Oxford: OUP.

Demsetz, H. (1993) The Theory of the Firm Revisited, in O.E. Williamson and S.G. Winter (eds), *The Nature of the Firm: Origins, Evolution and Development*, Oxford: Oxford University Press, pp. 159–78.

Driver, C. and P. Temple (2010) Why Do Hurdle Rates Differ from the Cost of Capital? *Cambridge Journal of Economics*, **34**(3), 501–23.

Fama, E.F. (1980) Agency Problems and the Theory of the Firm, *Journal of Political Economy*, **88**(2), 288–307.

Fama, E.F. and K. French (2002) Testing Trade-off and Pecking Order Predictions about Dividends and Debt, *Review of Financial Studies*, **15**(1), 1–33.

Foss, N.J., H. Lando and S. Thomsen (2000) The Theory of the Firm, in Boudewijn Bouckaert and Gerrit De Geest (eds), *Encyclopedia of Law and Economics*, vol. III, Cheltenham, UK and Northampton, MA, USA: Edward Elgar, pp. 631–58.

Frank, M.Z. and V.K. Goyal (2008) Trade Off and Pecking Order Theories of Debt, in E. Eckbo (2008), *Handbook of Corporate Finance: Empirical Corporate Finance*, Vol. 2, Chapter 12, Amsterdam: Elsevier.

Frey, B.S. and M. Osterloh (2005) Yes, Managers Should be Paid like Bureaucrats, *Journal of Management Inquiry*, **14**(1), 96–111.

Gibbons, R. (2001) Firms (and Other Relationships), Chapter 7 in P. DiMaggio (ed.), *The Twenty-first Century Firm: Changing Economic Organization in International Perspective*, Princeton, NJ: Princeton University Press.

Graham, J.R. and C.R. Harvey (2001) The Theory and Practice of Corporate Finance: Evidence from the Field, *Journal of Financial Economics*, **61**(2), 187–243.

Hart, O.D. (1995) *Firms, Contracts, and Financial Structure*, Oxford: Oxford University Press.

Hart, O.D. (2001) Financial Contracting, *Journal of Economic Literature*, **39**(4), 1079–100.

Hart, O.D. and J. Moore (1990) Property Rights and the Nature of the Firm, *Journal of Political Economy*, **98**(6), 1119–58.

Hermalin, B.E. and M.S. Weisbach (2003) Boards of Directors as an Endogenously Determined Institution: A Survey of the Economic Literature, *FRBNY Economic Policy Review*, **9**(1), 7–26.

Holmstrom, B. (1989) Agency Costs and Innovation, *Journal of Economic Behavior & Organization*, **12**(3), 305–27.

Holmstrom, B.R. and S.N. Kaplan (2001) Corporate Governance and Merger Activity in the US: Making Sense of the 1980s and 1990s, *Journal of Economic Perspectives*, **15**(2), 121–44.

Holmstrom, B.R. and P. Milgrom (1987) Aggregation and Linearity in the Provision of Intertemporal Incentives, *Econometrica*, **55**(2), 303–28.

Jensen, M.C. (1986) Agency Costs of Free Cash Flow, Corporate Finance, and Takeovers, *American Economic Review Papers and Proceedings*, **76**(2), 323–9.

Jensen, M.C. and W.H. Meckling (1976) Theory of the Firm: Managerial Behavior, Agency Costs and Ownership Structure, *Journal of Financial Economics*, **3**(4), 305–60.

Jensen, M.C. and K.J. Murphy (2004) Remuneration: Where We've Been, How We Go to Here, What Are the Problems, and How to Fix Them, ECGI Working Paper No.44/2004.

Lazear, E. and S. Rosen (1981) Rank Order Tournaments as Optimal Labor Contracts, *Journal of Political Economy*, **89**(5), 841–64.

Lazonick, W. (2007) The US Stock Market and the Governance of Innovative Enterprise, *Industrial and Corporate Change*, **16**(6), 983–1035.

Levin, J. (2003) Relational Incentive Contracts, *American Economic Review*, **93**(3), 835–57.

Matthews, R.C.O. (1991) The Economics of Professional Ethics: Should the Professions Be More Like Business?, *Economic Journal*, **101**(407), 737–50.

Menard, C. and M.M. Shirley (2005) *Handbook of New Institutional Economics*, the Netherlands: Springer.

Meng, R.J. and X.M. Zhou (2007) Managerial Promotions: The Determinants and Incentive Effects Working Paper, School of Economics and Finance, The University of Hong Kong.

Michie, J. and C. Oughton (2003) Comparative Corporate Governance: Beyond 'Shareholder Value', *Journal of Interdisciplinary Economics*, **14**(2), 81–111.

Michie, J. and M. Sheehan (2003) Labour Market Deregulation, 'Flexibility', and Innovation, *Cambridge Journal of Economics*, **27**(1), 123–43.

Murphy, K. (1999) Executive Compensation, in O. Ashenfelter and D. Card (eds), *Handbook of Labor Economics*, Amsterdam: North Holland, pp. 2485–563.

Myers, S.C. (2000) Outside Equity, *Journal of Finance*, **LV**(3), 1005–37.

Myers, S.C. (2003) Financing of Corporations, in G.M. Constantinides, M. Harris and R.M. Stultz (eds), *Handbook of the Economics of Finance*, Vol. 1A, *Corporate Finance*, Amsterdam: Elsevier.

Myers, S.C. and S. Majluf (1984) Corporate Financing Decisions When Firms Have Investment Information That Investors Do Not, *Journal of Financial Economics*, **13**(2), 187–220.

Olsen, W.K. (2006) Pluralism, Poverty and Sharecropping: Cultivating Open-mindedness in Development Studies, *Journal of Development Studies*, **42**(7), 1130–57.

Ortega, J. (2003) Power in the Firm and Managerial Career Concerns, *Journal of Economics and Management Strategy*, **12**(1), 1–29.

Osterloh, M. and B. Frey (2000) Motivation, Knowledge Transfer, and Organizational Forms, *Organization Science*, **11**(5), 538–50.

O'Sullivan, M. (2005) Finance and Innovation, in J. Fagerberg, D. Mowery and R. Nelson (eds), *The Oxford Handbook of Innovation*, Oxford: OUP.

Pagano, U. and M.A. Rossi (2009) The Crash of the Knowledge Economy, *Cambridge Journal of Economics*, **33**(4), 665–83.

Palley, T.I. (1997) Managerial Turnover and the Theory of Short-termism, *Journal of Economic Behavior & Organization*, **32**(4), 547–57.

Pitelis, C.N. (2004) Corporate Governance (Shareholder) Value and (Sustainable) Economic Performance, *Corporate Governance: An International Review*, **12**(2), 210–23.

Prendergast, C. (1999) The Provision of Incentives in Firms, *Journal of Economic Literature*, **37**(1), 7–63.

Prendergast, C. (2002) The Tenuous Trade-off Between Risk and Incentives, *Journal of Political Economy*, **110**(5), 1071–102.

Pugno, M. and S. Depedri (2009) Job Performance and Job Satisfaction: An Integrated Survey, Working Paper, No. 0904, Dipartimento di Economia Università degli Studi di Trento.

Rajan, R.G. and L. Zingales (1998) Power in a Theory of the Firm, *Quarterly Journal of Economics*, **113**(2), 387–432.

Rebérioux, A. (2007) Does Shareholder Primacy Lead to a Decline in Managerial Accountability? *Cambridge Journal of Economics*, **31**(4), 507–24.

Roberts, J. (2004) *The Modern Firm: Organizational Design for Performance and Growth*, Oxford: OUP.

Roberts, J. and E. van der Steen (2004) Shareholder Interests, Human Capital Investment and Corporate Governance, Research Paper No. 1631, Graduate School of Business, Stanford University.

Scharfstein, D.S. and J.C. Stein (1990) Herd Behavior and Investment, *American Economic Review*, **80**(13), 465–79.

Stiglitz, J. (1974) Risk Sharing and Incentives in Sharecropping, *Review of Economic Studies*, **41**(2), 219–56.

Taggart, R.A. Jr. (1987) Allocating Capital among a Firm's Divisions: Hurdle Rates vs. Budgets, *Journal of Financial Research*, **10**(3), 177–89.

Tirole, J. (1999a) Corporate Governance, *Econometrica*, **69**(1), 1–35.

Tirole, J. (1999b) Incomplete Contracts: Where Do We Stand?, *Econometrica*, **67**(4), 741–81.
Tirole, J (2006) *The Theory of Corporate Finance*, Princeton, NJ: Princeton University Press.
Williamson, O.E. (1985) *The Economic Institutions of Capitalism: Firms, Markets, Relational Contracting*, New York: Free Press.
Williamson, O.E. (1996) *The Mechanisms of Governance*, Oxford and New York: Oxford University Press.
Williamson, O.E. (2005) Transaction Cost Economics, in C.M. Ménard and M.M. Shirley (eds), *Handbook of New Industrial Economics*, Dordrecht: Springer.
Zwiebel, J. (1995) Corporate Conservatism and Relative Compensation, *Journal of Political Economy*, **103**(1), 1–25.

12 Hybrid governance
Albert Jolink and Eva Niesten

12.1 INTRODUCTION

As with all phenomena in real life, variety abounds in the real world of governance structures. The abstractions of hierarchies and markets, which have populated the binary universe of scholars of organizations, only faintly relate to their real-life counterparts. In many cases, the governance structures that have served the variety of transaction composites were neither market nor hierarchy, and often represented a category of their own.

In the economics of organization, this third category has been denoted as a hybrid governance structure, stressing both the difference with either market or hierarchy, as well as resembling both, at least partially, at the same time. Over the last 40 years, the studies of hybrids have served to identify and categorize the characteristics of this governance structure, but have only gradually come to grips with the complexities involved.

At least two theoretical perspectives within the economics of organization have studied hybrid governance structures. These are the capabilities perspective and transaction cost economics. Richardson (1972) was one of the first advocates of a capabilities perspective on inter-firm cooperation. He claimed that when we look at reality only in terms of the sharp dichotomy of firms and markets, we obtain a distorted view of how the industrial system works. The complex networks of cooperation between firms exist, because of the need to coordinate closely complementary but dissimilar activities and capabilities (ibid.). This capabilities perspective is much more conscious of the production side of the firm than is transaction cost economics, and it represents the nature of production in a way that is potentially complementary to the transaction cost approach (Langlois and Foss, 1999). Transaction cost economics is a comparative efficiency perspective that argues that firms, markets and hybrids exist in an industrial system for transaction cost economizing reasons. There is an efficiency place for each of these governance structures, which is determined by the attributes of the transactions. Hybrids are more efficient when the transactions are relatively uncertain and specific (Williamson, 1991).

In this chapter, the emphasis is on the theoretical perspective of transaction cost economics because, in line with the equilibrium direction of this part of the handbook, it is based on a comparative efficiency perspective, which may not be the case with other alternative approaches. Section 12.2 of this chapter presents the received view on hybrid governance structures. It provides a definition of hybrids, and discusses the attributes and the variety of hybrids. It illustrates which transactions are efficiently aligned with hybrid governance structures. This discussion on hybrids is based on the review by Grandori and Soda (1995), and the literature on hybrids by Williamson (1991) and Ménard (1996, 2000, 2004). This section concludes with some remarks by these authors on the status of the research on hybrids during the early days of the twenty-first century.

Section 12.3 provides a review of the recent literature (from 2005 until 2010) on hybrid governance structures. This review includes 40 articles from seven different journals in the field of the economics of organization. It demonstrates which new hybrid forms of governance have been identified in recent years, and which new areas of application for the study of hybrids have been chosen. It discusses which of the areas for potential research, as suggested by the received view, have eventually been addressed. These include among others the performance and the dynamics of hybrids, and the impact of the institutional environment on hybrids. This section also gives a detailed account of the new insights on hybrids in the literature, and illustrates how transaction cost economics is combined with other theoretical perspectives, such as the resource-based view, the economics of knowledge and learning, and the modularity theory. Hence, although transaction cost economics retains its characteristic flavour, the new developments in the research of hybrids illustrates a stronger tendency for theoretical alliances with previously seemingly incompatible approaches.

Section 12.4 provides a summary of the three novel developments in the literature on hybrids, and section 12.5 draws the final conclusions of this chapter.

12.2   A RECEIVED VIEW ON HYBRID GOVERNANCE STRUCTURES

12.2.1   Hybrids Defined

Within the economics of organization, and more specifically within transaction cost economics, 2009 Nobel Prize laureate Oliver Williamson was one of the first to analyse hybrid governance structures. In 1979, he referred to hybrids as 'intermediate forms of organization' (Williamson, 1979, p. 234). He associated these intermediate forms with long-term and flexible contracts, incentives of the contracting parties to sustain the relationship, and mechanisms to fill in the gaps of the flexible contracts. He argued that these intermediate forms of organization have an advantage over other governance structures when there is a substantial degree of uncertainty and the contracting parties have invested in specific assets. He distinguished between two types of intermediate forms: bilateral governance and trilateral governance. In trilateral governance structures, third-party assistance is employed to resolve disputes and to evaluate performance (ibid., pp. 249–50). Since 1991, Williamson has used the term hybrid to refer to these intermediate forms of organization (Williamson, 1991).

In 1995, Grandori and Soda published one of the first literature reviews on hybrid governance structures, which they termed 'inter-firm networks' (Grandori and Soda, 1995). In addition to studies within the economics of organization, they included other theoretical perspectives in their review, such as industrial economics, historical and evolutionary approaches, organizational perspectives, resource dependence views, population ecology and social network theory. They argued, however, that 'at present, organizational economics is one of the most widely used approaches in the analysis of networks' (ibid., p. 186). Grandori and Soda defined inter-firm networks as modes of organizing economic activities through inter-firm coordination and cooperation, and as modes of regulating interdependence between firms (ibid., p. 184).

In more recent years, Ménard (1996, 2000, 2004) has published extensively on hybrid governance structures from a transaction cost economics perspective. He has identified the minimum number of attributes of hybrid governance structures that still encapsulate the variety of hybrids. He has accordingly defined hybrids as 'legally autonomous entities doing business together, mutually adjusting with little help from the price system, and sharing or exchanging technologies, capital, products, and services, but without a unified ownership' (Ménard, 2004, p. 348).

In sum, we may define a hybrid as a type of governance structure that is located in between two other forms of governance: the market and the hierarchy. A governance structure is an organizational construction that coordinates the transactions between the parties to incomplete contracts. In a hybrid, the contracting parties retain their legal autonomy, but they are dependent upon each other to a substantial degree. The contracting parties in a hybrid have invested in specific assets, and when combined with the behavioural assumption of opportunism, these specific assets lead to the contractual hazard of bilateral dependency. The hybrid provides safeguards for this contractual hazard, as it combines a long-term contract with various administrative controls, such as information disclosure mechanisms and monitoring.

12.2.2   Attributes of Hybrid Governance Structures

Two elements of a hybrid governance structure stand out in its analytical refinements. These are the contractual agreements and the administrative mechanisms of hybrids. First, Ménard (2000) has categorized contracts along three attributes, such as the duration, the degree of completeness and the enforcement procedures of contracts (ibid., p. 237). The contracts in hybrid governance structures are long-term contracts with gaps in their planning. They include processes and techniques that create flexibility, and they are often assisted by a third party to evaluate performance and to resolve disputes. When disputes are resolved through arbitration, as is often the case in hybrids, the continuity of the contractual relation is presumed (Williamson, 1979, pp. 237–8). In 2004, Ménard has further added several attributes of contracts to this first categorization in 2000. The number of contracting parties is an additional distinguishing factor, leading to hybrid forms that are either bilateral or multilateral. Adaptation clauses are included in the contracts of hybrids, which do not only give the hybrid a degree of flexibility, but also allow for an information disclosure between the contracting parties. In addition, specifications in contracts differ, which in hybrids may include quality standards.

Second, the administrative control of a governance structure refers to the various mechanisms that support the functioning of the structure. Hybrid governance structures require administrative mechanisms to secure and monitor the incomplete contractual agreements, to reduce the risk of opportunistic behaviour by the contracting parties, to protect and share the rents and to solve disputes. The administrative control mechanisms of hybrids include information disclosure and information verification mechanisms, specialized dispute settlement machinery often involving a third party and penalties for premature termination of the contract (Williamson, 1996). Ménard (2004) referred to 'authorities' or 'private governments' as examples of administrative mechanisms in hybrids. These 'private governments' promote the transfer of (subclasses of) decisions of autonomous contracting parties to these authoritative entities (ibid., p. 366). Grandori and Soda (1995) identify ten different administrative mechanisms that are used in different combinations and varying degrees in different inter-firm networks. A first mechanism is the use of a common staff in a central agency, which is important when, for instance, the number of cooperating firms in a hybrid is high. Second, networks can make use of hierarchical and authority relations between firms, next to more parity-based mechanisms. Third, when performance is difficult to measure, inter-firm networks may use mechanisms that align objectives among the contracting parties. Such incentive systems may include property rights. Fourth, public support of inter-firm networks is relevant when cooperation is highly beneficial but very difficult to achieve. The final six mechanisms include communication, decision and negotiation mechanisms; social coordination and control; integration and linking-pin roles and units; planning and control systems; information systems; and selection systems (ibid., pp. 194–7).

Hybrids are thus characterized by long-term, flexible contracts and a variety of administrative control mechanisms. In addition to these main attributes of hybrid governance structures, Williamson and Ménard have identified a few additional attributes of hybrids. Williamson mentioned the intermediate degree of incentive intensity of hybrids. Incentive intensity is the degree to which changes in efforts expended by an economic actor have an immediate effect on his or her compensation or stream of revenues (Williamson, 1996, p. 99). An intermediate value on incentive intensity may mean that a part of the income to be earned cannot be influenced by the economic actor; or that the transaction itself may not directly earn an income, but is a prerequisite for earning an income with a consecutive transaction (Niesten, 2009). Hybrids are also characterized by cooperative adaptation, because contracting parties may consult each other when adapting to disturbances. This type of adaptation is intentional, or in Barnard's words, it is 'conscious, deliberate, and purposeful' (Barnard, 1938, p. 4). Ménard (2004) has illustrated that hybrids combine the attribute of contracting with 'pooling resources' and 'competing'. In pooling resources the contracting parties in hybrids plan jointly, make key investment decisions jointly, exchange information and share rents. In addition, contracting parties to a hybrid compete with each other, and they compete together with other hybrids and other governance structures.

12.2.3 Family of Hybrid Forms

Grandori and Soda (1995) make a distinction between three categories of inter-firm networks: social networks, bureaucratic networks and proprietary networks (Table 12.1). They make this distinction on the basis of the ten administrative mechanisms and on the degree of formalization of the networks. The latter refers to the extent to which networks are safeguarded by a contractual agreement (Grandori and Soda, 1995, p. 198). First, social networks are *not* safeguarded by a formal contractual agreement. These networks can be symmetric (parity-based) networks (e.g., personal networks, interlocking directorates, industrial districts), or they can be asymmetric and include elements of authority (e.g., putting-out systems, subcontracting). The asymmetric type of social networks coordinates vertical or transactional interdependencies between firms and is characterized by a central agent that has authority over the other firms. A contract may be present in the asymmetric social network to specify the terms of exchange, but the network itself, and thus the mode of coordination, is not formalized in a contract (ibid., p. 200). Second, in bureaucratic networks, formal contractual agreements specify the organizational relationships. Examples of symmetric bureaucratic networks are trade associations, cartels,

Table 12.1   Family of hybrids

	Social Networks	Bureaucratic Networks	Proprietary Networks
Symmetric	Personal networks, interlocking directorates, industrial districts	Trade associations, cartels, federations, consortia	Joint ventures
Asymmetric	Putting-out systems, subcontracting	Agency networks, licensing and franchising	Capital ventures

federations and consortia. The consortia, for instance, are characterized by the presence of public support, specified rights over the results of the consortium and monitoring and penalty systems (ibid., p. 202). Examples of asymmetric bureaucratic networks are agency networks, licensing and franchising. The latter is characterized by central personnel training, common central marketing and purchasing, a degree of hierarchical supervision and incentive systems that involve gain sharing (ibid., p. 203). Third, proprietary networks, such as joint ventures and capital ventures, are a bureaucratic form of formalized networks that are founded on some proprietary commitment. Joint ventures are symmetric and employ all the administrative mechanisms that have been described in the previous section. Capital ventures are an example of asymmetric proprietary networks (ibid., pp. 203–4).

The distinction above results in a family of six hybrid forms: the three categories and the symmetric or asymmetric variety of each. Within the economics of organization, and more specifically within transaction cost economics, the symmetric type of social network of Grandori and Soda is often not included in the analysis, because of the absence of a contractual agreement in this type of hybrid. Among the remaining forms Ménard (2004) has identified subcontracting, networks of firms, franchising, collective trademarks, partnerships, cooperatives and alliances as examples of hybrid governance structures. The family of hybrids is located in between markets and hierarchies, and ranges from contract-based approaches that are closer to the market to more integrated structures that are closer to the hierarchy. Ménard (ibid.) has placed hybrid governance structures on this range from contract-based approaches to more integrated structures. For instance, in increasing order towards more integrated structures, he has identified licensing, relational networks, leadership and formal government as hybrids.

12.2.4   Discriminating Alignment of Hybrids

The core argument of transaction cost economics is the discriminating alignment hypothesis, which claims that 'transactions, which differ in their attributes, are aligned with governance structures, which differ in their cost and competence, so as to effect a discriminating – mainly a transaction cost-economizing – result' (Williamson, 1996, p. 12). Transactions are characterized along three attributes: uncertainty, asset-specificity and frequency.

The use of the hybrid form of governance has an economizing effect when the transactions are characterized by an intermediate or high degree of uncertainty and mixed or idiosyncratic assets. It is only when the transactions occur frequently that the set-up costs of a specialized, bilateral governance structure can be recovered. A trilateral governance structure is more efficient when the transactions occur less often (Williamson, 1985, p. 79).

Ménard (2004) has applied the discriminating alignment hypothesis to the family of hybrids, by examining asset-specificity and uncertainty. He has claimed that, in particular, specific investments in human assets and in brand-name capital are relevant in hybrid governance structures. Contracting parties that each invest in specific assets and that only look for complementarities of these investments will be more inclined to adopt a contract-based approach within the hybrid family, while parties that invest together in specific assets will be more efficiently aligned with hybrids that are closer to integrated structures. This last type of investment increases the mutual dependence of the parties, and therefore necessitates greater forms of control. In addition to the specific investments, Ménard also considered uncertainty as a determining factor for the type of hybrid that is chosen. He has argued that when transactions are characterized by either asset-specificity or by uncertainty, the hybrid will be closer to a contract-based approach, but when both asset-specificity and uncertainty characterize the transactions, the hybrid will be closer to an integrated structure.

12.2.5   Loose Ends

In 2004 Ménard (2004, p. 370) identified several areas for future research on hybrids. He advocated a focus on the performance of different hybrid governance structures, an explanation of the dynamics of hybrids (i.e., their stability over time and the forces pushing towards change) and the creation of a typology of hybrid forms. In addition, the impact of the institutional environment on the choice of a specific hybrid and its characteristics should be studied. Finally, Ménard mentioned that hybrid governance structures represent a challenge to competition policies that are built on the simplistic trade-off between firms and markets, and that the transformations in competition policies remain an open question.

Grandori and Soda (1995, p. 205) have claimed that the framework that they have developed on the attributes and types of inter-firm networks should be used in future empirical research to develop testable comparative models of inter-firm coordination.

12.3   REVIEW OF RECENT LITERATURE ON HYBRIDS

We have reviewed the recent literature on hybrid governance structures to analyse the latest developments in the study of hybrids within the field of economics of organization. We have selected 40 articles for review from seven journals: *Cambridge Journal of Economics, Industrial and Corporate Change, Industry and Innovation, Journal of Economic Behavior & Organization, Journal of Institutional and Theoretical Economics, Journal of Law & Economics, and Journal of Law, Economics & Organization*. These journals are listed in the Social Sciences Citation Index, within the subject category of economics, and are selected because of their focus on governance, organizational forms, changing boundaries of firms and markets, the economics of organization, transaction cost economics and institutional economics, as is mentioned in the aims of the journals. The articles are selected when they refer to hybrid governance or to a specific form of hybrid governance, such as alliances, licensing, franchising and joint ventures. We include articles from the period 2005 until 2010, as these are published *after* the publication by Ménard (2004) on the 'economics of hybrid organizations', in which the areas for future research on hybrids were identified.

12.3.1   Attributes of Contracts and Administrative Control

The reviewed articles highlight similar attributes of the contracts and administrative mechanisms of hybrids, as were identified by Williamson, Ménard and Grandori and Soda. The contracts in the hybrid governance structures are long term and include standards on the quality of goods and services (Fink et al., 2006; Mayer and Teece, 2008; Zanarone, 2009). The contracting parties of the hybrids exchange information and knowledge, they make decisions jointly (Mayer and Teece, 2008), and in addition to being partners, they can be competitors (Elliot, 2006; Deakin et al., 2008; Hodgson, 2008). Property rights are used to align the objectives between the contracting parties in the hybrids (Andersen et al., 2007; Robinson and Stuart, 2007a). The administrative control mechanisms in the hybrids protect and share rents, reduce risks and solve disputes (Elliot, 2006; Fink et al., 2006; Mayer and Teece, 2008). A distinction is made between symmetrical and asymmetrical hybrids, or in other words, between parity-based hybrids and hybrids with hierarchical or authority relations (Andersen et al., 2007; Kalmi, 2007). Elliot (2006) refers to hybrid governance structures with a separate business model and separate operations from those of the partner organizations, which resembles Grandori and Soda's hybrids with a common staff, and marketing and purchasing in a central agency.

A few articles in the review focus specifically on analysing the contracts in hybrid governance structures. Cebrián (2009) explains why fixed payments or royalties are used in licensing contracts. When there is a technology gap between the licensee and the licensor and thus knowledge needs to be exchanged between the two parties, fixed payments in the contract mitigate the moral hazard of the licensee, whereas royalties mitigate the moral hazard of the licensor. The analysis of Robinson and Stuart (2007a) illustrates that the number of board seats in strategic alliance contracts varies with the size of the equity stake. In addition, a better reputation of a firm as an alliance partner leads to less detailed contracts, less project-level and firm-level oversight and larger upfront payments.

12.3.2   Extending the Family of Hybrids and Specific Areas of Application

The studies in the review analyse a variety of hybrids, ranging from trust, associations and licensing to franchising and joint ventures. The largest part of the reviewed studies focus on strategic alliances, and on inter-firm relationships and hybrids more generally. The review also includes new types of hybrids, and hybrids that were not mentioned by Ménard and Grandori and Soda. For instance, Elliot (2006) identifies the ambient organization as an emerging specialized organizational form. The ambient organization is a networked entity of organizations that, enabled by emerging technologies, exploits virtual resources, communication and collaboration schemes and defines an organizational structure and business model to create sustainable value (Elliot, 2006, p. 210). Antonelli (2006) refers to patent thicketing and constructed interactions, Blois (2006) to quasi-hierarchies, and Deakin et al. (2008) analyse quasi-markets. Kalmi (2007) refers instead to the disappearance of a discussion on cooperatives in economics textbooks. He argues that the main reason for this disappearance is the paradigm shift from institutional to neoclassical analysis in economics.

The study of this diverse set of hybrids has mainly been applied to technology, and more specifically to the governance of technology transfers and technological practices, and to the governance under technological uncertainty (Ernst, 2005; Zylbersztajn and Lazzarini, 2005; Filson and Morales, 2006; De Jong and Klein Woolthuis, 2008; Künneke, 2008; Cebrián, 2009). A few of the reviewed articles argue for the application of new institutional economics to specific fields of research, such as the study of healthcare provision (Hodgson, 2008), copyrights (Andersen et al., 2007), and employment (Grimshaw and Rubery, 2005), because the theory on hybrid systems in new institutional economics is better equipped to address the complexity in these fields than is, for instance, neoclassical economics.

12.3.3   Discriminating Alignment

The discriminating alignment hypothesis of Williamson that matches the governance structures to the attributes of transactions in a transaction cost economizing manner is confirmed by several of the reviewed articles. Brickley et al. (2006) find that contract duration is positively related to the franchisee's specific physical and human capital investments. This relation only holds in subsamples of the most established franchisors. The long-term relational exchanges, studied by Fink et al. (2006), are characterized by a great degree of specificity and product technological uncertainty. De Jong and Klein Woolthuis (2008) show that inter-organizational trust increases the performance of high-tech alliances that are subject to high levels of uncertainty.

Andersen et al. (2007) demonstrate that the governance of music copyrights was altered to reduce transaction costs. Deakin et al. (2008) find that the introduction of quasi-markets and networks in British broadcasting was associated with increased transaction costs. Ulset (2008) and Yvrande-Billon and Ménard (2005) show how governance structures change as a result of inefficient alignments between governance and transactions. Raynaud et al. (2009) link Williamson's efficient alignment of governance and transactions to branding strategies. They argue that firms carefully design the governance of the most critical and quality-relevant transactions, because a misalignment for these transactions may have higher consequences than misalignment for more peripheral ones. These transactions, which are relevant for the quality and thus the branding of the product, are more tightly controlled than the peripheral transactions.

Claude-Gaudillat and Quélin (2006), however, do not confirm the discriminating alignment hypothesis. They find that market transactions are used to access specific capabilities. In their study, the market may be used as a default mode, because firms do not have enough internal resources to engage in an alliance or acquisition. Ellman (2006) complements the existing theory on long-term contracting stressing the potential relevance of intentional specificity in a broad range of settings. Contrary to Klein (1980) and Williamson (1983), Ellman proves that long-term contracting does not preclude strategic explanations of specificity as a device for enhancing incentives.

12.3.4   Combination of Theoretical Frameworks and Focus on Modularity Theory

Several of the reviewed studies combine the theoretical perspective of transaction cost economics with the resource-based view in their analysis of hybrid governance structures (Claude-Gaudillat and Quélin, 2006; Fink et al., 2006; Mayer and Teece, 2008; Vega-Jurado et al., 2009). Others focus on the combination of transaction cost economics with learning theory (Wuyts et al., 2005), with information economics, economics of knowledge and the corporate strategy domain (Cozzi and Tarola, 2006; Reuer and Ragozzoni, 2008) and with an evolutionary perspective (Ulset, 2008). Antonelli (2006) provides an application of information economics to the economics of knowledge in his study of knowledge governance mechanisms. Andersen et al. (2007), Hodgson (2008) and Grimshaw and Rubery (2005) argue for the application of new institutional economics to the study of hybrids in the fields of copyright, healthcare and employment respectively.

Baldwin (2008) combines transaction cost economics with modularity theory. He constructs a theory of the location of transactions and the boundaries of firms. He makes a distinction between thick crossing points and thin crossing points of the task network. At thick crossing points, the transactions are more complex and relational contracts have an advantage over formal contracts or spot transactions. Transaction costs are low at thin crossing points, which signals the boundary of a module. Campagnolo and Camuffo (2009) use strategic alliances as a proxy for the rate of adoption of modular organizational forms. Strategic alliances are considered as organizational modules in a larger system. Langlois and Garzarelli (2008) also use the idea of modularity and apply it to the study of open source collaboration. They argue that open source software projects are hybrids that manifest both voluntary production and conscious planning, and are located in between innate modularity and integrality. Ernst (2005) claims that the enthusiasm for modularity has gone too far. With evidence from chip design, he illustrates how competitive dynamics and cognitive complexity create modularity limits.

12.3.5   New Studies Addressing the Loose Ends

The articles in the review address several of the loose ends that were mentioned by Ménard (2004). They focus on the performance and dynamics of hybrids, and on the impact of the institutional environment on hybrid governance structures. De Jong and Klein Woolthuis (2008) measure the performance of high-tech alliances, in terms of relational satisfaction, and they illustrate how inter-organizational trust fosters the performance of these alliances. Inter-organizational trust develops and is promoted when the partners to the strategic alliance have a shared past. Robinson and Stuart (2007b) studied a network of strategic alliances with social network analysis. They conclude that the success of relational contracting largely depends on the proximity of the joint ventures and the centrality of the firm in the network. In their study on external knowledge sourcing and innovation, Vega-Jurado et al. (2009) measure performance by the extent to which firms have introduced new or significantly improved products or processes. They find that science-based firms innovate more in products, as compared to supplier-dominated firms that innovate more in processes. The science-based firms cooperate more with external parties than supplier-dominated firms. In addition, Vega-Jurado et al. (ibid.) demonstrate that internal R&D activities are positively related to cooperation strategies and product innovations.

With respect to the dynamics of hybrids, Claude-Gaudillat and Quélin (2006) explain the choice between markets, acquisitions and alliances for entering an industry on the basis of market timing. The diminishing interest in signing an alliance over time is explained by the decreasing numbers of partners available. Evans and Guthrie (2006) demonstrate that the inefficiency of cooperatives can be understood when analysed over a longer period of time. Filson and Morales (2006) show on the one hand that equity links between parties to strategic alliances are less likely to be used when one party has had more previous successful alliances. On the other hand, they illustrate that equity links are more likely to be used when the contract is modified after the initial signing date and when the contract is signed during a period that involves a high risk of failure or a high investment. Ulset (2008) aims to develop an evolutionary transaction cost economics that is capable of explaining the rise and fall of global network alliances. The farsighted contracting of standard transaction cost economics is replaced by experiential contracting. After the contracting parties have set up an alliance, the relevant contractual hazards are disclosed, and the parties learn about the efficiency of other contractual designs and governance structures. This experiential contracting explains why alliances fail and subsequently are replaced by more appropriate markets or hierarchies. Künneke (2008) claims that incoherence between institutions and technological practice are the drivers for change in an industry. Elliot (2006) argues that the emerging organizational form, the ambient organization, provides a previously unrecognized linkage between organizational form and industry transformation.

Yvrande-Billon and Ménard (2005) and Zylbersztajn and Lazzarini (2005) illustrate how the institutional environment stimulates changes at the level of governance structures and contracts. In the article by Yvrande-Billon and Ménard, public policy-makers stimulate change in the rail industry by imposing a governance form that is not suited for the transactions at stake. Zylbersztajn and Lazzarini show that external uncertainty increases contract terminations, and that the value of an ongoing relationship may decline over time due to the obsolescence of the technology being exchanged.

Andersen et al. (2007) focus on the interplay between the regulation of copyrights and the institutional arrangements that organize the creation and distribution of value from copyrights. Zanarone (2009) illustrates that, after an EC regulation prohibited exclusive dealer territories, automobile franchise contracts were adjusted to include price ceilings and standards on verifiable marketing and service inputs. These contracts were adjusted to induce the desired dealer behaviour that was previously stimulated by the exclusive dealer territories. Hagedoorn et al. (2008) demonstrate that the higher the level of technological sophistication and the stronger the regime of appropriability of industries, the higher the likelihood that firms prefer partnership-embedded licensing to standard licensing contracts. Partnership-embedded licensing is broader than the standard licensing contracts, because it is not only concerned with the single act of transferring technology, but also with the sharing of resources and exploring joint R&D activities. The analysis of Ahmadjian and Oxley (2006) suggests that the robustness of different types of hostages depends on the value, durability and observability of the hostages involved and that these features in turn depend on the particulars of the institutional environment in which the relationship is embedded.

In an international context, Hainz (2007) and Norman (2009) study the impact of the institutional environment on hybrid governance structures. Hainz (2007) argues that business groups perform functions of missing institutions, such as enforcing contracts in emerging markets. Norman (2009) analyses the effect of geographical distance on licensing or franchising contracts, and concludes that licensing is preferred to internalization when there are few spillover effects from the licensee's market to the licensor's home market.

12.3.6   New Insights

In addition to these studies that address the research challenges, the reviewed articles have also extended the economics of organization and the analysis of hybrids in other ways. We will discuss four of these novel insights: the analysis of multiple transactions, alternative governance choices when timing is relevant, the role of litigation in hybrids, and a focus on ex post contract duration. First, Antonelli (2006) has provided an approach that highlights the key role of nested transactions and the need to go beyond the analysis of single transactions when indivisibility matters. The standard transaction cost economics has only focused on analysing the attributes of a single transaction, and on finding the comparative efficient governance structure for this transaction, without much consideration for the attributes of related transactions in the hybrid governance structure of the transacting parties. The modularity theory may also contribute to analysing the location of transactions and hybrids in a larger system (Baldwin, 2008; Campagnolo and Camuffo, 2009). Cooper and Ross (2009) extend this direction of research by examining the effect of the governance structure in one market on the governance structure in another market. They conclude that a strategic alliance of two firms in one environment is consequential for the market structure of these same firms in another environment.

Second, in 1991, Williamson addressed several problems with the analysis of innovation in transaction cost economics. One of the problems is that firms sometimes choose to adopt a governance structure, not for asset-specificity reasons, but for reasons of speed. Innovation often requires fast responses of firms to rapidly changing conditions, and firms may therefore prefer to use the market or a hybrid, as opposed to the hierarchy. Claude-Gaudillat and Quélin (2006) have now demonstrated such a preference for the market as a default mode in the case of disruptive innovations and market entry strategies. Dibiaggio (2007) concludes that collaboration is to be preferred over integration when there is a rapid change in technology. It then becomes difficult to determine the potential value of new knowledge, and speed of access to knowledge is critically important to improve time to market.

Third, in transaction cost economics, the contracts of market governance structures are claimed to be the least flexible and most complete of the incomplete contracts. When disputes arise, these contracts are ended, and courts are reserved as a forum for ultimate appeal. In hybrid governance structures, arbitration is preferred over courts to resolve disputes. Robinson and Stuart (2007a) have instead highlighted that contracting parties to an alliance include unobservable provisions in their contracts to allow for litigation as an enforcement tool. It may be desirable to include unverifiable provisions in a contract because doing so raises contracting surplus by more than it increases transaction costs.

Finally, Zylbersztajn and Lazzarini (2005) study ex post contract duration, and thus the survival of contractual relationships over time. Contract theory and transaction cost economics have mainly focused on ex ante contract duration, and thus the duration as specified in the contractual agreements. The study of ex post contract durations may provide better insights into the contractual relations. For instance, short-term contracts may in fact be long-term agreements when they are renewed every year.

12.4 DISCUSSION

The intellectual struggle over the last 40 years to come to grips with the concept of hybrid governance structures, has resulted in, on the one hand, a better understanding of the limits of the market and the hierarchy as distinct governance structures, and, on the other hand, a further refinement and variety of the concept of the hybrid itself. This latter development, as it seems, has not reached its final destination yet.

Earlier reviews conveyed an array of developments related to non-market and non-hierarchy types of governance structures. The initial attempts to categorize these types of hybrids served in this chapter to illustrate the most recent explorations along these categories, but also allowed for the exposition of novel mutations that have emerged.

At least three novel developments can be singled out in our review of the most recent literature on the hybrid governance structure, which appear to be promising for a further understanding of hybrid governance structures and transaction cost economics. First, the combination of transaction cost economics with other fields; second, the integration of transaction cost economics and modularity theory; third, the development of what may be referred to as a 'generalized' transaction cost economics.

The empirical studies in recent years on hybrids reveal the complexity and multifaceted nature of the object of study in practice. In dealing with these governance structures, transaction cost economics has proven a need to enlarge its theoretical basis or to find alliances with other fields of enquiry. The collaboration of transaction cost economics and social network analysis, which we have seen above, is a case in point in which fruitful new developments may be expected, leading to a further enlightenment of the hybrid organizations. This will lead to a better understanding of (bilateral) alliances and hybrids of some sort, which can be viewed as being part of a larger network.

In a similar vein, though quite distinct, are the recent attempts to integrate modularity theory and transaction cost economics. By taking modularity as a systems concept, in which components may be separated and recombined, transactions may be nested into a variety of clusters, separated by differing boundaries. This development expresses the necessity to search for the inter-relatedness of transactions in a larger whole, and the essential role for hybrids.

Third, the review reveals the awareness of the consequences of hybrid governance structures in one environment on the compound of transactions and governance in another environment. The case of the strategic alliance in one environment and its effect on the competition in another environment, which we presented above, may serve as an example. The case illustrates the relevance of the interaction of networks or clusters of governance structures with other networks or clusters of governance structures.

These three developments appear to move into the direction of a more *generalized transaction cost economics.* The 'generalization' with respect to transaction cost economics refers to the development in which transactions, governance structures and alignments are viewed in a larger context, involving a multitude of these items.

12.5   CONCLUSIONS

The last 40 years of studies on hybrids have offered ample new developments in terms of variety. One may acknowledge that the inclusion of the hybrid governance structure, as one of the three generic governance structures in transaction cost economics, has led to an avalanche of discoveries of new hybrids. The suggestions of previous reviewers of the literature on hybrid governance structures to promote the theoretical rigour of the concept of hybrids itself, still awaits being picked up. The recent developments in the literature seem to head towards the empirical requirements of governance structures, on the one hand, and towards a broader and richer perception of transaction cost economics with a pivotal role for hybrids.

REFERENCES

Ahmadjian, C. and J. Oxley (2006) Using hostages to support exchange: dependence balancing and partial equity stakes in Japanese automotive supply relationships. *The Journal of Law, Economics, & Organization,* **22**(1), 213–33.

Andersen, B., R. Kozul-Wright and Z. Kozul-Wright (2007) Rents, rights n'rhythm: cooperation, conflict and capabilities in the music industry. *Industry and Innovation,* **14**(5), 513–40.

Antonelli, C. (2006) The business governance of localized knowledge: an information economics approach for the economics of knowledge. *Industry and Innovation,* **13**(3), 227–61.

Baldwin, C. (2008) Where do transactions come from? Modularity, transactions, and the boundaries of firms. *Industrial and Corporate Change,* **17**(1), 155–95.

Barnard, C. (1938) *The Functions of the Executive.* Cambridge, MA: Harvard University Press.

Blois, K. (2006) The boundaries of the firm – a question of reinterpretation? *Industry and Innovation,* **13**(2), 135–50.

Brickley, J., S. Misra and L. van Horn (2006) Contract duration: evidence from franchising. *Journal of Law & Economics,* **49**(1), 173–96.

Campagnolo, D. and A. Camuffo (2009) What really drives the adoption of modular organizational forms? An institutional perspective from Italian industry-level data. *Industry and Innovation,* **16**(3), 291–314.

Cebrián, M. (2009) The structure of payments as a way to alleviate contractual hazards in international technology licensing. *Industrial and Corporate Change,* **18**(6), 1135–60.

Claude-Gaudillat, V. and B. Quélin (2006) Innovation, new market and governance choices of entry: the internet brokerage market case. *Industry and Innovation,* **13**(2), 173–87.

Cooper, R. and T. Ross (2009) Sustaining cooperation with joint ventures. *The Journal of Law, Economics, & Organization,* **25**(1), 31–54.

Cozzi and Tarola (2006) R&D cooperation, innovation, and growth. *Journal of Institutional and Theoretical Economics,* **162**(4), 683–701.

Deakin, S., A. Lourenco and S. Pratten (2008) No 'third way' for economic organization? Networks and quasi-markets in broadcasting. *Industrial and Corporate Change,* **18**(1), 51–75.

Dibiaggio, L. (2007) Design complexity, vertical disintegration and knowledge organization in the semiconductor industry. *Industrial and Corporate Change,* **16**(2), 239–67.

Elliot, S. (2006) Technology-enabled innovation, industry transformations and the emergence of ambient organizations. *Industry and Innovation,* **13**(2), 209–25.

Ellman, M. (2006) Specificity revisited: the role of cross-investments. *The Journal of Law, Economics, & Organization*, **22**(1), 234–57.

Ernst, D. (2005) Limits to modularity: reflections on recent developments in chip design. *Industry and Innovation*, **12**(3) 303–35.

Evans, L. and G. Guthrie (2006) A dynamic theory of cooperatives: the link between efficiency and valuation. *Journal of Institutional and Theoretical Economics*, **162**(2), 364–83.

Filson, D. and R. Morales (2006) Equity links and information acquisition in biotechnology alliances. *Journal of Economic Behavior & Organization*, **59**(1), 1–28.

Fink, R., L. Edelman, K. Hatten and W. James (2006) Transaction cost economics, resource dependence theory, and customer–supplier relationships. *Industrial and Corporate Change*, **15**(3), 497–529.

Grandori, A. and G. Soda (1995) Inter-firm networks: antecedents, mechanisms and forms. *Organization Studies*, **16**(2), 183–214.

Grimshaw, D. and J. Rubery (2005) Inter-capital relations and the network organisation: redefining the work and employment nexus. *Cambridge Journal of Economics*, **29**(6), 1027–51.

Hagedoorn, J., S. Lorenz-Orlean and H. van Kranenburg (2008) Inter-firm technology transfer: partnership-embedded licensing or standard licensing agreements? *Industrial and Corporate Change*, **18**(3), 529–50.

Hainz, C. (2007) Business groups in emerging markets: financial control and sequential investments. *Journal of Institutional and Theoretical Economics*, **163**(2), 336–55.

Hodgson, G. (2008) An institutional and evolutionary perspective on health economics. *Cambridge Journal of Economics*, **32**(2), 235–56.

Jong, G. de and R. Klein Woolthuis (2008) The institutional arrangements of innovation: antecedents and performance effects of trust in high-tech alliances. *Industry and Innovation*, **15**(1), 45–67.

Kalmi, P. (2007) The disappearance of cooperatives from economics textbooks. *Cambridge Journal of Economics*, **31**(4), 625–47.

Klein, B. (1980) Transaction cost determinants of unfair contractual relations. *American Economic Review Proceedings*, **70**(2), 356–62.

Künneke, R. (2008) Institutional reform and technological practice: the case of electricity. *Industrial and Corporate Change*, **17**(2), 233–65.

Langlois, R. and N. Foss (1999) Capabilities and governance: the rebirth of production in the theory of economic organization. *Kyklos*, **52**(2), 201–18.

Langlois, R. and G. Garzarelli (2008) Of hackers and hairdressers: modularity and the organizational economics of open source collaboration. *Industry and Innovation*, **15**(2), 125–43.

Mayer, K. and D. Teece (2008) Unpacking strategic alliances: the structure and purpose of alliance versus supplier relationships. *Journal of Economic Behavior & Organization*, **66**(1), 106–27.

Ménard, C. (1996) On clusters, hybrids and other strange forms: the case of the French poultry industry. *Journal of Institutional and Theoretical Economics*, **152**(1), 154–83.

Ménard, C. (2000) *Institutions, Contracts, and Organizations: Perspectives from New Institutional Economics*. Cheltenham, UK and Northampton, MA, USA: Edward Elgar.

Ménard, C. (2004) The economics of hybrid organizations. *Journal of Institutional and Theoretical Economics*, **160**(3), 345–76.

Niesten, E. (2009) *Regulation, Governance and Adaptation: Governance Transformations in the Dutch and French Liberalizing Electricity Industries*. Rotterdam: ERIM PhD Series Research in Management.

Norman, G. (2009) Internalisation revisited. *Journal of Institutional and Theoretical Economics*, **165**(1), 121–33.

Raynaud, E., L. Sauvée and E. Valceschini (2009) Aligning branding strategies and governance of vertical transactions in agri-food chains. *Industrial and Corporate Change*, **18**(5), 835–68.

Reuer, J. and R. Ragozzoni (2008) Adverse selection and M&A design: the roles of alliances and IPOs. *Journal of Economic Behavior & Organization*, **66**(2), 195–212.

Richardson, G.B. (1972) The organisation of industry. *The Economic Journal*, **82**(327), 883–96.

Robinson, D. and T. Stuart (2007a) Financial contracting in biotech strategic alliances. *Journal of Law & Economics*, **50**(3), 559–95.

Robinson, D. and T. Stuart (2007b) Network effects in the governance of strategic alliances. *The Journal of Law, Economics, & Organization*, **23**(1), 242–73.

Ulset, S. (2008) The rise and fall of global network alliances. *Industrial and Corporate Change*, **17**(2), 267–300.

Vega-Jurado, J., A. Gutiérrez-Gracia and I. Fernández-de-Lucio (2009) Does external knowledge sourcing matter for innovation? Evidence from the Spanish manufacturing industry. *Industrial and Corporate Change*, **18**(4), 637–70.

Williamson, O. (1979) Transaction-cost economics: the governance of contractual relations. *Journal of Law & Economics*, **22**(2), 233–61.

Williamson, O. (1983) The use of hostages as a credible commitment in bilateral exchange. *American Economic Review*, **73**(4), 519–40.

Williamson, O. (1985) *The Economic Institutions of Capitalism: Firms, Markets, Relational Contracting*. New York: Free Press.

Williamson, O. (1991) Comparative economic organization: the analysis of discrete structural alternatives. *Administrative Science Quarterly*, **36**(2), 269–96.

Williamson, O. (1996) *The Mechanisms of Governance*. Oxford: Oxford University Press.

Wuyts, S., M. Colombo, S. Dutta and B. Nooteboom (2005) Empirical tests of optimal cognitive distance. *Journal of Economic Behavior & Organization*, **58**(2), 277–302.

Yvrande-Billon, A. and C. Ménard (2005) Institutional constraints and organizational changes: the case of the British rail reform. *Journal of Economic Behavior & Organization*, **56**(4), 675–99.

Zanarone, G. (2009) Vertical restraints and the law: evidence from automobile franchising. *Journal of Law & Economics*, **52**(4), 691–700.

Zylbersztajn, D. and S. Lazzarini (2005) On the survival of contracts: assessing the stability of technology licensing agreements in the Brazilian seed industry. *Journal of Economic Behavior & Organization*, **56**(1), 103–20.

13 Transaction cost empirical work
Richard Carter

13.1 INTRODUCTION

The transaction cost theoretical framework has been exposed to substantial empirical testing: Macher and Richman (2008), in a recent review of the empirical literature, identified around 900 studies that tested some aspect of the transaction cost economics (TCE) theory in a broad range of circumstances.[1] TCE empirical work came to prominence with some early articles that are now landmark studies in the field (Monteverde and Teece, 1982; Anderson and Schmittlein, 1984; Masten, 1984). The focus of these studies and the many others that followed was on testing the transactional alignment predictions of TCE. More recently, a 'second generation' of studies has emerged that employs empirical methods that address some of the inherent limitations of the reduced-form analysis that has been employed in the majority of the TCE empirical work (Yvrande-Billon and Saussier, 2004).

Empirical work provides vital feedback on the TCE theoretical framework and hence to the theory of the firm debate. It has been claimed both that TCE is an empirical success story and that the empirical work is broadly corroborative of the predictions of TCE (Williamson, 1985, 1999, 2000). These claims are very significant for the academic debate and hence it is essential that they are well founded. This review argues that the empirical support for TCE is in fact rather mixed and that the more recent empirical work suggests that governance (or integration) decisions can be helpfully informed by TCE alongside alternative theoretical perspectives.

This review focuses on empirical studies in two areas that are of particular relevance to the theory of the firm: vertical integration and hybrid relationships. The review starts with a discussion of Williamson's TCE framework to establish its key elements and, importantly, the specific predictions of the framework. Section 13.3 provides a discussion of some of the most prominent and influential of the 'first generation' of empirical studies that have tested Williamson's discriminating alignment predictions. In section 13.4 the limitations of the standard empirical tests based on a reduced-form model are outlined, along with a discussion of the 'second generation' of empirical research that has arisen, at least in part, in response to these limitations. The final section considers the conclusions that can be drawn from the empirical work.

13.2 THE TCE THEORETICAL FRAMEWORK AND EMPIRICAL TESTING

It is Oliver Williamson's theoretical work that has been instrumental in the rise of TCE to prominence (Williamson, 1979, 1985). The introduction of the concept of asset specificity was crucial in the development of Williamson's approach, as it explained how a large numbers bargaining situation could be transformed into a small numbers bargaining situation, creating the possibility of hold-up by one of the contracting partners. Williamson (1979, p. 245) outlined clearly the importance of asset specificity (or transaction-specific investments), but only alongside the other elements of his framework:

> [T]he three critical dimensions for characterizing transactions are (1) uncertainty, (2) the frequency with which transactions recur, and (3) the degree to which durable transaction-specific investments are incurred. Of these three, uncertainty is widely conceded to be a critical attribute; and that frequency matters is at least plausible. The governance ramifications of neither, however, have been fully developed – nor can they be until joined with the third critical dimension: transaction-specific assets.

Williamson's framework sets out how specific governance mechanisms could be aligned with these three transaction dimensions to economize on transaction costs, resulting in better performance than would have been the case had an alternative misaligned governance mechanism been chosen.[2]

Williamson (1979) sets out the specific predictions for vertical integration and hybrid relationships. Vertical integration is the efficient governance mechanism where: (1) investments are idiosyncratic (high asset specificity), uncertainty is either medium or high and the transaction is recurrent; or (2) when investments are mixed (medium asset specificity), uncertainty is high and the transaction is recurrent.

The position is more complex for hybrid relationships, as Williamson (ibid.) outlines two forms of generic contractual governance mechanisms: bilateral, obligational contracting and trilateral, neoclassical contracting. Within a bilateral contract the emphasis is on the continuity of the relationship and hence the need for adaptability to changing circumstances (the focus being on quantity rather than price adjustments). The inclusion of a third party, or arbitrator, to deal with disputes arising from changes in trading circumstances is the key feature of a trilateral contract. Williamson's (1983, 1985) discussion of credible commitments identifies a number of mechanisms that could be used to support the contractual arrangements, including balancing investments in specific assets, hostages, take-or-pay procurement clauses and reciprocity arrangements. Williamson's (1991, p. 280) later discussion of hybrid relationships emphasizes the need for the support of formal 'contractual safeguards and administrative apparatus (information disclosure, dispute-settlement machinery)'.

His framework predicts: (1) bilateral contractual governance will be efficient for transactions that are recurrent, have intermediate levels of uncertainty and mixed investment characteristics; and (2) trilateral contractual governance will be efficient for transactions that are occasional, have intermediate levels of uncertainty and have either idiosyncratic or mixed investment characteristics.

Before Williamson developed this predictive framework the general concept of transaction costs had been difficult to test, both because transaction costs were difficult to observe and quantify and because of the selection problem, namely that transaction costs could only be observed for the governance mechanism chosen (Masten, 1996). By identifying how governance mechanisms should be aligned with transaction dimensions, Williamson provided the breakthrough necessary for empirical testing (ibid.). Empirical researchers were able to employ reduced-form models to test Williamson's predictions. This was a vital development, but at the same time a consequence of this has been that much of the empirical testing that followed contained some inherent weaknesses (ibid.). This issue is discussed later in section 13.4.

13.3   STANDARD EMPIRICAL TESTS OF THE TCE PREDICTIONS

The studies that are reviewed in this section are all prominent TCE empirical studies that have been influential in the debate on the empirical testing of the TCE framework. A minimum citations methodology was used to create a sample of the most influential studies that employ some element of Williamson's TCE framework in their empirical model.[3] The studies are separated into two categories: vertical integration and hybrid relationship studies.

13.3.1   Vertical Integration Studies

The results of these studies can be assessed in two ways: (1) by considering each individual variable in the TCE framework, and (2) against the complete predictions provided by the TCE framework. Empirical researchers typically test each variable separately and hence earlier reviews have typically reported and assessed the results in this way, but this does not provide a sufficient understanding of how the TCE predictive framework has stood up to empirical testing. It is, therefore, the latter assessment approach that receives the major focus here, although a very brief discussion of the findings for individual variables is provided.

The relevant results from 12 empirical studies of vertical integration are provided in Table 13.1. As the table and the discussion that follows in section 13.3.1.2 demonstrate, the results are actually quite mixed and not as overwhelmingly supportive of TCE as other reviews have suggested (Shelanski and Klein, 1995; Macher and Richman, 2008).

13.3.1.1   Assessment of the individual TCE variables

There is very strong support for the asset specificity variables tested in the 12 studies. Each of the studies finds support for at least one form of asset specificity, the support for human asset specificity being particularly notable. This accords with the findings of other review studies (David and Han, 2004; Lafontaine and Slade, 2007).

The support for the uncertainty variables tested was more mixed. Three studies found support for the uncertainty variables that they tested. Six of the studies found support for at least one uncertainty variable tested but also found no support for at least one uncertainty variable tested. Two studies did not test for uncertainty at all and one study found support for the opposite relationship to that expected (i.e., that uncertainty was negatively correlated with vertical integration). This again accords with the findings of David and Han (2004). Macher and Richman (2008) also note the uneven treatment of uncertainty in the empirical literature.

Only two of the 12 studies included a transaction frequency variable in their empirical models and in both of those cases no support was found for it. Macher and Richman (2008), in their very extensive review of the TCE empirical work, highlighted both the very limited testing and the very limited support for transaction frequency, as did David

Table 13.1 Vertical integration studies

Study	Dependent Variable	Asset Specificity	Uncertainty	Transaction Frequency	Results
Anderson (1985)	Internal sales force or independent sales representatives	*Human*	**Environmental interaction, behavioral**, environmental, behavioral	Transaction frequency	Partly consistent and partly inconsistent with TCE
Anderson and Coughlan (1987)	Internal sales force or independent sales representatives	**Human**	No uncertainty variable	No transaction frequency variable	Partly consistent with TCE
Anderson and Schmittlein (1984)	Internal sales force or independent sales representatives	**Human**	Environmental interaction, behavioral interaction, environmental, **behavioral**	Transaction frequency	Partly consistent and partly inconsistent with TCE
Balakrishnan and Wernerfelt (1986)	Degree of integration	**General**	*External (technological)*	No transaction frequency variable	Partly consistent and partly inconsistent with TCE
Erramilli and Rao (1993)	Full control or shared control entry mode	**Human, physical**	**External interaction**, internal interaction, external, *internal*	No transaction frequency variable	Partly consistent and partly inconsistent with TCE
Gatignon and Anderson (1988)	Wholly owned subsidiary or partnership	**Human, brand name**	External interaction, *external*, **internal**	No transaction frequency variable	Partly consistent and partly inconsistent with TCE

		Human	**Environmental, behavioral**		
John and Weitz (1988)	Percentage of sales through a direct channel	Human	Environmental, behavioral	No transaction frequency variable	Inconclusive
Klein et al. (1990)	Degree of channel integration	Human, **physical**	External interaction, **external (volatility)**, *external (diversity)*	No transaction frequency variable	Partly consistent and partly inconsistent with TCE
Masten (1984)	Internal production or external procurement	**General (design)**, site	**External (complexity)**	No transaction frequency variable	Partly consistent with TCE
Masten et al. (1991)	Internal production or external procurement	**Human**, physical, **temporal**	**External (complexity)**	No transaction frequency variable	Partly consistent with TCE
Monteverde and Teece (1982)	Majority internal production or external procurement	**Human, general (component)**	No uncertainty variable	No transaction frequency variable	Partly consistent with TCE
Walker and Weber (1984)	Internal production or external procurement	**General**	**External (volume)**, external (technological)	No transaction frequency variable	Partly consistent with TCE

Notes and explanations:

The evaluations in Table 13.1 are made according to Williamson's standard TCE model and not according to the expectations of the researchers, whatever these may be. The table records both the TCE variables employed in the individual studies and whether they were found to be in accord with TCE predictions. Where a word appears in **bold** it indicates a positive result. Where it is in ***bold italics*** it indicates that the results for this variable are mixed but that some are positive. Where the word appears in a normal typeface it means that the variable was not found to have any statistically significant relationship with the dependent variable. Where the word appears in *italics* it indicates that the opposite relationship to that predicted by TCE is found. In the uncertainty column, the term interaction refers to a test of an interaction effect between asset specificity and uncertainty. John and Weitz (1988) and Klein et al. (1990) explicitly reject the need to test for transaction frequency. Walker and Weber (1984) explicitly reject the need to test for an interaction effect between asset specificity and external uncertainty. Anderson (1985) and Anderson and Schmittlein (1984) perform different tests on the same dataset, and due compensation should be made for this.

Source: Carter and Hodgson (2006). Reprinted with permission.

and Han (2004). This neglect of transaction frequency may not appear particularly important, but each of the transaction dimensions in the TCE predictive framework is needed to determine the appropriate governance mechanism. For example, where there are idiosyncratic investments and a medium level of uncertainty a move from an occasional to a recurrent transaction should shift the governance mechanism from hybrid (trilateral) to vertical integration.

It is standard practice for empirical researchers to test individual elements of the TCE framework within an empirical model and then report on the statistical significance of each individual variable. No criticism can be attached to this approach, but there is a danger that insufficient attention is then given to the complete predictions of the TCE framework, with the focus instead being on the individual hypotheses into which it can be broken down.

13.3.1.2   Assessment of the TCE predictive framework

The precise predictions for when vertical integration will be the efficient governance mechanism were set out earlier in section 13.2. The empirical tests are categorized as being fully consistent, partly consistent, partly consistent and partly inconsistent, or inconsistent with the predictions of Williamson's TCE framework, or inconclusive. An explanation of these terms is provided in the discussion that follows, which focuses on aspects of the studies that require further explanation.

Fully consistent: *To be classified as fully consistent with Williamson's TCE an empirical study must (1) test all three of the transaction dimensions of Williamson's TCE framework (asset specificity; uncertainty; transaction frequency) and (2) produce results for the three dimensions that are all consistent with the relevant predictions of this framework.*

No study is fully consistent with Williamson's TCE as none tests successfully for all three of Williamson's dimensions.

Partly consistent: *A study is classified as being partly consistent with Williamson's analysis where it tests only a part of his complete framework, has some dimensional results that are consistent, and no dimensional result that is inconsistent, with Williamson's predictions.*

Five of the 12 studies are partly consistent with Williamson's TCE. None of these studies tests for transaction frequency and, additionally, neither Anderson and Coughlan (1987) nor Monteverde and Teece (1982) test for uncertainty. Interestingly, Walker and Weber (1984) highlight that comparative production costs (rather than asset specificity or uncertainty) are actually the strongest predictor of make-or-buy decisions.

Partly consistent and partly inconsistent: *A study is classified as being partly consistent and partly inconsistent with Williamson's TCE framework where it has some dimensional results that are consistent, and at least one dimensional result that is inconsistent, with Williamson's predictions.*

Six out of the 12 studies are categorized as partly consistent and partly inconsistent. It is the uncertainty variable that provides the most frequent reason for a study being characterized as partly inconsistent. A number of studies find conflicting results for uncertainty.

Anderson (1985) and Anderson and Schmittlein (1984) are the only two out of the 12 vertical integration studies that test for transaction frequency and neither finds support for the predicted relationship. Balakrishnan and Wernerfelt (1986) find that, contrary to Williamson's framework, technological uncertainty is negatively related to vertical integration.

The study of foreign market entry by Erramilli and Rao (1993) has very mixed results for uncertainty. The researchers find support for an external uncertainty interaction (with asset specificity). However, they find no support for an internal uncertainty interaction or for external uncertainty tested alone and actually find a negative relationship between internal uncertainty and full control entry mode. Erramilli and Rao (ibid., p. 33) also argue that strategic considerations come into play alongside transaction costs, thus explaining why 'many service firms establish full-control modes, even in low asset specificity situations'.

Gatignon and Anderson's (1988) study finds support for internal uncertainty, but it finds external uncertainty to have an inverse relationship with vertical integration. Consistent with Erramilli and Rao (1993), Gatignon and Anderson (1988) also note that even at low levels of asset specificity, integration seems to be the preferred option. Klein et al. (1990, pp. 205–6) argue that their study 'raises more questions than it answers'. They find support for an uncertainty (volatility) variable, but their other uncertainty (diversity) variable has a negative relationship with vertical integration.

Inconsistent: *A study is classified as being inconsistent with Williamson's TCE framework where it has no dimensional result that is consistent, and at least one dimensional result that is inconsistent, with Williamson's predictions.*

No vertical integration study fits this classification.

Inconclusive: *A study is categorized as inconclusive if it tests Williamson's TCE framework with no empirical result that contradicts or supports its predictions, in part or whole.*

The dependent variable in John and Weitz's (1988) empirical model is defined in a way that differs from Williamson's model and comparable empirical studies reviewed here, which means that the results are most accurately classified as inconclusive. In defining 'direct channel' they include both the internal sales force and independent sales representatives, whereas these are normally considered as internal versus external supply options.

13.3.2 Hybrid Relationship Studies

The hybrid relationship studies pose an extra challenge compared to the vertical integration studies. The central problem is that there is less of a consensus over their causes and the form that the relationships can take. This is reflected in the discussion of the studies below.

13.3.2.1   The developmental nature of the hybrid relationship studies

What constitutes a hybrid relationship is open to dispute (Hodgson, 2002; Ménard, 2004). It is unsurprising, therefore, that the empirical work on hybrid forms involves a highly eclectic range of empirical models, with less emphasis on directly testing the predictions of Williamson's TCE framework. Many of the empirical studies take as a starting point the view that Williamson's treatment of hybrids is inadequate. The initial concern is to develop his theoretical framework and then submit it to empirical test. This is a major contrast to the vertical integration empirical studies. For example Heide and John (1990, 1992) comment:

> Unfortunately, Williamson does not identify operational dimensions of governance structures. Researchers readily accept the notion that governance is a multidimensional phenomenon. . .but there is little consensus as to the dimensions that characterize the construct. (Heide and John, 1990, pp. 24–5)

> Of particular significance is the inability of the conventional wisdom in transaction cost analysis to account for complex nonmarket governance modes between nominally independent firms. It does not suffice to place markets and hierarchies at the ends of a continuum and interpolate between them. The underpinnings of such quasimarket modes differ fundamentally from both markets and hierarchies, and we see that the normative structure is one aspect that must be attended to more closely in analyzing such cases. (Heide and John, 1992, pp. 40–1)

Many of the empirical models in the studies analyzed here include developments and refinements beyond the TCE predictive framework, which means that they require careful interpretation to identify any implications for Williamson's theory.[4] These developments and refinements are not, however, of foremost interest here, as the central aim is to assess the empirical results in relation to Williamson's own predictions.

An interesting feature of the hybrid relationship studies is that, as with the vertical integration studies, there is significant support for asset specificity, that is to say that there is a correlation between asset specificity and the need for a specialist governance mechanism (of some form). However, as Table 13.2 shows, perhaps the most significant feature of the studies is that the results of ten out of 15 are inconclusive.

13.3.2.2   Assessment of the TCE predictive framework

The precise predictions for when a hybrid relationship will be the efficient governance mechanism were set out earlier in section 13.2. Given the developmental nature of many of the empirical studies, it is necessary to provide a more extensive discussion of the studies below than was required for the vertical integration studies. The same evaluative terms as defined earlier in the paper are adopted here.

Partly consistent: Three studies are categorized as being partly consistent. The first of these, Bucklin and Sengupta (1993), considers hybrid relationships from the perspective of power imbalances between partners. Their results show an interaction effect between expected transaction-specific investments and contractual governance terms in reducing power imbalance in the relationship, which suggests, albeit in an indirect way, that specific contractual terms are an appropriate governance mechanism when asset specificity is present in an alliance. Although no support is found for behavioral uncertainty this is a

Table 13.2 The hybrid relationship studies

Study	Characteristics of the Relationship	Circumstances of the Relationship	Results
Anderson and Weitz (1992)	Relationship commitment	**General asset specificity**	Inconclusive
Bucklin and Sengupta (1993)	Power imbalance	**General asset specificity, transaction frequency**, behavioral uncertainty	Partly consistent with TCE
Dyer (1996)	Relationship safeguards	**Numerous measures of asset specificity**	Partly consistent and partly inconsistent with TCE
Eccles (1981)	Quasi-firm	N/A – see discussion in main text	Inconclusive
Heide and John (1988)	Dependence balancing	**Human asset specificity**	Inconclusive
Heide and John (1990)	Joint action	**General asset specificity, internal uncertainty**, *technological uncertainty*, environmental uncertainty	Inconclusive
Heide and John (1992)	Relational norms	**General asset specificity**	Inconclusive
Joskow (1985)	Contract terms	**General asset specificity**	Partly consistent with TCE
Joskow (1987)	Contract terms	**General asset specificity**	Inconclusive
Noordewier et al.(1990)	Relational elements	**Environmental uncertainty**	Inconclusive
Nooteboom et al.(1997)	Relational risk	**General asset specificity**	Partly consistent with TCE
Osborn and Baughn (1990)	Informal arrangements, contractual agreements	**Technological uncertainty**	Inconclusive
Parkhe (1993)	Relationship context	**General asset specificity**	Inconclusive
Stump and Heide (1996)	Supplier opportunism	**General asset specificity**, *technological uncertainty*	Partly consistent and partly inconsistent with TCE
Zaheer and Venkatraman (1995)	Quasi-integration, joint action	**General asset specificity**, behavioral uncertainty	Inconclusive

Notes and explanations:
The evaluations in Table 13.2 are made according to Williamson's standard TCE model (where relevant and hence possible). The table records both the TCE variables employed in the individual studies and whether they were found to be in accord with TCE predictions. Where a word appears in **bold** it indicates a positive result. Where the word appears in a normal typeface it means that the variable was not found to have any statistically significant relationship with the dependent variable. Where the word appears in *italics* it indicates that the opposite relationship to that predicted by TCE is found. Joskow (1985) makes an explicit assumption about the presence of uncertainty and arguably an implicit assumption about the transaction being recurrent. Noordewier et al. (1990) explicitly reject the need to test for either asset specificity or transaction frequency.

Source: Carter and Hodgson (2006). Reprinted with permission.

very indirect test without any relation to a governance mechanism, so the lack of support is not deemed inconsistent with Williamson's predictions.

From Joskow's (1985) qualitative assessment of transactions between electric utilities and coal suppliers, he concludes that both price and non-price contractual safeguards will be employed in response to transaction-specific investments. Although Joskow (1985) makes an assumption about uncertainty and arguably also about transaction frequency, in the absence of actual tests the study is categorized as partly consistent with Williamson's TCE framework. Significantly, however, Joskow (ibid.) is unable to discriminate between the use of long-term contracts and vertical integration.

Nooteboom et al. (1997) incorporate trust into an extended TCE model. Their results show that asset specificity creates a governance concern and private and legal ordering act to decrease the probability of loss from a relationship. Of note, however, is their finding that asset specificity acts as a restraint on a trading partner's opportunism, which, they suggest, makes the net effect of specific investments ambiguous.

Partly consistent and partly inconsistent: Two studies are categorized in this way. Dyer (1996) has conflicting findings for the governance mechanism, making it particularly difficult to categorize. The results show that within the hybrid relationship idiosyncratic investments are protected by a variety of mechanisms. Financial hostages, which can be seen as a form of credible commitment, are one such mechanism. However, no support is found for formal contracts. A reasonable interpretation of Williamson's framework is that a credible commitment would be made in conjunction with a formal contract, hence, the categorization as being partly consistent and partly inconsistent with Williamson's TCE model.

The finding of balancing specific investments by the buyer and the supplier in Stump and Heide (1996) appears to be consistent with Williamson's framework but the finding of a negative correlation between technological uncertainty and balancing specific investments by the supplier appears to be contrary to the framework.

Inconclusive: Ten out of the 15 studies are categorized as inconclusive. A common reason for this is that many of these studies test a governance mechanism that does not fit within Williamson's classification of governance forms.

Although Anderson and Weitz (1992) draw on the TCE model the main concern of the study is to understand what creates commitment to a relationship, rather than to understand the circumstances in which such a relationship would be the efficient governance structure. Anderson and Weitz (ibid., p. 28) explain that they do not address the question of 'when is it advisable to develop a quasivertically integrated arrangement' and hence the results are inconclusive.

Eccles (1981) develops a model of the 'quasi-firm', which he locates within Williamson's TCE contracting framework. Although he demonstrates the longevity and stability of the contracting relationships, he does not demonstrate the specific contractual elements that facilitate this and he does not then attempt to map them on to particular transaction dimensions. As such the results are best categorized as inconclusive.

Heide and John (1988) find that sales agencies balance the specific investments they make in their relationship with a manufacturer by also making specific investments in their relationships with their customers. By bonding themselves to their customers they make it harder for manufacturers to change agencies and still retain access to these customers. As it is the same party that makes both investments, this is not a credible commitment as described by Williamson (1983). The researchers state that long-term contractual safeguards are not present in the environment they study (suggesting that the sales agency is able to protect its idiosyncratic investments in an arm's length market relationship) but they do not actually test this proposition. In the absence of an actual test of a specific Williamson TCE governance mechanism it is again necessary to categorize this study as inconclusive.

Heide and John (1990) find support for their proposition that specific investments made by both manufacturers and suppliers significantly increase the level of joint action in the relationship and that this joint action acts as a safeguard for the specific investments. They recognize that these specific investments from each side could be viewed as credible commitments (Williamson, 1983) that attenuate the need for safe-guards like joint action but they test for and reject this proposition. However, as the study does not identify a specific Williamson TCE governance mode the results are inconclusive.

Heide and John (1992) find that informal, non-contractual, relational norms are used to protect idiosyncratic investments in a relationship, although they do not test for uncertainty and transaction frequency. However, as they test a hybrid governance mechanism outside Williamson's taxonomy the results are also best categorized as inconclusive.

Joskow (1987) finds a correlation between asset specificity and contract length, but he explains that his database shows little variation in factors such as contractual methods for determining price and quantity adjustments, which do feature in Williamson's analysis of hybrids. It is not clear that contract length on its own accurately reflects Williamson's view that a hybrid relationship should be governed by contract terms that facilitate adaptability. Given that Joskow (1987) identifies a governance mechanism that is a form of hybrid relationship but which does not accurately reflect Williamson's perspective on hybrid forms of governance and maps this onto asset specificity alone (as the analysis does not deal with uncertainty or transaction frequency), a categorization of inconclusive seems reasonable.

Noordewier et al. (1990) focus on uncertainty only, making assumptions about both asset specificity and transaction frequency. Their results suggest that the problem of uncertainty (and by assumption asset specificity) can be attenuated by informal rela-tional structures rather than through formal contract terms. However, given that they do not actually test for asset specificity or transaction frequency and given that they focus on a non-Williamson governance mechanism a categorization of inconclusive is appropriate.

Although it draws on Williamson's TCE framework, Osborn and Baughn's (1990) empirical model focuses specifically on the influence of technological uncertainty in the choice of whether to select an agreement or a joint venture as the means for governing an alliance. Their definition of agreement incorporates a variety of different governance mechanisms: cooperative ties, developmental assistance programs, informal arrange-ments, licensing arrangements, and marketing and supply arrangements. Some of these appear to be closest to a market governance mechanism, but others appear to be more like formal contractual mechanisms. The researchers find that uncertainty is posi-tively correlated with the use of agreements but they do not test for asset specificity or transaction frequency. Given the nature of their definition of an agreement and given that they only test for uncertainty the results are best judged as inconclusive.

Parkhe (1993) clearly draws from the ideas of TCE but chooses to use and test them in an eclectic way. He finds that the level of commitment of non-recoverable investments is negatively related to the perception of opportunistic behavior, which suggests that potential opportunism is a crucial decision variable, rather than a fundamental constant (as in TCE). He also finds some support for a correlation between the level of contractual safeguards in a relationship and the extent of the perception of opportunistic behavior. However, although these elements of Williamson's framework appear in Parkhe's (ibid.) research hypotheses, they do so in a disjointed way and hence the results are best regarded as inconclusive.

Zaheer and Venkatraman (1995) find a positive correlation between a form of governance structure referred to as quasi-integration and asset specificity, but they find no correlation with behavioral uncertainty. They also find that quasi-integration and joint action are positively correlated. However, given that quasi-integration does not appear to reflect Williamson's view of a hybrid relationship governance mechanism, the results again can only be described as inconclusive.

13.4   SOME LIMITATIONS OF THE STANDARD EMPIRICAL TESTING AND EMPIRICAL RESPONSES

This section outlines a number of limitations in the approach that has been taken in many of the empirical tests of TCE and then goes on to discuss a range of studies that attempt to address these limitations.

13.4.1   Limitations of the Standard TCE Empirical Tests

As noted above, Williamson's predictive framework opened TCE up to empirical testing. Researchers were able to test the predictions using reduced-form models. This was a vital and significant breakthrough, but it also contained within it some inherent limitations, as tests based on the reduced-form model: (1) do not demonstrate the effects of organizational form on relative performance, and (2) do not, for example, identify whether relationship-specific assets lead to increased costs of contracting or whether they lead to reduced costs of internal organization (Masten, 1996). These are very real concerns, as the majority of empirical tests of the TCE framework have been based on reduced-form analysis (Yvrande-Billon and Saussier, 2004).

Even if an empirical test found strong support for the full predictions of Williamson's TCE framework, it would not give any indication of whether such discriminating alignment led to better performance (as TCE would suggest) than would result if the firm 'misaligned' the transaction. Additionally, although a study might find a strong correlation between human asset specificity and internal organization, it could not determine the 'role' that human asset specificity plays: it could create contracting hazards and hence higher costs of contracting or alternatively it could lead to lower costs of internal organization. Whilst the former would support a TCE explanation of vertical integration the latter would be more consistent with a resource-based view (RBV) of the firm. The basic problem, however, is that the results could be open to alternative interpretations.

In a related manner there has also been a call for empirical tests that explicitly consider alternative theoretical frameworks alongside TCE (Joskow, 1988; Shelanski and Klein, 1995; David and Han, 2004). Even when TCE hypotheses are found to be consistent with the data, in the absence of joint testing it cannot be ruled out that alternative theoretical frameworks might achieve a better fit with the data.

13.4.2 Empirical Tests of Governance Performance and Alternative Theoretical Frameworks

A number of empirical studies have now been undertaken, however, that address, at least to some degree (in each individual study) the limitations that have been outlined above. The studies that are discussed below are not straightforward to categorize, but they can be separated into two broad groups: (1) those that focus primarily on testing the performance effect of aligned governance, and (2) those that focus primarily on testing alternative theoretical frameworks. In fact some of the studies that address the performance issue also test TCE alongside other approaches.

13.4.2.1 Studies employing alternative empirical methods

The impact that governance decisions have on a firm's performance (with performance being measured in a variety of different ways) is the main issue that has been addressed within the studies discussed below. Does a firm that aligns its transactions in the manner suggested by TCE perform better than it would if it 'misaligned' its transactions? Alongside this two related issues have also been explored in some of the studies. First, what are the differential effects of misalignment? Is the performance penalty greater for internalizing a transaction that should be undertaken in the market or for a market transaction that should be integrated into the firm? Second, are firms able to realign their transactions to improve their performance? A final issue that is addressed is the role that human asset specificity plays in a firm's performance, that is to say, does the performance benefit stem from lower costs of internal organization or from avoiding higher costs of market contracting?

Discriminating alignment and performance The results from the studies discussed in this section provide general support for the relationship between transactional alignment and enhanced performance. However, when the results are examined in more detail the support for Williamson's framework is actually more mixed.

A number of the studies employ a two-stage modeling approach that first tests the discriminating alignment predictions (making it possible to categorize the results on the same basis as that employed in section 13.3) and then tests the performance effects of discriminating alignment.[5]

Masten et al. (1991) find support for the asset specificity and uncertainty variables tested, which, as outlined in section 13.3, leads to a categorization of partly consistent with TCE predictions. In their second stage modeling their results demonstrate significant organizational cost savings from selecting the appropriate form of governance, as would be expected by TCE. However, as discussed later, Masten et al. (ibid.) also find that human asset specificity is associated with lower costs of organization rather than higher cost of contracting as would be expected by TCE, hence posing a challenge to TCE rather than providing support for it. Nickerson et al.'s (2001) study of international courier services in Japan employs a three-stage modeling approach that integrates insights from Porter's strategic positioning framework (SPF) and TCE to investigate international courier services in Japan. They have three interrelated findings: (1) a firm's market position is supported by its resource profile (i.e., idiosyncratic investment in IT), as predicted by the SPF; (2) its idiosyncratic investments are aligned with an appropriate governance mechanism, making the results partly consistent with Williamson's TCE framework; and (3) that this resulting resource profile/organization pairing leads to performance advantages for the firm. The researchers argue that their results support a joint positioning–economizing perspective.

Leiblein et al. (2002) and Poppo and Zenger (1998) have mixed findings in their tests of TCE predictions on transactional alignment and hence are classified as partly consistent and partly inconsistent. Leiblein et al. (2002) find support for an asset specificity and uncertainty interaction term, however asset specificity and uncertainty when tested separately both have the opposite relationship to that predicted by TCE. Poppo and Zenger (1998) find support for asset specificity but they find no clear support for technological uncertainty. In their second stage modeling both studies find support for the performance benefits of transactional alignment. However, Leiblein et al. (2002) also highlight that the continued significance of the self-selection term in their modeling suggests that factors other than TCE that influence governance choice are also an influence on organizational performance and hence point to the value of contingency-based theoretical approaches.

Mayer and Nickerson (2005) consider the performance implications of contracting decisions for information technology services. Although they find support for the relationship between contractual hazards, governance choice, and profitability, their governance choice model does not appear to be based on Williamson's TCE framework. Indeed, the researchers explicitly draw attention to the importance of contracting hazards that arise for reasons other than asset specificity. This also appears to be the case with Sampson (2004). The organizational choice model is based on transaction cost considerations but these reflect contractual hazards generally rather than the specific elements of Williamson's TCE framework. The results of Sampson (ibid.) show that selecting a governance mechanism according to transaction cost considerations has performance benefits. However, given that neither study bases its governance choice model on Williamson's TCE the results of both are probably best categorized as inconclusive.[6] Nevertheless, although they do not provide support for Williamson's TCE framework, they do provide support for transaction cost considerations more generally.

Argyres and Bigelow (2007), Nickerson and Silverman (2003), and Silverman et al. (1997) employ a slightly different empirical approach: they construct a misalignment variable and then test for the performance effects of misalignment, making it difficult to categorize the studies according to a test of TCE's discriminating alignment predictions. All three studies do, though, include asset specificity considerations in their misalignment variable and hence are based on part of Williamson's framework. Argyres and Bigelow (2007) do not find support for their performance hypothesis that transactional misalignment leads to higher mortality regardless of the stage of the industry life cycle.

They do, however, find that the effect of misalignment is stronger in the shake-out rather than the fragmentation phase, suggesting that a combined TCE and industry life-cycle theory model achieves better support than TCE considerations alone.

In their study of the US trucking industry Nickerson and Silverman (2003) find that misalignment of the driver relationship (i.e., employee versus independent operator) does lead to lower profitability, as would be expected by TCE. By contrast, Silverman et al. (1997), in an earlier study of the of the US trucking industry, do not find support for their main TCE hypothesis that firms that align their use of employees and independent contractors with their specific investments and operational characteristics will have lower mortality rates than those that do not. Support is found, however, for a secondary TCE hypothesis on the lower mortality of firms that correctly align their debt/equity financing with their incidence of general/specific assets, as well as for four out of five of the organizational ecology hypotheses. The results lead the researchers to argue in favour of a hybrid model (blending efficiency-based[7] and ecologically based selection mechanisms).

Differential costs of misalignment   Some of the studies discussed above also explore the issue of the relative costs of transactional misalignment. The results, which differ between studies, raise interesting questions for TCE theory, though it is not possible to generalize from such a small number of studies.

The results of both Leiblein et al. (2002) and Poppo and Zenger (1998) suggest that performance is negatively affected by not integrating a transaction in the face of contracting hazards, but integrating a transaction where there are low contract hazards has no significant impact on performance.

The results from Masten et al. (1991) suggest that mistakenly subcontracting a component or mistakenly integrating the production of the component both increase the costs of organizing the transaction and hence have a negative impact on performance, although the results suggest the negative impact is greater from mistaken subcontracting. Mayer and Nickerson (2005) provide a similar finding, though, as noted earlier, their model is not based directly on Williamson's TCE framework.

Sampson (2004), again based on a broad contractual hazards model rather than drawing directly on Williamson's TCE model, finds the reverse to Leiblein et al. (2002) and Poppo and Zenger (1998). Firms that choose a joint venture when contract hazards are low suffer a high cost from misalignment, whereas there is only a minor cost to misalignment when a pooling contract is chosen in an environment of high contractual hazards, suggesting that it is high organization costs rather than high transaction costs that are the main problem.

Realignment of transactions   Nickerson and Silverman (2003) consider how firms adapt towards transactional alignment from a position of misalignment. They find that firms generally do attempt to realign their driver relationships, but that this realignment takes between three to five years and that firms that attempt to realign too quickly are more likely to exit the market. A number of factors have an impact on the speed of adjustment: (1) presence of specific investments and contractual commitments lessens the amount and speed of readjustment, (2) carriers with high profitability adjust more slowly, (3) carriers are slower to adjust if change makes them look less like their nearby firms.

Nickerson and Silverman (ibid.) argue that linking TCE and structural inertia theories offers a more complete theory of environmentally induced organizational change.

These results pose an interesting possible challenge to Williamson's TCE framework, as it has been argued that Williamson's framework does not accommodate the idea of adaptation, but rather is based on a static, once-for-all exercise in transaction alignment (Slater and Spencer, 2000).

Role of human asset specificity in firm performance   Masten et al. (1991) and Poppo and Zenger (1998) explicitly address the issue of whether human asset specificity leads to lower costs of internal organization or higher costs of market contracting and they provide conflicting results. This is an important issue that is worthy of further empirical investigation.

The results of Masten et al.'s (1991) second-stage modeling reveal that, contrary to expectations, human asset specificity is associated with a decrease in internal organization costs rather than an increase in external contracting costs. Masten et al. (ibid.) also suggest that the results of Monteverde and Teece (1982) and Masten et al. (1989) could be reinterpreted in this manner.[8] Extending this further, the 12 vertical integration studies discussed in section 13.3 could also be reassessed in this way: 11 employed reduced-form analysis and nine of those studies found support for a human asset specificity variable. Hence nine of the 12 studies could be reinterpreted to be consistent with a resource-based view of the firm.

Poppo and Zenger (1998) respond to the issues raised in Masten et al. (1991), devising an empirical approach that allows them to test the RBV reinterpretation of human asset specificity. Contrary to Masten et al. (ibid.) their results suggest that decisions to integrate when there are specific assets turn on the losses that would arise from using market governance rather than from increasing internal efficiency. The researchers, though, do offer a number of words of caution on their results. First, they argue that the rapid technological change in their research setting could cause internal routines to become rigidities, hence undermining the resource-based benefits of integration and rationalize their results with the results of Masten et al. (ibid.) on this basis. Second, they emphasize that they test only a very narrow version of the RBV (i.e., to address the issue raised by Masten et al.) and hence the study should not be viewed as providing a full joint test of the TCE and RBV frameworks. Finally, Poppo and Zenger (1998) also argue that their results show that a theory of the firm is likely to be complex, based on an integration of TCE, measurement and RBV approaches.

13.4.2.2   Studies testing TCE and alternative theoretical frameworks
The studies discussed in this subsection focus explicitly on the testing of multiple theoretical frameworks. As they only address the issue of governance choice and not the performance effects of governance (with the exception of Combs and Ketchen, 1999), they have the same limitations as the studies discussed in section 13.3. Although only five studies are discussed below and hence any conclusions must be very tentative, the results suggest that there is value in considering how alternative theoretical perspectives can be combined to gain a better understanding of integration decisions.[9]

Three studies, Argyres (1996), Combs and Ketchen (1999), and Mayer and Salomon (2006), in testing the TCE framework, focus primarily on asset specificity. They all find support for its role in governance decisions and hence, according to the approach taken in section 13.3, they are partly consistent with TCE.[10] Argyres (1996), in a qualitative case study, also tests firm capabilities (alongside TCE) explanations of vertical integration decisions. Numerous make-or-buy decisions are examined and the majority of decisions are assessed to be consistent with TCE reasoning. However, some decisions are explained jointly by asset specificity and relative capabilities considerations and one decision is inconsistent with TCE reasoning but is consistent with a capabilities explanation.

The empirical model in Combs and Ketchen (1999) blends TCE and RBV insights in an attempt to reconcile the differences between the two approaches. The results show support for both TCE and RBV considerations in governance decisions. They also find, though, that contrary to TCE but in line with RBV reasoning, firms with low resource levels enter into cooperative agreements (to gain access to critical resources) even in the face of adverse exchange conditions. However, and very importantly, the researchers then test the performance effects of governance decisions and find that low resource firms entering into alliances in adverse exchange conditions are actually the worst performers in the study. The researchers argue, though, that this weak performance is perhaps not to be unexpected, as firms may be willing to accept poor performance in the short term in exchange for the acquisition of needed resources that will generate medium- and longer-term benefits. The researchers find some support for this position, as further analysis of the data reveals that the performance difference is eliminated within a relatively short time span.

Mayer and Salomon (2006) also develop an empirical model that integrates TCE and RBV perspectives. Support is found for both TCE and RBV propositions and the researchers argue that their results show that both perspectives inform governance decisions but that the TCE variables explain a greater portion of the variance. However, perhaps the most interesting finding from this study is the possible role of strong capabilities in moderating governance decisions. Mayer and Salomon (ibid.) argue that their results show that strong technological capabilities allowed the firm to subcontract even in the face of higher levels of hold-up hazards. They go on to argue that this is consistent with Williamson's (1999) view that it is necessary to take a contingent view of governance decision-making.

Hoetker (2005) employs a model that blends insights from three different theoretical perspectives: TCE, capabilities, and the literature on interfirm relationships. Some caution is necessary in interpreting the results, as the study only focuses on uncertainty and does not address the issue of asset specificity (suggesting that the results should be categorized as partly consistent with TCE). The results show that suppliers employ different governance mechanisms at different levels of uncertainty. Although the results show that the greater a supplier's technical capabilities the greater the likelihood it will be selected, other factors become important as uncertainty increases. Prior transactions with a supplier are more important the higher the level of uncertainty, but ultimately at high levels of uncertainty internalization is the chosen governance option. As with many of the other studies discussed in this section, the results show that a model that integrates insights from different theoretical perspectives performs more effectively than each of the approaches taken individually.

The model in Leiblein and Miller (2003) blends insights from TCE, RBV, and real options theory. The asset specificity and uncertainty interaction variable is correlated with vertical integration, though there is no support for the individual asset specificity variable and the uncertainty variable has the opposite relationship to that predicted by TCE (so the results are partly consistent and partly inconsistent with TCE). Additionally, however, support is found for the two RBV variables and for the real options variable. The researchers argue that, as the results reveal both transaction and firm-level effects, there are benefits from blending insights from the three different theoretical frameworks.

13.5   CONCLUSIONS FROM THE EMPIRICAL WORK

The results of the studies discussed in section 13.3 suggest that the support for the full predictions of TCE theory is more mixed than other reviews have argued (Shelanski and Klein, 1995; Macher and Richman, 2008), though this position is broadly in line with the review by David and Han (2004). Half of the vertical integration studies are partly consistent and partly inconsistent with the predictive framework and the results of one are inconclusive. For the hybrid studies the major conclusion is that Williamson's framework does not address the sheer diversity of hybrid governance mechanisms and hence the results of ten of the 15 studies are inconclusive. That is not to argue, however, that important theoretical work on hybrid forms has not been undertaken (Ménard, 2004). Indeed, the studies discussed in section 13.3 provide very useful empirical data to inform theoretical developments.

One aspect of both the vertical integration and hybrid relationship studies that stands out, however, is the strong correlation between asset specificity and a specialist governance mechanism of some form. An interpretation of this is that the empirical work provides strong support for the basic TCE proposition that asset specificity transforms a large numbers into a small numbers bargaining situation, hence giving rise to the need for a specialist governance mechanism (Nooteboom, 2004). However, the precise circumstances in which a particular governance mechanism is chosen and the precise form that the governance mechanism takes (recognizing the diversity of possible hybrid relationships) is less well supported by the empirical work.

The 'second-generation' studies reviewed in section 13.4 provide a diverse set of results and it is important that further empirical studies are undertaken before any firm conclusions can be drawn. Two relatively common features can, however, be discerned at this stage. One is that governance choice matters for business performance and that although the support for Williamson's discriminating alignment predictions is quite mixed, general TCE reasoning is instructive in informing governance choice. The second is that TCE reasoning can be complemented by alternative theoretical perspectives to improve our understanding of the nature of the firm and specifically the decisions that determine the boundaries of the firm. Such a conclusion is entirely consistent with Williamson's (2007) discussion of the possibility of joining together several approaches to the theory of the firm, though Williamson's caution that this should not be done prematurely without their theoretical interrelationships having being worked through is very pertinent. The issue of whether human asset specificity leads to lower costs of internal organization or higher costs of market contracting and hence whether earlier TCE empirical studies should be reinterpreted from an RBV perspective requires further empirical investigation, as this remains a very important issue.

This latter conclusion, that integration decisions can be better understood from a 'hybrid' theoretical perspective, can be aligned with the general conclusion made on the tests of TCE's predictive framework. That the empirical work supports the argument that asset specificity gives rise to the possibility of hold-up and hence the need for some form of specialist governance mechanism, but does not support the precise predictions for when and in what form, is explained by Nooteboom (2004) as being due to the existence of other causal mechanisms that TCE disregards. Although a variety of alternative theoretical perspectives are advanced in the 'second-generation' empirical studies discussed above, they do provide support for the general argument that TCE factors need to be augmented by other considerations for a more comprehensive understanding of integration decisions.

The empirical work in TCE provides vital feedback to the theoretical debate and highlights specific areas for further consideration and development. These lessons should be heeded such that our understanding of the nature of the firm can be further refined and developed in the future.

NOTES

1. There have been more than 20 studies that review some aspect of the TCE empirical work including: Joskow (1988), Shelanski and Klein (1995), Masten (1996), Rindfleisch and Heide (1997), Masten and Saussier (2000), David and Han (2004), Yvrande-Billon and Saussier (2004), Klein (2005), Carter and Hodgson (2006), Lafontaine and Slade (2007) and Macher and Richman (2008).
2. This represents the core elements of Williamson's framework and this is reflected in the way that it has been tested empirically. However, Williamson has proposed a number of possible extensions or refinements to the framework, including incorporating the institutional environment (Williamson, 1991) and the concept of atmosphere (Williamson, 1999) as well as incorporating production costs into the economizing framework (Williamson, 1981). It is the core framework (or parts of it), however, that has typically been tested in the empirical studies.
3. The analysis in this section draws directly from Carter and Hodgson (2006). A minimum average citation level of five per year, based on a five-year average citation figure (1998–2002), was used to create the sample. Section 13.4 provides a discussion of more recent empirical studies that move beyond the focus of the 'first generation' of empirical work.
4. Some of the 'extended' TCE empirical models discussed in this section could possibly be viewed as tests of TCE alongside alternative frameworks and hence be included in section 13.4.2.2. There is inevitably some judgment required in determining how to separate studies for the purposes of assessment.
5. See Yvrande-Billon and Saussier (2004) for a comprehensive discussion of the econometric methods used in the empirical tests of governance performance.
6. Strictly speaking the study should attempt to provide a test of Williamson's framework to be categorized as inconclusive according to the definition used in section 13.3.
7. This hybrid model does not appear, however, to include the main TCE relationship between asset specificity and governance form.
8. Monteverde (1995a, 1995b) also takes up this issue of reinterpretation of TCE empirical results.
9. A number of the studies discussed in 13.4.2.1 also highlighted the value of blending insights from different theoretical perspectives and hence are supportive of this conclusion.
10. All three of these studies have specific findings that pose a challenge to the TCE framework, which could perhaps suggest that a categorization of partly consistent and partly inconsistent with TCE would be more appropriate.

REFERENCES

Anderson, E. (1985) 'The Sales Person as Outside Agent or Employee: A Transaction Cost Analysis', *Marketing Science*, **4** (3): 234–54.

Anderson, E. and A.T. Coughlan (1987) 'International Market Entry and Expansion via Independent or Integrated Channels of Distribution', *Journal of Marketing*, **51** (1): 71–82.

Anderson, E. and D.C. Schmittlein (1984) 'Integration of the Sales Force: an Empirical Examination', *RAND Journal of Economics*, **15** (3): 385–95.

Anderson, E. and B. Weitz (1992) 'The Use of Pledges to Build and Sustain Commitment in Distribution Channels', *Journal of Marketing Research*, **29** (1): 18–34.

Argyres, N.S. (1996) 'Evidence on the Role of Firm Capabilities in Vertical Integration Decisions', *Strategic Management Journal*, **17** (1): 129–50.

Argyres, N.S. and L. Bigelow (2007) 'Does Transaction Misalignment Matter for Firm Survival at All Stages of the Industry Life Cycle?', *Management Science*, **53** (8): 1332–44.

Balakrishnan, S. and B. Wernerfelt (1986) 'Technical Change, Competition and Vertical Integration', *Strategic Management Journal*, **7** (4): 347–59.

Bucklin, L.P. and S. Sengupta (1993) 'Organizing Successful Co-marketing Alliances', *Journal of Marketing*, **57** (2): 32–46.

Carter, R. and G.M. Hodgson (2006) 'The Impact of Empirical Tests of Transaction Cost Economics on the Debate on the Nature of the Firm', *Strategic Management Journal*, **27** (5): 461–76.

Combs, J.G. and D.J. Ketchen Jr. (1999) 'Explaining Interfirm Cooperation and Performance: Toward a Reconciliation of Predictions from the Resource-based View and Organizational Economics', *Strategic Management Journal*, **20** (9): 867–88.

David, R.J. and S.-K. Han (2004) 'A Systematic Assessment of the Empirical Support for Transaction Cost Economics', *Strategic Management Journal*, **25** (1): 39–58.

Dyer, J.H. (1996) 'Does Governance Matter? Keiretsu Alliances and Asset Specificity as Sources of Japanese Competitive Advantage', *Organization Science*, **7** (6): 649–6.

Eccles, R.G. (1981) 'The Quasifirm in the Construction Industry', *Journal of Economic Behavior and Organization*, **2** (4): 335–57.

Erramilli, M.K. and C.P. Rao (1993) 'Service Firms' International Entry-mode Choice: A Modified Transaction-cost Analysis Approach', *Journal of Marketing*, **57** (3): 19–38.

Gatignon, H. and E. Anderson (1988) 'The Multinational Corporation's Degree of Control over Foreign Subsidiaries: An Empirical Test of a Transaction Cost Explanation', *Journal of Law, Economics, & Organization*, **4** (2): 305–36.

Heide, J.B. and G. John (1988) 'The Role of Dependence Balancing in Safeguarding Transaction-specific Assets in Conventional Channels', *Journal of Marketing*, **52** (1): 20–35.

Heide, J.B. and G. John (1990) 'Alliances in Industrial Purchasing: the Determinants of Joint Action in Buyer–Supplier Relationships', *Journal of Marketing Research*, **27** (1): 24–36.

Heide, J.B. and G. John (1992) 'Do Norms Matter in Marketing Relationships?', *Journal of Marketing*, **56** (2): 32–44.

Hodgson, G.M. (2002) 'The Legal Nature of the Firm and the Myth of the Firm–Market Hybrid', *International Journal of the Economics of Business*, **9** (1): 37–60.

Hoetker, G. (2005) 'How Much You Know Versus How Well I Know You: Selecting a Supplier for a Technically Innovative Component', *Strategic Management Journal*, **26** (1): 75–96.

John, G. and B.A. Weitz (1988) 'Forward Integration into Distribution: An Empirical Test of Transaction Cost Analysis', *Journal of Law, Economics, & Organization*, **4** (2): 337–55.

Joskow, P.L. (1985) 'Vertical integration and Long-term Contracts: the Case of Coal-burning Electric Generating Plants', *Journal of Law, Economics, & Organization*, **1** (1): 33–80.

Joskow, P.L. (1987) 'Contract Duration and Relationship-specific Investments: Empirical Evidence from Coal Markets', *American Economic Review*, **77** (1): 168–85.

Joskow, P.L. (1988) 'Asset Specificity and the Structure of Vertical Relationships: Empirical Evidence', *Journal of Law, Economics, & Organization*, **4** (1): 95–117.

Klein, P.G. (2005) 'The Make-or-buy Decision: Lessons from Empirical Studies', in C. Ménard and M.M. Shirley (eds) *Handbook of New Institutional Economics*, Dordrecht: Springer, pp. 435–64.

Klein, S., G.L. Frazier and V.J. Roth (1990) 'A Transaction Cost Analysis Model of Channel Integration in International Markets', *Journal of Marketing Research*, **27** (2): 196–208.

Lafontaine, F. and M. Slade (2007) 'Vertical Integration and Firm Boundaries: The Evidence', *Journal of Economic Literature*, **45** (3): 629–85.

Leiblein, M.J. and D.J. Miller (2003) 'An Empirical Examination of Transaction- and Firm-level Influences on the Vertical Boundaries of the Firm', *Strategic Management Journal*, **24** (9): 839–59.

Leiblein, M.J., J.J. Reuer and F. Dalsace (2002) 'Do Make or Buy Decisions Matter? The Influence of Organizational Governance on Technological Performance', *Strategic Management Journal*, **23** (9): 817–33.

Macher, J.T. and B.D. Richman (2008) 'Transaction Cost Economics: An Assessment of the Empirical Research in the Social Sciences', *Business and Politics*, **10** (1): 1–63.

Masten, S.E. (1984) 'The Organization of Production: Evidence from the Aerospace Industry', *Journal of Law and Economics*, **27** (2): 403–17.

Masten, S.E. (1996) 'Empirical Research in Transaction Cost Economics: Challenges, Progress, Directions', in J. Groenewegen (ed.) *Transaction Cost Economics and Beyond*, Boston: Kluwer, pp. 43–64.

Masten, S.E. and S. Saussier (2000) 'Economics of Contracts: An Assessment of Developments in the Empirical Literature on Contracting', *Revue d'Economie Industrielle*, **92** (2/3): 215–36.

Masten, S.E., J.W. Meehan Jr. and E.A. Snyder (1989) 'Vertical Integration in the U.S. Auto Industry', *Journal of Economic Behavior & Organization*, **12** (2): 265–73.

Masten, S.E., J.W. Meehan Jr. and E.A. Snyder (1991) 'The Costs of Organization', *Journal of Law, Economics, & Organization*, **7** (1): 1–25.

Mayer, K.J. and J.A. Nickerson (2005) 'Antecedents and Performance Implications of Contracting for Knowledge Workers: Evidence from Information Technology Services', *Organization Science*, **16** (3): 225–42.

Mayer, K.J. and R.M. Salomon (2006) 'Capabilities, Contractual Hazards, and Governance: Integrating Resource-based and Transaction Cost Perspectives', *Academy of Management Journal*, **49** (5): 942–59.

Ménard, C. (2004) 'The Economics of Hybrid Organizations', *Journal of Institutional and Theoretical Economics*, **160** (3): 345–76.

Monteverde, K. (1995a) 'Applying Resource-based Strategic Analysis: Making the Model More Accessible to Practitioners', Working Paper, No. 95-1, College of Business and Administration, Saint Joseph's University, Philadelphia.

Monteverde, K. (1995b) 'Technical Dialog as an Incentive for Vertical Integration in the Semiconductor Industry', *Management Science*, **41** (10): 1624–38.

Monteverde, K. and D.J. Teece (1982) 'Supplier Switching Costs and Vertical Integration in the Automobile Industry', *The Bell Journal of Economics*, **13** (1): 206–13.

Nickerson, J.A. and B.S. Silverman (2003) 'Why Firms Want to Organize Efficiently and What Keeps Them from Doing So: Inappropriate Governance, Performance, and Adaptation in a Deregulated Industry', *Administrative Science Quarterly*, **48** (3): 433–65.

Nickerson, J.A., B.H. Hamilton and T. Wada (2001) 'Market Position, Resource Profile, and Governance: Linking Porter and Williamson in the Context of International Courier and Small Package Services in Japan', *Strategic Management Journal*, **22** (3): 251–73.

Noordewier, T.G., G. John and J.R. Nevin (1990) 'Performance Outcomes of Purchasing Arrangements in Industrial Buyer–Vendor Relationships', *Journal of Marketing*, **54** (4): 80–93.

Nooteboom, B. (2004) 'Governance and Competence: How Can They Be Combined?', *Cambridge Journal of Economics*, **28** (4), July: 505–25.

Nooteboom, B., H. Berger and N.G. Noorderhaven (1997) 'Effects of Trust and Governance on Relational Risk', *Academy of Management Journal*, **40** (2): 308–38.

Osborn, R.N. and C.C. Baughn (1990) 'Forms of Interorganizational Governance for Multinational Alliances', *Academy of Management Journal*, **33** (3): 503–19.

Parkhe, A. (1993) 'Strategic Alliance Structuring: A Game Theoretic and Transaction Cost Examination of Interfirm Cooperation', *Academy of Management Journal*, **36** (4): 794–829.

Poppo, L. and T. Zenger (1998) 'Testing Alternative Theories of the Firm: Transaction Cost, Knowledge-based, and Measurement Explanations for Make-or-buy Decisions in Information Services', *Strategic Management Journal*, **19** (9): 853–77.

Rindfleisch, A. and J.B. Heide (1997) 'Transaction Cost Analysis: Past, Present, and Future Applications', *Journal of Marketing*, **61** (4): 30–54.

Sampson, R.C. (2004) 'The Cost of Misaligned Governance in R&D Alliances', *Journal of Law, Economics, & Organization*, **20** (2): 484–526.

Shelanski, H.A. and P.G. Klein (1995) 'Empirical Research in Transaction Cost Economics', *Journal of Law, Economics, & Organization*, **11** (2): 335–61.

Silverman, B.S., J.A. Nickerson and J. Freeman (1997) 'Profitability, Transactional Alignment, and Organizational Mortality in the U.S. Trucking Industry', *Strategic Management Journal*, **18** (S1): 31–52.

Slater, G. and D.A. Spencer (2000) 'The Uncertain Foundations of Transaction Cost Economics', *Journal of Economic Issues*, **34** (1): 61–87.

Stump, R.L. and J.B. Heide (1996) 'Controlling Supplier Opportunism in Industrial Relationships', *Journal of Marketing Research*, **33** (4): 431–41.

Walker, G. and D. Weber (1984) 'A Transaction Cost Approach to Make-or-buy Decisions', *Administrative Science Quarterly*, **29** (3): 373–91.

Williamson, O.E. (1979) 'Transaction Cost Economics: the Governance of Contractual Relations', *Journal of Law and Economics*, **22** (5): 233–61.
Williamson, O.E. (1981) 'The Economics of Organization: The Transaction Cost Approach' *American Journal of Sociology*, **87** (3): 548–77.
Williamson, O.E. (1983) 'Credible Commitments: Using Hostages to Support Exchange' *American Economic Review*, **73** (4): 519–40.
Williamson, O.E. (1985) *The Economic Institutions of Capitalism*, New York: Free Press.
Williamson, O.E. (1991) 'Comparative Economic Organization: The Analysis of Discrete Structural Alternatives', *Administrative Science Quarterly*, **36** (2): 269–96.
Williamson, O.E. (1999) 'Strategy Research: Governance and Competence Perspectives', *Strategic Management Journal*, **20** (12): 1087–108.
Williamson, O.E. (2000) 'The New Institutional Economics: Taking Stock, Looking Ahead', *Journal of Economic Literature*, **38** (3): 595–613.
Williamson, O.E. (2007) 'An Interview with Oliver Williamson', *Journal of Institutional Economics*, **3** (3): 373–86.
Yvrande-Billon, A. and S. Saussier (2004) 'Do Organization Choices Matter? Assessing the Importance of Governance Through Performance Comparisons', in H.S. James Jr (ed.) *New Ideas in Contracting and Organizational Economics Research*, New York: Nova Science Publishers, pp. 71–87.
Zaheer, A. and N. Venkatraman (1995) 'Relational Governance as an Interorganizational Strategy: An Empirical Test of the Role of Trust in Economic Exchange', *Strategic Management Journal*, **16** (5): 373–92.

PART IV

THE MULTINATIONAL FIRM

14 The multinational firm: characteristics, activities and explanations in historical context
Grazia Ietto-Gillies

14.1 INTRODUCTION

The multinationals are firms that operate direct business activities and own assets in at least two countries. The words enterprise, company or corporation are often used instead of firm. The multi- or cross-countries nature of their activities is indicated by the adjective 'multinational' or 'international' or 'transnational'. I usually prefer to use the latter adjective because it highlights the fact that these companies strategically plan, organize and control business operations across several countries rather than just operate independently in each of them.[1] Transnational corporations (TNCs) is the term used by the United Nations Conference on Trade and Development (UNCTAD), the official international institution dealing with data, research and a range of publications on these firms.[2]

Transborder direct business activities date back a long time. The Medici bank in Renaissance Florence can be seen as conducting direct financial activities across frontiers well before the birth of the nation-states. Similarly, the British and Dutch chartered trading companies of the seventeenth and eighteenth centuries were conducting direct business activities abroad. However, the real forerunners of the TNC can be traced to the nineteenth-century joint stock companies, particularly those dealing with the development of railways that involved the organization of resources and control of operations at a distance. The issue of control has been seen as essential for operations spread across territories as first noted in the seminal work by Stephen Hymer ([1960] 1976), which will be discussed in section 14.5.

The chapter proceeds as follows. The next section deals with the issue of control and its relevance for the TNC. Sections 14.3 and 14.4 consider the activities and characteristics of TNCs, respectively. Section 14.5 presents a summary of the main theoretical approaches to the explanation of TNCs and their activities. Section 14.6 addresses the question of why we need a special study of the TNCs. Section 14.7 considers the main key issues in the study of TNCs and the last section summarizes.

14.2 THE TNC AND CONTROL

Within large companies we can identify two types of control, (1) *Ownership control* denotes the percentage of equity stake necessary for controlling an affiliate of a major company. This equity control is a necessary condition for the exercise of general control by the headquarters of the company. The percentage of equity stake necessary for the exercise of control varies from company to company and from sector to sector. In companies where the ownership is concentrated in few owners a higher stake is needed than in companies where ownership is very disperse. Nonetheless, a base line is needed for statistical and classificatory purposes underpinning international, sectoral and micro comparisons. The International Monetary Fund (1977) gives as 10 per cent the minimum equity ownership necessary for the foreign affiliate to be considered as part of the controlling interests of the parent company. (2) *Organizational control* refers to the ability to organize and manage business activities at a distance and is closely connected to the development of the transportation and communication systems. Only fairly developed systems allow a suitable organization and control of activities at a distance and this is why the forerunners of the modern TNCs are traced to the nineteenth century.

The early trading companies were set up under full equity control but could not be organizationally controlled and managed at a distance due to poor communication and transportation systems. The owners had to rely fully on trusted appointed local managers. These early forms of direct business in foreign countries have been classified not as TNCs but as *free-standing companies* by the historian Mira Wilkins (1988).

It is interesting to note how the internal organizational structure of companies evolved alongside the developments in the activities and geographical scope of companies as well as alongside developments in the technologies and costs of communication and transportation. Following Chandler (1962), Hymer (1970) sees the early single function, single sector company growing and changing organizational structure along several departments distinguished by function (the unitary U-form). This suited companies that were growing larger though still involved in uni-product business. The twentieth century saw the evolution into multi-product firms and a new structure was needed. The multi-divisional form (M-form) emerged with divisions established along product lines. This laid the foundations for the organization of companies that were growing along geographical lines. The TNC could be organized along geographical divisional lines. Product and geography lines could be taken into account simultaneously in the matrix structure developed later.

The last two decades have seen firms outsourcing and developing business activities with a variety of external partners ranging from subcontractors to suppliers to partners in research, development or production activities. New structures have been developed to take account of these external networks as well as of networks of affiliates internal to the company. Both types of networks can be within the same country or can extend to several. The *network company* has been more recently analysed particularly in relation to transnational direct activities (Ghoshal and Bartlett, 1990; Forsgren et al., 2005; Forsgren, 2008).

14.3   TNC ACTIVITIES

Business activities across frontiers go a long way back into history: millennia rather than centuries. However, this does not mean that we can trace back the object of our study in this chapter as far back as that. For a start the adjective referring to nations and national – be it international or multinational or transnational – is inappropriate before the existence of nation-states. Moreover, and most important, the nature of operations that defines our companies is specific. The very early type of business activities across frontiers, the one that goes back millennia, is trade, that is, import and export. But this type of activity is not what makes a firm a TNC.

The defining characteristic of the transnational corporation is *direct business activities via ownership of assets abroad*. So a firm must own assets abroad, those assets must be destined to business activities and the assets must be controlled by the parent company. The controlling element comes in again in terms of the classification of foreign investment. *Foreign direct investment (FDI)* in which the company owns at least 10 per cent of the foreign business is seen as part and parcel of TNCs' activities and assets. Foreign investment involving a lower percentage is classified as *portfolio investment* because it does not give a controlling interest in the business whose shares have been acquired. Portfolio investment can also take the form of acquisition of government and non-government bonds. TNCs are often involved in portfolio investment as well as in FDI, which is their defining type of investment.

Worldwide the largest transactions are due to international trade. Imports and exports of goods and services can be initiated by both uni- and multinational firms. However, in reality the vast majority of the world trade is the responsibility of TNCs. Moreover, about one-third of world trade takes place on an *intra-firm* basis. This means that trade across frontiers takes place between units belonging to the same company; it can be trade between two affiliates or between an affiliate and the parent company. So we are talking of trade that is external to countries but internal to firms. The TNCs are also responsible for much *intra-industry trade*. This is the importation and exportation of products belonging to the same industrial categories by the same country.[3] One of the reasons for the large and increasing volume of intra-industry and intra-firm trade is due to the strategy of international vertical integration across countries practised by many TNCs. As they locate segments of their production process in many countries they have to move the components from country to country. This gives rise to international trade that is both intra-firm and intra-industry because the components belong to the same industrial category.

There is another structural feature of international trade for which the TNCs are responsible: the geographical structure. The fact that they are responsible for most world trade and for all intra-firm and most intra-industry trade makes them also responsible for the geographical structure of trade: for which country trades with whom and for what amount. For example, the FDI by many western TNCs into China leads to considerable imports and exports by China from/into many countries including the ones that are home to the investing TNCs. Much of this trade is intra-firm and intra-industry. Countries not directly involved in the FDI transaction may also see their trade affected by TNCs' strategies. For example, following the establishment of the Single European Market many non-European companies – especially from the USA and Japan – invested in Britain with a view to exporting from Britain to other European countries. The latter were open to trade from Britain but subject to tariffs from outside the USA, Japan or other countries.

Other business activities across frontiers include collaborative partnerships such as alliances and joint ventures (Hagedoorn, 1996 and 2002) between partners located in different countries. They also take the form of franchising, licensing or subcontracting with companies located abroad. All these forms of *inter-firm partnerships* have been increasing in the last few decades. Most of these take place across national frontiers under the strategic direction of TNCs.

14.4   THE CHARACTERISTICS OF TRANSNATIONAL CORPORATIONS

In the popular view TNCs are huge, all powerful companies in charge of the world's destiny. Most TNCs are indeed very large and most large companies operate directly in several countries. However, the last 30 years have seen an increase in the number of smaller TNCs. Their emergence and growth is the effect of improvements in the systems of transportation and communication and of learning and imitation effects. Smaller companies learn from bigger ones. Often they start working with or for the bigger TNCs and learn from them; they then branch out on their own into the international arena.

Worldwide there are currently[4] some 103 786 companies classified as TNCs and together they have 892 114 affiliates in foreign countries. Most TNCs originate from developed countries (70 per cent) though the percentage originating from developing countries has been increasing and is currently 29. The pattern of location of affiliates differs from the pattern of location of headquarters. Some 57 per cent of affiliates are located in developing countries, with China hosting 49 per cent of the total worldwide foreign affiliates.

This pattern is reflected to some extent in the location of foreign direct investment. The largest percentage stock of FDI originates from developed countries and forms their outward FDI (82 per cent). Most of this FDI is directed towards other developed countries whose inward FDI stood at 65.3 per cent of the total in 2010 against 31.1 in developing countries (Table 14.1). The fact that developing countries host a large percentage of affiliates and a smaller percentage of inward FDI is an indication that many of the foreign affiliates in developing countries have low capital assets.

Though the developing countries absorb a smaller percentage of inward FDI than the developed countries, the impact on their domestic economies may be as big. The ratio of stock of inward FDI to GDP stands at 30.8 in 2010 for the developed countries and at 29.1 for the developing ones.

The historical pattern of inward FDI is of interest for its connection to the sectoral pattern of involvement by TNCs. Table 14.1 gives the evolution in the percentage of stock of inward FDI between developed, developing and Central and Eastern European

Table 14.1   Stock of inward FDI, developed market economies, developing countries and Central and Eastern Europe, selected years, 1914–2008, percentage shares

Host Region	1914	1938	1960	1971	1975	1980	1985	1990	1995	2010
Developed countries	37.2	34.3	67.3	65.2	75.1	75.5	71.4	78.4	71.7	65.3
Developing countries	62.8	65.7	32.3	30.9	24.9	24.5	28.6	21.4	27.0	31.1
Central and Eastern Europe	na	na	na	na	na	0.02	0.02	0.2	1.3	3.6
Unallocated	–	–	0.4	3.9	–	–	–	–	–	–

Note: na = not available.

Sources: For 1914, 1938, 1960, 1971, Dunning (1983, Table 5.2); also see Ietto-Gillies (2002, Table 2.3, p. 14); UNCTAD (2011).

(CEE) countries for selected years in the last 95 years. The years before World War II saw the developing countries absorbing the highest percentage of FDI: over 60 per cent. This was due to the fact that most FDI at the time was by companies seeking raw material resources abroad, in developing countries. After World War II we saw a big increase in TNCs operating in manufacturing and this led to increase in the share of FDI in developed countries.

The last few decades have seen growth in the share of inward FDI into developing countries as more manufacturing and services production is located into these regions. These decades have also seen a transformation in the strategies of TNCs, leading to closer integration of the economies of developed and developing countries via the TNCs' strategies of international vertically integrated production. The development of ICTs has made it possible to design production processes split into segments according to the type of labour and other resources necessary to produce the relevant component. The production of the different components is then located in different countries according to the local availability of skills and the local cost of labour: those requiring skilled labour are located in developed countries and those requiring unskilled cheap labour and/or specific raw materials are located in developing countries. These cost-minimization strategies have led to closer integration between countries as well as to some disintegration of the production process. They also have consequences for the structure of world trade and in particular for the growth of intra-firm and intra-industry trade as discussed in section 14.3.

So far we have analysed FDI as if it automatically leads to capital formation in the host country. In reality things are a little more complicated. A TNC can invest in a foreign country – be it developed or developing – in two ways: (1) by setting up a new factory and business where none existed before (*greenfield investment*);[5] or (2) by acquiring an existing business/factory (investment via *mergers and acquisitions – M&As*).[6] Both modalities of FDI result in the generation of new productive capacity for the company. However, only the first one – greenfield – leads to the creation of new productive capacity for the host country. This has considerable impact on the employment effects in the host country. Greenfield investment leads to positive employment effects while M&As do not. In fact, following restructuring of the acquired business some jobs may well be lost in the short to medium term. Productivity may increase due to cuts in jobs and also due to new organizational methods introduced by the TNC. In the longer term the TNC may increase capacity in the acquired business or it may reduce it depending on its strategies worldwide.

The TNCs are employing 77 million people worldwide, but the number of people directly employed by TNCs has been decreasing not because of a diminished relevance of TNCs, whose number worldwide has been increasing. The decrease in employment is likely to be due to the fact that in the last 30 years companies and TNCs worldwide have been following outsourcing strategies: they are contracting out segments of the production process. This is likely to lead to a reduction of employment for which they are directly responsible. However, the suppliers of components are usually under the strategic control of the larger companies/TNCs. In fact, one of the possible reasons for outsourcing is shedding responsibility and fixed costs for sections of the labour force while retaining control of production (Ietto-Gillies, 2012, Ch. 14).

14.5   THE ECONOMICS OF THE TRANSNATIONAL CORPORATION[7]

The years after World War II saw major developments in the TNC and in FDI. There was a big increase in foreign direct investment originating mainly from the USA and directed towards Europe, particularly the UK, and towards Canada and South America. This went hand in hand with a sectoral change in FDI, which moved from the primary to the secondary sector as we saw in the previous section.

These developments provoked interest on the part of a few economists. Prior to World War II there was no theory of foreign direct investment, indeed the term had not yet been introduced. Studies of investment activities abroad were made under the broad category of foreign investment with no distinction between those investments made for portfolio/speculative reasons and those made to gain control over production activities. The explanation for foreign investment did not touch on the theory of the firm and was along purely neoclassical lines in which differentials in interest rates played the major role in the explanation of movements of funds from country to country.

It fell to two economists from countries at the receiving end of US FDI to try to understand what was going on by analysing the firms rather than the movements of funds. John Dunning in the UK was puzzled by the differentials in productivity between British firms and affiliates of US firms operating in Britain in the same sectors; but it was a young Canadian economist working on his doctoral thesis at the Massachussets Institute of Technology (MIT) who started the ambitious project of developing a full theory – the first ever – of the international firm. His thesis was completed in 1960 but not published till 1976 after his premature death in a car accident. Stephen Hymer's work was path breaking in a variety of dimensions. It introduced the distinction between portfolio and direct investment, leading to the analysis of the two types of control we discussed in section 14.2. Moreover, it gave the first theory of why firms invest abroad and become 'international firms'. His approach was based mainly on looking at the industry's structural imperfections and at the firm's desire to use its existing advantages over rivals to increase its market power by investing abroad.

Hymer's work was seminal and gave life to a variety of interpretations and refinements of his own theory as well as to the possibility of new theories. The following two breakthroughs led to the realization that new theoretical approaches were needed: (1) the distinction between the two different types of foreign investment; and (2) the realization that the standard theory of the firm could not explain international production activities of firms.

From then on several theories were developed. The first in historical terms was published by Raymond Vernon (1966) not long after Hymer completed his thesis.[8] Vernon was working at the Harvard Business School just up the road from where Hymer had been a student. His 'international product life cycle' theory concentrated on the product rather than the firm as a whole. Product innovation is taken as a starting point for a theory that is highly dynamic since it involves changes through time in: (1) the geographical structure of trade and production; (2) the competitive position of the company and the product; and (3) the comparative position of countries. Both developed and developing countries become involved as the product moves from one group of countries to the other in terms of production location and/or trade. This has been a highly successful theory but it has also been much criticized. A very perceptive critique is by Vernon himself (1979) and a more recent one by Cantwell (1995).

After that two major contributions were made on the European side of the Atlantic. A group of economists were working on the multinational firm at Reading University in the UK. Peter Buckley and Mark Casson developed a theory of the multinational enterprise by focusing on the organization of activities internally or externally to the firm: the internalization theory of the multinational enterprise. They built on previous developments in the theory of the firm, specifically Coase's (1937) influential paper on why firms exist at all and why their activities are not taken over completely by market transactions. His explanation emphasized the role of transaction costs of operating in the market. This explanation was to prove seminal in a variety of applications to the theory of the firm, organization and markets (see Part III of this book). The first major contribution came from Oliver Williamson (1975 and 1981). Applications to the multinational enterprise were being made around the same time by McManus (1972), Buckley and Casson (1976) and Dunning (1977 and 1980).

Dunning broadened the scope of the internalization theory by adding to the organizational issues – and thus to transactional imperfections – others related to firm's specific advantages – and therefore to market imperfections as considered by Hymer – and others specific to the locality where investment is to take place. Both the internalization and Dunning's theories have been hugely successful; applications, refinements and critiques of these theories continue to be developed. These are also the theories taken as the basis for more recent developments in more mainstream literature. Several economists on both sides of the Atlantic have developed a theory of the MNC in the context of equilibrium analysis, taking as starting points the existence of transaction costs and internalization advantages as well as firms' ownership advantages. Their theory is known as 'new trade theory of the MNC' (Helpman, 1984 and 1985; Markusen, 1984, 1995 and 1998; Helpman and Krugman, 1985)[9] because it uses assumptions and maximization techniques based on increasing returns as in 'new trade theory' (Krugman, 1985, 1991a, 1991b and 1998).

Other interesting and successful theories are the following. First, an approach developed by the Scandinavian school, which focuses on the stages in the internationalization process (Johanson and Wiedersheim-Paul, 1975; Johanson and Vahlne, 1977 and 1990).[10] The authors see an 'establishment chain' in internationalization. It starts with exports by agents and then moves on to the setting up of sales subsidiaries and finally to local production subsidiaries. This is a very dynamic approach that analyses time sequences and developments of the firm and its internationalization strategies over time.

Another dynamic approach builds on developments in the theory of the firm (Penrose, 1959) and specifically on the evolutionary theory of the firm in Nelson and Winter (1982).[11] The emphasis is on the firm as locus of social knowledge (Kogut and Zander, 1993) and of technological innovation (Cantwell, 1989). There is interaction between knowledge and innovation developments, firms' advantages, location advantages and internationalization strategies.

One of the latest approaches developed is based on recent developments in the organization of production and the firm. In section 14.3 I mentioned briefly the trend towards outsourcing of some of the firms' activities. The outsourcing is often done in such a way as to allow the principal firm – usually the large TNC – to retain strategic control over the product and production process. Cowling and Sugden (1998, p. 67) view the scope of the firm as 'not primarily about a set of transactions' . . . but *'primarily about strategic decision-making'* (italics in original). The outsourcing strategies involve the firm into a series of networks with suppliers and distributors. Other networks are developed with customers. There are also the very important networks of affiliates that are internal to the firm and – in the case of foreign affiliates – are external to the home country. Thus several contributors see the major development in the TNC in the last two decades as being the so-called network firm. Theories about its motivations and effects have been developed by several authors largely, but not entirely, working on management and organization (Forsgren, 2008).

14.6   WHY A SPECIAL STUDY OF TRANSNATIONAL CORPORATIONS?[12]

The previous section gives a flavour of the main approaches developed to explain the TNC, its activities and organization. Prior to World War II economists did not see the need to have a special theory for firms operating across frontiers. This was mainly due to the fact that the numbers and activities of such firms were not very large. After World War II the numbers and activities increased and with this came developments of specific theories designed to explain direct business activities across frontiers.

It is now time to pause and ask ourselves why direct activities across national borders need special explanations. After all, direct business activities across regions of the same nation-state are not the subject of special theories even when the country is very large and has many regions/states like the USA. We do not see the need to develop theories of why a firm located in England invests in Northern Ireland or Scotland or why a firm located in Texas invests in Michigan or one located in Piemonte invests in Sicily. In seeking explanations for such patterns we work within theories of the firm and/or investment in general coupled with location theory. But we do see the need for special theories when firms operate across national frontiers. Why? What is special about national frontiers? Is it a matter of geographical distance? Or of cultural distance? Not quite. Distance tends to be higher between locations of different nation-states but this is not always the case. Cities near national borders may be closer in distance and indeed in culture to location in a nearby nation-state than to location within the same nation-state. Milan is closer in geographical distance and probably culture to Geneva than it is to Bari or Palermo.

National borders delimit nation-states as geographical territories and also as loci of regulatory regimes in relation to a variety of elements. Specifically relevant to business are the regulatory regimes related to: (1) currency regimes; (2) fiscal regimes; and (3) labour and social security regimes. They encompass all the laws, customs and regulations related to these three areas. The regulatory regimes for these three areas tend to be more uniform – though not completely uniform – between regions of the same state than between different nation-states.

The divergence between regulatory regimes across nation-states allows TNCs to develop location strategies that maximize their returns. It is the differentials in fiscal regimes that allows TNCs to develop strategies of location and movements of components leading to manipulation of transfer prices that minimizes the overall tax liabilities for the company as a whole.

A company that locates the production of segments of the value chain in various countries will have to move the components from country to country for further processing and eventually for placement into the final market. These movements take place across national frontiers but are internal to the firm, giving rise to intra-firm trade as discussed in section 14.3. The movements internal to the company could be material goods or services; for example, the services of managers exchanged between affiliates or headquarters and affiliates. The unit of the firm that supplies the component or service will invoice the unit of destination located in a different country. If the two countries have different tax rates it will be in the interest of the company as a whole for the invoice to be priced in such a way that most profits are declared in the country with the lowest tax rate. Thus location strategies, intra-firm trade strategies and pricing strategies can be coordinated to minimize the fiscal liabilities of companies that operate across national frontiers. Similar strategies could be applied between regions of the same nation-state if the tax regimes differ. However, in this case, the tax regimes are more likely to be uniform; moreover the company is more likely to be found out. The practice of manipulation of transfer prices is, in fact, illegal but known to be widely practised. It is difficult for governments' revenue departments to monitor the processes and query the set prices for internal transfers because many components and services do not have clear equivalents on the market.

Other areas in which differentials in regulatory regimes is of benefit to companies working across frontiers and thus across loci of different regulatory regimes, are labour and social security regimes. Companies can devise strategies to benefit from using different labour and its skills in various countries according to the cost of labour. Moreover, the labour force working for the same company but located in different countries is spatially and socially fragmented. It therefore finds it more difficult to organize and bargain together with management. This is in contrast with the TNCs that can plan, organize and control across national frontiers. Thus the TNCs have advantages towards their fragmented labour force and they can exploit them strategically for their own benefit.

It is interesting to note that the Confederation of British Industry has always opposed uniformity of fiscal and labour regimes within the European Union though it has welcomed the enlargement of markets and the abolition of obstacles to the movements of goods and services. Successive British governments have obliged.

The discussions in this section point to the relevance of strategic behaviour for TNCs. This means that the explanations of TNCs' motivation, activities and location patterns have to take account of strategic and not just efficiency elements. Strategies towards rival firms have often been incorporated into theories of the TNC, starting with Hymer and – to some extent Dunning – as well as others not considered above.[13] However, strategic behaviour can be also applied by companies to labour and to governments. And this is where the TNCs have an advantage over companies that operate within national frontiers only. It is the existence of different regulatory regimes across different nation-states that allows them to develop strategies designed to maximize their returns from operating in different countries.[14] It is thus the existence of different nation-states with their specific regulatory regimes that makes it necessary to develop specific theories of the TNCs.

14.7   KEY ISSUES IN THE STUDY OF TRANSNATIONAL CORPORATIONS

The activities of transnational corporations raise many issues for society, the economy and for economists. Many such issues have been touched on here and there in the previous sections either when discussing developments, activities and characteristics or when introducing some of the theories. I shall mention here some of the issues raised at the level of companies, industries and macroeconomies. The theoretical approaches – including those considered in section 14.5 – touch on some of the following issues.

At the company level the major issues are concerned with strategies in relation to the following:

- Diversification by product and/or geography.
- Internalization versus externalization of activities and related issue of local production versus production at home with servicing of foreign markets via exports.
- Collaborations with external firms as suppliers, distributors, licensees, franchisees, or partners in research, and/or product development.
- Strategies of international vertical integration across countries.
- Competitive strategies.
- Strategies towards labour and governments in various countries.
- Greenfield versus mergers and acquisitions type of investment: their comparative impact on the company's profitability and competitiveness.

At the level of sectors the following seem relevant:

- Impact of the activities of large TNCs on market structure and on smaller firms.
- Impact on the market structure of investment via greenfield or via M&As.
- Is the market characterized by follow-the-leader strategies regarding pricing, product innovation and location of FDI?[15]

At the macro level there are many effects and issues including the following:

- Effects of TNCs' activities and strategies on: trade, balance of payments, employment, labour relations, government revenue (Barba Navaretti and Venables, 2004; Ietto-Gillies 2012, Part IV).
- Effects on the spreading of knowledge and innovation across countries and industries (Cantwell, 1989; Castellani and Zanfei, 2002 and 2006; Frenz and Ietto-Gillies, 2007 and 2009).
- Effects on cross-countries integration particularly across developed and developing countries.
- Role of TNCs in the globalization process (Ietto-Gillies, 2002: Ch. 9 and 2011)
- TNCs and political power.

These issues involve both theoretical and empirical elements and on both fronts much research is still needed.

14.8   CONCLUSION

This chapter started by introducing the multinational company in its historical development. The issue of control is then discussed. Sections 14.3 and 14.4 are devoted to discussions on the range of activities of TNCs and on their evolving characteristics. The chapter then gives a summary of most of the theories developed in the last 50 years since the completion of the work by Stephen Hymer in which he developed the first theory of 'international operations of national firms'. The theories are discussed in historical sequence and they are very briefly commented on.

The chapter goes on to tackle the question of why we need special theories of the transnational corporations. The search for an answer in section 14.6 links the need for theories to the strategic behaviour of TNCs and the opportunities for strategic behaviour offered by the existence of different regulatory regimes in different nation-states. Finally, the work presents a list of issues – at the micro, meso and macro levels – in which empirical and theoretical studies are still very much needed.

NOTES

1. Nonetheless, the various terms will be used interchangeably in this chapter partly to reflect the terminology of the authors under discussion.
2. Regular publications include the annual *World Investment Report* and the quarterly research journal *Transnational Corporations*.
3. A full discussion of theories and empirical works is in Grimwade (2000). The concept and measurements were originally developed in Grubel and Lloyd (1975).
4. The data in this section come from UNCTAD (2011) and usually refer to the year 2010 or the latest available at the time.
5. The term *brownfield investment* is used to refer to investment on a site where old/disused capacity existed.
6. More on M&As in Part VII of this volume.
7. All the theories sketched in this section as well as others are discussed and analysed in Ietto-Gillies (2012, Parts II and III). For a summary of theoretical approaches see also Cantwell (2000).
8. As far as I know Vernon was not aware of Hymer's work, which had not yet been published.
9. A discussion of the 'new trade theories' applied to the TNCs as well as a critique of them is in Ietto-Gillies (2000 and 2012, Ch. 12). See also Barba Navaretti and Venables (2004) for applications.
10. Some of these papers have been reprinted in Buckley and Ghauri (1999).
11. See Part V of this volume.
12. The issues in this section are further developed in Ietto-Gillies (2012, Ch. 14).
13. See in particular Knickerbocker (1973) and Cowling and Sugden (1987).
14. A theory of international production that emphasizes strategic behaviour towards labour and governments is developed in Ietto-Gillies (2012, Ch. 14).
15. On the latter see Knickerbocker (1973) and Graham (1978 and 1990).

REFERENCES

Barba Navaretti, G. and A.J. Venables (2004), *Multinational Firms in the World Economy*, Princeton and Oxford: Princeton University Press.

Buckley, P.J. and M.C. Casson (1976), 'A long-run theory of the multinational enterprise', in P.J. Buckley and M.C. Casson (eds), *The Future of the Multinational Enterprise*, London: Macmillan, pp. 32–65.

Buckley, P.J. and P.N. Ghauri (1999), *The Internationalization of the Firm. A Reader*, London: ITBP, Ch. 6, pp. 61–79.

Cantwell, J. (1989), *Technological Innovation and Multinational Corporations*, Oxford: Blackwell.

Cantwell, J. (1995), 'The globalisation of technology: what remains of the product cycle model?', *Cambridge Journal of Economics*, **19**(1), 155–74.

Cantwell, J. (2000), 'A survey of theories of international production', in C.N. Pitelis and R. Sugden (eds), *The Nature of the Transnational Firm*, London: Routledge, Ch 2, pp. 10–56.

Castellani, D. and A. Zanfei (2002), 'Multinational experience and the creation of linkages with local firms. Evidence from the electronic industry', *Cambridge Journal of Economics*, **26**(1), 1–25.

Castellani, D. and A. Zanfei (2006), *Multinational Firms, Innovation and Productivity*, Cheltenham, UK and Northampton, MA, USA: Edward Elgar.

Chandler, A.D. (1962), *Strategy and Structure: Chapters in the History of the Industrial Enterprise*, Cambridge, MA: MIT Press.

Coase, R.H. (1937), 'The nature of the firm', *Economica*, **4**(16), 386–405. Reprinted in G.J. Stigler and K.E. Boulding (eds) (1953), *Readings in Price Theory*, London: Allen and Unwin, pp. 331–51.

Cowling, K. and R. Sugden (1987), *Transnational Monopoly Capitalism*, Brighton: Wheatsheaf.

Cowling, K. and R. Sugden (1998), 'The essence of the modern corporation: markets, strategic decision-making and the theory of the firm', *The Manchester School*, **66**(1), 59–86.

Dunning, J.H. (1977), 'Trade, location of economic activity and the MNE: a search for an eclectic approach', in B. Ohlin, P.O. Hesselborn and P.M. Wijkman (eds), *The International Allocation of Economic Activity*, London: Macmillan, pp. 395–431.

Dunning, J.H. (1980), 'Explaining changing patterns of international production: in defence of the eclectic theory', *Oxford Bulletin of Economics and Statistics*, **41**(4), 269–95.

Dunning, J.H. (1983), 'Changes in the level and growth of international production: the last 100 years', in M. Casson (ed.), *The Growth of International Business*, London: Allen and Unwin, pp. 84–139.

Forsgren, M. (2008), *Theories of the Multinational Firm. A Multidimensional Creature in the Global Economy*, Cheltenham, UK and Northampton, MA, USA: Edward Elgar.

Forsgren, M., U. Holm and J. Johanson (2005), *Managing the Embedded Multinational: A Business Network View*, Cheltenham, UK and Northampton, MA, USA: Edward Elgar.

Frenz, M. and G. Ietto-Gillies (2007), 'Does multinationality affect the propensity to innovate? An analysis of the third UK Community Innovation Survey', *International Review of Applied Economics*, **21**(1), 99–117.

Frenz, M. and G. Ietto-Gillies (2009), 'The impact on innovation performance of different sources of knowledge: evidence from the UK Community Innovation Survey', *Research Policy*, **38**(7), 1125–35.

Ghoshal, S. and C.A. Bartlett (1990), 'The multinational corporation as an interorganizational network', *Academy of Management Review*, **15**(4), 603–35.

Graham, E.M. (1978), 'Transatlantic investment by multinational firms: a rivalristic phenomenon?', *Journal of Post-Keynesian Economics*, **1**(1), 82–99.

Graham, E.M. (1990), 'Exchange of threats between multinational firms as an infinitely repeated non-cooperative game', *International Trade Journal*, **4**(3), 259–77.

Grimwade, N. (2000), *International Trade: New Patterns of Trade, Production and Investment*, 2nd edition, London: Routledge.

Grubel, H.G. and P.J. Lloyd (1975), *Intra-industry Trade*, London: Macmillan.

Hagedoorn, J. (1996), 'Trends and patterns in strategic technology partnering since the early seventies', *Review of Industrial Organization*, **11**(4), 601–16.

Hagedoorn, J. (2002), 'Inter-firm R&D partnerships: an overview of major trends and patterns since 1960', *Research Policy*, **31**(4), 477–92.

Helpman, E. (1984), 'A simple theory of international trade with multinational corporations', *Journal of Political Economy*, **92**(3), 451–71.

Helpman, E. (1985), 'Multinational corporations and trade structure', *Review of Economic Studies*, **52**(3), 443–58.

Helpman, E. and P. Krugman (1985), *Market Structures and Foreign Trade. Increasing Returns, Imperfect Competition and the International Economy*, Cambridge, MA: MIT Press.

Hymer, S.H. ([1960] 1976), *The International Operations of National Firms: A Study of Direct Foreign Investment*, Cambridge, MA: MIT Press.

Hymer, S.H. (1970), 'The efficiency (contradictions) of multinational corporations', *American Economic Review*, **60**(2), 411–8. Reprinted in R.B. Cohen, N. Felton, J. Van Liere and M. Nkosi (eds) (1979), *The Multinational Corporation: A Radical Approach, Papers by S. H. Hymer*, Cambridge: Cambridge University Press, pp. 41–53.

Knickerbocker, F.T. (1973), *Oligopolistic Reaction and Multinational Enterprise*, Cambridge, MA: Division of Research, Graduate School of Business Administration, Harvard University.

Ietto-Gillies, G. (2000), 'What role for multinationals in the new theories of trade and location?' *International Review of Applied Economics*, **14**(4), 413–26.

Ietto-Gillies, G. (2002), *Transnational Corporations. Fragmentation Amidst Integration*, London: Routledge.

Ietto-Gillies, G. (2011), 'The role of transnational corporations in the globalisation process', in Jonathan

Michie (ed.), *The Handbook of Globalisation*, 2nd edition, Cheltenham, UK and Northampton, MA, USA: Edward Elgar.

Ietto-Gillies, G. (2012), *Transnational Corporations and International Production. Concepts, Theories and Effects, Second Edition*, Cheltenham, UK and Northampton, MA, USA: Edward Elgar.

International Monetary Fund (IMF) (1977), *Balance of Payments Manual*, 4th edition, Washington, DC: IMF.

Johanson, J. and J-E. Vahlne (1977), 'The internationalization process of the firm – a model of knowledge development and increasing foreign market commitment', *Journal of International Business Studies*, **8**(1), 23–32.

Johanson, J. and J-E. Vahlne (1990), 'The mechanism of internationalization', *International Marketing Review*, **7**(4), 11–24.

Johanson, J. and F. Wiedersheim-Paul (1975), 'The internationalization of the firm: four Swedish cases', *Journal of Management Studies*, **12**(3), 305–22.

Kogut, B. and U. Zander (1993), 'Knowledge of the firm and the evolutionary theory of the multinational corporation', *Journal of International Business Studies*, **24**(4), 625–45.

Krugman, P. (1985), 'Increasing returns and the theory of international trade', *National Bureau of Economic Research Working Papers*, No. 1752.

Krugman, P. (1991a), *Geography and Trade*, Cambridge, MA: The MIT Press.

Krugman, P. (1991b), 'Increasing returns and economic geography', *Journal of Political Economy*, **99**(3), 483–99.

Krugman, P. (1998), 'What's new about the new economic geography?' *Oxford Review of Economic Policy*, **14**(2), 7–17.

Markusen, J.R. (1984), 'Multinationals, multiplant economies and the gains from trade', *Journal of International Economics*, **16**(3/4), 205–24. Reprinted in J.N. Bhagwati (ed.) (1981), *International Trade: Selected Readings*, Cambridge, MA: MIT Press, pp. 457–95.

Markusen, J.R. (1995), 'The boundaries of multinational enterprises, and the theory of international trade', *Journal of Economic Perspectives*, **9**(2), 169–89.

Markusen, J.R. (1998), 'Multinational firms, location and trade', *The World Economy*, **21**(6), 733–56.

McManus, J. (1972), 'The theory of the international firm', in Gilles Paquet (ed.), *The Multinational Firm and the Nation State*, Don Mills, Ontario: Collier-Macmillan, pp. 66–93.

Nelson, R.R. and S.G. Winter (1982), *An Evolutionary Theory of Economic Change*, Cambridge, MA: Harvard University Press.

Penrose, E.T. (1959), *The Theory of the Growth of the Firm*, Oxford: Blackwell.

United Nations Conference on Trade and Development (UNCTAD) (2011), *World Investment Report. Non-equity Modes of International Production and Development*, Geneva: United Nations.

Vernon, R. (1966), 'International investment and international trade in the product cycle', *Quarterly Journal of Economics*, **80**(2), 190–207.

Vernon, R. (1979), 'The product cycle hypothesis in a new international environment', *Oxford Bulletin of Economics and Statistics*, **41**(4), 255–67.

Wilkins, M. (1988), 'The Freestanding Company, 1817–1914', *Economic History Review*, **61**(2), 259–82.

Williamson, O.E. (1975), *Markets and Hierarchies: Analysis and Anti-trust Implications*, New York: Free Press.

Williamson, O.E. (1981), 'The modern corporation: origins, evolution, attributes', *Journal of Economic Literature*, **19**(4), 1537–68.

15 Internalization theory
Mark Casson and Nigel Wadeson

15.1 INTRODUCTION

Internalization is a theory of the boundaries of a firm. It does not claim to be a complete and self-sufficient theory of the firm, but rather a necessary component of any comprehensive theory of the firm. The basic principle is that there are two main ways of coordinating economic activity. One is through the market and the other is through management. Each mechanism tends to be preferred when it is the more efficient. Which mechanism is most efficient depends on specific circumstances. Identifying the circumstances that favour markets and those that favour management is one of the key contributions of internalization theory.

Internalization relates to both intra-plant coordination and inter-plant coordination. The need for intra-plant coordination arises when different resources are co-located within the same plant and are used in conjunction with each other. The resources might be different workers that make up a team, or different machines carrying out related activities, or a combination of machines and their operatives. The theory of intra-plant coordination explains the nature of the employment contract under which labour is hired, the terms under which capital equipment is rented or leased, and the arrangements under which other factors of production, such as land, are supplied. It is therefore concerned with arrangements that prevail in factor markets (Alchian and Demsetz, 1972; Demsetz, 1988).

The theory of inter-plant coordination, by contrast, is concerned with product markets – in particular, intermediate product markets. In this case the related resources are not co-located, but are spatially dispersed. Each intermediate product flow is generated by a plant at one location and utilized at a plant at another location. Internalization theory examines whether for any given set of plants the volumes of the flow between them at any given time is determined by arm's length negotiations between the managers of independently owned plants, or by managers working for a firm that owns all the plants involved. In the latter case the intermediate product flows are said to be internalized within the firm concerned (Casson, 1997).

The focus of this chapter is on inter-plant internalization. It examines the relative costs and benefits of coordinating intermediate product flow between plants that are separately owned and between plants that have a common owner. By explaining the conditions under which the common ownership of related plants is most efficient, internalization theory generates a simple theory of the multi-plant firm.

The theory of the multi-plant firm has many ramifications. Inter-plant internalization applies not only to production plants but also to other types of facility – in particular R&D laboratories (Grant, 1996). The distinction between production plants on the one hand and R&D laboratories on the other is that the former generate ordinary outputs – often of a tangible nature – whereas the latter generate knowledge – which is intangible and has strategic implications for the growth and diversification of the firm. There are significant advantages in internalizing knowledge flows, for reasons explained below. Many knowledge-intensive firms, therefore, own not only R&D laboratories but also production plants that exploit the knowledge generated by the R&D. These plants receive a steady flow of knowledge from their laboratories and use it to reduce production costs and improve the quality of their product.

Internalization is also relevant to entrepreneurship (Langlois and Robertson, 1993; Casson, 2005). In a world of unanticipated change, new opportunities constantly arise to alter the composition of output in the economy. New products need be introduced, and the outputs of some existing products expanded. In a fully employed economy the resources required for this expansion must be obtained by cutting back the outputs of some other products, or ceasing their production altogether. Opportunities therefore exist to acquire resources from declining activities and re-direct them into expanding ones. An entrepreneur who is the first to spot such an opportunity can, in principle, generate a profit by buying up the relevant resources and putting them to a better use.

Knowledge of opportunities may be regarded as an intermediate product, just like the technological knowledge generated by R&D. Knowledge of opportunities is, however, based on knowledge of market conditions rather than on knowledge of technology per se. Knowledge of opportunities is typically generated at the headquarters of the firm, at which the entrepreneur is based. Just like technological knowledge, entrepreneurial knowledge usually benefits from being exploited internally within the firm. As a result, a successful entrepreneur may own and control a series of separate plants from a single headquarters facility that generates the knowledge of opportunities that the individual plants exploit.

15.2   COASE'S SEMINAL CONTRIBUTION

The basic insights of internalization theory derive from the early work of Ronald Coase (1937). Coase observed that in economic theory markets are said to coordinate different activities that, in business studies, are said to be coordinated by managers instead. This apparent duplication of the coordination function led Coase to identify an ambiguity in the theory over whether a market or a manager coordinates a given set of activities. Coase resolved the indeterminacy by postulating that the two mechanisms of coordination incurred different costs, and that in any given situation the mechanism with the lowest level of cost would be chosen. Thus if theory could determine the relative costs of the two mechanisms in any given situation then it could predict which mechanism – market or management – would be used.

In principle either planners or the market could decide which inter-plant linkages were internalized and which were not. In a centrally planned state-run economy for example, the planners might decide that certain sets of activities would be privatized so that the intermediate product linkages within each set could be coordinated by market forces (Hayek, 1937). They would permit private ownership of the relevant activities in order to promote efficiency in the intermediate product markets. Coase, however, assumed that the process would work the opposite way round. He postulated a free market economy in which private owners were able to take over inter-related activities and coordinate them through a single managerial unit. According to Coase, therefore, the market would decide where planning was efficient – planners would not decide where markets were efficient. Both approaches can be observed in practice. Large firms are often formed by mergers or by takeovers of smaller firms, but they can also be formed by the privatization of industries – notably utilities – previously owned by the state.

Coase's conceptual innovation was not immediately taken up by the economics profession. It undermined two precepts of the economics of the time. The first was that markets were perfect, and the second was that all firms used the same production function. Coase's contention that markets incurred costs contradicted the professional view that competitive markets produced perfect results. If they did so then there could be no need for management, since managers could not improve upon the results generated by markets. Like conventional economists, Coase was in favour of markets, but for different reasons – though imperfect, markets were often superior to the best available alternative, namely management; furthermore, as explained above, markets offered the best way of deciding which activities should be coordinated by management and which should not.

The conventional notion that competitive markets produced perfect results was superficially endorsed by Alfred Marshall's 'scissors' analysis of supply and demand (Marshall, 1890). A close reading of Marshall, however, shows that he did not in fact deny the existence of the costs to which Coase later referred, but simply subsumed them into his demand and supply functions. The costs incurred by producers in selling their output were added to Marshall's supply price while the costs incurred by customers in buying products were subtracted from their demand price. In this context, therefore, the benefits of internalization could be expressed by simultaneously shifting down the supply curve to reflect lower selling costs and shifting up the demand curve to reflect lower buying costs – thereby increasing the volume of trade in the market.

In a more general setting, Leon Walras ([1874] 1954) had argued that competitive markets could be analysed as though they were intermediated by an auctioneer. This auctioneer quoted uniform prices that were adjusted to equilibrium levels before any trade took place. Buyers and sellers could be matched with perfect ease, and so no costs were incurred in operating the market. Furthermore, the auctioneer did not abuse his monopoly of intermediation by setting a margin between buying prices and selling prices, but rather passed on to buyers and sellers all the benefits of his costless activity by setting no margin between the prices at all. Walrasian theory was becoming very popular at the time that Coase wrote, and so Coase's attack upon its basic assumptions was not well received.

Coase's recognition that management matters also called the production function into question. The production function relates the output of a plant to its inputs, and in its simple form assumes that all plant owners have access to the same technology and the same information. Coase, however, implied that the owners of different plants might operate with different production functions due to differences in technology or information. Furthermore, most economists assumed that each industry involved just a single type of plant, whereas Coase implicitly assumed that each industry comprised an interrelated set of different types of plant, each of which had its own production function. Coase's analysis of production was therefore much more nuanced than that employed by most economists of his time.

The ideological objections of the economics profession were not the only barrier to the dissemination of Coase's ideas, however. Coase himself was vague on a crucial point - namely the exact nature of the costs incurred by markets. He referred in general terms to the costs of search and of bargaining, negotiating and forming contracts. Whilst this was an important move away from the model of perfect competition, it left considerable room for speculation about what he really meant. This chapter reviews the various attempts that have been made to refine Coase's analysis, but before doing so some general observations on this crucial issue may be helpful.

As already indicated, a key difference between internal and external coordination lies in the ownership of the resources being controlled (Grossman and Hart, 1986; Hart and Moore, 1990; Hart, 1995). Under internalization, interdependent resources are under common ownership, whereas under externalization they are not. It is important to be clear about what is meant by a resource in this context, however. In the case of labour, for example, the resource that is owned is not the worker themselves but rather the output that the worker produces whilst under the direction of the owner of the output. In effect, the owner of the output rents or leases the worker's time and acquires the right to direct the worker, during this time, to any activity the owner thinks fit, within certain limits agreed with the worker at the outset. The same applies, in principle, to capital equipment and other assets – it is not the ownership of the asset that is crucial but rather the ownership of the output of the asset. In the case of physical assets, however, the owner may choose to acquire the asset outright as a means of acquiring rights to future output as well as to current output – an option not usually available in the case of labour.

The reason why the right to output is so crucial is that the decision about what type of output to produce, and in what quantity, is the key to the successful ownership of a resource. If the owner of a resource has agreed to rent or lease the resource at a given price before any judgement has been made on how the resource is to be used then the owner of the resource (as opposed to the output) receives a payment that is independent of that use. If the judgement exercised by the owner of the output is correct then they stand to profit, because the high price of the output will be set against the fixed cost of the resource input. The only exception is when the owner of the resource contracts in advance to receive a payment that is contingent on the output produced or on the price for which it is sold. The owner of the output therefore receives a profit that rewards the quality of judgement that they bring to bear on how the resource is used. The owner of the resource, by contrast, receives a rental that reflects the scarcity of the resource in the light of the range of alternative uses to which it might conceivably be put. Unlike the owner of the output, who takes the key decision as to how the resource is used, the owner of the resource simply selects the buyer who offers the highest rent, and in an efficient market this involves a simple comparison of the alternative rents on offer. This means that when the theory of internalization speaks of the internalization of an intermediate product flow it refers to two plants that are either owned or leased by the same firm, and not just the case where both plants are owned outright.

15.3 MODELLING INTERNALIZATION: BASIC PRINCIPLES

The simplest way to understand internalization theory is to focus on the coordination of a single linkage (Williamson, 1971). In Figure 15.1 intermediate product flows from

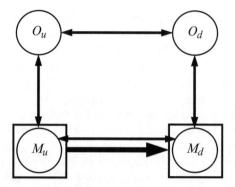

Figure 15.1   Schematic illustration of the coordination of a single linkage using an external market

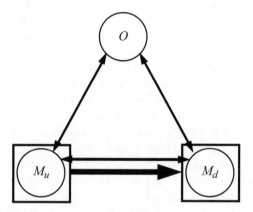

Figure 15.2   Schematic illustration of the internalization of a single linkage

an upstream production plant, *U*, to a downstream production plant, *D*; for example, metal flows from an upstream ore refinery to a downstream engineering plant. To begin with it is assumed for simplicity that all the output from the upstream plant is consigned to the downstream plant and that the downstream plant sources all its output from the upstream plant (Parmigiani, 2007). The plants are represented by square boxes, the flow between them by a thick black line, and the direction of flow by an arrow. This flow can be coordinated either through negotiation between independent firms, as illustrated in the figure, or through unified control by a single firm, as illustrated in Figure 15.2.

Intra-plant coordination is effected by a local manager. People are represented by circles. The upstream plant is managed by M_u and owned by O_u, while the downstream plant is managed by M_d and owned by O_d. In a small firm the roles of owner and manager may be combined, but in large firms they are normally distinct. In a joint stock company, ownership may be collective, for example, individual owners club together to employ a salaried manager to take decisions on their behalf.

Communication is represented by thin lines; it is normally two-way, as indicated by the twin arrows. Owners specify the rules and procedures, and managers apply these rules and report back to the owners. With an external market in the intermediate product, the owners of the two plants negotiate the terms on which they will trade, that is, they determine prices – whilst their managers fix the orders placed at these prices on a day-to-day basis. Thus strategic communications take place between the owners O_u and O_d (or senior managers who represent them) whilst tactical communications take place between the local managers M_u and M_d.

Under internalization, by contrast, there is a single owner, O, who controls both managers M_u, M_d, as shown in Figure 15.2. Internalization provides an opportunity to centralize control, although this option may not be exercised. For example, the owner O may establish a procedure for the negotiation of internal transfer prices at which the intermediate product is exchanged, and instruct the managers to negotiate deals that maximize the notional profits imputed to their respective plants.

A major advantage of decentralizing decisions is that it allows local managers to respond to local volatility. Where shocks are local, and occur independently at each of the plants, economies in communication may be achieved by allowing each manager to respond directly to changing local circumstances after consultation with the manager of the other plant, without communicating with a central decision-maker.

On the other hand, if shocks are general, and impinge on both plants simultaneously, then a central manager who monitors this source of volatility can instruct both plant managers on how to respond and thereby coordinate their decisions directly. A single source of volatility is often dominant when upstream and downstream activities need to be operated in fixed proportions (Alchian and Demsetz, 1972). For example, if the amount of metal that needs to be refined upstream is directly proportional to output of engineering products downstream then a change in the supply of metal ores, or a change in the demand for engineering products, requires the scale of both activities to be adjusted in the same proportion. A central manager that monitors the key source of volatility can then change the overall scale of activity whilst maintaining the requisite proportions.

By contrast, local responsiveness is most valuable when there are local substitution possibilities, for example, the upstream plant has alternative outputs that it can produce, and the downstream plant has alternative inputs that it can use. An upstream shock may encourage the production of a substitute output, whilst a downstream shock may encourage the use of a substitute input. Independent local shocks and the existence of local substitution possibilities therefore favour decentralization, whilst a common shock and lack of local substitution possibilities favours centralization (Casson, 1994).

If there is little incentive for either firm to default on a contract (see below) then local responsiveness can be achieved most easily through an external market. If, however, there is a significant risk of default, then ownership may be unified and local responsiveness achieved by allowing managers to negotiate internal prices. Where local responsiveness is not required, however, internalization with authority-based control is the best option.

Where local volatility is coupled with significant substitution possibilities, therefore, external markets are favoured, provided that the risks of default are low. By contrast, when complementarity is dominant, and volatility is driven by either upstream supply or downstream demand, then internalization is favoured whether or not there is a serious risk of default. Complementarities associated with a single source of risk therefore favour internalization, whilst substitution possibilities associated with multiple local shocks favour externalization instead, provided that the risk of default is low.

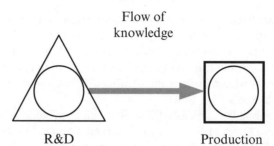

Figure 15.3   Single linkage involving knowledge flow

15.4   DEVELOPING THE INTERNALIZATION MODEL: THE ROLE OF KNOWLEDGE

Complementarities, substitution possibilities and patterns of volatility are not the only factors that influence internalization. To appreciate the significance of other factors, however, it is useful to examine internalization in a wider context. The first step in this direction is to recognize that internalization involves not only commodity flows of the type analysed above, but knowledge flows as well (Buckley and Casson, 1976; Loasby, 1998). An important example of knowledge flow is the flow of new technology generated by R&D.

R&D may be regarded as the upstream stage of knowledge flow, with its application to production being the downstream stage, as illustrated in Figure 15.3. While the owner of a new technology may be the best person to develop it, they are not necessarily the best person to exploit it, as exploitation may require rather different skills. The owner of a technology can, in principle, license its exploitation to an independent producer, and a market can be created in the right to use the technology. This is not necessarily the best solution from the owner's point of view, however. There are two problems, both of which are special cases of general problems that influence internalization decisions.

The first is the limited scope of intellectual property rights and the practical difficulty of enforcing them. Patents only cover certain types of invention, and suing for infringement is an expensive and uncertain business. This is a special case of the general problem that the scope of property rights is limited, even in a sophisticated market economy, and that contracts for the transfer of property rights are often difficult to enforce at law, as noted above (Maskin and Tirole, 1999). In the absence of intellectual property rights, the value of knowledge is often best appropriated through secrecy. Instead of transferring its knowledge to other parties, the firm exploits the information itself.

The second problem is the difficulty of convincing other people of the value of the technology. There is an asymmetry in the information available to the licensor and licensee. The licensor knows how the knowledge was discovered. They know whether they have been honest and they know how the knowledge was generated. The licensee knows neither; the licensor's claims could be wrong because they are deliberately false, or because the licensor is incompetent. The evidence required to investigate these concerns is not available unless the licensor agrees to divulge it. But in divulging such evidence an honest licensor may give away the knowledge itself; once the licensee has acquired the knowledge in this way, they may no longer be willing to pay for it. This is a special case of the general problem that buyers cannot always trust the claims that are made by sellers, and honest sellers cannot afford the cost of reassuring them. Internalization solves this problem too. By integrating forward into the exploitation of knowledge, the firm avoids the need to convince an independent buyer of its value. It is possible to keep the knowledge secret and exploit the knowledge itself, as explained above.

This is also a special case of a general problem, namely quality control. Many goods can be produced in two versions – the genuine article, which matches the specification contained in the contract with the buyer, and an inferior alternative. If the producer is dishonest then the alternative will be cheaper, in order to increase the profit margin, and will be made to look as much as possible like the genuine article, in order to deceive the buyer. If the producer is merely incompetent, however, then the alternative may actually be more expensive to produce and its defects may be easily detected. In the case of knowledge both possibilities need to be taken seriously. Inventors, for example, may deliberately make bogus claims, or they may simply be over-confident of their ability.

A distinction is often drawn between 'inspection' and 'experience' goods. The quality of the former can be ascertained from inspection, or by testing a small proportion of a batch, but the quality of the latter can only be ascertained through use. A buyer may be able to reject inferior inspection goods before they have paid for them, but this does not apply to experience goods. In some cases experience goods can be paid for in instalments, according to how they perform in use, or they can be supported by warranties – perhaps underwritten by independent brokers. All of these arrangements can be problematic to enforce at law, however. Under these conditions, it may pay a buyer to internalize their supplies by owning the plant that produces them. This gives the buyer the opportunity to monitor the process of production and thereby to detect and rectify problems at an early stage. The benefits to the buyer are greater:

- the greater the cost of using poor-quality items;
- the more difficult it is to monitor quality once the product has been produced;
- the easier it is to monitor quality whilst the product is being produced and;
- the greater the risk that the supplier is incompetent or deceitful.

It is possible, of course, that a supplier might consent to the buyer supervising their production process. They would be unlikely to do so, however, if they were exploiting trade secrets in production, for the buyer might then imitate their methods using a plant of their own instead. A deceitful supplier would also be unlikely to consent – in which case they would disguise their intent by claiming that they were protecting trade secrets instead. Where trade secrets are used, or there is intent to deceive, therefore, the advantage of internalization is greatest.

Quality control can also apply to deceitful or incompetent buyers who abuse the products they purchase. Where a supplier issues a warranty to insure a buyer against defective production they expose themselves to risks arising from misuse, for example, fashion garments may be returned with spurious defects once they have been worn. If buyers cannot be trusted then warranties become expensive, and in the absence of warranties sellers have an increased incentive to cheat.

Writers who emphasize 'opportunism' exaggerate the importance of deceit and correspondingly underestimate the significance of incompetence (Williamson, 1975, 1985, 1996). The same writers tend to assume that information asymmetry always favours the buyer rather than the seller, and is always exploited strategically. Where a producer is incompetent rather than dishonest, however, the buyer may know more than the seller, and even if the seller knows more than the buyer they may not exploit this advantage. An assumption of opportunism therefore confuses the analysis. It is perhaps for this reason that opportunism was not a component of Coase's original analysis. Nevertheless, deceit is potentially a more serious problem than incompetence, as the preceding discussion shows; thus while opportunism does not cause the problem of quality control, it certainly exacerbates it.

15.5   DEVELOPING THE INTERNALIZATION MODEL: THE IMPORTANCE OF CONTEXT

So far the discussion has focused on the analysis of a single linkage – between upstream and downstream production or between production and R&D. The economy, however, consists of a complex web of linkages, and interactions between different linkages have an important influence on patterns of internalization. The activities internalized by a large firm often involve multiple linkages. These multiple linkages frequently involve interactions between knowledge flows and commodity flows.

Figure 15.4 illustrates a situation in which both upstream and downstream production draw upon a common source of R&D. To provide added realism, the figure illustrates not only a flow of new technology from R&D to production, but the feedback of experience from production to R&D. It illustrates the important point that internalization

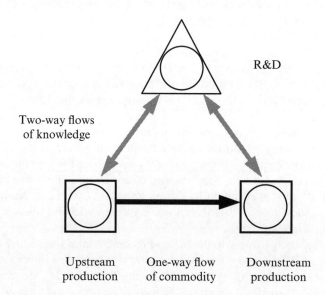

Figure 15.4   Joint outputs of knowledge from R&D, with feedback of experience from production

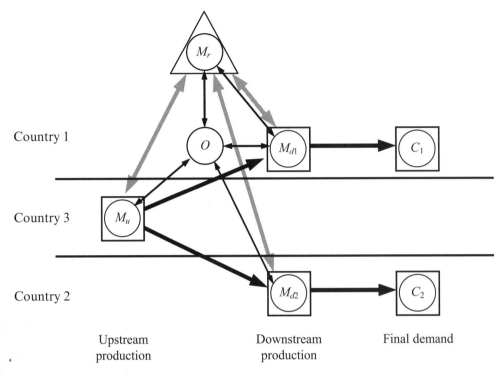

Figure 15.5   Multinational enterprise internalizing production in three countries

of knowledge flow can lead to internalization of commodity flow, even when there are no economies of internalizing commodity flow itself. To internalize knowledge flow to and from upstream production the firm will bring both R&D and upstream production under common ownership and control, and to internalize knowledge flow to and from downstream production it will bring R&D and downstream production under common ownership and control as well. Thus upstream and downstream production will come under common ownership and control simply because of their mutual dependence on the same source of knowledge. This shows that the explanation of the internalization of commodity flow may lie in the internalization of knowledge flows. Focusing the theory on the internalization of commodity flows, as some authors have done, may therefore be misleading, because the explanation of internalization lies elsewhere. Complicated arguments for internalizing commodity flow are concocted when a much simpler argument based on knowledge flow would prove more satisfactory.

A wider context also reveals the significance of knowledge as a public good. General knowledge has many uses, and in so far as scientific laws are universal, technological knowledge has potential global application. This means that R&D in one country may be simultaneously linked to many production plants in different countries. This is particularly important in understanding the connection between internalization and multinational enterprise. Figure 15.5 illustrates the 'market sourcing problem' in a three-country world. It focuses on a special case where two developed country markets, 1 and 2, are sourced by local downstream production, whilst upstream production is concentrated in a less developed country, country 3, that exports raw materials. The knowledge generated by R&D is shared not only between the stages of production (as in Figure 15.4) but also between the downstream plants in each market. Because of their common dependence on the same source of R&D, and the internalization of knowledge flow, both downstream plants are owned by the same firm. The owner, O, controls not only the manager of R&D, M_r, but also the managers of the plants M_{d1}, M_{d2}. These two plants operating at the same stage of production (but in different markets) are horizontally integrated because of their common dependence on R&D. At the same time upstream and downstream production are vertically integrated (as before) because of common dependence on R&D (i.e., O controls M_u). As a result, trade in raw materials is intra-firm – it is internalized, not just within any firm, but within the firm that carries out the R&D.

The public good nature of knowledge increases the risks of piracy, and provides additional reasons for internalization where new technology is concerned. If the technology is licensed in just a single market, the local licensee may attempt to sub-license producers in other countries, thereby undermining the market for licences in other countries and creating competition for the firm's foreign subsidiaries world-wide. If, for example, the firm were to license technology in country 1 then the licensee in country 1 could sub-license the producer in country 2, and thereby undermine the firm's overall profitability. In the long run independent sub-licensees might invade each other's markets by exporting, and thereby dissipate most of the rents that would otherwise have accrued to the owner of the technology.

There is a 'dark side' to internalization, however. Horizontal integration benefits a multinational firm by limiting competition in local markets. It facilitates the enforcement of a producer cartel. Cartels are well-known to be unstable because individual members have a strong incentive to secretly undercut the cartel price. Unifying the ownership of cartel members through horizontal integration eliminates the incentive to under-cut. Where a firm is exploiting a new technology, limiting local price competition may be necessary in order to prevent competitive erosion of the monopoly rents from R&D. In this respect internalization facilitates innovation by the multinational firm. Where no new technology is involved, however, there is no social case for monopoly rents and internalization is against the public interest – hence the case for anti-trust regulation to be applied on an international basis.

15.6   MARKET STRUCTURE: THE IMPACT OF FIXED COSTS AT THE INDUSTRY LEVEL

In the early 1970s many industrial economists believed that market structure held the key to internalization. More specifically, they argued that monopoly power encouraged vertical integration. This focus was subsequently criticized by transaction cost theorists, who argued that individual transactions, rather than an industry as a whole, was the appropriate unit of analysis. This misguided argument has led to an unwarranted neglect of market structure theory.

It has long been recognized that different stages of production in an industry may have different minimum efficient scales. These minimum efficient scales are measured by the capacities of the plants that afford minimum average cost of production. Where a plant incurs fixed costs (i.e., costs that are independent of output), but operates under diminishing returns, the average cost curve is U-shaped and there is generally a unique minimum efficient scale. Suppose, for example, that upstream production has a minimum efficient scale of 7000 units and downstream production a minimum efficient scale of 3000 units. For the number of units produced at each stage to match up, the number of plants at the upstream stage must be in the ratio of 3:7 compared to the downstream stage. Thus if there is final demand for 42 000 units then there will be 42 000/7000 = six upstream plants and 42 000/3000 = 14 downstream plants.

With an industry cost structure of this type, vertical integration will tend to be wasteful. A single upstream plant cannot be matched up with a single downstream plant because their efficient scales are so different. Even if each upstream plant were matched with two downstream plants the upstream plant would not be fully utilized, whilst if each upstream plant were matched with three downstream plants then the downstream plants would not be fully utilized. This point is often overlooked by modern transaction costs theorists. They assume that the size of a transaction is conveniently matched to the sizes of the upstream and downstream plants, when there is no guarantee that these plants will be of equal size.

To implement vertical integration on an efficient scale in this example, three upstream plants need to be matched to seven downstream plants, and so the firm as a whole must have a capacity of 21 000 units. The internal market would not involve a single transaction of 21 000 units, but an entire network of transactions in which each upstream plant supplied at least three different downstream plants.

Implementing integration under these circumstances would undermine competition. Instead of three upstream plants competing with each other, and seven downstream plants doing the same, there would be scope for just two large firms of equal size. Rivalry between these firms would discourage them from trading with each other, as each would be afraid that the other would act disruptively if they became dependent on them. If one of the upstream plants encountered problems and had to be shut down, and the same happened to one of the downstream plants, then a competitive market would reshuffle resources throughout the industry to match up capacity in the most efficient way. But if the upstream plant belonged to one integrated firm, and the downstream plant to the other integrated firm, and the two firms did not trade with each other, then both would experience disruption and output would be much lower as a result. Overall, therefore, internal markets would work badly.

Under a different cost structure, however, internalization may become efficient. Suppose, for example, that there are substantial economies of scale upstream, whilst the cost structure downstream remains unchanged. Upstream there are large fixed costs and constant marginal costs. As a result, average costs throughout the industry are minimized by having a single large plant upstream, with a capacity of 42 000 units and 14 small plants downstream, each with a capacity of 3000 units as before. In the absence of industry regulation, the large upstream firm will set a monopoly price in the intermediate product market. Because it sells to 14 different downstream firms, it will charge a uniform price to all of them. The price will overstate the marginal cost of upstream production, and the intermediate product will therefore acquire an artificial scarcity. If the downstream firms combine the intermediate product with another input, such as labour, in their production process then they will increase the amount of the other input in order to conserve the scarce intermediate product. This will distort the allocation of resources downstream and increase average costs throughout the industry as a whole. The price of the final product is increased not only by the upstream monopolistic mark-up but by the cost of larger downstream inputs too.

Higher downstream costs erode some of the profit that the monopolist could otherwise extract from the industry. Internalization can eliminate waste because when the upstream monopolist also owns all the downstream plants then they no longer need to charge a monopoly price for the intermediate product, for it is of no consequence whether profit is imputed to the upstream or downstream stage. The internal price of the intermediate product is equated to its marginal cost of production that, because of economies of scale, is lower than its average cost. Thus upstream production makes a notional loss, but this is more than covered by the notional profit earned downstream.

The resultant allocation of resources in the industry is not fully efficient, because consumers pay a monopoly price for the final product, and so demand is artificially restrained. However, the monopoly price is not so high as before, and so demand is not so restrained. Both profit and consumer surplus are therefore higher, and overall social welfare is increased.

There is an important qualification, however. The distortion of intermediate product prices arises only because the upstream monopolist does not impose a two-part tariff on downstream buyers. Using a two-part tariff the upstream producer could extract all its monopoly rents by charging downstream producers a fixed sum for a right to buy, and then supplying individual units at marginal cost. In response to such a strategy, however, downstream firms could merge in order to pay the fixed sum only once, and the monopolist would then have to respond by adjusting the fixed sum to the number of independent downstream firms. Implementing this strategy therefore requires more knowledge of the downstream firms than the upstream firm may possess.

A similar point applies to the final product market. If the final product were sold to consumers using a two-part tariff in which the marginal consumer paid only marginal cost then there would be no restraint of demand. This policy may be difficult for competitive downstream firms to implement, however. An advantage of internalization, therefore, is that by confronting consumers with a monopolist it is easier to implement a two-part tariff in the final product market. If this arrangement proves effective then the industry-wide profit of the monopolist will exceed the sum of profit and consumer surplus generated under the uniform price regime. Ironically, therefore, total monopoly becomes the socially optimal outcome.

15.7   SUNK COSTS

Fixed costs are not necessarily sunk costs. In the previous example, it may be possible to recover fixed costs by shutting down production and re-deploying resources to alternative uses. Such re-deployment is impossible where sunk costs are concerned. While most sunk costs are fixed, fixed costs are not necessarily sunk.

It is risky to commit sunk costs on the basis of promises made by other people. Consider again the case of a firm that has developed a new technology. This firm will already have sunk costs into R&D by the time that it is considering investment in production. Suppose that production requires specific assets that are useful only in conjunction with the new technology. The owner of the technology would like to license production to an independent firm, or to subcontract production whilst retaining control over distribution. In either case the independent producer needs to invest in specific equipment whose value is underpinned only by the innovator's optimistic assessment of the technology. Suppose that there is no decisive evidence on the value of the technology. If a producer does not share the innovator's optimism then the innovator will need to insure them against the risk that the technology is worthless. Unlike the previous case, differences of opinion cannot be resolved by appeal to objective evidence, whether secret or not.

It is characteristic of innovators that they are often more optimistic about their technology than anyone else; this partly explains why they often face little competition in the early phases of exploitation. But if no one shares their optimism then the insurance premium they face may be very high. They may have to loan the funds with which to purchase the capital equipment themselves; indeed, if they retain the equipment as collateral for the loan then they effectively own the equipment. Alternatively, they may offer a forward contract to the producer, guaranteeing to buy a fixed amount of product at a stipulated price. The profit from this stream of output may be sufficient for the producer to repay the loan they take out to buy the equipment. Once again, the producer is effectively purchasing the equipment on behalf of the producer – this time by making promises in kind.

Forward contracts have a number of practical limitations, however. The first is that they can be very rigid. At the time the contract is made there may be considerable uncertainty on the buyer's part, for example, the innovator may be unsure precisely how large the market is and therefore how much product they wish to buy. One solution to this is to make the contract contingent – more like a conventional insurance contract, in other words. Thus the innovator may agree to buy a large quantity only on condition that future trading conditions are good. Such conditions complicate the contract, however. The more conditions that are stipulated, the more finely tuned is the insurance, but the greater is the complexity in writing and comprehending the contract (Arrow, 1975; Bernhardt, 1977; Carlton, 1979, 1983).

Furthermore, some of the contractual conditions may be ambiguous. This may allow each party to put a different interpretation on the contract, and where these rival interpretations are each self-serving, conflict may result. These differences may prove difficult to resolve through social arbitration or legal process.

A further risk is that one of the parties reneges on the contract. Recovery of consequential losses will be difficult if they have limited liability and are insolvent. In seeking to manage one set of risks, therefore, other risks are incurred, and sometimes the solution may turn out to be worse than the problem it attempts to solve.

Forward contracts can also be used to coordinate exploration and exploitation of new energy sources and raw materials. Once a new source has been identified, inter-related investments may be required in upstream extraction and downstream processing. If these investments are made by independent firms then each is exposed to the risk that the other may not make the complementary investment that is required to make the entire project work. Investments can in principle be coordinated through forward contracts in which the downstream party agrees to buy a stipulated amount of product and the upstream party agrees to supply it. If, however, a forward contract is difficult to enforce, then opportunities for strategic behaviour arise. This typically involves deferring investment until the other party has invested themselves. The greater the sunk costs, the greater the potential gains from such a strategy.

There are two main reasons for such behaviour, and they have rather different implications. The first is that each believes that the other knows something about the project that they do not, so that the other party's strategy signals their hidden knowledge. Each party can therefore free ride on the other's knowledge by being the last to invest.

The second possibility is that behaviour is purely strategic, in the sense that each party hopes to improve their negotiating position. Each party hopes to remain flexible whilst the other invests, with a view to re-negotiating the forward contract once the other party is in a vulnerable position. Unlike the previous case, the advantage of this strategy depends not so much on the sunk costs of the party that defers as on the sunk costs of the party that does not, since the latter determines how vulnerable the party is in the event of a forced renegotiation.

This second possibility has become known in the literature as the 'hold up' problem (Klein et al., 1978). It is often cited as though it were a generic phenomenon, and a major factor in most internalization decisions. In the light of the preceding discussion, however, it can be seen that it represents a very special motive for internalization and that there are many other motives that seem to be of equal, or even greater, practical importance.

The propensity of sunk costs to amplify subjective risks is a general feature of a market economy. For example, an innovator contemplating R&D could attempt to finance their R&D by raising funds from prospective buyers of the novel product. They would sell the product forward, contingent on it going into production, and use the payments to fund the R&D. In practice, though, the risks are potentially so high, and so difficult to assess, that few customers are willing to participate in such arrangements, and so instead the capital is typically provided by equity investors – such as private equity firms and venture capitalists – who specialize in vetting R&D programmes.

15.8   INSTITUTIONAL INFRASTRUCTURE: LAW, SOCIETY AND REPUTATION

The discussion of sunk costs highlights the importance of trust in the choice of contractual arrangements. A similar point emerged from the earlier analysis of quality control. It is important not only to be able to trust people, but also to know who can be trusted. Institutions can make an important contribution in both respects (Podolny and Page, 1998; Kranton and Minehart, 2001).

Trust is to some extent a subjective issue – it is a belief that other people are predictable – and in particular that they can be expected to do the right thing, in terms of the contract they have made. There is no advantage in being gullible, however, and believing that people can be trusted when they cannot. It is warranted trust that is valuable, that is, trust that accords with the way people actually behave. Warranted trust is an equilibrium concept, in the sense that people whose trust is warranted have no reason to change their behaviour in the light of actual outcomes. In the following discussion, therefore, trust signifies warranted trust.

In the discussion of quality control a distinction was drawn between honesty and competence, and this distinction can also be applied to trust. Trusting in someone's honesty does not imply trusting in their competence, and vice versa. It is generally necessary to trust in both honesty and competence in order to rely on a person doing the right thing.

Where there is trust, a wider range of contractual arrangements becomes viable (Blois, 1972; Richardson, 1972). 'Relational contracts' can be made, in which there is a tacit agreement that certain aspects of a contract can be renegotiated if unforeseen circumstances arise (Baker et al., 2002). This makes long-term contracts – such as the forward contracts described above – more attractive because it is no longer necessary to specify explicitly all the contingencies that might arise.

Trust also makes joint ventures viable. Superficially, a 50:50 joint venture, in which two firms each own half the equity in a venture, creates enormous risks because of the ambiguity of control. Joint ventures can offer significant benefits, however, which will be lost if the risks created by ambiguity cannot be resolved. Joint ventures allow two firms, each of whom is engaged in several different activities, to integrate their operation with regard to one of these activities whilst maintaining independence in respect of others. They also provide a forum in which dominant firms can cooperate without being penalized by anti-trust authorities. Finally, each firm acquires an option to increase their commitment by buying out their partner, or reducing their commitment by selling out to them. Investing in sufficient trust to manage ambiguity can therefore provide handsome dividends to joint venture partners. These are particularly significant for pre-competitive R&D partnerships in innovative global industries.

A person who is trusted by one person may well be trusted by another. This is for two reasons. The first is that different people may all have direct experience of the way that a given person behaves; this is likely where the person concerned is high profile and acts in a public arena. The second is that the person concerned has acquired a reputation, so that trust is based upon second-hand information, for example, people with direct knowledge of the person share their experiences with others.

Since it is risky to acquire reputation from a potentially unreliable source, reputations tend to be made by specialized reputation brokers – namely people who have a reputation for knowing how other people behave. These people are often the leaders of social groups. People seeking to enhance their reputations may compete to join elite social groups. Membership may therefore be regulated to preserve the members' rents and the leader's perks. Access to a group may be regulated by wealth, for example, where high subscriptions are charged; by competence, for example, where entry is by examination; or by existing reputation, for example, where election is concerned. A similar point applies to firms or other organizations seeking to improve their reputation who apply for membership of trade associations, for royal patronage, and government endorsement and so on.

People are often concerned much more about their reputation with certain types of people or institutions than with others. This is mainly for instrumental reasons – a person's reputation with someone they are never likely to meet or to do business with has little direct impact on welfare. Concern with reputation need not be purely instrumental, however. People may value reputation in its own right as well as a means to material ends. In particular people may be concerned with their reputation with themselves. They may seek to be honest and competent simply to preserve or enhance their own self-esteem. Advocates of opportunism often suggest that such incentives are weak, despite the historical evidence of their strength amongst religious groups such as Quakers and

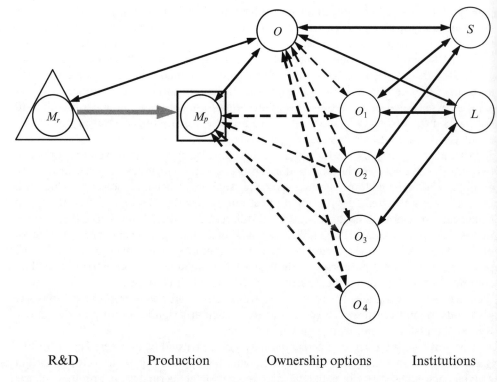

R&D   Production   Ownership options   Institutions

Figure 15.6   Influence of social group membership and legal jurisdiction on
*   internalization strategy*

Methodists. They also overlook the fact that the 'founding father' of modern economics
– Adam Smith – emphasized the role of self-reputation, in the form of conscience, in his
earliest analysis of market behaviour.

  Because of their disdain for social institutions, many transaction cost theorists emphasize the role of law rather than society in the enforcement of contracts. Legal mechanisms
are often very expensive, however, and are often limited in their coverage too (as noted
in the earlier discussion of intellectual property rights). Furthermore, legal systems are
restricted territorially because they are products of individual states. Despite the prolifer-
ation of treaties and inter-governmental organizations, it remains more costly to enforce
international contracts than purely national ones. Historically, international traders
have exploited family and community networks by trading within diaspora where contracts can be enforced through social conventions instead. International trade and investment flows continue to be concentrated between culturally similar communities despite
the harmonization of international laws and cheaper transport and communications.
Evidence suggests, therefore, that both social and legal institutions are important in
enforcing contracts, and are therefore a significant influence on internalization decisions.

  The interaction of social and legal institutions is illustrated schematically in Figure
15.6, which is an extension of Figure 15.3. The figure illustrates the production options
available to the owner, *O*, of a new technology. Five options are illustrated; one involves

internalizing production and the other involves a choice of independent licensees. Licensee 1 is a low-risk choice because they belong to the same social group, S, as the owner, and also operate under the same legal system, L. Licensee 2 affords moderate risk because although they belong to the same social group they operate under a different legal system (like the foreign members of a diaspora). Licensee 3 also affords moderate risk because although they operate under the same legal system they belong to a different social group. Licensee 4 is the highest risk option because they neither belong to the same social group nor operate under the same system of law. So far as the internalization decision is concerned, therefore, the critical choice is between internalization and the best of the external options, which is likely to be option 1.

The differences between these options means that they cannot easily be compared in terms of price alone. Thus licensee 4 might offer the best terms for a licence, but only because they plan to default because an agreement with them will be difficult to enforce. There may, of course, be differences between these licensees in terms of competence as well as honesty, and the owner of the technology must take account of such differences in reaching a final judgement. This judgement may prove difficult if it involves a trade-off between the competency and the honesty of alternative licensees.

15.9   OTHER INSTITUTIONAL FACTORS

The enforcement of contracts is not the only role of institutions. Institutions also reduce communication costs and structure the flow of information (Casson and Wadeson, 1996). In an economy that possesses effective market institutions a firm requiring intermediate inputs or seeking buyers for intermediate outputs can advertise, or can scan the advertisements placed by others. To compare the prices and products offered by alternative suppliers the firms can go to a central place – perhaps a trade fair or a specialized industrial district. This not only informs the firm of the different varieties of products available but also facilitates the negotiation of a competitive price. Having struck a deal, the firm can pay for its inputs, or receive payment for its outputs, in a stable currency. In the absence of effective market institutions, advertising media, such as trade publications, may not be available; trade associations may be too weak to sponsor trade fairs, and the size of markets may be so small that specialized centres fail to emerge. The currency may be prone to inflation (so that contracts have to be index-linked), whilst weaknesses in the banking system may create a shortage of large-denomination currency in which payments can be made. Given the difficulties of searching out a customer or supplier, negotiating a deal and making payment, a firm may prefer to internalize instead.

Where markets are ineffective, prices are likely to be more volatile because it is difficult for buyers and sellers to make alternative arrangements when temporary scarcities or gluts develop for specific commodities. Short-run prices may deviate considerably from long-run equilibrium levels. Government may therefore intervene to control prices. This, however, may only exacerbate the problem in the long run. When prices are fixed at disequilibrium levels, and quantities are consequently rationed, the incentive to internalize is further increased.

The problems of using the market may be reinforced by differences in language, culture, currency and trading standards – differences that are particularly acute in international markets. Even in a well-developed market economy there may be prob lems in marketing certain types of intermediate product. Where a firm requires a nove input, there may be no one available that can produce it. If an input is highly different ated, there may be no one who possesses the relevant production skills. Even if ther is, it may be difficult to make contact with them and explain to them precisely what i required. The natural response is to 'do it yourself', that is, for the buyer to internaliz production.

Novel and specific inputs are characteristic of the early stages of the development c an industry. This suggests that internalization will be characteristic of the early stages o industry growth, and that 'disintegration' will occur as an industry matures. As produc designs become more standardized, competitive markets for intermediate product emerge, and so 'disintegration' occurs as the industry matures. Firms begin to 'out source' products they previously produced 'in house'. This process is sometimes referrec to as the 'hollowing out' of the firm.

Firms can internalize by either taking over existing firms or setting up a 'greenfield operation of their own. Where the minimum efficient scale of production is large rela tive to the size of the market, merger or acquisition involving an existing facility has the advantage that it does not add to industry capacity. Neither does it intensify competitio because it simply changes the ownership of one of the competing firms. Firms may resis takeover, however; family firms may resent the loss of independence, whilst manage of joint stock companies may resist because their jobs are at risk. These factors raise the cost of takeover and thereby discourage internalization in cases where greenfield investment is not a viable option.

Fiscal factors can also influence internalization. The best-known example concerns transfer pricing. Where two related activities are located in different countries and are subject to different marginal rates of profits tax, overall tax liability is minimized by imputing all profit to the low tax activity. This can be effected by manipulating the internal transfer for intermediate products. In some cases a virtual intermediate product – such as 'management services' – may be invented for this purpose. Internalization is normally required for this purpose. To avoid confusing managerial decisions, two sets of accounts need to be produced: the tax accounts and a set of management accounts in which intermediate products are priced at their true opportunity costs. The incentives for transfer pricing are greatest where tax rates differ most and where there are no external market prices that tax authorities can use to benchmark internal prices.

A related point is that internalization allows firms to by-pass rigidities in market prices imposed by government regulation, since internal prices cannot be regulated so easily as external ones. This view is supported by evidence that highly regulated national economies are often dominated by large integrated firms.

15.10   INTERNALIZATION THEORY AND TRANSACTION COST THEORY: A COMPARISON

Internalization theory is superficially similar to transaction cost theory, as developed by Williamson (1985, 1991, 1996) and his followers, but in practice there are several important differences.

Internalization theory develops a pure Coasian tradition, whilst transaction cost theory integrates Coase's ideas with those of the behaviourist Herbert Simon and the traditional American institutionalist John Commons (Williamson, 1975). Following Simon, 'bounded rationality' plays a major role in transaction cost theory, whereas in internalization theory it plays no role at all (Foss, 2003). Internalization theory uses information costs to explain the phenomena that transaction costs impute to bounded rationality. Variations in information costs explain why certain decisions deviate more from the full information ideal than others, whereas bounded rationality implicitly assumes the same amount of deviation everywhere. In addition, internalization theory assumes that individuals are aware of information costs and respond to them in a rational way, whereas bounded rationality theory is often ambiguous on this point.

Transaction cost theory introduces the concept of 'opportunism' – using the term to signify self-seeking with guile (Williamson, 1985). This concept is missing from Coase and from internalization theory. Transaction cost theory treats opportunism as a pervasive phenomenon. Internalization theory, by contrast, does not assume self-seeking behaviour, although it recognizes the importance of profit-maximization in the survival and growth of firms. Internalization theory follows mainstream economics in assuming that individual decision-makers can rank perceived alternatives in a consistent logical order, but it does not assume that this ordering necessarily reflects a narrow materialistic self-interest. This allows internalization theory to analyse the boundaries, not only of firms, but of all institutions, including non-profit and charitable institutions that do not have self-seeking objectives.

Internalization theory identifies a wide range of factors that influence the boundaries of the firm. Transaction cost theory, by contrast, emphasizes just a small subset of these factors. Early versions of the theory emphasized the frequency of transacting (Williamson, 1975), which evidence suggests has limited significance, and which plays no role in internalization theory. Later versions have emphasized the 'hold up' problem, which is deemed to be particularly significant in bilateral monopolies with large sunk costs (Williamson, 1983, 1985; Macher and Richman, 2008). However, such cases represent only a small proportion of the actual cases in which internalization occurs. In so far as internalization theory highlights specific factors, it emphasizes the limited scope of property rights and the problems of quality control. It also highlights knowledge flows, on the grounds that commodity flows are often internalized because of common dependence on knowledge, and that the global exploitation of knowledge explains the emergence of multinational enterprise.

Internalization theory thus adopts a holistic view of the economy, in which the boundaries between firms are constantly being re-drawn as knowledge accumulates and the structure of the economy adjusts to recurrent shocks. Such a system cannot be adequately analysed by focusing on a single transaction, and ignoring all the volatility in the environment within which that transaction takes place, as transaction cost theory attempts to do. As Wadeson (2009) has recently shown, contracts entered into by firms constrain the subsequent contractual options available to the firms in respect of other parties, and so a change in the conditions under which other parties operate can trigger changes in seemingly unrelated parts of the economy. Casson (2010) makes a similar point regarding the global economy: changes in the contractual arrangements by which a firm serves one foreign market may lead to changes in the way that its other markets are served. These interdependencies were fundamental to Coase's early thinking, but have been lost sight of in much recent analysis.

15.11   CONCLUSIONS

When Coase first set out the principles of internalization, he did so in the context of a national economy. This context was suggested by contemporary debate on the relative merits of capitalism and socialism, and the relative advantages of 'planning' and 'prices' in the allocation of resources. Coase's genius was to recognize that a market economy could evolve privately owned planning units – namely firms – in direct response to market forces. In contrast to government, which is funded by taxes, firms were funded by sales revenue. It was therefore the 'votes' of individual consumers that determined which firms came into being and which products they produced. Internalization explained the boundaries of these firms.

In today's world it is the global economy rather than the national economy that is the natural unit of analysis (Casson, 2000). Focusing on the global economy not only draws attention to international political rivalries but also highlights the fact that production and knowledge generation are spatially distributed. Modern internalization theory reflects this view by analysing the economy as a collection of interdependent specialized activities connected by a web of intermediate product flows. By explaining which types of flow will be internalized, it predicts the pattern of firms that will emerge and locates the boundaries between these firms. It thereby makes a major contribution to our understanding of the modern global economy.

REFERENCES

Alchian, A. and H. Demsetz (1972) Production, information costs, and economic organization, *American Economic Review*, **62**(5), 777–95.
Arrow, K.J. (1975) Vertical integration and communication, *The Bell Journal of Economics*, **6**(1), 173–83.
Baker, G., R. Gibbons and K. Murphy (2002) Relational contracts and the theory of the firm, *Quarterly Journal of Economics*, **117**(1), 39–84.
Bernhardt, I. (1977) Vertical integration and demand variability, *The Journal of Industrial Economics*, **25**(3), 213–29.
Blois, K.J. (1972) Vertical quasi-integration, *Journal of Industrial Economics*, **20**(3), 253–72.
Buckley, P.J. and Mark Casson (1976) *The Future of Multinational Enterprise*, London: Macmillan.
Carlton, D.W. (1979) Vertical integration in competitive markets under uncertainty, *The Journal of Industrial Economics*, **27**(3), 189–209.
Carlton, D.W. (1983) Equilibrium fluctuations when price and delivery lags clear the market, *Bell Journal of Economics*, **14**(2), 562–72.
Casson, M. (1994) Why are firms hierarchical? *Journal of the Economics of Business*, **1**(1), 47–76.
Casson, M. (1997) *Information and Organization: A New Perspective on the Theory of the Firm*, Oxford: Oxford University Press.
Casson, M. (2000) *Economics of International Business: A New Research Agenda*, Cheltenham, UK and Northampton, MA, USA: Edward Elgar
Casson, M. (2005) Entrepreneurship and the theory of the firm, *Journal of Economic Behavior & Organization*, **58**(2), 327–48.
Casson, M. (2010) Towards a general theory of international business: extending internalization theory, *University of Reading Discussion Papers in Economics and Management*.

Casson, M. and N. Wadeson (1996) Information strategies and the theory of the firm, *International Journal of the Economics of Business*, **3**(3), 307–30.

Coase, R. (1937) The nature of the firm, *Economica*, **4**(16), 386–405.

Demsetz, H. (1988) The theory of the firm revisited, *Journal of Law, Economics & Organization*, **4**(1), 141–61.

Foss, N. (2003) Bounded rationality in the economics of organization: 'Much cited and little used', *Journal of Economic Psychology*, **24**(2), 245–64.

Grant, R. (1996) Toward a knowledge-based theory of the firm, *Strategic Management Journal*, **17**, 109–22.

Grossman, S. and O. Hart (1986) The costs and benefits of ownership: a theory of vertical and lateral integration, *Journal of Political Economy*, **94**(4), 691–719.

Hart, O. (1995) *Firms, Contracts, and Financial Structure*, Oxford: Oxford University Press.

Hart, O. and J. Moore (1990) Property rights and the nature of the firm, *Journal of Political Economy*, **98**(6), 1119–58.

Hayek, F.A. (1937) Economics and knowledge, *Economica*, **4**(13), 33–54.

Klein, B., R.G. Crawford and A.A. Alchian (1978) Vertical integration, appropriable rents, and the competitive contracting process, *Journal of Law & Economics*, **21**(2), 297–326.

Kranton, R.E. and D.F. Minehart (2001) A theory of buyer–seller networks, *The American Economic Review*, **91**(3), 485–508.

Langlois, R.N. and P.L. Robertson (1993) Business organization as a coordination problem: towards a dynamic theory of the boundaries of the firm, *Business and Economic History*, **22**(1), 31–41.

Loasby, B.J. (1998) The organisation of capabilities, *Journal of Economic Behavior & Organization*, **35**(2), 139–60.

Macher, J.T. and B.D. Richman (2008) Transaction cost economics: an assessment of empirical research in the social sciences, *Business and Politics*, **10**(1), Article 1.

Marshall, A. (1890) *Principles of Economics*, London: Macmillan.

Maskin, E. and J. Tirole (1999) Two remarks on the property-rights literature, *The Review of Economic Studies*, **66**(1), 139–49.

Parmigiani, A. (2007) Why do firms both make and buy? An investigation of concurrent sourcing, *Strategic Management Journal*, **28**(3), 285–311.

Podolny, J. and K. Page (1998) Network forms of organization, *Annual Review of Sociology*, **24**(1), 57–76.

Richardson, G.B. (1972) The organisation of industry, *Economic Journal*, **82**(327), 883–96.

Wadeson, N.S. (2009) Market disequilibrium: the firm and the coordination of productive resources, paper presented at the DRUID Summer Conference, available at: www2.druid.dk/conferences/viewpaper.php?id=5567&cf=32; accessed 19 January 2012.

Walras, L. ([1874] 1954) *Elements of Pure Economics* (trans. W. Jaffe), London: George Allen & Unwin.

Williamson, O.E. (1971) The vertical integration of production: market failure considerations, *American Economic Review*, **61**(2), 112–23.

Williamson, O.E. (1975) *Markets and Hierarchies: Analysis and Antitrust Implications*, New York: The Free Press.

Williamson, O.E. (1983) Credible commitments: using hostages to support exchange, *American Economic Review*, **73**(4), 519–40.

Williamson, O.E. (1985) *The Economic Institutions of Capitalism: Firms, Markets and Relational Contracting*, New York: The Free Press.

Williamson, O.E. (1991) Comparative economic organization: the analysis of discrete structural alternatives, *Administrative Science Quarterly*, **36**(2), 269–96.

Williamson, O.E. (1996) *The Mechanisms of Governance*, Oxford: Oxford University Press.

16 The Japanese firm: from the analysis of a model to the understanding of its increasing heterogeneity
Sébastien Lechevalier

16.1 INTRODUCTION

From the mid-1980s to the mid-1990s, many papers with different backgrounds investigated the specificities of Japanese firms in comparison to their American or European counterparts, from the perspectives of both the internal structure and the external relationships. These studies have shown that Japanese firms are significantly different from their American and European counterparts in some aspects of their organization and strategy, such as: corporate governance (Aoki, 1994), corporate finance (Sheard, 1989), objectives of the firm (Odagiri, 1994), internationalization strategies (Belderbos, 1997), and resort to subcontractors (Nishiguchi, 1994). Moreover, these characteristics seemed to lead to better performance (for a critical survey of this literature, see Aoki, 1990). This last stylized fact has indeed been the starting point of the research agenda on the Japanese firm, more than some specific practices that may have been explained by cultural reasons.

More than 20 years later, after almost 15 years of stagnation during the so-called 'Lost "Decade"' (1992–2005), we are far from that time, when the 'Japanese model of the firm' (J model) was celebrated as representing a new form of organization leading at the same time to higher performance and to better satisfaction for workers. It is fair to say that the Japanese firm is no longer at the top of the research agenda of researchers specializing in the theory and the empirics of the firm, outside Japan, the only exception being Toyota, which still attracts the interest of researchers, especially in the field of management studies. It leads us to raise the following questions. What do we know now about the Japanese firm? Did this model vanish? Is it a concept of the 1980s? Has this mode of organization not adapted to the new context since the mid-1990s?

What appears from the above is that the theories of the Japanese firm cannot be analyzed by abstracting them from the macro-context of the Japanese economy; they also cannot be separated from reflections in terms of diversity of capitalism. At the same time, the theories of the Japanese firm go much beyond the case of the Japanese economy or Japanese capitalism. One reason is that while the Japanese economy was facing economic stagnation, some of the organizational characteristics of the Japanese firm have been diffused: for example, the flexible organization mentioned in Thesmar and Thoenig (2000) is nothing but inspired by the J model. More generally and more importantly, the Japanese firm, as it has been theorized, has contributed to showing more than anything else the limits of the neoclassical theory of the firm as well as of some institutionalist theories. As emphasized by Aoki (1990):

The model that emerges to answer these questions turns out to be somewhat at odds with the standard contractual model of the firm that now prevails in the Anglo-American theoretical literature. . . . [There is] a need to broaden the scope and reorder the focus of the theory of the firm.

In this chapter, we will argue this is detrimental to our understanding of what a firm is for two reasons. First, the various theories of the Japanese firm have been deeply articulated to more general discussion on the theory of the firm and have important impacts on it. Second, Japanese firms experienced an important evolution from the late 1990s, which can be summarized as an increasing heterogeneity, which has important implication from empirical and theoretical points of view.

This chapter focuses on the theoretical dimension of the Japanese firm. However, as the various theories of the Japanese firm (including the ones by Aoki) were initially based on some stylized facts, which have evolved over time, it will also review various empirical contributions. Because of lack of space, this chapter will not deal specifically with the characteristics of the Japanese firm regarding innovation and global engagement, but rather focus on the classical theory of the Japanese firm and its aftermath, characterized by an increasing heterogeneity. However, these two dimensions will inevitably be discussed in the course of our argument. The rest of the chapter is organized as follows: in section 16.2, we introduce and discuss the classical model of the Japanese firm; in section 16.3, we introduce the most recent research on the increasing heterogeneity of the Japanese firm.

16.2   THE CLASSICAL MODEL OF THE JAPANESE FIRM

It is fair to say that there are at least as many theories of the Japanese firm as there are theoreticians (some of them have indeed proposed more than one theory. . .). Among these numerous theories of the Japanese firm, we have selected the ones proposed by Aoki and Fujimoto, because of their influence, their common points (the analysis of Toyota system), and their differences, as will be emphasized later.

The basic idea of this section is that the various theories of the Japanese firm are directly connected to more general theories of the firm. For example, Aoki and Fujimoto's theories are respectively connected to the transaction cost approach and to the resource-based view of the firm. At the same time, some of their hypotheses and results are at odds with the general theories to which they refer. It means that they are not a simple extension of previous models. Their contribution to general theories should be considered seriously. According to us, their originality comes at the same time from new facts that have not been considered by other theories (typically some characteristics of the Japanese firm) and by fresh ideas (for example, the analysis of technology and operations management or the tentative link between historical and functional analyses in Fujimoto's approach). In return, their ambition is to generalize existing theories or subsume them under more general approaches. It is worth noting that both theories are inspired by the very specific case of Toyota, which is maybe the archetype of manufacturing companies in the second half of the twentieth century.

16.2.1   From Paradoxical Facts to the Search for a Rational Model of the Japanese Firm

The starting point of all the attempts to propose theories of the J firm is the recognition of the existence of various characteristics that seem to be specific to the Japanese firm and sometimes at odds with the conventional understanding of the firm. Among them, one can cite the *kanban* system (just-in-time method) and other practices of manufacturing operations, the long-term employment, the seniority wage, the enterprise unionism, the bonus system, the Main Bank system, the *keiretsu*, the subcontracting system.[1] It means that all theories of the Japanese firm are deeply rooted in the concrete observation of firms' characteristics and behaviors.[2]

Having identified these characteristics and their apparent contradiction with mainstream theories of the firm, the next question is to know whether they are the outcome of cultural practices or the result of rational choices in specific environments and contexts. This question can be formulated even more simply as follows: is the J model rational? A very classical cultural explanation is the one proposed by Michio Morishima (1988). His approach is not a theory of the firm but it has some implications for understanding the characteristics above. To put it briefly, from his perspective, the Japanese firm is the result of cultural practices emphasizing the group orientation, the long-term perspective, and the respect for hierarchy. With this model, it is possible to explain such characteristics as the long-term employment, the implication of workers, and so on.

However, this kind of cultural explanation, focusing on structural invariants to explain some key features of the Japanese firm does not pass the empirical test provided by business and economic history works. It is even possible to say that these works play the same role for the theories of the Japanese firm as do Chandler's works in the case of the American firm. The J firm, as it is analyzed in the 1980s, is essentially a historical construction. Economic historians such as Okazaki (in Okazaki and Okuno-Fujiwara, 1999), social historians (Gordon, 1988), labor economists (Koike, 1988) or financial specialists (Hoshi and Kashyap, 2001) have shown that most of the characteristics of the J firm in the 1980s were absent before World War II, when all the institutions of J capitalism were much more market oriented. For example, in the interwar period, the Japanese labor market was characterized by a high turnover and external flexibility; as for corporate finance, it was resting on capital markets, not on institutions such as the Main Bank. The Japanese firm, as we know it in the 1980s, emerged from the war; it was then stabilized during the long-term growth period (1950s–80s). These historical works lead us to confirm that the J model of the firm does not exist in the middle of nowhere but is strongly determined by its institutional environment (see, for example, Okazaki and Okuno-Fujiwara, 1999; Hoshi and Kashyap, 2001).

To summarize, it is possible to say that both this question about the rationality of the Japanese firm and the criticism of the culturalist answer are at the origin of the various theories of the Japanese firm, which will be presented below.

16.2.2 Towards a Unified Theory of the J Firm, Beyond the Transaction Cost Approach: How Did the Work of Masahiko Aoki Deeply Change our Understanding of What a Firm Is?

Again, the starting point of the theories of the Japanese firm is the statement of its differences with conventional practices or models. Then, two questions are addressed. How much are these differences rational? Do they lead to superior performance?

Aoki's theory has changed over the years and depending on the context. It should be understood as various attempts to integrate the model of the Japanese firm in various more general models (e.g., the agency model in Aoki, 1990, the transaction cost theory in Aoki, 1994). Aoki's main purpose is indeed to establish the rationality of the model of the J firm. Despite these changes, the core of the theory has remained stable and can be characterized by the horizontal nature of the coordination and the hierarchical nature of the incentives system. To understand these specificities of the Japanese firm, Aoki systematically introduces them by contrasting them to the characteristics of the A(merican) firm or the H(ierarchical) mode.

More generally, according to Aoki (1990, 1994), the main features of the J firm are the information system, the rank hierarchy (part of the incentive structure) and the associated employment relationship, the subcontracting relationship, and the Main Bank relationship. The starting point of this theory is the recognition that firms are information systems. The organizational schemes differ, depending on how these information processing activities are structured within the firm. To summarize, whereas the H mode has two essential features – the hierarchical separation between planning and implemental operation and the emphasis on the economies of specialization, the J mode is characterized by the horizontal coordination among operating units based on the sharing of ex post on-site information (learned results). Coordination of operations across workshops is often performed horizontally without managerial intervention. It means that operational workers also participate in considerable collective decision-making. Strategic corporate decisions are not made unilaterally by top management on the basis of centralizing relevant information but are rather formed inductively through intensive vertical exchange of information and opinions across various levels of administrative hierarchy. Those characteristics defy the usual modeling of the internal information system as a hierarchy, as in Williamson (1985).

What type of incentive structure is compatible with the information system as described above? When and how are workers motivated to cooperate in decentralized problem-solving as well as horizontal communications/coordination? The primary incentive device of the Japanese firm is an internal rank hierarchy along which employees compete for faster promotion. Rank hierarchy is status–wage differentiation that is not based on job classification. After entry at an identical starting point for a certain educational credential, employees compete for promotion in rank throughout their careers. The criteria for promotion are years of service and merit, with the latter not specifically related to particular jobs but to broadly defined problem-solving abilities, communication skills, and so on.

Due to lack of space, we skip the next step of the analysis, the one dedicated to the subcontracting relation, which is characterized by hierarchical transaction structuring (Nishiguchi, 1994). We focus rather on the Main Bank (MB) system, which plays a decisive role in the J model (Sheard, 1989). The MB is not the main lender (whose share is strictly limited by regulation). It plays the role of manager of a loan consortium of banks and is responsible for closely monitoring the business affairs of the company. If the company suffers a business crisis, the MB assumes major responsibility for various rescue operations. In the normal course of events, however, the MB exercises explicit control neither in the selection of management nor in corporate policy-making: well-run companies that incur little or no debt from banks appear to be virtually free from banks' intervention, and their management enjoys the highest degree of autonomy. Moreover, a second characteristic of the financial structure of the Japanese firm is that their management is insulated from takeover raids through the open market, because a large portion of the equities held by banks and other corporate entities are extremely stable.

After having analyzed these various characteristics, Aoki focuses on complementarities between these different dimensions, which are essential to understanding the coherence of this system of attributes. Complementarities are defined as follows: they describe relationships in which 'an attribute of one characteristic enhances the effectiveness (productivity) of attributes of other characteristics and vice versa' (Aoki, 1994, p. 22). For example, the hierarchical nature of the incentive scheme complements the non-hierarchical tendency of operational coordination and helps maintain organizational effectiveness and integrity.

Having determined the characteristics and the logic of the J model in contrast to the A model, is it possible to compare their respective performance and outcomes? Aoki's main conclusion is that their respective performance depends on the environment: to put it briefly, if it is extremely volatile or uncertain, or, on the contrary, very stable, the decentralized organization is not superior; in the intermediate case, where external environments are continually changing but not too drastically, the J mode is superior. This conclusion holds for different macroenvironments but also for different industries. Moreover, the J model is characterized by some specific outcomes. First, it pursues a higher growth rate in investment than the stockholder-controlled firm, mainly because the growth of the firm is favorable to the employees from the point of view of their promotion opportunities. Second, the level of employment security is higher but the expansion of the workforce relative to the growth of value-added tends to be limited. Third, the J firm seeks innovative opportunities by developing an in-house knowledge base rather than pursuing breakthrough innovation requiring an entirely new organization of its R&D team.

16.2.3   Transition: Transaction Cost Versus a Production-oriented Theory of the Firm?

What Langlois and Foss wrote in 1999 (p. 202) about the 'general' theories of the firm is also true in the case of the Japanese firm:

> [T]he one-sided concentration on incentive conflicts has left something out. Specifically, the economics of organization literature has tended to overlook the production side of the firm. . . . The emergence of what we call the capabilities view. . .represents a revitalized attention to the importance of production costs for understanding the problem of economic organization.

As recalled in Chapter 20 of this volume, the 'competence approach' (or 'capabilities', or 'dynamic capabilities') emerged in the first half of the 1990s with seminal papers such as

Langlois and Robertson (1995) or Teece and Pisano (1994). This approach focuses on the idea that much knowledge is tacit and can be acquired only through a time-consuming process of learning by doing. In this world, firms will not confront the same production costs for the same type of productive ability. This is a key point for the understanding of the source of firm heterogeneity, which we will go back to later.

In the context of the Japanese firm, the assessment of Langlois and Foss (1999) sounds particularly pertinent. Partly in relation to this theoretical trend, partly independently of it, Takahiro Fujimoto develops, a little later than Aoki, a theory of the capabilities of the Japanese firm. The contribution of Fujimoto in various papers and books (Fujimoto, 1999, 2003) clearly reintroduces the production side at the center of the theory of the firm, in an approach that owes a lot to management studies – Fujimoto is first of all a specialist of management and production design in the car industry, and his most representative contribution in this field is the book published in 1991 with K.B. Clark (Clark and Fujimoto, 1991) – and to the evolutionary theories of the firm. Like Aoki, the main source of inspiration is Toyota (and the car industry in general) but the path followed by the theory is quite different, because the basic research question is not the same.[3]

16.2.4   Toyota and Beyond: The Contribution of Takahiro Fujimoto and the Resource-capability-based Theory of the Japanese Firm with an Evolutionary Flavor

The initial question addressed by Fujimoto is indeed about neither the nature/boundaries of the Japanese firm nor the rationality of the organizational mode of the J firm. Rather, it concerns the source of its competitive strength and of the evolution of its organization. More precisely, the starting point is the following: how do manufacturing companies such as Toyota, despite uncertain and highly competitive markets consistently outperform their rivals over a long period of time? There is now a consensus that the Toyota production system (TPS) and total quality control (TQC) have provided a definite source of competitive advantage to Toyota, along with the company's product development capabilities and its effective relationships with suppliers. What underlies this explanation is the idea that a company such as Toyota possesses a set of firm-specific and difficult to imitate resources and routines on which is based its high competitive performance. These characteristics are called 'organizational capabilities', in reference to the resource-capability-based approaches.

However, the next question is the following: from where do these capabilities come? How were they formed in the first place: by chance, or through a deliberate and rational plan? The originality of the answer by Fujimoto lies in the introduction of three layers:

- The *routinized manufacturing capability*, with typical examples being the just-in-time or the *kanban* system.
- The *routinized learning capability*, the best example being the *kaizen*, the routinized ability for continuous improvements. More generally, it includes routines for problem identification, for problem-solving and for solution retention.
- The *evolutionary learning capability*, which describes an organization's overall ability to evolve competitive routines even in a highly uncertain environment. It refers to a firm's ability to build a competitive set of routine capabilities as the system emerges. Companies such as Toyota, which durably outperform other

companies, not only implement the right systems or routines at a certain point of time but also have a long-term ability to produce effective routines in changing environments.

This leads Fujimoto to specify his understanding of the organizational change within firms such as Toyota. His basic point is that it is neither the result of rational planning nor a purely random matter, but rather of a *multi-path emergence* of the system, which gives place to random trials, rational calculation, environmental constraints, entrepreneurial vision, knowledge transfer, and so on. An important implication of this is that it would be completely misleading to study the Toyota system from a static point of view, as it is a historical construction. The key to understanding why it has outperformed other corporate systems lies in the non-routinized learning capability, namely the third layers analyzed by Fujimoto.

This analysis of organizational routines and change within a single firm is a convincing answer to the question of long-term higher performance of some firms over others. However, as Fujimoto himself recognizes in his 1999 book, *The Evolution of a Manufacturing System at Toyota*, the main limitation of this approach focusing on one particular company is that it does not allow us to understand the interfirm heterogeneity in industry dynamics, contrary to the results of more classical evolutionary theories.

This limitation is related to a more general problem, the fact that theories until the late 1990s have tended to emphasize the differences between firms of different types of capitalism and to underestimate the heterogeneity of firms within a type of capitalism (Deeg and Jackson, 2006; Lechevalier, 2007). What we have learnt from the last 15 years is that the homogeneity of the Japanese firm has been exaggerated. Generally speaking, theories of the variety of capitalism are unable to analyze the diversity of firms within a type of capitalism. In the case of Japanese capitalism, Lechevalier (2007) reviews three theories (varieties of capitalism; comparative institutional analysis; and the regulation theory) and shows their tendency to characterize each form of capitalism by a dominant type of firm. The evolution in the 1990s, which is the object of the next section, shows that it is more than urgent to combine this kind of theory with approaches taking into account interfirm heterogeneity. Fujimoto does not say anything else beyond mentioning researches that go beyond his own approach, namely the various by GERPISA, which emphasize the heterogeneity of firms' profit strategies within the car industry (Boyer et al., 1998; Freyssenet et al., 1998).

16.2.5   Epilog: After Aoki and Fujimoto, the Aftermath of the Classical Theories of the Japanese Firm

Before turning to reviewing the most recent research on the Japanese firm, it is worth briefly mentioning the impact of the 1980s to early 1990s' theories of the Japanese firm outside Japan, after the height of the theory of the Japanese firm. A first point concerns the increasing importance of Toyota, not only for the theory of the Japanese firm, not only for management studies, but also much beyond. It has become common to refer to *Toyotism*, without reference to the J firm or to Toyota, to describe a post-Fordist organization of work, being characterized as flexible, 'stakhanovist' or 'lean' (Askhenazy, 1998; Thesmar and Thoenig, 2000). This fact cannot only be explained by the strength of the theory of the Japanese firm but also by the success of this leading manufacturing company, whose work organization has been the object of numerous transfer attempts in other companies or countries (Lechevalier, 2005).

A second point concerns more specifically the fate of Aoki's approach. Two trends can be distinguished. On the one hand, this theory has been criticized by such 'revisionist' authors as Miwa (1996), who have argued that Aoki has exaggerated the specificities of the Japanese firm and the differences with the American firm. On the other hand, more positively, it is worth noting that the cultural explanations of the Japanese mode of organization have lost their influence. It means that Aoki and others have convincingly shown that, whatever the type and degree of differences between the American and European firm, the organization of the Japanese firm is rational.

However, the most important trend is that the number of studies aiming at analyzing some characteristics of the Japanese firm, at both theoretical and empirical levels, decreased sharply, after the mid-1990s. The reasons are easy to find in the crisis that the Japanese economy has faced from the early 1990s, after the collapse of the 'Bubble'. As the explanations of the Japanese 'miracle' from the 1950s to the 1980s – that is, a long period of high growth and much better performance than the US and the European economies even after the oil shocks – have very often referred to the very specific model of the firm, it is understandable that this model has been interpreted as the cause of the crisis.[4] Suddenly, the long-term perspective of the Japanese firm, once celebrated as a new model, has been criticized, as well as the lack of respect for such golden principles as shareholder value. A common idea is that the Japanese firm has lost its comparative/competitive advantage (and therefore the Japanese economy) in a new context characterized by two new waves of globalization and technical progress.

In fact, from the mid-1990s, some important evolutions have been observed in Japan to the point that it is possible to ask whether the Japanese firm converges towards the American model, after 20 years of institutional change. This evolution and this question do not only concern the Japanese firm. Japan shares with Germany increasing pressures to adapt its model to a new context (Aoki et al., 2007). These pressures particularly concern corporate governance and interfirm relations (*keiretsu*, Japanese style of sub-contracting system, cross-shareholding). These evolutions are of importance for our general theory of the firm. If one effectively observes a convergence of the J firm towards the A firm, it does not mean that all the theories of the J firm were wrong in the 1980s. However, it would fair to say that, in this case, the differences between the A and the J firm, which were at the origin of most of the theories, did in fact correspond to a time lag before the full convergence to the equilibrium, that is, the A model.

16.3 CONVERGENCE TOWARDS THE 'A' MODEL OR EVOLVING DIVERSITY OF FIRMS? THE CASE OF JAPANESE FIRMS

After a gap in the interest in the Japanese firm, we observe a revival from the early 2000s. However, the focus has shifted from international comparison to the analysis of the heterogeneity of Japanese firms. This diversity is not specific to them but its contrast with previous analyses emphasizing the homogeneity of the Japanese model and the fact that this heterogeneity has significantly increased explains this new trend in the research on the Japanese firm (Lechevalier, 2011a). While it is more empirical than the research in the 1980s and early 1990s, it shares with previous analyses a high interest for our general understanding of firms.

16.3.1 The Empirical Evidence: Increasing Heterogeneity of Performance and Organization of Japanese Firms

We start this section by addressing two related empirical issues. What are the micro-foundations of the poor macro-performance of the Japanese economy? Did uniform organizational changes characterize Japanese firms from the mid-1990s?

As for the performance dimension, it would be of course misleading to consider that all firms necessarily perform poorly in a context of economic stagnation or crisis. However, what is surprising in the context of the late 1990s in Japan, in the midst of a macro-downturn, is that companies such as Toyota or Canon, which were considered the archetype of the J model, not only were not in crisis but were also enjoying record profits, whereas one observed at the same time a significant increase in the number of bankruptcies (Lechevalier, 2007). More generally, the stylized fact that has been uncovered by various studies is an increasing dispersion of productivity among Japanese firms during the 'Lost Decade' (Fukao and Kwon, 2006; Ito and Lechevalier, 2009). Moreover, this heterogeneity is observed for firms of similar size and belonging to the same narrowly defined sectors.

This increasing heterogeneity of firms also concerns their forms of organization and their strategies. Most of the studies could not find any convergence towards the American model but, rather, diverging evolution of the Japanese model of the firm (Aoki et al., 2007).[5] Because of the lack of space, we focus here on human resource management. The common picture regarding the HRM is that Japanese firms are moving away from the 'traditional' practices of long-term employment and seniority wages. An often-cited example concerns the rising share of 'non-regular' workers (e.g., temporary and part-time workers), which represent today more than one-third of the total workforce. However, some studies have shown that this overall increase in the use of non-regular workers does not concern all the firms (Lechevalier, 2007). Another employment-related dimension concerns the flexibility mode and the practice of downsizing. In the late 1990s to early 2000s, the simultaneous restructuring of firms in the electrical machinery sector has been interpreted as a sign of the convergence towards US-style downsizing practices. However, Hurlin and Lechevalier (2003) compare two periods of restructuring, the late 1970s and the late 1990s and show that the average speed of employment adjustment has been very stable, whereas the standard deviation of the individual speeds has increased. It confirms the increasing heterogeneity of HRM practices in Japan.

16.3.2 Looking for 'Models'

This growing diversity for each element of the firm's organization and strategy makes it particularly difficult to define the competing 'models' and therefore to check whether there is an emerging 'model' that performs better than others. The underlying issue is indeed to know whether this heterogeneity is temporary and corresponds to the path towards a new equilibrium with one dominant model of the firm, or if it is more structural and may last. This implies that, in looking for the roots of the competing models, we have to identify what makes them coherent. It can be basically found in the complementarities between the different elements of organization and strategy. This investigation regarding the complementarities has to be done in relation with the analysis of the micro-performance. The difficulty here is to conduct the analysis, without referring to any a priori classification, such as small versus large firms.

To achieve this research agenda, it is indeed preliminarily necessary to determine the nature of the line of cleavage among firms, which has potentially evolved. One attractive tool of analysis is the cluster analysis (Aoki et al., 2007). A first advantage of this approach is to go beyond a priori classification. A second one is to test the persistence of complementarities between various dimensions of the firm's organization (e.g., between human resource management and corporate finance) and to leave open the possibility of a *hybridization*, which can be interpreted as the sign of a weakening of previous complementarities. What are the main findings of Aoki et al. (2007), who focus on corporate governance? Their cluster analysis of about 900 firms listed on the Tokyo Stock Exchange reveals that Japanese corporations have grown remarkably diverse, forming three distinct clusters. The first one (67 percent of total employment but only 23 percent of firms, including Toyota and Canon) is comprised of corporations that combine market-based financing and long-term employment practices, in contradiction to predictions of the initial versions of Aoki's theory. They earn comparatively high profits and occupy a predominant position among Japanese firms. The second cluster (21 percent of all firms, and 10 percent of total employment) is comprised of firms that have managed to combine relational financing and market-based employment practices. Most of these firms are newly established and led by founders. They also record relatively high levels of performance. The third cluster (26 percent of all firms, and 11 percent of the workforce) encompasses traditional Japanese firms that combine relational financing with long-term employment practices. Finally, it is worth noting that the authors did not find any cluster corresponding to the A type of firm (even if a few firms did have practices that conform to this model).

To summarize, despite some methodological limitations of the cluster analysis, it is possible to find some emergent competing models. However, it does not allow us to determine whether one of them performs better than the others.

16.3.3 Why Some Firms Persistently Out-perform Others? The Japanese Case

This issue goes much beyond the Japanese case. Analyzing the relations between organization and performance is still at the frontier of the research on the heterogeneity of firms.[6] It is indeed fair to recognize that our theoretical understanding of this stylized fact is still very limited. We know that technology and governance explain many observed differences.[7] However, we have not fully identified the origin of this heterogeneity. Economic models generally assume that performance differences are exogenous, making it difficult to explain how firms' endogenous strategic choices interact. On the contrary, if significant complementarities are found to exist between different organizational or strategic dimensions of the firm, they may help to define coherent alternative *productive models*. An important task is therefore to identify coherent and viable strategies.

Ito and Lechevalier (2010) take up this challenge by investigating innovation and internationalization strategies of Japanese firms. They confirm the existence of complementarities between investments in R&D and exporting. They show that firms' endogenous choices regarding innovation and exports affect their performance, both in terms of productivity and survival. It is possible to establish a stable ranking of performance based on the strategies of firms, the best firms being characterized by both international engagement and R&D investment.[8]

16.3.4   Understanding the Determinants of the Evolving Heterogeneity of Firms

Finally, the recognition of the increasing diversity of Japanese firms, both in terms of performance and organization leads to the investigation of the determinants of the evolving heterogeneity. The most advance research concerns the analysis of the evolving dispersion of productivity. Among the various theoretical explanations, the impact of innovation is certainly the most popular. For example, Caselli (1999) built a model in which increasing productivity dispersion is generated by differences in the rate of technology adoption. Other theoretical explanations focus on the impact of internationalization (Melitz, 2003), market competition (Syverson, 2004), or institutional factors (Aoki, 2000). Let us specify this last explanation, which concerns not only the performance but also the organization and which has not been yet investigated by the mainstream literature. As emphasized by the theories of comparative capitalisms, the institutional changes that occurred in the 1980s and 1990s have affected the organizational diversity of firms and therefore their performance dispersion (Deeg and Jackson, 2006; Lechevalier, 2007). More precisely, the process of liberalization in the most developed economies did not lead to the disappearance of rules but rather to the coexistence of old and new rules. This institutional layering has led to the differential adoption of old and new business practices according to firm-specific characteristics.

On the empirical side, studies have tended to confirm the technology explanation (e.g., Dunne et al., 2004 for the case of the USA and Faggio et al., 2010 for the case of the UK). However, as for the Japanese case, Ito and Lechevalier (2009) find that the introduction of information and communication technologies (ICT) decreased the within-industry labor productivity dispersion, while internationalization and the trend toward a more oligopolistic market structure in some industries increased it. What their empirical study shows is that we cannot account for the increasing dispersion of productivity in Japanese firms by considering only the introduction of new technology. An empirical perspective that links the evolution of productivity dispersion to the evolution of organizational heterogeneity appears particularly promising, as it would further our understanding of the chain of causality. This is a possible direction for future research.

16.3.5   Putting the Heterogeneity of Firms at the Center of the Theory

Most of this section has dealt with the empirical evidence on the increasing heterogeneity of Japanese firms since the mid-1990s. In a final stage, we would like to draw some tentative conclusions regarding the theoretical implications of this empirical evidence.

What emerges is an unsatisfied feeling with regard to our theories of the firm, especially concerning our understanding of interfirm heterogeneity and its integration with a more general theory of the diversity of capitalism. However, it is fair to recognize that various evolutionary theories of the firm are more satisfying from this regard (Lechevalier, 2007). What we need is an alternative theory of the firm that allows us to combine the variety of capitalism and the diversity of firms. Evolutionist theories of the firm may be good candidates. Indeed, they are fundamentally interested in *discretionary* differences across firms. A part of evolutionist explanations lies in the statement of the considerable variation among firms in the technology they create and adopt and in the large gap between average practice and best practice. Another part of the explanation relates to the considerable range of flexibility left by technology and managerial instructions; that is why the internal organization of the firm matters. Beyond the Japanese case, the evolutionist approach appears to conciliate the heterogeneity of firms and the diversity of capitalism and it is not by chance that the most recent work by Aoki has a more pronounced evolutionary flavor (Aoki, 2010).[9]

16.4   CONCLUSION: DEFINING A NEW RESEARCH AGENDA ON THE JAPANESE FIRM

In this chapter, we have tried to show that the 1980s to early 1990s' theories of the Japanese firm have had an impact that went much beyond the understanding of Japanese capitalism. It is not exaggerating to say that they had a long-term impact on general theories of the firm. Although they are less fashionable in the USA and in Europe, these theories are still active and are in the process of generalization as shown by most recent work by Aoki (2010) or by Fujimoto (1999, 2003) (on design-based comparative advantage).

However, from our point of view, the most promising research agenda is not about the comparison between Japanese, American, and European firms. It should rather concern the analysis of the increasing heterogeneity of Japanese firms, in terms of performance and organization. The question of heterogeneity does not concern only the Japanese firm but the stylized facts that have been presented in the second part of this chapter show that it is a particularly interesting case. Questions that should be addressed as priority concern the origin of the heterogeneity of firms and the determinants of the evolution of this heterogeneity.

Moreover, another related issue concerns the generalization of theories of the diversity of capitalism, which should directly address this issue of interfirm heterogeneity within a given form of capitalism (Lechevalier, 2011b). The Japanese example shows that it is misleading to define a type of capitalism based on a homogeneous model of firm. This point also has important implications for our understanding of institutional change, which should be micro-founded in a specific way. Institutional change fundamentally depends on its mediation by firms and on the evolving composition of the economy in terms of 'models' at the firm level. However, this relation between the composition of the economy and the institutional change is characterized by important non-linearities and is therefore far from being mechanical. The concept of coordination provides a tool to analyze the complex process of dynamic aggregation and of articulation between the micro- and the aggregate levels of change (Lechevalier, 2007). These are directions for further research on the Japanese firm.

NOTES

1. Aoki (1990) gives usual references to studies that have specifically studied each of these dimensions.
2. For example, Aoki himself has conducted a number of interviews and field studies, before elaborating hi theory.
3. We will focus in this presentation on the capabilities perspective that Fujimoto adopts in this book however, we should not forget to mention that in Chapter 4, he adopts an alternative framework very clos to the one by Aoki. It shows that these two views are not in opposition but complementary.
4. It is important to understand that the 'Lost Decade' does not mean that the Japanese firm as a real entity (not as a concept) has failed. The Lost Decade is a macro- and institutional crisis, not a micro-crisis. On proof that we will emphasize later is that at the time the Japanese economy was stagnating such companie like Toyota or Canon were enjoying record profits.
5. The critical point here does not concern the static heterogeneity of the firm but its evolution, as it will b emphasized later.
6. See 'Inter-firm heterogeneity: nature, sources and consequences for industrial dynamics', *Industrial an Corporate Change*, **20**(1), February 2011, Special Issue edited by G. Dosi and S. Lechevalier.
7. As for technology, see, for example, Nelson (1991). Furthermore, Bloom and Van Reenen (2007) hav recently analyzed the impact of diverse modes of organization (including governance) on performance. Le et al. (2009) have replicated this study in the case of Japanese and Korean firms.
8. It means that international engagement and R&D investment far from concern all the Japanese manu facturing firms. As mentioned in the introduction, we will not develop further the discussion regarding the international engagement and the innovation strategies of the Japanese firm, due to lack of space Let us mention here only a few points. First, Ito and Lechevalier (2010) show the share of innovating firms is larger than the share of exporting, which is different from what is observed in other cases (e.g. Taiwan). As for R&D, some studies have shown the R&D investment behavior of Japanese firms is very similar to other types of investment (Hall et al., 1999). As for international engagement, the literature on FDI and export have followed different paths. The former has focused on *keiretsu* behavior whereas the latter is characterized as following exporting behavior (respectively Belderbos, 1997 and Head and Ries, 2003).
9. However, it is also characterized by two drawbacks that are discussed in Lechevalier (2007). the uni dimensional understanding of the determinants of the heterogeneity of firms, which is itself rooted in a restrictive vision of the firm, focusing almost exclusively on technology and innovation; and second, its simplistic normative evaluation of that heterogeneity.

REFERENCES

Aoki, Masahiko (1990), Toward an economic model of the Japanese firm, *Journal of Economic Literature*, **28**(1), 1–27.
Aoki, Masahiko (1994), The Japanese firm as a system of attributes: a survey and research agenda, in A. Masahiko and R. Dore (eds), *The Japanese Firm: Sources of Competitive Strength*, Oxford and New York: Oxford University Press.
Aoki, Masahiko (2000), *Information, Corporate Governance, and Institutional Diversity. Competitiveness in Japan, the USA, and the Transitional Economies*, Oxford and New York: Oxford University Press.
Aoki, Masahiko (2010), *Corporations In Evolving Diversity: Cognition, Governance, Institutional Rules*, Clarendon Lectures in Management Studies Series, Oxford: Oxford University Press.
Aoki, Masahiko, Gregory Jackson and Hideaki Miyajima (2007), *Corporate Governance in Japan. Institutional Change and Organizational Diversity*, Oxford and New York: Oxford University Press.
Askhenazy, Philippe (1998), The neo-Stakhanovism, DELTA Working Papers, No. 98-16.
Belderbos, René (1997), *Japanese Electronics Multinationals and Strategic Trade Policies*, Oxford and New York: Oxford University Press.
Bloom, Nick and John Van Reenen (2007), Measuring and explaining management practices across firms and countries, *The Quarterly Journal of Economics*, **122**(4), 1351–408.
Boyer, Robert et al. (eds) (1998), *Between Imitation and Innovation: The Transfer and Hybridization of Productive Models in the International Automobile Industry*, Oxford and New York: Oxford University Press.
Caselli, Francesco (1999), Technological revolutions, *American Economic Review*, **89**(1), 78–102.
Clark, K.B. and Takahiro Fujimoto (1991), *Product Development Performance*, Cambridge, MA: Harvard Business School Press.

Deeg, Richard and Gregory Jackson (2006), Towards a more dynamic theory of capitalist variety, King's College London – Department of Management Research Papers No. 40.

Dunne, Timothy, Lucia Foster, John Haltiwanger and Kenneth Troske (2004) Wage and productivity dispersion in US manufacturing: the role of computer investment, *Journal of Labor Economics*, **22**(2), 397–430.

Faggio, G., K.G. Salvanes and J. Van Reenen (2010), The evolution of inequality in productivity and wages: panel data evidence, *Industrial and Corporate Change*, **19**(6), 1919–51.

Freyssenet, Michel, Andrew Mair, Koichi Shimizu and Giuseppe Volpato (eds) (1998), *One Best Way? Trajectories and Industrial Models of the World's Automobile Producers*, Oxford and New York: Oxford University Press.

Fujimoto, Takahiro (1999), *The Evolution of a Manufacturing System at Toyota*, Oxford and New York: Oxford University Press.

Fujimoto, Takahiro (2003), *Nôryoku kôchiku kyôsô: nihon no jidôsha Sangyô ha naze tsuyoinoka* [*The competition of capabilities building: why are Japanese firms in the car industry so strong?*], Chuô koron shinsha (in Japanese).

Fukao, Kyoji and Hyeog Ug Kwon (2006), Why did Japan's TFP growth slow down in the lost decade? An empirical analysis based on firm-level data of manufacturing firms, *Japanese Economic Review*, **57**(2), 195–228.

Gordon, Andrew (1988), *The Evolution of Labor Relations in Japan (1853–1955)*, Cambridge, MA: Harvard University Press.

Hall, B.H., J. Mairesse, L. Branstetter and B. Crepon (1999), Does cash-flow cause investment and R&D? An exploration using panel data for French, Japanese, and United States scientific firms, in D.B. Audretsch and R. Thurik (eds), *Innovation, Industry Evolution, and Employment*, New York: Cambridge University Press: pp.129–56.

Head, Keith and John Ries (2003), Heterogeneity and the FDI versus export decisions of Japanese manufacturers, *Journal of the Japanese and International Economies*, **17**(4), 448–67.

Hoshi, Takeo and Anil K. Kashyap (2001), *Corporate Financing and Governance in Japan. The Road to the Future*, Cambridge, MA: MIT Press.

Hurlin, Christophe and Sébastien Lechevalier (2003), The heterogeneity of employment adjustment across Japanese firms. A study using panel data, CEPREMAP Working Papers (Couverture Orange) No. 0310.

Ito, Keiko and Sébastien Lechevalier (2009), The evolution of productivity dispersion of firms. reevaluation of its determinants in the case of Japan, *Review of World Economics*, **145**(3), 404–29.

Ito, Keiko and Sébastien Lechevalier (2010), Why do some firms persistently out-perform others: investigating the interactions between innovation and exporting strategies, *Industrial and Corporate Change*, **19**(6), February, Special Issue edited by G. Dosi and S. Lechevalier.

Koike, Kazuo (1988), *Understanding Industrial Relations in Modern Japan*, London: Macmillan.

Langlois, Richard N. and Nicolaï Foss (1999), Capabilities and governance: the rebirth of production in the theory of economic organization, *Kyklos*, **52**(2), 201–18.

Langlois, Richard N. and Paul L. Robertson (1995), *Firms, Markets, and Economic Change: A Dynamic Theory of Business Institutions*, London: Routledge.

Lechevalier, Sébastien (2005), Will Toyota save Japan (and the world. . .)?', HEC Eurasia Institute.

Lechevalier, Sébastien (2007), The diversity of capitalism and heterogeneity of firms. A case study of Japan during the lost decade, *Evolutionary and Institutional Economics Review*, **4**(1), 113–42.

Lechevalier, Sébastien (2011a), The increasing heterogeneity of firms in Japanese capitalism: facts, causes, consequences and implications, in R. Boyer, A. Isogai and H. Uemura (eds), *Diversity and Transformations of Asian Capitalisms*, London: Routledge.

Lechevalier, Sébastien (2011b), *La grande transformation du capitalismes japonais*, Paris: Presses de Sciences Po, Paris.

Lee, Keun, Tustomu Miyagawa, Shigesaburo Kabe, Junhyup Lee, Hyoungjin Kim and YoungGak Kim (2009), Management practices and firm performance in Japanese and Korean firms. An empirical study using interview surveys, JCER Discussion Paper No. 120.

Melitz, Marc J. (2003), The impact of trade on intra-industry reallocations and aggregate industry productivity, *Econometrica*, **71**(6), 1695–725.

Miwa, Yoshiro (1996), *Firms and Industrial Organization in Japan*, Basingstoke: Macmillan Press.

Morishima, Michio (1988), Confucianism as a basis for capitalism, in Daniel I. Okimoto and Thomas P. Rohlen (ed.), *Inside the Japanese System*, Stanford, CA: Stanford University Press.

Nelson, Richard R. (1991), Why do firms differ, and how does it matter?, *Strategic Management Journal*, **12**(Winter), 61–74.

Nishiguchi, Toshiaki (1994), *Strategic Industrial Sourcing: The Japanese Advantage*, Oxford and New York: Oxford University Press.

Odagiri, Hiroyuki (1994), *Growth Through Competition. Competition Through Growth*, Oxford: Clarendon Press.

Okazaki, Tetsuji and Masahiro Okuno-Fujiwara (eds) (1999), *The Japanese Economic System and its Historical Origin*, Oxford and New York: Oxford University Press.

Sheard, Paul (1989), The main bank system and corporate monitoring and control in Japan, *Journal of Economic Behavior & Organization*, **11**(3), 399–422.

Syverson, Chad (2004), Product substitutability and productivity dispersion, *The Review of Economics and Statistics*, **86**(2), 534–50.

Teece, David J. and Gary Pisano (1994), The dynamic capabilities of firms: an introduction, *Industrial and Corporate Change*, **3**(3) 537–56.

Thesmar, David and Mathias Thoenig (2000), Creative destruction and firm organization choice, *The Quarterly Journal of Economics*, **115**(4), 1201–37.

Williamson, Oliver E. (1985), *The Economic Institutions of Capitalism*, New York: Free Press.

17 The European firm

Alessandra Colombelli and Francesco Quatraro

17.1 INTRODUCTION

The organization of production has represented a key issue to economics scholars since Adam Smith's *Wealth of Nations* (1776). The example of the pin factory or the one concerning the improvements in steam engines already called for the importance of division of labor, organization of production and the relationships between process and organizational innovations. Later on, Alfred Marshall's *Principles of Economics* (1890) and *Industry and Trade* (1919) provided an analysis of the organization of production within different industrial contexts, comparing different national systems.

However, business organization began to be included in a well-defined field of enquiry only in the late 1930s, that is, the theory of the firm. While the former approaches (Coase, 1937) were much interested in establishing a neoclassical basis to the theory of the firm, in the 1960s there was a change in the intellectual climate influencing the development of the discipline, leading to the introduction of the so-called managerial and behavioral theories, and then to the transaction costs approach proposed by Williamson.

The shift away from the neoclassical approach to the theory of the firm was much influenced by the increasing awareness that the post-war international economy was farther and farther from a perfect competition situation. The use of markets ceased to appear as costless, and it was clear that in many countries, like France, Germany, and the United States, firms appeared more as large corporations carrying out many, if not all, of the stages of the production process, rather than as tiny and non-influential productive units. The evidence provided by Alfred Chandler (1962 and 1977) demonstrated that the industries that benefited from the technological system characterizing the so-called Second Industrial Revolution showed larger and capital-intensive production units, able to pursue scale and scope economies so as to gain higher profit margins. The US large and diversified corporation, organized as a multidivisional hierarchy, was seen as a sort of optimum towards which all industrial systems should have converged sooner or later in order to retain competitiveness and stay in the market.

Such a stream of literature represents the first attempt to identify an ideal type of firm, on the basis of which clear prescriptions could have been formulated. In the mid-1980s the interest of business historians began to move towards the analysis of the distinctive features characterizing Japanese firms (Aoki, 1990; Aoki and Dore, 1994). The phenomenology of the Japanese firm has then been studied under different perspectives, emphasizing the specificity of their internal structure as well as the structure of the network of relationships in which they operate, made up of both economic and institutional actors. A pretty interesting picture has then emerged that on the one hand shed light, at least in part, on the reasons underlying their success, and on the other hand provided new challenges to the theory of the firm (see Chapter 16 by Lechevalier in this book).

More recently, a new stream of literature appeared, following the increasing integration of European countries and globalization of European firms. The emergence and the gradual hardening of the Single European Market raised the important issue of what should be the future of business organization for European firms. On the one hand, scholars have maintained that the chance to confront larger and larger markets should lead to the establishment of a sort of US-like European multidivisional firm, able to get significant rents due to market power and technical economies of scale. On the other hand, the increasing literature showing the advantages of outsourcing and of networking firms proposed flexible and specialized firms as the model towards which industrial systems in Europe should have converged. A different approach to the issue has been synthesized in a recent volume edited by Richard Withley and Hull Krinstensen (1996), the contributions to which set out a framework based on social contingency and social choice. According to this strand of literature, a unique ideal-type of European firm can hardly be devised, due to the social, political, and institutional variety that characterizes the different European countries. Moreover, similar economic agents in different economic contexts may be motivated by different objectives, so that the analysis of economic choices would not necessarily be the same.

The purpose of this chapter is to provide an extended overview on the debate on the European firm, by articulating it against the backdrop of more traditional theories of the firm. The chapter also proposes a different interpretation of the issue by grafting the discussion onto the interpretative framework of complexity theory, so as to provide a new and possibly richer heuristic. The rest of the chapter is organized as follows. Section 17.2 provides a review of main theories of the firm, from early neoclassical to more recent evolutionary approaches. In section 17.3 we go into the debate about the perspectives for a European firm, emphasizing the importance of local idiosyncratic factors in shaping the technology of production. We will argue that key economists like Alfred Marshall, Simon Kuznets, and Joseph Schumpeter already provided the bases for a contingency-based approach. Section 17.4 develops a complexity approach to the issue of the European firm from a dynamic viewpoint, while Section 17.5 presents the conclusions and suggests possible avenues for future research.

17.2   THEORIES OF THE FIRM: AN OVERVIEW

17.2.1   The Neoclassical Theory of the Firm

In the neoclassical theory, the firm is conceptualized as a black box rational entity. The theory builds upon production and demand functions where the firm is described as a production function that transforms inputs into outputs. According to this theory, the firm maximizes its profit under the assumption of perfect rationality.

The main limit of this theory is that it does not take into account the internal structure of the firm conceived as a black box. It does not help to explain how production is organized and governed or how profit maximization is achieved. Moreover, traditional economic analysis neglects the boundaries of the firm and, consequently, does not help to explain what determines vertical or horizontal integration. It also neglects the conflict of interests between economic actors arising from asymmetries of information as it assumes complete information. Finally, it mainly deals with static equilibrium analysis and thus does not account for firms' dynamics.

17.2.2 The Transaction Costs Theory of the Firm

In transaction costs economics the firm is not described as a production function but is conceptualized as a governance structure. This theory is based on the assumption of bounded rationality and opportunism. One of the main contributions of the transaction costs view is that it tries to go inside the black box and understand the firm's internal structure. In particular, the transaction costs theory focuses on the make-or-buy decision in the context of vertical integration.

In his pioneering article 'The nature of the firm' Coase developed the approach to the theory of the firm based on transaction costs. According to Coase, within a firm, market transactions based on price mechanisms are eliminated and the production is coordinated by the entrepreneur. 'A firm consists of the system of relationships which comes into existence when the direction of resources is dependent on an entrepreneur' (Coase 1937, p. 393). In this view, the entrepreneur coordinates transactions with the aim of minimizing his or her costs function. Thus, a firm emerges when the costs of production factors are lower if a certain transaction is carried out within the firm rather than in the open market. Yet, the exact nature of transactions is not well specified by Coase.

The contribution of Oliver Williamson to this theory is important in that it has gone in depth into the analysis of transaction costs that determine the decision to make or buy and has described the main governance structures of transactions. According to Williamson, three main attributes help in describing transactions: 'the frequency with which transactions recur, the uncertainty – disturbances – to which they are subject, and the condition of asset specificity' (Williamson, 1998, p. 36). In this view, a firm decides to vertically integrate when transactions are frequent, have high uncertainty because of information asymmetries, and involve highly specific assets. Williamson also identifies three broad types of governance structures: (1) the market, which is non-transaction-specific, (2) transaction-specific governance that is adapted to the special needs of the transactions, and (3) transaction-semi-specific, which falls in between. According to Williamson, transactions and governance structures are aligned in order to economize transaction costs.

Although the transaction costs theory addresses some of the weaknesses of the neoclassical theory, it is not without its critics. First, it begs the question of how profit maximization, that is, costs minimization, is achieved. Even if transaction costs theory assumes asymmetries of information, it still neglects the conflict of interests between economic actors and agency costs. Finally, it does not allow for firm evolution.

17.2.3 The Principal–Agent Theory of the Firm

In the principal–agent theory (Jensen and Meckling, 1976), the firm is conceived as a nexus for a set of contracting relationships among individuals. As a neoclassical theory, it is based on the principle of maximizing behavior on the part of all individuals. Yet, an individual aims at maximizing his or her own utility and this may generate conflicts of interest between different economic actors.

In particular, the principal–agent theory focuses on the contracts between the owners and managers of the firm and investigates the efficiency of the separation of ownership and control as a form of organization. The agency relationship involves the principal, which is the owner and risk-bearer of the firm, and the agent, which is the manager and the decision-maker. As both of them are utility maximizers, the theory assumes that the manager will not always act in the best interests of the owner. The divergence between the agent's decision and the optimal decision from the principal's perspective of profit maximization engenders the agency costs related to the losses in profits and the monitoring expenditures by the principal, and to the bonding expenditures by the agent. Under these conditions, the principal–agent theory investigates the incentives faced by both the principal and the agent within their contractual relationship. In particular, the literature has mainly focused on the incentive schemes that align the manager's objectives with the owner's interests.

This theory has some weaknesses. As the neoclassical theory of the firm, it still fails to define the boundaries of the firm. Moreover, it still mainly deals with static equilibrium analysis and thus does not allow for firm evolution.

17.2.4   The Resource-based View and the Evolutionary Theory of the Firm

The resource-based theory analyses the firm from the resource side rather than the product side. The idea of looking at the firm as a set of resources has its roots in the work by Penrose (1959) and emphasizes the role of critical resources in shaping firms' evolution and growth (Rumelt, 1984; Teece, 1984; Wernerfelt, 1984; Dierickx and Cool, 1989; Barney, 1991). As with the transaction costs theory, the resource-based view looks inside the black box, in particular, by focusing on the resources it owns and assumes bounded rationality. Yet, it is based on the knowledge-based approach rather than the opportunistic-based view (Conner and Prahalad, 1996).

According to the resource-based view of the firm a critical resource can be either a person or a specific asset that cannot be easily imitated and differentiates a firm from its competitors. A number of works have pointed out that knowledge, skills, and experience are the major source of sustainable competitive advantage and new opportunities exploitation (Winter, 1987; Prahalad and Hamel, 1990).

In line with this theory, Teece et al. (1997) have developed the concept of dynamic capabilities referring to the ability of adapting organizational skills, resources, and competences to changing environment. 'Dynamic capabilities thus reflect an organization's ability to achieve new and innovative forms of competitive advantage given path dependencies and market positions' (ibid., p. 516).

The evolutionary theory of the firm offers an alternative definition of the firm based on routines. In the evolutionary theory proposed by Nelson and Winter (1982), the firm is still motivated by profit as in the neoclassical view yet it is not analyzed in equilibrium conditions but it is assumed to operate in an open-ended dynamic process. In this view a firm can be defined through the set of routines and competencies that the firm encompasses. As routines and competences are firm-specific and differ among different firms, the evolutionary theory conceives firms as heterogeneous economic agents. In order to survive, heterogeneous firms compete in the market by employing new techniques and producing at lower costs than their competitors. Firms' evolution is thus driven by technological competition and selection mechanisms, on one hand, and innovation processes, on the other hand.

While addressing some of the issues related to the more traditional theories, the resource-based and the evolutionary theories have their own limitations. Although the resource-based view looks inside the black box in terms of the resources it owns, in the evolutionary theory the firm is still a black box. The boundaries of the firm are still not defined and the issues related to the separation of ownership and control are not accounted for.

17.3   THE EUROPEAN FIRM: AN OPEN DEBATE

Most of the theories of the firm reviewed so far share a common limit, which has somehow influenced the debate on the more appropriate organization of production in modern capitalistic societies. They indeed end proposing, more or less explicitly, a sort of ideal organizational structure in the continuum between markets and hierarchies, on the basis of the comparison between specific advantages and disadvantages.

On the one hand, earlier approaches view the firm as a nexus of contracts. The main pillars of the production process are therefore transactions carried out within market dynamics. In this direction, firms take the typical form expected in competitive markets and predicted by traditional neoclassical theories. On the other hand, subsequent schools of thought have emphasized the importance of information asymmetries and the risk for moral hazard and adverse selection in favoring the development of larger and vertically integrated production units (Williamson, 1975). In addition, the focus on differential objectives featuring owners and managers led to stressing the advantages of managerial firms, as different from those in which ownership and control are concentrated in the same persons (Jensen and Meckling, 1976).

The search for an archetypical organizational form also inspired empirical works in business history. The main reference is in this respect the voluminous works by Alfred Chandler (1962 and 1977). In his analysis of the co-evolution of organizational forms and western capitalism, Chandler stressed that the emergence of the diversified and multidivisional form could have been regarded as the heyday of the evolution of modern economies. While single and family-owned businesses were mainly typical of the industries featured in the First Industrial Revolution, the second one was instead characterized by the rise of chemical and pharmaceutical productions as well as the introduction of new technologies, like electricity, that made production processes much faster and cheaper. The new industries also showed peculiar technical features according to which the minimum efficiency scale was pretty high, partly as an effect of the sunk costs needed to implement effective factories. The prospects for scale and scope economies were therefore one of the main factors leading to emergence of large corporations in the Second Industrial Revolution.

Both Chandler and Williamson tended to represent the multidivisional form (M-form) typical of American capitalism as a superior form of organization. The former in particular proposed that there clearly was an increasing diffusion of such a kind of organization amongst most advanced economies. A convergence process was about to display its effects, concerning the 'type of enterprise and system of capitalism used by all advanced economies for the production and distribution of goods' (Chandler, [1984] 1992, p. 156). This process of convergence was likely to interest both European and the Japanese governance of firms' groups.

Williamson, however, offered some years later the chance to extend and reshape the ongoing debate. The evidence about the peculiar organization of Japanese firms' groups typical of *keiretsu* systems did cast some doubts on the pretended universality of the American multidivisional firm. The virtues of this governance scheme grounded on outsourcing, informal ties, and the emphasis of core businesses were so evident that Williamson himself had to admit that the *keiretsu* organization could have been regarded as effective as the M-form (Williamson, 1993).

On this basis, the *discourse* on the nature of European firms began to assume a different perspective, along with increasing awareness that different varieties of capitalism were possible (Hall and Soskice, 2001) and hence that different ways of organizing the production process could have co-existed at the same historical time, as an effect of different idiosyncratic characteristics featuring local contexts.

17.3.1   Role of the Industrial Structure

Such awareness could hardly be regarded as brand new achievement in economic theory. The link between the organization of production and industrial peculiarities was indeed already emphasized, for example, in the works by Alfred Chandler. International differences were regarded as sort of out-of-equilibrium situations, which, however, would have ended up as the ideal form. The seminal contributions by two founding economists, that is, Alfred Marshall and Simon Kuznets, may help enrich the framework.

Marshall's masterpiece, *Principles of Economics* (1890), is famous for having set up the principles of partial equilibrium analysis as well as for having analyzed in detail the British production environment during the First Industrial Revolution. The celebrated concept of industrial districts originated therein, and has represented, and still represents, for some economists the best possible world towards which local production systems ought to converge, though Marshall's analysis was positive rather than normative. His other important contribution, *Industry and Trade* (1919), has been less fortunate, despite the richness and the broad empirical context of analysis. In this work Marshall carries out an interesting comparison among the sources of industrial leadership in Great Britain, France, Germany, and the United States, emphasizing the co-existence of different forms of business organization in different countries, as well as the importance of the institutional setting, like the access conditions to financial resources, fiscal policies, and the degree of competition, besides the traditional influence of technical factors. Marshall's work in sum contained all the ingredients for a 'relativist' theory of the firm, appreciating the importance of the specific features of industrial and geographical contexts.

A few years later Simon Kuznets (1930) proposed an interesting analysis of the cyclical behavior of industries, able to explain how the economic leadership moved from some countries to others according to the relative stage of life cycles that characterizes the industries they are specialized in. Such evolution, mainly grounded on technological factors, is likely to explain, for example, the gradual shift of industrial leadership and the related effects on economic growth. Kuznets's analysis enables us to appreciate the dynamic character of economic structure. The performance of industries exhibit a cyclical behavior, and some countries are likely to take the lead at a given historical time, while others are likely to replace them when their core industries undergo the phase of growth. Structural change is a key element of economic life. Along with Marshall's remark on the close relationship between the organization of production and the peculiarities of industrial sectors, such contributions allow us to understand how hard it is to discover a unique firm model. On the contrary, there is a changing variety of industries, both across countries at the same time and over time within the same country. Each industry is likely to be characterized by a form of business organization that better fits with the features of production. This was explicitly advanced by Kuznets, who emphasized how in modern economies 'Major aspects of structural change include the shift away from agriculture to non-agriculture pursuits and, recently, away from industry to services; a change in the *scale of production units*, and a related *shift from personal enterprise to impersonal organization of economic firms*' (Kuznets, 1973, p. 248, italics added). For this reason the search for an ideal firm form would appear to be an abstraction too far from what can be empirically observed.

17.3.2   Innovation and Path-dependence

The interest in the dynamics of structural change can be regarded as a distinctive feature of the intellectual climate established in the 1930s in the field of economics. Shortly after Kuznets's book, Joseph Schumpeter published *Business Cycles* (1939), in which he treated to a great extent the intertwining between industrial and technological life cycles. The dynamics of technological change is at the same time both a determinant and an outcome of economic dynamics. As a scholar of economics of innovation, Schumpeter provided both theoretical and empirical contributions that are pretty consistent with the criticism of the universalist approach typical of the supporters of the M-form.

In his *Theory of Economic Development* ([1912] 1934), he proposed a taxonomy of innovations, out of which process innovations and, more explicitly, organizational innovation bear precisely on the way in which firms carry out the production process. Schumpeter maintained that the organization of production is subject to change, and that the changes in the institutional and economic environment in which firms operate are likely to influence such dynamics. Further, his works are a clear clue to this process. Indeed, in the above-mentioned book Schumpeter identifies the entrepreneur as the main engine of economic growth. The small family-owned company, built around an innovative idea, represents the desirable organizational form. The access to credit, in particular thanks to the bank system, is in turn a key enabling condition. Later on, in *Capitalism, Socialism and Democracy* (1942), Schumpeter changed his mind, stressing how it is the large and monopolistic firm that provides the economy with the necessary impulse to change and grow. A temporary monopoly is necessary according to Schumpeter in order to guarantee sufficient extra profits for firms having invested large amounts to resource research and development. The financing of innovation becomes more an internal business rather than an activity sustained by external credit.

Schumpeter's works therefore show how interpretative lenses are strictly related to the *esprit du temps*. Different organizational forms appear to be equally effective, depending on the features of the actual economic and institutional environments. His works also point to the importance of history in economics, and therefore to the need for an evolutionary approach to economics. The conditions in which economic agents operate are far from static and immutable, but economic agents make their plans on the basis of the actual observed parameters. Therefore, when conditions change, agents react by introducing different kinds of innovation in their daily business (Schumpeter, 1947). Organizational innovation is one of the possible outcomes.

In this direction the M-form is only one of the possible organizational forms, which is strictly related to the set of idiosyncratic features impinging upon specific industrial and geographical contexts at given moments in time. The economics of path-dependence provides insightful complementary inputs in this respect. A path-dependent process is one in which remote events, both systematic and stochastic, can exert important influences on the final outcome. Stochastic processes not converging to single equilibrium are called non-ergodic. Within this framework, the set of historical accidents needs to be accounted for, for the purpose of economic analysis. A path-dependent process is therefore one in which multiple equilibria are possible, due to the essentially historically character of the dynamic process under scrutiny (David, 1985).

The economics of path-dependence has been successfully applied to the analysis of innovation and integrated in the localized technological change approach (Antonelli, 1995 and 1999). The basic ingredients of this framework are well suited to providing further theoretical support to the idea that it is quite difficult to expect business organization to converge to a fixed-point distribution of outcomes. On the contrary, the dynamics of economic processes is such that the observed outcome at a given point in time is the result of a sequence of actions, according to which each action at time t is likely to shape actions at time $t+1$, raising a chain of unpredictable events. Social actions happen in time and space, so that the observed mix of path-dependent outcomes observed in a specific place is likely to be different from others in places elsewhere. Localization matters along with history. Different regions may therefore be characterized by idiosyncratic factors, within which one can also include the prevalent organizational form of enterprises.

It is clear that in this context the concept of the ideal type firm is meaningless. The question as to what should be the organizational form towards which European firms should converge can only be solved by accepting that there may be a variety of locally optimal equilibria, which are difficult to predict ex ante as they are the result of a long-lasting evolutionary process.

17.3.3   Societal Contingency and Societal Choice

The discussion conducted so far has shown that, besides more traditional approaches proposing the adoption of a 'Pareto superior' business form, different approaches grounded in economic history and economics of innovation articulated a set of arguments that implicitly questioned the idea of a globally optimum organization of production, and therefore the idea itself of a possible European firm. However, such an issue has been explicitly tackled only recently by economic scholars.

The volume by Withley and Krinstensen (1996) represents a key reference in this respect. The book collects together different chapters developing a theoretical framework supporting a contingent approach to the issue in the first part, and then provides an application to the investigation of the main organizational forms characterizing different European countries.

The arguments set forth in *The Changing European Firm* are grounded on an institutional approach to economics. Economic agents are therefore not characterized by complete rationality and profit-maximizing behavior. On the contrary, the economy is viewed as a web of relationships between different kinds of institutional actors with diverging interests, in which agents' rationality is bounded to a limited portion of the whole set of knowledge. Learning plays a key role in order to fill relevant gaps, so that individuals are able to adapt to changing conditions of economic environment.

Within this framework, the baseline hypothesis impinges upon two main pillars. On the one hand, the *societal-contingency approach* (Sorge, 1991; Withley, 1994) represents an application of the general contingency theory, according to which effectiveness depends on fit with critical contingencies. In this direction, firms may develop specific organizational forms due to the peculiar features of main institutions affecting economic behavior, like local labor markets, the rigidity of financial markets, and the quality of ownership and management systems. The design of such institutions may be such to override more universalistic industry or technological factors. It follows that it would be pretty difficult to observe a shared consensus on the most effective organizational form amongst heterogeneous contexts such as European countries. It is indeed more reasonable to expect that dominant patterns of business organization vary widely from country to country, or from one business system to another.

On the other hand, within the institutionalist approach, the *societal-choice* view argues that while societal-contingency correctly focuses attention on the key role of institutional variety, this is not sufficient to gain a full understanding of the economic reality. The persistence of the holding company across different countries indeed calls for additional explanations, to explain the reasons why different institutional contexts might be characterized by similar dominant organizational forms. In particular, scholars within this framework put forth the need for a more pluralistic approach, focusing also on the features of economic agents besides those of the institutional settings in which they operate (Whittington, 1992).

Each context is characterized by a variety of actors, which differ on the basis of motivations and targets, as well as in terms of their relative power within the local socio-economic system. The distribution of power amongst economic actors may engender choices that do not follow exactly capitalistic rules. Different 'sociological' groups may be identified, like the entrepreneurs, the banks, the families and the state. On the basis of their relative strength, these actors may choose strategies better suited to their own purposes, even at the cost of economic efficiency. This is a possible explanation for the survival of some specific organizational forms the institutional setting of which would be better suited to hosting different designs.

It is clear that such a set of arguments is enriched by a multidisciplinary approach in which institutionalism is blended with economic sociology. The concept of *embeddedness* seems to be particularly appropriate in this context (Granovetter, 1985). According to this, economic action is likely to be influenced by concrete personal relations and by their structures. The structure of relations is represented as a network in which economic agents are connected to one another. If one allows for variety, rather than assuming a representative economic agent, such networks turn out to be made of different actors, pursuing different objectives and with different relative weight.

The European firm issue can therefore be framed in the light of embeddedness theory.

This would allow for better understanding of the bidirectional flow of interactions from the network to the agent and vice versa. The relationships between the structure of the network and the features of the nodes it is made of, opens up a new perspective on the topic implemented on concepts and methodologies typical of complexity theory.

17.4   A COMPLEXITY PERSPECTIVE TO ADDRESSING THE EUROPEAN FIRM ISSUE

Complexity is emerging as a new unifying theory to help understand endogenous change and transformation across a variety of disciplines, ranging from mathematics and physics to biology. The application of the basic tools of complex system analysis to social sciences has recently led to increasing attempts to implement an actual economics of complexity (Arthur et al., 1997). A complex system may be defined as a system that comprises many elements that interact richly (Simon, 1966; Kauffman, 1993).

One can articulate the idea that the organizational form taken by firms is an emergent property of a system characterized by organized complexity. According to the theory of complexity, emergence is a phenomenon whereby aggregate behaviors that arise from the organized interactions of localized individual behaviors, provide both the system and the agents with new capabilities and functionalities. By organized complexity we mean a system in which 'interactions are not independent, feedback can enter the system. Feedback fundamentally alters the dynamics of a system. In a system with negative feedback, changes get quickly absorbed and the system gains stability. With positive feedback, changes get amplified leading to instability' (Miller and Page, 2007, p. 50).

The implementation of such views allows us to appreciate the important role of the properties of the system into which firms originate and develop. In other words, considering the organizational form as an emergent property of socioeconomic systems is strictly related to the issue of embeddedness. An analysis of the complex dynamics of European firms should move from a clear definition of the system in which firms operate. In this system:

- Economic agents are heterogeneous, which are interconnected and networked with other agents in the system in order to exploit complementarities and interdependence.
- The heterogeneous agents are firms and also public and private institutions and organizations.
- Each agent is a network of resources and competences.
- The emergence of organizational forms stems from intentional choices by economic agents.
- The structure of the system changes endogenously.

Consistent with the institutionalist approaches discussed in the previous section, the quality of institutions, as well as the different features characterizing economic agents are likely to explain the persistence of different types of firms across different countries in Europe. Institutions, families, banks, financial and factor markets, are the typical nodes of a network of relationships within which firms carry out their business. The architecture of such networks, in terms of both distribution of links and relative importance of nodes, is likely to shape emergent properties of system dynamics.

The complexity view may be pushed even further, by adopting the competence view of the firm, as introduced by Penrose and further implemented in the capability approach. The firm itself can be viewed as a bundle of networked resources, out of which there are production resources, management, ownership, and so on and so forth. The way in which these components are linked to one another, as well as the relative weight of some of them, can be thought of as features characterizing the structure of the firm as a network.[1]

The system dynamics of the components that constitute the firms leads to emergent properties that are the performances of firms themselves. Firms' performances are, however, a sort of feedback that the firms send to the system in which they operate, which in turn shape the organization of the firm and eventually its performance again. It follows a circular process, shaped by powerful self-enhancing dynamics.

The issue would be relatively simple if one would assume the structure of the networks, the socioeconomic system and the bundle of firms' capabilities, as stable over time, or at most affected by exogenous change, like most of the complexity thinking assumes. Yet, the architecture of a complex system may well change over time, and so may the structure of epistatic relationships. This may occur either due to a change in the relative weight of some elements in the system, these elements switching from a non-influential to an influential position, or by means of introduction of new elements within the system. This is in turn likely to alter the existing structure of relationships. Within this context, the pleiotropy represents the number of elements in the system that are affected by the appearance of new elements. It is clear that the higher the pleiotropy, the greater the change in the architecture of the system that the inclusion of new elements may engender.

The model of constructional selection by Altenberg (1994 and 1995) represents one of the few attempts to cope with the issue of changing architectures of complex systems. Such class of models is well suited to investigate the evolution of organizational forms considered as artifacts made of interdependent elements (Lane and Maxfield, 2005). The viewpoint of endogenous complexity makes the analysis of organizations particularly appealing and challenging. The structure of the firm can indeed be represented as an emergent property stemming from *multi-layered complex dynamics* (see Figure 17.1). In other words, the adoption of an endogenous complexity made possible by this approach allows for the combination of the view of the firm as an artifact with the view of firm as an act, that is, as the product of collective actions involving agents with converging incentives and aligned interests (Arthur, 2009; Lane et al., 2009).

The structure of the network of relationships amongst interacting agents represents therefore a crucial factor able to shape the ultimate layout of organizational forms. Constructional selection matters, in that new institutions entering the network need first of all to choose which incumbents they want to be linked with. The concept of preferential attachment applies to this situation. In a wide number of contexts, the new nodes in a network generally end up linking with those 'old' nodes already characterized by a large number of connections (Barabási and Albert, 1999). As a consequence, the entrance of new actors in the network is likely to reshape the relative weight of nodes, and hence modify the structure and the balance of relationships.

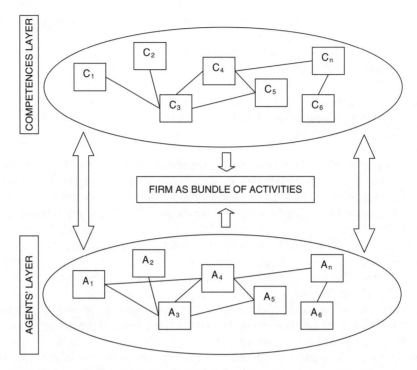

Figure 17.1   The multi-layered complexity of the firm

Organizations so achieved stem from the combination of competences dispersed among socioeconomic agents. They may be thought of as a collection of elements linked to one another. The firm can be therefore be imagined as a network in which the nodes are competences or organizational units and the links represent their actual combination. Organizational forms in this sense turn out to be an emergent property of complex dynamics featuring the interdependent elements of the system.

This is a quite unexplored consequence of the approach to the European firm as an emergent property stemming from qualified interactions, which provides further richness to its dynamics. Each organizational form may be represented as a network, the nodes of which are smaller units while the edges stand for their actual combination. Hence each organization is characterized by a structure with its own architecture. This in turn may evolve over time, as an effect of the introduction of new nodes and the consequent change in their relative weight within the network.

Dynamic irreversibility and path-dependence represent a channel through which the topology of organization structure affects the dynamics at the level of agents' networks. The organization of production is localized as an effect of the interactions between the complex dynamics at the agents' level. However, the topology of the structure of the socioeconomic system is in turn shaped by the choices made at the competence level as to which resources combine together and in which way. A self-sustained process is likely to emerge, according to which the organization of production tends more and more towards a local attractor in which they are locked in. The changing European firm

an be therefore represented as a distribution of local attractors across different local-
zed contexts shaped by idiosyncratic factors, wherein the changing conditions both in
he socioeconomic system and in the architecture of firms' structure itself are likely to
>roduce variations over time.

At a given time, firms can choose among multiple outcomes. Their location choice
:an be directed towards different places and is influenced by both their internal charac-
•eristics that include the preceding path and external characteristics that depend on the
•ocation strategies of other agents carried out in the past. Hence the concentration of dif-
'erent forms of organizations in different places stemming from the idiosyncratic factors
>f the local attractor is a path-dependent process.

A number of emergent properties or conditions of the local system can make a place
n space more attractive than others. The interaction and networks of local actors that
•llow for the exploitation of complementarities and interdependences, reinforced by the
:echnological and industrial specialization of the area, the institutional endowment, and
>y a common local culture of trust, based on shared practices and rules, are centripetal
'orces that make a base of attraction of the local system. However, it is not only the local
•ttributes or conditions but rather the sequence of cumulative interactions between them
•nd positive feedback that give rise to a local complex system. Both local attractiveness
•nd accidental historical order of choice generate agglomerations (Arthur, 1989, 1994).

Once the local attractor has emerged following a path-dependent process, heterogeneous agents within it are subject to self-reinforcing mechanisms. The process of increasing
•returns is self-reinforcing since the benefits of remaining in the current path are higher
•than the cost of switching to an alternative path. Localized increasing returns operate as
•a selection mechanism and favor the survival of firms and forms of organization that are
•well established in the local system. Thus, the generation of different forms of organiza-
•tions is a persistent process.

The persistence of the actual forms of organization takes place when the internal capabilities accumulated by means of learning processes lead to the generation and exploitation
•of new knowledge. Another fundamental condition for organizational success is when the
external context provides the access to complementary and indispensable inputs in terms
of external knowledge and capabilities. The generation of new knowledge requires both
internal learning and the acquisition of external tacit and codified knowledge.

Firms are attracted towards and remain locked into the local attractor until the profits
stemming from their activities are above the equilibrium one. The selection mechanism depends on the profits realized by each firm. Extra profits and increasing returns
engender positive feedback and self-reinforcing mechanisms that sustain firms' creative
behavior and competitive advantage. The attractiveness of a place persists as long as
the returns stemming from complementarities and interdependence of capabilities and
agents are positive.

New forms of organization can emerge when firms within the local attractor understand that the benefits of remaining in the current organizational path, which in turn
has engendered the current local attractor, are lower than the cost of shifting to an
alternative path and, thus, to an alternative attractor. Firms are induced to react creatively to changing local conditions. The collective process of the search for new capabilities may finally engender radical changes in the organizational paradigm and leads
to Schumpeterian gales of creative destruction. Radical changes in the organizational

paradigm make the system move unpredictably and irreversibly away from the old local attractor. Positive feedback and network externalities sustain this process of change and define the basis of attraction of the new attractor.

17.5   CONCLUSIONS

The debate about the European firm has recently attracted the attention of economic scholars specializing in the theory of the firm. The baseline argument of the institutionalist approach to the issue states that it is very difficult and somewhat simplistic to expect firms in the European context to converge towards a universalistic organization of production. The gradual thickening of the Single European Market, along with globalization of production, does not lead necessarily to the establishment of a sort of European version of the American M-form corporation.

The institutionalist approach, drawing upon contingency theory, shows how the evolution of firms' structure is embedded in the contexts in which they operate. The quality of institutions like capital markets, banks, rules and norms, labor markets, and financial resources, is likely to exert a strong influence on the actual configuration of the organization of the production process. Moreover, the heterogeneity of economic agents, in terms of motivation and objectives, provides explanation for the observation of organizational forms hardly fitting with the environment in which they are placed. Economic agents, consistently with behavioral assumptions, are not characterized by perfect rationality and may want to pursue objectives that are different from profit maximization. That is why organizational forms that are not effective from an economic viewpoint may persist over time.

In this chapter, after having provided an overview on the 'theories' of the firm, we have shown that former contributions of main pillars of economic theory enable us to reach the same conclusions. Both Marshall's and Kuznets's works, as well as those by Schumpeter, show that the evolution and diffusion of specific organizational forms are strictly related to industrial peculiarities and to the features of the context in which firms originate and develop. Such works appeared well before Chandler's analyses supporting the idea of a universalistic organizational form, and yet have been mostly neglected by theorists of the firm.

The basic idea that different organizational forms may prove to be equally efficient, according to the nature of the contexts in which they operate, is very related to the concepts of multiple equilibria, dynamic irreversibilities, and path-dependence. We have therefore proposed to extend to the theory of the firm the recent tendency to apply the tools and concepts of complexity theory to the understanding of the origins and evolution of organizational form. We have articulated an interpretative framework in which organizational forms are emergent properties stemming from qualified interactions at the agent level. Organizations are in turn characterized by internal qualified interactions that feed back to agent levels. A multi-layered representation has been proposed, with two-way feedback flows, in which organizational change and institutional change are the endogenous result of complex system dynamics. We think this approach may be far-reaching for a theory of the firm able to integrate both the variety of resources and activities that make up a firm and the variety of agents with which firms interact in their environment.

NOTE

The concept of firm as a network is not new (see, for example, Antonelli, 1987), but it has not received adequate consideration from a theoretical viewpoint. The grafting of the complexity theory in the theory of the firm could take great advantage from such a conceptualization.

REFERENCES

Altenberg, L. (1994) Evolving Better Representations Through Selective Genome Growth, in J.D. Schaffer, H.P. Schwefel and H. Kitano (eds) *Proceedings of the IEEE World Congress on Computational Intelligence*, Piscataway, NJ: IEEE, pp. 182–7.

Altenberg, L. (1995) Genome Growth and the Evolution of the Genotype–Phenotype Map, in W. Banzhaf and F.H. Eckman (eds) *Evolution and Biocomputation*, Berlin and Heidelberg: Springer-Verlag, pp. 205–59.

Antonelli, C. (1987) L'impresa reta: cambiamento tecnologico, internalizzazione e appropriazione di quasi rendite, *Annali di storia dell'impresa*, III, pp. 79–119.

Antonelli, C. (1995) *The Economics of Localized Technological Change and Industrial Dynamics*, Boston: Kluwer Academic Press.

Antonelli, C. (1999) *The Microdynamics of Technological Change*, London and New York: Routledge.

Aoki, M. (1990) Toward an Economic Model of the Japanese Firm, *Journal of Economic Literature*, **28**(1), 1–27.

Aoki, M. and R. Dore (1994) *The Japanese Firm: The Sources of Competitive Strength*, Oxford: Oxford University Press.

Arthur, B. (1989) Competing Technologies, Increasing Returns and Lock-in by Small Historical Events, *Economic Journal*, **99**(394), 116–31.

Arthur, B. (1994) *Increasing Returns and Path Dependence in the Economy*, Ann Arbor: Michigan University Press.

Arthur, W.B. (2009), *The Nature of Technology*, New York: Free Press.

Arthur, W.B., S.N. Durlauf and D.A. Lane (eds) (1997), *The Economy as an Evolving Complex System II*, Redwood City, CA: Addison-Wesley.

Barabási, A.L. and R. Albert (1999), Emergence of Scaling in Random Networks, *Science*, **286**(5439), 509–12.

Barney, J.B. (1991) The Resource Based View of Strategy: Origins, Implications, and Prospects, *Journal of Management*, **17**(1), 97–211.

Chandler, A.D. (1962) *Strategy and Structure: Chapters in the History of the Industrial Enterprise*, Cambridge, MA: MIT Press.

Chandler, A.D. (1977) *The Visible Hand: The Managerial Revolution in American Business*, Cambridge, MA and London: The Belknap Press of Harvard University Press.

Chandler, A.D. ([1984] 1992) The Emergence of Managerial Capitalism, in M. Granovetter and R. Swedberg (eds) *The Sociology of Economic Life*, Boulder, CO: Westview Press.

Coase, R. (1937) The Nature of the Firm, *Economica*, **4**(16), 386–405.

Conner, K.R. and C.K. Prahalad (1996) A Resource-based Theory of the Firm: Knowledge versus Opportunism, *Organization Science*, **7**(5), 477–501.

David, P.A. (1985) Clio and the Economics of QWERTY, *American Economic Review*, **75**(2), 332–7.

Dierickx, I. and K. Cool (1989) Asset Stock Accumulation and Sustainability of Competitive Advantage, *Management Science*, **35**(12), 161–84.

Granovetter, M. (1985) Economic Action and Social Structure: The Problem of Embeddedness, *American Journal of Sociology*, **91**(3), 481–93.

Hall, P.A. and D. Soskice (2001) *Varieties of Capitalism: The Institutional Foundations of Comparative Advantage*, Oxford: OUP.

Jensen, M.C. and W.H. Meckling (1976) Theory of the Firm: Managerial Behavior, Agency Costs and Ownership Structure, *Journal of Financial Economics*, **3**(4), 305–60.

Kauffman, S. (1993) *Origins of Order: Self-organization and Selection in Evolution*, Oxford: Oxford University Press.

Kuznets, S. (1930) *Secular Movements in Production and Prices*, Boston: Houghton Mifflin.

Kuznets, S. (1973) Modern Economic Growth: Findings and Reflections, *American Economic Review*, **63**(3), 247–58.

Lane, D. and R. Maxfield (2005) Ontological Uncertainty and Innovation, *Journal of Evolutionary Economics*, **15**(1), 3–50.

Lane, D.A., S.E. Van Der Leeuw, D. Pumain and G. West (eds) (2009), *Complexity Perspectives in Innovatio and Social Change*, Berlin: Springer.

Marshall, A. (1890) *Principles of Economics*, London: Macmillan.

Marshall, A. (1919) *Industry and Trade*, London: Macmillan.

Miller, J.H. and S.E. Page (2007), *Complex Adaptive Systems*, Princeton: Princeton University Press.

Nelson, R.R. and S.G. Winter (1982) *An Evolutionary Theory of Economic Change*, Cambridge, MA: Belknap Press.

Penrose, E.G. (1959) *The Theory of the Growth of the Firm*, New York: Wiley.

Prahalad, C.K. and G. Hamel (1990) The Core Competence of the Corporation, *Harvard Business Review* **68**(3), 79–91.

Rumelt, R.P. (1984) Towards a Strategic Theory of the Firm, in R.B. Lamb (ed.) *Competitive Strategi Management*, Englewood Cliffs, NJ: Prentice Hall.

Schumpeter, J.A. ([1912] 1934), *The Theory of Economic Development*, Oxford: Galaxy Books.

Schumpeter, J.A. (1939) *Business Cycles. A Theoretical, Historical and Statistical Analysis of the Capitalis Process*, New York and London: McGraw Hill.

Schumpeter, J.A. (1942) *Capitalism, Socialism and Democracy*, London: Unwin.

Schumpeter, J.A. (1947) The Creative Response in Economic History, *Journal of Economic History*, **7**(2) 149–59.

Simon, H. (1966) *The Sciences of the Artificial*, Cambridge, MA: MIT Press.

Smith, A. (1776) *An Inquiry into the Nature and Causes of the Wealth of Nations*, London: W. Strahan anc T. Cadell.

Sorge, A. (1991) Strategic Fit and Societal Effect: Interpreting Cross-national Comparisons of Technology Organization and Human Resources, *Organization Studies*, **12**(2), 161–90.

Teece, D.J. (1984) Economic Analysis and Strategic Management, *California Management Review*, **26**(3) 87–110.

Teece, D.J., G. Pisano and A. Shuen (1997) Dynamic Capabilities and Strategic Management, *Strategic Management Journal*, **18**(7), 509–33.

Wernerfelt, B. (1984) A Resource Based View of the Firm, *Strategic Management Journal*, **5**(2), 171–80.

Whittington, R. (1992) Putting Giddens into Action: Social Systems and Managerial Agency, *Journal of Management Studies*, **29**(6), 693–712.

Williamson, O.E. (1975) *Markets and Hierarchies: Analysis and Antitrust Implications*, New York: The Free Press.

Williamson, O.E. (1993) Transaction Cost Economics and Organization Theory, *Industrial and Corporate Change*, **2**(1), 107–56.

Williamson, O.E. (1998) Transaction Cost Economics: How it Works; Where it is Headed, *De Economist*, **146**, 23–58.

Winter, S. (1987) Knowledge and Competence as Strategic Assets, in D.J. Teece (ed.) *The Competitive Challenge: Strategies for Industrial Innovation and Renewal*, Cambridge, MA: Ballinger.

Withley, R. (1994) Dominant Forms of Economic Organization in Market Economies, *Organization Studies*, **15**(2), 153–82.

Withley, R. and H. Krinstensen (1996) *The Changing European Firm – Limits to Convergence*, London: Routledge.

PART V

DYNAMIC APPROACHES TO THE FIRM

18 Edith Penrose and George Richardson
Brian J. Loasby

18.1 INTRODUCTION

Edith Penrose and George Richardson met only twice: in Oxford at his invitation at about the time that *The Theory of the Growth of the Firm* was published (Penrose, 1959), and at her invitation in Waterbeach after its republication in 1995. The topics discussed at the first meeting are now forgotten; at the second they ranged widely but did not include economics (Richardson, 2002, p. 37). Richardson's analysis of the organization of industry in terms of complementarities and similarities between the capabilities that are required to undertake particular activities seems a natural development of Penrose's account of the evolution of the specific sets of activities undertaken by each firm that succeeds in growing, and extends it to the evolution of interfirm relationships. Both add valuable detail to Marshall's theory of the interlinked evolution of economic systems and human knowledge, in which essential roles are played by the specific internal and external connections that are developed, consciously and unconsciously, by each firm.

It may therefore seem surprising that the direct contacts between the two were so slight. However, this absence of contacts between people whose ideas (and attitudes) seem in retrospect to be closely connected is not so uncommon as one might imagine; and in this instance there is a good reason that is worth exploring for its historical, methodological and substantive interest. In summary, the eventual convergence was the unintended consequence of attempts to deal with what have often been conceived as distinct problems: the coordination of economic activities, or efficient allocation, and economic growth. These different topics are readily associated with the distinctive analytical concepts of equilibrium and process: the former naturally requires some means of handling interactions between agents, while the latter directs attention to the role of individual agents, especially firms. The symbolic figures for these topics are Walras and Schumpeter; and the latter emphasized the disjunction between the two kinds of enquiry. Penrose explicitly followed his example.

What originated the convergence was Richardson's unfashionable interest in the neglected aspect of equilibrium theory: how is equilibrium attained? This question prompted an inquiry into credible processes, and therefore into the knowledge and the characteristics of the agents whose actions drive these processes. It was Richardson's later recognition that Penrose's conception of the firm was directly relevant to his own enquiries into the practical working of an economic system that led him to increasing emphasis on the interdependence between allocative efficiency and growth, which he saw was consilient with his early studies of Smith, Menger, Marshall and Hayek. Knight and Hayek had both observed that economic problems arise only because of change, either externally generated or internally created; and external factors may elicit a creative response. The most fundamental conclusion from this history, which is exemplified in the practice of Adam Smith and Alfred Marshall and the subject of an explicit warning by

Marshall (1920, p. 382), is that theories of coordination that ignore the context of growth are liable to be seriously misleading.

18.2   PENROSE

By her own account, in an interview with David King (Parkin and King, 1992, quoted in Penrose and Pitelis, 2002, p. 19), Penrose came to the study of firms simply as a means of earning money. Her supervisor at Johns Hopkins University, Fritz Machlup, had become co-director of a substantial research project on the growth of firms and invited her to join the team. Machlup's orientation to 'Austrian' economics would have impressed him with the importance of entrepreneurship – unlike most conventional economists; but although he agreed with Mises and Hayek that purposeful human action supplied the microfoundations for economic theory he did not consider detailed analysis of what happened inside firms to be part of that theory. 'We are not primarily interested in business men, business decisions, business routine and business reactions' (Machlup, 1974, p. 277). However, business behaviour was a proper subject for a research study, and a source of income, and so he was prepared to be co-director of such a study.

After 'nine months of reading and especially thinking' how to apply to the empirical studies of her colleagues the traditional theory of the firm in which she had been trained, Penrose had convinced herself that this theory had no relevance to this research project (Parkin and King, quoted by Penrose and Pitelis, 2002, p. 19). She therefore decided to develop a new theory for this particular purpose, which should not be constrained by the assumptions, methods or content of the existing theoretical system; and in presenting her conclusions she explicitly disclaimed any implications for the established role of 'the firm' in price theory. All this was consistent with Machlup's views. Nevertheless it was an astonishingly bold ambition, even when compared with many of the research objectives that have led to Nobel Prizes in economics.

Penrose begins her exposition by defining her protected theoretical space. She claims that the growth of the firm and efficient resource allocation are incommensurable theoretical domains; thus, formally incommensurate theories may be applied to these domains without creating conflict. '[T]he economist's firm in the "theory of the firm" is not at all the economic institution that ordinary people would think of as a firm' (Penrose, 1959, p. 7); it is an abstraction intended to analyse the overall coordination of activities within an economic system. Her alternative conception of the firm as an administrative system is presented as a different kind of abstraction that is appropriate for explaining the introduction of specific novelties in particular parts of that system (ibid., pp. 15–16). There is a double contrast; between equilibrium and process and between a comprehensive theory and an analytical method that is applicable to domain-specific processes of growth in particular firms.

Her treatment often implicitly violates the boundaries that she prescribes – and is the more valuable for doing so; but it was rhetorically effective. Even though the firm as an administrative organization is explicitly a system for allocating resources that does not simply reflect the dictates of the market, her theory appeared to be less threatening than the 'managerial theories' that were being developed more or less contemporaneously by Baumol (1959) and Williamson (1964), because these directly challenged the assumption of profit maximization as an analytical principle while preserving the assumption of individual optimization. Penrose's firms are profit-seekers, and their managers are not seeking personal objectives. However, the compatability with price theory is strictly limited. Although firms are assumed to be trying to do the best they can, they cannot escape uncertainty – and their attitudes to uncertainty may be important (Penrose, 1985, p.12). Their opportunity sets are not natural givens; they are self-created and may be illusory. This is not just a problem; it is the essential basis for her theory of growth:

> Once it is recognized that the very processes of operation and of expansion are intimately associated with a process by which knowledge is increased, then it immediately becomes clear that the productive opportunity of a firm will change even in the absence of any change in external circumstances or in fundamental technological knowledge. (Penrose, 1959, p.56)

Her claim (ibid., p.56 fn.) that this 'in no way interferes with the usefulness for price and output analysis of the "static" assumptions' might seem plausible if, like Machlup (1946), one treats price theory as an instrument for explaining and predicting price and quantity changes for a single commodity; it clearly 'interferes' with general equilibrium theory, and undermines its extension to supposedly 'endogenous' growth.

Penrose's three foundational propositions are first, that the growth of the firm, exemplified by the firms studied in the research programme that prompted her theory-building, and in particular by the Hercules Powder Company (Penrose, 1960), is driven by the growth of knowledge within the firm; second that the particular knowledge that is generated within each firm is a consequence, sometimes targeted and sometimes incidental, of its particular activities; and third, that firms are a major source of the growth of knowledge within an economy – substantially because the combination of purposeful activity and diversity across firms tends to produce such a variety of potentially useful knowledge. All three propositions are entirely outside the scope of conventional theory; hence the professional and personal advantage of presenting them as propositions that belong to a new realm of discourse.

That opportunity sets within an economy change as the direct result of the activities and ideas of economic agents was a revolutionary idea within contemporary economics. However, it was also a reinvention: that economic development is primarily a consequence of the creation and application of knowledge within a population of differentiated firms is the theme of Marshall's (1920) Book IV, though this was barely recognized at the time when Penrose was developing her analysis, or if recognized was dismissed as marginal to the study of efficient allocation. To appreciate the quality of Penrose's achievement, we may consider how her theoretical system might have been developed by integrating elements from earlier sources, the existence or relevance of which had been concealed by her orthodox training. We should not, however, assume that such an integration might have produced an even better synthesis. First, no one else perceived the opportunity: Austin Robinson, who understood Marshall's analysis better than anyone else in Cambridge, and recognized the firm as an administrative system (Robinson, 1931), had perhaps the best preparation, but Cambridge was no longer a supportive environment, while Coase – a notably thoughtful economist – demonstrated the difficulty of making connections that later seem obvious by failing to use his investigations into what happens in firms to explore what is involved in 'running a business' (Coase, 1991a, p.65). Second, Penrose's explicit rejection, not just of a theoretical system but of the questions to which it was directed, was a declaration of independence, constrained only by the detailed evidence of managers at work, and supported by the sympathetic criticism that Penrose acknowledged in her preface. Could anyone else have made so much of that opportunity?

If it is possible for knowledge to grow, it must always be incomplete: not only are probabilities unknown, so is the possibility set. Knight (1921) had identified uncertainty as a necessary condition for the existence of both firms and entrepreneurship, but though Penrose cites Knight twice she does not make this connection – as Coase did, but without exploring the implications for economic growth. (We should remember that opportunities do not reveal themselves, even to thoughtful economists.) Shackle is not mentioned, but she makes effective use of two pervasive Shacklean themes. First, the consciousness of uncertainty causes people to reject whole classes of actions: thus managers and entrepreneurs – in Penrose's analysis these roles are often combined – will at any time refuse to contemplate many projects, but increased knowledge in particular fields will encourage new ventures. Thus each firm's range is always limited, but these limits may recede as a direct consequence of its own activities (Penrose, 1959, pp. 60–63). (That people are changed by what they do was the basis of Marshall's hopes for progress.) Second, uncertainty is not only a constraint: to adapt Shackle's (1979, p. 26) phrase, it gives scope for 'the imagined, deemed [capable of being made] possible' – which is the briefest possible summary of what drives the growth of a Penrosian firm. Though Penrose (1959, p. 36n.) observes that Schumpeter's concept of entrepreneurship is a more dramatic version of her own, she does not cite Schumpeter's (1934, p. 85) invocation of imagination as an essential element in the distinction between theories of allocative efficiency and theories of growth. Nevertheless in adopting Boulding's (1956) term 'image', she clearly recognized the significance of imagination as a beneficial consequence of uncertainty (Penrose, 1959, p. 5). This image is different for every firm (ibid., p. 217); and entrepreneurs believe that they can act in ways that will change their environment (ibid., p. 42). The result is the 'tendency to variation' that Marshall (1920, p. 355) identified as 'a chief cause of progress'.

We may find appropriate, though unused, microfoundations for her theory in Knight's (1921, p. 348) reflections on the extremely unattractive features of a world without uncertainty, and his corresponding theme of uncertainty as opportunity – in particular for the development of intelligence. In a world of certainty, automata would suffice (ibid., p. 268), but intelligent action requires us to construct our own knowledge by forming categories on the basis of similarities that appear to be consistent with 'the purpose or problem in view' (ibid., p. 206), and then to make domain-specific connections, of cause and effect, or of perception and action, between categories. Karl Popper (1972, pp. 420–21) likewise observes that similarity is always restricted to '*certain respects*' and presupposes 'the adoption of *a point of view*' (original emphasis). Knight notes that people differ in their ability to construct useful categories, and that for each individual this ability will vary substantially between fields. The notion that knowledge and the ability to construct and apply knowledge are both context-dependent is crucial to Penrose's theory; each firm provides a distinctive context and therefore distinctive opportunities for the development and application of knowledge. (This variation is quite different from the concept of 'information asymmetry', which does not recognize that the information content of any message depends on the receiver's structure of knowledge into which it is fitted.) That the firms in an industry should not be homogeneous but diverse is a quintessentially Marshallian theme; and the contemporary association of diversity with imperfect competition and its pervasive welfare losses provided a substantial justification for Penrose's insistence on her protected theoretical space.

Penrose's principle of the development of distinctive knowledge within each firm may now be seen as an application of Adam Smith's universal rule of economic progress set down in the opening sentence of Book 1, Chapter 1, of the *Wealth of Nations*. 'The greatest improvement in the productive powers of labour, and the greater part of the skill, dexterity and judgement with which it is anywhere directed, or applied, seem to have been the effects of the division of labour' (Smith [1776] 1976b, p. 13). This rule, in turn, is derived from Smith's theory of the growth of knowledge through the imaginative creation of new combinations to impose patterns on apparent disorder within a particular class of phenomena, which he first used to explain the emergence of science as a distinctive, and later subdivided, domain in his 'History of Astronomy' (Smith [1795] 1980). Specialization provides multiple foci for the development of effective knowledge for particular purposes, and leads directly to a theory of endogenous – and inherently competitive – technological change, based on a combination of incentive and more detailed understanding (Smith [1776] 1976b, pp. 19–22). Smith supplies the components of the cumulative process elaborated by Penrose, but he does not develop it. We should, however, note for future reference that his economic theory, which combines coordination and growth, is founded on the creation and application of increasingly diversified knowledge.

Economic development through the creation and application of differentiated knowledge by many people in many contexts is Alfred Marshall's justification for his suggestion that organization should be considered alongside land, labour and capital as a factor of production (Marshall, 1920, pp. 138–9). For this role it has a far better claim than 'total factor productivity', because it provides the basis for explaining in detail (using Penrose's theory) the essential relationships that the undecomposable aggregate labelled 'total factor productivity' conceals. If knowledge and its application are always context-limited, then the creation, modification and connection of contexts is a major determinant of the rate at which knowledge is generated and of the kinds of knowledge that are produced. Marshall indicates the importance of different forms of organization, each with their internal variations, in providing distinctive and complementary kinds of environment for knowledge creation.

Penrose's analysis of the operations of individual firms and of their collective significance provides an extensive elaboration of one particular category of Marshall's treatment. The commonalities deserve attention. Variation between firms is essential, and is a natural consequence of local differences in context. Raffaelli (2003) has traced this emphasis on the development of domain-specific knowledge, especially practical knowledge, to Marshall's (1994) early thought experiment of a mechanical brain. Any firm may introduce novelty, including 'showing people things which they had never thought of having before; but which they want to have as soon as the notion is suggested to them' (Marshall, 1920, p. 280); compare Penrose's (1959, p. 80) proposition that 'it is reasonable to suppose that consumers' tastes are formed by the range of commodities which is available to them, or, at least, about which they know' and that an entrepreneur may therefore consider demand 'as something he ought to be able to do something about'.

No new goods will be created without a deliberate decision to take some of the opportunities that are inherent, though often not obvious, in the new knowledge that is created within the firm; and that requires purposive behaviour to drive imagination and convert what is imagined into a practical and profitable line of business. In this process logic may play a valuable supporting role. Thus the scope of Penrose's theory, like Schumpeter's, is deliberately limited to those firms whose owners and managers wish their firm to grow. Neither author has any use for the notion of a 'representative firm' as an analytical device. Marshall's [1920, pp. 317–8, 342–3] 'representative firm' was invoked as a summary statistic to indicate the changing supply price of an industry as a consequence of the evolving activities of a diverse and changing population of firms. Her belief in the importance of purposive behaviour had been signalled by her criticism of Alchian's (1950) argument that the usefulness of neoclassical theory did not depend on the rationality of business decisions, because a moderately severe selection environment would generally produce roughly the results predicted, even if business people had neither interest nor skill in profit-making. Penrose (1952) insisted that there was no equivalent in economic systems to the urge to reproduce that guaranteed excess entry in biological systems. Without purposive behaviour, it was far from certain that firms that took economically perverse actions would disappear, both because their rivals might be even less competent and because 'the environment is not independent of their own activities' (Penrose, 1959, p. 42). Human motivation could not be bypassed in economics.

It is therefore no surprise that the motivation of those within the firm receives explicit attention in her exposition (ibid., pp. 26–30, 34–7, 183–6). As she recognizes (ibid., p. 36n.), this is a generalization of Schumpeter's perspective. 'All the evidence we have indicates that the growth of a firm is connected with attempts of particular groups of people to do something; nothing is gained and much is lost if this fact is not explicitly recognized' (ibid., p. 2). In the context of incomplete and expandable knowledge, however, profit maximization has no clear meaning. This perspective helps to assimilate growth and long-run profitability as objectives, and entrepreneurial imagination with both. Though her theory deals only with successful firms, there is no suggestion that all their expansion plans succeed; moreover it is as clear as in Kirzner's (1973) theory of entrepreneurship that some opportunities remain unrecognized.

The consequences for the economy of the desire for profits and growth are examined in the final chapter, but though this is the equivalent of the welfare appraisal that was then a standard feature of books on industrial economics it makes no reference to the concept of optimality. What concerns her is the maintenance of the process of competition that delivers continual improvement, through growth based on the cycle of resources applied to new services that are then directed towards new productive opportunities, the active management of which eventually settles into routine while creating new resources for which profitable uses may be imagined once managers are no longer preoccupied with the most recent innovation. As with Herbert Simon, in explaining business behaviour the scarce resource of attention is a crucial factor; hence the prime significance of the administrative framework in shaping the deployment of this resource and therefore the development of knowledge and the perception of opportunities. Evidence that major changes in this framework may be essential to continued growth was being collected and explained by Alfred Chandler (1960) while Penrose was developing her theory; both subsequently recognized the complementarities. This process embodies a dialectical relationship between routine and innovation resembling that to which Raffaelli (2003) has drawn attention in Marshall's work.

Like Marshall, Penrose bases her analysis on the limitations and extendability of human knowledge. Though her discussion of this is brief (Penrose, 1959, pp. 53–4) it includes a distinction between objective and experiential knowledge that corresponds to Ryle's (1949) distinction between 'knowledge that' and 'knowledge how'. 'Knowledge how' evolves with idiosyncratic experience as well as through organized learning, and we should not expect that either the capabilities or the perceptions of firms will relentlessly converge. The distinctiveness of organizational capabilities was a persistent theme in the work of Peter Drucker, the outstanding twentieth-century practical analyst of management: for example, he noted that General Motors had been consistently successful in developing businesses that it had acquired whereas General Electric had an excellent record in creating new businesses, but neither seemed able to do what the other could (Drucker, 1964, pp. 107–8). Penrose (1959, pp. 118, 132, 139) emphasizes the importance of a technological base, which requires continued investment in order to make possible adaptation and diversification.

It is a central theme of Penrose's theory (as of Marshall's) that organization matters. It matters essentially because the development and application of different kinds of knowledge must be differently organized, and because, as we shall see in the following section, complementary capabilities must be combined in ways that respect the dissimilarities between them. Penrose's firm conforms to Coase's (1937, p. 393) definition of 'a system of relationships which comes into existence when the direction of resources is dependent on an entrepreneur'. However, in a notable example of the effects of different foci of attention, Coase explained this system of relationships as an efficient response to the costs of relying on markets in a context of Knightian uncertainty but did not enquire how it worked, whereas Penrose, whose problem was not the existence but the operation of firms, explains how this 'autonomous administrative planning unit' (Penrose, 1959, p. 15) becomes an area of 'authoritative communication' (ibid., p. 20), in which the basis of coordination is the compatibility of decision premises. As Ménard (1994) has emphasized, in a successful organization these authoritative communications flow up and across as well as down formal channels; they also flow between members of different organizations. Since Penrose appears to endorse Barnard's (1938, p. 163) view that authority is granted by the recipient of the communication, she naturally argues that the effectiveness of this coordination depends on experience within the firm and its external connections.

That is why, as Coase ([1972] 1988, p. 63) later observed, 'the costs of organizing an activity within any given firm depend on what other activities the firm is engaged in'. Penrose explains this relationship by the degree of compatability between the capabilities that are required to conduct these activities, and extends this explanation to the sequence of growth. In a successful business, the patterns of thinking, the criteria for identifying occasions for decisions, and the characteristics of a satisfactory response provide a set of institutions that are superior to market contracting within a domain that is never precisely defined. (This is Simon's crucial elaboration of Coase's [1937] explanation of the firm.) These institutions lead and direct the growth of the firm; if the institutions cease to match the environment they lead and direct its decay, as has been repeatedly demonstrated. That most formal organizations sooner or later fail to maintain this equilibrium prompted Barnard's (1938) study of the role of the executive, which extends far beyond decision-making, and Drucker (1969, p. 293) noted that a crucial virtue of private enterprise is its potential to 'go bankrupt and disappear' in case of failure, which should be expected to be common since 'business. . .is designed to make and to manage change' (ibid.). The firm's capabilities provide its option value, though there is no reliable means of determining that value. Since the justification for all moves is conjectural, firms, like scientists and economic theorists, make many mistakes, and some mistakes are fatal. Penrose does not discuss mistakes, but her theory readily encompasses them. Indeed, there is still no better foundation for pursuing the joint development of institutional and evolutionary economics in the tradition of Adam Smith.

In recent years, the value of Penrose's work has been increasingly recognized among writers on evolutionary economics and business strategy. In both fields her signal contribution is the crucial combination of imagination and heterogeneity. Because they lend themselves more readily to formal modelling, selection processes and replication have tended to receive most attention among evolutionary theorists; but neither of these can be of lasting interest unless there is some process that continually replenishes the variety on which selection and replication can act; and many academic analysts of business strategy have been so influenced by equilibrium theorizing in their attempts to identify the possible sources of sustainable advantage that they have tended to forget that a competitive advantage can be sustained only through the creation of new productive opportunities. A company may be able to sustain an equilibrium in terms of its theory and policy, but not an equilibrium set of activities. 'The enterprise, by definition, must be capable of producing more or better than all the resources that comprise it' and that requires 'a transmutation of the resources', which is the continuing task of management (Drucker, 1955, p. 12). What Penrose has to offer those who seek to understand economic evolution or business strategy is a thorough analysis of transmutation through the imagination of new services that these resources can provide, leading to new opportunities, the process of exploiting which creates new resources, together with analysis of the crucial importance of the administrative framework in facilitating (or impeding) and shaping this sequence, and of the need to modify this framework to allow it to continue.

18.3   RICHARDSON

George Richardson's academic journey started very differently (Richardson, 1998, pp. ix–xix). After a wartime two-year degree in mathematics and physics at the University of Aberdeen, followed by three years in naval and then political intelligence, he read PPE at Oxford, where what he described as a gratuitous display of mathematics caused his tutor to pass him on to John Hicks. This turned out to be a crucial event, for entirely non-mathematical reasons. Hicks was an effective educator, and encouraged him to stay on; after a year in the Foreign Office, Richardson took this advice and returned to Oxford to read for a PhD. He was soon elected as the first Economics Fellow at St John's College (presumably with Hicks's support) where he was persuaded to abandon the doctorate as an unnecessary qualification and an undesirable constraint on original thought – not an uncommon view in both Oxford and Cambridge at the time. In extreme contrast to Penrose who, at a later stage of her career, felt compelled to cope with the specific problem of constructing a theory to fit the evidence about the ways in which firms grew, Richardson could think about anything he liked. Moreover, he did almost all of his thinking alone.

However, his relationship with Hicks had given him one great advantage, in addition to his own example. Hicks had advised him in preparing his weekly essay not to read recent articles but to go directly to the relevant works of the great economists, such as Walras, Edgeworth, Menger and Marshall (Richardson, 1990, p. xviii); that this was congenial advice is suggested by his enjoyment of Bertrand Russell's *The Problems of Philosophy* and G.E. Moore's *Ethics* during his time-compressed course in Aberdeen (Richardson, 1998, p. xiv). So he began his thinking with a very broad view of the subject matter of economics and of the ways in which it might be analysed; he also believed that he 'knew economics and enough physics to know the difference' – and that the core difference was the essential role in economics of individual 'intention, expectation [and] knowledge' (ibid., p. xii) – a principle that was also emphasized, though in explicit contrast to evolutionary biology, by Penrose.

As Richardson considered the contemporary style of equilibrium theorizing, the close association between perfect competition and ideal economic organization, and the resultant pronouncements on economic policy, he became increasingly convinced of the potential for substantial error in our understanding of economic systems because of the failure to incorporate the basic principle that knowledge is both fragmented and uncertain. Hayek's (1937) 'Economics and Knowledge' seemed to offer the best insight, which he later realized was closely related to Adam Smith's vision (Richardson, 1998, p. xi), and gave the initial direction to a sequence of thinking and writing that culminated in the recognition that the allocation problem, as normally defined, is actually secondary to the problem of organizing the improvement and application of the knowledge that is available within the system. This conclusion may be matched with Penrose's theory of growth, which embedded intra-firm allocation within a theory of the development and application of firm-specific knowledge.

In his first published article, Richardson (1953) began his investigation of business behaviour on more realistic assumptions about knowledge. This includes a connection, of great potential, from Knight's (1921) distinction between risk and uncertainty to Gilbert Ryle's (1949) distinction between 'knowing that' and 'knowing how'. Richardson (1953, p. 139) points out that an understanding of the principles of probabilistic reasoning is not easily convertible into the skills that are required to form an estimate of the particular probability function that is appropriate to a specific problem (thus incidentally providing support for Keynes's [1937, p. 214] warning about the fragility of expectations). The application to production knowledge was to come much later.

This article 'attracted no interest whatever' (Richardson, 1998, p. xi). The attitude to Hayek would have been sufficient proof of its irrelevance in Cambridge; and its suggestion that what appear to be obvious imperfections may sometimes be very helpful in making the system work was unwelcome to most defenders as well as critics of 'the market', few of whom were interested in market institutions. Nevertheless he embarked on a thorough exploration (Richardson, 1959, 1960) of the central problem that Hayek (1937, p. 45) had identified in the theory of perfect competition: how are the individuals within an economy to make the specific decisions that will lead to the equilibrium that in theoretical models is directly derived from the supposed data about goods, resources, technology and preferences, and how is each of them to acquire the information that will lead inevitably to those decisions? Perfect competition requires complete independence of action; but the correct action for each depends on the aggregate effects of the actions of everyone else; therefore what is optimal for each depends on what others will do, as in models of oligopoly (Richardson, 1960, p. 35). The consequences of investment in new capacity will become apparent only when this capacity comes into use, but they need to be accurately foreseen by everyone contemplating decisions about future production if the result is to be the equilibrium supposedly inherent in the data. Shackle has explored the macroeconomic implications, identified by Keynes, of this problem, as well as incorporating it in his own textbook theory of the firm (Shackle, 1970).

Plans depend on beliefs, and how are these beliefs to be formed (Richardson, 1959, p. 224)? Within the theory, the answer was given by the supply curve, but this curve is claimed to summarize individual responses and cannot legitimately be used to predict them. In an earlier paper Richardson (1956, pp. 114–15) had elaborated his argument that there is no justification for the standard practice in long-period analysis of assuming that the curve showing marginal cost as a function of current output, which is a physical relationship dependent on technology and input prices, can be transmuted into the curve showing future output as a function of the price expected (by whom?) at a time when expansion plans come into effect, which is a relationship between individual expectations and the sum of their consequences.

Richardson rejects the argument that the record of reasonably satisfactory adjustment demonstrates that there is no problem: apart from the less satisfactory episodes in that record he argues that satisfactory adjustment relies on what, in relation to perfect competition, are 'essential imperfections', and that attempts to remove these imperfections in the search for Pareto improvements may have unfortunate consequences. (We may now see this as a particular example of the general principle that all knowledge requires structure, which is a particular pattern of connections, not the universally connected system that is postulated in general equilibrium theory.) One possibility is explicit collusion; much more common are shared assumptions about what is appropriate behaviour. Both the significance of such institutional support for social coherence and its possible origins in human characteristics and the limitations of individual knowledge may be traced back to Adam Smith's ([1759] 1976a) *Theory of Moral Sentiments*: Richardson (1960, p. 54) cites Hume but not Smith.

A nearly ubiquitous helpful imperfection is firm heterogeneity: this implies differential awareness of any particular opportunity (which is crucial to Kirzner's [1973] theory of entrepreneurship), differences in the ability to obtain finance, equipment, or workers, or to cope with the additional demands on management, and limitations imposed by the established market connections of other firms. Although Richardson (1960, p. 30) draws attention to the importance of technical knowledge in restricting the set of firms to be considered, in this analysis he does not consider the implications of variations between firms in 'knowledge how', but focuses on the problems of obtaining the appropriate market information.

All these elements are relevant to Penrose's theory, which is not surprising because they are problems of growing a business. However, Richardson is here concerned to expose the limitations of a theory of efficient allocation that cannot explain how this allocation is achieved (ibid., pp. 49–71); he is not yet thinking about growth. He then turns o the problems, peculiar to each firm, of obtaining from other firms all the additional goods and services that it needs to increase its own production, recognizing that some of these other firms are likely to be trading with some of its rivals (ibid., pp. 72–87): these problems are invisible in a conceptual scheme of anonymous exchange. Next he drops the assumption of a fixed list of goods, and extends the concept of efficient adjustment to include the assortment of production, which he calls 'the filling up of uncharted economic space' (ibid., p 102). This is close to Penrose's theme, and his proposal to switch attention to satisfactions that may be met in various ways (ibid., pp. 102–4) helps us to understand the differential perception of productive opportunities that is essential to her theory. He briefly discusses Chamberlin's (1933) attempt to expand equilibrium theory in this way, concluding that its failure to deal with the problem of change is its most serious deficiency (Richardson, 1960, p. 112). Penrosian dynamics could have released the great potential of Chamberlin's ideas.

Richardson's analysis left him sceptical of any simple rules for competition policy. Many kinds of arrangements, formal and informal, might contribute to efficient adjustment, but they might not deliver efficient outcomes. In retrospect, he suggested considering the economy as similar to a natural system that sometimes malfunctioned; when it did, intervention was in order, but should be appropriate to our limited knowledge of how things worked (Richardson, 1998, p. xvi). He therefore approved the British preference for a formal investigative system, and served on the Monopolies Commission for some years. This experience, preceded by some consultancy work, brought him closer to the internal working of firms. One consequence was a paper on a firm's limits to growth, which includes his first reference to Penrose's work (Richardson, 1964, p. 11) in support of the reality of a managerial limit to expansion. This he argues is essentially an organizational limit: people have to build relationships, and develop ways of identifying problems and framing solutions. However, there is no reference to the work of Herbert Simon and his colleagues at Carnegie Tech, in which he has never shown much interest – a productive opportunity not perceived.

This line of reasoning suggested the need for a framework in which to explain the great diversity of forms taken by 'contrived coordination' (Richardson, 1998, p. xvi) to complement the wider ranging spontaneous coordination emphasized by Hayek; and he realized that Penrose's (1959) detailed examination of how firms operate, and the interactions between their administrative framework and their operations, supplied the basis for explaining why firms need 'outside' as well as 'inside' systems of communication and cooperation, as Marshall had so well understood. The result was his most famous paper (Richardson, 1972). Without invoking his earlier criticism of perfect competition theory for its inability to explain adjustment to change, he focuses on the simplifying assumptions in the theory of the firm that the set of products is well defined, that every product has its production function from which the optimal input combination may be calculated for every situation, and that the performance of productive operations is never problematic. Though this is highly convenient for choice theory, it is not an adequate basis for a theory of industrial organization, which must begin with an explicit recognition that 'production has to be undertaken (as Mrs Penrose has so very clearly explained) by human organizations embodying specifically appropriate human experience and skill' (ibid., p. 888). Ryle is cited again (ibid., p. 895).

Had he then been aware of Ronald Coase's address at the National Bureau of

Economic Research's fiftieth anniversary colloquium in 1970, he might have observee that the continuing neglect of Penrose's work was a major reason why, as Coase com plained, what is commonly called industrial organization 'tells us almost nothing abou the organization of industry' (Coase, 1972, p. 58). It should be noted that what Coas proposed was 'a large-scale systematic study' that 'would endeavour to discover th characteristics of the grouping of activities within firms' (ibid., pp. 71, 73–4), not th development of a theory, and that he still seemed to regard firms and markets as func tioning in sharply differentiated ways – relying on planning or prices. There still seem to be little recognition that Penrose and Richardson offer major contributions to wha Coase (1991b) called 'the institutional structure of production'; but since the institutiona structure of production is ignored in most economic reasoning that is not surprising.

Richardson replaces Penrose's distinction between resources and services by a distinc tion between capabilities and activities (presumably because of their more specificall human associations), but retains the two-way relationship: capabilities develop as a resul of activities, and developed capabilities may be applied to new activities. In a subsequen paper (Richardson, 1975) this interaction is traced back to Adam Smith's explanatior of growth through the interacting effects of the division of labour on knowledge and o knowledge on the division of labour, generating increasing returns as markets expand this provides 'the essentials of a self-sustaining theory of economic growth' (ibid., p. 352) Increasing return is a process, not a property of a production function: this is explicit in Marshall's (1920, p. 318) definition, which follows Adam Smith by incorporating organi zational change as an essential element. Richardson (1975, p. 353) observes that the theoretical insistence on perfect competition at the expense of increasing returns 'might reasonably be regarded as a denial of Smith's central principle erected into a system of political economy', and draws attention (ibid., p. 352) to the elaboration of this process by Allyn Young (1928). Penrose (1959, p. 71) refers to Young and argues that the growth of knowledge induces changes in industrial organization precisely because of limits to the rate at which knowledge can be absorbed and applied within existing administrative frameworks.

Richardson had become deeply impressed by the extreme complexity of industrial organization, which could not be adequately represented by a formal model but could be interpreted by an appropriate conceptual scheme. The elements of this scheme are taken directly from Penrose; what he adds are two kinds of relationships between capabili ties: those of similarity and complementarity. Both are matters of degree; recalling the observations of Knight and Popper cited earlier, we may add that they are also matters of perspective – and changes of perspective may be the key to new combinations, of both knowledge and organizational arrangements.

Richardson's basic principle, like many valuable principles, is conceptually simple but requires both skill and specific knowledge to apply successfully: this applies to both analysts and practitioners. (Richardson had later experience of a comprehensive failure by consultants during his time at Oxford University Press.) Adding additional activities ('productive services') that require similar capabilities provides an expansion path for Penrose's firms; that similarity is a matter of degree and perception allows firms within an industry to create different expansion paths and so to maintain Marshall's 'tendency to variation'. However, the appropriate criterion of similarity depends on context; and there is ample evidence of firms getting this wrong. Many products require a combina-

on of substantially different activities, and if these require substantially different capabilities they are best assigned to different organizations in order to secure the advantages
of the division of labour – probably assisted by the kind of 'external organization' that
Marshall recognized.

The hard cases, in practice even more than theory, arise when activities that are highly
specific to particular products, and that therefore need to be closely coordinated, require
very different capabilities, indicating powerful advantages in strict differentiation.
Richardson gives examples of the great variety of arrangements in place in response to
such situations. The 'dense network of cooperation and affiliation' (Richardson, 1972,
p. 883) includes stable market relationships supported by goodwill, formal contracts or
shareholding, subcontracting and collaboration of various kinds in design, development
and marketing, sometimes in very complex combinations. We may note the multifarious
possibilities for 'holdups', and at the same time the dubious effectiveness of the instruments of control that have been presented as remedies; and we may conclude, as Simon
suggested, that the most effective remedy – which cannot be guaranteed – may lie in the
difficulties, and challenges, of the operational task that leave little cognitive or emotional
energy for ingenious opportunism.

Penrose (1995, pp. ix, xvi) enthusiastically endorsed Richardson's contribution, and
it is now widely recognized within a substantial – but not mainstream – research community. But his 1975 paper was intended to be his last. Since few economists showed
any interest, not only in his work, but in the significance of the questions to which it was
addressed, he decided to make a definitive break, signalled by disposing of his economics
books. He became Chief Executive of Oxford University Press, with 3000 employees –
one of the very few academic economists to run a major business. While there he experienced Penrosian problems and perceived Penrosian opportunities, and applied his own
analysis in divesting the company's printing and paper-making businesses because these
complementary activities required different capabilities and did not match the diversity of the Press's needs, requiring the managers of both to deal extensively with other
businesses. Richardson explained this to Oliver Williamson at a conference in 1998.

Of potentially greater interest are his reflections on the role of the chief executive in
supporting and developing a set of institutional arrangements that is appropriate to
running each particular business and that allows major decisions to be 'arrived at rather
than taken, and by a process to which rational calculation [is] not central' (Richardson,
1998, p. xviii). His limited reflections seem consistent with Chester Barnard's (1938)
analysis of the functions of senior management, which he has not read; but there is no
basis for any systematic discussion.

Increasing interest in Richardson's ideas was indicated by a second edition of
Information and Investment in 1990 and a set of collected papers in 1998, for which he
chose the title that he was not allowed to use for *Information and Investment* in 1960
(Richardson, 1998), a conference in his honour (Foss and Loasby, 1998), and an invitation to the inaugural conference of the Danish Research Unit for Industrial Dynamics
in 1995, which began an influential and happy relationship. He responded by writing
several more papers, most of them unpublished, mainly on particular industrial issues.
His paper on 'Competition, Innovation and Increasing Returns' shows how an industry of Penrosian firms may use their subjective perceptions and evolving capabilities to
compete in time as well as product space, how demand and cost may therefore not be

independent, and how established firms may often take advantage of their establishe connections and specific knowledge but may sometimes fail to perceive opportunitie that do not emerge from their own experience and underrate the prospects of outsider (Richardson, 1998, pp. 168–77).

18.4   CONCLUSION

The most fundamental message from Penrose and Richardson is the significance of time 'The universe exists by happening' (Kelly, 1963, p. 7). Time brings change in both cir cumstances and knowledge, much of it as a consequence of human activity. This activity is often directed to a particular purpose, but things rarely turn out precisely as intended Moreover, change is often qualitative, not simply a rearrangement or augmentation o the original data; and that may not be accurately reflected in statistics and is rarely wel represented in economic theory. All this is especially true of knowledge. Knowledge i structured, being composed of categories and relationships, and grows by amending either or both in ways that seem appropriate to particular situations or problems. It i therefore not surprising that different people know different things and have differen thoughts. Moreover, analysts tend to systematically underrate the significance of 'knowl edge how', even though this is the primary content of their own education.

Structures of knowledge and of economic systems may develop in ways that were no predicted, and indeed may be inherently unpredictable; closely related ideas and activities may diverge, and unrelated ideas and activities may converge, as contexts of similarity are redefined to cope with unfamiliar situations and newly imagined possibilities. The intellectual histories of Penrose and Richardson illustrate such an unplanned convergence; it is beyond the scope of this chapter to explore comparable 'new combinations' of productive capabilities developed by firms engaged in apparently unrelated activities.

Both the development and application of knowledge depends on, but is not determined by, context; and all knowledge systems, such as economies, are complex structures combining, as Marshall said, many forms of organization – notably administrative frameworks and interfirm relations. The architecture of complexity relies on quasidecomposability (Simon, 1969); and it is the 'quasi' that causes the trouble for analysts, system designers and participants alike. As Richardson realized, making judgements about the desirability of particular forms, or of variants within a form, is far more difficult than economists hoped in the mid-twentieth century.

These issues have attracted the attention of some of the greatest economists, who have made major contributions to our understanding. Among recent economists Penrose and Richardson merit special consideration because of the inspiration and direction they offer, not least in their methods and their attitudes.

REFERENCES

Alchian, Armen A. (1950) Uncertainty, evolution and economic theory. *Journal of Political Economy* **58**(3): 211–21.
Barnard, Chester I. (1938) *The Functions of the Executive*. Cambridge, MA: Harvard University Press.

Baumol, William J. (1959) *Business Behavior, Value and Growth*. New York: Harcourt, Brace and World.

Boulding, Kenneth E. (1956) *The Image*. Ann Arbor: University of Michigan Press.

Chamberlin, Edward H. (1933) *The Theory of Monopolistic Competition*. Cambridge, MA: Harvard University Press.

Chandler, Alfred D. (1960) *Strategy and Structure*. Cambridge, MA and London: MIT Press.

Coase, Ronald H. (1937) The nature of the firm. *Economica* N.S. **4**(16): 386–405. Reprinted in Coase (1988), pp. 33–56.

Coase, Ronald H. (1972) Industrial organization: a proposal for research. In Victor R. Fuchs (ed.) *Policy Issues and Research Opportunities in Industrial Organization*. New York: National Bureau of Economic Research, pp. 59–73. Reprinted in Coase (1988), pp. 57–74. (References are to this reprint.)

Coase, Ronald H. (1988) *The Firm, the Market, and the Law*. Chicago and London: University of Chicago Press.

Coase, Ronald H. (1991a) The nature of the firm: influence. In O.E. Williamson and S.G. Winter, pp. 61–74.

Coase, Ronald H. (1991b) The institutional structure of production. In O.E Williamson and S.G. Winter, pp. 227–35.

Drucker, Peter F. (1955) *The Practice of Management*. London: Heinemann.

Drucker, Peter F. (1964) *Managing for Results*. London: Heinemann.

Drucker, Peter F. (1969) *The Age of Discontinuity*. London: Heinemann.

Foss, Nicolai J. and Brian J. Loasby (1998) *Economic Organization, Capabilities and Cooperation: Essays in Honour of G.B. Richardson*. London and New York: Routledge.

Hayek, Friedrich A. (1937) Economics and knowledge. *Economica* N.S. **4**(1): 33–54.

Kelly, George A. (1963) *A Theory of Personality*. New York: W.W. Norton.

Keynes, J. Maynard (1937) The general theory of employment. *Quarterly Journal of Economics* **51**(2): 209–23.

Kirzner, Israel M. (1973) *Competition and Entrepreneurship*. Chicago: University of Chicago Press.

Knight, Frank H. (1921) *Risk, Uncertainty and Profit*. Boston: Houghton Mifflin.

Machlup, Fritz (1946) Marginal analysis and empirical research. *American Economic Review* **36**(4): 519–54.

Machlup, Fritz (1974) Situational determinism in economics. *British Journal for the Philosophy of Science*, **25**(3): 271–84.

Marshall, Alfred (1920) *Principles of Economics*. London: Macmillan.

Marshall, Alfred (1994) 'Ye Machine'. *Research in the History of Economic Thought and Methodology, Archival Supplement 4*. Greenwich CT: JAI Press, pp. 116–32.

Ménard, Claude (1994) Organizations as co-ordinating devices. *Metroeconomica* **45**(3): 224–47.

Parkin, M. and David King (2002) *Economics*. London: Addison Wesley.

Penrose, Edith T. (1952) Biological analogies in the theory of the firm. *American Economic Review* **42**: 804–19.

Penrose, Edith T. (1959) *The Theory of the Growth of the Firm*. Oxford: Basil Blackwell.

Penrose, Edith T. (1960) The growth of the firm – a case study: the Hercules Powder Company. *Business History Review* **34**(1): 1–23.

Penrose, Edith T. (1985) The theory of the growth of the firm twenty-five years after. *Acta Universitatis Upsaliensis*: *Studia Oeconomiae Negotiorum* **20**(1): 1–16.

Penrose, Edith (1995) *The Theory of the Growth of the Firm*, 3rd edn. Oxford: Oxford University Press.

Penrose, Perran and Christos Pitelis (2002) Edith Elura Tilton Penrose: life, contribution and influence. In C. Pitelis (2002), pp. 17–36.

Pitelis, Christos (ed.) (2002) *The Growth of the Firm: The Legacy of Edith Penrose*. Oxford and New York: Oxford University Press.

Popper, Karl R. (1972) *The Logic of Scientific Discovery*. 6th impression. London: Hutchinson.

Raffaelli, Tiziano (2003) *Marshall's Evolutionary Economics*. London and New York: Routledge.

Richardson, George B. (1953) Imperfect knowledge and economic efficiency. *Oxford Economic Papers* **5**(2): 136–56. Reprinted in G.B. Richardson (1998), pp. 1–21.

Richardson, George B. (1956) Demand and supply reconsidered. *Oxford Economic Papers* **8**(2): 113–26. Reprinted in G.B. Richardson (1998), pp. 37–50.

Richardson, George B. (1959) Equilibrium, expectations and information. *Economic Journal* **69**(274): 223–37.

Richardson, George B. (1960) *Information and Investment*. Oxford: Oxford University Press.

Richardson, George B. (1964) The limits to a firm's rate of growth. *Oxford Economic Papers* **16**(1): 9–23. Reprinted in G.B. Richardson (1998), pp. 66–80.

Richardson, George B. (1972) The organisation of industry. *Economic Journal* **82**(327): 883–96. Reprinted in G.B. Richardson (1998), pp. 143–56.

Richardson, George B. (1975) Adam Smith on competition and increasing returns. In Andrew S. Skinner and Thomas Wilson (eds) *Essays on Adam Smith*. Oxford: Oxford University Press, pp. 350–60. Reprinted in G.B. Richardson (1998), pp. 157–67.

Richardson, George B. (1990) *Information and Investment*, 2nd edn. Oxford: Clarendon Press.

Richardson, George B. (1998) *The Economics of Imperfect Knowledge*. Cheltenham, UK and Northampton MA, USA: Edward Elgar.

Richardson, George B. (2002) Mrs Penrose and neoclassical theory. In C. Pitelis (2002), pp. 37–44.

Robinson, E. Austin G. (1931) *The Structure of Competitive Industry*. Cambridge: Cambridge University Press

Ryle, Gilbert (1949) *The Concept of Mind*. London: Hutchinson.

Schumpeter, Joseph A. (1934) *The Theory of Economic Development*. Cambridge MA: Harvard University Press.

Shackle, George L.S. (1970) *Expectation, Enterprise and Profit*. London: Allen and Unwin.

Shackle, George L.S. (1979) *Imagination and the Nature of Choice*. Edinburgh: Edinburgh University Press.

Simon, Herbert A. (1969) The architecture of complexity. In *The Sciences of the Artificial*. Cambridge, MA and London: MIT Press, pp. 84–118.

Smith, Adam ([1759] 1976a) *The Theory of Moral Sentiments*, ed. D.D. Raphael and A.L. Macfie. Oxford Oxford University Press.

Smith, Adam ([1776] 1976b) *An Inquiry into the Nature and Causes of the Wealth of Nations*, ed. R.H Campbell, A.S. Skinner and W.B. Todd. 2 volumes. Oxford: Oxford University Press.

Smith, Adam ([1795] 1980) The principles which lead and direct philosophical enquiries: illustrated by the history of astronomy. In *Essays on Philosophical Subjects*, ed. W.P.D. Wightman. Oxford: Oxford University Press.

Williamson, Oliver E. (1964) *Economics of Discretionary Behavior: Managerial Objectives in a Theory of the Firm*. Englewood Cliffs, NJ: Prentice-Hall.

Williamson, Oliver E. and Sidney G. Winter (eds) (1991), *The Nature of the Firm: Origins, Evolution and Development*. New York and Oxford: Oxford University Press.

Young, Allyn (1928) Increasing returns and economic progress. *Economic Journal* **38**(152): 527–42.

19 Nelson and Winter revisited*

Markus C. Becker and Thorbjørn Knudsen

19.1 INTRODUCTION

In this chapter, we consider Richard R. Nelson and Sidney G. Winter's work within the context of dynamic approaches to the firm. We first review how Nelson and Winter provided the foundation of evolutionary economics and the evolutionary theory of the firm. Then we identify how their work was developed further and finally, point to some avenues for research that emerge on the basis of their work.

19.2 FOUNDATIONS

There is a long history of conceiving of economic change as a selection process (Veblen, [1899] 1970; Schumpeter, [1911] 1934; Alchian, 1950),[1] but the full treatment of the evolutionary argument that makes it a serious contender to standard theory first came with Nelson and Winter's (1982) foundational work.

Winter's (1964) critique of Milton Friedman's (1953) natural selection argument decisively paved the way for modern evolutionary economics. Friedman (ibid.) argued that it does not matter whether the behavior of economic actors is determined by utility maximization or follows other rules. If the firm does not exhibit behavior that in effect is like that of utility maximizers, the firm will perform less well than its competitors. Because of this, it will sooner or later go out of business. Managers would therefore seem to act as if they played out the predictions of textbook economics. For Friedman, this constitutes a process of 'natural selection': only those firms that act as if they maximize utility will survive.

For a couple of reasons this is not a compelling argument. Winter's counter-argument was that Friedman's logic is incomplete: assuming that there is something like a selection of firms, the theory must explain why the distribution of available strategies (including those that firms hit upon through learning processes) would necessarily contain the neoclassical alternative.[2] And even if the selection process led some firms to accidentally stumble over the neoclassical solution, there is the problem of explaining why these firms would continue to behave as if they were profit-maximizers:

> A theory of natural selection must characterize the basic sources of continuity in the evolutionary process. In the biological case, this basic source is the genetic transmission of characteristics. If there were no causal link between the characteristics of the n-th generation and the characteristics of the n+1st, there could be no natural selection and no evolution. (Winter, 1975, p. 96)

However, contrary to Friedman's claims, even if such a mechanism existed, it would not necessarily establish an argument for the utility-maximization hypothesis. Problems relating to intermediate selection processes creep in (Levinthal and Posen, 2007). The selection process must reliably favor the neoclassical solution along the entire trajectory of the evolution of industry configuration, or it must at least come up with it at the end of time.[3] Also at intermediate points in time, the selection process must be able to identify the proposed members of the final equilibrium configuration.

With his critique, Winter demonstrated that an application of evolutionary theory does not necessarily guarantee convergence to the neoclassical solution, or to a steady state that would have appealing welfare implications. That is, evolutionary theory cannot be viewed as license to apply a laissez-faire doctrine. And without his early and forceful objections, 'evolutionary' theorizing in economics could have turned out to be no more than an appendix in the tomes that lay out standard theory. This would have been a serious drawback since there is a need to understand the dynamics that drive economic progress in many sectors of the modern economy.

Even if selection processes would lead to industry configurations that asymptote the characterizations provided by standard theory, usual scientific standards dictate that the theory allows derivation of transition effects, in particular if the process is assumed to unfold on time-scales that exceed available data. While standard theory might get the asymptotic characterization of market structures right as time goes to infinity, it is a useless foundation for comparing predictions with empirical cases if the only available evidence reflects transient effects at early stages of this dynamics.[4] According to this argument, it is critical to analyze the process rather than an assumed end state. This suggests a theoretical program that allows derivation of interesting transient effects from a general set of assumptions. Ideally, such a program would encompass the predictions of standard theory as statements about the asymptotic state that the dynamics would tend to under special conditions. Many have overlooked that Nelson and Winter's (1982) formal model actually came with this attractive feature. Thereby, Nelson and Winter (ibid.) established the importance of analyzing process, rather than just the assumed end state that the processes might tend to. By anchoring their baseline solutions in an analytical model, Nelson and Winter (ibid.) pioneered a standard that defines an ideal for the use of computational models in economics and organization studies.

19.3   ESSENTIAL BUILDING BLOCKS – ROUTINES AND THEIR REPLICATION

In his critique, Winter had focused attention on the 'causal link between the characteristics of the n-th generation and the characteristics of the n+1st' (Winter, 1975, p. 96). Working on this missing link in the evolutionary explanation of economic behavior, Winter provided two building blocks of an evolutionary theory of the firm. First, he considered the mechanism of inheritance, or retention, that any evolutionary explanation needs to specify: in order for selection to operate effectively, there has to be a certain degree of stability (Winter, 1971). In other words, the unit of selection (firm behavior) has to be somewhat stable. Nelson and Winter subsequently identified possible candidates for such units of selection and inheritance, that is, the 'routine application of established rules, procedures, and policies' (ibid., pp. 240–41), where 'the decision rules themselves are the economic counterpart of genetic inheritance' (ibid., p. 245). In an early joint paper, Nelson and Winter (1973, p. 441) acknowledge that 'these decision rules may be quite complex patterns of routinized behavior, keyed to market prices or other environmental signals'. In other words, routines are the missing link and the equivalent to genes in biological theory:

> Our general term for all regular and predictable behavioral patterns of firms is 'routine'. . . In our evolutionary theory, these routines play the role that genes play in biological evolutionary theory. They are a persistent feature of the organism and determine its possible behavior (though actual behavior is determined also by the environment); they are heritable in the sense that tomorrow's organisms generated from today's have much of the same characteristics, and they are selectable in the sense that organisms with certain routines may do better than others, and, if so, their relative importance in the population (industry) is augmented over time. (Nelson and Winter, 1982, p. 14)

Winter also identified a second building block. Having argued that the unit of selection needs to have stability, and pointing to organizational routines as possible units of selection, Winter subsequently identified a mechanism of transmission, that is, the replication of organizational routines. In work with colleagues, Winter started to cast some light on how the replication of routines in organizations works (Szulanski, 1999; Winter and Szulanski, 2001; Szulanski and Winter, 2002; Baden-Fuller and Winter, 2007).

Nelson and Winter's idea that routines embody behavioral continuity of firms is one of the pillars of evolutionary economics. This idea has been the subject of intense scrutiny and extensive empirical research. Scholars have pursued different avenues, which at times appeared to point in different directions. Many scholars have considered repeated behavior patterns for accomplishing tasks to be organizational routines (e.g., Pentland and Rueter, 1994; Pentland, 2003a, 2003b). Other scholars thought of organizational routines in terms of standard operating procedures or rules (Cyert and March [1963] 1992; March et al., 2000). Finally, some authors understand organizational routines as dispositions to engage in previously adopted or acquired behavior, triggered by an appropriate stimulus or context (Hodgson and Knudsen, 2004a and 2004b; Cohen, 2007). These authors emphasize that routines as well as (stable) rules are stored behavioral capacities or capabilities, while their expression can be observed as actual patterns of behavior. These capacities involve knowledge and memory. They involve organizational structures and individual habits that, when triggered, lead to sequential behaviors (Hodgson and Knudsen, 2004a and 2004b). Although those three ideas might seem contradictory, they fit neatly into an overall conception of organizational routines: the concept of organizational routines provides a perspective on organizations that focuses on regularities and stability in how organizational tasks are accomplished jointly by several actors. Such a perspective provides a concept for describing stable multi-person *behavior* (recurrent interaction patterns), and two different potential *causes* of the stability of such behavior (standard operating procedures and dispositions). Standard operating procedures are an instance of conventions while dispositions are an instance of individual-level causes. The two potential causes of stable behavior therefore comprise both macro- (top-down) and micro- (bottom-up) causes. The three perspectives on behavioral continuity jointly offer a perspective on the sources and nature of the pool of stable repertoires that characterize firm behavior.

19.4   THE INNOVATING FIRM AND ECONOMIC GROWTH

In essence, evolutionary theory views firm behavior as a disequilibrium phenomenon and therefore makes more cautious and rather different predictions about economic data than those derived from the assumption of profit maximization (Simon et al., 1987). But even if Nelson and Winter's (1982) evolutionary program formulated the basic principles of an evolutionary theory of the firm, their book was as much about technological advance and economic growth. While these two aspects of reasoning seem to be natural complements, they have stimulated two rather distinct strands of literature. One is the huge literature on firms and organizational capabilities and the other is the equally impressive literature on technological change.

The evolutionary theory of the firm sees the innovating firm as the main unit of analysis. Sidney Winter's (2006) article, written many years ago, but recently published in *ICC*, first described the main elements of an evolutionary theory of the firm. By a 'theory of the firm' Winter (ibid., p. 126) referred to:

> a plausible, logically correct, and complete model setting forth what are alleged to be the main determinants of the economic transactions of the firm – the quantities and prices of inputs bought and outputs sold, the amounts and interest rates involved in its borrowing and lending activities, and so forth.

Such a theory would identify determinants of firm behavior, taking into account the fundamental problem that technological change and a multiplicity of unobservable factors shape what firms are actually doing.

Winter's (2006) analysis was inspired by Schumpeter's (1934) book, *Theory of Economic Development*. As is well known, Schumpeter established that conventional economic theory is only valid under static assumptions and assumes that the economy can be described as a stationary process, a 'circular flow'. The static type of the economy is most importantly characterized by the fact that nothing new ever happens. The same goods are produced, year in and year out, in essentially the same way. Demand and supply match each other and whatever capital is needed is available in the system. This is roughly the picture found in textbook economics. Against the ideal type of the static type of economy, Schumpeter posits another type: the dynamic economy where entrepreneurs introduce innovations. The challenge (or drawback if you wish) from the point of view of theory is that in a dynamic economy no analysis of equilibrium behavior is possible at the level of the individual firm.

As Winter (2006) pointed out, disequilibrium at the level of the individual firm and behavioral plausibility are inseparable features. A plausible description of firm behavior implies that the distinction between routine and innovative behavior is a continuous gradation, that is, no sharp distinction can be made between 'techniques known to the firm and those that are unknown' (ibid., p. 139). One way to see this is that firms incrementally improve their operations through organizational learning. The typical description of such processes is that experience will teach firms to assess more precisely how to utilize different techniques – knowledge gradually becomes more precise as firms gain experience. This implies that firm behavior changes as a function of the cumulative effect of incremental adjustments, which in turn affect the viability of other firms that are themselves adjusting their course of action.[5] As Winter (ibid., p. 140) noted, 'the standard conclusions of received price and allocation theory can be preserved, if at all, only as theorems describing equilibrium configurations of dynamic systems in which the histories of all the firms are jointly determined'. What then?

The logical conclusion was to suggest an evolutionary theory of the firm grounded in a plausible description of firm behavior, a quest that has spawned a huge literature on capabilities and firm behavior (e.g., Burgelman, 1994; Collis, 1994; Teece et al., 1997; Eisenhardt and Martin, 2000; Winter, 2000, 2003; Zollo and Winter, 2002). Thanks to this literature, we now have a fairly coherent picture of how firms actually behave: firms engage in path-dependent learning processes involving myopic choices, imperfect adaptation and mistake-ridden discoveries. The literature is truly enormous and it is impossible to adequately summarize the rich insights gained from empirical studies of firm capabilities within the space of this chapter. Suffice it to say that studies of firm capabilities both support and enlighten the behavioral foundations provided by Nelson and Winter (1982). Complementing the literature on firm behavior that came out of Nelson and Winter (ibid.), their work stimulated an equally rich stream of research on technological advance that has shed light on the fundamental relation between innovation and economic growth. We have gained a much sharper understanding of industry dynamics and technology cycles, a development that has informed science studies and economic geography. This literature is also truly enormous and it is impossible to even begin to summarize it within the perimeter of the present article, but see Dosi (1997) and Nelson (1995) for useful reviews.

If we recognize that the economics of technological change is a subject that is inseparable, in principle, from the economics of production (Winter, 2008), it is rather strange to see that the two streams of literature that came out of Nelson and Winter (1982) have not yet been connected. After all, the literature on capabilities provides a detailed and rich set of data on firm behavior that would seem to have immediate implications for technical advance and economic growth. It is hard to understand the deeper reasons why these two dots have not been connected, even if is clear that they lived well in isolation. Perhaps the reason is simply that each stream of literature has had more than enough to do with managing its own success. Or it could be that the many detailed descriptions of firm behavior are too rich to summarize in a simple way. But there are nevertheless promising ways to forge ahead and assess potential gains from trade. For example, Winter (2008) suggests a promising path by connecting important stylized facts about state- and time-dependent firm behavior (such as the differential scalability of production factors and the path-dependent nature of innovation) to variables that can be examined in models of technological advance. The benefit? In this example, Winter (ibid.) points to potential gains from an advanced analytical representation of scale-related technological trajectories. For another example, Knudsen et al. (2010) recently pointed to slow scale-adjustment at the firm level (a notable empirical fact) as an important determinant of industry structure, profitability and, ultimately, economic growth.

It is our hope that the capabilities literature can serve to advance models of technological change by supplying stylized facts about the innovating firm that can be translated into characteristic properties of industries populated by such firms. Central to that endeavor is the parallel reform of the theory of production that Nelson and Winter (1982) began a while ago.

19.5   ROAD AHEAD

Nelson and Winter have provided an evolutionary theory of economic and organizational change that is rooted in profit-induced selection processes among firms. Its core mechanisms are variation, selection and retention. Selection mechanisms are fairly well documented. Empirical studies spanning a large number of industries have established that industry dynamics is a selection process where entry and exit of firms change the industry-wide properties of firms, including product technology, efficiency and size (Utterback and Abernathy, 1975; Dunne et al., 1989; Dosi, 1990; Klepper and Graddy, 1990; Geroski, 1995; Klepper, 1997). We also know that there is widespread and amazingly persistent behavioral continuity in the social world. For example, historical research shows that habits and routines transplanted from England to North America during the great migrations around the beginning of the seventeenth century persist even into the present day (Fischer, 1989). Diffusion research shows, right from the first empirical studies, that it can take years, even decades before new habits and routines replace old ones (Rogers, 1983; Attewell, 1992), and management research provides a striking illustration of the impact of inherited strategies (Tripsas and Gavetti, 2000).

We also know how behavioral repertoires are replicated in particular firms whose growth strategy is based on the idea of copying a tried and tested working template. Examples of such replicator organizations include McDonald's, Marriott, Ikea and many other firms that are active in retail settings (Szulanski, 1999; Winter and Szulanski, 2001; Szulanski and Winter, 2002). Even if we do know how routines are replicated in such replicator organizations, it is unclear exactly how they are replicated in the general case. Nevertheless, we can observe that the economy is characterized by a pool of fairly stable repertoires such as accounting practices. It is therefore highly likely that selection forces systematically shape distributions of the behavioral repertoires that account for vital properties of economic organization.

Despite advances in our understanding of selection processes, the general problem of the existence and replenishment of variety remains a vital question of evolutionary research in the social and technological domain (Nelson, 1991; Saviotti, 1996; Metcalfe, 1998). Innovations are a common source of new variation and so are the many unintended consequences of conscious effort, but the determinants of such novelties are not fully understood. That points to variation as a particular focus on the research agenda of an evolutionary theory of economic and organizational change. For a perspective on organizations that views their behavioral repertoires as bundles of routines (Nelson and Winter, 1982), an important challenge is to explain how variety is generated in routine-based organizations. Burgelman's (1994) analysis of how Intel became a microprocessor firm is illuminating in that regard. According to the argument there, a series of smaller decisions generated new variation by jointly altering the informal organization structure and the allocation of production capacity. In effect, the accumulation of minor changes in a multitude of daily routines systematically changed the way Intel operated and ultimately led to the dramatic final outcome – Intel dropped its memory business and became a microprocessor company.

More specifically, an evolutionary theory of the firm requires a theory that accommodates three rather different kinds of changes: (1) incremental changes in vital properties of existing routines; (2) inter-firm and intra-firm diffusion of routines; and (3) the generation of distinctively novel routines. While theories of learning address the first and diffusion theories the second problem, what is missing is a theory that can explain the generation of distinctively novel routines. Where do we look for mechanisms of such variation? As suggested in recent work (Becker et al., 2006), the combinatorics of routines and unreliable routine replication are plausible sources of new variation in economic evolution, including distinctively novel routines.

Considering the combinatorial space of extant behavioral repertoires suggests practically unlimited variation, including variations with rather extreme potential. In addition, unreliable routine replication is very likely a source of a random walk in the realized performance of organizations. An important unsolved problem in this regard is whether unreliable routine replication is predominantly state-dependent or time-dependent. Does routine replication become more reliable as a function of time independent of the state of firm-specific variables, or are firm-specific variables more important in this regard than the passing of time?

19.6 HOW DOES EVOLUTIONARY THEORY EXPLAIN THE STRUCTURE, BOUNDARIES, AND EXISTENCE OF FIRMS?

The evolutionary perspective developed by Nelson and Winter (1982) has turned out to be very fruitful in stimulating empirical research that accounts for firm and industry and organization in terms of selection processes. Why do some firms and industries perform better than others? This question is of fundamental importance for strategy and management scholars. From an evolutionary perspective, the answer to such questions begins from an understanding of the selection processes that are shaping distributions of firms and industries. The evolutionary economist would therefore quickly add that selection processes are characterized by the particular selection criteria (fitness components) that are present in a particular context (e.g., entry barriers, cost distributions, and demand conditions) at a particular point in time. Can insights about the selection process indicate which attractors the dynamics is likely to tend to? Do we expect industry structures with dominant firms and do we expect dramatic oscillation in firm size even if the industry structure remains stable? Could it be that the selection process is driven by the way behavioral repertoires influence firm-specific growth rates?[6] Are there permanent cycles in vital properties of economic organization as commonly observed in the fashion industry?

The general answer to such essential questions pertaining to the structure, boundaries, and ultimately the existence of particular organizational forms would be that they are determined by selection forces. The difficult part of the problem is: exactly how does this occur? Consider organizational structure. The evolutionary explanation would examine a population of firms, starting from a fitness function that captured how environmental factors would alter the distribution of structural properties in firms. The fitness function would map hypothesized antecedents onto observable changes in the distribution of firm properties. The antecedents in question are likely to capture specific hypothesized sources of new variation (from entry and experiential learning) as well as existing variants (from exit and imitation). The emergent structure of a population of firms would

thereby be explained in terms of an evolutionary process reflecting the kinds of properties that a local selection environment favors (a fact that has been documented in empirical studies such as Barnett et al., 1994).[7] The explanation would rarely identify globally
optimal structures, but rather structures that would have more (or less) support in a
particular context. To the extent that the context is generated by the firms that live in it,
we have a well-known possibility of unpredictable changes in firm-level structures. Note
also that the evolutionary explanation would provide an answer to the essential question
of the theory of the firm in plural. It is a theory that can explain a distribution of properties (structure and boundary), including the possible occurrence of a uniquely optimal
type of firm.

The huge amount of empirical research on firm evolution indicates that the theory has
been an important stimulant for advancing our knowledge about the origins and evolution of firm structure and boundaries. Nelson and Winter's work also points to further
opportunities for advancing our knowledge on important open questions. One question
relates to intra-firm selection processes. It would seem obvious to extend the evolutionary explanation to understand how the expectation of the market translates into a
selection environment that shapes the distribution of routines within the firm (Knudsen,
2002). While the size distribution of industries and how these evolve over time has been
fairly well documented, there is little evidence on the way internal selection processes
shape the properties of firm-specific routines. This is not a minor oversight. In order
to understand how evolutionary forces shape industry dynamics and market structure,
it would seem obvious to understand how intra-firm selection processes constrain firm
growth.

As an example of one of the few empirical studies on internal selection processes,
consider Burgelman's (1994) study of how Intel became a microprocessor firm. This
article provides a detailed description of how Intel's internal selection environment was
constituted, in part, by its organization structure, its resource allocation process, and its
culture of information sharing. A critical component of the selection process was a rule
(to maximize margin-per-wafer-start) that guided manufacturing resource allocation.
Since this rule would systematically lead niche markets to be selected over commodity
markets, it effectively translated external selection pressures into an internal selection
environment that altered the distribution of routines inside the firm.

Another fundamental problem that may be illuminated by jointly considering internal
and external selection pressures is the evolution of ownership structures. For example,
internal selection pressures often generate interfaces among various business functions
(e.g., defined by profit centers) that external selection forces eventually break up into
independently owned businesses.[8] Jacobides's (2005) analysis of the US mortgage bank
nicely illustrates this point.[9] More generally, it seems promising to translate stylized facts
about internal selection processes into variables that can be used in our models of industry evolution. For example, there have been a number of studies that, within the context
of a broadly defined industry, show how productive establishments tend to grow while
less productive ones decline and exit (see, e.g., Geroski, 1995). But these same studies also
show that there is little relationship between the *rate* of growth and productivity.[10] This
puzzle invites further examination of the relation between industry dynamics and the rate
at which firms adjust their scale of operations (Knudsen et al., 2010). An important item
on the evolutionary agenda is, in brief, the need to combine Nelson and Winter's (1982)

theory of industry evolution with an updated account of Edith Penrose's (1959) theory of the growth of the firm. The further pursuit of this problem calls for an evolutionary theory of economic change that operates on multiple levels of economic organization, and involves multiple interdependent selection criteria (fitness components).

A further call for expansion of the evolutionary agenda points to an ambitious research agenda for developing a theory of the market to complement the body of literature on the theory of the firm.[11] If we move one level up in the level of analysis, from considering distributions of firms within industries, to considering distributions of market forms within the broader local and global context, it would be interesting to consider how macro-forces have shaped the evolution of particular market forms.[12] How are distributions of communication technologies, matching principles, negotiation rules, profit-sharing rules, and the many other pieces of market design[13] shaped by selection forces? How are different market forms tipping the balance between viable organization by hierarchy and market?

Recent work on financial trading shows that new electronic trading ventures are often unviable even if they lower costs and increase market transparency (Weber, 2006). For example, Optimark, Tradepoint, Jiway, and BondConnect did not develop sufficient trading volume to survive. In contrast, the International Securities Exchange (ISE) has succeeded in attracting a critical mass of volume and liquidity even if it was facing competition with four incumbent markets including the Chicago Board Options Exchange (ibid.). According to Weber's analysis, the presence of electronic technology, careful designation of membership roles, and network externalities were important factors contributing to the success of this new market. The examples from electronic trading are striking illustrations of the way selection processes favor some types of market design over others. But little is known about the way selection processes more generally generate distributions of market forms.

What we are interested in is a particular agenda relating to Richard Nelson's (2008b) recent call for connecting the literature on institutions with the literature on technical advance. The question we are asking is simply: given a market's 'context', how would the evolutionary process alter its boundary, structure, and viability? By 'context' we mean the actual and potential exchange partners (sellers and buyers) as well as other parties that are able to influence how the market actually works. We would be interested in assessing how altered properties of communication technologies, matching principles and so on would incrementally change the way markets actually work. Would the advent of alternative communication technologies improve the informational properties of the market? Would this increase the share of activities that are allocated through the market mechanism? If so, would we expect the evolutionary process (perhaps aided by some clever market designer) to hit upon incremental improvements? Since the evolution of markets and the evolution of firms are both likely to go through a path of incremental improvements, it is a co-evolutionary process. The boundaries, organization and viability of particular market 'designs' are therefore likely to reflect the boundaries, organization, and viability of the particular economic agents that are active in the market, and vice versa. For an illustrative example, consider how new communication technologies completely change the timing and quality of signals that suppliers receive. Does that mean that some of the activities that are currently organized in firms are likely to be outsourced, does it mean that the rules for bidding are likely to be altered, or shall we see both things happening simultaneously? From an evolutionary perspective, the theory of the firm could turn out to produce a complementary theory of market evolution.

Nelson and Winter's (1982) evolutionary theory has been decisive in advancing our knowledge about the origins and evolution of firm structure and boundaries. We envision that the further pursuit of this research agenda shall lead to a multi-level theory of economic evolution spanning the micro-level of selection processes inside firms, the meso-level of industry evolution, and the macro-level of evolving market forms. A further item on the evolutionary agenda is the possibility of informing welfare analysis by working out how the operative selection criteria would often seem to favor solutions that are superior in the current local context but perhaps seriously inferior from the perspective of a broader definition of time and space. While the literature on market design has led to important new insights about the welfare properties of particular markets (Roth, 2008), much is still unknown about the welfare properties of co-evolving firms and markets. The evolutionary approach seems to have an important unfulfilled role in addressing this problem.

NOTES

*   The authors thank Stephan Billinger, Ulrik Nash, Kannan Srikanth, Nils Stieglitz as well as Richard R. Nelson and Sidney G. Winter for comments on earlier drafts.
1.   Hodgson and Knudsen (2010) provide a comprehensive assessment of the past history and future challenges of evolutionary theories in the social domain.
2.   Lucas (1986, p. S402) further developed the neoclassical defense in an article featured in *The Journal of Business*: 'I think of economics as studying decision rules that are steady states of some adaptive process, decision rules that are found to work over a range of situations and hence are no longer revised appreciably as more experience accumulates'. In the same issue Winter (1986, p. S429) replied: 'To be willing to limit the aspirations of the study of economic science to the study of steady states of adaptive processes is presumably to view vast realms of apparent rapid change as either unimportant or illusory'.
3.   Introducing learning presumably expands the available set of behaviors but does not alter the argument with respect to this (expanded) set of behaviors. Of course, learning can also be used to assume the problem away so that we can concentrate on analyzing steady states (or equilibrium configurations).
4.   It is obviously important for the evolutionary program to explain the trajectory of observed distributions of vital firm properties (Nelson, 1991, 2008a). But there is a question about the importance one should impute to observed firm heterogeneity (Nelson, 1991). Does such heterogeneity reflect heterogeneous demand, short-term equilibria or truly robust steady states?
5.   Strategy research typically portrays actual firm behavior as deviant from planned strategies. An added nuance is that the net effect of emergent behavior can be a source of radical reorientation and innovation (Burgelman, 1994).
6.   See Rothblum and Winter (1985) for a penetrating analysis of this question.
7.   For example, Barnett et al. (1994) found that selection forces in retail banks favor multi-unit structures over single-unit banks. The exposure to more severe selection pressures in single-unit banks in turn stimulated a more effective adaptive response in single-unit banks that engaged in learning processes to cope with competitors.
8.   A similar argument may account for the integration of independent businesses.
9.   See also Jacobides and Winter (2005).
10. Nelson (2008a) provides a number of plausible reasons why empirical estimates of the correlation between successful innovation and firm are usually rather weak.
11. We are aware that there is a huge body of literature on the (general) equilibrium properties of markets, that the literature on industrial organization considers a theory of strategic interaction in markets, and that industry life-cycle theory is concerned with explaining the properties of alternative industry configurations across time (e.g., size distributions of firms and propensity to innovate) and so on. While industry life-cycle theory in particular considers the evolution of size distributions of firms, what we are interested in is a theory that can explain the gradual evolution of the defining features of market forms (such as

matching principles) as a function of a selection processes. A useful way to conceive of this process is the evolution of a sequence of momentary equilibria (Radner, 1970).

2. Jacobides's (2005) study of market formation in mortgage banking illustrates some of the dynamics that are involved in market evolution. Consideration of the broader (institutional, economic and technological) context and its influence on the functioning of the (mortgage) market would further enlighten this analysis.

3. See, for example, McMillan (2002), Milgrom (2004), and Roth and Sotomayor (1990) for an account of the many features that characterize market design.

REFERENCES

Alchian, Armen A. 1950. Uncertainty, Evolution, and Economic Theory. *Journal of Political Economy* **68**: 211–21.

Attewell, Paul. 1992. Technology Diffusion and Organizational Learning: The Case of Business Computing. *Organization Science* **3**(1): 1–19.

Baden-Fuller, Charles and Sidney G. Winter. 2007. Replicating Organizational Knowledge: Principles or Templates? SSRN Working Paper, SSRN ID 1118013.

Barnett, William P., Henrich R. Greve and Douglas Y. Park. 1994. An Evolutionary Model of Organizational Performance. *Strategic Management Journal* **15**(Special Issue): 11–28.

Becker, Markus C., Thorbjørn Knudsen and James G. March. 2006. Schumpeter, Winter, and the Sources of Novelty. *Industrial and Corporate Change* **15**(2): 353–71.

Burgelman, Robert A. 1994. Fading Memories: A Process Theory of Strategic Business Exit in Dynamic Environments. *Administrative Science Quarterly* **39**(1): 24–56.

Cohen, Michael D. 2007. Reading Dewey: Reflections on the Study of Routine. *Organization Studies* **28**(5): 773–86.

Collis, David J. 1994. Research Note: How Valuable Are Organizational Capabilities? *Strategic Management Journal* **15**(5): 143–52.

Cyert, Richard M. and James G. March. [1963] 1992. *A Behavioral Theory of the Firm.* 2nd edition. Oxford: Blackwell.

Dosi, Giovanni. 1990. Finance, Innovation and Industrial Change. *Journal of Economic Behavior & Organization* **13**(3): 299–319.

Dosi, Giovanni. 1997. Opportunities, Incentives and the Collective Patterns of Technological Change. *The Economic Journal* **107**(444): 1530–47.

Dunne, Timothy, Mark J. Roberts and Larry Samuelson. 1989. The Growth and Failure of U.S. Manufacturing Plants. *The Quarterly Journal of Economics* **104**(4): 671–98.

Eisenhardt, Kathleen M. and Jeffrey A. Martin. 2000. Dynamic Capabilities: What Are They? *Strategic Management Journal* **21**(10/11): 1105–121.

Fischer, David Hackett. 1989. *Albion's Seed – Four British Folkways in America.* Oxford: Oxford University Press.

Friedman, M. 1953. *Essays in Positive Economics.* Chicago: University of Chicago Press.

Geroski, P.A. 1995. What Do We Know About Entry? *International Journal of Industrial Organization* **13**(4): 421–40.

Hodgson, Geoffrey M. and Thorbjørn Knudsen. 2004a. The Complex Evolution of a Simple Traffic Convention: The Functions and Implications of Habit. *Journal of Economic Behavior & Organization* **54**(1): 19–47.

Hodgson, Geoffrey M. and Thorbjørn Knudsen. 2004b. The Firm as an Interactor: Firms as Vehicles for Habits and Routines. *Journal of Evolutionary Economics* **14**(3): 281–307.

Hodgson, Geoffrey M. and Thorbjørn Knudsen. 2010. *Darwin's Conjecture. The Search for General Principles of Social and Economic Evolution.* Chicago: University of Chicago Press.

Jacobides, Michael G. 2005. Industry Change Through Vertical Disintegration: How and Why Markets Emerged in Mortgage Banking. *Academy of Management Journal* **48**(3): 465–98.

Jacobides, Michael G. and Sidney G. Winter. 2005. The Co-evolution of Capabilities and Transaction Costs: Explaining the Institutional Structure of Production. *Strategic Management Journal* **26**(2): 395–413.

Klepper, Steven. 1997. Industry Life Cycles. *Industrial and Corporate Change* **6**(1): 145–82.

Klepper, Steven and Elizabeth Graddy. 1990. The Evolution of New Industries and the Determinants of Market Structure. *The RAND Journal of Economics* **21**(1): 27–44.

Knudsen, Thorbjørn. 2002. Economic Selection Theory. *Journal of Evolutionary Economics* **12**(4): 443–70.

Knudsen, Thorbjørn, Daniel A. Levinthal and Sidney G. Winter. 2010. The Role of Scale Adjustment I Industry Dynamics. Working Paper. Philadelphia, PA: Wharton School.
Levinthal, Daniel and Hart E. Posen. 2007. Myopia of Selection: Does Organizational Adaptation Limit th Efficacy of Population Selection? *Administrative Science Quarterly* **52**(4): 586–620.
Lucas, Robert E. 1986. Adaptive Behavior and Economic Theory. *The Journal of Business* **59**(4): S401–S426.
March, James G., Martin Schulz and Xueguang Zhou. 2000. *The Dynamics of Rules – Change in Writte Organizational Codes.* Stanford: Stanford University Press.
McMillan, John. 2002. *Reinventing the Bazaar. A Natural History of Markets.* New York and London: W.W Norton & Company.
Metcalfe, J. Stanley. 1998. *Evolutionary Economics and Creative Destruction.* London: Routledge.
Milgrom, Paul. 2004. *Putting Auction Theory to Work.* Cambridge: Cambridge University Press.
Nelson, Richard R. 1991. Why Do Firms Differ, and How Does it Matter? *Strategic Management Journe* **12**(S2): 61–74.
Nelson, Richard R. 1995. Recent Evolutionary Theorizing About Economic Change. *Journal of Economi Literature* **33**(1): 48–90.
Nelson, Richard R. 2008a. Why Do Firms Differ, and How Does it Matter? A Revisitation. *Seoul Journal c Economics* **21**(4): 607–19.
Nelson, Richard R. 2008b. What Enables Rapid Economic Progress: What are the Needed Institutions *Research Policy* **37**(1): 1–11.
Nelson, Richard R. and Sidney G.Winter. 1973. Toward an Evolutionary Theory of Economic Capabilities *American Economic Review (Papers and Proceedings)* **68**(2): 440–49.
Nelson, Richard R. and Sidney G. Winter. 1982. *An Evolutionary Theory of Economic Change.* Cambridge MA: Belknap Press of Harvard University Press.
Penrose, Edith T. 1959. *The Theory of the Growth of the Firm.* Oxford: Basil Blackwell.
Pentland, Brian T. 2003a. Conceptualizing and Measuring Variety in the Execution of Organizational Worl Processes. *Management Science* **49**(7): 857–70.
Pentland, Brian T. 2003b. Sequential Variety in Work Processes. *Organization Science* **14**(3), 528–40.
Pentland, Brian and Henry Rueter. 1994. Organizational Routines as Grammars of Action. *Administrativ Science Quarterly* **39**(3): 484–510.
Radner, Roy. 1970. Problems in the Theory of Markets under Uncertainty. *The American Economic Review* **60**(2): 454–60.
Rogers, Everett M. 1983. *Diffusion of Innovations.* New York: The Free Press.
Roth, Alvin E. 2008. What Have We Learned from Market Design? *The Economic Journal* **118**(527): 285–310
Roth, Alvin E. and Marilda A. Oliveira Sotomayor. 1990. *Two-sided Matching: A Study on Game-theoretic Modelling.* Cambridge: Cambridge University Press.
Rothblum, Uriel G. and Sidney G. Winter. 1985. Asymptotic Behavior of Market Shares for a Stochastic Growth Model. *Journal of Economic Theory* **36**(2): 352–66.
Saviotti, Pier Paolo. 1996. *Technological Evolution, Variety and the Economy.* Cheltenham, UK and Brookfield, VT, USA: Edward Elgar.
Schumpeter, Joseph Alois. [1911] 1934. *The Theory of Economic Development: An Inquiry into Profits, Capital, Interest, and the Business Cycle.* Cambridge, MA: Harvard University Press.
Simon, Herbert A., George B. Dantzig, Robin Hogarth, Charles R. Plott, Howard Raiffa, Thomas C. Schelling, Kenneth A. Shepsle, Richard Thaler, Amos Tversky and Sidney Winter. 1987. Decision Making and Problem Solving. *Interfaces* **17**(5): 11–31.
Szulanski, Gabriel. 1999. Appropriability and the Challenge of Scope: Banc One Routinizes Replication. In Giovanni Dosi, Richard R. Nelson and Sidney G. Winter (eds), *Nature and Dynamics of Organizational Capabilities,* Oxford: OUP, pp. 69–97.
Szulanski, Gabriel and Sidney Winter. 2002. Getting it Right the Second Time. *Harvard Business Review* **80**(1): 62–71.
Teece, David J., Gary Pisano and Amy Shuen. 1997. Dynamic Capabilities and Strategic Management. *Strategic Management Journal* **18**(7): 509–33.
Tripsas, Mary and Giovanni Gavetti. 2000. Capabilities, Cognition and Inertia: Evidence from Digital Imaging. *Strategic Management Journal* **21**(10/11): 1147–61.
Utterback, J. and W. Abernathy. 1975. A Dynamic Model of Process and Product Innovation. *Omega* **3**(6): 639–56.
Veblen, Thorstein. [1899] 1970. *The Theory of the Leisure Class – An Economic Study of Institutions.* London: Unwin.
Weber, Bruce W. 2006. Adoption of Electronic Trading at the International Securities Exchange. *Decision Support Systems* **41**(4): 728–46.
Winter, Sidney G. 1964. Economic 'Natural Selection' and the Theory of the Firm. *Yale Economic Essays* **4**(1): 225–72.

inter, Sidney G. 1971. Satisficing, Selection, and the Innovating Remnant. *Quarterly Journal of Economics* **85**(2): 237–61.

Vinter, Sidney G. 1975. Optimization and Evolution in the Theory of the Firm. In R. Day and T. Groves (eds), *Adaptive Economic Models*. New York: Academic Press, pp. 73–118.

Vinter, Sidney G. 1986. Comments on Arrow and on Lucas. *The Journal of Business* **59**(4): S401–S426.

Vinter, Sidney G. 2000. The Satisficing Principle in Capability Learning. *Strategic Management Journal* **21**(10/11): 981–96.

Vinter, Sidney G. 2003. Understanding Dynamic Capabilities. *Strategic Management Journal* **24**(10): 991–5.

Vinter, Sidney G. 2006. Toward a Neo-Schumpeterian Theory of the Firm. *Industrial and Corporate Change* **15**(1): 125–41.

Vinter, Sidney G. 2008. Scaling Heuristics Shape Technology! Should Economic Theory Take Notice? *Industrial and Corporate Change* **17**(3): 513–31.

Vinter, Sidney G. and Gabriel Szulanski. 2001. Replication as Strategy. *Organization Science* **12**(6): 730–43.

ollo, Maurizio and Sidney G. Winter. 2002. Deliberate Learning and the Evolution of Dynamic Capabilities. *Organization Science* **13**(3): 339–51.

20 Modern resource-based theory(ies)
Nicolai J. Foss and Nils Stieglitz

20.1 INTRODUCTION

Almost since its inception, strategic management has been heavily indebted to economics, particularly mainstream economics (Porter, 1981; Camerer, 1994; Rumelt et al., 1994; Hoskisson et al., 1999; Foss, 2000; Lockett and Thompson, 2001; Gavetti and Levinthal, 2004; Agarwal and Hoetker, 2007). This is hardly surprising: central, arguably *the* central, constructs of strategic management – namely, value creation, value appropriation and sustained competitive advantage – lend themselves directly to an economics interpretation. The notion that all of strategic management ultimately boils down to creating and appropriating more value than the competition (e.g., Peteraf and Barney, 2003) can be usefully addressed in terms of the established economics corpus of applied price theory, industrial organization theory, game theory and bargaining theory. Not surprisingly, modern strategic management theory is often presented as beginning from some 'competitive imperfection' (Knott, 2003): ultimately, *some* deviation from the Walrasian general equilibrium model, or, in some formulations, from the zero transaction cost setting of the Coase theorem (Foss and Foss, 2005), leading to imperfect factor and/or product markets, explains strategy's central dependent variable, sustained competitive advantage. As Knott (2003, p.929) argues, '[t]he field of strategy is concerned with the conditions under which the microeconomic equilibrium of homogeneous firms with zero profits can be overcome'.

All modern economics-based approaches have taken this approach, beginning with Michael Porter's (1980, 1985) work, essentially an application of the industrial organization economics of Bain (1956) and Scherer (1980) (cf. Porter, 1981). Later currents in industrial organization, such as contestable markets theory (Baumol et al., 1982), game-theoretical new industrial organization (Tirole, 1989) and the Chicago-UCLA approach (Demsetz, 1973) have also had enormous influence on strategic management. More specifically, contestable markets theory and new industrial organization have dominated the commitment approach (Ghemawat, 1991), and the Chicago-UCLA approach to industrial organization as well as ideas from Penrose ([1959] 1995) and Schumpeter (1911) have motivated the resource-based view (Lippman and Rumelt, 1982; Rumelt, 1984; Barney, 1986, 1991; Peteraf, 1993; Foss, 2000) – the key focus of the present chapter.

From the perspective of economics, the resource-based view (RBV) is in many ways a half-way house. On the one hand, it revitalized the concern with firm heterogeneity, innovation and dynamics associated with such heterodox economists as Thorstein Veblen (see Foss, 1998), Joseph Schumpeter (1911), Edith Penrose ([1959] 1995), and George Richardson (1972) (see Jacobson, 1992). On the other hand, what is perhaps the RBV core model (Demsetz, 1973; Lippman and Rumelt, 1982; Barney, 1986, 1991; Peteraf, 1993; Peteraf and Barney, 2003) is essentially a competitive equilibrium model with (at least one) heterogeneous firms. This tension has been manifest in the RBV from its inception in the beginning of the 1980s, and has led commentators to speak of 'Demsetzian' and 'Penrosian' (Foss, 2000) or 'high church' and 'low church' versions of the RBV (Gavetti and Levinthal, 2004) (cf. also Mathews, 2006, 2010). These distinctions boil down to the same thing: is use made in the relevant RBV contribution of an equilibrium model with underlying strong assumptions of rationality, or does a process model with underlying behavioural assumptions closer to bounded rationality underpin the contribution? The high church RBV, or the 'RBV proper' is perhaps best associated with the VRIN (valuable/rare/inimitable/non-substitutable) framework of Barney (1991) (we discuss this later), while the low church RBV may be associated with ideas on core competences (Hamel and Prahalad, 1994), capabilities (Denrell et al., 2003) or dynamic capabilities (Teece et al., 1997).

In this chapter we also adopt this distinction and use it to organize our presentation and discussion of the RBV. However, as we point out, the high and the low churches within the RBV make frequent contact, and, consistent with Gavetti and Levinthal's overall argument that the strategy field as a whole is manifesting a 'movement toward the middle' (2004, p. 1312) there are signs of an emerging synthesis of the two.

20.2   ORIGINS AND KEY TENETS OF THE 'HIGH CHURCH' RESOURCE-BASED VIEW

20.2.1   Origins

The dominant contemporary approach in strategic management is the RBV, whether in its high or low church versions (Acedo et al., 2006; Newbert, 2007; Heimriks et al., 2010). Although part of the marketing effort of the RBV has been to point to its roots in Edith Penrose's thinking on firm growth (Penrose [1959] 1995; Kor and Mahoney, 2000), the RBV does not become established in the strategy field until the seminal contributions by Lippman and Rumelt (1982), Wernerfelt (1984), Rumelt (1984) and Barney (1986). As already mentioned, resource-based scholars have relied heavily on fundamental insights and theories of various fields and branches in economics, such as the economic theory of the entrepreneur (Knight, 1921; Barney, 1986; Rumelt, 1987); efficient markets theory (Barney, 1986; Fama, 1970); theories of input heterogeneity and its consequences for firm growth (Penrose [1959] 1995; Wernerfelt, 1984); property rights economics (Coase, 1960; Teece, 1986; Foss and Foss, 2005; Kim and Mahoney, 2005); the theory of competitive equilibrium (Debreu, 1959; Lippman and Rumelt, 1982); and, arguably, particularly Chicago-UCLA industrial organization economics (Demsetz, 1973, 1974; Peltzman, 1977; Klein et al., 1978). Thus, the base of economics from which the RBV has drawn nourishment is one of applied microeconomics and efficient markets theory.

20.2.2   Chicago Industrial Economics as the Foundation for the High Church RBV

Applied microeconomics and efficient markets theory are, of course, equilibrium theories. Not surprisingly, economic equilibrium, particularly in the form of competitive equilibrium, is central in the high church RBV. Indeed, the dominance of the RBV has meant that the key issue of strategic management is routinely defined as the problem of achieving sustained competitive advantage in the sense of earning (efficiency) rents in equilibrium. The intellectual pedigree of this lies in the Chicago approach to industrial organization (Brozen, 1971; Demsetz, 1973, 1982; Peltzman, 1977). Briefly, a central aim of this approach is to explain long-lived performance differences in terms of efficiency rents existing under competitive conditions rather than in terms of monopolistic abuse of market power. In the Chicago view, entry barriers are informational, concentration is a result of efficiency, and high returns are returns to efficient underlying assets rather than monopoly profits stemming from restriction of supply (e.g., Demsetz, 1973, 1982). Such returns may be long-lived because of the complexity of the assets that cause them (Demsetz, 1973). Moreover, assets are not necessarily priced according to their value, because of informational asymmetries (ibid.). Thus, the Chicago view is one that stresses efficiency in a world constrained by informational scarcity. The appeal of the Chicago approach it that it promises to reconcile the emphasis on idiosyncratic and firm-specific factors that is characteristic of the strategic management field with economic equilibrium theory. As we shall see, many of these key ideas have been taken over lock, stock and barrel by the high church RBV.[1]

20.2.3 Key Tenets

The RBV is often presented as a 'theory of the firm'. Given the now dominant Coasian conception of what such a theory entails (Coase, 1937; Williamson, 1996), it is more correct to say that the RBV is first and foremost a theory of (firm-level) sustained competitive advantage that makes ample use of price theory. Sustained competitive advantage refers to the potential of a firm to create and appropriate more value than the competition (in some formulations, simply more than the marginal firm, for example, Peteraf and Barney, 2003), that is, the ability to capture a large share of the sum of producers' and consumers' surpluses than other firms (in the same industry). Thus, sustained competitive advantage is an antecedent to financial performance, not the same thing. In turn, this potential is traced to the resource endowments of firms and the characteristics of these resources. The crowning achievement of the high church RBV – and its main predictive context – has been the formulation of criteria that must be jointly met for resources to give rise to sustained competitive advantage (Barney, 1991; Peteraf, 1993; Peteraf and Barney, 2003).

Thus, in Barney's seminal 1991 paper, one of the most cited strategic management texts ever, and among a handful of social science papers with more than 10 000 Google Scholar hits, sustained competitive advantage can be enjoyed by firms that control resources that are valuable, rare and costly to imitate and substitute (i.e., the 'VRIN framework'). Barney (1991, p. 102) explains that:

> A firm is said to have a competitive advantage when it is implementing a value creating strategy not simultaneously being implemented by any current or potential competitors. A firm is said to have a sustained competitive advantage when it is implementing a value creating strategy not simultaneously being implemented by any current or potential competitors and when these other firms are unable to duplicate the benefits of this strategy.

Thus, sustained competitive advantage is defined in terms of situations in which all attempts by competitor firms at imitating or substituting a successful firm have ceased, that is, equilibrium obtains.[2]

Barney (1991) is not entirely forthcoming about the precise meaning of these criteria (Foss and Knudsen, 2003), but value may be linked to the existence of a span between the reservation price of the products made possible by the relevant resource and the costs of production of those products; 'rare' should be understood in a simple counting sense (implying that not 'too many' other firms can implement the same strategy(ies) as the firm enjoying a sustained competitive advantage), and the two remaining criteria refer to the costliness of imitating or substituting the resource or bundle of resources that give rise to the competitive advantage.

Earlier work by Barney (1986) established the necessary condition for sustained competitive advantage that the relevant underlying resources or the services thereof are acquired or rented at a price that is lower than their net present value. Otherwise, any competitive advantages will be offset by supply prices on 'strategic factor markets'. This is explicitly included in Peteraf's (1993) closely related contribution, which also introduces a condition of relative immobility of resources: essential but highly mobile resources can appropriate most or all of the value they contribute to the firm.

20.2.4 Empirical Work

Despite its broad theoretical appeal and strong influence on managerial education and practice, the empirical track record of the key tenets of the RBV has so far been rather modest (Priem and Butler, 2001a). Hoopes and Madsen (2008) argue that the RBV lacks a cumulative body of work showing how firms differ in their resource bases. In survey articles on the empirical support for the RBV, Armstrong and Shimizu (2007) and Newbert (2007) find only modest support for the key tenets of the RBV that connect resource characteristics to sustained profitability (cf. Crook et al., 2008 for a meta-study that finds more robust support). Arend (2006, p.410) even argues that:

> there are no satisfactory empirical tests of the RBV. No paper or collection of related papers measures the benefits specified by RBV theory; adjusts for the costs of the resources; provides evidence that resources meet the RBV criteria; and controls for the influence of higher-level resources. Moreover, the adequacy of testing has not improved over the last 10 years. If empirical testing does not alter its approach, the RBV will be in increasing jeopardy.

More broadly, Arend also argues that (1) resources that meet the VRIN criteria are usually identified only ex post, making the explanation circular (empirical tests handle this problem, however); (2) the RBV is mainly used as a convenient framing device and specific implications of the view are seldom tested; (3) the link between resources and performance is not carefully examined, for example, in terms of organizational variables that mediate this link; (4) key resources are hard to measure, particularly those 'socially complex' and 'tacit' resources that the view often focuses on (e.g., Dierickx and Cool, 1989; Barney, 1991); and (5) the gains from superior resources may not be captured at the firm level – but rather be captured by individual resources (Coff, 1999; Lippman and Rumelt, 2003a) – in which case firm performance cannot be the dependent variable.

20.2.5   Later Work

Much subsequent research has consisted in elaborating, refining, extending and testing the core ideas of the RBV as well as refining the more specific criteria for sustained competitive advantage. We briefly survey this work here.

20.2.5.1   Resource accumulation

A central question in the RBV is what factors make resources hard to imitate. The seminal contribution here is the resource accumulation model advanced by Dierickx and Cool (1989) that was highly influential for subsequent work. Dierickx and Cool (ibid.) argue that competitive advantages stem from firm-specific resource stocks that need to be accumulated internally. Strategists are mainly concerned with the building of valuable stocks of resources (like brand reputation, manufacturing capabilities, technological expertise) by making appropriate choices about strategic investments flows. The imitability and sustainability of competitive positions result from the characteristics of the mapping of investment flows onto resource stocks. Dierickx and Cool argue that time compression diseconomies explain early mover advantages, since higher investment outlays over a shorter period of time by a follower are required to catch up with an early mover. Asset mass efficiencies confer an advantage to a firm that has already accumulated a critical mass of a resource (cf. Cohen and Levinthal, 1990). However, in the presence of asset erosion, Knott et al. (2003) argue and show empirically that time compression diseconomies and asset mass efficiencies are not sufficient to gain sustainable competitive advantages.

Rather, the interconnectedness of asset stocks and causal ambiguity appear to be necessary to explain long-term differences in resource stocks (Lippman and Rumelt 1982; Barney, 1991). The interconnectedness of asset stocks relate to complementarities among two or more resources (Stieglitz and Heine, 2007). The value of an asset stock depends on the presence of complementary resources, sharply increasing the investment costs for an imitator (Ghemawat, 1991). Causal ambiguity obfuscates the link between resources and firm performance. It points to the tacitness, complexity and specificity of the resource base (Reed and De Fillippi, 1990). Recent work has particularly highlighted the complexity of a firm's resource base as an effective barrier to imitation (Rivkin, 2000, 2001; Winter, 2000). However, causal ambiguity of its resources may also restrict the strategic options of a firm, since it may find it impossible to transfer or to replicate the competitive advantage in a different context (King and Zeithamel, 2001; Winter and Szulanski, 2001). These characteristics also impact the tradability of resources. Thus, while generic resources may be acquired in factor markets, the firm-specific and idiosyncratic resources underpinning competitive advantages result from internal accumulation processes. Lippman and Rumelt (2003a, p.1082) succinctly summarize RBV's insistence on the primacy of internal resource accumulation: 'The resource-based view predicts that firms will focus their energies on the development of complex "home-grown" resources, taking time and care to develop knowledge, know-how, social capital, and other socially complex, difficult-to-transfer resources'. However, Makadok (2001) argues that resource development may not constitute the only causal mechanism to explain competitive advantages. Firms may also be better than others at picking undervalued resources in the market for resources. Resource-picking points to the role of strategic factor markets in explaining firm behaviour and competitive advantage.

20.2.5.2 Strategic factor markets

Barney (1986) characterized markets for resources as strategic factor markets. Apart from luck, firms may only acquire resources below their net present value by forming heterogeneous expectations about resource value. Otherwise, prospective buyers bid up the price to the resource's net present value and the seller appropriates the value from the resource (e.g., Capron and Shen, 2007). Much subsequent research on strategic factor markets has focused on the origins of differential expectations about resources. Chi (1994), Makadok (2001) and Makadok and Barney (2001) analyse differences in the information acquisition strategies of firms. Denrell et al. (2003) point to entrepreneurial serendipity to explain the acquisition of undervalued resources. A second line of inquiry has focused on co-specialization among heterogeneous resources (Teece, 1986; Lippman and Rumelt, 2003a; Adegbesan, 2009). Even with perfect information, heterogeneous firms may place differential values on a complementary resource in a strategic factor market. With resource heterogeneity among buyers, gains from resource trade are not dissipated in a competitive bidding process and at least some of the resource value is appropriated by the buyer.

One of the traditional differentiating characteristics of the RBV is its focus on factor markets – to the exclusion of a concern with product markets. RBV scholars sometimes explain this as a simple intellectual division of labour, the positioning approach handling product imperfections (e.g., Porter, 1980), the RBV handling factor market imperfections (e.g., Barney, 1991). Accordingly, product markets are often treated as perfectly competitive in the RBV (e.g., Lippman and Rumelt, 1982; Peteraf, 1993). However, it seems fundamentally odd for reasons of basic symmetry to invoke highly imperfect factor markets and perfect products at the same time, particularly given that one firm's product market is another firm's factor market. Priem and Butler (2001a and 2001b) argued that there are demand-side aspects of value creation that the RBV abstracts from. Thus, for any transaction, created value is the difference between the reservation price and the underlying costs of production. To the extent that the RBV essentially abstracts from the demand side by only focusing on competitive product markets, it also neglects an important part of value creation, as well as those resources (e.g., advertising capabilities) that are valuable because they can influence demand-side value creation.

Moreover, if product market conditions (i.e., what game forms characterize interaction in product markets) significantly influence factor market behaviours, it would seem odd to separate factor and product markets. In fact, recent work shows that there are close connections between product market and factor market behaviours (Asmussen, 2010; Makadok, 2010), which suggests that focusing on only upstream or downstream markets may lead analysis astray.

Work on strategic factor markets points to the more general problem of bargaining and rent-sharing among resource owners (Peteraf, 1993) (although small numbers bargaining on strategic factor markets still have to be modelled in the literature). Bargaining among resource owners has attracted a great deal of attention in recent contributions to the RBV.

20.2.5.3   Bargaining

Coff (1999) argues that rent-sharing and value appropriation among resource owners (e.g., employees, shareholders, suppliers) fundamentally depends on the bargaining power of each resource owner. Following in the tradition of Peteraf (1993), he shows how various instantiations of constrained resource mobility systematically influence the bargaining position of resource owners (cf. Jacobides et al., 2006). Lippman and Rumelt (2003a) and Adegbesan (2009), drawing on cooperative game theory, analyse how co-specialization among resources systematically changes the outside options for resource owners and thereby determines their relative bargaining positions. MacDonald and Ryall (2004) add to this emerging stream of literature by establishing the necessary conditions for value appropriation. They highlight the importance of competition for a scarce resource among different resource coalitions for value appropriation. Blyler and Coff (2003) add a social dimension to the bargaining problem by stressing the role of social capital for attaining and leveraging bargaining power. However, recent research has also begun to point to the dynamic properties of bargaining power. That is, expectations about value appropriation drive investments into resources (Stieglitz and Heine, 2007) as well as the entrepreneurial search for new resource combinations (Lippman and Rumelt, 2003b; Stieglitz and Foss, 2009). Explicit bargaining costs have yet to be considered within the RBV, however. Such costs are a part of the broader category of transaction costs.

20.2.5.4   Transaction costs and property rights

Some proponents of the RBV have tried to separate it from the more mainstream economics of the firm (e.g., Conner, 1991; Conner and Prahalad, 1996), and have argued that the RBV has the potential to develop into a distinct theory of the firm. It has become increasingly clear, however, that not only are the RBV and mainstream economics insights in transaction costs and property and how these shape economic organization highly complementary, there is also a very significant overlap (Foss, 1996; Silverman, 1999; Nickerson and Zenger, 2004). More generally, it is arguable that the RBV relies on competitive imperfections that are essentially in the nature of transaction costs or at least information costs, notably costs of imitation (Foss, 2003).

Foss and Foss (2005) argue that transaction costs are present right at the heart of the RBV. Thus, the basic unit of analysis in the RBV is the discrete resource. The notion of resource has a direct intuitive appeal because it can be so associated with real entities, like machines, buildings, experts, and so on. However, what firms ultimately demand are the *services* that resources yield (Penrose, [1959] 1995). In fact, resources are really collections of 'attributes', that is, services, functionalities, and so forth. In a world without transaction costs, all these attributes could be identified and traded, and there would be no reason to trade discrete resources. To the extent that such resources are actually traded, it is because it pays in terms of transaction costs to bundle attributes in resources. The other side of the coin is that resources are really endogenous results of economizing with transaction costs. Relatedly, resource value is intimately related to transaction costs. Thus, the lower the costs of defining and enforcing property and ownership rights to resources, the higher the value of the relevant resource (all else equal) (Foss and Foss, 2005; Kim and Mahoney, 2005). Finally, some resources are valuable because they are capable of reducing transaction costs. Contracts, credit rating systems, organizational structures and so on may be analysed in this light.

20.2.5.5   Path-dependent theoretical development

As the above brief review of RBV work within the last 15 years indicates, the high church RBV has been a progressive research programme in a number of ways: the understanding of the workings of strategic factors have been much improved; a better understanding of bargaining and value appropriation has been reached; adding transaction costs to the basic model has yielded an increased understanding of value creation and impediments to such value creation; and a deeper understanding of the value of resources has been developed by incorporating demand-side factors and transaction costs into the analysis.

Still, the core model has changed rather little as a result of this work, which has tended to refine and elaborate already existing insights rather than yielding fundamentally novel insights. And core RBV theorizing continues to be wedded to a model that originated in mainstream economics in the context of industrial economics. In this sense, a strong intellectual path-dependence has obtained in the history of the RBV.

Although borrowing from the Chicago approach in some ways furthered strategic management, the set of phenomena relevant to strategic management that can be framed by relying on this approach is rather limited. This follows from the basic Chicago research methodology, which casts virtually any social phenomenon in terms of competitive equilibrium – what Chicago school insider Melvin Reder (1982) characterized as the 'tight prior equilibrium' assumption. The core of this approach is that 'in the absence of sufficient evidence to the contrary, one may treat observed prices and quantities as good approximations to their long-run competitive equilibrium values' (Reder, 1982, p. 12). The resulting notion of competitive equilibrium may not entirely be of the perfect competition (Walrasian) textbook variety, but it is very close. The famous Lippman and Rumelt (1982) paper starts from the standard assumptions of independent profit-maximizing decision-makers and competitive markets with free entry. New industry entrants' production processes are assumed to be subject to an ex ante uncertainty (causal ambiguity) in the specific sense that entrants' post-entry cost function is randomly drawn from a known probability distribution after paying a fixed non-retrievable entry investment cost. This produces an equilibrium in which rents persist. Key to generating the desired results is the isolation of new firm production processes – which are assumed to be subject to ex ante uncertainty – from an otherwise frictionless (competitive) economic environment. Though not cast in formal terms, later key contributions to the RBV adopt essentially this model as the founding model.[3] The low church RBV very clearly differs with respect to intellectual pedigree, and its emergence can to a certain extent be understood in the context of the constraining nature of the equilibrium-based high church RBV (Foss, 2000; Mathews, 2010).

20.3   THE LOW CHURCH RESOURCE-BASED VIEW

20.3.1   Origins

Encompassing the 'knowledge-based view of the firm' (Kogut and Zander, 1992), the 'evolutionary theory of the firm' (Nelson and Winter, 1982), the 'capabilities view of the firm' and the 'dynamic capabilities view' (Teece et al., 1997), the origins of the low church RBV are more diverse than is the case of the high church RBV, some of its pedigrees lie outside of economics and many lie within heterodox economics. Thus, the low church RBV draws on the product development and knowledge management literatures in management, evolutionary economics, Schumpeterian thought, the organizational learning literature, work on leadership and alliances, business history, as well as Penrose's thought. Thus, the low church RBV is the contemporary heir to Penrose who stressed that 'One of the primary assumptions of the theory of the growth of firms is that "history matters"; growth is essentially an evolutionary process and based on the cumulative growth of collective knowledge, in the context of a purposive firm' ([1959] 1995, p.xiii). What is more, in light of only modest empirical support for the RBV, Newbert (2007) argues that a firm's organizing context and its dynamic capabilities rather than its static resources are essential for understanding competitive positions and superior profitability. Hence, the low church approach to the RBV might not only offer a different theoretical perspective, but may also help to address certain empirical shortcomings of the RBV.

20.3.2   Key Tenets

Whereas the high church version of the RBV is founded on economic equilibrium and maximizing behaviour, and generates its predictions in the time-honoured manner of selectively introducing imperfections in an otherwise perfect world, the low church RBV is a much more amorphous collection of insights that in some dimensions overlap with the high church RBV. Thus, overall there is the same emphasis on firms as collections of heterogeneous resources.

However, the high church RBV focuses on given resources that, moreover, tend to be seen as efficiently organized within a firm. In contrast, the low church RBV focuses on building, accumulating, transforming, managing, learning about, combining and recombining resources, and, in particular, the services that can be derived from such resources. Dynamics and learning are key in the low church RBV. Moreover, whereas the high church RBV is hesitant to privilege any specific resource category, the low church RBV unambiguously concentrates on resources or assets that are knowledge-based, social in the sense that they are somehow linked to a collectivity of interacting agents (Felin and Foss, 2005), and tend to put much emphasis on the tacit nature of the knowledge that is alleged to reside in such interaction. Notions of 'capabilities', 'dynamic capabilities', 'routines' and the like capture these characteristics.

Though clearly anticipated in Nelson and Winter's (1982) notion of 'dynamic routines' and in the innovation literature (e.g., notions of 'dynamic efficiency', Klein, 1977), research on (dynamic) capabilities was rejuvenated by Teece et al. (1997) who argued that superior performance comes from a firm's capacity to change its resource base in the face of Schumpeterian competition and environmental change. Dynamic capabilities are defined as the firm's ability to integrate, build and reconfigure internal and external competences to address rapidly changing environments (ibid., p.516). Importantly, dynamic capabilities reflect past learning processes, as they are a learned pattern of collective activity through which the organization systematically generates and modifies its operational routines in pursuit of improved performance. This basic definition has been subsequently refined and extended (e.g., Eisenhardt and Martin, 2000; Winter, 2000; Zollo and Winter, 2002; Teece, 2007). What unites different approaches and definitions is the insistence on an organizational ability to alter its resource base. Thus, Helfat et al. (2007, p. 4) synthesize prior conceptual work by defining a dynamic capability as 'the capacity of an organization to purposefully create, extend, and modify its resource base'. Accordingly, dynamic capabilities may perform different tasks that alter the resource base, such as new product development, alliance formation, or post-acquisition integration (Eisenhardt and Martin, 2000). According to the dynamic capability (DC) approach, a firm's capacity to alter its resource base indirectly influences economic profitability (Helfat and Peteraf, 2009). Superior dynamic capabilities enable firms to adapt more quickly and effectively to a changing business environment, creating a stream of temporary competitive advantages over time (Teece et al., 1997; Zott, 2003; Helfat et al., 2007).

Recent work on dynamic capabilities has increasingly stressed the role of organizational processes for understanding how firms alter their resource base. Teece (2007) opens up the black box of dynamic capabilities by relating the concept to organizational processes of sensing and seizing business opportunities and the constant (re)alignment of resources (cf. Helfat and Peteraf, 2009). A firm's sensing ability critically depends on the organizational systems and individual capacities to learn and to identify, filter, evaluate and shape opportunities. Once a business opportunity is identified, the organizational structure, procedures and incentives influence whether and how a firm seizes the opportunity and creates a new strategic path. What is more, governance and organizational structures shape how firms align their specific resources over time. These 'microfoundations' of dynamic capabilities (Teece, 2007) link the DC approach to extant research on organizational design and adaptation and on transaction costs and governance structures.

However, despite the popularity of the low church approach to the RBV in general and dynamic capabilities in particular, many open questions and unresolved issues remain. Williamson (1999), for example, argues that the definition of dynamic capabilities remains overly inclusive and elastic. While most of the DC literature seems to imply that dynamic capabilities are a fundamental precondition for resource alterations, Helfat and Peteraf (2003) argue that dynamic capabilities are not required for capability-building and strategic change. Furthermore, Salvato (2003) and Felin and Foss (2005) point to the lack of proper microfoundations, since extant research fails to demonstrate how individual behaviour (i.e., individual skills) aggregates into collective outcomes (i.e., organizational capability). In a recent critique, Arend and Bromiley (2009) argue that the current DC approach offers unclear additional insights relative to existing concepts in the management literature, lacks a coherent theoretical foundation, receives only weak empirical support and offers diffuse practical implications. Helfat and Peteraf (2009) respond to these criticisms by pointing to the complexity of the research questions, which is matched by the complexity of the theoretical underpinnings. What is more, they also claim that the DC approach is still in a state of flux and in its formative stage. According to Helfat and Peteraf (2009, p. 99), 'dynamic capabilities are not yet a theory'.

20.4   MOVEMENT TOWARDS THE MIDDLE?

Changes within the high church as well as the low church RBV have brought them closer to each other. Thus, the low church RBV has become increasingly formal, and although it does not have a core model in the sense that the high church does, it may be reaching for one. Thus, Gavetti and Levinthal (2004, p. 1310) explicitly argue that the

> framework of evolutionary economics (Nelson and Winter 1982, 2002) rests on a conceptual apparatus that is quite consistent with the nature of this movement. More specifically, we view it as an emerging archetype, a paradigm, which has the potential to unify this growing middle ground and provide the coherence that is key to the cumulative development of any field of intellectual inquiry.

In its turn, the high church RBV may have reached the point where further reliance on patched-up competitive equilibrium models no longer yields progress. In fact, recent advances within this branch of the RBV make use of the language of game theory (Lippman and Rumelt, 2003a; MacDonald and Ryall, 2004; Adegbesan, 2009) that has supplanted the reliance on competitive equilibrium in economics as the main vehicle of analytical development.[4] In fact, it is arguable that many RBV contributions have already been pushing the envelope quite significantly. Thus, as Gavetti and Levinthal (2004, p. 1311) point out, it is arguable that the seminal Dierickx and Cool (1989) paper can be read as a low church contribution:

> Within their perspective, actions were not necessarily rational and there was not a presumption of equilibrium. . . Although not explicitly linked to the Carnegie School tradition of characterizing organizations as engaged in problemistic search, Dierickx and Cool drew a picture of a firm's capability development that was certainly compatible with such a viewpoint.

Indeed, the question of how new resources and capabilities are developed is arguably becoming a common theme in both approaches to the RBV. Recent theorizing has stressed that competitive advantage usually does not stem from access to a single, unique resource. Rather, what underpins competitive advantage are complex combinations of co-specialized resources (Peteraf, 1993; Levinthal, 1997; Rivkin, 2000; Winter, 2000; Denrell et al., 2003; Knott et al., 2003; Lippman and Rumelt, 2003b). The fundamental question then becomes how firms search for new, valuable resource combinations. The line of inquiry connects RBV thinking to the substantial literature on organizational search and learning. An important theme there is that the search for new resource combinations is not a purely random process, even though luck and serendipity play an essential role in explaining heterogeneous firm performance (Lippman and Rumelt, 1982; Rumelt, 1984; Denrell et al., 2003; Denrell, 2004). The effectiveness of organizational search is influenced by internal factors such as a firm's internal structure (Siggelkow and Levinthal, 2003; Siggelkow and Rivkin, 2005; Knudsen and Levinthal, 2007) and external linkages (Rosenkopf and Nerkar, 2001; Holmqvist, 2004). What is more, goal-setting and performance feedback shape an organization's breadth of search. As many empirical studies have shown, negative performance feedback stimulates explorative search for new resource combinations (see Greve 2003 for an overview).

Recent theoretical and empirical research on organizational search similarly suggests that agents use specialized mental models to navigate the vast space of possible resource combinations (cf. Nickerson and Zenger, 2004; Gavetti, 2005; Gavetti and

Rivkin, 2007). In a simulation model, Gavetti and Levinthal (2000) show how the effectiveness of organizational search may be substantially enhanced by cognitive representations of the resource space. A cognitive representation is a simplified picture of the resource space. A well-informed cognitive representation provides guidance in opportunity discovery and allows firms to identify attractive regions in a problem space. Because the cognitive representation is just a coarse-grained depiction of the resource space, an entrepreneur engages in local adaptation to refine the initial business idea. After the discovery of a potentially value-creating resource combination, firms proceed to its refinement and modification (Siggelkow and Levinthal, 2003; Stieglitz and Heine, 2007; Stieglitz and Foss, 2009). Hence, what the cognitive representation fundamentally represents is the entrepreneurial expectation and speculation about more attractive regions in the resource space, what Foss et al. (2007) call 'judgment'.

The key question then is where cognitive representations come from. For technological innovations, an obvious source for a cognitive representation is basic science (Fleming and Sorensen, 2004). Basic science offers an understanding of causal laws and how certain resources combine and interact in principle. Scientific understanding leads entrepreneurs more directly to useful resource combinations, eliminates fruitless paths of research, and motivates them to press on even in the face of negative feedback (ibid., pp. 911–12). Likewise, a cognitive representation of the resource space may also be informed by analogies (Gavetti et al., 2005; Gavetti and Rivkin, 2007; Gavetti and Warglien, 2007). Analogies allow human agents to take insights developed in one context and apply it to a new setting. More generally, an important source of competitive advantage is the heterogeneity of expectations and cognitive representations held by human agents in an economy.

Such a reading is developed by Foss and Foss (2008) who, drawing on the resource-based view, argue that firm-level entrepreneurial opportunities emerge along paths shaped by the firm's experience. However, they also argue that property rights and transaction cost considerations are important to understanding the discovery and exploitation of opportunities. Two mechanisms link transaction costs and opportunity discovery. First, transaction costs determine how well defined and enforced property rights to resource attributes are; in turn, this influences the value that entrepreneurial resource owners expect to appropriate, and therefore their incentives to engage in opportunity discovery. This is the 'appropriability mechanism'. Second, entrepreneurial experience influences opportunity discovery (e.g., Shane, 2000). However, experience (also) emerges from resource learning, that is, entrepreneurs' learning about the attributes of resources (Mahoney, 1995). Such learning entails transaction costs, for example, the costs of measuring the productivity potential of employees. The transaction costs that entrepreneurs face influence their resource learning, introduce path-dependence in such learning, and therefore influence which opportunities will be discovered (the 'resource learning mechanism'). In other words, the mental models that firms (managers) adopted from their learning experience of available opportunities are influenced by transaction costs and property rights. Although embedded in the resource-based view and property rights economics, the approach of Foss and Foss is thus akin to recent attempts to include learning mechanisms in transaction cost economics (Mayer and Argyres, 2004; Argyres and Mayer, 2007).

20.5 CONCLUSIONS

As we have argued the various contributions that make up modern resource-based theory draw from a large and heterogeneous set of influences. To be sure, many of the key ideas can be found in the work of the matriarch of the resource-based view, Edith Penrose ([1959] 1995), but not all of them, and in certain ways her work contains insights that are still to be addressed in modern theory. Thus, the key idea of heterogeneity as key to understanding phenomena of strategic interest is, of course, in Penrose's work. However, Penrose stressed the role of heterogeneous services rather than of resources per se, and the role of the administrative framework of the firm as well as management in shaping the kind of services that the resources under the control of the firm can yield. In fact, a key concern in her book is management's actions with respect to resources, that is, processes of acquiring, bundling, leveraging resources (cf. Kraaijenbrink et al., 2010). This is not a concern in modern theory to the same extent. As Barney and Arikan (2001, p. 174) admit, the (high church) RBV has 'a very simple view about how resources are connected to the strategies that a firm pursues'. Relatedly, Crook et al. (2008) argued that contingencies related to managerial choice should be a major research area within the RBV. More generally, Felin and Foss (2005) argued that action and interaction in general should be more prominently featured in the RBV in order to understand the emergence, maintenance, and change of firm-level capabilities. A potentially fruitful avenue of research that fulfils some of these more 'individual-centric' concerns is represented by a string of recent contributions that link the RBV to research on entrepreneurship (Alvarez and Barney, 2005).

In certain key ways, these ideas also hark back to the other important ancestor of the RBV, Harold Demsetz. Demsetz (1973, p. 3) attributes superior performance to the 'combination of great uncertainty plus luck or atypical insight by the management of a firm'. What is more, if information acquisition is costly, managers and their ability to sense and seize business opportunities and effectively recombine resources, becomes more specialized over time (Alchian and Demsetz, 1972; Demsetz, 1988). This line of thinking places more emphasis on decision-making and the individual ability to search and evaluate resource combinations. A number of contributions highlight individual cognition in structuring the search for new resource combinations (e.g., Amit and Schoemaker, 1993; Foss, 1993; Gavetti and Levinthal, 2000, Gavetti et al., 2005; Knudsen and Levinthal, 2007), but these ideas do not seem to be well integrated into the core of the RBV. In addition, the decision-making process about resource allocation and capability development is structured by the organization design (Adner and Levinthal, 2004; Gavetti, 2005; Foss et al., 2007; Christensen and Knudsen, 2010). Lastly, the incentive system of a firm influences where and how a firm searches for new resource combinations (Manso, 2008). In a nutshell, it appears that the RBV stands to gain from a more careful consideration of individual and organizational factors that influence how a firm searches and evaluates resource combinations and allocates resources. In terms of drawing on neighbouring fields, the operational implications seem to be that the RBV may stand to gain from linking up more explicitly with research on strategic human resource management and top management teams.

Finally, another area for further research is the development of (formal) models that would facilitate the cumulative build up of theoretical knowledge and careful development of empirical hypotheses. While the RBV has a long tradition of formal models (e.g., Lippman and Rumelt, 1982, 2003a; Makadok, 2001; Denrell, 2004; MacDonald and Ryall, 2004), these contributions appear to represent a fringe rather than a widely accepted theoretical core of RBV thinking. For example, it is unclear how a standard model in the RBV looks that connects differential resource advantage to product market competition (e.g., Klepper and Simons, 2000), although this issue is beginning to be explored (Asmussen, 2010; Makadok, 2010). Does the NK model (Kauffman, 1993), widely applied to problems of organizational search and adaptation, represent an adequate model platform to study how firms engage in resource learning, recombine resources and protect them from competition? To what extent can RBV theory draw on formal theories of the firm that link resource investments to the bargaining positions of resource owners and other factors (Gibbons, 2005)? It is noteworthy that formal arguments have been brought to bear on issues both within the high and the low church RBV. Perhaps the movement towards the middle that we have diagnosed will be prompted by formal developments, and the long-standing schism within the RBV will finally be overcome.

NOTES

1. The Chicago legacy is perhaps most clearly present in an often cited paper by Peteraf (1993), which explicitly casts the RBV in terms of rents in competitive equilibrium, using the basic demand and supply apparatus of economics textbooks to graphically illustrate this.
2. In terms of the earlier point about the debt that the RBV owes to the Chicago-UCLA industrial economics tradition, Barney's analysis of the conditions under which such situations obtain is entirely in line with the Chicago school in its emphasis on resources (i.e., input factors) being costly to copy, and so on (compare Brozen, 1971; Demsetz, 1973, 1974, 1982, 1989; Peltzman, 1977). His argument that all performance differences are explainable in terms of differential efficiencies of the resources that underlie the strategies, and that, therefore, superior returns are fully compatible with social welfare, is straight out of the Chicago book (e.g., Demsetz, 1974, 1989). Barney's (1986) earlier emphasis on factor market rather than product market imperfections as a condition of competitive advantage is also vintage Chicago (e.g., Demsetz, 1973).
3. The Lippman and Rumelt model and its later verbal RBV counterparts are instances of a specific economic modelling methodology in which imperfections are introduced in a piecemeal manner into a world that is otherwise perfect in order to generate a specific result. As an example, the foundational RBV high church models take factor markets to be imperfect, while product markets are assumed to be perfect (i.e., competitive).
4. Although game-theoretical work on the RBV tends to be cast in a cooperative mould, rather than the non-cooperative approach that dominates economics.

REFERENCES

Acedo, F.J., C. Barroso and J.L. Galan. 2006. The Resource-based Theory: Dissemination and Main Trends. *Strategic Management Journal* **27**(6) 621–36.
Adegbesan, A.J. 2009. On the Origins of Competitive Advantage: Strategic Factor Markets and Heterogeneous Resource Complementarity. *Academy of Management Review* **34**(3) 463–75.
Adner, R. and D.A. Levinthal. 2004. What is Not a Real Option: Considering Boundaries for the Application of Real Options to Business Strategy. *Academy of Management Review* **29**(1), 74–85.
Agarwal, R. and G. Hoetker. 2007. A Faustian Bargain? The Growth of Management and its Relationship with Related Disciplines. *Academy of Management Journal* **50**(6), 1304–22.
Alchian, Armen A. and Harold Demsetz. 1972. Production, Information Costs, and Economic Organization. *The American Economic Review* **62**(5), 777–95.

Alvarez, S. and J.B. Barney. 2005. How Do Entrepreneurs Organize Firms Under Conditions of Uncertainty. *Journal of Management* **31**(5), 776–93.
Amit, R. and P. Schoemaker. 1993. Strategic Assets and Organizational Rent. *Strategic Management Journal* **14**(1), 33–46.
Arend, R.J. 2006. Tests of the Resource-based View: Do the Empirics Have Any Clothes? *Strategic Organization* **4**(4), 409–21.
Arend, R.J. and P. Bromiley. 2009. Assessing the Dynamic Capabilities View: Spare Change, Everyone? *Strategic Organization* **7**(1), 75–90.
Argyres, N.S. and K.J. Mayer. 2007. Contract Design as a Firm Capability: An Integration of Learning and Transaction Cost Perspectives. *Academy of Management Review* **32**(4), 1060–77.
Armstrong, C.E. and K. Shimizu. 2007. A Review of Approaches to Empirical Research on the Resource-based View of the Firm. *Journal of Management* **33**(6), 959–86.
Asmussen, C.G. 2010. Chicken, Stag, or Rabbit? Strategic Factor Markets and the Moderating Role of Downstream Competition. Working Paper, Center for Strategic Management and Globalization, Copenhagen Business School.
Bain, J.S. 1956. *Barriers to New Competition*. Cambridge, MA: Harvard University Press.
Barney, J.B. 1986. Strategic Factor Markets: Expectations, Luck, and Business Strategy. *Management Science* **32**(10), 1231–41.
Barney, J.B. 1991. Firm Resources and Sustained Competitive Advantage. *Journal of Management* **17**(1), 99–120.
Barney, J.B. and A.M. Arikan. 2001. The Resource-based View: Origins and Implications. In M.A. Hitt, R.E. Freeman and J.S. Harrison (eds) *Handbook of Strategic Management*, Oxford: Basil Blackwell.
Baumol, W.J., J.C. Panzar and R.D. Willig. 1982. Contestable Markets: An Uprising in the Theory of Industry Structure: Reply. *The American Economic Review* **73**(3), 491–6.
Blyler, Maureen and Russell W. Coff. 2003. Dynamic Capabilities, Social Capital, and Rent Appropriation: Ties That Split Pies. *Strategic Management Journal* **24**(7), 677–86.
Brozen, Y. 1971. The Persistence of 'High Rates of Return' in High-Stable Concentration Industries. *Journal of Law and Economics* **14**(2), 501–12.
Camerer, C. 1994. Does Strategy Research Need Game Theory? In R.P. Rumelt, D. Schendel and D.J. Teece (eds) *Fundamental Issues in Strategy*. Boston: Harvard Business School Press.
Capron, Laurence and Jung-Chin Shen. 2007. Acquisitions of Private vs. Public Firms: Private Information, Target Selection, and Acquirer Returns. *Strategic Management Journal* **28**(9), 891–911.
Chi, T. 1994. Trading in Strategic Resources: Necessary Conditions, Transaction Cost Problems, and Choice of Exchange Structure. *Strategic Management Journal* **15**(4), 271–90.
Christensen, Michael and Thorbjørn Knudsen. 2010. Design of Decision-making Organizations. *Management Science* **56**(1), 71–89.
Coase, R.H. 1937. The Nature of the Firm. *Economica* **4**(16), 386–405.
Coase, R.H. 1960. The Problem of Social Cost. *Journal of Law and Economics* **3**(October), 1–44.
Coff, R.W. 1999. When Competitive Advantage Doesn't Lead to Performance: The Resource-based View and Stakeholder Bargaining Power. *Organization Science* **10**(2), 119–33.
Cohen, Wesley M. and Daniel A. Levinthal. 1990. Absorptive Capacity: A New Perspective on Learning and Innovation. *Administrative Science Quarterly* **35**(1), 128–52.
Conner, K.R. 1991. A Historical Comparison of Resource-based Theory and Five Schools of Thought Within Industrial Organization Economics: Do We Have a New Theory of the Firm? *Journal of Management* **17**(1), 121–54.
Conner, K.R. and C.K. Prahalad. 1996. A Resource-based Theory of the Firm: Knowledge versus Opportunism. *Organization Science* **7**(5), 477–501.
Crook, T.R., D.J. Ketchen Jr, J.G. Combs and S.Y. Todd. 2008. Strategic Resources and Performance: A Meta-analysis. *Strategic Management Journal* **29**(11), 1141–54.
Debreu, G. 1959. *Theory of Value*. New York: Wiley.
Demsetz, H. 1973. Industrial Structure, Market Rivalry, and Public Policy. *Journal of Law and Economics* **16**(1), 1–10.
Demsetz, H. 1974. Two Systems of Belief About Monopoly. In idem. 1989. *Efficiency, Competition, and Policy*. Oxford: Basil Blackwell.
Demsetz, H. 1982. Barriers to Entry. In idem. 1989. *Efficiency, Competition, and Policy*. Oxford: Basil Blackwell.
Demsetz, Harold. 1988. The Theory of the Firm Revisited. *Journal of Law, Economics, & Organization* **4**(1), 141–61.
Demsetz, H. 1989. The Indivisibility Rent Theory of Measured Oligopoly Profit. In idem. 1989. *Efficiency, Competition, and Policy*. Oxford: Basil Blackwell.
Denrell, Jerker. 2004. Random Walks and Sustained Competitive Advantage. *Management Science* **50**(7), 922–34.

enrell, J., C. Fang and S.G. Winter. 2003. The Economics of Strategic Opportunity. *Strategic Management Journal* **24**, 977–90.
ierickx, I. and K. Cool. 1989. Asset Stock Accumulation and the Sustainability of Competitive Advantage. *Management Science* **35**(1), 1504–11.
senhardt, Kathleen M. and Jeffrey A. Martin. 2000. Dynamic Capabilities: What Are They? *Strategic Management Journal* **21**(10/11), 1105–21.
ama, E.F. 1970. Efficient Capital Markets: A Review of Theory and Empirical Work. *Journal of Finance* **25**(2), 383–417.
elin, T. and N.J. Foss. 2005. Strategic Organization: A Field in Search of Microfoundations. *Strategic Organization* **3**(4), 441–55.
eming, L. and O. Sorenson. 2004. Science as a Map in Technological Search. *Strategic Management Journal* **25**(8–9), 909–28.
oss, Nicolai J. 1993. Theories of the Firm: Contractual and Competence Perspectives. *Journal of Evolutionary Economics* **3**(2), 127–44.
oss, N.J. 1996. Knowledge-based Approaches to the Theory of the Firm: Some Critical Comments. *Organization Science* **7**(5), 470–76.
oss, N.J. 1998. The Competence-based Approach: Veblenian Ideas in the Modern Theory of the Firm. *Cambridge Journal of Economics* **22**(4), 479–96.
oss, Nicolai J. 2000. Equilibrium vs Evolution in the Resource-based Perspective. In Nicolai J. Foss and Paul L. Robertson (eds) *Resources, Technology, and Strategy*. London: Routledge.
oss, N.J. 2003. The Strategic Management and Transaction Cost Nexus: Past Debates, Central Questions, and Future Research Possibilities. *Strategic Organization* **1**(2), 139–69.
oss, K. and N.J. Foss. 2005. Resources and Transaction Costs: How Property Rights Economics Furthers the Resource-based View. *Strategic Management Journal*, **26**(6), 541–53.
oss, K. and N.J. Foss. 2008. Understanding Opportunity Discovery and Sustainable Advantage: The Role of Transaction Costs and Property Rights. *Strategic Entrepreneurship Journal* **207**(2), 191–207.
oss, N.J. and T. Knudsen. 2003. The Resource-based Tangle: Towards a Sustainable Explanation of Competitive Advantage. *Managerial and Decision Economics* **24**(4), 291–307.
oss, K., N.J. Foss and P.G. Klein. 2007. Original and Derived Judgment: An Entrepreneurial Theory of Economic Organization. *Organization Studies* **28**(12), 1893–912.
avetti, G. 2005. Cognition and Hierarchy: Rethinking the Microfoundations of Capabilities' Development. *Organization Science* **16**(6), 599–617.
avetti, G. and D.A. Levinthal. 2000. Looking Forward and Looking Backward: Cognitive and Experiential Search. *Administrative Science Quarterly* **45**(1), 113–37.
avetti, G. and D.A. Levinthal. 2004. The Strategy Field from the Perspective of Management Science: Divergent Strands and Possible Integration. *Management Science* **50**(10), 1309–18.
avetti, Giovanni and Jan W. Rivkin. 2007. On the Origin of Strategy: Action and Cognition over Time. *Organization Science* **18**(3), 420–39.
avetti, G. and M. Warglien. 2007. Recognizing the New: A Multi-agent Model of Analogy in Strategic Decision-making. Harvard Business School Working Paper, No. 08-028.
avetti, G., D.A. Levinthal and J.W. Rivkin. 2005. Strategy Making in Novel and Complex Worlds: The Power of Analogy. *Strategic Management Journal* **26**(8), 691–712.
hemawat, P. 1991. *Commitment: The Dynamic of Strategy*. New York: The Free Press.
ibbons, Robert. 2005. Four Formal(izable) Theories of the Firm? *Journal of Economic Behavior & Organization* **58**(2), 200–245.
reve, H.R. 2003. *Organizational Learning from Performance Feedback*. Cambridge: Cambridge University Press.
amel, G. and C.K. Prahalad. 1994. *Competing for the Future*. Boston: Harvard Business School Press.
eimriks, K.H., T. Fellin, N.J. Foss and M. Zollo. 2010. A Comparative Review of the Resource, Routines, and Capabilities Literatures: Similarities, Differences and a Proposed Agenda. Working Paper.
elfat, C.E. et al. 2007. *Dynamic Capabilities: Understanding Strategic Change in Organizations*. Oxford: Blackwell.
elfat, C.E. and M.A. Peteraf. 2003. The Dynamic Resource-based View: Capability Lifecycles. *Strategic Management Journal* **24**(10), 997–1010.
elfat, Constance E. and Margaret A. Peteraf. 2009. Understanding Dynamic Capabilities: Progress Along a Developmental Path. *Strategic Organization* **7**(1), 91–102.
olmqvist, M. 2004. Experiential Learning Processes of Exploitation and Exploration Within and Between Organizations: An Empirical Study of Product Development. *Organization Science* **15**(4), 70–81.
oopes, David G. and Tammy L. Madsen. 2008. A Capability-based View of Competitive Heterogeneity. *Industrial and Corporate Change* **17**(3), 393–426.
oskisson, R.E., M.A. Hitt, W.P. Wan and D. Yiu. 1999. Theory and Research in Strategic Management: Swings of a Pendulum. *Journal of Management* **25**(3), 417–56.

Jacobides, M.G., T. Knudsen and M. Augier. 2006. Benefiting from Innovation: Value Creation, Valu Appropriation and the Role of Industry Architectures. *Research Policy* **35**(8), 1200–221.

Jacobson, R. 1992. The Austrian School of Strategy. *Academy of Management Review* **17**(4), 782–807.

Kauffman, S.A. 1993. *The Origins of Order: Self-organization and Selection in Evolution*. Oxford/New York OUP.

Kim, J. and J.T. Mahoney. 2005. Property Rights Theory, Transaction Costs Theory, and Agency Theory: A Organizational Economics Approach to Strategic Management. *Managerial and Decision Economics* **26**(4) 223–42.

King, Adelaide Wilcox and Carl P. Zeithaml. 2001. Competencies and Firm Performance: Examining the Causal Ambiguity Paradox. *Strategic Management Journal* **22**(1), 75–99.

Klein, B.H. 1977. *Dynamic Economics*. Cambridge, MA: Harvard University Press.

Klein, Benjamin, Robert G. Crawford and Armen A. Alchian. 1978. Vertical Integration, Appropriable Rents and the Competitive Contracting Process. *Journal of Law and Economics* **21**(2), 297–326.

Klepper, Steven and Kenneth L. Simons. 2000. Dominance by Birthright: Entry of Prior Radio Producer. and Competitive Ramifications in the U.S. Television Receiver Industry. *Strategic Management Journa* **21**(10/11), 997–1016.

Knight, F.H. 1921. *Risk, Uncertainty, and Profit*. New York: Augustus M. Kelley.

Knott, A.M. 2003. The Organizational Routines Factor Market Paradox. *Strategic Management Journa* **24**(8), 929–43.

Knott, Anne Marie, David J. Bryce and Hart E. Posen. 2003. On the Strategic Accumulation of Intangible Assets. *Organization Science* **14**(2), 192–207.

Knudsen, T. and D.A. Levinthal. 2007. Two Faces of Search: Alternative Generation and Alternative Evaluation. *Organization Science* **18**(1), 39–54.

Kogut, B. and U. Zander. 1992. Knowledge of the Firm, Combinative Capabilities, and the Replication of Technology. *Organization Science* **3**(3) 383–97.

Kor, Y.Y. and J.T. Mahoney. 2000. Penrose's Resource-based Approach: The Process and Product of Research Creativity. *Journal of Management Studies* **37**(1), 109–39.

Kraaijenbrink, J., J.-C. Spender and A.J. Groen. 2010. The Resource-based View: A Review and Assessment of its Critiques. *Journal of Management* **36**(1), 349–72.

Levinthal, D. 1997. Adaptation on Rugged Landscapes. *Management Science* **43**(7), 934–50.

Lippman, S.A. and R.P. Rumelt. 1982. Uncertain Imitability: An Analysis of Interfirm Differences in Efficiency Under Competition. *The Bell Journal of Economics* **13**(2), 418–38.

Lippman, S.A. and R.P. Rumelt. 2003a. A Bargaining Perspective on Resource Advantage. *Strategic Management Journal* **24**(11), 1069–86.

Lippman, S.A. and R.P. Rumelt. 2003b. The Payments Perspective: Micro-foundations of Resource Analysis. *Strategic Management Journal* **24**, 903–27.

Lockett, A. and S. Thompson. 2001. The Resource-based View and Economics. *Journal of Management* **27**(6), 723–4.

MacDonald, G. and M.D. Ryall. 2004. How Do Value Creation and Competition Determine Whether a Firm Appropriates Value? *Management Science* **50**(10), 1319–34.

Mahoney, J.T. 1995. The Management of Resources and the Resource of Management. *Journal of Business Research*, **33**(2), 91–101.

Makadok, R. 2001. Toward a Synthesis of the Resource-based and Dynamic-capability Views of Rent Creation. *Strategic Management Journal* **22**(5), 387–401.

Makadok, R. 2010. The Interaction Effect of Rivalry Restraint and Competitive Advantage on Profit: Why the Whole is Less Than the Sum of the Parts. *Management Science* **56**(2), 356–72.

Makadok, R. and J.B. Barney. 2001. Strategic Factor Market Intelligence: An Application of Information Economics to Strategy Formulation and Competitor Intelligence. *Management Science* **47**(12), 1621–38.

Manso, G. 2008. Motivating Innovation. MIT Working Paper.

Mathews, J.A. 2006. *Strategizing, Disequilibrium and Profits*. Stanford, CA: Stanford University Press.

Mathews, J.A. 2010. Lachmannian Insights into Strategic Entrepreneurship: Resources, Activities and Routines in a Disequilibrium World. *Organization Studies* **31**(2), 219–44.

Mayer, Kyle J. and Nicholas S. Argyres. 2004. Learning to Contract: Evidence from the Personal Computer Industry. *Organization Science* **15**(4), 394–410.

Nelson, R.R. and S.G. Winter. 1982. *An Evolutionary Theory of Economic Change*. Cambridge, MA: Belknap Press.

Nelson, Richard R. and Sidney G. Winter. 2002. Evolutionary Theorizing in Economics. *The Journal of Economic Perspectives* **16**(2), 23–46.

Newbert, S.L. 2007. Empirical Research on the Resource-based View of the Firm: An Assessment and Suggestions for Future Research. *Strategic Management Journal* **28**(2), 121–47.

Nickerson, Jackson and Todd Zenger. 2004. A Knowledge-based Theory of the Firm: The Problem-solving Perspective. *Organization Science* **15**(6), 617–32.

Peltzman, S. 1977. The Gains and Losses from Industrial Concentration. *Journal of Law and Economics* **20**(2), 229–63.

Penrose, Edith T. 1959. *The Theory of the Growth of the Firm*. Oxford: Oxford University Press. 1995 edition.

Peteraf, M.A. 1993. The Cornerstones of Competitive Advantage: A Resource-based View. *Strategic Management Journal*, **14**(3), 179–91.

Peteraf, M.A. and J.B. Barney. 2003. Unraveling the Resource-based Tangle. *Managerial and Decision Economics* **24**(4), 309–23.

Porter, M. 1980. *Competitive Strategy*. New York: The Free Press.

Porter, M.E. 1981. The Contribution of Industrial Organization to Strategic Management. *Academy of Management Review* **6**(4), 609–20.

Porter, M.E. 1985. *Competitive Advantage*. New York: The Free Press.

Priem, R.L. and J.E. Butler. 2001a. Is the Resource-based 'View' a Useful Perspective for Strategic Management Research? *The Academy of Management Review* **26**(1), 22–40.

Priem, R.L. and J.E. Butler. 2001b. Tautology in the Resource-based View and the Implications of Externally Determined Resource Value: Further Comments. *The Academy of Management Review* **26**(1), 57–66.

Reder, M.W. 1982. Chicago Economics: Permanence and Change. *Journal of Economic Literature* **20**(1), 1–38.

Reed, Richard and Robert J. De Fillippi. 1990. Causal Ambiguity, Barriers to Imitation, and Sustainable Competitive Advantage. *The Academy of Management Review* **15**(1), 88–102.

Rivkin, Jan. 2000. Imitation of Complex Strategies. *Management Science* **46**(6), 824–44.

Rivkin, Jan W. 2001. Reproducing Knowledge: Replication Without Imitation at Moderate Complexity. *Organization Science* **12**(3), 274–93.

Rosenkopf, Lori and Atul Nerkar. 2001. Beyond Local Search: Boundary-spanning, Exploration, and Impact in the Optical Disk Industry. *Strategic Management Journal* **22**(4), 287–306.

Rumelt, R.P. 1984. Towards a Strategic Theory of the Firm. In Richard B. Lamb (ed.) *Competitive Strategic Management*. New Jersey: Englewood Cliffs.

Rumelt, R.P. 1987. Theory, Strategy, and Entrepreneurship. In D.J. Teece (ed.) *The Competitive Challenge: Strategies for Industrial Innovation and Renewal*. Cambridge, MA: Ballinger, pp. 137–58.

Rumelt, R.P., D. Schendel and D.J. Teece (eds). 1994. *Fundamental Issues in Strategy*. Boston: Harvard Business School Press.

Salvato, C. 2003. The Role of Micro-strategies in the Engineering of Firm Evolution. *Journal of Management Studies* **40**(1), 83–108.

Scherer, F.M. 1980. *Industrial Market Structure and Economic Performance*. Boston: Houghton Mifflin.

Schumpeter, Joseph A. 1911. *The Theory of Economic Development: An Inquiry into Profits, Capital, Credit, Interest, and the Business Cycle*. Translated by Redvers Opie. Cambridge, MA: Harvard University Press, 1934.

Shane, Scott. 2000. Prior Knowledge and the Discovery of Entrepreneurial Opportunities. *Organization Science* **11**(4), 448–69.

Siggelkow, N. and D.A. Levinthal. 2003. Temporarily Divide to Conquer: Centralized, Decentralized, and Reintegrated Organizational Approaches to Exploration and Adaption. *Organization Science* **14**(6), 650–69.

Siggelkow, N. and J.W. Rivkin. 2005. Speed and Search: Designing Organizations for Turbulence and Complexity. *Organization Science* **16**(2) 101–22.

Silverman, Brian S. 1999. Technological Resources and the Direction of Corporate Diversification: Toward an Integration of the Resource-based View and Transaction Cost Economics. *Management Science* **45**(8), 1109–24.

Stieglitz, N. and N.J. Foss. 2009. Entrepreneurship and Transaction Costs. *Advances in Strategic Management* **26**, 67–96.

Stieglitz, N. and K. Heine. 2007. Innovations and the Role of Complementarities in a Strategic Theory of the Firm. *Strategic Management Journal* **28**(1), 1–15.

Teece, D.J. 1986. Profiting from Technological Innovation: Implications for Integration, Collaboration, Licensing and Public Policy. *Research Policy* **15**(6), 285–305.

Teece, D.J. 2007. Explicating Dynamic Capabilities: The Nature and Microfoundations of (Sustainable) Enterprise Performance. *Strategic Management Journal* **28**(13), 1319–50.

Teece, David J., Gary Pisano and Amy Shuen. 1997. Dynamic Capabilities and Strategic Management. *Strategic Management Journal* **18**(7), 509–33.

Tirole, Jean. 1989. *The Theory of Industrial Organization*. Cambridge, MA: MIT Press.

Wernerfelt, Birger. 1984. A Resource-based View of the Firm. *Strategic Management Journal* **5**(2) 171–80.

Williamson, O.E. 1996. *The Mechanisms of Governance*. Oxford: Oxford University Press.

Williamson, O.E. 1999. Strategy Research: Governance and Competence Perspectives. *Strategic Management Journal* **20**(12), 1087–108.

Winter, Sidney G. 2000. The Satisficing Principle in Capability Learning. *Strategic Management Journal* **21**(10/11), 981–96.
Winter, Sidney G. and Gabriel Szulanski. 2001. Replication as Strategy. *Organization Science* **12**(6), 730–43.
Zollo, Maurizio and Sidney G. Winter. 2002. Deliberate Learning and the Evolution of Dynamic Capabilities. *Organization Science* **13**(3), 339–51.
Zott, Christoph. 2003. Dynamic Capabilities and the Emergence of Intra-industry Differential Firm Performance: Insights from a Simulation Study. *Strategic Management Journal* **24**(2), 97–125.

21 Cognitive theory of the firm: a pragmatist perspective
Bart Nooteboom

21.1 INTRODUCTION

Why a cognitive turn in theory of the firm? We talk of the knowledge economy, organizational learning, knowledge management and the like, and we should then know what we are talking about, and rather than reinventing wheels let us employ insights from cognitive science that are available. This chapter will adopt what is known as an 'embodied cognition' view, which has roots in philosophical pragmatism. This yields a constructivist, interactionist view of cognition. Cognition is internalized action. Goals, ideas, dispositions are largely unconscious and when they are exercised in action they run into obstacles and novel opportunities that cause them to shift. This view goes against rationalist assumptions of autonomous, pre-established goals for which optimal use of means is sought. This has important implications for theory of the firm and of inter-firm relationships.

21.2 EMBODIED COGNITION

When we turn to cognitive science the problem is that there are different schools of thought. I opt for the 'embodied cognition' school, in the work of Damasio (1995, 2003), Lakoff and Johnson (1999) and Hendriks-Jansen (1996). It rejects Cartesian separation of body and mind and recognizes that cognition is rooted in largely unconscious bodily processes of perception, feelings and emotions. In this, Damasio (2003) goes back to the insights of Spinoza (in the second part of his *Ethics*). The embodied view is also found in the work of Merleau-Ponty (1964). In this embodied view, cognition is a wide concept, including knowledge as well as feelings and normative evaluations.

The roots of cognition in the body and in feelings allow the theory to connect with neural science and with social psychology respectively. In neural science it connects with the work of Edelman (1987, 1992), who proposed a 'neural Darwinism' where neural structures develop in analogy to evolution, with variety generation by connections between existing structures and selection by reinforcement of structures that generate conduct that is experienced as successful.

In social psychology embodied cognition connects with the notion of mental framing and with decision heuristics in which unconscious psychological mechanisms, emotions and rational evaluation mix (see, e.g., Kahneman and Tversky, 1979; Kahneman et al., 1982; Bazerman, 1998). The decision heuristics can be interpreted as making sense from a perspective of evolutionary psychology (Barkow et al., 1992). While they may be substantively irrational by the standards of rational choice, taking into account survival conditions that require fast perception, interpretation and response to opportunities and threats they are adaptive and in that sense procedurally rational.

Cognition and action are situated. People develop repertoires of mental frames, forms of perception and dispositions to interpretation, judgement and action, and it depends on the situation how selections and combinations from those repertoires are made. From the situation, people adopt cues that trigger mental frames and perceptions of events are assimilated into them to make sense. In the process people attribute characteristics to situations and people according to mental schemas triggered by situational cues even when the characteristics are not observed. That yields prejudice but is also functional in fast response and the efficient use of experience.

21.3   PRAGMATISM

Embodied cognition has roots in the American school of pragmatic philosophy of James, Peirce (1957), Dewey, G.H. Mead (1934) and related to more contemporary philosophers, such as Hans Joas (1992). This reference to pragmatism is tricky since in everyday language pragmatism is misleadingly seen as a shedding of principles and ideals in a muddling through with compromises. Philosophical pragmatism holds that cognition, in a wide sense including normative judgements and goals, occurs on the basis of mental dispositions and categories that are developed in interaction with the physical and especially the social environment. Intelligence is internalized practice. Questions of truth soon lead to questions of workability. There is a cycle of interaction between on the one hand cognition and language, and on the other hand action, in which knowledge and meaning are applied (or better: exercised) in action and there run into limitations and novel challenges that lead to an adaptation or transformation of knowledge and meaning. For an elaboration of that in earlier work (Nooteboom, 2000) I have been inspired by the work of the developmental psychologist Jean Piaget.

Expression is not literally expression of pre-established contents of consciousness. In expression we surprise ourselves. What we mean becomes more determinate and emerges in expression and the action in which expression takes place. This process acquires powerful leverage by expression in a language that we share with others, who in their response contribute to the forming and shifting of what we mean. We cannot have private language. This idea emerges in the philosophy of Wittgenstein but goes back to the eighteenth-century German philosopher Herder (Joas, 1992).

The pragmatic perspective has important implications for notions of rationality, uncertainty, knowledge, learning, innovation, entrepreneurial behaviour and innovation policy, as I will elaborate in this chapter. The economic doctrine of rational choice of means to achieve pre-established goals according to given preferences is fundamentally misleading. According to pragmatism, goals, means and action interact. We do have goals, preferences and largely subconscious dispositions to action but they are revised as the result of discovery of means and of results of actions, especially when action encounters problems or new opportunities are found. That happens especially in innovation but on a lower scale also in ordinary life. The dynamics of cognition and action is not an add-on to statics as the base case, it is the base case. Situations and institutions not only condition goal achievement but also are constitutive of goals. Entrepreneurs engage in what Lévi-Strauss called 'bricolage'. They do have some initial view of where they want to go, but on the way they shift targets as they encounter new problems and opportunities. This has important implications for innovation policy, as I will indicate later.

It has to be noted that, more or less implicitly, this pragmatic perspective of cognition was also the perspective employed by Penrose (1959). As managers employ resources and act according to existing goals they discover new uses for existing resources and new goals.

Since goals, intentions, perceptions and meanings become determinate and shift in interaction with other people, action and cognition are inherently social, and the methodological individualism of economic theory fails fundamentally. This not only has cognitive and economic implications but also moral ones. Creativity requires interaction with others, enabled by empathy and benevolence, so that other-directedness is not an obstacle but a condition for creativity, while self-centredness holds it back.

21.4 ABSORPTIVE AND EXPRESSIVE CAPACITY

The well-known notion of absorptive capacity requires a two-fold conceptual widening. First, it needs to encompass the wider notion of cognition indicated above. We should include not only the competence side of substantive understanding but also the governance side of insight and empathy concerning styles of thought, action, communication, conflict resolution, motives, and moral views and predilections (Nooteboom, 2004). In the literature on the firm, competence and governance run in largely separate streams, in on the one hand studies of competence, learning, innovation and the like, and on the other hand studies of governance, as in transaction cost economics.

On the organizational level absorptive capacity includes institutionalized ways of communication and knowledge sharing, organizational memory, and cultural features concerning views and attitudes towards the outside world. This is elaborated later with the notion of 'organizational cognitive focus'.

Absorptive capacity also needs to be widened as follows. It refers to the receiver side in communication and needs to be complemented by expressive capacity on the sender side, in the ability to be clear, to explain and to give clever examples and metaphors that trigger understanding on the receiver side.

This can be connected with the notion of 'relational signalling' (Lindenberg, 2003). In their actions people send signals concerning the mental frames they are in, and they should be aware of such signals and their effects, while the other side should learn to interpret the signals. Together, the wider notion of absorptive capacity in combination with expressive capacity yield a wider notion of 'collaborative capacity': the ability to both understand and clarify both intellectual and moral aspects of cognition.

21.5 COGNITIVE DISTANCE

Cognitive construction on the basis of interaction with physical and social conditions entails cognitive distance: different people develop different cognitive structures along different life paths in different environments. Cognitive distance entails difference in

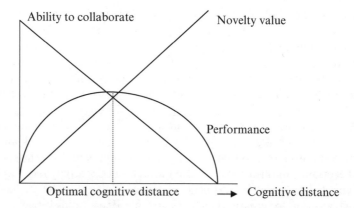

Figure 21.1   Optimal cognitive distance

cognition in the narrow sense of knowledge but also difference in moral perceptions and views.

In economics and society cognitive distance yields both a problem and an opportunity. The problem is that to the extent that cognitive distance is larger people understand each other more imperfectly, have different normative views and inclinations, and have less empathy, less ability to imagine themselves in the position of the other, which all limit ability to collaborate. The positive side of cognitive distance is that it provides an opportunity for learning and innovation. Hence cognitive distance can be too small to generate novelty or too large to utilize its opportunities.

This may be modelled as follows. If we model the decline with cognitive distance of ability to collaborate as a downward sloping straight line, the increase of novelty potential as an upward sloping straight line, and performance of innovation by interaction as the mathematical product of the two, the result is an inverted U-shaped parabola. This yields the notion of 'optimal cognitive distance'. For a specification of the mathematical model, see Appendix A. The model is illustrated in Figure 21.1. The upward sloping line for novelty value reflects the potential for learning and innovation while the downward sloping line for collaborative ability reflects the ability to realize that potential. Thus the product is expected performance in learning and innovation. The lines could conceivably be curved, not straight, but they are, in the first instance, assumed to be linear for reasons of parsimony.

The optimum may be seen as resulting from a trade-off between consensus and dissensus. With the term 'optimal' I do not wish to suggest that the optimum can be calculated prior to choice of partners, but rather that it is approximated by trial and error, with initial hunches based on experience or reputation.

The location of the optimum depends on how radical innovation involved in the interaction is meant to be. If we adopt the well-known distinction (March, 1991) between exploitation, defined as improvements within a basic design, set of principles or architecture, and exploration as the breaking of such frames, then in exploitation the marginal disutility of lack of understanding and agreement (slope of the downward sloping line) is higher, and the marginal utility of novelty (slope of the upward sloping line) is lower than in exploration, resulting in a lower optimal distance.

The notion of cognitive distance entails a distinction between reducing and crossing cognitive distance. Reducing cognitive distance entails alignment of cognition, with people thinking similarly. Crossing cognitive distance is making partial understandings and agreements while continuing to think differently. Reducing cognitive distance is equalization of capability, crossing it is connecting capabilities. When people who think differently continue interaction, starting from surface agreements, they may in time come to think more similarly, that is, share underlying cognition, in a reduction of cognitive distance. Connecting capabilities may lead to sharing them.

The optimum is not fixed in time. It depends, in particular, on the ability to collaborate at any level of cognitive distance, and this may increase as a function of the accumulation of knowledge and experience in collaboration. This will be discussed later.

21.6   ORGANIZATION

Clearly, for a theory of the firm we must open the black box and see how firms operate as organizations. In this it makes sense to also employ sociology, which is, after all, the study of interactions between people that constitute organizations. Not only people but also organizations are boundedly rational. Max Weber's (1864–1920) view of rational bureaucracies that implement means–end logics is a caricature. Since Luhmann (1927–98) organizations and the people working in them are seen more as having multiple, partly informal, hidden and even contradictory goals. There are also undirected processes, unintended consequences, and reasons for actions are often rationalizations post hoc. In all this a certain coherence and direction of action can be achieved by rules and regulations and by organizational culture.

As pointed out in transaction cost theory an advantage of organizations over markets is that within them one can demand more information, exert more monitoring and control, give orders and resolve conflicts, under the authority relation of an employment contract, than would be possible under transactional contracts between firms. As a result, organizations can deal with transaction costs more easily than markets can. However, there are also possibilities to deal with transaction costs and relational risks between firms, in alliances, as a large literature on inter-organizational relations has shown. For example, apart from using contracts one can govern by balancing mutual dependence and by the use of reputation mechanisms, hostages, development of trust and the use of go-betweens. Within firms, with hierarchical control and incentives one can further efficiency but the incentive is not as 'high powered' as responsibility for survival in an independent firm. Nevertheless, in the longer duration of relations within a firm on the basis of organizational culture one can develop identification, commitment and loyalty. That can yield intrinsic motivation next to motivation in money and career prospects. To some extent that is also possible in more durable inter-organizational relationships.

The distinction between market and organization and the separation between organizations are legally sharp (Hodgson, 2002) but in form and method of collaboration organizations can resemble markets in far-reaching decentralization of authority, responsibility for profit and internal transactions on the basis of transfer pricing. That is more needed as an organization grows larger and includes activities that are difficult to assess and coordinate with sufficient speed and knowledge. Markets can have elements of organization in alliances with a high degree of mutual investment, dependence, agreements for the distribution of tasks, responsibilities and revenues, mutual understanding and ability to collaborate, in more durable relationships. There is no overarching authority of legal ownership and liability but there may be coordination with the help of third parties or go-betweens.

Of course all this is standard organization theory. The question here is how cognitive considerations matter.

21.7   COGNITIVE TRANSACTION COSTS

Next to the standard transaction costs and relation-specific investments there are additional transaction costs and investments related to cognition. This includes the costs and problems of mutual understanding indicated above. Specific investments beyond the usual ones in machinery, installations, instruments, buildings and training are investments in mutual understanding and in building trust. Those may be highly relation specific, particularly when collaboration is highly specialized and distinctive from what others do. This applies, in particular, when collaboration is aimed at high added-value on the basis of specialized products. Trust building is particularly important when contracting and monitoring are problematic due to specialized professional labour and/or uncertainty of conditions of market and technology, competencies, goals and intentions, as in innovation.

It is part of the standard logic of transaction cost theory that specific investments require sufficient ex ante expectation of continuity of the relationship for the investment to be recouped, or else they will not be made. In debates on innovation there is a widespread claim, in rhetoric of flexibility, that relationships should be maximally flexible to allow for Schumpeterian novel combinations. That seems plausible, but also, even especially, for innovation specific investments are needed and then we need to aim not for maximum but for optimal flexibility of relationships, durable enough to elicit the specific investments needed for mutual understanding and trust but not so durable as to yield rigidity that obstructs novel combinations (Nooteboom, 1999). This applies within as well as between organizations, in labour relations and ownership of firms as well as in inter-firm alliances.

21.8   MARKET AND ORGANIZATION

Next to transaction cost theory for an explanation of the purpose and boundaries of the firm we can propose a theory based on cognitive distance, as set out in Nooteboom (2009). In this line, firms serve primarily for exploitation, to utilize opportunities for combining complementary resources and capabilities, with limited internal cognitive distance, while markets serve to offer larger cognitive distance, in a wider scope of possible novel combinations. This view is related to Hayek's view of 'competition as a discovery process' and the market as opening up a wide variety of localized knowledge (Hayek, 1945). There is a trade-off involved in cognitive distance. At small distance one can come to mutual agreement and understanding more quickly, which favours efficiency and speed of exploitation. Larger distance allows for more variety for innovation but takes more time to build up mutual understanding and capability to collaborate.

In the more durable relationships and the authority of an employment relationship within firms one can build and employ rules and procedures for formal coordination and organizational culture as a basis for more informal coordination. Such coordination is cognitive in the narrow sense of mutual understanding but also in the wider sense of an alignment of views, goals, priorities, ethical or moral principles and styles of thought and action as a basis for joint purpose and conflict resolution.

Within firms cognitive distance cannot and should not become zero. Some distance is required to maintain specialization of labour (in inseparable economy of scope); variety needed to match variety of operation across contexts (e.g., different customers or markets for a product) and needed for incremental innovations in efficiency and product differentiation. To the extent that the firm conducts exploration, internal cognitive distance must be larger.

Within larger organizations there are different levels of cognitive distance, with the lowest distance within communities of practice, larger distance between such communities, within divisions of a firm, and yet larger distance between divisions, subsidiaries and so on. However, as cognitive distance increases, investment in developing and maintaining collaborative capability increases and limits the variability of competence in order to preserve collaborative ability and its stability. In the trade-off between on the one hand speed and efficiency of coordination, and on the other hand cognitive distance, one reaches a point where it is better to surrender stable ability to coordinate, in order to allow for greater cognitive distance, accepting that coordination will have to be organized more ad hoc as the need arises. And then there is no longer an argument to combine activities within the firm, and variety and distance are surrendered to the market. Thus there are limits to the size of the firm, not only to the rate of growth of the firm, as Penrose (1959) suggested.

There are two ways to achieve collaborative capability between people with complementary capabilities. One is to limit cognitive distance, thus reducing innovative capability, and the other is to raise the level of collaborative capability (Postrel, 2002). The latter takes a higher level of training and/or experience that is more costly and takes time. Also, larger collaborative capability widens the scope for people to find employment elsewhere. This point will be discussed again.

21.9   ORGANIZATIONAL FOCUS

The limitation of cognitive distance is achieved by means of an organizational 'cognitive focus', based on organizational culture (Nooteboom, 2009). The focus can be narrow and wide, constraining cognitive distance more or less. The content and extent of cognitive alignment may vary.

In addition to the distinction between the competence and governance sides of focus, there are five dimensions for both. First, there is *width*, that is, the range of different activities or areas of competence and governance to which focus applies. This depends on the range of capabilities that a firm encompasses. Second, there is *reach*, that is, the number of aspects within each area covered by the focus. Does it cover all or only some key aspects of a given capability? A third dimension is *tightness* versus *looseness*, that is narrowness of tolerance levels of standards or rules imposed by focus, versus allowance for improvised, unforeseen meanings, actions, and so on.

Fourth, focus may have different *content*. In particular, on the governance side, there may be formal, that is, depersonalized, norms of legitimacy, which regulate what managers and workers can do and can expect from each other. Such formal norms render relations more impersonal and thereby reduce tensions associated with the exercise of personal power, and they enlist workers' participation in the control of their colleagues (Scott, 1992, p.306). The content of focus may also be more cultural, in the sense of offering guidance by more emotion-laden underlying values, expressed in symbolic entities, behaviours, events or processes. The two types of content are related, since norms of legitimacy may be expressed culturally, but can nevertheless be distinguished. One can have norms of legitimacy that are specified rigorously and formally, and one can have more informal, ambiguous, cultural features that do not express norms of legitimacy. The cultural side of focus will be discussed in more detail later.

Fifth, focus may relate to *surface regulations* concerning specific actions or to underlying more fundamental notions, in a *deep structure* of logic, principles, convictions or cognitive categories that form the basis for surface regulation. Simon (1976) already acknowledged that an organization controls not decisions but their premises. Nelson and Winter (1982) made a similar distinction, between routines and 'meta-routines' that guide the development of routines. Mintzberg (1989) allowed for 'missionary' organizations that align actions on the basis of purpose and ideals. Schein (1985) made a similar distinction in organizational culture. Below the surface features such as specific rules, practices, symbols, myths, rituals, at the basis of organizational culture lie fundamental views and intuitions regarding the relation between the firm and its environment ('locus of control': is the firm master or victim of its environment), attitude to risk, the nature of knowledge (objective or constructed), the nature of man (loyal and trustworthy or self-interested and opportunistic), the position of man (individualistic or part of a community), and relations between people (rivalrous or collaborative), which inform content and process of strategy, organizational structure, and styles of decision-making and coordination. Schein also allowed for an intermediate level, connecting the fundamental cognitive categories with the surface level of specific structures and rules, in the form of general principles that express fundamental cognitive categories but are yet general and generic rather than specific to certain activities and contexts.

The difference between activities, surface regulation and deep structure is schematically illustrated in Figure 21.2. Here, for simplicity of exposition the intermediate level is left out. A given surface regulation enables a bundle of potential actions. An underlying cognitive category in deep-level structure enables a bundle of surface-level regulation. The establishment of coordination on the surface level (routines, if one wants to use that term) leaves freedom for a variety of underlying cognitive categories, but has to be set up ad hoc each time, and requires the solution of complications due to differences in underlying cognition. The establishment of coordination on the deep level yields more ex ante agreement for setting up surface regulation, and thus enhances speed of action, but it reduces variety of cognition on the deep level. It entails more indoctrination and thereby is more *invasive*, impinging on a deeper, more emotion-laden level and a wider range of

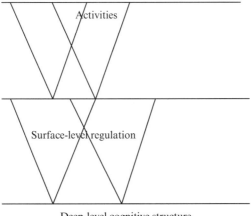

Deep-level cognitive structure

Figure 21.2   Levels of coordination

the life world of people. I will argue that organizations serve especially to coordinate on the deep level, with an advantage of easier and faster understanding and agreement and the disadvantage of less cognitive variety, while collaboration between organizations operates more on the surface level, with the advantage of greater variety on the deep level and the disadvantage of more limited or slower agreement.

If we take an evolutionary view of markets and firms, cognitive focus arises as an imprint of goals and style of conduct from the original founder of the firm, which survives if it is sufficiently aligned with selection conditions of technology, markets and institutions. Focus may be adapted to changing conditions to the extent that the ability to make such adaptations is part of the focus. People working in the firm enact and reconstruct the focus until a major crisis arises, where the firm fails or its leadership is replaced, with a shift of focus, which itself jeopardizes survival of the firm. Next to intellectual and behavioural coordination organizational focus also has functions of *selection* and *adaptation*. In selection, it selects people, in recruitment and often on the basis of self-selection of personnel joining the organization because they feel affinity with it. In adaptation, organizational focus socializes incoming personnel, with initiation processes, and focuses their capabilities, in training.

21.10   EXAMPLES

On the competence side of organizational focus, surface regulations may be codified standards, in the form of definitions, formulae, standard operating procedures, 'performance programmes' (March and Simon, 1958), manuals, blueprints, job descriptions, or, when knowledge is more tacit, training programmes to develop tacit understanding from shared practice. In the deep structure it may be basic notions of process or structure, knowledge, action, the relation between the two, principles of mathematics, physics, and so forth. On the intermediate level it may be more specific but still general principles of organization or design, such as parallel vs sequential processing, simultaneous or sequential design and implementation, degree of systemic integration vs decomposition, principles of planning-push or demand-pull in production, and so on.

An example is the basic 'Fordist' notion of a production system oriented towards high volume, mass production of standard products, on the basis of a 'push' principle. Here production is planned on the basis of demand forecasts, and resulting production schedules are handed down in a hierarchy of planning and execution, and production takes place in isolated steps of specialized work, with stocks as buffers between them. The basic underlying cognitive categories are those of hierarchy, centralized planning, a whole as designed from separate parts, efficiency as economy of scale and specialization, and individuality of action and work. By contrast, consider the Toyota system, oriented towards small volume production of differentiated products, on the basis of a 'pull' system (Coriat, 2000). Here, volume and configuration of production are guided by demand, in teams of workers jointly responsible for an integrated whole of quality, scheduling and execution of tasks, seen as an integrated flow of activities, without stocks between steps in the sequence, in 'just in time' production, de-specialization and integration of skills. The basic underlying cognitive categories are those of work as a collective, not individual activity, the whole as a flow between connected parts, efficiency as economy of time and flow, and work as an integration of skills.

On the governance side, surface regulations may be labour contracts, incentive schemes, reporting and evaluation procedures, labour conditions, hiring/firing and career policies. In the deep structure it may be underlying, more fundamental norms and values of conduct, concerning trust, loyalty, commitment, intrinsic or extrinsic motivation, reciprocity, consensus vs command and control, individuality or collectivity, hierarchy or autonomy, rivalry or mutual support, ambition or quality of life, and so on. On the intermediate level we find structural principles of (de)centralization, levels of hierarchy, density of connections, centrality of positions, and so forth, and procedural principles of authority sharing, accountability and control, communication, decision-making, amongst others, and human resource principles such as lifetime vs ad hoc employment, specialization versus integration of skills, and segmentation vs integration of tasks. Note again that while surface regulation allows for variety on the deep level, regulation on the deep level entails more ideology and indoctrination, especially in regulation on the governance side. The more fundamental, durable, generic elements of focus, in organizational culture, constitute the core of organizational identity.

21.11   COHESIVENESS

One property of focus that derives from its basic dimensions is *cohesiveness* of focus, which increases with the number of activities or capabilities that fall under the focus (width), the extent to which each activity or capability is regulated (reach), and the tightness of regulation. Cohesiveness denotes the extent to which people are tied *together* under the focus. *Inclusiveness* of focus denotes the extent to which an *individual* is tied up in the focus. It relates to the range of people's life world covered by organizational focus. It increases with the extent that people are involved in more activities in the firm, have more roles, contribute more capabilities, each falling under the focus (width), with greater reach, greater tightness and greater depth (yielding greater indoctrination).

Organizations have a *strong* culture to the extent that it is more inclusive, that is, more cohesive and deeper. In other words, whatever people do in the organization (whether they have few or many roles), it is regulated with great reach, tightness and depth. Paragon examples of strong cultures are those of 'primitive' families and tribes, and clans and cliques, which encompass the full life world of their members.

With the dimensions of organizational focus we can be more precise about the contrast between firms and markets. Markets yield minimum width, reach, tightness and depth of focus, in both competence and governance. That would be impossible to coordinate, in central planning, and when tried would yield stagnation: the fixing of ideas, meanings, standards and division of labour to maintain exploitation would disastrously limit the scope for exploration.

The notion of inclusiveness of focus connects with the distinction that Simmel ([1917] 1950) made between a person's function in an organization, which takes up only part of his or her personality, and his or her full personality, and Ring and van de Ven's (1994) distinction between roles that people play in organizations and behaviour 'qua persona'. In an inclusive focus, role and persona get closer. Variety among people is constrained, in small cognitive distance. Extremes of this are found in cliques, and especially in clandestine, secluded or secret societies (Simmel [1917] 1950, pp. 345–76). Outside freedom, to engage in external relationships, is constrained by high inclusiveness of organizational focus, with few dimensions of the life world left that are not in some way already regulated within the group. Inside freedom is constrained by the tightness of focus, with little room to deviate from narrow norms. Both inside and outside sources of variety, and hence of innovation, are highly constrained.

Under an inclusive focus, tightness may become self-imposed. When high inclusiveness forms an obstacle to outside relationships, and people are cut off from sources of fresh, different ideas, they will tend to gravitate towards meanings shared inside the organization, which increases tightness, not because it is imposed by focus, but because it emerges from decreasing cognitive distance. Thus inclusiveness and tightness together tend to reinforce themselves. We see this in fundamentalist religious groups, sects and top management teams.

21.12   ORGANIZATION BETWEEN ORGANIZATIONS

Organizational focus by definition yields organizational myopia. To repair for this organizations require complementary outside cognition, connecting with other firms at a greater cognitive distance than inside the firm. In this way cognitive theory of the firm incorporates a theory of inter-firm relationships.

It has been well documented, over many years of research, that mergers and acquisitions fail more often than they succeed. Part of the reason lies in organizational focus: it is problematic to merge different foci with their attendant cultures. We should acknowledge, however, that alliances also succeed in less than half the cases. There the problem is that there is no overarching formal authority to manage conflicts. Cognitive distance also plays an important role.

In a modified form, cognitive distance also applies at the higher aggregation level of organizations, if we then define it as difference in organizational focus, that is, differences

in shared knowledge, language, meanings, perceptions, understandings and values an
norms of behaviour.

Cognitive distance, whether on the individual or organizational level, is not amenabl
to any simple, one-dimensional measure of distance, since cognition has many dimen
sions, including both rational and emotion-based inference, judgement and decision
making, as shown in social psychology. In particular, cognition has dimensions relate
to understanding and dimensions related to moral judgement, which interact but ca
be distinguished conceptually. In spite of this multidimensionality, measurement o
cognitive distance is possible.

In empirical work, proxy measures of the cognitive distance between firms hav
been constructed on the basis of indicators from organizational data and technologica
profiles derived from patent data, and distance was calculated in terms of correlatioi
between profiles (Wuyts et al., 2005; Nooteboom et al., 2007). An alternative is to locat
technological position in a multidimensional space of characteristics, and calculate th
Euclidean distance between them. However, depending on the context, distance in som
dimensions of knowledge may matter more than in other dimensions. Here, there i:
room and a requirement for further elaboration, and for a consideration of alternative
measures.

In a refinement of the distance model we could separate competence and governance.
as follows. The downward sloping line of collaborative capability would then split intc
a line for ability to share knowledge (competence), that is, absorptive capacity, and a
line for ability and willingness to collaborate (governance), and distance would split intc
distance in knowledge/skills and distance in practices, rules and norms of conduct, oi
underlying moral values.

Then it is plausible to assume that for governance distance mostly has a negative effect.
and little positive effect of novelty value. In other words, the slope of the novelty line
would be lower than for competence. While it is useful to have different, complementary
knowledge, difference in views on how to behave in relationships is mostly bothersome.
Intuitively, one would expect optimal distance in views on collaboration to be small
relative to optimal distance in substantive knowledge.

21.13   DURATION

What is the effect of ongoing collaboration on innovative performance? Familiarity no
doubt breeds trust, as Gulati (1995) claimed. However, while trust is certainly good for
the ability to collaborate, too much familiarity and trust may reduce variety in competence too much and thereby take the innovative steam out of collaboration. More precisely, cognitive distance will decline, and the curve of performance in Figure 21.1 will be
traversed from right to left, as the duration of exclusive collaboration increases. In other
words, surface alignment between cognitively diverse partners may in time lead to more
similarity in underlying cognition.

Thus, there is a derived hypothesis of an inverted U-shaped relationship between
performance, particularly innovative performance, and the duration of exclusive collaboration. Wuyts et al. (2005) empirically confirmed this for inter-firm collaboration for
innovation in the pharmaceutical industry.

Note the qualification that the effect obtains for the duration of collaboration that is exclusive, that is, excludes the contribution from other parties beyond the dyad. To the extent that the partners in the focal relationship also have non-overlapping ties of collaboration with others, their knowledge and competence base may be continually renewed from different sources, maintaining cognitive distance between them. The argument brings us close to the argument of 'structural holes', propounded by Burt (1992), which indicates the value for learning of access to sources of knowledge not accessed by others, by bridging holes in the network of connections between them.

21.14 LEARNING TO COLLABORATE

In the preceding analysis, the model was static in the sense that ability and value of collaboration, analysed as functions of cognitive distance, were taken as given, so that the organization could only reduce or increase distance to achieve its given optimal level. Another possibility to consider is a change of the parameters. One option is to try to shift absorptive capacity upwards, with an increased ability, at any distance, of people to understand and accept, in collaboration, people who see, think and act differently. That is one type of organizational dynamic capability. It applies to collaboration within as well as between organizations.

Postrel (2002) asked when communities of practice should invest in knowing about each other, and when they should go their own way. On the face of it, the answer is that they should invest in knowing about each other when activities of different communities are strongly coupled, or, in other words, when activities are 'systemic', and that one should go one's own way when activities are not or only loosely coupled, or 'stand-alone'. Only in the first case is it necessary to mutually adapt activities. Postrel shows that this intuition is not necessarily correct. If by going their own way, and investing only in their own knowledge and skill, specialist communities can extend the scope and flexibility of their activities, then they can thereby achieve fit to whatever other communities do. In terms of the present analysis, they increase their absorptive capacity and ability to collaborate.

Nevertheless, even here there are some things they have to agree on, and some views, often tacit, that they need to share, on goals, norms, values, standards, outputs, competencies and ways of doing things, even if those are achieved not by coordination but by an extension of the scope and flexibility of activities, as showed by Postrel. The question then is how allowance for full variety between communities, with no interference from organizational focus, might ensure that sufficient bridging between them arises. Some connection, in some cognitive proximity, must somehow be ensured, if activities are dependent upon each other. If not, why should those communities be part of the same firm? Penrose also proposed that purely financial holdings can hardly count as firms, for lack of coordination.

An upward shift of ability to collaborate, in competence and governance, allows an organization to cope with more cognitive variety, and to thereby increase innovative capacity, while maintaining the coordination needed to utilize complementarities of competence. Such a shift may be achieved by a greater scope and depth of both intellect and skill, on the competence side, and ability to collaborate, on the governance side, as a

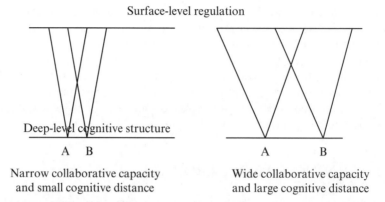

Figure 21.3   Absorptive and collaborative capacity

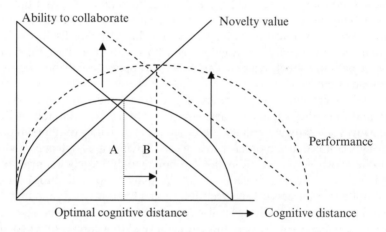

Figure 21.4   Upward shift of ability to collaborate

result of past learning, either by analysis or by experience. In particular, increased ability to collaborate arises from experience in collaborating with people with different world views, behaviour and morality. Let us call the first competence capital (as an extension of intellectual capital, to include skills) and the latter behavioural capital. An increase of such capital increases optimal cognitive distance and collaborative performance.

The principle is illustrated in Figure 21.3, which is derived from Figure 21.2. Here, an increased absorptive capacity, or ability to collaborate more widely, entails that categories on the deep level of cognition have an increased range of applications, with more opportunities for surface-level regulations. With a narrow range, distance between categories of A and B has to be small, in order to create overlap for the sake of coordination, in the left part of the figure. With a wide range, on the right part of the figure, with a wider scope of understanding and ability to collaborate, overlap in surface regulation (crossing cognitive distance) is achieved at greater cognitive distance on the deep level. The effect of the upward shift of ability to collaborate is illustrated in Figure 21.4. The mathematics are specified in Appendix B.

Complications arise when two parties have different absorptive capacities or more generally different abilities to collaborate. Let us assume that novelty value as a function of cognitive distance is the same for both. The party with the lowest ability to collaborate (A) has a lower optimal cognitive distance than the other party (B). The distance at which A can adequately collaborate is too small to be fully interesting for B. This complication may to some extent be resolved if B has the additional capability to 'draw' A out of its limitations. This requires didactic and rhetorical skills, such as the clever use of metaphor to shift sense-making, and the use of examples or illustrations to trigger understanding. This relates to the extension of the notion of absorptive capacity with expressive or explanatory capacity discussed before. When this fails, one may still seek recourse to intermediaries that help cross cognitive distance. They must then have requisite absorptive capacity and experience in cognitive bridge building. This is one of several roles that intermediaries or go-betweens can play.

21.15   INCREASING AND DECREASING RETURNS TO KNOWLEDGE

In inter-firm collaboration for innovation, the inverse U-shaped effect of cognitive distance on innovative performance, in terms of patent production, and the effect of knowledge accumulation on absorptive capacity, as an important part of ability to collaborate, illustrated in Figure 21.4, was tested and confirmed empirically in an econometric study by Nooteboom et al. (2007). There was also an unexpected but easy to understand additional effect of knowledge accumulation. In addition to its effect on ability to collaborate, higher knowledge accumulation, yielding a wider scope of technological competence, also yielded a lower slope of the line for novelty value. As illustrated in Figure 21.5 this means that at a higher level of knowledge accumulation, one has to go further afield, at higher cognitive distance, to achieve a given level of novelty, and this effect increases with the level of novelty sought. This can be interpreted as a principle of decreasing returns to knowledge, or as a 'boredom effect': the more one knows, the more one has to seek out exotic, distant sources of knowledge to learn something new. This effect, when applied to

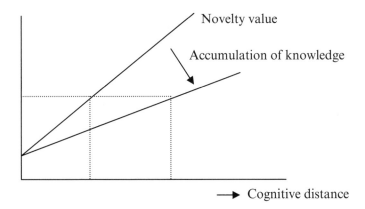

Figure 21.5   Decreasing returns to knowledge

combinations within a firm, has implications for limits to the size of a firm, in decreasing returns to the range of capabilities (Nooteboom, 2009).

In sum, there are both increasing and decreasing returns to knowledge. Increasing returns in the increased ability to collaborate with others, decreasing returns in an increasing difficulty to still find partners that can offer something new.

21.16   CONCLUSION

Cognitive theory, in the form of the embodied cognition view, related to the American philosophical stream of pragmatism, connects with the perspective taken by Penrose in her pioneering work on the theory of the firm, and yields a basis for a view of the firm and its boundaries that may serve as complementary to transaction cost economics. The key concept is cognitive distance and the logic of making a trade-off between cognitive proximity for the sake of efficient coordination for the sake of exploitation, and cognitive distance for the sake of variety needed for exploration. The first favours the firm and the second favours the market. The limitation of cognitive distance is achieved by organizational cognitive focus, established by means of organizational culture. Since organizational focus by definition causes organizational myopia, to repair for that firms need outsider relations with other organizations at greater cognitive distance. Thus, the cognitive theory of the firm includes, as an integral part, a theory of inter-firm relations. The view of the market as a source of cognitive variety connects with that of Hayek. Among other things, the analysis leads to the conclusion that there are both increasing and decreasing returns to knowledge. The theory has many more aspects and applications than can be discussed within the confines of this chapter (see Nooteboom, 2009).

REFERENCES

Barkow, J., L. Cosmides and J. Tooby (1992), *The adapted mind: evolutionary psychology and the generation of culture*, Oxford: Oxford University Press.
Bazerman, M.H. (1998), *Judgement in managerial decision making*, New York: Wiley.
Burt, R. (1992), 'Structural holes: the social structure of competition', in N. Nohria and R. Eccles (eds), *Networks and organizations: structure, form and action*, Boston: Harvard Business School Press, pp. 57–91.
Coriat, B. (2000), 'The abominable Ohno production system. Competences, monitoring, and routines in Japanese production systems', in G. Dosi, R.R. Nelson and S.G. Winter (eds), *The nature and dynamics of organizational capabilities*, Oxford: Oxford University Press, pp. 213–43.
Damasio, A.R. (1995), *Descartes error: emotion, reason and the human brain*, London: Picador.
Damasio, A.R. (2003), *Looking for Spinoza*, Orlando: Harcourt.
Edelman, G.M. (1987), *Neural Darwinism; the theory of neuronal group selection*, New York: Basic Books.
Edelman, G.M. (1992), *Bright air, brilliant fire; on the matter of mind*, London: Penguin.
Gulati, R. (1995), 'Familiarity breeds trust? The implications of repeated ties on contractual choice in alliances', *Academy of Management Journal*, **38**(1), 85–112.
Hayek, F.A. (1945), 'The use of knowledge in society', *American Economic Review*, **35**(4) September, 519–30.
Hendriks-Jansen, H. (1996), *Catching ourselves in the act: situated activity, interactive emergence, evolution and human thought*, Cambridge MA: MIT Press.
Hodgson, G.M. (2002), 'The legal nature of the firm and the myth of the firm–market hybrid', *International Journal of the Economics of Business*, **9**(1), 37–60.
Joas, Hans (1992), *Die Kreativität des Handelns*, Frankfurt a.M.: Suhrkamp.
Kahneman, D. and A. Tversky (1979), 'Prospect theory: an analysis of decision making under risk', *Econometrica*, **47**(2), 263–91.

Kahneman, D., P. Slovic and A. Tversky (eds) (1982), *Judgment under uncertainty: heuristics and biases*, Cambridge, UK: Cambridge University Press.

Lakoff, G. and M. Johnson (1999), *Philosophy in the flesh*, New York: Basic Books.

Lindenberg, S. (2003), 'Governance seen from a framing point of view: the employment relationship and relational signalling', in B. Nooteboom and F.E. Six (eds), *The trust process; empirical studies of the determinants and the process of trust development*, Cheltenham, UK and Northampton, MA, USA: Edward Elgar, pp. 37–57.

March, J.G. (1991), 'Exploration and exploitation in organizational learning', *Organization Science*, **2**(1), 101–23.

March, J.G. and H.A. Simon (1958), *Organizations*, New York: Wiley.

Mead, G.H. (1934), *Mind, self and society; from the standpoint of a social behaviorist*, Chicago: Chicago University Press.

Merleau-Ponty, M. (1964), *Le visible et l'invisible*, Paris: Gallimard.

Mintzberg, H. (1989), *Mintzberg on management*, New York: The Free Press.

Nelson, R.R. and S. Winter (1982), *An evolutionary theory of economic change*, Cambridge, UK: University Press.

Nooteboom, B. (1999), 'Innovation and inter-firm linkages: new implications for policy', *Research Policy*, **28**(8), 793–805.

Nooteboom, B. (2000), *Learning and innovation in organizations and economies*, Oxford: Oxford University Press.

Nooteboom, B. (2004), 'Governance and competence, how can they be combined?', *Cambridge Journal of Economics*, **28**(4), 505–26.

Nooteboom, B. (2009), *A cognitive theory of the firm; learning, governance and dynamic capabilities*, Cheltenham, UK and Northampton, MA, USA: Edward Elgar.

Nooteboom, B., W.P.M. Van Haverbeke, G.M. Duijsters, V.A. Gilsing and A. V.d. Oord (2007), 'Optimal cognitive distance and absorptive capacity', *Research Policy*, **36**(7), 1016–34.

Peirce, C.S. (1957), *Essays in the philosophy of science*, Indianapolis: Bobbs-Merrill.

Penrose, E. (1959), *The theory of the growth of the firm*, New York: Wiley.

Postrel, S. (2002), 'Islands of shared knowledge: specialization and mutual understanding in problem-solving teams', *Organization Science*, **13**(3), 303–20.

Ring, P. and A. van de Ven (1994), 'Developmental processes of cooperative interorganizational relationships', *Academy of Management Review*, **19**(1), 90–118.

Schein, E.H. (1985), *Organizational culture and leadership*, San Francisco: Jossey-Bass.

Scott, W.R. (1992), *Organizations; rational, natural, and open systems*, 3rd edition, Englewood Cliffs, NJ: Prentice-Hall.

Simmel, G. ([1917] 1950), *The sociology of Georg Simmel*, translation Kurt Wolff, Glencoe IL: The Free Press.

Simon, H.A. (1976), *Administrative behavior*, 3rd edition, New York: Free Press.

Wuyts, S., M.G. Colombo, S. Dutta and B. Nooteboom (2005). 'Empirical tests of optimal cognitive distance', *Journal of Economic Behavior & Organization*, **58**(2), 277–302.

APPENDIX A   OPTIMAL COGNITIVE DISTANCE

The mathematical specification of the model is as follows:
The downward sloping line for ability to collaborate (A):

$$A = a_1 - a_2.CD, a_1, a_2 > 0 \tag{A21.1}$$

where CD is cognitive distance.
The upward sloping line for value (N):

$$N = b_1 + b_2.CD, b_1, b_2 > 0 \tag{A21.2}$$

Multiplying (A21.1) and (A21.2) results in the performance (L):

$$L = A.N = a_1.b_1 + (a_1.b_2 - b_1.a_2).CD - a_2.b_2.CD^2 \tag{A21.3}$$

If $a_1.b_2 - b_1.a_2 > 0$, this yields a parabolic, inverse U-shaped function of cognitive distance, with some optimal level of distance.
From (A21.3) it follows that optimal cognitive distance (CD^*) is:

$$CD^* = (a_1.b_2 - b_1.a_2)/2\,a_2.b_2 = \tfrac{1}{2}(a_1/a_2 - b_1/b_2) \tag{A21.4}$$

And corresponding optimal performance (L^*) is:

$$L^* = a_1.b_1 + (a_1.b_2 - b_1.a_2)^2/4a_2.b_2 \tag{A21.5}$$

From (A21.4) it follows that for optimal distance to be positive, we must again have $a_1.b_2 - b_1.a_2 > 0$.

APPENDIX B   INCREASING COLLABORATIVE CAPACITY

In terms of the model in cognitive distance, an upward shift of collaborative ability entails an increase of the intercept (a_1) of the corresponding declining line in Figure 21.1. Suppose that:

$$a_1 = c_1 + c_2.TC, c_1, c_2 > 0 \qquad \text{(A21.6)}$$

where TC is competence and/or behavioural capital accumulated from past learning from collaboration.

Then, from (A21.3) we find for collaborative performance:

$$L = c_1.b_1 + c_2.b_1.TC + (c_1.b_2 - b_1.a_2).CD + c_2.b_2.TC.CD - a_2.b_2. CD^2 \qquad \text{(A21.7)}$$

For optimal cognitive distance, this yields:

$$CD* = \tfrac{1}{2}(c_1/a_2 - b_1/b_2) + \tfrac{1}{2}(c_2/a_2)TC \qquad \text{(A21.8)}$$

This shows how optimal cognitive distance increases with competence and behavioural capital (TC). That yields lasting competitive advantage, in the ability to deal with larger cognitive distance and hence innovate more radically, since that capital takes time to build up and is cumulative.

PART VI

MODERN ISSUES

22 Revisiting Chandler on the theory of the firm
Steven Toms and John F. Wilson

22.1 INTRODUCTION

In three influential books, *Strategy and Structure* (1962), *The Visible Hand* (1977) and *Scale and Scope* (1990), Alfred Chandler (1918–2007) made a seminal contribution to the development of the theory of the firm in the second half of the twentieth century. Specifically, Chandler's theory of the firm was developed from detailed empirical observation, rather than formal model building, providing a commentary on the rise of the large managerial corporation. Although Chandler's contribution to the theory of the firm is therefore somewhat implicit, it is clear from subsequent work by a range of social scientists that he is regarded as one of the key twentieth-century influences on this and other dimensions of economic and management theory. A great deal of subsequent theory-building in organizational economics, transaction cost theory, new institutional economics and the resource-based view of the firm has accordingly acknowledged a debt to Chandler's earlier empirical work. His theory of the firm is a theory of the large firm, or a theory of why large firms are successful. It is controversial, and implies a universally applicable model of business organization, as a consequence of which he has attracted considerable criticism.

To describe these theories, accommodating this critique, and to suggest extensions, the chapter is structured as follows. We first describe the economic components of Chandler's model. These components require extraction from Chandler's work, in view of the strong empirical orientation of most of his writings. These are also characterized by interlinkages to antecedent and contemporaneous theoretical developments, which are described in section 22.3. We offer a critique of the Chandlerian perspective as a whole, from a theoretical and empirical point of view in section 22.4. In the light of this critique, we briefly discuss possible extensions of the Chandlerian perspective in section 22.5, incorporating elements of capital market transaction cost theory. We then summarize and draw conclusions.

22.2 THE ECONOMIC COMPONENTS OF CHANDLER'S MODEL

The origins of Chandler's thinking lie in a deep-rooted analysis of corporate America, centred on four case studies of large organizations in the inter-war period, typified by Du Pont (Chandler, 1962). While 'Chandler developed most of this early thinking in a theoretical vacuum' (Whittington, 2008, p. 267), his detailed historical investigation into the responses of managers to the challenges of market and technology-led growth in America's largest firms resulted in his influential thesis that the structure of an organization is determined by its strategy towards products and markets. Accordingly, the multidivisional structure is a response to diversification across product and or geographical markets.

Chandler's concept of the 'visible hand' explains the origins of the firm and its subsequent growth. Firms exist because they can achieve coordination more effectively than the market so that investment in managerial hierarchy achieves productivity gains. Such gains are more easily realizable when the market for the firm's output creates sufficient scale economies. Some of these gains arise from decentralization of decision-making within the managerial hierarchy. To achieve them most effectively, firms adopt the multidivisional form (Chandler, 1962). The term M-form is also used to describe this structure, and although commonly ascribed to Chandler, it was introduced and defined more precisely by Williamson (1971, p. 382). According to this definition, the key features are, first, centralized control over strategic decision-making and investment in new products and markets, and, second, delegation of operational decision-making to divisions monitored as profit centres. Chandler complements rather than rejects the conventional theory of the firm. So, on the one hand, estimation of market demand remains one of the key challenges facing managers of hierarchical and M-form enterprises, notwithstanding their expanded scale and market dominance. At the same time, his theory offers a detailed analysis of the organization of supply.

Chandler also offers a theory of the growth of the firm. His ideas developed in parallel to Rostow's (1960) stages theory of economic growth, which in the Cold War period underpinned a universalizing alternative to Marxism. Chandler's large managerial enterprise represented a progression from prior stages of less efficient forms of organization (Whittington and Mayer, 2000, pp. 26–7), whereby managers are empowered by the increasing complexity of the organization and the technical content of its routines. Ownership is thereby divorced from control, since family and investor groups could not provide the managerial capacity or the technical understanding to exercise direct control over the management process. Much of the impetus to growth arises from the perpetuation of managerial hierarchies. Management constitutes a new business class whose incentives are predicated on growth rather than profit and on reinvestment rather than shareholder dividends.

In *Scale and Scope* (1990), Chandler examined the nature of such investment more specifically. First, investment in production facilities realizes economies of scale and scope embedded in technological development. Second, investment in a marketing and distribution network delivers sales volume equivalent to the production capacity. Third, investment in managerial hierarchy is required in order to coordinate production and sales and to plan for future investment in these functional activities (Chandler, 1990, p. 8). Such investments, Chandler argues, create first-mover-based competitive advantage. The American model of business organization is offered as an example in contrast to the British, where such investments occurred less extensively. British relative economic decline is therefore often cited as proof of the Chandler hypothesis. In this sense, it is empirically testable and has given rise to a number of studies, discussed below, that raise opportunities for further refinement, as well as the inevitable question marks.

22.3   ANTECEDENT AND ASSOCIATED ECONOMIC THEORIES

As can be observed from this brief review of Chandler's ideas, there are some obvious debts to other economic theorists. Coase's (1937) transaction cost explanation of the firm as an alternative to costly market coordination provides a consistent theoretical justification for Chandler's managerial hierarchy. Penrose's (1959) analysis also contained similar elements to Chandler's model, linking growth, structure and the management function. She was the first to suggest that resources determine growth rate and profit level, in that limits on the firm's growth rate arise from managerial and capacity constraints. Penrose and others writing in the 1960s recognized the growing influence of managerial hierarchy on firm behaviour, and like Chandler, utilized objectives other than profit maximization to explain firm behaviour. Baumol (1959) proposed revenue maximization, Williamson (1964) managerial utility maximization and Marris (1964) growth maximization. The notion of maximization itself was also challenged at around the same time by the behaviouralists, building on the work of Simon (1955, 1959) and Cyert and March (1963), who applied the theory of bounded rationality to explain firm behaviour, in terms of satisfactory rather than optimal outcomes. The notion of 'satisficing' is more attuned to a managerial theory of the firm since it can more readily accommodate the multiple objective functions that managers in large productive enterprises typically face. It is also more likely to replace profit maximization where capital market imperfections impose monitoring costs on outside shareholders (Jensen and Meckling, 1976). Taken together, these new economic assumptions about managerial behaviour provided important building blocks for Chandler's model.

These parallel theoretical developments have evolved along with Chandler's own writings, with the consequence that his model has become firmly embedded in the wider institutional and transaction cost economics literature. In addition to the conventional economic category of economies of scale, building on these literatures, Chandler (1990, pp. 17–18, fn. 2–3) adds economies of joint production and distribution, economies of scope (Coase, 1937; Teece, 1980; Willig, 1981; Bailey and Friedlaender, 1982), and transaction cost economies (Coase, 1937; Williamson, 1981). By the same token, Williamson (1981) acknowledges the work of Chandler, which he develops to provide an economic, transaction cost explanation of inter alia the rise of the multidivisional firm. Whilst relying upon and assimilating with these literatures, Chandler's emphasis differs in some important respects. Chandler (1990) stresses the active role of entrepreneurs in creating first-mover competitive advantage, by making investments in plants of sufficient size to realize scale and scope economies. In contrast, theories that contain behavioural dimensions assume negative attributes such as shirking (Alchian and Demsetz, 1972), opportunism (Williamson, 1975), or passivity (Cyert and March, 1963). Although more similar, institutional theories of the firm tend to offer more deterministic explanations of firm behaviour, in the form of isomorphism (DiMaggio and Powell, 1991), evolution and routine (Nelson and Winter, 1982) and population ecology models of the firm and industry life cycle (Hannan and Freeman, 1989).

There are also some important similarities between Chandler and parallel developments in organizational economics. Nelson (1991) extends Chandler's strategy and structure relation to include organizational capabilities, which when integrated with

Nelson and Winter's (1982) evolutionary perspective forms the basis of a new dynamic capability-based approach to strategy. Chandler (1992) aligns himself with this perspective in preference to three other classes of theories of the firm: neoclassical, principal agent and transaction cost (Teece, 1993). A crucial element of difference in these theories is that in evolutionary approaches what happened in the past matters, instead of what is expected to happen in the future. Reflecting the influence of Chandler (Teece, 1993, p. 220), the dynamic capabilities framework (Teece et al., 1997) has become influential in our understanding of how internal processes can create competitive advantage assets with associated path dependencies.

Chandler's positive and active view of corporate leadership is manifest in other branches of organizational economics. Most prominent of these is the resource-based view (RBV) of the firm. Tracing its roots back to Penrose (1959), the RBV explains competitive advantage, or delivery of sustained above-normal returns (Peteraf, 1993) or economic profit (Barney, 2001), in terms of firms' bundles of resources (Rumelt, 1984; Amit and Schoemaker, 1993), which are valuable, rare, inimitable and non-substitutable (VRIN) (Barney, 2001). Resources, including managerial talent and leadership create competitive advantage and access to superior profits. In this sense, the RBV has been constructed in part on Chandler's pioneering work, even if Penrose's work preceded his by several years. Although associated with dynamic capabilities framework, there are differences, for example in the RBV's description of superior returns as rents. These rents are Ricardian (Peteraf, 1993; Teece et al., 1997, p. 513), since Schumpeterian rents (Foss and Knudsen, 2002), as synergies, or economies of scope are imitable, except in the short run (Barney and Peteraf, 2003). These differences aside, it is clear that through the RBV and dynamic capabilities literatures, Chandler's influence continues to be felt.

22.4   CRITIQUE

In common with much of institutional economics, Chandler presents us with an organization that is efficient by virtue of cost minimization. Whilst offering a useful alternative to the branch of economics that relies on profit maximization, it offers no commensurate theory of value. In this sense, it is incomplete as a theory of the firm. For example, consider a firm making a Chandlerian investment in large-scale plant with the objective of securing first-mover competitive advantage. There is no theoretically consistent discount rate that can be used to appraise such investments, because such rates are derived from equilibrium-based capital market models that assume rational maximizing behaviour. If the firm uses a discount rate that is regarded as 'satisfactory' by the manager, but suboptimum by the capital market, the value of the firm's assets will nonetheless be downgraded by the market. As a consequence, the manager will face the threat of removal from the operation of the market for corporate control. A similar result arises from the information asymmetry inherent in corporate investment decisions of this character. The manager can counter the risk of devaluation from these two sources by applying the market discount rate, in other words, becoming a shareholder value maximizer, and by supplying more complete information to market monitors. Chandler (1977) acknowledges that under such circumstances managerial control is partially relinquished and is replaced by finance capitalism. As Wu (1989, p. 11) puts it, capital market imperfections create an entrepreneurial role for capitalists, but as capital markets become more developed, financiers shed their entrepreneurial role and entrepreneurs shed their financing function in favour of corresponding groups of professional managers. Chandler does not, however, enter into a discussion of these theoretical trade-offs.

A further problem arising from the absence of a Chandlerian theory of value is how to price the assets that give rise to first-mover competitive advantage. In essence, this is the same as the problem of heterogeneous asset valuation that has remained unresolved in the wider field of economics since the close of the Cambridge controversies in the early 1980s (Cohen and Harcourt, 2003).[1] Conventionally, the asset value is the present value of the future cash flows it is likely to generate, presupposing a discount rate and therefore a rate of profit. However, in the case of a first-mover competitive advantage asset, as in neoclassical economics, the rate of (abnormal) profit follows from the possession of (heterogeneous) valuable assets.

There are, though, more specific additional problems with the Chandlerian model. First, as the firm is a managerially controlled non-maximizer, higher rates of profit relative to other firms are not its objective, so cannot be used to infer competitive advantage. Second, even if the firm is an efficient cost minimizer, the benefits of minimization are unobservable. If the cheaper firm controls some but not all of the market, the price of output is regulated by the less efficient firm that can nonetheless satisfy some of the demand. The difference will constitute a rent for the more efficient firm. As the firm is managerially controlled, the rent may be absorbed by higher executive salaries or in managerial perquisites, which can manifest themselves as organizational slack. If the rent is absorbed in such fashion, in monetary terms the efficiency from lower-cost production is exactly counterbalanced by the generation of managerial rents. Of course, the rent can be used to fund further investment in productive capacity, such that the firm can capture a greater share of the market. The realization of monopoly places an upward limit on this process, creating greater incentive for diversification. However, because the portfolio investor can diversify at a lower transaction cost, the cost minimization rationale for diversification can no longer apply.[2] In summary, even if efficiencies arising from investment in scale and scope economies can be generated, there are trade-off allocative efficiency problems in the absence of an efficient capital market.

Arising from this, while economies of scale and scope have an obvious influence on organizational form and business strategy, they cannot by themselves account for general categories such as 'personal' and 'managerial' capitalism. The processes of allocating and distributing resources must also be considered. Notwithstanding the title of Chandler's 1990 work, *Scale and Scope*, all the economies of scale and scope referred to are internal, and external economies of scale and scope are only directly dealt with insofar as the distribution system is controlled by the firm to reduce associated unit and joint costs. Other external economies of scope are left out of the analysis, notwithstanding their potential importance for the understanding of economic performance and competitive advantage. These include district or local-level economies associated with physical infrastructure, access to services, or pools of knowledge and expertise that lie outside the direct control of individual firms, as originally described by Alfred Marshall (Kamien et al., 1992; Oughton and Whittam, 1997). Clustering of firms in industrial districts, trade associations and other networked organizations are promoted through sharing trade secrets and drawing on local pools of experience and skilled labour. Such economies are of course important in regions and industries where the Chandlerian model appears to be less applicable, for example the successful Lancashire textile industry of the nineteenth century (Toms, 1998), the networked craft industries of Italy (Rinaldi, 2005), and the knowledge-driven industries of Silicon Valley (Lecuyer, 2001).

The fragmentation of the computer industry in recent decades is a good illustration of how specialization in certain periods of history and stages of economic development promotes flexibility, potentially replacing standardization and scale economies (Piore and Sabel, 1984). Flexible specialization does not, however, presuppose small scale; indeed, the computer industry, in the USA at least, continues to sustain very large firms. Rather, competitive advantage comes from the fluidity of the boundaries of the firm (Zeitlin, 2008, p. 129). As a result, the coordinating mechanism is adjusted quickly according to circumstance, for example from market to hybrid (subcontract, franchise, lease, etc.) to hierarchy and back again, perhaps corresponding to the phase of the industry life cycle (Toms and Filatotchev, 2004). Managerial structure accordingly plays a reduced role and its importance varies through time.

By emphasizing managerial structure as the key mechanism for unlocking productivity, Chandler also neglects institutional factors that might promote managerial hierarchy or limit its scope for strategic action. As the literature on varieties of capitalism suggests (Whitley, 1994), the ownership of businesses and their capital structure are a function of the configuration of financial institutions and can be very important as constraints or enablers of managerial activity.

The pattern of corporate development in the face of these changes in institutional structures presents a strong empirical challenge to Chandler's model. That challenge has been responded to most notably in the field of business history (Wilson, 1995, pp. 3–8), where Chandler's influence continues to be strongly felt. Indeed, the Chandlerian thesis remains a widely accepted view of British business history (Elbaum and Lazonick, 1986). Empirical surveys have documented the extent of the diffusion of the M-form model, in Britain (Channon, 1973; Toms and Wright, 2002; Toms and Wilson, 2003), in France and Germany (Dyas and Thanheiser, 1976) and in all three countries (Whittington and Mayer, 2000). The latter evidence suggests that M-form adoption has indeed been widespread amongst the very large firms at least, but that there is a parallel and increasing trend towards sell-offs, buy-outs and parent to parent sales of subsidiaries (Toms and Wright, 2002).

A further empirical test of the Chandler hypothesis is its prediction of British relative economic decline as a consequence of failure to adopt the efficiency features of the American model. For Chandler (1990) and Elbaum and Lazonick (1986), it was the absence of the large firm that undermined economic competitiveness. Again, this notion has been subjected to considerable empirical scrutiny by business historians. Whereas the Chandler hypothesis has remained influential in the USA, historians of British business have stressed the vibrancy of alternative forms of business organization (Lamoreaux et al., 2008, p. 44), including family businesses (Church, 1993; Jones and Rose, 1993), smaller and non-integrated firms. Others have argued that large firms have always been a feature of the British economy (Wardley, 1999), and that these were controlled by dispersed shareholders, in contrast to the family groups that dominated US big business (Hannah, 2007). Because the Chandler model most obviously applies to manufacturing, and most would concede that British manufacturing has declined post-1945 (Matthews,

007), other historians have pointed to the relative success of other sectors, particularly
services and financial services over the longer run (Rubinstein, 1993), and pointed out
that where success has been achieved, it has been more a function of market competition
than managerial hierarchy (Broadberry and Crafts, 2001).

As suggested in the theoretical critique above, the rationale for the Chandlerian firm,
with its managerially determined objective function, depends to a certain extent on the
absence of capital market scrutiny. Hence, the state of development of the capital market
is likely to mediate the observed organizational form. Although Chandler highlights the
importance of dividends in limiting capital accumulation in family businesses as part
of his critique of British personal capitalism, he has little to say about capital markets
and corporate governance (Toms and Wilson, 2003). If capital markets were to become
more efficient at scrutinizing the actions of managers, then the Chandlerian firm might
be expected to become less prominent.

Such a proposition can be subjected to empirical scrutiny. For example, the absence
or presence of a market for corporate control might have an important impact on the
motivation and character of diversification. Similarly, the presence or absence of liquid
capital markets and legal rules on creditor and minority protection, accounting disclosure and insider trading might constitute further examples of market, governance and
regulatory influences on corporate strategy and structure. Indeed, these aspects appear
to have become more important in recent decades and many key developments have
followed the high-water mark of the large Chandlerian organization of the 1980s. Since
then the steady growth of the managerial firm and its associated hierarchy has been
supplanted by waves of divestment and delayering in Britain (Toms and Wright, 2002)
and the USA (Toms and Wright, 2005). Chandler's model has not yet been adapted to
the wave of downsizing and sell-offs that has transformed M-form US businesses into
newer structures befitting the later twentieth century, including networks, joint ventures,
multilayered subsidiary organizations (Prechel, 2000; Zey and Swenson, 2001; Toms
and Wright, 2005). According to these authors, corporate restructuring away from
the M-form model has been a consequence in substantial part of the liberalization and
greater transparency of financial markets.

As this brief review of empirical evidence suggests, the Chandlerian model lacks universal appeal because, as Whittington and Mayer suggest (2000, p. 10), there is a need
to accommodate both 'territory – national cultures and national institutions', as well as
'the constant ebb and flow of power or fashion' in our understanding of business evolution. From a historical point of view, the more the institutional environments of other
countries and periods beyond the first half of the twentieth century are considered, the
less sustainable Chandler's model becomes (Wilson, 1995, pp. 3–8). Similarly, there is
no provision for the political power of big business in explaining the success of corporate America. Nonetheless, as a model designed to explain an important episode in US
corporate history, Chandler's model has enduring appeal.

22.5   CAN THE CHANDLER MODEL BE DEVELOPED?

As the critique above has suggested, Chandler's work might be developed by an engagement with capital market and valuation theory. At first sight, this is a contradictory

project, since managers and capital markets are concerned with maximizing different things, or as we have seen in the case of managerial hierarchies, avoiding maximization altogether. However, Chandler's paradigm and capital market theory both operate with and accommodate transaction costs, in the latter case, for example, information costs where outside investors cannot monitor managerial insiders without incurring costs. At the same time, managerial insiders face resource dependency vis-à-vis the capital market, creating incentives to share information at certain stages of the product life cycle. Meanwhile, capital markets undergo institutionally determined changes in their ability to monitor resource use by managerial groups, and hence the transaction-based monitoring cost involved. Consequently, whereas the Chandlerian firm minimizes internal transaction costs, for example by using an internal capital market in an M-form structure, there is no reason why the minimization of all transaction costs, including the governance aspects of the organization, should not be accommodated into the model. Organizational evolution then becomes a function of the relative importance of internal and external transaction costs, according to the conditions of economic development. Such a synthesis also offers the opportunity to build upon the seminal empirical work of Chandler, adding dimensions of corporate governance and accountability to explain the long-run evolution of business organizations (Toms and Wilson, 2003).

22.6   CONCLUSIONS

Chandler's work forms part of a significant managerial economics literature going back to the 1930s and the contemporaneous writing of Edith Penrose. For the reasons discussed above, Chandler's importance stretches beyond managerial economics and the theory of the firm, and has been influential in the strategy[3] and management literature for similar reasons, and a dominant figure in business and economic history. There are strands of Chandler's influence in all these areas that are of consequence for the theory of the firm, themes that this chapter has endeavoured to extract and summarize. As a consequence of such an engagement with Chandler's writings, a deeper understanding of the growth and development of the large-scale corporate organization can be acquired. In this sense, Chandler's empirical contribution is as important as his theoretical contribution. As Bartlett and Ghoshal (1993, p. 25) concluded, the theory of the firm ought to be developed according to Chandler's (1962, p. 7) suggestion 'from the point of view of busy men responsible for the destiny of the enterprise', rather than deduced from the premises of social scientists.

That said, as the above discussion has shown, the Chandler model, in common with all theories, has shortcomings that prevent it operating as a fully integrated theory of the firm. Chandler's contribution is therefore to complement other theories to provide a more detailed understanding of the economics of the firm, to understand what Coase (1937, p. 386) called the 'real world firm' (Dietrich and Krafft, 2005, p. 2). He does so by building a theoretical framework from case studies, in contrast to other theories of the firm such as agency theory, which elaborate general models that are tested in different applications.

From an empirical standpoint, Chandler's model works better in some contexts than others, for example as an explanation of the development of US big business in the first ialf of the twentieth century. Even so, according to some, the large Chandlerian firm is of continuing importance and is developing in line with the global economy (Cassis, 2008). Meanwhile, the experience of managerial delayering, outsourcing and downsizing has shown that the large corporation is vulnerable to market pressures and capital market scrutiny. Where managers champion shareholder value, it is clear that to some extent they have lost sight of the managerially determined objectives of investment in scale and scope economies. If Chandler offers a view of productive efficiency, it needs to be reconciled with the question of allocative efficiency. In other words, for the economist, the crucial contingent questions remain: what is the optimum number of firms in a market and what is the optimum level of competition? Chandler's analysis poses these questions rather than resolves them. In that sense, his theory of the firm remains to be developed.

NOTES

1. For a recent analysis of the problem of heterogeneous assets valuation, see Toms (2010).
2. Exceptions to this rule, notably external economies of scale and under-utilized capacity, are analysed by Teece (1980). Chandler (1962 – see p. 453, fn. 1) also points out that excess capacity arising from indivisible assets leads to diversification.
3. Chandler is credited with bringing the word 'strategy' into the business vocabulary, replacing the rather antiquated 'business policy', as well as offering a definition of the term that has stood the test of time (Whittington, 2008, p. 267).

REFERENCES

Alchian, A.A. and H. Demsetz (1972), 'Production, information costs, and economic organization', *American Economic Review*, **62**(5), 777–95.

Amit, R. and P.J.H. Schoemaker (1993), 'Strategic assets and organizational rents', *Strategic Management Journal*, **14**(1), 33–46.

Bailey, E.E. and A.F. Friedlaender (1982), 'Market structure and multi-product industries', *Journal of Economic Literature*, **20**(3), 1084–148.

Barney, J.B. (2001), *Gaining and sustaining competitive advantage*, 2nd edition, Reading, MA: Addison Wesley.

Barney, J.B. and M. Peteraf (2003), 'Unravelling the resource-based tangle', *Managerial and Decision Economics*, **24**(4), 309–23.

Bartlett, C.A. and S. Ghoshal (1993), 'Beyond the M-form: towards a managerial theory of the firm', *Strategic Management Journal*, **14**(Special Issue), 23–46.

Baumol, W. (1959), *Business behavior, value and growth*, New York: Macmillan.

Broadberry, S. and N. Crafts (2001), 'Competition and innovation in 1950s Britain', *Business History*, **43**(1), 97–118.

Cassis, Y. (2008), 'Big business', in G. Jones and J. Zeitlin (eds), *The Oxford handbook of business history*, Oxford: Oxford University Press, pp. 171–93.

Chandler, A.D. (1962), *Strategy and structure: chapters in the history of the industrial enterprise*, Cambridge, MA: MIT Press.

Chandler, A.D. (1977), *The visible hand*, London: Belknap.

Chandler, A.D. (1990), *Scale and scope*, London: Belknap.

Chandler, A.D. (1992), 'Organizational capabilities and the economic history of the industrial enterprise', *Journal of Economic Perspectives*, **6**(3), 79–100.

Channon, D.F. (1973), *The strategy and structure of British enterprise*, London: Macmillan.

Church, R. (1993), 'The family firm in industrial capitalism: international perspectives on hypotheses and history', *Business History*, **35**(4), 17–43.

Coase, R. (1937), 'The nature of the firm', *Economica*, **4**(16), 386–405.

Cohen, A.J. and G.C. Harcourt (2003), 'Whatever happened to the Cambridge capital theory controversies?', *Journal of Economic Perspectives*, **17**(1), 199–214.

Cyert, R. and J.G. March (1963), *A behavioral theory of the firm*, Englewood Cliffs, NJ: Prentice-Hall.

Dietrich, M. and J. Krafft (2005), 'The firm in economics and history: towards an historically relevant economics of the firm', ENEF Working Paper, University of Sheffield.

DiMaggio, P. and W. Powell (1991), 'The iron cage revisited: institutional isomorphism and collective rationality in organizational fields', in Walter Powell and Paul DiMaggio (eds), *The New Institutionalism in Organizational Analysis*, Chicago: Chicago University Press.

Dyas, G.P. and H. Thanheiser (1976), *The emerging European enterprise*, London: Macmillan.

Elbaum, B. and W. Lazonick (eds) (1986), *The decline of the British economy*, Oxford: Oxford University Press.

Foss, N.J. and T. Knudsen (2002), 'The resource-based tangle: towards a sustainable explanation of competitive advantage', *Managerial and Decision Economics*, **24**(4), 291–307.

Hannah, L. (2007), 'The "divorce" of ownership from control from 1900 onwards: re-calibrating imagined global trends', *Business History*, **49**(4), 404–38.

Hannan, M.T. and J.H. Freeman (1989), *Organizational ecology*, Cambridge, MA: Harvard University Press.

Kamien, M., E. Mueller and I. Zang (1992), 'Research joint ventures and R&D cartels', *American Economic Review*, **82**(5), 1293–306.

Jensen, M.C. and W.H. Meckling (1976), 'Theory of the firm: managerial behavior, agency costs and ownership structure', *Journal of Financial Economics*, **3**(4), 305–60.

Jones, G. and M. Rose (1993), 'Family capitalism', *Business History*, **35**(4), 1–16.

Lamoreaux, N., D. Raff and P. Temin (2008), 'Economic theory and business history', in G. Jones and J. Zeitlin (eds), *The Oxford handbook of business history*, Oxford: Oxford University Press, pp. 37–66.

Lecuyer, C. (2001), 'Making Silicon Valley: engineering culture, innovation and industrial growth, 1930–1970', *Enterprise and Society*, **2**(4), 666–72.

Marris, R. (1964), *The economic theory of 'managerial' capitalism*, New York: Macmillan.

Matthews, D. (2007), 'The performance of British manufacturing in the post-war long boom', *Business History*, **49**(6), 763–79.

Nelson, R.R. (1991), 'Why firms differ, and how does it matter?', *Strategic Management Journal*, **12**(Special Issue), 61–74.

Nelson, R. and S. Winter (1982), *An evolutionary theory of economic change*, Cambridge, MA: Belknap.

Oughton, C. and G. Whittam (1997), 'Competition and co-operation in the small firm sector', *Scottish Journal of Political Economy*, **44**(1), 1–30.

Penrose, E. (1959), *The theory of the growth of the firm*, Oxford: Oxford University Press.

Peteraf, M.A. (1993), 'The cornerstone of competitive advantage: a resource-based view', *Strategic Management Journal*, **14**(3), 179–91.

Piore, M. and C. Sabel (1984), *The second industrial divide*, New York: Basic Books.

Prechel, H. (2000), *Big business and the state: historical transitions and corporate transformation, 1880s–1990s*, Albany: State University of New York Press.

Rinaldi, A. (2005), 'The Emilian model revisited: twenty years after', *Business History*, **47**(2), 244–66.

Rostow, W.W. (1960), *The stages of economic growth: a non-communist manifesto*, Cambridge: Cambridge University Press.

Rubinstein, W. (1993), *Capitalism, culture and decline in Britain, 1750–1990*, London: Routledge.

Rumelt, R. (1984), 'Toward a strategic theory of the firm', in R. Lamb (ed.), *Competitive Strategic Management*, Englewood Cliffs, NJ: Prentice-Hall, pp. 556–70.

Simon, H. (1955), 'A behavioral model of rational choice', *Quarterly Journal of Economics*, **69**(1), 99–118.

Simon, H. (1959), 'Theories of decision making in economics', *American Economic Review*, **49**(3), 253–83.

Teece, D. (1980), 'Economies of scope and the scope of the enterprise', *Journal of Economic Behavior & Organization*, **1**(3), 223–47.

Teece, D. (1993), 'The dynamics of industrial capitalism: perspectives on Alfred Chandler's *Scale and Scope*', *Journal of Economic Literature*, **31**(1), 199–225.

Teece, D., G. Pisano and A. Shuen (1997), 'Dynamic capabilities and strategic management', *Strategic Management Journal*, **18**(7), 509–33.

Toms, S. (1998), 'Growth, profits and technological choice: the case of the Lancashire cotton textile industry', *Journal of Industrial History*, **1**(1), 35–55.

Toms, S. (2010), 'Value, profit and risk: accounting and the resource based view of the firm', *Accounting, Auditing and Accountability Journal*, **23**(5), 647–70.

Toms, S. and I. Filatotchev (2004), 'Corporate governance, business strategy, and the dynamics of networks: a theoretical model and application to the British cotton industry, 1830–1980', *Organization Studies*, **25**(4), 629–51.

Toms, S. and J. Wilson (2003), 'Scale, scope and accountability: towards a new paradigm of British business history', *Business History*, **45**(4), 1–23.

Toms, S. and M. Wright (2002), 'Corporate governance, strategy and structure in British business history, 1950–2000', *Business History*, **44**(3), 91–124.

'oms, S. and M. Wright (2005), 'Corporate governance, strategy and refocusing: US and British comparatives, 1950–2000', *Business History*, **47**(2), 267–95.

Vardley, P. (1999), 'The emergence of big business: the largest corporate employers of labour in the United Kingdom, Germany and the United States', *Business History*, **41**(4), 88–116.

Vhitley, R. (1994), 'Dominant forms of economic organization in market economies', *Organization Studies*, **15**(2), 153–82.

Vhittington, R. (2008), 'Alfred Chandler, founder of strategy: lost tradition and renewed inspiration', *Business History Review*, **82**(2), 267–77.

Vhittington, R. and M. Mayer (2000), *The European corporation*, Oxford: Oxford University Press.

Villiamson, Oliver E. (1964), *The economics of discretionary behavior: managerial objectives in a theory of the firm*, Englewood Cliffs, NJ: Prentice Hall.

Villiamson, Oliver E. (1971), 'Managerial discretion, organization form, and the multi-division hypothesis', in R. Marris and A. Wood (eds), *The corporate economy, growth, competition, and innovation potential*, London: Macmillan.

Villiamson, Oliver E. (1975), *Markets and hierarchies*, London: The Free Press.

Villiamson, Oliver E. (1981), 'The modern corporation: origins, evolution and attributes', *Journal of Economic Literature*, **19**(4), 1537–68.

Willig, R. (1981), 'Economies of scope', *American Economic Review*, **71**(2), 268–72.

Wilson, John F. (1995), *British business history, 1720–1994*, Manchester: Manchester University Press.

Wu, S. (1989), *Production, entrepreneurship and profits*, Oxford: Blackwell.

Zeitlin, J. (2008), 'The historical alternatives approach', in G. Jones and J. Zeitlin (eds), *The Oxford handbook of business history*, Oxford: Oxford University Press, pp. 120–40.

Zey, M. and T. Swenson (2001), 'The transformation and survival of Fortune 500 industrial corporations through mergers and acquisitions, 1981–1995', *The Sociological Quarterly*, **42**(3), 461–86.

23 Financialization and the firm
Michel Aglietta and Antoine Rebérioux

23.1 INTRODUCTION

Over the last two decades, stock market activity has grown sharply, in the USA as well as in Europe, while there has been a continuous increase of equity holdings by financial investors, to the detriment of households, cross-holdings by non-financial companies, families or the state. These evolutions have caused deep transformations at the corporate level: in particular, stock price has become a crucial metric for corporate management in listed companies, whose shares are traded on regulated markets. This process of 'financialization' of the business firm has had, and still has, dramatic consequences in terms of corporate governance and human resource management practices. This chapter intends to examine the extent and consequences of this financialization process. In addition, it offers an assessment of the way the 2008 global financial crisis might affect this process, by favouring the rise to power of long-term investors with specific asset management practices and corporate governance requirements. The chapter is ordered as follows. We document the rise to power of institutional holdings and the related consequences on corporate governance. We set out in greater detail the impact of financialization on labour. We analyse the emergence of a new class of long-term investors, as a probable response to the subprime mortgage crisis.

23.2 FINANCIALIZATION AND CORPORATE GOVERNANCE

23.2.1 The Anglo-American Case

At the end of the first decade of the twenty-first century, institutional (financial) investors own about half of the shares listed in the USA, the other half being owned by households. The rise in institutional holdings has been a long-term process, starting after World War II: in 1950, pension funds and mutual funds alone owned less than 3 per cent of US listed shares, against more than 40 per cent today. In the UK, this 'institutionalization' process started later, but is even more remarkable: including insurance companies, the holdings of institutional investors represent more than 70 per cent of listed shares. Although these investors manage large volumes of assets, they usually diversify their portfolios – with the exception of private equity funds (see below). They are, most of the time, minority shareholders, who can easily play an 'exit' strategy by selling their holdings in any given firm. Two immediate consequences should be emphasized. On the one hand, stock market prices, which in theory capture expectations of dividends and determine the possibilities of making capital gains, are the best indicator of the interests of these investors. On the other hand, the dispersion of equity ownership resulting from portfolio diversification makes direct control of managers by stockholders difficult, or even impossible – as early noted by Berle and Means ([1932]1967). However, shareholder activism, formal (through the submission of proposals at annual shareholder meetings) or informal, has gained in importance since the beginning of the 1980s. It is now common practice among institutional investors in the United States and also, to a lesser extent, in Great Britain (Black, 1998; Becht et al., 2009). In addition, and probably more importantly, a certain number of devices that encourage the managers to behave in line with the interests of the minority shareholders started to develop over the same period, favoured by regulators and/or pressure by institutional investors' associations. In the UK, a flexible regime for hostile takeover bids favours stock market discipline (Deakin et al., 2003), while in the USA, share option schemes have become a common attribute of corporate executives' compensation pay package (Jensen et al., 2004).

Both mechanisms sensitize managers to the stock market price that guarantees the 'prioritization' of shareholders' interests in business conduct. Shareholder primacy has thus become the norm in terms of corporate governance (Lazonick and O'Sullivan, 2000; O'Sullivan, 2000; Fiss and Zajac, 2004; Aglietta and Rebérioux, 2005).

23.2.2 The Continental European Case

In the academic field, interest in corporate governance has prompted a number of studies, at the beginning of the 1990s, comparing 'national' models. This comparative literature has contrasted continental Europe with the USA and the UK (see, for example, Prowse, 1995). The Anglo-American system is usually referred to as 'outsider control', because it relies first and foremost on players from outside the company (minority shareholders). As argued earlier, the main characteristic of this model is that it takes the stock market price as a central indicator in the management of listed companies.

In continental Europe, the importance of institutional investors is lower – notably due to the lesser presence of pension funds. The possession of shares by non-financial companies and/or founder family is relatively substantial, with large block holdings. The concentration of ownership is therefore quite high (Faccio and Lang, 2002). It tends to protect or insulate listed companies from the stock market. In addition, employees' rights to information and consultation, particularly through works councils, constitute an internal counterweight (Rebérioux, 2002). In Germany, these rights are made even more substantial by the system of codetermination, where employee representatives of certain companies are given seats on the supervisory board (with the same rights as the shareholder representatives). This general pattern of corporate control is referred to as 'insider control', giving significant voice to agents committed to stable relations with the company (block-holders and employees).

However, the above typology is being overturned: the shift of the continental European model of shareholding towards the Anglo-Saxon model is now widely described in the comparative literature (see, for example, Denis and McConnell, 2003). Taking as an example the French case, it is possible to identify certain developments that undeniably play a part in shifting the insider model of governance towards a more market-based (outsider) one, as part of a larger, global process of financialization.

The first evidence is the growth in stock market activity and capitalization, directly related to the growing presence of financial investors, not only national but also non-resident. In 2005, for the largest companies (included in the CAC40 French stock market index), 46.4 per cent of the equity capital was held by non-residents, with more than 20 per cent for British and US funds looking for international diversification of their portfolios (Poulain, 2006). This increase in the power of minority shareholders in the equity capital of French listed companies has been accompanied by a decline, but not a collapse, in block holdings (Thomsen, 2004). In 2010, institutional investors, French and foreign, represent by far the most important category of shareholders in listed companies. In Germany, we observe a dramatic, yet smaller, increase in institutional holding. A plausible explanation is that Anglo-Saxon mutual funds favoured investment in France, given the weaker level of worker involvement as compared to German codetermination (Rebérioux, 2002; Goyer, 2006).

This financialization process deeply influenced corporate governance and conduct. A series of corporate governance codes, promoting the interests of minority shareholders through 'best practices', have been published since the mid-1990s.[1] Concerning dividend policy, Batsch (2007) observes that the dividend per share practically doubled on average (multiplied by 1.9) between 1999 and 2005, for the 30 industrial groups of the CAC40. Also, Ginglinger and L'Her (2006) point out that share buybacks, by which some of the cash flow can be transferred to shareholders, have become commonplace, encouraged by a change in the regulation in 1998. The standard use of stock options by French listed companies is another marker of this financialization process: according to a study by consultancy firm Towers Perrin, France is the European country in which the proportion of stock options and free shares in executive pay is the highest (50 per cent, compared with less than 30 per cent in Great Britain, and more than 65 per cent in the United States).

Altogether, and just like in the USA or the UK, these evolutions have increased the sensitivity of corporate executives to the interests of minority shareholders, promoting a shareholder-value-oriented approach to managing a business.

23.2.3 Firms, Markets and Information

The financialization process has deeply modified the relationships of the firm with its environment, most notably with stock markets. On the one hand, demand for higher informational transparency, through greater and better reporting, has significantly increased the importance of information flows running from inside (the firm) to the outside (to the market). On the other hand, financialization implies a greater sensitivity of the firm to stock market signals, therefore increasing the magnitude of information flows running from the outside (the stock market) to the inside (the firm): here, so-called 'independent' directors have played a decisive role.

Minority shareholders (whether financial investors or households) need reliable information on company past performance and future prospects. Listed companies are thus under strong pressure to periodically disclose financial and non-financial information, contrary to private, non-listed companies. Such disclosure is a priori the most direct way to lower the cost of capital arising from information asymmetries and to promote managerial accountability.

Accordingly, listed companies are more and more inclined to 'voluntarily' disclose information, so as to please investors and to secure the value of their shares. In addition, regulators have strengthened disclosure requirements both in the USA and in Europe, as a perceived solution to managerial abuses and corporate scandals that have multiplied since the beginning of the 2000s. A conspicuous example is the Sarbanes-Oxley Act of 2002, whose principal objective was the protection and enhancement of the integrity of financial disclosure for listed companies. The same movement can be observed in France, with important changes in securities law and, to a lesser extent, in corporate law, which have strongly enhanced minority shareholder protection and, more specifically, information disclosure requirements (Cioffi and Cohen, 2000; Lele and Siems, 2006).

Regarding board composition, inside directors have steadily declined, to the benefit of outsiders, so-called 'independent directors'. In the mid-2000s, independent members accounted for 75 per cent of directors in large US listed companies, and for 50 per cent in France. Board independence was primarily advocated in the beginning of the 1980s by US activist shareholders and, in particular, by public pension funds grouped in the Council of Institutional Investors. In turn, independence has become a central requisite in the many corporate governance codes since published. In addition, depending on the jurisdiction, company law and/or stock market regulations now usually require the presence of some independent directors.

The basic idea common to a number of existing definitions of 'independence' is to identify some *objective* criteria that minimize conflicts of interests between directors and corporate officers. Generally speaking, independence is assumed to be compromised if the director of a company (1) is, or has been, a corporate executive of that company or of its affiliates, (2) is, or has been, employed by that company or by its affiliates, (3) is employed as an executive of another company where any of that company's executives sit on the board, (4) is a large block-holder of that company or (5) has a significant business relationship with that company or its affiliates. Clearly, the promotion of independent directors tends to discard worker involvement at the board level: codetermination is therefore at odds with shareholder value and independency requirements.

It is now increasingly recognized that independent directors, at a distance from the company and its business model, have a cognitive disadvantage as compared to non-independent directors (Osterloh and Frey, 2006). However, this disadvantage is usually not perceived as crucial: 'independent' directors are considered to be less captured by the internal (managerial) perspective, and in a better position to favour stock market evaluation in corporate conduct. Put differently, the role of independent directors is to make corporate insiders sensitive to external pressure and information. To do so, a director does not necessarily need firm-specific information. This point is most clearly presented in an influential article by Gordon (2007, p.1563):

> Stock prices are taken as the measure of most things. In this environment, independent directors are more valuable than insiders. They are less committed to management and its vision. Instead, they look to outside performance signals and are less captured by the internal perspective, which, as stock prices become more informative, becomes less valuable.

23.2.4   Limits of the Financial, Stock-based Model of Corporate Governance

In sum, and according to shareholder primacy proponents, market-induced mechanisms (stock-based remuneration schemes and hostile takeover threats), together with an independent board, are likely to evolve so as to ensure that: (1) relevant information is incorporated rapidly into corporate securities prices; and (2) managers in turn respond quickly to stock market signals in a manner conducive to the minimization of agency costs. However, a series of well-publicized accounting scandals such as the Enron and WorldCom collapses at the turn of the twenty-first century and, more recently, the subprime mortgage crisis and ensuing implosion of major Anglo-American financial institutions have conspired to undermine public and academic confidence in the reliability of this market model of corporate governance. While commentators and regulators have specifically emphasized the responsibility of auditors and securities analysts (in 2001–02) and of rating agencies (in 2008), it is striking that neither independent boards, nor equity-based compensation plans prevented highly risky behaviour. It might even be argued that those devices have favoured those behaviours, as exemplified by the Enron and Lehman Brothers cases – the two biggest bankruptcies in US history at the moment they occurred.

The utility of stock options as a managerial remuneration scheme is unsurprisingly open to debate. While the empirical literature is, by and large, inconclusive on the performance impact of stock option compensation plans, an increasingly prominent view is that such devices have served primarily to benefit corporate insiders, in the absence of (or, worse still, to the positive detriment of) other corporate participant groups such as employees or even minority shareholders themselves.[2] Concerning the market for corporate control, meanwhile, the empirical evidence is rather inconclusive. The extensive literature on the effects of takeovers, whilst pointing to the (positive) short-term implications of takeover bids in terms of market value, suggests that those operations do not have, on average, any positive effect on either market value or operating performance over the long run. Indeed, an extensive series of empirical studies actually suggests that takeover bids have an overall *negative* impact in the above respects (see, e.g., Burkart and Panunzi, 2008). Finally, regarding the board of directors, a number of studies have focused on the impact of independence. Empirical evidence generally shows a negligible or negative effect on firm performance (see, e.g., Bhagat et al., 2008).

Doubts as to the ability of stock-market-based mechanisms to ensure proper control over public corporations have led law and finance scholars to consider an opposite form of governance, namely joint ownership and control by means of private equity (see Jensen, 1989 and 2007). Private equity in the form of leveraged buyouts (LBOs) expanded in popularity and significance throughout the 1980s to become a relatively mainstream practice of US corporate finance and governance by the end of the decade. The first decade of the twenty-first century witnessed the onset of a larger-scale and more globalized LBO movement, against the background of very low interest rates, buoyant equity markets after they had recovered from the ICT crash and a (temporary) revival in the international junk bond market.

LBOs typically entail the acquisition of control by one or more specialist financial firms over a formerly listed corporation, by means of intensive recourse to borrowed funds. Normally at least 70 per cent of a target company's purchase price will be financed in the form of debt from third parties, with at most only 30 per cent of that figure comprising equity from the buyout fund itself. As collateral for the loan(s), the private equity fund will pledge the assets and/or future cash flows of the target company's business(es). Lending banks will thereafter typically 'spread' their risk exposure amongst the investing public by issuing a large number of liquid asset-backed securities (ABSs) on the internaional debt markets. From a corporate governance perspective, LBOs directly reconnect the dual ownership and control dimensions of the (formerly) public corporation, whilst, at the same time, preserving one important benefit of the public corporation: the specialization between risk-bearing (through the wide dispersion of liquid securitized debt) and management. Following successful completion of the LBO, the acquired corporation will typically be de-listed from the relevant public equity market and re-registered as a private company.

The typical board of directors of a private equity-controlled company will be comprised mainly of representatives of the private equity fund, who will work closely with the firm's management team on an ongoing basis. In a sense then, the archetypal director in a private equity-controlled company is the exact opposite of the 'independent' board member in a public company, whose inevitable lack of direct connection with the firm arguably reduces his or her ability to monitor corporate executives robustly. In this way, the decision-making process at board level is redesigned specifically for the purpose of resolving 'internal' strategic problems rather than on ensuring perfunctory 'external' accountability to financial market actors. Academic advocates of LBOs argue that such devices are an antidote to the aforementioned 'agency problem' that is endemic to the structure of public corporations. In providing what is arguably the most well-known academic justification of LBOs, Jensen ([1989] 1997, p. 1) argued:

> By resolving the central weakness of the large public corporation – the conflict between owners and managers over the control and use of corporate resources – these new organizations are making remarkable gains in operating efficiency, employee productivity, and shareholder value.

Yet LBOs raise serious concerns that cast doubt on the pretension of private equity to constitute a coherent, alternative model of corporate governance for large business firms (Moore and Rebérioux, 2011). First, there is the significant concentration of power that private equity governance necessarily entails. Although the same charge of concentrated power could be levelled at the hegemonic managerialist corporation, the fact that residual 'ownership' rights in public companies are spread amongst a multitude of minority shareholders vests the process of public company governance with a formally pluralist character. In contrast, within private equity-controlled companies there occurs an amalgamation of both managerial and proprietary governance rights. If corporate governance is concerned primarily with the proper way to mitigate the concentration of power within public (widely held) companies, it may well be the case that, as a medicine to cure this concentration, LBOs are often worse than the putative disease. Second, there is the issue of private equity's lack of transparency, as compared to listed company. By virtue of their de-listed status, private equity-controlled firms are exempt from the standard public company disclosure requirements. This has bred concern as to a possible 'accountability deficit' within the private equity sector, whereby the activities of firms with high socioeconomic impact can be effectively 'veiled' from public inspection simply by means of removing their securities from the investment marketplace. In particular, worker unions worry about the implications of LBO operations in terms of employee security and welfare. Last but not least, the fact that LBOs are by definition heavily dependent on debt, 'leverage' renders their continuing operation and success contingent to a significant extent on the maintenance of favourable macro-conditions and, in particular, the preservation of low interest rates. It is therefore unsurprising to witness a sharp contraction in large-scale public-to-private LBO activity as a result of the subprime mortgage crisis and ensuing 'credit crunch' on the international debt markets. The final part of this chapter envisages an alternative, third model of corporate governance, beyond the stock-based model and the private equity model: namely, long run shareholder value creation through long-term investors.

23.3   FINANCIALIZATION AND HUMAN RESOURCE MANAGEMENT

A growing attention is now paid to the implications of the financialization process for employment (see, e.g., Gospel and Pendleton, 2004). For example, one might suspect that the prioritization of shareholder interests has altered the distribution of value-added between shareholders and workers, to the detriment of the latter – even if we lack empirical evidence on this point. Also, while shareholders' and workers' interests might be opposed considering the distribution of value, it is not the case in terms of information. It is likely that they align their interests vis-à-vis management: both parts share a common interest for greater transparency, inviting managers to disclose reliable information (Jackson et al., 2004). Hence workers have (indirectly) benefited from increased disclosure requirements, as a positive externality of the financialization process (Perraudin et al., 2012).

Some studies have explored the influence of corporate governance and ownership structure on human resource management (HRM) practices (Black et al., 2007; Conway et al., 2008).

In a capitalist system, every company has to achieve a level of profitability, allowing it to cover the cost of capital. Over and above this level, the requirements of profitability will be more or less intense according to the macro-institutional context that underlies the variety of capitalism. The process of 'financialization' tends to accentuate these requirements. Value-based management models, which first appeared in the 1990s, are all founded on the same principle (see, e.g., Froud et al., 2000b): there is 'creation of shareholder value' when the return on equity (ROE, i.e., the net result divided by the book value of equity capital) achieved by the company is higher than the profitability expected by the market (the cost of equity capital for the firm, k). The most widely used tool of shareholder value creation, the economic value added (EVA), expresses this approach most clearly: the market equilibrium return (k) is considered as the minimum return, a benchmark, on the basis of which the real creation of value can be appreciated. Managers are invited to maximize shareholder value in each financial period, and this should guarantee them a favourable evaluation in the stock market. From an operational point of view, as managers have no direct influence over the cost of capital (k), the requirement of shareholder value creation ultimately comes down to a requirement for the maximization of financial profitability (ROE).

This approach might influence human resource management practices at two distinct levels. First, a strategy of labour costs minimization might be put in place, as they are the primary component in operating costs. In its most direct form, this may be achieved by reducing the workforce, through downsizing. Company restructuring over the last two decades has often appeared to be guided by the desire to reduce the proportion of value-added devoted to labour, in order to satisfy the profitability constraints imposed by financialization (see, for example, Froud et al., 2000a for the British case and O'Sullivan, 2000 for the case of the USA during the 1980s and 1990s). For a given size of the workforce, such a strategy can also take the form of a restrictive pay policy or the limitation of training expenditures. This hypothesis is envisaged by Black et al. (2007), who use macroeconomic data to test the impact of stock market activity on the training effort of firms – without obtaining any significant results.

Second, a prominent effect of stock market pressure is to strengthen the damaging consequences in case of poor short-term financial results. As the EVA definition makes clear, any 'destruction' of shareholder value (financial profitability that is *positive but below* the cost of capital) runs the risk of provoking a fall in the price of the company's shares. Accordingly, listed companies might seek greater control over the variations in profit than non-listed companies. Here, the flexibility of operating costs might be exploited. Labour costs then might be adjusted through the use of flexible forms of employment and flexible pay practices. By using temporary labour arrangements, through employment contracts (fixed-term contracts) or commercial contracts (temporary agency workers and subcontracting), the company can resort to a workforce without any long-term commitment. It can adjust the quantity of labour used over the very short term. Pay policy is another tool of labour cost flexibility. Beyond the wages, employers have the possibility of implementing, on a selective and reversible basis, individual bonus schemes (linked to attendance or individual performance appraisal, for example) or collective bonus schemes (linked to financial performance or sales notably). An indication of this effect is provided by Jackson et al. (2004) who observe, in a series of case studies, the massive use of performance-related pay schemes by German firms pursuing shareholder value-based management strategies. On micro-, firm-level data, Perraudin et al. (2008) and Conway et al. (2008) find similar results for France and the UK. Stock market pressure can lead to downwards adjustments of labour costs, achieved through wage flexibility (individual and collective bonus) and the substantial use of temporary contracts. Among the latter, the use of commercial contracts (agency workers or subcontractors) is favoured rather than the use of fixed-term employment contracts.

For workers in listed companies, the outcome of such flexibility is ambiguous, depending on whether it has been (implicitly) exchanged against participation to future value creation, or simply imposed by employers. A few studies provide some insight. In particular, Perraudin et al. (2008) observed, on French enterprise data, that net (hourly) wage levels were higher in establishments belonging to listed companies, controlling for a large set of observable firm-level characteristics (including the occupational structure of the workforce). This result rather suggests that increased volatility in remuneration has been traded off against higher compensation. Again, this result echoes Jackson et al. (2004) for German firms. Although they observed that the pressure exerted by financial markets led companies to reduce their workforce, they also found that the wages paid to the remaining employees tended to rise.

23.4   LONG-TERM INVESTORS AND THE FUTURE OF FINANCIAL CAPITALISM

Long-term financial investors are likely to rise to prominence after the shock wave of the financial crisis has abated. The Wall Street model of unfettered and unregulated market finance, which has magnified both credit and liquidity risk, has lost its lustre (Buiter, 2007). Upcoming regulation will raise the cost of credit and limit the scope for leverage and private equity (Blundell-Wignall and Atkinson, 2008). Meanwhile world growth will not be driven any more by unsustainable debt-financed and bubble-induced consumption in affluent countries. A sustainable world growth regime will require capital and technology transfers to finance the catching-up of emerging market countries, strategic asset allocation to finance the ageing of mature economies and project finance to substitute for non-renewable resources and to mitigate the adverse impact of climate change. Banks alone are not well-suited to take the long-maturity, non-financial risks inherent in those environment-structuring and innovative investments, where public initiatives and private saving will be associated. The role of long-term financial investors will be enhanced (Committee on the Global Financial System, 2007).

23.4.1   The Virtues of Long-term Investors in Principle

Long-term investors are financial actors with long-standing commitments that impinge upon their liabilities. It follows that mutual funds, subject to redemption constraints at short notice and defined-contribution pension funds that transfer risks on individual households, are not long-term investors. Following those restrictions, the size of assets under the management of long-term investors worldwide was $32 100bn at 2006 year end according to the McKinsey 2007 Global Institute Report. Insurance companies made the most with $18 500bn, defined-benefit pension funds mustered $10 800bn, sovereign wealth funds and public reserve funds (designed to mitigate the shock-wave of the baby boom) reached $2 500bn and endowment funds $300bn.

Amongst this population, institutional investors (insurance companies and defined-benefit investors) have contractual commitments. The others are assigned goals by governments (sovereign wealth funds and reserve funds) or by boards of trustees (endowment funds). They are committed to preserving the long-run real value of their funding with a probability defined by their supervisory board or the guarantees implied in their liabilities. Over this paramount goal, they aim at long-run real returns compatible with their liability commitments. Their objective function leads those investors to financial management starkly different from, even opposed to, financial dealers (investment banks and hedge funds). Their incentives entail a business at odds with short-term speculative arbitrage.

Because they collect long-term saving or get perennial capital from the state or from private donors, they do not indulge in excess leverage, indeed in any leverage. Because they pay benefits over their asset returns on predefined schedules, they are not trapped into unexpected liquidity needs that trigger distress sales on liquid markets and disturb a whole range of asset prices with adverse consequences on other institutions' balance sheets. They exert no systemic pressures on third parties. Therefore they do not spread endogenous risk (Aglietta and Rigot, 2009).

Not being destabilizing, they can be stabilizing if they actually pursue long-term strategies. Given their long horizons, they gain nothing and even lose fees while they indulge in market timing. On the contrary, they can thrive on contrarian dynamic rebalancing of their portfolios in exploiting mean-reverting forces in stock price paths. Furthermore, mean-reverting processes in long stock price cycles entail negative correlations between high (low) short-term expected returns and the returns that might be expected five years or more ahead (Balvers et al., 2000). It follows that the volatility of stock returns is the lower the longer the horizon. These characteristics of equity prices allow long-term financial investors to account for intertemporal hedging in their portfolio diversification. As a consequence, long-term investors should have a higher share of equities in their portfolios than other investors conditional to the same price expectations (Campbell and Viceira, 2002). This is a definite advantage because the post-crisis growth regime will require more equity investment.

23.4.2   Project Financing and the Ability to Take Risk

Long-term investors have a comparative advantage in investing in illiquid assets because they can hold the assets to maturity, warding off liquidity risk. For them the higher return due to the liquidity premium embodied into the price of the assets is a risk-adjusted return, as far as liquidity risk is concerned.

Two types of productive investment that will be made to enhance productivity in the post-crisis growth regime are highly illiquid. The first category encompasses greenfield projects in infrastructures. They will be associated with urbanization in emerging market countries. China and India are prime candidates for heavy investments. Those projects are structured in public–private partnerships whereby a public entity (a development bank or a state financial agency) makes an initial capital funding and guarantees costs and future incomes against building, operational and environmental risks that markets are unable to hedge beyond five years ahead. With public backing, private investors are able to bring in capital participation and buy long infrastructure bonds issued by tranches to finance the project.

Infrastructures are diversifying assets to own while built. The stream of incomes is public-utility-like, thus is inflation-linked in the long run and has low correlation with equity income. However, since they are not quoted, they require an active management. They enter the so-called real alternative asset class in combination with real estate and primary commodities (Swensen, 2000).

The second category of investment belongs to the projects of innovating enterprises. There is uncertainty on both the maturity and the level of industrial risk. Bank credit is badly suited to financing such projects, because lenders bear losses if the project fails but do not participate in the extra return if it succeeds. Venture capital is the best way to finance innovation provided that the investor does not resort to debt, because debt finance forces the investor to shorten the horizon of investment dramatically. Private equity funds boasted that they were long-term investors. However, because they went heavily into debt in order to obtain absurdly high returns, they shortened their horizon to three to five years. In the 2000s they abandoned the field of venture capital to indulge exclusively in leveraged buyouts in order to extract the goodwill of the target firms. At the time it was caught up by the financial crisis that swept it out, private equity performed essentially value extraction that was a mockery of long-term investment.

The big question for sustainable growth is a new generic innovation wave taking roc in technologies substituting for non-renewable energy sources and reducing greenhous gases. New technologies have the potential to reach all industrial sectors, from energ production to smart grids in energy distribution, from thermal insulation of housing t low-carbon means of transport and domestic appliances (Aghion et al., 2009). The dif fusion stage that entails fast-growing demand and high returns can only stem from gov ernment initiative. Radical changes in economic policy would overhaul both the revenu side and the expenditure side of the budget. A common carbon tax all over Europe designed on the model of the value-added tax, should pilot a steady increase in the pric of carbon emissions (Laurent and Le Cacheux, 2010). The proceeds of the tax shoulc partly feed investment subsidies to give proper incentives to venture capital and partl substitute for wage taxes to foster Europe's competitiveness.

Under proper government policies aiming at giving impetus to innovation and selec tion of projects pursued at the European level and gauged to criteria of sustainable growth, long-term investors can participate in project financing. In Europe a group o qualified long-term investors have taken an initiative to work together. In 2009 they jointly created the 'Marguerite' Fund, which was able to invest €30–50bn as early a 2010. Other types of arrangements are conceivable if governments act according tc what they boast, for example, building the best performing knowledge economy in the world. For projects with the approval of the EC Council, it would be possible that the EC issues European innovation bonds with guarantees from the EC budget that would be held by long-term investors. Another arrangement might be cooperation with the European Investment Bank. The EIB would provide seed money to venture projects, taking development risks and attracting private investors to obtain a strong multiplier effect in financing.

Whatever the financing arrangements, long-term investors need proper prudential and accounting rules. Those alternative investments are not for trading. They are for enrich-ing the holding of diversified portfolios with assets weakly correlated to more traditional assets. They should be registered as capital investments so that they are not impacted by fluctuations in market values. If they are accounted at fair value, variations in value should not impact profit and loss statements, but be treated as 'other comprehensive income', unless the underlying asset is impaired (suffers heavy and prolonged losses). If the securities bought by the investors are assimilated to a debt instrument held to maturity, they are accounted at amortized historical value.

23.4.3　Long-term Investors and the Liability Side

Pension funds and insurance companies make up the bulk of potential long-term inves-tors. They have contractual liabilities to ultimate savers. The liability side of their balance sheet is their benchmark. The risks on contractual liabilities are intergenera-tional risks that the asset side should immunize (Sharpe and Tint, 1990). It is what insti-tutional investors are all about. They should manage their asset portfolio in such way that they mutualize intergenerational risks in order to offer collective protection to indi-viduals. For pension funds with corporate sponsors, the corporation is not impacted by s pension fund, albeit in its planned contribution to contractual funding, if the pension und immunizes the liabilities correctly. However, immunization is far from perfect. Eventual underfunding of the pension fund due to a slump in asset value directly impacts the financial health of corporations, as the tribulations of General Motors and many other US companies have made plain. Gaps in funding can come from severe uncertainties in the actuarial valuation of liability risks and from incompleteness in financial markets in hedging such risks. It can also come from deliberate and careless underfunding by the corporations themselves, which count on optimistic asset price appreciation to boost the value of the pension fund to fill the gap.

Contractual liabilities are commitments to deliver future retirement income. For the individuals who save contractually to feed their pension fund or life insurance contract, their contractual saving makes part or the whole of their financial wealth. This is a component of their total wealth that interacts with their human wealth over their life cycle. The latter is sensitive to two main variables: the variation of labour income in the course of their working life on the one hand, the age that increases then decreases human wealth along the life cycle on the other hand. Pension fund managers should run an asset liability process to ultimately immunize the total wealth of their customers, meaning that they should adjust asset portfolios to offset the variations in human wealth.

If the stream of labour income is predictable over the working life of the individuals, the risk on human wealth is low. The pension fund should strengthen the weight of risky assets to raise yield. Alternatively, if labour income is uncertain and correlated with equity returns, the financial portfolio should be biased towards riskless assets. To make allowance for ageing, the portfolio of assets should be modulated with the age of the individuals. Young adults have childcare spending and housing financing, making them indebted. They are unable or unwilling to invest their spare personal savings in equities. It is why their contractual saving should be designed to tilt to a high weight of equities. Conversely when individuals belong to the mature high-saving age group they are able and willing to save more personally. Their contractual saving should be managed according to the size of their financial wealth and the need to decorrelate from their personal portfolio (Blake et al., 2008).

23.4.4 Governance of Long-term Investors

From what has been said above, it appears that long-term investors have social responsibilities, both to the intergenerational sharing of rights and obligations and to the financing of the economy. However, the financial crisis has amply shown that they work in a market environment where greed, irresponsibility and the search for power by market intermediaries (investment banks, hedge funds, private equity) are dominant features. Financial globalization has promoted the Wall Street model of unlimited leverage and risk transfer. Institutional investors have passively absorbed the toxic products sold by the arrangers of structured credit with the complacent advice of the rating agencies. In no way have they performed with due diligence. At no time before the crisis have they exerted their right to control bank management as shareholders via boards of directors, risk control and compensation committees. Abysmal losses have been the result of such lax behaviour. One may hope that the losses will act as a wake-up call to overhaul their governance in the dual dimensions of their responsibilities: managing their asset allocation to protect future retirement income of the people on the one hand, providing finance for risky corporate investments or the other.

There is a first cardinal rule that trustees and administrators of pension funds and sovereign wealth funds should follow. The strategic allocation process should be entirely run in-house. Therefore administrators must hire teams of experts with capabilities to structure a portfolio between broad categories of assets. The second cardinal rule is to prohibit investment in assets whose risk is not understood. Risk control is one of the most important tasks of governance, chiefly in alternative asset classes deprived of market benchmarks. Resort to delegation should be mandated only to well-known specialists in specific areas. Contracting with hedge funds should be very restrictive and agreed upon only with the most extreme care.

The usual dichotomy between strategy and tactic, where the strategic part is conventional and rigid, gives rise to the practice of market timing for the pursuit of illusory capital gains. It should be abolished in favour of a time-flexible strategic allocation (Davanne and Pujol, 2005). A review every year and an in-depth reshaping every three years, based on macroeconomic prospective scenarios built on a five to ten year horizon, helps determine a target portfolio. Well-designed scenarios induce in-depth analysis and judgmental assessment that try to distinguish structural changes in asset prices from cyclical fluctuations and market anomalies (bubbles, amplified volatility and price distortions between asset classes). This is the background to running a contrarian strategy that has stabilizing features in financial markets. The more long-term investors act as such, the less volatile the markets will be.

The other side of due diligence that long-term investors should perform is their direct implication in corporate governance in their capacity of activist shareholders. Because they are not leveraged, these investors can be at odds with private equity funds that have incentives to boost short-term cash flows of their target firms in selling assets and saving on intangible investments for the sake of quick returns. However, institutional investors are neither entitled to take majority participation, nor to hold shares for a long time in a given company. Institutional investors have a long horizon in the search for steady returns on diversified portfolios of equities in a large array of firms. They are not majority owners or even stable investors who immobilize capital in any particular firm. Therefore activist corporate governance is a question of principles and countervailing powers that should be imposed in the corporate sector generally to remedy the utter failure that has led to the financial crisis. The obstacle to achieving a common view and to pressuring corporate management is the fragmentation of the pension fund industry that has difficulty in organizing as a counter-lobby.

Shareholder value has made trustees and managers of pension funds mute instead of alive to their fiduciary duties to the ultimate beneficiaries. In so doing, they have invited governance capture by a financial elite of executives, lawyers and counsellors. They have behaved like absentee owners, letting corporate executives run their business in their own interests, not the interests of the shareholders. Correcting this bias is very difficult. It depends on strong governance rules that institutional shareholders as a group should want to be implemented. The rules are made to foster countervailing powers. They include a board of directors whose chairmanship should be strictly separated from the CEO and committees of risk control, compensation and recruitment that report directly to the chairman of the board and that are sheltered from the intimidation exerted by corporate executives. In addition, independence should also be (re)defined in cognitive terms, with directors competent enough to fulfil their monitoring role, rather than being entirely dependent on the information provided by the firm's executive management. Nothing will happen in this direction if the supervisory bodies of the institutional investors themselves are not converted to a long-term view of shareholder value.

NOTES

1. In France, the Viénot I (1995) and Viénot II (1999) reports, and the Bouton report (2002).
2. Enron and Lehman Brothers provide some striking examples here: the last CEOs of each company – Jeffrey Skilling for Enron and Richard Fuld for Lehman – respectively pocketed $300 and $250 million over a comparable period (1998–2001 in the first case, 2004–07 in the second case) through the exercise of share options schemes.

REFERENCES

Aghion, P., D. Hemous and R. Veugelers (2009), 'No Green Growth Without Innovation', *Bruegel Policy Brief*, November.
Aglietta, M. and A. Rebérioux (2005), *Corporate Governance Adrift. A Critique of Shareholder Value*, Cheltenham, UK and Northampton, MA, USA: Edward Elgar.
Aglietta, M. and S. Rigot (2009), *Crise et rénovation de la finance*, Paris: Odile Jacob.
Balvers, R., Y. Wu and E. Gilliland (2000), 'Mean Reversion across National Stock Markets and Parametric Contrarian Investment Strategies', *Journal of Finance*, **55**(2), 745–72.
Batsch, L. (2007), 'Variations empiriques autour des groupes du CAC40, 2000–2005', paper presented at the CEPN seminar (University Paris Nord), 9 February 2007.
Becht, Marco, Julian R. Franks, Colin Mayer and Stefano Rossi (2009), 'Returns to Shareholder Activism: Evidence from a Clinical Study of the Hermes UK Focus Fund', *The Review of Financial Studies*, **22**(8), 3093–129.
Berle, A. and G. Means ([1932] 1967), *The Modern Corporation and Private Property*, New York: Harcourt, Brace and World.
Bhagat, S., B. Bolton and R. Romano (2008), 'The Promise and Pitfalls of Corporate Governance Indices', *Columbia Law Review*, **108**(8), 1803–82.
Black, B. (1998), 'Shareholder Activism and Corporate Governance in the United States', in *The New Palgrave Dictionary of Economics and the Law*, vol. 3, pp. 459–65.
Black, B., H. Gospel and A. Pendleton (2007), 'Finance, Corporate Governance, and the Employment Relationship', *Industrial Relations*, **46**(3), 643–50.
Blake, David, Andrew Cairns and Kevin Dowd (2008), 'Turning Pension Plans into Pension Planes: What Investment Strategy Designers of Defined Contribution Pension Plans Can Learn from Commercial Aircraft Designers', Pensions Institute, Discussion Paper, PI-0806, April.
Blundell-Wignall, A. and P. Atkinson (2008), 'The Subprime Crisis: Causal Distortions and Regulatory Reform', OECD and Sciences Po, Paris.
Buiter, W. (2007), 'Lessons from the 2007 Financial Crisis', *CEPR Policy Insight*, No. 18, December.
Burkart, M. and F. Panunzi (2008), 'Takeovers', in X. Freixas, Ph. Hartmann and C. Mayer (eds), *Handbook of European Financial Markets and Institutions*, Oxford: Oxford University Press, pp. 265–97.
Campbell, J. and L. Viceira (2002), *Strategic Asset Allocation*, Oxford: Oxford University Press.
Cioffi, J. and S. Cohen (2000), 'The State, Law and Corporate Governance: The Advantage of Forwardness', in S. Cohen and B. Gavin (eds), *Corporate Governance and Globalization. Long Range Planning Issues*, Cheltenham, UK and Northampton, MA, USA: Edward Elgar, pp. 307–49.
Committee on the Global Financial System (2007), 'Institutional Investors, Global Saving and Asset Allocation', *CGFS Papers*, No. 27, February.

Conway, N., S. Deakin, S. Konzelmann, H. Petit, A. Rebérioux and F. Wilkinson (2008), 'The Influence of Stock Market Listing on Human Resource Management: Evidence for France and Britain', *British Journal of Industrial Relations*, **46**(4), December, pp. 631–73.

Davanne, O. and T. Pujol (2005), 'Allocations d'actifs, variation de primes de risque et benchmarks', *Revue d'Economie Financière*, No. 79, pp. 95–110.

Deakin, S., R. Hobbs, D. Nash and G. Slinger (2003), 'Implicit Contracts, Takeovers and Corporate Governance: In the Shadow of the City Code', in D. Campbell, H. Collins and J. Wightman (eds), *Implicit Dimensions of Contract*, Oxford: Hart Publishing.

Denis, D. and J. McConnell (2003), 'International Corporate Governance', ECGI - Finance Working Paper, No. 05/2003.

Faccio, M. and H. Lang (2002), 'The Ultimate Ownership of Western European Corporations', *Journal of Financial Economics*, **65**(3), 365–95.

Fiss, Peer C. and Edward J. Zajac (2004), 'The Diffusion of Ideas over Contested Terrain: The (Non)Adoption of a Shareholder Value Orientation in German Firms', *Administrative Science Quarterly*, **49**(4), 501–34.

Froud, J., C. Haslam, S. Johal and K. Williams (2000a), 'Restructuring for Shareholder Value and its Implications for Labour', *Cambridge Journal of Economics*, **24**(6), 771–98.

Froud, J., C. Haslam, S. Johal and K. Williams (2000b), 'Shareholder Value and Financialization: Consultancy Promises, Management Moves', *Economy and Society*, **29**(1), 80–110.

Ginglinger, E. and J.-F. L'Her (2006), 'Ownership Structure and Open Market Stock Repurchases in France', *European Journal of Finance*, **12**(1), 77–94.

Gordon, J. (2007), 'The Rise of Independent Directors in the United States, 1950–2005: Shareholder Value and Stock Market Prices', *Stanford Law Review*, **59**(6), 1465–568.

Gospel, H. and A. Pendleton (eds) (2004), *Corporate Governance and Labour Management: An International Comparison*, Oxford: Oxford University Press.

Goyer, M. (2006), 'Varieties of Institutional Investors and National Models of Capitalism: The Transformation of Corporate Governance in France and Germany', *Politics and Society*, **34**(3), 399–430.

Jackson, G., M. Höpner and A. Kurdelbusch (2004), 'Corporate Governance and Employees in Germany: Changing Linkages, Complementarities, and Tensions', in H. Gospel and A. Pendleton (eds), *Corporate Governance and Labour Management: An International Comparison*, Oxford: Oxford University Press, pp. 84–121.

Jensen, M.C. (1989), 'Eclipse of the Public Corporation', *Harvard Business Review*, **67**(6), 61–74; revised version published 1997, pp. 1–31.

Jensen, M.C. (2007), 'The Economic Case for Private Equity (And Some Concerns)', pdf of keynote slides, *Harvard NOM research paper*, No. 07-02, available at: http://ssrn.com/abstract=963530; accessed 1 February 2012.

Jensen, M., K. Murphy and E. Wruck (2004), 'Remuneration: Where We've Been, How We Got to Here, What are the Problems, and How to Fix Them', Harvard NOM Working Paper No. 04-28; ECGI Finance Working Paper No. 44/2004.

Laurent, E. and J. Le Cacheux (2010), 'Taxe carbone: et maintenant?', Open Access publication from Sciences Po, Lettre de l'OFCE, No. 316, 15 February.

Lazonick, W. and M. O'Sullivan (2000), 'Maximising Shareholder Value: A New Ideology of Corporate Governance', *Economy and Society*, **29**(1), 13–35.

Lele, P. and M. Siems (2006), 'Shareholder Protection: A Leximetric Approach', *Journal of Corporate Law Studies*, **17**, 17–50.

McKinsey Global Institute Report (2007), *The New Power Brokers: How Oil, Asia, Hedge Funds, and Private Equity are Shaping Global Capital Markets*, October.

Moore, M. and A. Rebérioux (2011), 'Revitalizing the Institutional Roots of Anglo-American Corporate Governance', *Economy and Society*, **40**(1), 84–111.

Osterloh, M. and B. Frey (2006), 'Shareholders Should Welcome Knowledge Workers as Directors', *Journal of Management and Governance*, **10**(3), 325–45.

O'Sullivan, M. (2000), *Contests for Corporate Control. Corporate Governance and Economic Performance in the United States and Germany*, Oxford: Oxford University Press.

Perraudin, C., H. Petit and A. Rebérioux (2008), 'The Stock Market and Human Resource Management: Evidence from a Survey of French Establishments', *Louvain Economic Review*, **74**(4–5), 541–86.

Perraudin, C., H. Petit and A. Rebérioux (2012), 'Worker Information and Firm Disclosure. Analysis on French Linked Employer Employee Data', *Industrial Relations* (forthcoming).

Poulain, J.-G. (2006), 'La détention du capital des société françaises du CAC40 par les non-résidents fin 2005', *Bulletin de la Banque de France*, May, No. 149.

Prowse, S. (1995), 'Corporate Governance in an International Perspective: A Survey of Corporate Control Mechanisms among Large Firms in the U.S., U.K., Japan and Germany', *Financial Markets, Institutions and Instruments*, vol. 4, 1–61.

Rebérioux, A. (2002), 'European Style of Corporate Governance at the Crossroads: The Role of Worker Involvement', *Journal of Common Market Studies*, **40**(1), 111–34. Reprinted in T. Clarke (ed.) (2005), *Corporate Governance, Volume III: European Corporate Governance*, London: Routledge, pp. 64–87.

Sharpe, W. and L. Tint (1990), 'Liabilities: A New Approach', *Journal of Portfolio Management*, Winter, **16**(2), 5–10.

Swensen, D. (2000), *Pioneering Portfolio Management. An Unconventional Approach to Institutional Investment*, New York: The Free Press.

Thomsen, S. (2004), 'Convergence of Corporate Governance during the Stock Market Bubble: Towards Anglo-American or European Standards?', in A. Grandori (ed.), *Corporate Governance and Firm Organization. Microfoundations and Structural Forms*, Oxford: Oxford University Press, pp. 297–317.

24 Firm growth: empirical analysis
Alex Coad and Werner Hölzl

24.1 INTRODUCTION

Firm growth and decline is at the core of economic dynamics. Since the beginning of research in economics there has been an interest in firm growth. Especially in Marshall's (1920) version of neoclassical economics, heterogeneous firms and their organization are the driving forces behind economic change. However, the failure of the Marshallian integration of evolution and equilibrium was the ultimate reason for the redefinition of the representative firm into the language of static competition by Pigou (Moss, 1984). Empirical work began to flourish with the availability of representative and comprehensive data sets. As a result, much work has been done, usually taking the form of regressions in which the growth rate of a firm is the dependent variable, and attempts are made to explain this in terms of a long list of other variables. This new literature on firm growth confirms the important role of heterogeneity and shows that firm growth is highly idiosyncratic and difficult to predict. At the same time new empirical regularities were discovered, such as the finding that those growth rate distributions follow a 'tent-shaped' pattern.

The chapter starts with definitions of firm growth used in the empirical literature, before discussing the growth rate distribution and research into the determinants of growth rates. We also discuss the contribution of fast-growth firms to economic growth.

24.2 MEASURING FIRM GROWTH

The number of possible indicators of firm size is rather vast. Most commonly employment or total sales are used in empirical analysis (Delmar, 1997). While sales growth may mirror best the short- and long-term changes in the firm and may be the most common indicator to measure growth by managers and entrepreneurs, employment has advantages as an indicator of firm growth. First, sales may overstate the size of the firm as sales not only reflect the value-added of a company but also material purchases. Second, measuring size in terms of employment reduces measurement problems compared to financial measures such as sales, as it does not require deflation. Thus measuring firm size in employment is useful in multi-industry and cross-country analyses. Third, for measuring the growth of small firms employment may be more robust than misreporting reported sales and profits. On the other hand, indivisibilities of employment growth are substantial for very small firms with only a few employees.

There are two basic approaches to measuring growth: absolute or relative. Measures of absolute growth examine the actual difference in firm size. Absolute growth is used relatively frequently in the literature on the growth of small entrepreneurial firms, while growth rates are predominantly used in the industrial organization and the labour economics literature. Relative growth rates are best measured by taking log-differences of size (Tornqvist et al., 1985), that is:

$$g_{it} = \log(S_{it}) - \log(S_{i,t-1}) \tag{24.1}$$

where S_{it} is the size of firm i at time t.

Measuring growth in absolute or relative terms can lead to different results (Almus, 2002). Measures of absolute and proportional growth are biased towards larger and smaller firms, respectively. To reduce the impact of firm size on the growth indicator Birch (1987) used a combination of both the relative and absolute growth rates. This growth indicator, also known as the 'Birch index', can be presented as:

$$m = (E_{it} - E_{it-1}) \frac{E_{it}}{E_{it} - 1} \tag{24.2}$$

where E_{it} is the employment of firm i at time t.

Firms can grow organically through expansion of their activities or by acquiring existing firms. Growth by organic expansion and growth by acquisition are likely to be different both in terms of the processes underlying the types of growth and the economic implications (Davidsson and Wiklund, 2000). In a study of high-growth firms Davidsson and Delmar (2006) show that for younger and smaller high-growth firms most of the growth is organic, while for larger and older firms most of the expansion comes from growth by acquisition.

24.3 THE GROWTH RATE DISTRIBUTION

A relatively recent finding is that the Laplace (or symmetric exponential) distribution is a good approximation to the empirical density (Stanley et al., 1996; Bottazzi and Secchi, 2006). While most firms hardly grow at all, a handful of firms experience very large growth rates. Figure 24.1 shows the distribution of the growth rates of sales (top) and employment (bottom). Most firms have a growth rate close to zero, while a small number of firms experience accelerated growth and decline. The 'tent-shaped' distribution of growth rates has been found in data sets from a number of countries, industries and years, making it a robust feature of the firm growth process. Indeed, even in a recession in a declining industry, there will always be some firms growing fast and others simultaneously experiencing fast decline.

When firm growth rates are calculated as growth rates, small firms are observed to grow particularly fast, with a higher growth rate variance than for larger firms. For example, it is easier for a firm of five employees to experience a growth rate of 100 per cent (i.e., grow to ten employees in the following year), than for a firm of 500 employees to grow by 100 per cent by taking on an additional 500 employees. As a result, the growth rate distributions observed in samples of small firms are even more heavy-tailed than the Laplace (Fu et al., 2005).

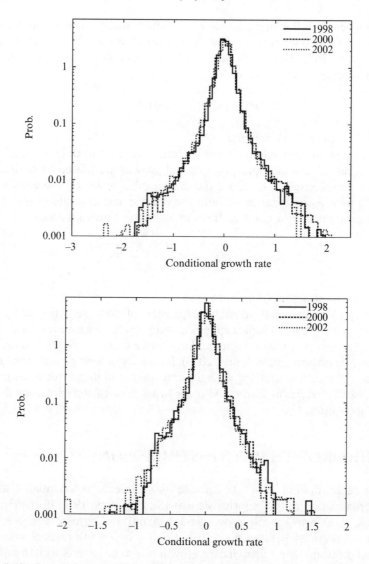

Note: Top: distribution of sales growth rates of French manufacturing firms (Bottazzi et al., 2011). Bottom: distribution of employment growth rates of French manufacturing firms (Coad, 2007a). Note the log scale on the y-axis.

Figure 24.1   Growth rate distributions

Higson et al. (2002, 2004) study the evolution of the cross-sectional distribution of the growth rate of sales for large US and UK firms over the business cycle. They observe that the distribution remains heavy-tailed but that the moments of the distribution of sales growth have cyclical patterns. The mean and kurtosis are procyclical while standard deviation and skewness are countercyclical.

24.4 GIBRAT'S LAW

24.4.1 Gibrat's Model

Empirical investigations into firm growth have been guided by a simple stochastic model devised by Gibrat (1931), who observed the log normal firm size distribution[1] and then proposed a model of firm growth capable of reproducing this distribution. Gibrat's model of firm growth can be represented as follows. Let x_t be the size of a firm at time t, and let ε_t be the random variable representing an iid idiosyncratic, multiplicative growth shock over the period $t - 1$ to t, with mean $\bar{\varepsilon}$. We have:

$$x_t - x_{t-1} = \varepsilon_t x_{t-1} \tag{24.3}$$

which can be developed to obtain:

$$x_t = (1 + \varepsilon_t) x_{t-1} = x_0 (1 + \varepsilon_1) (1 + \varepsilon_2) \ldots (1 + \varepsilon_t) \tag{24.4}$$

It is then possible to take logarithms in order to approximate $(1 + \varepsilon_t)$ by ε_t to obtain:[2]

$$\log (x_t) \approx \log (x_0) + \varepsilon_1 + \varepsilon_2 + \ldots + \varepsilon_t = \log (x_0) + \sum_{s=1}^{t} \varepsilon_s \tag{24.5}$$

In the limit, as t becomes large, the $\log (x_0)$ term will become insignificant, and we obtain:

$$\log (x_t) \approx \sum_{s=1}^{t} \varepsilon_s \tag{24.6}$$

Central limit theorem implies that $\log (x_t)$ is normally distributed, which means that firm size (i.e., x_t) is log normally distributed.

Gibrat's model therefore 'explains' growth events in terms of purely random shocks. This model has become the workhorse of empirical research into firm growth, because random growth is taken as a null hypothesis in attempts to discover factors that systematically affect firm growth rates. Although empirical work has made progress in our understanding of the determinants of growth rates, Gibrat's model remains a useful benchmark of the growth process for a population of firms.

24.4.2 Size and Age

Gibrat's stochastic model of firm growth led to what is known as Gibrat's law, which holds that firm growth rates are independent of firm size. Gibrat's law is often observed to fail, under closer examination, because of a negative dependence of growth rates on size: smaller and younger firms have higher expected growth rates than older and larger firms (some classic references include Mansfield, 1962; Singh and Whittington, 1975; Evans, 1987a, 1987b; Hall, 1987; Hart and Oulton, 1996; see also Lotti et al., 2003 and Coad, 2009, Chapter 4 for surveys). However, some authors have suggested that a negative dependence of growth rates on size holds only for samples of small firms, while growth rates are independent of size for large firms above a certain size threshold (Hart and Oulton, 1996). Given the close relationship between firm size and firm age, researchers have also considered the effect of firm age on expected growth rate. A firm's age has also been observed to have an influence on its growth, with the majority of studies reporting that older firms experience slower growth (see among others Evans, 1987a and Dunne and Hughes, 1994). Lotti et al. (2009) show that Gibrat's law cannot be rejected once they account for learning and selection processes of young small firms.[3] Caves (1998) concludes his survey of the topic by writing that, above a certain size threshold, the negative relation between size and growth disappears.

24.4.3   The Persistence of High Growth

One difficulty in investigating Gibrat's law, and measuring the impact of size on growth rates, is the fact that annual growth rates are autocorrelated (Chesher, 1979). Some early studies focusing on samples of large firms found a positive autocorrelation in annual growth rates, in the order of around +30 per cent (Ijiri and Simon, 1967; Singh and Whittington, 1975). More recently, however, work on larger samples has found autocorrelation that is smaller in magnitude (Kumar, 1985; Dunne and Hughes, 1994), and often even taking negative values (Goddard et al., 2002; Bottazzi et al., 2007). Capasso et al. (2009) highlight the heterogeneity of growth behaviour by pointing out that some persistent high-growth firms coexist with firms that have one-time extreme growth events. More specifically, it seems that the growth of small firms is a rather erratic phenomenon characterized by negative autocorrelation in annual growth rates, whereas the expansion of larger firms is much smoother, displaying positive autocorrelation (Coad, 2007a). Indeed, small firms that grew very fast in the previous period are particularly unlikely to repeat this growth performance (Coad, 2007a; Coad and Hölzl, 2009). For longer time horizons the autocorrelation of growth rates vanishes. Controlling for growth rate autocorrelation does not lead us to reject the negative relationship between size and growth rate, however.

24.5   DETERMINANTS OF FIRM GROWTH

Gibrat's model of firm growth presented in section 24.4.1 is provocative in the sense that it sets a challenge to empirical researchers to find regularities in firm growth rates that would allow us to go beyond this purely random benchmark. We have already seen how growth rates vary with firm size and age. In this section we summarize the other main factors that have been put forward as determinants of firm growth, such as innovation and financial performance.

24.5.1   Innovation and Growth

A number of theoretical models have posited a positive relationship between innovation and firm growth. Empirical work into firm-level innovation has investigated these intuitions, usually measuring innovation in terms of R&D expenditure, number of patents owned by the firm, or in terms of responses to innovation questionnaires such as the

Community Innovation Surveys (CIS). Empirical work on the matter has had difficulty confirming the theoretical intuitions, however. On average, innovation doesn't have much of an impact for firm growth, and some studies fail to find a significant effect of innovation on subsequent growth of sales (Geroski et al., 1997; Bottazzi et al., 2001). One explanation for this lack of empirical confirmation can be given by referring to the growth rate distributions discussed in section 24.3 – the average firm doesn't grow by very much, and so it might not be useful to search for the determinants of growth of the average firm. Instead, we should go beyond the average to look at the determinants of growth for the fastest-growing firms. Empirical results from quantile regressions has shown that, while innovation has a limited impact on the sales growth rates of average firms, it is much more important for the fastest-growing firms (e.g., Coad and Rao, 2008). This characterization of the relationship between innovation and firm growth is consistent with the characterization of innovation as a highly uncertain activity, with the returns to innovation being remarkably unequal (some firms benefit greatly from innovation while many others are less fortunate).

Another facet of the relationship between innovation and firm growth concerns the phenomenon of technological unemployment – whether innovative firms have a lower demand for labour because they apply new technologies (such as robots) to reduce their labour requirements. The aggregate analysis of the impact of technical change on employment is particularly tricky, however. There may well be many indirect feedback effects operating through numerous 'substitution channels' – for instance, new technologies may lead to changes in employment elsewhere in the economy (upstream sectors), and they may affect demand by lowering prices, or increasing wages and investment (see Spiezia and Vivarelli, 2000). That said, investigations at the firm level have generally found a positive influence of innovation on employment growth. Many authors have found it useful to distinguish between product innovation, which is usually associated with employment creation via increased demand, and process innovation, which is often characterized as labour-saving. While process innovation is usually found to be associated with employment growth at the firm level, the effect of process innovation is less clear, being associated with job destruction in some cases (Harrison et al., 2005; Hall et al., 2008).

24.5.2 Profits and Growth

A large number of theoretical models take it for granted that the more profitable firms will grow while less profitable firms will decline (e.g., Nelson and Winter, 1982 and Metcalfe, 1998).[4] In this view, selection pressures operate to redistribute market share to the more profitable firms. Indeed, one would expect that profitable firms have not only the means to finance expansion, but also the motivation to grow, since they can obtain a larger amount of profits from a larger sales base. It is puzzling, therefore, that empirical work only offers weak support to this idea. Growth rates do not seem to increase with profits. It is also surprising that this issue has not received much attention in empirical work despite the theoretical interest in the relationship.

To begin with, it has been observed that, while profit rates are heterogeneous across firms, they display a high degree of persistence (Mueller, 1977; Dosi, 2007), while firm growth rates do not display much persistence. This in itself leads us to question the expected relationship between profits and growth (Geroski and Mazzucato, 2002). Further investigation based on regression analysis has generally shown that firm growth rates cannot be explained in terms of financial performance, whether the latter is measured in terms of profit rates (e.g., Coad, 2007b) or growth rates of the amount of profits (Coad, 2010; Coad and Rao, 2010). While there may be a statistically significant relationship between financial performance and growth, the magnitude of the effect is so low that it would be a valid approximation to view the two variables as independent. Furthermore, advanced econometric techniques also show that profits have a negligible causal effect on firm growth rates (Coad, 2007b; Moneta et al., 2010). Instead, it appears that growth has more of a positive effect on profits, than does profits on growth (Coad, 2007b, 2010).

This puzzling absence of the expected relationship between profits and firm growth seems to us to be one of the most pressing challenges for empirical work on firm growth. Whence this chasm between theoretical intuitions and empirical findings? It seems that financial performance has little effect on growth (measured in terms of either employment or sales) even in subsamples of younger or older firms, in subsamples of shrinking and growing firms, and also when specific industries and years are considered. Just as fluctuations in market value are difficult to predict, it is also difficult to predict firm growth. (However, although firm growth and market value are both indicators of relative performance, firm growth is not strongly related to market value [Geroski et al., 1997].)

24.5.3   Other Determinants of Firm Growth

24.5.3.1   Firm-level variables
A number of other factors have been identified and investigated as being associated with firm growth rates. Some of these factors concern the personality of the entrepreneur. For example, the education of the entrepreneur has been observed to have a positive effect on a firm's growth rate (McPherson, 1996). The sex of the entrepreneur may also play a role, because firms led by female entrepreneurs have been observed to experience slower growth (Mead and Liedholm, 1998).

Some other characteristics of the firm have been linked to growth rates. Evidence suggests that higher growth rates can be expected for multiplant firms (Variyam and Kraybill, 1992; Coad, 2008), for limited liability firms (Harhoff et al., 1998), and also for exporting firms (Robson and Bennett, 2000). On the other hand, government-owned firms seem to grow more slowly (Beck et al., 2005). The effect of foreign ownership is ambiguous and depends on the type of FDI (foreign direct investment; either greenfield or acquisition), learning effects and country of origin of the firm (Bellak, 2004).

It is also interesting to consider that managerial growth aspirations do not go very far in explaining variation in firm growth rates across firms. Wiklund and Shepherd (2003) find a small positive relationship between growth aspiration and growth rate, but the magnitude of this effect rises somewhat if growth aspirations are interacted with the entrepreneur's education and experience. Stam and Wennberg (2009) find that growth aspirations are positively and significantly associated with the growth of low-tech firms, but not for high-tech firms. These results indicate that even a strong desire for growth is not a sufficient requirement for actually achieving high growth rates. Instead, growth would appear to be the combination of both a readiness to grow and also the availability of growth opportunities and managerial resources (Penrose, 1959).

24.5.3.2   Industry-level variables

At the industry level, Audretsch (1995) reports a positive correlation between the minimum efficient scale (MES) and the growth of new firms. The degree of competition faced by firms is not always observed to have an impact on growth rates (Geroski and Gugler, 2004). Interestingly enough, Sutton (2007) shows that the growth rate of an industry leader is virtually independent of the growth rate of the second largest firm in the same industry.

24.5.3.3   Macroeconomic variables

The interaction between firm-level growth dynamics and the business cycle has received considerable attention over the last two decades. Modern business cycle theory highlights the importance of the distribution of variables at the microeconomic level for macroeconomic dynamics (Caballero and Hammour, 1994). The main lesson from this literature is that employment adjustment at the firm and plant level is lumpy and occasional (Davis et al., 1996). Nilsen and Schiantarelli (2003) show that fixed costs to employment adjustment do not vary with firm size. Therefore, smaller firms have lower adjustment frequencies than larger firms and react less strongly to changes in macroeconomic conditions.

The evidence regarding secular trends in industrial dynamics is mixed. Comin and Philippon (2006) and Comin and Mulani (2006) document an increase in microeconomic volatility over the last decades for the USA. But Davis et al. (2007) show that there is an important distinction between publicly traded and privately held firms. For privately held firms (that constitute the majority of US firms) they find a decline in the growth rate dispersion.

Systematic comparative evidence across countries on the growth of firms is scarce. However, such evidence is necessary in order to assess the importance and working of institutions and regulation on the processes of firm growth. Geroski and Gugler (2004) show that the growth behaviour of large firms is not affected by the firm's country of origin. Bartelsman et al. (2009) document that while entry and exit dynamics and survival patterns seem to follow quite similar patterns across EU countries and the USA, there are remarkable differences regarding the average post-entry performance of surviving firms across the USA and EU-15 countries. Surviving US firms have on average a two or three times higher growth rate than European firms measured over a period of seven years from entry. Bravo-Biosca (2010) confirms this view by studying the growth rate distribution across ten countries.

24.5.3.4   Discussion

Many different factors have been included as explanatory variables in growth rate regressions. Although in many cases the effects might be statistically significant, we are still far from providing a thorough explanation of the growth rates experienced by firms. In statistical terms, this is made evident by the low R^2 statistics obtained from regressions featuring growth rates as the dependent variable. The R^2 usually takes values of around 5 per cent, although in some cases it may reach up to 20–30 per cent (Coad, 2009, Table 7.1).

The limited success achieved in finding the determinants of growth rates reflects the difficulties in generalizing across firms. Firms are indeed heterogeneous and differ from each other in many ways, including their growth patterns. However, even within firms it is difficult to find the determinants of growth rates. Longitudinal data reveal that the majority of the variance in growth rates is within individual firms over time, rather than between different firms.

24.6   FAST-GROWING FIRMS

A large part of the empirical work on firm growth comes from the entrepreneurship and small firms' literature.[5] Within this field of research, much attention has been attached to the phenomenon of high-growth firms, also called 'gazelles'. The special interest in gazelles is motivated by the fact that they are perceived as important drivers of economic dynamics, diffusion of innovations and employment generation. In popular discussions of the superior innovative performance and job creation of innovative small firms, there are many references to high-technology firms such as Google, Apple and Microsoft.[6] But the available evidence shows that high-growth firms are found in all sectors of the economy and that there is no clustering in specific industries.

24.6.1   High-growth Firms and Employment Generation

Henrekson and Johansson (2010) provide a survey of 19 studies that use a variety of methods to identify high-growth firms.[7] They find that despite all differences in method and measurement results are remarkably robust in the details of definition of high-growth firms, time period and coverage of firms. The following stylized facts emerge:

- Gazelles, that is, the few most rapidly growing firms, create most new jobs within cohorts of firms of the same age.
- In relation to aggregate numbers, such as total job growth in the economy, the results are less clear-cut. For some countries (especially the USA), studies find that gazelles are the central driver of overall job generation, while other studies (especially for Scandinavian countries) find more moderate effects.
- Although most gazelles are SMEs, there is also an important subset of large gazelles. Acs et al. (2008) report that job creation is almost evenly split between small and large firms.
- Gazelles tend to be younger than the average firm in the industry. However, Acs et al. (2008) report for the USA that less than ten per cent of high impact firms were born in the previous four-year period, a fraction that is declining with firm size.
- There is no evidence to support the view that gazelles are overrepresented in high-tech industries. Gazelles exist in all industries. If anywhere, high-growth firms are overrepresented in knowledge-intensive service industries (Almus, 2002). Being a high-growth firm is primarily an economic and not a strictly technological phenomenon (Hölzl, 2009).
- Being a gazelle is a temporary phenomenon in the life of an enterprise (ibid.), especially if they are small firms.

Table 24.1 *The allocation of gross job creation and gross job destruction in the Austrian private sector between 1995 and 2000, and 1995 and 2005*

	1995–2000	2000–05	1995–2000	2000–05
Gross job creation	670 209	749 370	100.0	100.0
Entries	350 070	434 019	52.2	57.9
Surviving firms	320 139	315 351	47.8	42.1
Of which				
Top 5% gazelles	248 847	242 461	37.1	32.4
Others	71 292	72 890	10.6	9.7
Gross job destruction	617 736	723 278	100.0	100.0
Exits	320 113	463 978	51.8	64.1
Surviving firms	297 623	259 300	48.2	35.9
Of which				
Bottom 5%	215 057	181 280	34.8	25.1
Others	82 566	78 020	13.4	10.8
Net job creation	52 473	26 092		
Of which				
Surviving firms	22 516	56 051		
Turbulence	29 957	−29 149		

Source: Hölzl et al. (2007).

Overall, the findings confirm that a small number of high-growth firms have a high impact on the economy. In order to provide some more intuition Table 24.1 reports the gross job creation, gross job destruction and net job creation for five-year periods for Austrian private sector employment. Firms that increased employment are allocated to gross job creation, and enterprises that decreased employment to gross job destruction. Firms that did not exist in 1995 (2000) are classified as entrants in the calculation of gross job creation. Firms that did exist in the year 1995 (2000) but no longer existed in the year 2000 (2005) are considered as exits. The numbers for entry and exit show that turbulence is a significant element in the process of job creation and job destruction. Surviving firms account for less than 50 per cent of gross job creation and gross job destruction.[8] Within the group of surviving firms the top 5 per cent of performers account for more than 75 per cent of the job creation of surviving firms and the bottom 5 per cent for more than 70 per cent of their job destruction. Thus, both turbulence and gazelles are important for the creation of new jobs and that the job generation of surviving firms is heavily concentrated.

Henrekson and Johansson (2010) argue on this basis that it is 'misleading to narrowly focus on a particular piece of this process and to claim that it alone contributes a dispro-portionally large share of net job growth' (p. 241). However, this view stands somewhat in conflict with a perspective on 'turbulence' that refers to the evidence that there is a large number of firms of suboptimal size that enter and exit the markets (e.g. Hölzl and Reinstaller, 2009). In this context Santarelli and Vivarelli (2007) call for a distinction between 'turbulence' and true 'entrepreneurship' and remind us that Schumpeter (1926) already observed that the entry of new firms is due to a large majority of 'imitators' and a tiny minority of innovators.

24.6.2   Which Firms Grow Fast?

In general, it is difficult to make ex ante predictions about which firms will experience fast growth. Some combination of innovative behaviour, managerial capacities and growth inclination is the basis for the success of high-growth firms. However, given the importance of the phenomenon it is surprising how little is known about what are the determinants of high-growth firms.

Firm strategies might play an important role. The concept of entrepreneurial orienta-tion (EO) in the strategy literature has been conceptualized as strategy comprising three dimensions: innovativeness, 'risk taking', and proactiveness, which require extensive investments by a firm (Covin and Slevin, 1991). Entrepreneurial orientation has been shown to be an important factor for the success of small firms (Wiklund, 1999; Wang 2008). However, as the evidence presented in section 24.5 shows, persistence in profit-ability does not translate into persistent growth. This is also confirmed by Parker et al. (2010) in their study of a sample of 100 UK high-growth firms. Nevertheless Parker et al. (2010) advanced the explanation that management strategies are central. However, following static 'best practices' might be counterproductive, as routine application of 'best practice' strategies is unlikely to foster firm growth in changing economic environ-ments. Moreno and Casillas (2008) emphasize that the particularity of high-growth firms is the nature and timing of the change process. Sims and O'Regan (2006) identify agility as the most important characteristic of gazelles. R&D is one of the elements of a flexible entrepreneurial strategy. Most of the evidence regarding high-growth firms comes from advanced industrialized countries, where R&D and innovation are impor-tant sources of competitive advantage. In one of the few cross-country studies Hölzl (2009) shows that the technological and economic position of a country has a substan-tial influence on the success and choice of innovation and R&D-based growth strategies at the firm level.

24.7   CONCLUSION

We began this chapter by observing that the growth rate distribution is heavy-tailed, a stylized fact that is remarkably robust across different data sets. The implication is that in each industry and overall in the economy most firms have a growth rate close to 0 per cent, while there are a few firms that experience spectacular rates of growth and decline. These differences in growth rates are not persistent however – fast growth in one period in no way guarantees superior performance in the long run. In fact, firm growth rates are particularly difficult to predict. Persistent differences in productivity, profitability or innovative capacity do not translate into persistent differences in growth. Firm growth appears instead to be well approximated by a random process once one controls for size and age of the firms. This is also reflected in the fact that even though growth rate regressions may find statistically significant results, they nonetheless have a low R^2 sta-tistic. Although there are regularities at the population level, individual firms have idi-osyncratic reasons for growing, and it is difficult to generalize across firms. Furthermore, there is great variation in growth rates over time even within individual firms. The finding that growth rates are predominantly random is not just due to heterogeneity etween firms, but also because growth rates have little persistence over time and vary a ot even for individual firms over time.

ACKNOWLEDGEMENTS

A preliminary version of the paper was presented at the 2010 Ratio Colloquium for Young Social Scientists: Understanding Firm Growth. In addition we wish to thank Albert Bravo-Biosca, Michael Pfaffermayr and the editors of this book Jackie Krafft and Michael Dietrich for important comments that helped to improve the paper.

NOTES

1. For surveys of the firm size distribution, see de Wit (2005) and Coad (2009, Chapter 2).
2. This logarithmic approximation is only justified if ε_t is 'small' enough (i.e., close to zero), which can be reasonably assumed by taking a short time period (Sutton, 1997).
3. In a similar vein Pfaffermayr (2007) provides evidence for the fact that the predicted variance in firm size decreases for younger firms once sample selection is taken into account. For the older age cohorts the hypothesis of no change in the variance either cannot be rejected or increasing variances are found in accordance with a Gibrat's law behaviour.
4. See Chapter 38 by Antonelli and Teubal in this handbook for a survey of venture capital financing.
5. The growth of large firms is not discussed in this chapter. See, however, Chapter 22 by Toms and Wilson in this handbook.
6. Note, however, that these are not examples of small firms but large firms! Had they remained small firms, they would not have received as much attention. Indeed, the interest in the job creation of small firms is in those small firms that quickly stop being small.
7. Some methods include, for example, the 10 per cent fastest-growing firms (Schreyer, 2000) using the Birch index, firms doubling sales turnover in real terms between 1990 and 1997 (Littunen and Tohomo, 2003), average growth in employees greater than 20 per cent p.a. over a three-year period (Deschryvere, 2008).
8. The contribution of firms that were set up later than 1995 (2000) and closed down before 2000 (2005) is not included in these numbers.

REFERENCES

Acs, Z., J. Parsons and W. Tracy (2008): 'High-impact firms: gazelles revisited', discussion paper, SBA Office of Advocacy: Washington, DC.

Almus, M. (2002): 'What characterizes a fast-growing firm?', *Applied Economics*, **34**(12), 1497–508.

Audretsch, D.B. (1995): 'Innovation, growth and survival', *International Journal of Industrial Organization*, **13**(4), 441–57.

Bartelsman, E., J. Haltiwanger and S. Scarpetta (2009): 'Measuring and analyzing cross-country differences in firm dynamics', in T. Dunne, J. Jensen and M. Roberts (eds), *Producer Dynamics: New Evidence from Micro Data*, Chicago: University of Chicago Press.

Beck, T., A. Demirgüç-Kunt and V. Maksimovic (2005): 'Financial and legal constraints to growth: does firm size matter?' *Journal of Finance*, **60**(1), 137–77.

Bellak, C. (2004): 'How domestic and foreign firms differ and how does it matter?', *Journal of Economic Surveys*, **18**(4), 483–514.

Birch, D. (1987): *Job Creation in America: How Our Smallest Companies Put the Most People to Work*, New York: Free Press.

Bottazzi, G. and A. Secchi (2006): 'Explaining the distribution of firm growth rates', *Rand Journal of Economics*, **37**(2), 234–63.

Bottazzi, G., E. Cefis, G. Dosi and A. Secchi (2007): 'Invariances and diversities in the patterns of industrial evolution: some evidence from Italian manufacturing industries', *Small Business Economics*, **29**(1), 137–59.

Bottazzi, G., A. Coad, N. Jacoby and A. Secchi (2011): 'Corporate growth and industrial dynamics: evidenc from French manufacturing', *Applied Economics*, **43**(1), 103–16.

Bottazzi, G., G. Dosi, M. Lippi, F. Pammolli and M. Riccaboni (2001): 'Innovation and corporate growth in the evolution of the drug industry', *International Journal of Industrial Organization*, **19**(7), 1161–87.

Bravo-Biosca, A. (2010): 'Exploring firm growth across countries', mimeo, NESTA.

Caballero, R.J. and M. Hammour (1994): 'The cleansing effect of recessions', *American Economic Review* **84**(5), 1350–68.

Capasso, M., E. Cefis and K. Frenken (2009): 'Do some firms persistently outperform?' Tjalling Koopmann Research Institute Discussion Paper No. 09-28.

Caves, R. (1998): 'Industrial organization and new findings on the turnover and mobility of firms', *Journal o Economic Literature*, **36**(4), 1947–82.

Chesher, A. (1979): 'Testing the law of proportionate effect', *Journal of Industrial Economics*, **27**(4), 403–11.

Coad, A. (2007a): 'A closer look at serial growth rate correlation', *Review of Industrial Organization*, **31**(1) 69–82.

Coad, A. (2007b): 'Testing the principle of "growth of the fitter": the relationship between profits and firm growth', *Structural Change and Economic Dynamics*, **18**(3), 370–86.

Coad, A. (2008): 'Firm growth and scaling of growth rate variance in multiplant firms', *Economics Bulletin* **12**(9), 1–15.

Coad, A. (2009): *The Growth of Firms: A Survey of Theories and Empirical Evidence*, Cheltenham, UK and Northampton, MA, USA: Edward Elgar.

Coad, A. (2010): 'Exploring the processes of firm growth: evidence from a vector autoregression', *Industrial and Corporate Change*, **19**(6), 1677–703.

Coad, A. and W. Hölzl (2009): 'On the autocorrelation of growth rates', *Journal of Industry, Competition and Trade*, **9**(2), 139–66.

Coad, A. and R. Rao (2008): 'Innovation and firm growth in high-tech sectors: a quantile regression approach', *Research Policy*, **37**(4), 633–48.

Coad, A. and R. Rao (2010): 'Firm growth and R&D expenditure', *Economics of Innovation and New Technology*, **19**(2), 127–45.

Comin, D. and S. Mulani (2006): 'Diverging trends in aggregate and firm volatility', *Review of Economics and Statistics*, **88**(2), 374–83.

Comin, D. and T. Philippon (2006): 'The rise in firm level volatility: causes and consequences', in M. Gertler and K. Rogoff (eds), *NBER Macroeconomics Annual 2006*, Cambridge, MA: MIT Press, pp. 167–201.

Covin, J. and D. Slevin (1991): 'A conceptual model of entrepreneurship as firm behavior', *Entrepreneurship Theory and Practice*, **16**(1), 7–25.

Davidsson, P. and F. Delmar (2006): 'High-growth firms and their contribution to employment: the case of Sweden 1987–96', in P. Davidsson, F. Delmar and J. Wiklund (eds), *Entrepreneurship and the Growth of the Firm*, Cheltenham, UK and Northampton, MA, USA: Edward Elgar.

Davidsson, P. and J. Wiklund (2000): 'Conceptual and empirical challenges in the study of firms', in D. Sexton and H. Landstrom (eds), *The Blackwell Handbook of Entrepreneurship*, Oxford: Blackwell, pp. 26–44.

Davis, S.J., J.C. Haltiwanger and S. Schuh (1996): *Job Creation and Destruction*, Cambridge, MA and London: MIT Press.

Davis, S.J., J. Haltiwanger, R. Jarmin and J. Miranda (2007): 'Volatility and dispersion in business growth rates: publicly traded versus privately held firms', in D. Acemoglu, K. Rogoff and M. Woodford (eds), *NBER Macroeconomics Annual 2007*, Cambridge, MA: MIT Press, pp. 107–56.

Delmar, F. (1997): 'Measuring growth: methodological considerations and empirical results', in R. Donckels and A. Miettinen (eds), *Entrepreneurship and SME Research: On its Way to the Next Millennium*, Aldershot: Avebury, pp. 190–216.

Deschryvere, M. (2008): 'High-growth firms and job-creation in Finland', Discussion Paper No. 1144, ETLA, Helsinki.

de Wit, G. (2005): 'Firm size distributions: an overview of steady-state distributions resulting from firm dynamics models', *International Journal of Industrial Organization*, **23**(5–6), 423–50.

Dosi, G. (2007): 'Statistical regularities in the evolution of industries: a guide through some evidence and challenges for the theory', in F. Malerba and S. Brusoni (eds), *Perspectives on Innovation*, Cambridge, UK: Cambridge University Press.

Dunne, P. and A. Hughes (1994): 'Age, size, growth and survival: UK companies in the 1980s', *Journal of Industrial Economics*, **42**(2), 115–40.

Evans, D.S. (1987a): 'The relationship between firm growth, size and age: estimates for 100 manufacturing industries', *Journal of Industrial Economics*, **35**(4), 567–81.

Evans, D.S. (1987b): 'Tests of alternative theories of firm growth', *Journal of Political Economy*, **95**(4), 657–74.

Fu, D., F. Pammolli, S. Buldyrev, M. Riccaboni, K. Matia, K. Yamasaki and H. Stanley (2005): 'The growth of business firms: theoretical framework and empirical evidence', *Proceedings of the National Academy of Sciences*, **102**(52), 18801–6.

Geroski, P.A. and K. Gugler (2004): 'Corporate growth convergence in Europe', *Oxford Economic Papers*, **56**(4), 597–620.

Geroski, P. and M. Mazzucato (2002): 'Learning and the sources of corporate growth', *Industrial and Corporate Change*, **11**(4), 623–44.

Geroski, P.A., S.J. Machin and C.F. Walters (1997): 'Corporate growth and profitability', *Journal of Industrial Economics*, **45**(2), 171–89.

Gibrat, R. (1931): *Les inégalités économiques*, Paris: Recueil Sirey.

Goddard, J., J. Wilson and P. Blandon (2002): 'Panel tests of Gibrat's law for Japanese manufacturing', *International Journal of Industrial Organization*, **20**(3), 415–33.

Hall, B.H. (1987): 'The relationship between firm size and firm growth in the US manufacturing sector', *Journal of Industrial Economics*, **35**(4), 583–600.

Hall, B.H., F. Lotti and J. Mairesse (2008): 'Employment, innovation and productivity: evidence from Italian microdata', *Industrial and Corporate Change*, **17**(4), 813–39.

Harhoff, D., K. Stahl and M. Woywode (1998): 'Legal form, growth and exits of West German firms – empirical results for manufacturing, construction, trade and service industries', *Journal of Industrial Economics*, **46**(4), 453–88.

Harrison, R., J. Jaumandreu, J. Mairesse and B. Peters (2005): 'Does innovation stimulate employment? A firm-level analysis using comparable micro data on four European countries', mimeo, Universidad Carlos III, Madrid.

Hart, P.E. and N. Oulton (1996): 'The growth and size of firms', *Economic Journal*, **106**(3), 1242–52.

Henrekson, M. and D. Johansson (2010): 'Gazelles as job creators – a survey and interpretation of the evidence', *Small Business Economics*, **35**(2), 227–44.

Higson, C., S. Holly and P. Kattuman (2002): 'The cross-sectional dynamics of the US business cycle: 1950–1999', *Journal of Economic Dynamics and Control*, **26**(9–10), 1539–55.

Higson, C., S. Holly, P. Kattuman and S. Platis (2004): 'The business cycle, macroeconomic shocks and the cross-section: the growth of UK quoted companies', *Economica*, **71**(282), 299–318.

Hölzl, W. (2009): 'Is the R&D behaviour of fast-growing SMEs different? Evidence from CIS III data for 16 countries', *Small Business Economics*, **33**(1), 59–75.

Hölzl, W. and A. Reinstaller (2009): 'Market structure: sector indicators', in M. Peneder (eds), *Sectoral Growth and Competitiveness in the European Union*, Luxembourg: European Commission.

Hölzl, W., P. Huber, S. Kaniovski and M. Peneder (2007): 'WIFO-Weissbuch: Gründungen, Schliessungen und Entwicklung von Unternehmen. Evidenz für Österreich', *WIFO Monatsberichte*, **80**, 233–47.

Ijiri, Y. and H.A. Simon (1967): 'A model of business firm growth', *Econometrica*, **35**(2), 348–55.

Kumar, M. (1985): 'Growth, acquisition activity and firm size: evidence from the United Kingdom', *Journal of Industrial Economics*, **33**(3), 327–38.

Littunen, H. and T. Tohomo (2003): 'The high growth in new metal-based manufacturing and business service firms in Finland', *Small Business Economics*, **21**(2), 187–200.

Lotti, F., E. Santarelli and M. Vivarelli (2003): 'Does Gibrat's law hold among young, small firms?' *Journal of Evolutionary Economics*, **13**(3), 213–35.

Lotti, F., E. Santarelli and M. Vivarelli (2009): 'Defending Gibrat's law as a long-run regularity', *Small Business Economics*, **35**(2), 227–44.

Mansfield, E. (1962): 'Entry, Gibrat's law, innovation, and the growth of firms', *American Economic Review*, **52**(5), 1023–51.

Marshall, A. (1920): *Principles of Economics*, 8th edition, London: Macmillan.

McPherson, M.A. (1996): 'Growth of micro and small enterprises in Southern Africa', *Journal of Development Economics*, **48**(2), 253–77.

Mead, D.C. and C. Liedholm (1998): 'The dynamics of micro and small enterprises in developing countries', *World Development*, **26**(1), 61–74.

Metcalfe, J.S. (1998): *Evolutionary Economics and Creative Destruction*, London: Routledge.

Moneta, A., D. Entner, P. Hoyer and A. Coad (2010): 'Causal inference by independent component analysis with applications to micro- and macroeconomic data', mimeo.

Moreno, A.M. and J. Casillas (2008): 'Entrepreneurial orientation and growth of SMEs: a causal model', *Entrepreneurship Theory and Practice*, **32**(3), 507–28.

Moss, S. (1984): 'The history of the theory of the firm from Marshall to Robinson and Chamberlin: the source of positivism in economics', *Economica*, **51**(203), 307–18.

Mueller, D.C. (1977): 'The persistence of profits above the norm', *Economica*, **44**(176), 369–80.

Nelson, R.R. and S.G. Winter (1982): *An Evolutionary Theory of Economic Change*, Cambridge, MA: Belknap Press.

Nilsen, O. and F. Schiantarelli (2003): 'Zeros and lumps in investment: empirical evidence on irreversibilities and nonconvexities', *Review of Economics and Statistics*, **85**(4), 1021–37.

Parker, S., D. Storey and A. van Witteloostuijn (2010): 'What happens to gazelles? The importance of dynamic management strategy', *Small Business Economics*, **35**(2), 203–26.

Penrose, E.T. (1959): *The Theory of the Growth of the Firm*, Oxford: Basil Blackwell.

Pfaffermayr, M. (2007): 'Firm growth under sample selection: conditional σ-convergence in firm size?' *Review of Industrial Organization*, **31**(4), 303–28.

Robson, P. and R. Bennett (2000): 'SME growth: the relationship with business advice and external collaboration', *Small Business Economics*, **15**(3), 193–208.

Santarelli, E. and M. Vivarelli (2007): 'Entrepreneurship and the process of firms' entry, survival and growth', *Industrial and Corporate Change*, **16**(3), 455–88.

Schreyer, P. (2000): 'High-growth firms and employment', OECD Science, Technology and Industry Working Papers, 2000/3.

Schumpeter, J. (1926): *Theorie der Wirtschaftlichen Entwicklung*, 2nd edition, Leipzig: Duncker & Humblot.

Sims, M.A. and O'Regan, N. (2006): 'In search of gazelles using a research DNA model', *Technovation*, **26**(8), 943–54.

Singh, A. and G. Whittington (1975): 'The size and growth of firms', *Review of Economic Studies*, **42**(1), 15–26.

Spiezia, V. and M. Vivarelli (2000): 'The analysis of technological change and employment', in M. Vivarelli and M. Pianta (eds), *The Employment Impact of Innovation: Evidence and Policy*, London: Routledge, pp. 12–25.

Stam, E. and K. Wennberg (2009): 'The roles of R&D in new firm growth', *Small Business Economics*, **33**(1), 77–89.

Stanley, M.H.R., L.A.N. Amaral, S.V. Buldyrev, S. Havlin, H. Leschhorn, P. Maass, M.A. Salinger and H.E. Stanley (1996): 'Scaling behavior in the growth of companies', *Nature*, **379**(6568), 804–6.

Sutton, J. (1997): 'Gibrat's legacy', *Journal of Economic Literature*, **35**(1), 40–59.

Sutton, J. (2007): 'Market share dynamics and the "persistence of leadership" debate', *American Economic Review*, **97**(1), 222–41.

Tornqvist, L., P. Vartia and Y.O. Vartia (1985): 'How should relative changes be measured?', *American Statistician*, **39**(1) 43–6.

Variyam, J.N. and D.S. Kraybill (1992): 'Empirical evidence on determinants of firm growth', *Economics Letters*, **38**(1), 31–36.

Wang, C. (2008): 'Entrepreneurial orientation, learning orientation, and firm performance', *Entrepreneurship Theory and Practice*, **32**(4), 635–57.

Wiklund, J. (1999): 'The sustainability of the entrepreneurial orientation – performance relationship', *Entrepreneurship Theory and Practice*, **24**(1), 37–48.

Wiklund, J. and D. Shepherd (2003): 'Aspiring for, and achieving growth: the moderating role of resources and opportunities', *Journal of Management Studies*, **40**(8), 1919–41.

25 Corporate governance, innovative enterprise, and executive pay
William Lazonick

25.1 MAXIMIZING SHAREHOLDER VALUE

Since the early 1980s corporate executives have justified their stock-based compensation as well as the corporate financial behavior that increases it by the dominant ideology that the role of the corporate executive is to 'maximize shareholder value' (MSV) (Rappaport, 1981 and 1983). At the same time, through agency theory, academic economists have supported this ideology by propounding a shareholder-value perspective on corporate governance that is consistent with the neoclassical theory of the market economy (Fama and Jensen, 1983a and 1983b). Especially in the United States, MSV remains the dominant ideology of corporate governance not only in business schools and economics departments but also in executive suites and corporate boardrooms.

This chapter critiques agency theory and its MSV ideology by arguing that its basic tenets are contradicted by the theory of innovative enterprise (see Lazonick, 2002, 2010b, and 2010c). Indeed we contend that in the United States the use of stock-based compensation, and in particular stock options, to motivate corporate executives to have a strong personal interest in the performance of their companies' stock prices has resulted in not only an inequitable distribution of income but also reduced investment in innovation and unstable economic performance. In the next section, we make the intellectual argument that, given the way the real world actually works, innovation theory trumps agency theory as a theory of superior economic performance. In the following section we show that in the corporate economy of the United States, the implementation of the incentives advocated by agency theory for the sake of MSV have over the past three decades resulted in an explosion of top executive pay. In the final section of the chapter we document the importance of stock buybacks in the United States as an instrument for MSV that, by manipulating a company's stock price, helps to boost executive pay. In the real-world process of US corporate resource allocation, agency theory has trumped innovation theory, with inferior economic performance as the result.

25.2 INNOVATION THEORY VERSUS AGENCY THEORY

For adherents of the theory of the market economy, 'market imperfections' necessitate managerial control over the allocation of resources, thus creating an 'agency problem' for those 'principals' who have made investments in the firm. These managers may allocate corporate resources to build their own personal empires regardless of whether the investments that they make and the people whom they employ generate sufficient profits for the firm. They may hoard surplus cash or near-liquid assets within

the corporation, thus maintaining control over uninvested resources, rather than distributing these extra revenues to shareholders. Or they may simply use their control
over resource allocation to line their own pockets. According to agency theory, in the
absence of corporate governance institutions that promote the maximization of shareholder value, one should expect managerial control to result in the inefficient allocation
of resources.

The manifestation of a movement toward the more efficient allocation of resources, it
is argued, is a higher return to shareholders. But why is it shareholders for whom value
should be maximized? Why not create more value for creditors by making their financial
investments more secure, or for employees by paying them higher wages and benefits,
or for communities in which the corporations operate by generating more corporate
tax revenues? Neoclassical financial theorists argue that among all the stakeholders
in the business corporation only shareholders are 'residual claimants'. The amount of
returns that shareholders receive depends on what is left over after other stakeholders,
all of whom it is argued have guaranteed contractual claims, have been paid for their
productive contributions to the firm. If the firm incurs a loss, the return to shareholders
is negative, and vice versa.

By this argument, shareholders are the only stakeholders who have an incentive to
bear the risk of investing in productive resources that may result in superior economic
performance. As residual claimants, moreover, shareholders are the only stakeholders
who have an interest in monitoring managers to ensure that they allocate resources efficiently. Furthermore, by selling and buying corporate shares on the stock market, public
shareholders, it is argued, are the participants in the economy who are best situated to
reallocate resources to more efficient uses.

Within the shareholder-value paradigm, the stock market represents the corporate
governance institution through which the agency problem can be resolved and the
efficient allocation of the economy's resources can be achieved. Specifically, the stock
market can function as a 'market for corporate control' that enables shareholders to
'disgorge' – to use Michael Jensen's evocative term – the 'free cash flow'. As Jensen
(1986, p. 323), a leading academic proponent of maximizing shareholder value, put it in
a seminal article:

> Free cash flow is cash flow in excess of that required to fund all projects that have positive net
> present values when discounted at the relevant cost of capital. Conflicts of interest between
> share-holders and managers over payout policies are especially severe when the organization
> generates substantial free cash flow. The problem is how to motivate managers to disgorge the
> cash rather than investing it at below cost or wasting it on organization inefficiencies.

How can those managers who control the allocation of corporate resources be motivated, or coerced, to distribute cash to shareholders? If a company does not maximize
shareholder value, shareholders can sell their shares and reallocate the proceeds to what
they deem to be more efficient uses. The sale of shares depresses that company's stock
price, which in turn facilitates a takeover by shareholders who can put in place managers
who are willing to distribute the free cash flow to shareholders in the forms of higher dividends and/or stock repurchases. Better yet, as Jensen argued in the midst of the 1980s'
corporate takeover movement, let corporate raiders use the market for corporate control
for debt-financed takeovers, thus enabling shareholders to transform their corporate

equities into corporate bonds. Corporate managers would then be 'bonded' to distribute the free cash flow in the form of interest rather than dividends (ibid., p. 324).

Additionally, as Jensen and Murphy (1990), among others, contended, the maximization of shareholder value could be achieved by giving corporate managers stock-based compensation, such as stock options, to align their own self-interests with those of shareholders. Then, even without the threat of a takeover, these managers would have a personal incentive to maximize shareholder value by investing corporate revenues only in those 'projects that have positive net present values when discounted at the relevant cost of capital' (Jensen, 1986, p. 323) and distributing the remainder of corporate revenues to shareholders in the form of dividends and/or stock repurchases.

During the 1980s and 1990s, maximizing shareholder value became the dominant ideology for corporate governance in the United States. Top executives of US industrial corporations became ardent advocates of this perspective; quite apart from their ideological predispositions, the reality of their stock-based compensation inured them to maximizing shareholder value. The long stock market boom of the 1980s and 1990s combined with the remuneration decisions of corporate boards to create this pay bonanza for corporate executives.

To some extent, the stock market boom of the 1980s and 1990s was driven by New Economy innovation. By the late 1990s, however, innovation had given way to speculation as a prime mover of stock prices. Then, after the collapse of the Internet bubble at the beginning of the 2000s, corporate resource allocation sought to restore stock prices through manipulation in the form of stock buybacks. This massive disgorging of the corporate cash flow manifests a decisive triumph of agency theory and its shareholder-value ideology in the determination of corporate resource allocation.

Has this financial behavior led to a more efficient allocation of resources in the economy, as the proponents of maximizing shareholder value claim? Quite apart from the empirical evidence that I present later, there are a number of critical flaws in agency theory's analysis of the relation between corporate governance and economic performance. These flaws have to do with (1) a failure to explain how, historically, corporations came to control the allocation of significant amounts of the economy's resources; (2) the measure of free cash flow; and (3) the claim that only shareholders have residual claimant status. These flaws stem from the fact that agency theory, like the neoclassical theory of the market economy in which it is rooted, lacks a theory of innovative enterprise (see Lazonick, 2002 and 2010b).

Agency theory makes an argument for taking resources out of the control of inefficient managers without explaining how, historically, corporations came to possess the vast amounts of resources over which these managers could exercise allocative control (see Lazonick, 1992). From the first decades of the twentieth century, the separation of share ownership from managerial control characterized US industrial corporations. This separation occurred because the growth of innovative companies demanded that control over the strategic allocation of resources to transform technologies and access new markets be placed in the hands of salaried professionals who understood the investment requirements of the particular lines of business in which the enterprise competed. At the same time, the listing of a company on a public stock exchange enabled the original owner-entrepreneurs to sell their stock to the shareholding public. Thereby enriched, they were able to retire from their positions as top executives. The departing owner-entrepreneurs left control in the hands of senior salaried professionals, most of whom had been recruited decades earlier to help to build the enterprises. The resultant disappearance of family owners in positions of strategic control enabled the younger generation of salaried professionals to view the particular corporations that employed them as ones in which, through dedicated work effort over the course of a career, they could potentially rise to the ranks of top management.

With salaried managers exercising strategic control, innovative managerial corporations emerged as dominant in their industries during the first decades of the century. During the post-World War II decades, and especially during the 1960s' conglomerate movement, however, many of these industrial corporations grew to be too big to be managed effectively. Top managers responsible for corporate resource allocation became segmented, behaviorally and cognitively, from the organizations that would have to implement these strategies. Behaviorally, they came to see themselves as occupants of the corporate throne rather than as members of the corporate organization, and became obsessed by the size of their own remuneration. Cognitively, the expansion of the corporation into a multitude of businesses made it increasingly difficult for top management to understand the particular investment requirements of any of them (Lazonick, 2004).

In the 1970s and 1980s, moreover, many of these US corporations faced intense foreign competition, especially from innovative Japanese corporations (also, it should be noted, characterized by a separation of share ownership from managerial control). An innovative response required governance institutions that would reintegrate US strategic decision-makers with the business organizations over which they exercised allocative control. Instead, guided by the ideology of maximizing shareholder value and rewarded with stock options, what these established corporations got were managers who had a strong personal interest in boosting their companies' stock prices, even if the stock-price increase was accomplished by a redistribution of corporate revenues from labor incomes to capital incomes and even if the quest for stock-price increases undermined the productive capabilities that these companies had accumulated in the past.

Agency theory also does not address how, at the time when innovative investments are made, one can judge whether managers are allocating resources inefficiently. Any strategic manager who allocates resources to an innovative strategy faces technological, market, and competitive uncertainty. Technological uncertainty exists because the firm may be incapable of developing the higher-quality processes and products envisaged in its innovative investment strategy. Market uncertainty exists because, even if the firm succeeds in its development effort, future reductions in product prices and increases in factor prices may lower the returns that can be generated by the investments. Finally, even if a firm overcomes technological and market uncertainty, it still faces competitive uncertainty: the possibility that an innovative competitor will have invested in a strategy that generates an even higher-quality, lower-cost product that enables it to win market share.

One can state, as Jensen did, that the firm should only invest in 'projects that have positive net present values when discounted at the relevant cost of capital' (1986, p. 323). But, quite apart from the problem of defining the 'relevant cost of capital', anyone who contends that, when committing resources to an innovative investment strategy, one can foresee the stream of future earnings that are required for the calculation of net present value knows nothing about the innovation process. It is far more plausible to argue that if corporate managers really sought to maximize shareholder value according to this formula, they would never contemplate investing in innovative projects with their highly uncertain returns (see Baldwin and Clark, 1992; Christensen et al., 2008).

Moreover, it is simply not the case, as agency theory assumes, that all the firm's participants other than shareholders receive contractually guaranteed returns according to their productive contributions. Given its investments in productive resources, the state has residual-claimant status. Any realistic account of economic development must take into account the role of the state in (1) making infrastructural investments that, given the required levels of financial commitment and inherent uncertainty of economic outcomes, business enterprises would not have made on their own; and (2) providing business enterprises with subsidies that encourage investment in innovation. In terms of investment in new knowledge with applications to industry, the United States was the world's foremost developmental state over the course of the twentieth century (see Lazonick, 2008). As a prime example, it is impossible to explain US dominance in computers, microelectronics, software, and data communications without recognizing the role of government in making seminal investments that developed new knowledge and infrastructural investments that facilitated the diffusion of that knowledge (see, for example, National Research Council, 1999).

The US government has made investments to augment the productive power of the nation through federal, corporate, and university research labs that have generated new knowledge as well as through educational institutions that have developed the capabilities of the future labor force. Business enterprises have made ample use of this knowledge and capability. In effect, in funding these investments, the state (or more correctly, its body of taxpayers) has borne the risk that the nation's business enterprises would further develop and utilize these productive capabilities in ways that would ultimately redound to the benefit of the nation, *but with the return to the nation in no way contractually guaranteed.*

In addition, the US government has often provided cash subsidies to business enterprises to develop new products and processes, or even to start new firms. The public has funded these subsidies through current taxes, borrowing against the future, or by making consumers pay higher product prices for current goods and services than would have otherwise prevailed. Multitudes of business enterprises have benefited from subsidies without having to enter into contracts with the public bodies that have granted them to remit a guaranteed return from the productive investments that the subsidies help to finance.

Workers can also find themselves in the position of having made investments without a contractually guaranteed return. The collective and cumulative innovation process demands that workers expend time and effort now for the sake of returns that, precisely because innovation is involved, can only be generated in the future, which may entail the development and utilization of productive resources over many years. Insofar as workers involved in the innovation process make this investment of their time and effort in the innovation process without a contractually guaranteed return, they have residual claimant status.

In an important contribution to the corporate governance debate, Margaret Blair (1995) argued that, alongside a firm's shareholders, workers should be accorded residual-claimant status because they make investments in 'firm-specific' human capital at one point in time with the expectation – but without a contractual guarantee – of reaping returns on those investments over the course of their careers. Moreover, insofar as their human capital is indeed firm-specific, these workers are dependent on their current employer for generating returns on their investments. A lack of interfirm labor mobility means that the worker bears some of the risk of the return on the firm's productive investments, and hence can be considered a residual claimant. Blair goes on to argue that if one assumes, as shareholder-value proponents do, that only shareholders bear risk and residual-claimant status, there will be an underinvestment in human capital to the detriment of not only workers but the economy as a whole.

Investments that can result in innovation require the strategic allocation of productive resources to particular processes to transform particular productive inputs into higher-quality, lower-cost products than those goods or services that were previously available at prevailing factor prices. Investment in innovation is a direct investment that involves, first and foremost, a strategic confrontation with technological, market, and competitive uncertainty. Those who have the abilities and incentives to allocate resources to innovation must decide, in the face of uncertainty, what types of investments have the potential to generate higher-quality, lower-cost products. Then they must mobilize committed finance to sustain the innovation process until it generates the higher-quality, lower-cost products that permit financial returns.

What role do public shareholders play in this innovation process? Do they confront uncertainty by strategically allocating resources to innovative investments? No. As portfolio investors, they diversify their financial holdings across the outstanding shares of existing firms to minimize risk. They do so, moreover, with limited liability, which means that they are under no legal obligation to make further investments of 'good' money to support previous investments that have gone bad. Indeed, even for these previous investments, the existence of a highly liquid stock market enables public shareholders to cut their losses instantaneously by selling their shares – what has long been called the 'Wall Street walk'.

Without this ability to exit an investment easily, public shareholders would not be willing to hold shares of companies over the assets of which they exercise no direct allocative control. It is the liquidity of a public shareholder's portfolio investment that differentiates it from a direct investment, and indeed distinguishes the public shareholder from a private shareholder who, for lack of liquidity of his or her shares, must remain committed to his or her direct investment until it generates financial returns. The modern corporation entails a fundamental transformation in the character of private property, as Adolf Berle and Gardiner Means (1932) recognized. As property owners, public shareholders own tradable shares in a company that has invested in real assets; they do not own the assets themselves.

Indeed, the fundamental role of the stock market in the United States in the twentieth century was to transform illiquid claims into liquid claims on *the basis of investments that had already been made*, and thereby separate share ownership from managerial control. Business corporations sometimes do use the stock market as a source of finance for new investments, although the cash function has been most common in periods of stock market speculation when the lure for public shareholders to allocate resources to new issues has been the prospect of quickly 'flipping' their shares to make a rapid speculative return. Public shareholders want financial liquidity; investments in innovation require financial commitment. It is only by ignoring the role of innovation in the economy, and the necessary role of insider control in the strategic allocation of corporate resources to nnovation, that agency theory can argue that superior economic performance can be chieved by maximizing the value of those actors in the corporate economy who are the ultimate outsiders to the innovation process.

25.3 SPECULATION AND MANIPULATION IN THE EXPLOSION OF EXECUTIVE PAY

The ideology of maximizing shareholder value is an ideology through which US corporate executives have been able to enrich themselves. In this they were aided in the 1980s and 1990s by academic proponents of the ideology such as Michael Jensen who argued that aligning the interests of top executives with those of public shareholders would result in a mode of resource allocation that would result in superior performance in the economy as a whole (Jensen, 1986 and Jensen and Murphy, 1990). The result has been an explosion and re-explosion of executive pay over the past three decades, fueled by stock-based compensation.

According to AFL-CIO Executive Paywatch (2009), the ratio of the average pay of CEOs of 200 large US corporations to the pay of the average full-time US worker was 42:1 in 1980, 107:1 in 1990, 525:1 in 2000, and 319:1 in 2008. As shown in Table 25.1, the average annual real compensation in 2008 dollars of the 100 highest-paid corporate executives named in company proxy statements was $20.7 million in 1992–95, $78.2 million in 1998–2001, and $62.0 million in 2004–07.

As can be seen in Table 25.1, large proportions of these enormous incomes of top executives have come from gains from cashing in on the ample stock-option awards that their boards of directors have bestowed on them.[1] The higher the 'top pay' group, the greater the proportion of the pay of that group that was derived from gains from exercising stock options. For the top 100 group in the years 1992–2008, this proportion ranged from a low of 57 percent in 1994, when the mean pay of the group was also at its lowest level in real terms, to 87 percent in 2000, when the mean pay was at its highest. In 2000 the mean pay of the top 3000 was, at $10.8 million, only 10 percent of the mean pay of the top 100. Nevertheless, gains from exercising stock options accounted for 67 percent of the total pay of the top 3000 group.

Note in Table 25.1 how the average pay of the highest-paid corporate executives has risen and fallen with the fluctuations of major stock market indices. In the 1980s and 1990s, as shown in Table 25.2, high real stock yields characterized the US corporate economy. These high yields came mainly from stock-price appreciation as distinct from dividend yields, which were low in the 1990s despite high dividend payout ratios.[2] With the S&P 500 Index rising almost 1400 percent from March 1982 to August 2000, the availability of gains from exercising stock options became almost automatic. Given the extent to which the explosion in US top executive pay over the past three decades has been dependent on gains from exercising stock options, there is a need to understand the drivers of the stock-price increases that generate these gains.

The gains from exercising stock options depend on increases in a company's stock price. There are three distinct forces – *innovation*, *speculation*, and *manipulation* – that may be at work in driving stock-price increases. Innovation generates higher-quality, lower-cost products (given prevailing factor prices) that result in increases in earnings per share,

Table 25.1   Total compensation of top executives of US-based corporations, average for 100, 500, 1500, and 3000 highest-paid executives, and the proportion of total compensation derived from gains from exercising stocks options (mean compensation in millions of 2008 US dollars)

	S&P 500 Index	NAS-DAQ Index	NAS-DAQ/ S&P	Top 100 Mean $m.	% SO	Top 500 Mean $m.	% SO	Top 1500 Mean $m.	% SO	Top 3000 Mean $m.	% SO
1992	100	100	1.00	22.8	71	9.2	59	4.7	48	2.9	42
1993	109	119	1.10	21.0	63	9.0	51	4.7	42	3.1	36
1994	111	125	1.13	18.3	57	8.0	45	4.3	35	2.9	29
1995	131	155	1.18	20.6	59	9.6	48	5.2	40	3.4	34
1996	162	195	1.20	31.9	64	13.7	54	7.1	47	4.5	41
1997	210	243	1.16	43.5	72	18.3	61	9.3	55	5.8	49
1998	261	300	1.15	77.2	67	26.9	65	12.5	59	7.5	54
1999	319	462	1.45	69.0	82	27.5	71	13.2	63	7.9	57
2000	341	614	1.80	104.1	87	40.4	80	18.7	73	10.8	67
2001	284	332	1.17	62.3	77	23.7	66	11.3	58	6.8	53
2002	237	252	1.06	37.4	57	16.8	49	8.6	43	5.4	38
2003	232	275	1.18	48.4	64	21.0	55	10.7	48	6.7	43
2004	272	330	1.21	54.6	75	24.6	62	12.8	55	8.0	50
2005	290	348	1.20	66.5	78	28.2	63	14.3	56	8.9	51
2006	316	463	1.47	67.3	68	29.0	58	15.1	51	9.5	46
2007	354	428	1.21	59.6	69	27.4	58	14.6	50	9.3	45
2008	291	356	1.22	39.2	62	16.6	48	8.3	38	5.0	33

Notes:
a.   S&P 500 Index and the NASDAQ Composite Index set to 100 in 1992 for purposes of comparison.
b.   Total compensation (TDC2 in the Compustat database) is defined as 'Total compensation for the individual year comprised of the following: Salary, Bonus, Other Annual, Total Value of Restricted Stock Granted, Net Value of Stock Options Exercised, Long-term Incentive Payouts, and All Other Total').
c.   % SO means the percentage of total compensation that the whole set (100, 500, 1500, or 3000) of highest-paid executives derived from gains from exercising stock options.
d.   Note that company proxy statements (DEF 14A SEC filings) report the compensation of the company's CEO and four other highest-paid executives. It is therefore possible that some of the highest-paid executives who should be included in each of the 'top' categories are excluded. The mean compensation calculations are therefore lower bounds of actual average compensation of the highest-paid corporate executives in the United States.

Sources: Standard and Poor's Compustat database (Executive Compensation, Annual); Yahoo! Finance at http://finance.yahoo.com (Historical Prices, Monthly Data).

which in turn lift the stock price of the innovative enterprise. Speculation, encouraged perhaps by innovation, drives the stock price higher, as investors assume either that innovation will continue in the future (which, given that innovation is involved, is inherently uncertain) or that there is a 'greater fool' who stands ready to buy the stock at a yet higher price. Manipulation occurs when those who exercise control over corporate resource allocation do so in a way that increases earnings per share despite the absence of innovation.

Figure 25.1 charts the roles of innovation, speculation, and manipulation as *primary* drivers of US stock-price movements from the mid-1980s to the late 2000s. In the last

Table 25.2 Average annual US corporate stock and bond yields (%), 1960–2009

	1960–69	1970–79	1980–89	1990–99	2000–09
Real stock yield	6.63	−1.66	11.67	15.01	−3.08
Price yield	5.80	1.35	12.91	15.54	−2.30
Dividend yield	3.19	4.08	4.32	2.47	1.79
Change in CPI	2.36	7.09	5.55	3.00	2.57
Real bond yield	2.65	1.14	5.79	4.72	3.41

Notes: Stock yields are for Standard and Poor's Composite Index of 500 US corporate stocks. Bond yields are for Moody's Aaa-rated US corporate bonds.

Sources: Updated from Lazonick and O'Sullivan (2000, p. 27), using US Congress (2010, Tables B-62, B-73, B-95, B-96).

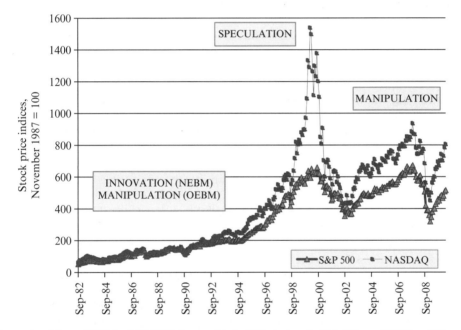

Note: As of August 2009 the S&P 500 Index consisted of 500 stocks, of which 410 were NYSE and 90 NASDAQ; and the NASDAQ Composite Index consisted of 2809 stocks. NEBM= New Economy Business Model; OEBM = Old Economy Business Model.

Source: Yahoo! Finance at http://finance.yahoo.com (Historical Prices, Monthly Data).

Figure 25.1 S&P 500 and NASDAQ Composite Indices, September 1982–April 2010 (monthly data, standardized for the two indices to 100 in November 1987)

half of the 1980s Old Economy companies that had run into trouble because of conglomeration in the United States and/or competition from the Japanese sought to manipulate stock prices through a 'downsize-and-distribute' resource-allocation strategy (Lazonick, 2004). This redistribution of corporate revenues from labor incomes to capital incomes often occurred through debt-financed hostile takeovers, with post-takeover downsizing enabling the servicing and retirement of the massive debt that a company had taken on. In addition, from the mid-1980s, many Old Economy companies engaged for the first time in large-scale stock repurchases in an attempt to support their stock prices. In the 1990s and 2000s stock buybacks would become a prime mode of corporate resource allocation. The main, and for most major US corporations only, purpose of stock buybacks is to manipulate stock prices (Lazonick, 2009b).

While Old Economy companies were manipulating stock prices in the 1980s and early 1990s, New Economy companies such as Intel, AMD, Microsoft, Oracle, Solectron, EMC, Sun Microsystems, Cisco Systems, Dell, and Qualcomm were reinvesting virtually all of their incomes to finance the growth of their companies, neither paying dividends nor, once they had gone public, repurchasing stock (Lazonick, 2009a, Ch. 2). It was *innovation* by New Economy companies, most of them traded on NASDAQ, that culminated in the Internet revolution that provided a real foundation for the rising stock market in the 1980s and first half of the 1990s.

These New Economy companies had broad-based stock-option programs that extended to non-executive employees. In the speculative boom of 1999–2000, the gains from exercising stock options of the average worker could be enormous. The most extreme example is Microsoft; in 2000 alone the gains across about 39000 employees (not including the five highest-paid executives) averaged an estimated $449000 (see Lazonick, 2009b). During the same year, the gains from exercising stock options of the five highest-paid Microsoft executives averaged $50.7 million – a ratio of 'top five' gains to average worker gains of 113:1.

In the late 1990s speculation took over, driving the stock market to unsustainable heights. As Figure 25.1 shows, the speculation in companies listed on NASDAQ was much more pronounced than in the companies that make up the S&P 500 Index, over 80 percent of which are listed on the New York Stock Exchange (NYSE). In 2000 the average compensation of the top 100 NASDAQ executives was 19 percent higher than that of the top 100 NYSE executives, while in 2007 the compensation of the top 100 NYSE executives was 11 percent higher than that of the top 100 NASDAQ executives. In both years the proportion of the compensation that came from exercising stock options was higher for NASDAQ executives than for NYSE executives. Still, even for the NYSE executives, this proportion was 78 percent for the top 100 and 53 percent for the top 3000 in 2000, and 65 percent for the top 100 and 43 percent for the top 3000 in 2007. Whether their companies are listed on NASDAQ or NYSE, stock options give the top executives of US corporations a huge personal financial stake in a rising stock market.

In the 2000s the stock-option gains of these executives have come primarily through manipulation as distinct from innovation and speculation. The key instrument of stock-market manipulation is the stock repurchase. A stock repurchase occurs when a company buys back its own shares. In the United States, the Securities and Exchange Commission (SEC) requires stock repurchase *programs* to be approved by the board of directors. These programs authorize a company's top executives to do a certain amount of buybacks over a certain period of time. It is then up to the top executives to decide whether the company should actually do repurchases, when they should be done, and how many shares should be repurchased at any given time. Repurchases are almost always done as open market transactions through the company's broker. The company

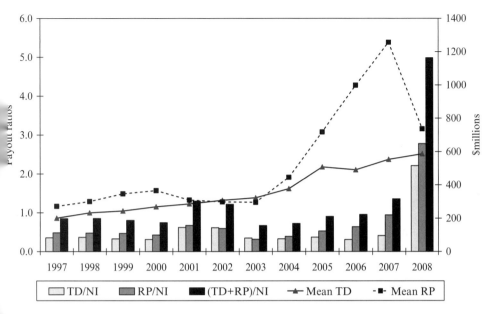

Notes:
a. Data for 438 corporations in the S&P 500 Index in January 2008 publicly listed 1997 through 2008.
b. RP, stock repurchases; TD, total dividends (common and preferred); NI, net income (after tax with
    inventory evaluation and capital consumption adjustments).

Sources: S&P Compustat database (North America, Fundamentals Annual, 1997–2008); company 10-K
filings for missing or erroneous data from the Compustat database.

Figure 25.2   *Ratios of cash dividends and stock repurchases to net income, and mean
              dividend payments and stock repurchases among S&P 500 (438 companies),
              1997–2008*

is not required to announce the buybacks at the time they are actually done, although
since 2004 it has been an SEC rule that, in their quarterly financial reports, companies
must state the amount of repurchases in the past quarter and the average purchase price.

Data on 373 companies in the S&P 500 Index in January 2008 that were publicly listed
in 1990 show that they expended an annual average of $106.3 billion (or $285 million per
company) on stock repurchases in 1995–99, representing 44 percent of their combined
net income. These figures represented a significant increase from $25.9 billion in repur-
chases (or $69 million per company) in 1990–94, representing 23 percent of their com-
bined net income. Yet in the late 1990s the stage was being set for an even more massive
manipulation of the market through stock repurchases, especially from 2003. Figure 25.2
shows the payout ratios and mean payout levels for 438 companies in the S&P 500 Index
in January 2008 that were publicly listed from 1997 through 2008.[3]

From 1997 through 2008 these 438 companies expended $2.4 trillion on stock repur-
chases, an average of $5.6 billion per company, and distributed a total of $1.7 trillion in
cash dividends, an average of $3.8 billion per company. Stock repurchases by these 438
companies averaged $323 million in 2003, rising to $1256 million in 2007. Combined, the
500 companies in the S&P 500 Index in January 2008 repurchased $436 billion of their

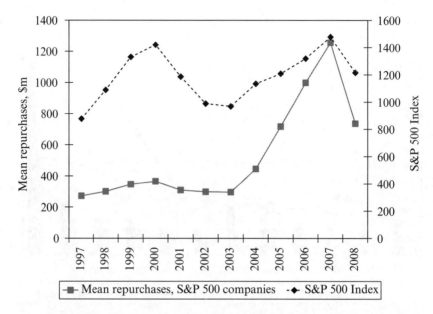

Sources: Standard and Poor's Compustat database (North America, Fundamentals Annual); Yahoo!
Finance at http://finance.yahoo.com (Historical Prices, Monthly Data).

*Figure 25.3   Stock repurchases by the S&P 500 (438 companies) and the movement of
the S&P 500 Index, 1997–2008*

own stock in 2006, representing 64 percent of their net income, and $549 billion in 2007
representing 94 percent of their net income.

Figure 25.3 shows how the escalating stock repurchases from 2003 through 2007
helped to boost the stock market, driving the S&P 500 Index even higher in 2007 than
its previous peak in 2000 before the 2008 financial debacle. In 2008 repurchases fell substantially for these 438 companies, constrained by a dramatic decline in combined net
income from $583 billion in 2007 to $132 billion in 2008. Nevertheless, their combined
repurchases only declined from $523 billion to $369 billion. As a result, the repurchase
payout ratio more than tripled from 0.90:1 to 2.80:1. In addition, these companies paid
out $5 billion more in dividends in 2008 than in 2007, with the result that the dividend
payout ratio leapt from 0.41:1 to 1.86:1. Allocated differently, the billions spent on buybacks could have helped stabilize the economy. Instead, collectively, these companies not
only spent all their profits on repurchases but also ate into their capital.

Why do corporations repurchase stock? Executives often claim that buybacks are
financial investments that signal confidence in the future of the company and its stock-
price performance (Vermaelen, 2005, Ch. 3; Louis and White, 2007). In fact, however,
companies that do buybacks never sell the shares at higher prices to cash in on these
investments. To do so would be to signal to the market that its stock price had peaked.
According to the 'signaling' argument, we should have seen massive sales of corporate
stock in the speculative boom of the late 1990s, as was in fact the case of US industrial
corporations in the speculative boom of the late 1920s when corporations took advantage of the speculative stock market to pay off corporate debt or bolster their corporate

reasuries (O'Sullivan, 2004). Instead, in the boom of the late 1990s corporate executives s *personal investors* sold their own stock to reap speculative gains (often to the tune of ens of millions). Yet, if anything, these same corporate executives as *corporate decision-makers* used corporate funds to repurchase their companies' shares in the attempt to bolster their stock prices – to their own personal gain. Given the extent to which stock repurchases have become a systematic mode of corporate resource allocation, and given the extent to which through this manipulation of their corporations' stock prices top xecutives have enriched themselves personally in the process, there is every reason to believe that, in the absence of legislation that restricts both stock repurchases as well as speculative and manipulative gains from stock options, executive behavior that places personal interests ahead of corporate interests will continue in the future.

There are a number of ways in which stock options as a mode of executive compensation can be abused. A company might reprice options that are underwater by canceling an existing option and replacing it with a new option with a lower exercise price (Chance et al., 2000; Ellig, 2007, pp. 434–5). As a result, an executive may be able to reap gains from stock-option grants even when the company's stock price declines. In 2006 a scandal broke out over the practice of backdating stock options – that is, granting option awards today as if they were granted at an earlier date when the market price of the stock and hence the exercise price of the options were lower (Lie, 2005; Forelle and Bandler, 2006; Bernile and Jarrell, 2009). Abuses can also occur in the timing of the exercise of options. Given the fact that in the United States companies are not required to announce the dates on which they actually do open market repurchases, there is an opportunity for top executives who have this information to engage in insider trading by using this information to time option exercises and stock sales (see Fried, 2000 and 2001).

The more fundamental problem with US-style stock options, however, is that they are unindexed; that is, they virtually never carry any performance criteria that would only permit an executive to gain from the exercise of stock options when the company's stock-price increases are greater than those warranted by productive performance (Bebchuk and Fried, 2004). As a result, an executive, or any other employee with stock options, can gain from a speculative stock market as distinct from an improvement in the company's productive performance. In addition, as I have argued, executives can augment their stock-option gains by allocating corporate resources to do buybacks, the sole purpose of which is to manipulate the company's stock price. Some of the stock-based compensation of US executives is undoubtedly attributable to innovation, although even then there is the question of whether the stock-based compensation that executives secure is equitable relative to other contributors to the innovation process. Be that as it may, since the last half of the 1990s it has been speculation and manipulation that have been the main drivers of the explosion in the pay of US corporate executives.

25.4   STOCK BUYBACKS AS 'WEAPONS OF VALUE DESTRUCTION'

The ideology of maximizing shareholder value is an ideology through which US corporate executives have been able to enrich themselves. In this they were aided in the 1980s and 1990s by academic proponents of the ideology such as Michael Jensen who argued that aligning the interests of top executives with those of public shareholders would result in a mode of resource allocation that would result in superior performance in the economy as a whole. The result has been an explosion and re-explosion of executive pay over the past three decades, fueled by stock-based compensation.

In his 2008 book, *Supercapitalism*, Robert Reich (2008, pp. 105–14), former Secretary of Labor in the Clinton administration, justifies the explosion in executive pay by arguing that intense competition makes it much more difficult to find the talent who can manage a large corporation than it used to be. Without going so far, others might argue that while this concentration of income at the top is highly inequitable, its impact on the performance of the US economy is neutral. The problem with these arguments is that they do not actually analyze the relation between the incentives inherent in different types of executive compensation – in this case, stock-based compensation, particularly in the form of stock-option grants – and the ways in which the executives who receive these incentives allocate resources.

My analyses of different industries (some of which I have studied in more depth than others) strongly suggest that the explosions in executive pay are coming at the expense of innovation and the upgrading of employment opportunities in the US economy. In what follows, I present some pertinent evidence from key sectors of the US economy.

Among the biggest stock repurchasers in the years prior to the financial crisis were many of the banks that were responsible for the meltdown and were bailed out under the Troubled Asset Relief Program. They included Citigroup ($41.8 billion repurchased in 2000–07), Goldman Sachs ($30.1 billion), Wells Fargo ($23.2 billion), JP Morgan Chase ($21.2 billion), Merrill Lynch ($21.0 billion) Morgan Stanley ($19.1 billion), American Express ($17.6 billion), and US Bancorp ($12.3 billion). In the eight years before it went bankrupt in 2008, Lehman Brothers repurchased $16.8 billion, including $5.3 billion in 2006–07. Washington Mutual, which also went bankrupt in 2008, expended $13.3 billion on buybacks in 2000–07, including $6.5 billion in 2006–07. Wachovia, ranked 38th among the Fortune 500 in 2007, did $15.7 billion in buybacks in 2000–07, including $5.7 billion in 2006–07, before its fire sale to Wells Fargo at the end of 2008. Other financial institutions that did substantial repurchases in the 2000s before running into financial distress in 2008 were AIG ($10.2 billion), Fannie Mae ($8.4 billion), Bear Stearns ($7.2 billion), and Freddie Mac ($4.7 billion). By spending money on buybacks during boom years, these financial corporations reduced their ability to withstand the crash of the derivatives market in 2008, thus exacerbating the jeopardy that they created for the economy as a whole.

Among the top ten repurchasers of stock in 2000–08 were five of the leading ICT companies: Microsoft (the No. 2 repurchaser with $94.3 billion in buybacks), IBM (No. 3, $72.9 billion), Cisco Systems (No. 5, $53.6 billion), Intel (No. 8, $48.8 billion), and Hewlett-Packard (No. 10, $43.3 billion). All of these companies spent more on buybacks than they spent on R&D in 2000–08. In the 2000s, all of these companies have been globalizing employment, and profiting through the creation of high-tech jobs in lower-wage parts of the world such as China and India while using the profits of globalization to do stock buybacks at home (Milberg, 2008; Lazonick, 2009b).

Meanwhile, US high-tech companies lobby the US government for more public investment in the US high-technology knowledge base, even as the companies allocate their own profits to huge stock buybacks. For example, in the 2000s Intel along with the Semiconductor Industry Association (SIA) has been lobbying the US Congress for more spending on the National Nanotechnology Initiative (NNI). At a press conference that the SIA organized in Washington DC in March 2005, Intel CEO Craig Barrett warned: 'U.S. leadership in the nanoelectronics era is not guaranteed. It will take a massive, coordinated U.S. research effort involving academia, industry, and state and federal governments to ensure that America continues to be the world leader in information technology' (*Electronic News*, 2005). In 2005 the annual NNI budget was $1.2 billion, just 11 percent of the $10.6 billion that Intel spent on stock repurchases in that year alone. Indeed, Intel's 2005 expenditures on stock buybacks exceed the total of $10.1 billion that has been spent on NNI since its inception in 2001 through 2009.[4] Given the extent to which the ICT industry in general, and a company like Intel in particular, has benefited from decades of government investments in the high-tech knowledge base, one might ask whether a portion of the massive funds that Intel allocates to buying back its own stock could not be more productively allocated 'to ensure that America continues to be the world leader in information technology' (ibid.).

Among the largest repurchasers of stock in the 2000s have been pharmaceutical companies. For 2000–08 Pfizer was the No. 7 repurchaser with $50.6 billion in buybacks, Johnson & Johnson No. 12 with $33.3 billion, Amgen No. 24 with $22.6 billion, and Merck No. 31 with $18.7 billion. These and other US pharmaceutical companies charge higher drug prices in the United States than in other rich nations such as Japan, Canada, and France because, their executives argue, they need the higher earnings to fund their R&D efforts in the United States. Yet the very same companies do massive stock buybacks for the sole purpose of manipulating their stock prices. Meanwhile, the United States is the world leader in biopharmaceuticals in large part because of $31 billion per annum that the National Institutes of Health spend in support of the life sciences knowledge base, as well as numerous government subsidies to the pharmaceutical industry, including those under the Orphan Drug Act of 1983 (see Lazonick and Tulum, 2009). Instead of doing stock buybacks, the pharmaceutical companies could be contributing to the national life sciences effort, or lowering their drug prices to make their products more affordable to the American public.

There has been virtually no public policy debate in the United States over the practice of buybacks, its acceleration in recent years, or the implications for innovation, employment, income distribution, and economic growth. Exceptionally, in the summer of 2008 four Congressional Democrats took aim at stock repurchases by the big oil companies, after Exxon Mobil, by far the largest repurchaser of stock ($144 billion in 2000–08), had announced record second quarter profits of $11.7 billion, of which $8.8 billion went to stock buybacks (US Congress, 2008). In a letter to oil industry executives, the Congressmen asked them to

> pledge to greatly increase the ratio of investments in production and alternatives to the amount of stock buybacks this year and next by investing much more of your profits into exploration and production on the leases you have been awarded in the U.S., and in the research and development of promising alternative energy sources. (US Congress, 2008)

Exxon Mobil did not pay much attention to this plea; in the last half of 2008 it repurchased another $17.5 billion for a total of $35.7 billion, or 79 percent of its net income, on the year. In the first three quarters of 2009 Exxon Mobil did another $17.3 billion in buybacks, equivalent to 131 percent of its net income.

Recently, the United States engaged in a debate over health care reform, with the companies that provide health insurance in the forefront of opposition to progressive change, including the availability of a 'public option' that would provide households with an alternative source of health insurance to that offered by the business corporations. Among the top 50 repurchasers for 2000–08 were the two largest corporate health insurers: UnitedHealth Group at No. 23 with $23.7 billion in buybacks and Wellpoint at No. 39 with $14.9 billion (Lazonick, 2010a). For each of these companies, repurchases represented 104 percent of net income for 2000–08. Over this period, repurchases by the third largest insurer, Aetna, were $9.7 billion, or 137 percent of net income, and the fifth largest, Cigna, $9.8 billion, or 125 percent of net income. Meanwhile the top executives of these companies typically reaped millions of dollars, and in many years tens of millions of dollars, in gains from exercising stock options. A serious attempt at health care reform would seek to eliminate the profits of these health insurers, given that these profits are used solely to manipulate stock prices and enrich a small number of people at the top.

In the United States, the problem of exploding executive pay has been around for a long time, and virtually nothing has been done about it. The one attempt in the 1990s by Democrats to control the rise of executive pay ended up doing just the opposite. In 1993, after Bill Clinton became President of the United States, his administration implemented a campaign promise to legislate a cap of $1 million on the amount of non-performance-related, top-executive compensation that could be claimed as a corporate tax deduction. One perverse result of this law was that companies that were paying their CEOs less than $1 million in salary and bonus *raised* these components of CEO pay toward $1 million, which was now taken as the government-approved 'CEO minimum wage'. The other perverse result was that companies increased CEO stock-option awards, for which tax deductions were not in any case being claimed, as an alternative to exceeding the $1 million salary-and-bonus cap (Byrne, 1994 and 1995).

A further irony of the Clinton legislation was that the high-tech lobby at the time was fighting against an attempt by the Financial Accounting Standards Board (FASB) to require companies to expense stock options. Especially for companies with broad-based stock-option plans, this prospective regulatory change would have resulted in lower reported earnings that, it was thought, would result in lower stock prices. Hence, even though the proposed FASB regulation (which was ultimately decreed in 2004) would have reduced the corporate tax bill, corporate executives were against it. Why would these same executives have given much thought to the fact that there would be no *corporate* tax deductions for personal pay that exceeded the million-dollar cap?

Then as now, it is futile to talk about placing restrictions on executive compensation without limiting the extent to which executives can reap gains from stock options that result from either speculation or manipulation. Besides making manipulative stock repurchases illegal, legislation is needed to place limits on stock-option grants to individuals and to make the gains from the exercise of stock options dependent on achieving a variety of performance goals, including first and foremost ongoing contributions to high-quality job creation in the United States.

Economic activity entails both the creation of value, as goods and services are produced, and the extraction of value, as goods and services are consumed. Investment in innovation creates the potential for higher standards of living for those who contribute to the innovation process. Inequity occurs when certain groups in the economy – for example, top corporate executives – use their control over resource allocation to extract more than they create. Instability occurs when this excessive value extraction undermines innovation, and with it the potential for higher standards of living for the broader population. It is my contention that in the United States in the 2000s the stock-based compensation of corporate executives is a prime source of this instability, and the stock buyback is their most powerful 'weapon of value extraction'. Indeed, my research suggests that, by undermining innovation, stock repurchases have become 'weapons of value destruction'. Corporate stock repurchases should be banned, and stock-based compensation should be controlled so that executives cannot gain from speculation on and manipulation of the stock market. If not, we can expect that executive pay will continue to explode, and that, for lack of innovation and high-quality job creation, American prosperity will continue to erode.

NOTES

1. A stock-option award gives an employee the non-transferable right to purchase a certain number of shares of the company for which he or she works at a pre-set 'exercise' price between the date the option 'vests' and the date it 'expires'. Typically in US option grants, the exercise price is the market price of the stock at the date that the option is granted; vesting of the option occurs in 25 percent installments at each of the first four anniversaries from the grant date; and the expiration date of the option is ten years from the grant date. Unvested options usually lapse 90 days after termination of employment with the company.
2. In the 1980s dividends paid out by US corporations increased by an annual average of 10.8 percent while after-tax corporate profits increased by an annual average of 8.7 percent. In the 1990s these figures were 8.0 percent for dividends (including an absolute decline in dividends of 4.0 percent in 1999, the first decline since 1975) and 8.1 percent for profits. The dividend payout ratio – the amount of dividends as a proportion of after-tax corporate profits (with inventory evaluation and capital consumption adjustments) – was 48.9 percent in the 1980s and 55.0 percent in the 1990s compared with 39.5 percent in the 1960s and 41.6 percent in the 1970s. From 2000 to 2009 the dividend payout ratio was 61.5 percent, including a record 70.4 percent in 2007.
3. I treat data for companies with fiscal years ending June 30–January 1 as representing the previous calendar year, and for fiscal years ending December 31– July 1 as representing the current calendar year.
4. In 2008 the NNI budget was $1554 million with an estimated budget for 2009 of $1657 million, and a proposed $1640 million for 2010 (www.nano.gov/html/about/funding.html).

REFERENCES

AFL-CIO, 2009, 'Executive Paywatch,' available at http://www.aflcio.org/corporatewatch/paywatch/pay/index.cfm; accessed 5 Feburary 2012.
Baldwin Carliss and Kim Clark, 1992, 'Capabilities and Capital Investment: New Perspectives on Capital Budgeting,' *Journal of Applied Corporate Finance*, **5**, 2: 67–87.
Bebchuk, Lucian and Jesse Fried, 2004, *Pay without Performance: The Unfulfilled Promise of Executive Compensation*, Cambridge, MA: Harvard University Press.
Berle, Adolf A. and Gardiner C. Means, 1932, *The Modern Corporation and Private Property*, New York: Macmillan.
Bernile, Gennaro and Gregg A. Jarrell, 2009, 'The Impact of the Options Backdating Scandal on Shareholders,' *Journal of Accounting and Economics*, **47**, 1–2: 2–26.
Blair, Margaret M., 1995, *Ownership and Control: Rethinking Corporate Governance for the Twenty-first Century*, Washington, DC: Brookings Institution.

Byrne, John A., 1994, 'That's Some Pay Cap, Bill,' *Business Week*, 25 April.
Byrne, John A., 1995, 'CEO Pay: Ready for Takeoff,' *Business Week*, 24 April.
Chance, Don M., Raman Kumar and Rebecca B. Todd, 2000, 'The "Repricing" of Executive Stock Options,' *Journal of Financial Economics*, **57**, 1: 129–54.
Christensen, Clayton M., Stephen P. Kaufman and Willy C. Shih, 2008, 'Innovation Killers: How Financial Tools Destroy Your Capacity to Do New Things,' *Harvard Business Review*, **86**, 1: 98–105.
Electronic News, 2005, 'US Could Lose Race for Nanotech Leadership, SIA Panel Says,' *Electronic News*, 16 March.
Ellig, Bruce R., 2007, *The Complete Guide to Executive Compensation*, New York: McGraw-Hill.
Fama, Eugene F. and Michael C. Jensen, 1983a, 'Agency Problems and Residual Claims,' *Journal of Law and Economics*, **26**, 2: 327–49.
Fama, Eugene F. and Michael C. Jensen, 1983b, 'Separation of Ownership and Control,' *Journal of Law and Economics*, **26**, 2: 301–25.
Forelle, Charles and James Bandler, 2006, 'The Perfect Payday: Some CEOs Reap Millions by Landing Stock Options When they are Most Valuable; Luck – or Something Else?' *Wall Street Journal*, 18 March, A:1.
Fried, Jesse M., 2000, 'Insider Signaling and Insider Trading with Repurchase Tender Offers,' *University of Chicago Law Review*, **67**, 2: 421–77.
Fried, Jesse M., 2001, 'Open Market Repurchases: Signaling or Market Opportunism,' *Theoretical Inquiries in Law*, **2**, 2: 1–30.
Jensen, Michael C., 1986, 'Agency Costs of Free Cash Flow, Corporate Finance, and Takeovers,' *American Economic Review*, **76**, 2: 323–9.
Jensen, Michael C. and Kevin J. Murphy, 1990, 'Performance Pay and Top Management Incentives,' *Journal of Political Economy*, **98**, 2: 225–64.
Lazonick, William, 1992, 'Controlling the Market for Corporate Control: The Historical Significance of Managerial Capitalism,' *Industrial and Corporate Change*, **1**, 3: 445–88.
Lazonick, William, 2002, 'Innovative Enterprise and Historical Transformation,' *Enterprise & Society*, **3**, 1: 35–54.
Lazonick, William, 2004, 'Corporate Restructuring,' in Stephen Ackroyd, Rose Batt, Paul Thompson and Pamela Tolbert, eds, *The Oxford Handbook of Work and Organization*, Oxford: Oxford University Press, pp. 577–601.
Lazonick, William, 2008, 'Entrepreneurial Ventures and the Developmental State: Lessons from the Advanced Economies,' World Institute of Development Economics Research Discussion Paper No. dp2008-01.
Lazonick, William, 2009a, *Sustainable Prosperity in the New Economy? Business Organization and High-tech Employment in the United States*, Kalamazoo, MI: Upjohn Institute for Employment Research.
Lazonick, William, 2009b, 'The New Economy Business Model and the Crisis of U.S. Capitalism,' *Capitalism and Society*, **4**, 2.
Lazonick, William, 2010a, 'Insurance Executives: A Big Part of Our Healthcare Problem,' *The Huffington Post*, 16 March; available at http://www.huffingtonpost.com/william-lazonick/insurance-executives-a-bi_b_501093.html; accessed 4 February 2012.
Lazonick, William, 2010b, 'The Chandlerian Corporation and the Theory of Innovative Enterprise,' *Industrial and Corporate Change*, **19**, 2: 317–49.
Lazonick, William, 2010c, 'The Explosion of Executive Pay and the Erosion of American Prosperity,' *Entreprises et Histoire*, No. 57: 141–64.
Lazonick, William and Mary O'Sullivan, 2000, 'Maximizing Shareholder Value: A New Ideology for Corporate Governance,' *Economy and Society*, **29**, 1: 13–35.
Lazonick, William, and Oner Tulum, 2009, 'US Biopharmaceutical Finance and the Crisis of the Biotech Industry,' University of Massachusetts Lowell Center for Industrial Competitiveness, July.
Lie, Erik, 2005, 'On the Timing of CEO Stock Option Awards,' *Management Science*, **51**, 5: 802–12.
Louis, Henock and Hal White, 2007, 'Do Managers Intentionally Use Repurchase Tender Offers to Signal Private Information?: Evidence from Firm Financial Reporting Behavior,' *Journal of Financial Economics*, **85**, 1: 205–33.
Milberg, William, 2008, 'Shifting Sources and Uses of Profits: Sustaining U.S. Financialization with Global Value Chains,' *Economy and Society*, **37**, 3: 420–51.
National Research Council, 1999, *Funding a Revolution: Government Support for Computing Research*, Washington, DC: National Academies Press.
O'Sullivan, Mary, 2004, 'What Drove the U.S. Stock Market in the Last Century?' INSEAD Working Paper.
Rappaport, Alfred, 1981, 'Selecting Strategies that Create Shareholder Value,' *Harvard Business Review*, **59**, 3: 139–49.
Rappaport, Alfred, 1983, 'Corporate Performance Standards and Shareholder Value,' *Journal of Business Strategy*, **3**, 4: 28–38.

Reich, Robert B., 2008, *Supercapitalism: The Transformation of Business, Democracy, and Everyday Life*, New York: Vintage Books.

US Congress, 2008, 'Democrats Tell Big Oil: Spend More on Production and Renewable Energy, Less on Stock Buybacks Before Making Demands for New Drilling Leases,' *US Congressional Documents and Publications*, 31 July, available at http://menendez.senate.gov/newsroom/press/release/?id=3a97a346-d592-46a9-9844-bc27ab1ec279; accessed 5 February 2012.

US Congress, 2010, Economic Report of the President, US Government Printing Office.

Vermaelen, Theo, 2005. *Share Repurchases: Foundations and Trends in Finance*, Hanover, MA: Now Publishers.

26 Innovation platforms, complexity and the knowledge-intensive firm
Pier Paolo Patrucco

26.1 INTRODUCTION

Economic approaches have evolved in parallel with the firm, acquiring an increasing centrality in the dynamics of innovation. As a matter of fact, only in quite recent years technological advances – long considered an exogenous variable, uncontrollable and not influenced by economic actors – has taken a leading role in the economic literature, so that it is now considered a factor crucial to the competitive positioning of business organizations and the key to growth of modern post-industrial societies (Aghion and Howitt, 1997; Acemoglu, 2008).

The black box of standard economic theory (a production function that transforms inputs into outputs through strategies not investigated with the tools of economists), has been gradually redefined thanks to the insights of different approaches that have taken place in the history of economics. These led to a new understanding of the firm as a learning organization that adopts intentional strategies for the improvement and expansion of its technological capabilities, and ultimately, to strengthen its innovative potential.

While throughout most of the twentieth century the large company that innovates through vertical integration of R&D, taking advantage of economies of scale and scope, has been regarded as the locus par excellence of the production of technological knowledge and innovation, a range of factors have emerged recently – such as the increasing environmental turbulence, the intensification of competition and the increasing complexity of the innovation process. These factors have radically changed the framework and questioned the viability of the vertically integrated model as the more appropriate strategy for the production and coordination of innovation.

The economic literature is in fact showing a new, growing interest in cooperative relations as governance mechanisms for the innovation process, helping to reopen the debate on the virtues of decentralized organization of innovative and productive activities. Innovation studies (e.g., Powell, 1990; Uzzi, 1997; Burt, 2000; Helper et al., 2000; Kogut, 2000; Ozman, 2009) gathered a growing consensus on the idea that networks are loci of innovation because they favour interactions between different firms, and support the access to a wide range of complementary technologies and expertise, which becomes an opportunity to recombine existing resources held by individual firms in new knowledge. Combining the flexibility of markets with the visible hand of organization, inter-firm ties reduce the costs of access to dispersed and diverse sources of knowledge, which is then considered the main driver of innovation and new knowledge generation.

This chapter traces the main characteristics of the shift in the organization of innovative and knowledge-intensive activities from the vertically integrated R&D model to the distributed and networked model. In particular, it integrates the contributions of the economics of innovation about the importance of knowledge sourced externally as an input in the knowledge production of the firm, with recent insights provided by complexity theory about the importance of changing patterns of interactions among organizations. It highlights the characteristics and virtues of the 'innovation platform' (Consoli and Patrucco, 2008 and 2011; Gawer, 2009a) as a model for the governance of innovation in which scholarly research is showing a growing interest because it combines some of the advantages of managerial control with the benefits of distributed resources and collective action typical of the network.

26.2 INNOVATION AS A CLOSED ACTIVITY AND THE DEMISE OF THE VERTICALLY INTEGRATED COMPANY AS LOCUS OF TECHNOLOGICAL KNOWLEDGE

The traditional approach in industrial economics and economics of innovation during the last century supported the argument about the superiority of the Fordist firm, considered the most efficient organizational model for the production of technological innovation because of the benefits stemming from R&D economies of scale and scope, and internal economies of learning (e.g., Penrose, 1959; Chandler, 1990).

This view rested on a model of knowledge production that can be described as 'closed' (Chesbrough, 2003), strongly oriented within the firm, which was based on the principle that successful innovation requires control. According to this view, firms compete on the basis of their ability to internally generate, develop, market and appropriate new ideas and new products.

The logic of closed innovation creates a powerful virtuous circle, already identified and described by Schumpeter (1942), based upon the following factors: (1) R&D laboratories internal to the firm producing new knowledge, inventions and discoveries; (2) ideas that have emerged from R&D are filtered and selected, and then developed, leading to the introduction of new products and services; (3) the introduction of new products and services to achieve higher sales volumes and therefore higher profit margins; (4) extra profits generate greater availability of resources that firms can invest in new R&D, which in turn leads to new discoveries, renewing the virtuous circle.

The strategy of internal R&D accumulation was so efficient in creating economies of scale and scope in the twentieth century that in many industrial sectors natural monopolies emerged (Chandler, 1990). Using the knowledge produced through their R&D labs, firms increased their ability to develop new products, as well as new properties and applications for existing products, thus benefiting from economies of scope. Economies of scale achieved through extensive R&D provide important entry barriers against potential entrants. Internal R&D was, in this context, a strategic asset that supports a cumulative production of innovations and consequently the strengthening of competitive positions. Only large firms with considerable resources available to invest in large-scale and long-term research programmes could in fact compete on such markets for innovation, appropriating at the same time – as an effect of the application of intellectual property rights – the greatest part of the returns stemming from their private R&D investments. The benefits of economies of scale and scope have thus encouraged the growth of a model, typical of the American economy, of proprietary innovation, in which large firms internalize firm-specific R&D and subsequently market the results of such knowledge production process (Herrigel and Zeitlin, 2004).

Henry Chesbrough (2003) recently described the pattern of production and organization of knowledge resulting from these dynamics in an image of fortified castles, mostly self-sufficient, set in an arid and poor landscape. Through this metaphor Chesbrough stresses a situation where knowledge is closely protected and developed within the boundaries of firms, while contacts with the external environment (universities and other centres for technological and scientific research) are very infrequent.

For most of the twentieth century this paradigm and the corresponding organization of industrial R&D work efficiently, leading to important discoveries and significant commercial successes. Since the 1990s, however, different factors have emerged that led to a rapid and radical transformation of the environment in which firms compete, raising questions about the applicability of this model to the new innovation landscape. First, the increasing environmental turbulence (for instance, due to greater instability in prices, the cost of inputs, demand) and the intensification of global competition reduces the effectiveness of managerial planning and command. In other words, it is increasingly difficult for management to predict with a sufficient degree of confidence the evolution of all variables, and is therefore less easy to organize their activities in a coherent and rational way. Second, the increased complexity of the innovative dynamics, the acceleration in the process of obsolescence of technology and the significant increase in development costs of innovation reduce the degree of autonomy of enterprises. No company is able to completely dominate all technological and organizational skills and have all the necessary financial resources to develop new knowledge on its own. Finally, and consequently, the firm, in order to search for new knowledge to apply to its innovative activity should explore an increasing range of sources. As highlighted, for instance, by Davenport and Prusak (1998) new and different players are emerging in the innovation system: in addition to public research laboratories and private, large R&D labs, other organizations are involved in the production of new knowledge, such as science parks, non-profit centres, university laboratories, start-ups, incubators, as well as supranational research networks (Foray, 2004).

The generation of knowledge is more and more seen as a widespread and distributed phenomenon, where firms search, select and integrate external knowledge as a strategic activity. This new context challenges the viability of the closed innovation model to access, develop and commercialize new ideas to market and contribute to undermine the 'knowledge monopolies' built in the twentieth century through centralized R&D (Chesbrough et al., 2006).

The progressive vanishing out (Langlois, 2004) of the vertically integrated model of R&D implies that the closed and linear logic, which saw innovation as a direct and almost automatic result of internal R&D investment and learning by doing, should be replaced: not only should firms reorganize their innovative strategy in order to benefit from external sources of knowledge and effectively integrate these with that produced internally (Chesbrough et al., 2006), but entire industries, such as recently in the case of the car sector (Enrietti and Patrucco, 2011), should also reconfigure their borders and their structures to benefit from expertise and technologies developed elsewhere, for instance in other sectors.

26.3 COLLECTIVE KNOWLEDGE AND THE THEORY OF COMPLEXITY: OPENING THE BOUNDARIES OF THE FIRM

In this context, the theory of complexity is gaining momentum in the economics of innovation. Complexity theory seems to emerge as a new paradigm able to explain the structural properties and dynamic processes of generation and dissemination of knowledge and innovation. Complexity theory seems to be a useful theoretical framework for understanding the characteristics of the processes of creation and dissemination of knowledge, as well as the characteristics and effects of structures for the coordination of knowledge between different organizations (Antonelli, 2008 and 2011; Lane et al., 2009).

Complex systems consist of a set of heterogeneous actors that interact to create new knowledge and organize their activities over time. In particular, within a complex system (Barkley-Rosser, 1999; Foster, 2005; Hanusch and Pyka, 2007):

- The players are heterogeneous with respect to their skills and the knowledge they possess.
- Each player has access to specific pieces of knowledge, and therefore is characterized by limited cognitive resources, so the creation of new knowledge takes place by trial and error and constant reviews of the conduct.
- The interaction between the actors involved in the system plays a crucial role as it is through interactions that actors can learn, access new skills and change their behaviour, thus creating mutual adaptation processes between individuals and between these and their environment.
- Complex systems are non-decomposable: aggregate dynamics cannot be reduced to micro-behaviours but are instead precisely the result of the interaction between the constituent elements of the system. A change in the composition of the system, that is, a change in one of its elements, implies a change in the aggregate dynamics.

The evolutionary dynamics of complex systems thus depends on the interactions that occur between individual actors and between micro- and macro-elements. Precisely because of this non-decomposability, these systems are: (1) inherently dynamic (Consoli and Patrucco, 2011): indeed, the actions of individual agents and the evolution of the environment affect each other, therefore can only be understood in historical perspective; (2) characterized by simultaneous changes and reconfigurations at different stages of production that make the existing know-how obsolete, requiring new skills and forcing organizations to acquire and develop new skills (Patrucco, 2011).

Recent advances provided by studies on innovation dynamics can fruitfully enrich this perspective. Indeed, in a complex environment characterized by continuous changes in product features and technologies, radical uncertainty and increasing specialization, individual firms can hardly manage all the technological capabilities needed in the process of generation of new knowledge. Each agent has specific and limited cognitive resources, and therefore dominates specialized modules and complementary technology and knowledge; each firm is therefore unique in relation to its ability to innovate (Cohen and Levinthal, 1989).

In line with the pioneering contribution of Nelson and Winter (1982), who viewed economic change as the product of the actions of actors who possess idiosyncratic skills and abilities, technological knowledge, because of high specialization and differentiation, is therefore characterized by very limited levels of interchangeability and substitutability, and high levels of complementarity.

The portions of knowledge sourced externally may largely differ from those possessed by the firm. The implementation of screening processes and strategies of absorption is a necessary condition for access to existing external knowledge, as well as for the efficient exploitation of externalities in the creation of new knowledge. This implies that the R&D conducted internally takes on new functions: its role is no longer limited to the production of new knowledge, but includes the identification and understanding of external knowledge available, the selection and integration of the relevant portions with internal knowledge in order to produce more complex combinations of technologies and capabilities.

Some authors (Cohen and Levinthal, 1989 and 1990) have in fact stressed the 'two faces' of R&D and the importance of investing in internal R&D in order to be able to use knowledge sourced externally. It has been suggested, in other words, that the function of R&D is more and more to conduct research that enhances the ability of the firm to identify, assimilate, integrate and ultimately exploit external knowledge, thereby developing absorptive capacity.

In this regard, the process of creating new technological knowledge is increasingly understood as a collective process based on a high degree of complementarity between internal R&D and learning and technological resources acquired externally from other firms (e.g., clients and suppliers, competitors) as well as research organizations (e.g., universities, public labs, technology transfer centres). The integration of the skills and knowledge produced externally requires the implementation of specific strategies for the identification, transaction, acquisition and absorption of external knowledge. Technological communication is therefore a key strategy for the firm to be able to exploit the complementarities between internal and external innovative resources and achieve increasing returns in the innovative process. In this sense, the collective nature of knowledge is not only the effect of a static distribution or sharing of resources, but necessarily requires mutual and intentional participation of different actors in order to take advantage of the interdependencies and the spillovers arising from the well-known indivisibility and complementarity that characterize the knowledge production processes. It is, in conclusion, a process that requires the dynamic coordination between heterogeneous actors, as opposed to the idea of static allocation of resources. Effective distribution of knowledge and opportunities for recombination can in fact take place only if the costs of assimilation of external knowledge are low and with the active communication between agents (Patrucco, 2008).

In short, the production of new knowledge requires the implementation of specific activities aimed at coordinating activities (Richardson, 1972), and thus requires a collective effort aimed at creating and maintaining dynamic complementarity between skills otherwise scattered, fragmentary and incomplete (Consoli and Patrucco, 2008). It is thus a process that takes shape through the interaction between the individual initiatives of specialized and heterogeneous and collective mechanisms that are implemented to align the objectives and incentives of the different actors (Antonelli, 2010; Consoli and Patrucco, 2011).

What was previously described as a process essentially closed, implemented within the boundaries of large firms, is now viewed as an open environment within which firms can create new ideas and knowledge by making their boundaries less defined and subject to continuous redefinition in order to be able to exploit both internal and external technological competencies (Chesbrough, 2003; Chesbrough et al., 2006). In this respect a growing empirical evidence (e.g., Schilling, 2008; Love and Roper, 2009; Ozman, 2009) views the single knowledge-intensive and innovative firm as part of a wider network of organizations that collectively operate according to collaborative innovation. It is clear that firms need to rethink their organizational structures in order to define new models of coordination of knowledge production capable of managing the current complex dynamics of innovation.

26.4   MODULARITY AND NETWORKS IN THE ORGANIZATION OF KNOWLEDGE AND INNOVATION

The perspective outlined above leads us to consider innovation as the result of collaborations developed between various knowledge-intensive organizations. Networks have been analysed by an established tradition of scholars from different disciplines with different interests and research approaches, which have in turn focused on different aspects of inter-firm relations. Some authors, for example, adopted a sociological perspective, emphasizing the non-economic basis of social exchange and the importance of interpersonal relationships for cooperation, efficiency production and innovativeness (Granovetter, 1973). Others have instead focused on the institutional network defined as a third alternative with respect to the market and the vertically integrated firm (Williamson, 1975). Other perspectives have also analysed the impact of inter-organizational networks on the probability of survival of firms (Uzzi, 1997), the competitive dynamics and organizational performance (Lorenzoni and Lipparini, 1999), the development of new skills and organizational learning process (McEvily and Zaheer, 1999), and last but not least the process of technological innovation (Freeman, 1991).

In particular, in the late twentieth century a broad and intense debate developed on which is the more efficient organizational form for managing and organizing the processes of knowledge creation and dissemination, and ultimately the organization of innovative activities within complex systems (Consoli and Patrucco, 2011).

In order to broaden their knowledge base and coordinate their innovative activity, firms can choose among a continuum of organizational solutions, which can be summarized in three main categories:

- vertically integrated firms focused on managerial command and authority;
- modular organizations based on outsourcing and market transactions;
- hybrid solutions such as collaborative networks between complementary partners.

A wide range of economic contributions offers many insights on the benefits and challenges that each of these solutions entails, and as we have already emphasized, the closed innovation model, based on the vertical integration of R&D and learning has dominated for much of the twentieth century.

Recently, however, there has been growing consensus among innovation scholars on the idea that if companies are not able to develop a sufficient level of innovative capacity by means of internal investments, they can implement hybrid solutions based on different forms of strategic alliances and inter-organizational ties aimed at minimizing the costs of external coordination and maximizing the creative contributions of individual partners. This finding has paved the way for the analysis of various forms (more or less radical) of decentralization, specialization and division of labour in production and innovation.

Thus, a wide stream of studies on the organization of innovation and technological knowledge has turned attention to modular solutions, based on market transactions and outsourcing. In these models, innovative activities and production are not closely integrated and coordination between the two processes takes place through adherence to shared goals and common standards. In these circumstances, the adoption of mechanisms such as standard interfaces ensures the integration of several components designed and made by different and separated units, avoiding specific and strict coordination mechanisms as the interface itself provides an implicit form of communication between all the different units involved in the innovation process (Schilling, 2008).

Studies on modularity are based on some classic contributions of Herbert Simon (e.g., 1962 and 2002) on complexity. Simon describes complex systems as hierarchical entities, that is, architectures consisting of a plurality of ordered items, where the position of each unit in the architecture determines interactions between the elements. In particular, Simon defines complex systems as loosely coupled systems, that is, the interactions between different subsystems are much weaker than the interactions within the individual elements of the same subsystem. In other words, in these systems individual elements remain fundamentally separate and independent from each other, and the characteristics and actions of an element can change without causing changes in the properties of other elements of the system (Consoli and Patrucco, 2011). In sum, according to Simon, near-decomposability identified the ultimate property of complex systems.

From this perspective, the literature on modular organizations has deepened the conditions in which they are preferable to integration (Baldwin and Clark, 1997; Arora et al., 1998; Langlois, 2002). For when a system is extended and the connections between elements and subsystems become especially numerous, coordination through an integrated structure is almost impossible. Modular organizations are most efficient in these cases, since by definition they involve breaking the system into subsystems that interact almost independently on the basis of weak connections through common interfaces. In particular, Baldwin and Clark (1997) and Langlois (2002) consider that the organization of production and innovation through modular strategies, that is, an approach that considers the quasi-decomposable system, represents the most appropriate and efficient way to organize and coordinate complex technologies and systems.

According to this approach, firms, in order to innovate, can decide to adopt an integrated organizational structure or modular according to the characteristics of technology and knowledge they rely upon: the more articulated and interconnected is the knowledge and technological expertise necessary to innovate, the more efficient it is to adopt a modular architecture and the use of formal contracts and market transactions, and conversely, the lower the number of elements that must interact to generate innovation, the easier is their coordination through vertical integration of R&D (Chesbrough and Teece, 1996).

The loose coupling strategy, however, has limitations. In particular, activities that require frequent exchanges of tacit knowledge or complex mechanisms also require the presence of more rigid integration than generally a modular organization can produce Schilling, 2008). If the task requires a form of intense and continuous coordination in time, the development process is conducted more efficiently within an integrated company, which maintains a closer integration between the partners involved.

Moreover, it has been highlighted that complex systems, by definition, are not decomposable into discrete and separate components as stated in the modular approach (Consoli and Patrucco, 2011). A key feature of complex systems relies on the non-decomposability of its individual components and subsystems, as changes in the behaviours or characteristics of a given firm – through feedback processes arising from the interaction between the elements – induce transformations in the interconnected organizations belonging to the system. Finally, the empirical evidence shows that, when dealing with decisions related to the organization of innovative activity, firms are not only swinging between purely modular or purely integrated models. Rather, firms are also able to use a wide range of inter-organizational solutions in order to combine the advantages of both solutions (ibid.).

The literature shows a growing emphasis on networks as a place of innovation. Networks facilitate coordination and integration of complementary pieces of knowledge in contexts characterized by complexity, uncertainty and dispersion of knowledge among heterogeneous sources, avoiding the costs and inefficiencies often related to complete integration. Much of the analysis focuses on the nature of the relationship and the roles played by different actors within the networks. The structure of the network received much attention in particular and two opposite configurations emerge: one characterized by strong and redundant ties, and one network characterized by structural holes and weak ties.

According to some authors, for example, networks characterized by strong ties were generally associated with intensive exchange of information, effective mechanisms to transfer tacit knowledge, and mutual trust between partners. Therefore, those links would be more efficient for the exchange and communication of complex knowledge, by enabling the establishment of cooperative behaviours through more efficient and repeated interactions as well as a balanced distribution of power within the network (Coleman, 1990). In contrast, other authors argued that networks characterized by weak connections and structural holes, that is, firms that act as brokers, directing and coordinating the flow of knowledge between companies or business groups not directly connected with each other, represent the most efficient solutions because of the benefits arising from a (partially) hierarchical organizational form (Burt, 1992).

Empirical evidence shows that both configurations are related to an improvement in innovation performance of firms and Orton and Weick (1990) and Brusoni and Prencipe (2009) tried to reconcile the two streams of literature by developing a somewhat different notion of loosely coupled networks.

Orton and Weick describe inter-firm networks based on two parameters: first, distinctiveness, namely the ability to manage and produce a range of complementary technological skills to innovate; second, responsiveness, that is, the intentional and active management of inter-organizational structures in order to provide the necessary cohesion of the network and coordinate learning from different and dispersed sources of knowledge. Under this conceptualization, 'if there is responsiveness without distinctiveness, the system is tightly coupled. If there is distinctiveness without responsiveness, the system is decoupled. If there is both distinctiveness and responsiveness, the system is loosely coupled' (Orton and Weick, 1990, p. 205).

It is precisely in this context that the notion of innovation platforms may yield it analytical scope. System integrators that through a hierarchical structure govern and coordinate the interactions between organizations not directly connected to each other characterize innovation platforms. In this sense, companies that act as system integrators are specific forms of structural holes at the centre of the flows of different portions of knowledge that are the basis of complex technological innovations.

Innovation platforms are specific organizational forms through which economic agents and their organizations acquire and coordinate innovative capabilities and new knowledge (Patrucco, 2011). The concept of platform expresses the view that innovation occurs when effective partnerships are implemented, based on the convergence of incentives, on the structured complementarity between the skills of a variety of heterogeneous actors, and when a clear direction of mutual interactions emerges, enhancing group cohesion and organization of the intrinsic complexity of the system around a common purpose and shared goals (Antonelli, 2010).

Efficient platforms appear when the various incentives and complementary capabilities of a multiplicity of actors involved in a heterogeneous network are organized and aligned to ensure cohesion and coordination of the network of knowledge exchanges that characterizes the innovation process. As we will argue below, innovation platforms, combining elements of hierarchical coordination and elements of decentralization of skills and innovative activities, are emerging in many areas where innovation is the result of processes and activities carried out collectively.

26.5 INNOVATION PLATFORMS AS GOVERNANCE FORMS FOR THE ORGANIZATION OF COMPLEX INNOVATION SYSTEMS

As already mentioned, in a context of strong specialization and differentiation economic actors possess portions of idiosyncratic and highly specific knowledge. This implies a high degree of complementarity between the technological expertise and a low degree of substitutability, and consequently some difficulty and stickiness (von Hippel, 1994) to exchange knowledge between firms. In this context, it is essential for the individual firm to be able to expand the range of internal portions through the accessing and integration of external knowledge (Consoli and Patrucco, 2011). The crucial problem for economic analysis therefore becomes to understand how firms can acquire and coordinate new technological knowledge.

In this context, innovation platforms are receiving much attention. The empirical evidence shows the emergence of this type of coordination structure in many areas where innovation and production of new knowledge are the result of the integration of complementary and heterogeneous skills, widespread and dispersed among specialized actors (such as automotive, banking, electronics, and software firms). One of the key points of the logic behind the creation of platforms is in fact to maximize the variety of contribu-

ons from heterogeneous sources of knowledge, although accompanied by the scope
f coherence and consistency through a hierarchical structure (Consoli and Patrucco,
011).

Innovation platforms in this sense represent a significant organizational innovation
lternative to the integrated firm, the market and the network themselves. Rather, plat-
orms constitute a new and specific form of governance of knowledge that emerges as a
esult of the dynamics of complex systems (ibid). In particular, they can be defined as a
ierarchical network, that is, a network in which interactions do not emerge and evolve
pontaneously, as, for instance, in the traditional literature on industrial districts, or as
uggested by the theory of complexity, but where the key nodes (organizations) exert an
ffect on directing the behaviour of other actors, influencing and leading such behaviour
nd the evolution of the system as a whole (Consoli and Patrucco, 2008).

The distinctive feature of these organizational forms is the active search for the exploi-
ation of complementarity between different activities. In other words, innovation plat-
orms are structured and designed to achieve precise and specific innovative targets. In
his context, as mentioned above, they play their key role as platform leaders.

Given the increasing spread of this phenomenon in different industries, platforms have
ecently been the object of numerous studies of the economics and management of innovation (see also for a review of this literature, Gawer and Cusumano, 2002; Consoli and
Patrucco, 2008; Gawer, 2009a; Gawer, 2009b; Patrucco, 2011). It is now recognized that
he emergence of platforms profoundly impacts on industrial dynamics, creating new
orms of competition and paving the way for the creation of new cooperative relations
nd inter-organizational innovation processes (Gawer, 2009a).

Interestingly, despite that the notion of platform has been used and tested in different
ields of scholarly research, the meaning of the term varies considerably among different research areas. It is therefore useful to refer to the typology recently elaborated by
Annabelle Gawer (2009b), which identifies three basic types of platforms, characterized
by several features related to the context in which they develop and the objectives for
which they are created:

- *Internal platforms* are basically product platforms that develop within the boundaries of the firm. In this sense, these can be defined as organizations to produce
  goods designed for specific markets, though designed to be easily modified and
  transformed through the addition, replacement or removal of certain components
  or characteristics (ibid.). In other words they consist of a set of interfaces designed
  intentionally to produce a common structure from which can be efficiently developed a bundle of products. The advantages of this platform lie in a reduction of
  fixed costs, greater efficiency and flexibility in developing new products through
  reuse of common parts, and particularly the capacity to produce a wide range of
  products. Furthermore, internal platforms promote economies of scope across different products, thus reducing the exploration of new technological solutions, particularly long especially in the case of complex products (as evidenced by the wide
  use of such platforms in the automotive or aerospace industries). The literature on
  product platforms then implicitly assumes that the firm (usually identified with a
  large manufacturing company that handles both in-house design and production)
  is able to determine in advance the ultimate use of the product, and therefore has

the required expertise for the development of new goods, services or technologies. This approach does not take into account the problem of access and integration of knowledge and innovative capabilities of enterprises and organizations.

- *Supply chain platforms* are made up of a set of subsystems and interfaces that form a common structure from which various partners along the supply chain can develop and produce a range of products. These are, in other words, product platforms shared between different providers or between providers and the firm that integrates the final complex products. In short, while the architecture remains almost unchanged compared to product platforms (the basic design rules are the systematic reuse of modular components and stability of the system architecture), the participation of different economic actors introduces inter-organizational specific collaborative and competitive dynamics.

- In *industry platforms* the products, services or technologies are developed by one or more firms, on the basis of which a large number of other organizations (loosely coupled within the so-called industrial ecosystem) produce and develop complementary products, services or technologies. A clear difference from the supply chain platforms is that, in the case of industry platforms, firms that develop complementary products do not necessarily belong to the same supply chain. Moreover, this type of platform is characterized by the presence of leading firms that introduce innovation into the industry through the coordination and integration of products and components developed separately and independently from each other. The different contributions on industry platforms have shown that such structures affect the competitive dynamics and the level of innovativeness of the sectors in which they are implemented. Indeed, the emergence of a platform can change the balance of power between assemblers and suppliers or can even damage leadership positions. At the same time, these types of platform increase the degree of innovation in complementary products and services. The greater the degree of innovation in components, the greater the value created for the platform and its users through direct and indirect network effects. Regarding the design rules, industry platforms share with other categories previously described the stability of architecture, which represents a milestone in every platform. However, the latter category has some important differences compared to previous ones. Indeed, the logic of design in this case is reversed. In other words, there is no one firm that is configured as master designer (and that in previous cases always coincided with the final assembler), but rather there exist one or more core components that are part of a larger modular structure, and the result of their final integration is unknown or only partially known ex ante. In fact, within industry platforms the precise use and characteristics of the final product is not predetermined. This means that the fundamental design rules for these platforms is the principle that the interfaces must allow the incorporation of new components, as well as the innovation of existing components.

The different characteristics and types shown above demonstrate that platforms may actually take different forms. However, some contributions have also highlighted the key features of platforms.

First, all platforms are based on the reuse and sharing of some core components n complex products or production systems (Baldwin and Woodard, 2009). Thus, for example, Meyer and Lehnerd (1997) describe product platforms as a set of components or modules from which can be effectively created a new line of products. In a broader sense, Robertson and Ulrich (1998) describe them as the set of assets (components, processes and knowledge) shared by a set of products.

One of the most useful definitions for the purposes of this discussion, however, has been provided by Bresnahan and Greenstein (1999), who describe the industry platform as 'a bundle of standard components around which buyers and sellers coordinate efforts' (p.4).

The rationale behind the reuse of some core components is simple but powerful (Baldwin and Woodard, 2009): the fact that some elements are fixed implies that it is often possible to achieve economies of scale by increasing production volumes, spread fixed costs over several product classes and use complementary assets (such as distribution channels and support services) more efficiently. At the same time, firms can create economies of scope at the system level by reducing development costs of variants of products aimed at different target markets.

Baldwin and Woodard (2009) then identify the essential feature of all platforms in their architecture. It is the system architecture that allows obsolete components to be removed and new ones to be involved in setting up new products for specific market niches. It can be argued, therefore, that at the architectural level all types of platforms are equivalent (ibid.), insofar as all platforms are characterized by specific modularity. The overall innovation system is divided into two sets of components: the first characterized by low variability and high reusability, the other by high variability and low reusability. The former are the platform itself, while the others are additional elements and complements. Interoperability is made possible by the creation of interfaces or design rules that specify the mode of interaction between the two elements of the overall innovation process.

The components of the platform are therefore essentially three:

- A core set of components that remain relatively stable over time.
- A set of complementary components characterized by high diversity and high rates of change over time.
- Interfaces that represent the set of rules – or design rules – that govern the relationships between components and allow the core and complementary elements to operate as a coherent system. In particular, interfaces specify the direction and nature of relationships between system elements, and are therefore also stable and long-lasting.

While the core components can evolve over time, under competitive pressure or in response to changes in the external environment, interfaces that govern the interaction between the components represent a stable element, which does not change over time as they are based on identity and internal coherence of the platform. The combination of stability and variability – which allows the creation of novelty without leading to the redefinition of the entire system as a whole or the construction of a new system from the beginning – is achieved through these tools.

The existence of stable, yet versatile, interfaces creates a fundamental property of the platforms, which makes them a particularly useful tool in a complex and constantly changing environment: the ability to evolve. In other words, the platforms are able to evolve, adapting to unexpected changes in the external environment (Baldwin and Woodard, 2009). It has been already mentioned that the architecture divides the system into core components, relatively stable, and peripheral components, variables. The principle of reusing core components reduces the cost of innovation at the systemic level. This means that, under this approach, to generate a new product or to meet a changing external environment does not require a radical change in the whole system, but simply a change in the peripheral components. Consequently, platforms as a whole can be adapted at relatively low cost without losing or changing their identity and their own design incorporation.

For these reasons it has been argued that innovation platforms are particularly advantageous when technological developments are uncertain, and the system must adapt to unpredictable changes (ibid.). In particular, major contributions (Meyer and Lehnerd, 1997; Robertson and Ulrich, 1998; Bresnahan and Greenstein, 1999; Baldwin and Clark, 2000; Gawer and Cusumano, 2002; Baldwin and Woodard, 2009; Gawer, 2009a, 2009b) identify platforms as a means of particularly efficient coordination for the organization of innovative activities in the case of modular technology, managed through loosely coupled structures, that is, that allow the insertion or removal of some peripheral components without affecting the architecture of the system as a whole. According to these approaches modularity plays a fundamental role in the creation of platforms, as the decomposition of complex products or technologies into simpler forms can establish standardized interfaces for components, which in turn enables and facilitates the introduction of new modules (Baldwin and Clark, 2000).

However, as we have already stressed, according to the central assumption of complexity theory, systems are complex precisely because they are irreducible to their constituent elements, which are interconnected with each other and only to a very limited extent interchangeable and replaceable. In other words, their evolution is determined by the interaction between a plurality of heterogeneous actors and in which the conduct and actions of an element can affect and change the trend and characteristics of other elements as well as the system as a whole (Consoli and Patrucco, 2011).

Those approaches that consider innovation as a collective process stressed that the development of a new technology is the result of a sequence of actions and user–producer relations brought forward in time by a number of additional actors. The rate and direction of the innovative process, therefore, are not predetermined but they can develop at any time according to a range of options, precisely affected by the relationships between actors and their behaviours.

The exclusion or inclusion of actors with different profiles in terms of skills and abilities, with different and idiosyncratic innovative capabilities, change the behaviour of the platform strategy, as well as the objectives and actions that can be achieved through a distributed organization of innovation. In this perspective, platform leaders play a crucial role. Concepts such as 'architectural knowledge' (Henderson and Clark, 1990) or 'architectural capability' (Jacobides, 2006) have been introduced precisely to describe the ability, owned by the network leader to coordinate and direct the work of complex organizations, and more precisely to combine elements of traditional integrated models (such as authority and control), with characteristics of modularity (as a sufficient degree f openness) to select the firms, skills and knowledge relevant to be included in the etwork (Gawer, 2009b; Consoli and Patrucco, 2011).

Only intentional convergence and alignment of the different incentives and capabili- es to common goals and strategies can shape the direction and speed of the innovation rocess. Innovation is thus the product of endogenous coalitions organized around spe- ific platforms (Antonelli, 2010). The specialization requires a wider knowledge base of ystem integrators to understand and integrate knowledge and innovations from outside nd to manage outsourced network components and subsystems. Therefore, the core ompetencies of the company acting as system integrators include the ability to govern he processes by which innovation is produced and shared collectively.

In this context the concept of innovation platforms as specific forms of coalitions is merging (Consoli and Patrucco, 2011). In other words, hierarchical networks, focusing on key firms whose strategic conduct directs and coordinates the behaviours and con- ributions of a number of parties, appears as the most appropriate form – as opposed o extreme solutions such as vertical integration or modularization of organizational tructures – for the management of innovative activities in complex environments.

26.6   CONCLUDING REMARKS

According to the seminal work by David Teece (1984), a radical or 'systemic' innovation can be defined as a new product or technology that requires changes in different and connected elements of the system in which it will be placed, in contrast to 'autonomous' innovations that easily fit into the already existing system without calling for consequent, diffused and simultaneous changes elsewhere in the system. Following this contribution, in the literature about the organization and management of innovation, it is often pre- sumed that the more radical or 'systemic', to use Teece's words, innovation is, the more appropriate and efficient is vertical integration and the coordination of the change within a single organization.

Instead, the contributions on innovation platforms point to the fact that, from both a conceptual and practical viewpoint, the crucial element that makes a distributed innova- tion model more desirable rather than vertical integration is not necessarily the novelty of the technology or the knowledge being implemented, but rather how closely comple- mentary are the activities and capabilities required to innovate. Scholars interested in both the governance of innovation and the theory of the firm would do well to rediscover the classical work of G.B. Richardson (1972) about the 'organization of industry' (see also Langlois and Foss, 1999; Langlois, 2004). Richardson argued that systemic produc- tive and technological capabilities are closely related or complementary, and require close coordination and reciprocal adaptation to ensure the success of the innovation. When the firm is not able to acquire and organize such capabilities on its own, some intermediate forms of coordination may emerge, such as licensing, equity agreement and joint venture. More generally, in these cases the governance of innovation relies upon forms of collaboration and networking.

This seems precisely to be the case for innovation platforms, where large coalitions have been implemented with the scope of learning and acquiring technological and pro- ductive competencies sourced externally. Yet, some elements of a hierarchy characterize such models since some directedness is required in order to both guarantee the cohesion of the network and the convergence of the complex system of goals, incentives and inter actions that characterizes such articulated innovation processes.

ACKNOWLEDGEMENTS

I acknowledge the financial support of the European Union D.G. Research with grant number 266959 for the research project 'Policy Incentives for the Creation of Knowledge Methods and Evidence' (PICK-ME), within the context Cooperation Program/Theme 8 Socio-economic Sciences and Humanities (SSH) of the Collegio Carlo Alberto and the University of Turin.

REFERENCES

Acemoglu, D. (2008), *Introduction to Modern Economic Growth*, Princeton, NJ: Princeton University Press.
Aghion, P. and P. Howitt (1997), *Endogeous Growth Theory*, Cambridge, MA: MIT Press.
Antonelli, C. (2008), *Localized Technological Change: Towards the Economics of Complexity*, London Routledge.
Antonelli, C. (2010), From population thinking to organization thinking: Coalitions for innovation, *Regional Studies* **44** (4), 513–18.
Antonelli, C. (2011), The economic complexity of technological change: An introductory frame, in C. Antonelli (ed.), *System Dynamics of Technological Change*, Cheltenham, UK and Northampton, MA, USA: Edward Elgar.
Arora, A., A. Gambardella and E. Rullani (1998), Division of labour and the locus of inventive activity, *Journal of Management and Governance* **1** (1), 123–40.
Baldwin, C.Y. and K.B. Clark (1997), Managing in an age of modularity, *Harvard Business Review* **75** (5), 84–93.
Baldwin, C.Y. and K.B. Clark (2000), *Design Rules: The Power of Modularity*, vol. I, Cambridge, MA: MIT Press.
Baldwin, C.Y. and C.J. Woodard (2009), The architecture of platforms: A unified view, in A. Gawer (ed.), *Platforms, Markets and Innovation*, Cheltenham, UK and Northampton, MA, USA: Edward Elgar.
Barkley-Rosser Jr., J. (1999), On the complexities of complex economic systems, *Journal of Economic Perspectives* **13** (4), 169–92.
Bresnahan, T.F. and S. Greenstein (1999), Technological competition and the structure of computer industry, *Journal of Industrial Economics* **47** (1), 1–40.
Brusoni, S. and A. Prencipe (2009), Design rules for platform leaders, in A. Gawer (ed.), *Platforms, Markets and Innovation*, Cheltenham, UK and Northampton, MA, USA: Edward Elgar.
Burt, R.S. (1992), *Structural Holes: The Social Structure of Competition*, Cambridge, MA: Harvard University Press.
Burt, R. (2000), The network structure of social capital, in S.I. Sutton and B.M. Staw (eds) *Research in Organizational Behavior*, Greenwich, CT: JAI Press.
Chandler, A.D. (1990), *Scale and Scope: The Dynamics of Industrial Capitalism*, Cambridge, MA: Belknap Press.
Chesbrough, H.W. (2003), *Open Innovation: The New Imperative for Creating and Profiting from Technology*, Cambridge, MA: Harvard Business School Press.
Chesbrough, H.W. and D.J. Teece (1996), When is virtual virtuous? Organizing for innovation, *Harvard Business Review* **74** (1), 65–73.
Chesbrough, H.W., W. Vanhaverbeke and J. West (eds) (2006), *Open Innovation: Researching a New Paradigm*, Oxford: Oxford University Press.
Cohen, W. and D. Levinthal (1989), Innovation and learning: The two faces of R&D, *Economic Journal* **99** (397), 569–96.
Cohen, W. and D. Levinthal (1990), Absorptive capacity: A new perspective on learning and innovation, *Administrative Science Quarterly* **35** (1), 128–52.

Coleman, J. (1990), *The Foundations of Social Theory*, Cambridge, MA: Harvard University Press.

Consoli, D. and P.P. Patrucco (2008), Innovation platforms and the governance of knowledge: Evidence from Italy and the UK, *Economics of Innovation and New Technology* **17** (7), 699–716.

Consoli, D. and P.P. Patrucco (2011), Complexity and the coordination of technological knowledge: The case of innovation platforms, in C. Antonelli (ed.), *System Dynamics of Technological Change*, Cheltenham, UK and Northampton, MA, USA: Edward Elgar.

Davenport, T.H. and L. Prusak (1998), *Working Knowledge: Managing What Your Organization Knows*, Cambridge, MA: Harvard Business School Press.

Enrietti, A. and P.P. Patrucco (2011), Systemic innovation and organizational change in the car industry: Electric vehicle innovation platforms, *Journal of Industrial and Business Economics* **38** (1), 85–106.

Foray, D. (2004), *The Economics of Knowledge*, Cambridge, MA: MIT Press.

Foster, J. (2005), From simplistic to complex systems in economics, *Cambridge Journal of Economics* **29** (6), 873–92.

Freeman, C. (1991), Networks of innovators: A synthesis of research issues, *Research Policy* **20** (5), 499–514.

Gawer, A. (2009a), Platforms, markets and innovation: An introduction, in A. Gawer (ed.), *Platforms, Markets and Innovation*, Cheltenham, UK and Northampton, MA, USA: Edward Elgar.

Gawer, A. (2009b), Platform dynamics and strategies: From product to services, in A. Gawer (ed.), *Platforms, Markets and Innovation*, Cheltenham, UK and Northampton, MA, USA: Edward Elgar.

Gawer, A. and M.A. Cusumano (2002), *Platform Leadership: How Intel, Microsoft, and Cisco Drive Industry Innovation*, Cambridge, MA: Harvard Business School Press.

Granovetter, M. (1973), The strength of weak ties, *American Journal of Sociology* **78** (6), 1360–80.

Hanusch, H. and A. Pyka (2007), Principles of neo-Schumpeterian economics, *Cambridge Journal of Economics* **31** (2), 275–89.

Helper, S., J.P. MacDuffie and C. Sabel (2000), Pragmatic collaborations: Advancing knowledge while controlling opportunism, *Industrial and Corporate Change* **9** (3), 443–88.

Henderson, R.M. and K.B. Clark (1990), Architectural innovation: The reconfiguration of existing systems and the failure of established firms, *Administrative Science Quarterly* **35** (1), 9–30.

Herrigel, G. and J. Zeitlin (eds) (2004), *Americanization and its Limits: Reworking US Technology and Management in Postwar Europe and Japan*, Oxford: Oxford University Press.

Jacobides, M.G. (2006), The architecture and design of organizational capabilities, *Industrial and Corporate Change* **15** (1), 151–71.

Kogut, B. (2000), The network as knowledge: Generative rules and the emergence of structure, *Strategic Management Journal* **21** (3), 405–25.

Lane, D., D. Pumain, S. van der Leew and G. West (eds) (2009), *Complexity Perspectives on Innovation and Social Change*, Berlin: Springer.

Langlois, R.N. (2002), Modularity in technology and organization, *Journal of Economic Behavior & Organization*, **49** (1), 19–37.

Langlois, R.N. (2004), Chandler in a larger frame: Markets, transaction costs, and organizational form in history, *Enterprise & Society* **5** (3), 355–75.

Langlois, Richard N. and Nicolai J. Foss (1999), Capabilities and governance: The rebirth of production in the theory of economic organization, *Kyklos* **52** (2), 201–18.

Lorenzoni, G. and A. Lipparini (1999), The leveraging of interfirm relationships as a distinctive organizational capability: A longitudinal study, *Strategic Management Journal* **20** (4), 317–38.

Love, J.H. and S. Roper (2009), Organizing the innovation process: Complementarities in innovation networking, *Industry and Innovation* **16** (3), 273–90.

McEvily, B. and A. Zaheer (1999), Bridging ties: A source of firm heterogeneity in competitive capabilities, *Strategic Management Journal* **20** (12), 1133–56.

Meyer, M.H. and A.P. Lehnerd (1997), *The Power of Product Platforms: Building Value and Cost Leadership*, New York: Free Press.

Nelson, R. and S.G. Winter (1982), *An Evolutionary Theory of Economic Change*, Cambridge, MA: Harvard University Press.

Orton, J.D. and K.E. Weick (1990), Loosely coupled systems: A reconceptualization, *Academy of Management Review* **15** (2), 203–23.

Ozman, M. (2009), Inter-firm networks and innovation: A survey of literature, *Economics of Innovation and New Technology* **18** (1), 39–67.

Patrucco, P.P. (2008), The economics of collective knowledge and technological communication, *Journal of Technology Transfer* **33** (6), 579–99.

Patrucco, P.P. (2011), Changing network structure in the organization of knowledge: The innovation platform in the evidence of the automobile system in Turin, *Economics of Innovation and New Technology* **25** (2), 477–93.

Penrose, E. (1959), *The Theory of the Growth of the Firm*, Oxford: Oxford University Press.

Powell, W. (1990), Neither market nor hierarchy: Network forms of organization, *Research in Organizationa* *Behavior* **12** (2), 295–336.

Richardson, G.B. (1972), The organization of industry, *Economic Journal* **82** (327), 883–96.

Robertson, D. and K. Ulrich (1998), Planning for product platforms, *Sloan Management Review* **39** (4), 19–31

Schilling, M.A. (2008), *Strategic Management of Technological Innovation*, 2nd edition, New York McGraw-Hill.

Schumpeter, J.A. (1942), *Capitalism, Socialism and Democracy*, New York: Harper and Brothers.

Simon, H.A. (1962), The architecture of complexity, *Proceedings of the American Philosophical Society* **10€** (6), 467–82.

Simon, H.A. (2002), Near decomposability and the speed of evolution, *Industrial and Corporate Change* **1** (3), 587–99.

Teece, D.J. (1984), Economic analysis and strategic management, *California Management Review* **26** (3) 87–110.

Uzzi, B. (1997), Social structure and competition in interfirm networks: The paradox of embeddedness, *Administrative Science Quarterly* **42** (1), 35–67.

von Hippel, E. (1994), 'Sticky information' and the locus of problem solving: Implications for innovation, *Management Science* **40** (4), 429–39.

Williamson, O. (1975), *Market and Hierarchies: Analysis and Antitrust Implications*, New York: Free Press.

27 Small firms and industrial districts
Marco Bellandi and Lisa De Propris

27.1 INTRODUCTION

Industrial districts (IDs) are dense centres of life and work, characterized by one or a few related localized industries tightly intertwined with the local society and the local institutional set-up (Becattini et al., 2009b). The agglomeration of firms, and thereby industries, in specific places when it coincides with the concentration and integration of related specializations, may generate positive external economies. The persistent variety of localized industries illustrates the widespread importance of such advantages over times and across places. Nevertheless, the same variety suggests that the 'agglomeration of firms' is not a sufficient condition to guarantee sustainable beneficial effects. Instead, it requires a complex mechanism that involves a broad set of local public and private agents. IDs illustrate, in general terms, that sustainable competitive strengths and collective advantages are associated with the overlap of an industrial agglomeration with a local society. In particular, this overlap has an autonomous meaning when local social-cultural and institutional relations exceed the possibility of control by a few powerful economic agents, and ensure an aggregate stability and a sense of identity. Drawing on their localized strengths, IDs are adapting to confront the open space of the current global networks. This mechanism is exemplified at best by IDs that are characterized by the evolving populations of locally embedded small-sized firms together with a local society. In line with this, we would argue that *IDs thrive on small firms*, namely they grow thanks to the dynamism and interaction of small firms.

At the same time, there is ample evidence suggesting that small firms find in IDs an ideal context to blossom and be valued, in other words *small firms thrive in IDs*.[1] The increasing importance of large-sized firms due to markets and technology requirements was at the core of industrial paradigms of the 1970s and 1980s – the golden age of mass production and mass marketing.[2] Nevertheless, small firms did not disappear in that context, but their survival was underplayed as expression of businesses that had peripheral or transient roles. However, since the 1990s, the Fordist paradigm showed its intrinsic weaknesses partly as a result of the demand sophistication and technological advancement it promoted. The demur of mass production led to a renewed interest in the role that smaller sized firms could have when market conditions require diversity and flexibility as new competitive advantages (Piore and Sabel, 1984). Market and technological niches proliferated, and the capacity of small firms especially when clustered to achieve sets of related economies of specialization became again a core competitive lever (after the nineteenth century wave described by Marshall). The recognition that this model of organizing production was here to stay came from large firms changing their own structure and becoming lean and modular, with a dramatic shift that lasted a long time and took nothing away from the advantages that small firms organized in local systems of production were reaping. Such tendencies placed centre stage small firms that, when embedded in systemic local forces, were no longer peripheral, interstitial or transitional players in the economy, but engines of competitive advantages, engines of growth and drivers of innovation.

The literature on IDs advocates for IDs and small firms to simultaneously thrive thanks to their mutual support. We will discuss later how the very nature of IDs is changing as the role of small firms is adapting to respond to external shocks, whilst, the evolution of the systemic infrastructure of IDs is itself impacting on the sustainability of the smaller firms.

Small firms correspond with many different types of organization, however, they are more broadly intended as business organizations whose small size[3] allows for a flat governance where ownership coincides with control. Further, their system of decision-making and communications is exercised more through personal relationships than codified procedures; and their entrepreneurial drive tends to coincide with one individual or a group of individuals tied together by regular contacts and trust-based personal linkages. Indeed, small firms also rely on strong (even if not always exclusive) social relations and economic resources that are embedded in the place where they emerge and live. Finally they are specialized in one or very few categories of products or services.[4] In terms of organizational complexity, they combine entrepreneurial leadership with the operational running of the business, as in artisan firms, with a moderate internal functional specialization, as in medium-sized firms. Sections 27.2 and 27.3 will expand on the synergies between small firms and IDs; section 27.4 will illustrate the heterogeneous and evolving nature of small firms and IDs. Finally, sections 27.5 and 27.6 present some thoughts on the perspectives of IDs as they adjust and adapt to the ever-changing nature and complexity of the current production and social relations, that is, globalization and the knowledge economy.

27.2   IDs THRIVE ON SMALL FIRMS

IDs are compact centres of dense life and working patterns, IDs present networks whose set-up, inter-penetration, as well as disaggregation depend on the complexity of many sets of connections related to the local production activities. Industry location could be explained by simple advantages of geographical proximity. However, the persistent overlap between a local society and a localized industry creates a high degree of embeddedness and tends to generate more complex forms of proximities, such as cognitive and organizational proximity (De Propris et al., 2008). Common attitudes and values, knowledge and norms are shared. Marshall wrote that such local identity supports local projects and investments in technical, human and social capital within the same or related sets of production activities; in this way, the advantages of geographical proximity are amplified by the spread of collective knowledge sharing and collective processes of learning (Becattini et al., 2003). It is well known that systemic processes of innovation are able to produce collective productivity gains and ultimately to determine the competitive advantage of IDs, especially when operating in certain worlds of production, that is, within a certain mix of market and technological as well as institutional tendencies (Lester and Piore, 2004). Nevertheless, such virtuous local interplay runs within a larger frame of territorial scales and relations, where it may be further strengthened but also altered,

eakened or even disrupted.[5] Yet, such local forces of economic growth can potentially
e autonomous from other more overarching factors of industrial development, related,
or instance, to the current challenges of globalization, such as the accumulation and use
f knowledge and economic power within large firms and public institutions.

The contemporary debate on IDs suggests that IDs require small firms to emerge and
evelop in ways that help the transformation of the talent and initiative naturally embed-
ed in the local socioeconomic fabric into entrepreneurial projects and investment.[6] In
particular, there are three main aspects of such a mutually reinforcing relation that is
worth exploring: entrepreneurship as a life project, artisanship as an expression of talent
nd skill, and the formation of teams of complementary producers.

First, in IDs the entrepreneur is the person who:

> invests in the firm not only her/his personal savings and those eventually entrusted to her/him
> by the parental and friendship networks, but also and more her/his reputation in terms of tech-
> nical and managerial competence, leadership and energy on the job, trade acumen, etc. who
> s/he has been able to build in the course of time within her/his community of life. This human
> and relational capital is much less transferable to different contexts than the financial capital
> at the core of the particle firm. Also the returns are measured not only in economic terms, but
> also in terms of the realization of a life project, or of some revision of it. (Becattini et al., 2009b,
> p. xxviii)

In other words, entrepreneurial ventures emerge as expressions of individual ambitions
but also as an integral part of a social mesh of personal relations where social and economic networks tend to overlap. The firm is therefore an individual's participation in the
local economy, and the returns are often both monetary and non-monetary (e.g., social
status or civic engagement), with the former more easily re-invested in the same context.

Second, in IDs small firms can take the form of artisanship as expressions of individuals' talent and skill. The many workshops and laboratories nested in an economically
active local society contribute to the local activities with unique and customized services
and products in a flexible and adjustable manner, meeting the needs of multi-geometry
markets (Becattini et al., 2009b, p. xxii). Small firms as embodiment of artisanship can
culminate in entrepreneurial ventures that translate expertise and specializations into
products and services that can be projected to external markets. Despite the extension
of the final markets, entrepreneurs find themselves well anchored in the local socioeconomic terrain from which they draw innovative ideas and processes, or where they find
all sorts of cooperative links that expand their ability to innovate, or again where they
test, and experiment with novelties coming from contacts with the external markets.

Third, IDs thrive when entrepreneurial dynamism and talent can be combined with a
socioeconomic context where formal or informal teams of producers emerge as collective players that are able to pursue a joint investment in shared resources.[7] These teams
are able to replace or supplement market or hierarchical transactions, since they are
underpinned by what economic theory refers to as quasi-market or hybrid transactions
(Williamson, 1991). Teams are formed ad hoc to bring together knowledge and skills that
support an entrepreneurial venture – that reflects a life project – for which the required
resources are likely to extend beyond the single network of the entrepreneur, but within
the broader IDs' system. IDs can therefore be seen as a temporary meta-network, where
each member has its roots in a different network but come together for a particular

project. More recently, teams support firms' ambitions to expand their productio
and trade capacities internationally whilst still maintaining strong links with the hom
locality. Current studies have looked at the impact of these collective initiatives on th
home system of socioeconomic relations and it has been found that in some cases the
can achieve functional upgrading for local firms without social disruption and full-sca
de-localization (Bellandi and Caloffi, 2008; De Propris et al., 2008). In this perspectivε
trans-local firms appear to be a recent and interesting phenomenon that would somehov
support the renewal and persistence of IDs.[8]

The demise of Fordism did not necessarily coincide with the death of large-sizε
firms, and to some extent their role in the economy and in IDs in particular cannot b
completely neglected. The three aspects just described (entrepreneurship as a life project
artisanship as an expression of talent and skill, and the formation of teams of comple
mentary producers) do not necessarily prevent larger firms from playing a role. In ID
(medium to) large firms can be the remains of an even larger firm that had downsized o
be the outcome of a small firm growing internally into a larger one – although curren
evidence shows that IDs' leaders tend to grow externally by creating groups (Cainell
and Iacobucci, 2007). In fact, recently, if globalization and technology were to be seizec
as opportunities rather than feared as threats, the costs, riskiness and exposure that arε
required have favoured firms' growth and created local leaders.[9]

In IDs the presence of large firms can be ambiguous. Large firms can play an analo-
gous role to aggregations of small firms in business teams, mobilizing social network:
and industrial platforms, thanks to their position in international value chains and thε
extensive relations with local smaller partners. For this, large firms can be quite strongly
embedded in the local society (Piore and Sabel, 1984). On the other hand, of course,
large firms can predate and leave the district after having depleted rich local resources or
generous public aid. Some of these issues will be discussed in section 27.5.

27.3   SMALL FIRMS THRIVE IN IDs

Small firms thrive in IDs: this is one of the main arguments and findings of a literature
in the 1980s (Brusco, 1986; Goodman and Bamford, 1989; Pyke et al., 1990) that has
reflected on the renewed role of small firms in the flexible organizations of production
that post-Fordism was advocating.

There are well-known intrinsic constraints that small firms face, for example, inability
to reach significant scale economies; limited financial resources; lack of managerial and
marketing skills; difficulties in exporting or in major risky and costly investments. Some
of these are particularly problematic in the current context. In fact, the globalization of
trade, production, as well as knowledge flows, together with the pace and the nature of
technological change, both require ability to take risks, to raise the necessary finance,
and to adjust, which exposes small firms' dramatic shortcomings. However, the presence and role of small firms has not weakened in the turmoil of the 1980–90s and the
emergence of the knowledge economy.

It could be argued that small firms have always been there, thriving or surviving
– usually somewhere within a short cycle of birth, maturity and decay or transformation – in worlds of production dominated by big companies (Sylos Labini, 1962). They

may have been: (1) marginal (sunk in insulated and poor markets), (2) satellite (inserted within networks controlled by big firms), or again (3) interstitial (suppliers in market niches at the side of mass consumption dominated by big firms), or finally, (4) highly innovative, creative to the point of growing in size.

The first two models illustrate the result of empirical constraints to the free exercise of the so-called 'principle of asymmetry' (Steindl, 1945), according to which all the economies achieved by a small firm can be internalized by a large firm. However, not all the economies achieved by a large firm are realized on a smaller scale. The other two models have illustrated peripheral or transitional exceptions to the above-mentioned principle of asymmetry, in so far as they recognize that there are efficiencies that only small firms can achieve: this stresses the importance of the economies of specialization in niche markets or infant industries (Penrose, 1959). In particular, as an exception to the presumed superior efficiency of large firms, the economies of specialization draw on the opportunity costs of organizing resources within a hierarchical organization of increasing size. Those costs are limited when market demand requires mass production and mass marketing so that production can be standardized. However, in case of specialized activities aimed at market niches, the opportunity costs for large firms devoted to mass markets are high. In this case, it is more convenient for large firms to leave such niches to smaller and specialized firms, sometimes controlled and sometimes just independent. The same is true of inventions that come more or less randomly from scientific knowledge spilling over from the main lines of R&D controlled by big firms or big public research entities. The opportunity costs of following all those knowledge threads are too high for large firms, but small innovative enterprises may try, and sometimes succeed in pursuing them successfully; this leads them to create new markets that can then be scaled up exponentially. In this case, either small innovative firms grow rapidly and become large firms (as is the case of Microsoft some decades ago), or they end up being acquired by large firms already incumbent in traditional markets and willing to enter new and more importantly expanding markets (as was the case of Innocent acquired by Coca-Cola in 2009).

One of the main features of post-Fordism has been the volatility and segmentation of demand as consumers have become more sophisticated in the way they have wanted their personalized needs to be satisfied. This has led to the creation of market niches especially at the top end of demand where price is quite inelastic. These niches have forced producers to expand product ranges as well as to offer customized solutions. In so doing, the range of variations has become more and more dense. This has increased the competitive advantage of organizations of production able to combine, within the same or across complementary *filières*, economies of specialization in activities related to product and knowledge differentiation, with economies of scale and stock for those production and service activities reliant on cost savings. The organization of production that emerged as being able to respond to such challenges was not necessarily under the same roof.

The combination of specialization and scale economies was made possible by the divisibility of the production process and thereby the possibility to have it segmented and dis-integrated across a number of complementary stage-specialized producers (Tani, 2009). Those modular and flexible organizations of production took the form of 'local systems' of independent, specialized and above all, small firms, which not only found a role to play in these contexts but became the repository of their competitive advantage. Crucial to the renewed role of small firms was the possibility for them to be part of a

system underpinned by specific public goods, and in particular, accessible shared indivisible resources that often, but not necessarily, are organized and accessed locally. These
shared resources enable individual firms to overcome the limits of their size and knowledge, by integrating across the value chain with other small firms, so that the collective
output is more than the sum of the parts. In fact, the joint economies of specialization
and scale, coordinated at the local level by the appropriate governance of specific public
goods, realize what at an aggregate level may be seen as agglomeration economies, that
is, competitive advantages that small firms could only achieve collectively thanks to
proximity. Indeed, the inter-penetration of a localized industry of small specialized firm
with a local society is able to support the governance of specific public goods with the
help of embedded socio-cultural and institutional relations. The same relations work as
hotbeds for the birth of new entrepreneurial ventures, which replace failing ones and/or
diversify the scope of the cluster's specializations. More importantly, they increase the
opportunities for inventing and innovating thanks, for instance, to cross-sector fertiliza-
tion, serendipity, and multiple inter-firm feedbacks with experience-based knowledge.

Ample evidence suggests that small firms thrive in IDs. Case studies have been able to
unearth the complex web of interdependent relations sketched above, while large-scale
econometric models have measured, for instance, the 'district effects'.[10] Such empirical
investigations have looked at IDs in Italy (Sforzi, 2009), as well as internationally. In
fact, as shown, in the *Handbook of Industrial Districts* (Becattini et al., 2009a), studies on
IDs cover a much larger geographical and historical scope, with recent studies looking at
IDs in emerging and developing countries (Posthuma, 2009).

The revival of Marshallian IDs and the role of small firms are linked to the distinction between external and internal economies. Advancements in our understanding of
the opportunities for small firms in IDs should have been easier and more widespread in
industrial and political economy if a correct interpretation of new institutional economics had prevailed, suggesting the centrality of heterogeneity of organizational solutions to
the problems of integration of evolving fabrics of division of labour (Dietrich and Krafft,
2008). This would lead to a 'theoretical', as well as an empirical, getaway from the trap
set by the asymmetry principle. Becattini and Bellandi (2002, p. 380) in fact argue that:

> For some products, everything that a large firm can do in terms of efficiency can be done by
> a population of small firms specializing in single phases, provided that they are contiguously
> located and operate in a socially, culturally and institutionally congenial environment. This
> shifts the emphasis, in seeking to explain the relative efficiency of production, from company
> size to the congeniality between type and organizational form of the main product in any local
> system and the social and cultural configuration of the community.

So, as much as the local factors of competitive advantage embodied in IDs have
enabled small firms to thrive, small firms are the repositories of IDs' efficiencies and
economic dynamism. Successful IDs typify the effective coming together of these factors.
However, as living and ever-changing forms, IDs themselves have been characterized by
heterogeneity and are prone to life cycles. Indeed, changes in the relations between small
firms and IDs may occur in sequence, and not always in a mutually reinforcing way or
through simultaneous virtuous circles (see, for example, Dei Ottati, 2009 and Robertson
et al., 2009). The makeup and evolution of IDs combine with other forces of industrial
development as recalled in the introduction, producing various models of local develop-

ıent (Becattini et al., 2003). In the next section some aspects of such heterogeneous and ʋolving entities are detailed.

27.4   THE HETEROGENEOUS NATURE OF SMALL FIRMS IN IDs

The nature of small firms within an ID tends to vary, especially so over time when IDs ɛvolve along trajectories of change shaped by internal and external factors. There is a ʋide literature on processes of 'districtualization' – district life cycle – describing embryɔnic, growing, mature and transitional states through which IDs go as dynamic forms of ɔrganization (Belussi, 2005).

The dis-integration of the division of labour described above leads to a pool of firms ʂpecialized in many tasks and functions. Such specializations coincide with specific ʂector niches related to each other by the role and position along the value chain. Some ıirms are more product-oriented, including micro-firms that are artisan in nature, as well ıs others that have internally integrated some processes because of technological constraints. At the same time, there are firms that provide a wide range of district-specific ʊusiness support services.

The systemic integration of firms' task specializations takes place through the functioning of a multitude of internal markets for intermediate goods. Many firms would act in these intermediate markets as both sellers and buyers; however, some would also engage with outside markets, albeit still in relation with the same intermediate or final products. Such 'bridging' firms act as intermediaries between the ID and the outside markets. Some firms act as subcontractors; a few act as integrators of sets of subcontractors and are, thereby, connectors with external markets. The constant buying and selling in the intermediate local markets creates stable networks of exchanges as firms maintain low transaction costs thanks to recurrent relations. Sometimes such networks of related specialized firms behave according to formal or informal teams. Teams may vary in origin and form, spanning from networks underpinned only by social relations, to more formal business groups with varying degrees of ownership interlocking, to hierarchical formal groups.

Among the more established and mature ones, some small firms succeed in reaching a position of leadership – more or less stable – within a certain internal network and in local and external markets. Leadership positions are more likely to coincide with larger size – firms becoming therefore medium-sized – or with the creation of business groups. The degree of vertical integration varies in the latter developments, depending on organizational strategies, market access and technology constraints, the position of the firms along the value chain and the position of the ID in its life cycle (Cainelli and Iacobucci, 2007, pp. 71–9; Robertson et al., 2009, pp. 274–6).

Some firms are young, weak, and dependent on more mature and established small firms, from which they have possibly spun out. Among the young ones, many are doomed to be short-lived due to the natural process of natural selection especially at the start of a business when a weak business plan or an underestimated business risk could be lethal.

The drive behind newborn firms in IDs can vary, although they all germinate from the local social networks. In addition to the life project entrepreneurs already mentioned small firms could start from a pure financial calculus and as an opportunity of capital investment; alternatively, they can represent a survival option whereby self-employment becomes a way out from unemployment. Many small start-ups are incremental innova tors, and venture in a new business picking up from an existing and well-known route They concentrate on products and services that present marginal improvements or small adaptations since their motivation is filling market niches their experience has identified Indeed, they build their entrepreneurial idea on their personal experience, known trade contacts, and the informal circulation of ideas within the ID. On the other hand, other small firms, usually fewer, are more risk-takers and really radical innovators. They might stumble across new technologies or see the opportunity to create new markets, and in this case, the entrepreneurial venture can push the knowledge frontier forward not only for the firm, but also for the ID. The capacity of the ID to favour the germination of the radical entrepreneur is one of the most dynamic features of its sustainability.[11] In IDs such risk-taking ventures – which could still fall under the life project entrepreneurship category – are facilitated by the thick social network; the personal and multifaceted relationships between people and business partners; and the sharing of information knowledge and market intelligence. Finally, more recently, IDs have attracted multi national firms that have located there – more or less temporarily – for instance to seek technology and knowledge (De Propris et al., 2005) that is anchored and immersed in the tacit know-how of specific places. These multinational firms might be large or small to-medium-sized; as leader firms, they can have a bridging role between the ID and the outside; however, they could also have predatory strategies that damage the ID.

The heterogeneity in business organizational forms in IDs is related to the extent of the internal system of markets and resources allocation (referring to Smith's well-known dictum that the division of labour is limited by the extent of the market), to the tight inter-penetration between businesses and the local society, as well as to the fact that small firms intrinsically reflect more directly the individual traits of their entrepreneurs and the contingencies of their foundation. For this reason IDs, especially mature ones, tend be ideal environments for observing variations in industrial organization.

27.5   MEDIUM-SIZED FIRMS, BUSINESS GROUPS AND TRANS-LOCAL FIRMS IN IDs

The nature of firms in IDs is undergoing significant changes against external challenges – namely, technology and globalization. The impact of these changes may take two forms. One relates to the internal and external growth of lead firms, which still maintains deep roots in the ID (Cainelli and Iacobucci, 2007; Coltorti, 2009). The other relates to the geographical extension of production activities of ID firms across localities, that is, trans-local firms (Bellandi and Caloffi, 2008). These cases were quite rare in the past, but are becoming more frequent especially in product sectors where the contribution of scale economies to specialization economies is particularly relevant.

ID firms that have been successful in building a competitive advantage have in some cases also been able to secure growing markets. These firms tend usually (but not neces- sarily) to be positioned downstream and therefore nearer to demand and to have many, omplex and diversified production links upstream with other firms in the ID – as already mentioned. In these circumstances, such lead firms have found themselves confronted with the incentive and the opportunity both to expand markets, for instance abroad, and to invest in product development. Both initiatives require significant risk capital and would greatly benefit from scale economies, forcing the typical ID firm to grow in size internally, with small firms growing into medium-sized firms (Coltorti, 2009). The increased scale has been congenial to firms that have had to maximize the benefits reaped by the combination of specialized economies on some function of its production, and internal scale economies on others, for instance product development, marketing, or export. At the same time, a larger scale has strengthened the ability of firms to raise risk capital to undertake innovation and to explore new product and geographical markets.

Alternatively to internal growth, some lead firms have chosen to grow externally, through the formation of business groups, via the acquisition of existing firms within the ID. A business group is driven by various motivations: to increase control over strategic complementary production stages; to extend the product range; to acquire frontier knowledge or complementary knowledge; to gain and secure access to product or geographical market; to gain access to venture capital and risk finance (Cainelli and Iacobucci, 2007). Through a business group, a lead firm can therefore realize risk projects (like innovation or market expansion) that small size would disallow.

In both cases, we witness a small entrepreneurial firm growing into a larger organization of production. Whilst their activities are similarly embedded in the local socioeconomic terrain, they are more vertically integrated and better able to manage systemic investments for radical innovation and discontinuous change (Becattini et al., 2003, pp. 138–46). If successful, their innovations may spill over to the entire ID and open up not only new technologies but also new markets and opportunities. Such positive impact on the local economy can involve dedicated public and private institutions able to catalyse collective actions and initiatives. However, current studies are also warning of the risks derived from an increased *hierarchization* of the system of relations between firms, that results from the vertical integration of production, creating unbalanced power between firms; increased competition coupled with reduced cooperation and more control; and preferential or exclusive relations with intermediary firms. In extreme cases, the leading firm can cease to invest (monetarily and relationally) in the locality and uproots itself from it, in so doing causing the dis-integration of the ID (Garofoli, 2009, pp. 494–9).

More generally, the role of medium-sized and large firms as key players in intra-systemic local and regional dynamics has been acknowledged in various streams of current literature, more or less explicitly related to ID studies.[12] This debate tends to consider examples of systems in countries like the USA where firm size is endemically larger than in Europe, and sectors where the high degree of industrial concentration tends to create large players as well as multinational firms, such as biotechnologies, pharmaceutical, aerospace or IT.

In the same way as the forces of globalization and technological change are altering the ID internal division of labour with a larger number of small firms growing internally and externally, a parallel phenomenon has been the de-localization of some production activities outside the ID borders. Indeed, ID lead firms have also started shifting some functions abroad, or engaging in international joint ventures or hosting foreign capital in search of efficiency, new knowledge or markets (Tattara, 2009). By and large the inter nationalization process has been gradual following a process of learning and adaptatio not by the single firm but by the system of firms. The impact of these *trans-local firm* (Bellandi and Caloffi, 2008) is unclear. They can have a positive impact if they act as II gateways by activating two-way channels for the flows of goods, services, knowledge an technology between the ID and the rest of the world. However, if they re-locate noda tasks for the ID or a critical mass of tasks, the impact on the socioeconomic system o activities is negative. The outcome can be the breakdown of the socioeconomic net works, the interruption of the circulation of information and the hollowing out of it know-how (De Propris, 2008).

The recent debate on forms of proximity (De Propris et al., 2008) helps us to under stand that district firms will not choose to embark in footloose international operations but instead they would prefer to develop and strengthen common patterns of behaviour common practices and routines together with informal communications. Even if the tie of geographical proximity might become loosened, the softer but nevertheless binding ties of cognitive and social proximity seem to still characterize inter-firm relations across multi-local value chains. Benefits from internationalization would come from an ID being able to maintain a critical mass of its embedded know-how, together with 'bridging' actors (rather than gatekeepers) able to search, read, understand, translate and finally integrate external knowledge inside the framework of the local know-how.

27.6   SOME CONCLUDING VARIATIONS ON SMALL FIRMS AND IDs IN A KNOWLEDGE ECONOMY

Heterogeneity and variation in organizational forms can be an effective lever to evolutionary change; in particular, entrepreneurial firms that reflect a life project are the constant germination of the fertile terrain that IDs are. In fact, especially in the face of difficult market and social challenges, the survival of IDs often depends on the constant regeneration of its pool of firms, especially on the constant emergence of radical innovators and their truly entrepreneurial ventures. Langlois (2007, pp. 1120–21) helps describe such ventures:

> What is common to the entrepreneurial firm. . .is that it involved self-conscious design. . . This is so because, rather by definition, they do not draw on existing unselfconscious repositories of knowledge and capability, whether these be existing market patterns or existing systems of rules of conduct within organizations. . . This is why entrepreneurial firms are sources of systemic novelty. . . If we mean by an entrepreneurial firm a firm in Coase's sense not just in Knight's, then design also involves direction of the effort of others. . . Knight reminds us, however, that the 'effort' the entrepreneur must direct, actually involves the exercise of judgment. This complicates the problem somewhat, since, even in a small entrepreneurial firm, there may be a good deal of delegation of judgment, and that judgment may cover a wide ground.

However, as the challenges of technological change and globalization assume more stable patterns, and IDs embrace or lead the transition to the knowledge economy, the local capacities of IDs in handling these forces need to be upgraded with a wide diffusion of organizational platforms and cultural attitudes that promote the emergence of a different generation of small entrepreneurial firms. In particular, thriving IDs would require a larger presence of small firms embodying a business culture that enables boundary-spanning activities and the integration of diverse fields of judgement. In such firms a common orientation in decision practices is shared within an entrepreneurial team of highly skilled people, thanks to a consistent cognitive and motivational framework. The knowledge and the strategic considerations of the team's members and their different perspectives and fields of operation and decision-making are integrated, so as to facilitate the ability of the firm to liaise with and evaluate in a coordinated way a variety of external opportunities (Best, 2009).

The diffusion of such types of firms within IDs, even mature ones with a record of past successes and evolutionary capacities, is, however, far from granted, although desirable, even within well established IDs with a dynamic population of active entrepreneurs. Consider, for example, that in many Italian IDs that emerged in the mid-1960s and that contributed to create the 'Made in Italy' brand internationally, the prevailing business culture saw business leadership coincide with small successful entrepreneurs who were self-made business people and a sort of stand-alone genius who coordinates paternalistically very small ventures and possibly small teams of related producers.

One key concern is what are the conditions, and perhaps the policies, that may enable IDs and district-like systems to upgrade their business culture and trigger again virtuous circles of local socioeconomic forces based on systems of small (to medium-sized) firms (possibly in interaction with local entities of big firms and public institutions)?

Referring to American cases of university-centric industrial districts and of high-tech regions, Lester and Piore (2004), Patton and Kenney (2009) and Best (2009) cautiously suggest some factors that might play a decisive role. These include: (1) open attitudes to networking for knowledge enhancement and discovery, featuring good and dynamic universities and other scientific and technical communities partly embedded in a territory, (2) appropriate business and knowledge services infrastructures; and (3) a rich entrepreneurial environment with attitudes, competencies and support institutions somehow related to the business trajectories that may develop from the areas of excellence of the local research communities.

The delicate balance that traditionally enables IDs and small firms to thrive jointly seems somewhat altered by the pace and nature of globalization and technological change. Open systems of local and global relationships combining tacit knowledge with codified stimuli are increasingly requested. Entrepreneurship in this dynamic context becomes an opportunity-seeking and boundary-spanning activity. The sustainable local development of places rests therefore on IDs maintaining socioeconomic embedded cohesion across the population of small businesses whilst opening gateways to multi-local synergies.

NOTES

1. Becattini et al. (2009a).
2. See Chapter 22 by Toms and Wilson in this volume.
3. In the EU context, small firms are defined operationally as businesses with less than 50 employees.
4. See Acs, Chapter 36 in this volume.
5. See Bellandi (2011) on Marshall's views on this point.

6.　See, for instance, Brusco (1986), Becattini and Bellandi (2002) on entrepreneurship dynamics in IDs.
7.　See also Buchmann and Pyka on innovation networks, in Chapter 33 of this volume.
8.　We would refer to De Propris and Crevoisier (2011) on anchoring and local development more broadly.
9.　See Coad and Hölzl, Chapter 24 in this volume on firms' growth.
10.　See De Blasio et al. (2009) for a critical survey; and Bellandi and Ruiz Fuensanta (2010) for an econometric analysis of district external economies.
11.　For a critical survey of entrepreneurship, see Mwuara et al. (2010).
12.　See for examples Porter's cluster model (Porter and Ketels, 2009); the innovative milieu (Maillat, 1998); regional innovation systems (Cooke et al., 2004); learning regions (Asheim, 1996); cultural clusters and cities (Cooke and Lazzeretti, 2007).

REFERENCES

Asheim, Björn (1996), 'Industrial districts as "learning regions": a condition for prosperity?', *European Planning Studies*, **4** (4), 379–400.
Becattini, Giacomo and Marco Bellandi (2002), 'Mighty pygmies and feeble Watutsis. Consideration on Italian industry', in *Review of Economic Conditions in Italy*, No. 3, 375–405.
Becattini, G., M. Bellandi and L. De Propris (2009a), *A Handbook of Industrial Districts*, Cheltenham, UK and Northampton, MA, USA: Edward Elgar.
Becattini, Giacomo, M. Bellandi and L. De Propris (2009b), 'Critical nodes and contemporary reflections on industrial districts: an introduction', in G. Becattini, M. Bellandi and L. De Propris (eds), *A Handbook of Industrial Districts*, Cheltenham, UK and Northampton, MA, USA: Edward Elgar, pp. xv–xxxv.
Becattini, Giacomo, Marco Bellandi, Gabi Dei Ottati and Fabio Sforzi (eds) (2003), *From Industrial Districts to Local Development. An Itinerary of Research*, Cheltenham, UK and Northampton, MA, USA: Edward Elgar.
Bellandi, Marco (2011), 'Regions, nations and beyond in Marshallian external economies', in T. Raffaelli, T. Nishizawa and S. Cook (eds), *Marshall and Marshallians on Industrial Economics*, Oxford and New York: Routledge.
Bellandi, Marco and Annalisa Caloffi (2008), 'District internationalisation and trans-local development', *Entrepreneurship and Regional Development*, **20** (6), November, 517–32.
Bellandi, Marco and Maria J. Ruiz Fuensanta (2010), 'An empirical analyis of district external economies based on a structure-conduct-performance framework', *Papers in Regional Science*, **89** (4), 801–18.
Belussi, F. (2005), 'Are industrial districts formed by networks without technologies? The diffusion of internet applications in three Italian clusters', *European Urban and Regional Studies*, **12** (3), 247–68.
Best, Michael H. (2009), 'Massachusetts high tech: a manufactory of species', in G. Becattini, M. Bellandi and L. De Propris (2009a), pp. 648–65.
Brusco, Sebastiano (1986), 'Small firms and industrial districts: the experience of Italy', in D. Keeble and E. Wever (eds), *New Firms and Regional Development in Europe*, London: Croom Helm, pp. 184–201.
Cainelli, Giulio and Donato Iacobucci (2007), *Agglomeration, Technology and Business Groups*, Cheltenham, UK and Northampton, MA, USA: Edward Elgar.
Coltorti, Fulvio (2009), 'Medium-sized firms, groups and industrial districts: an Italian perspective', in G. Becattini, M. Bellandi and L. De Propris (2009a), pp. 441–56.
Cooke, Philip and Luciana Lazzeretti (eds) (2007), *Creative Cities, Cultural Clusters and Local Economic Development*, Cheltenham, UK and Northampton, MA, USA: Edward Elgar.
Cooke, Philip, Martin Heidenreich and Hans-Joachim Braczyk (eds) (2004), *Regional Innovation Systems. The Role of Governance in a Globalized World*, London: Routledge.
De Blasio, Guido, Massimo Omiccioli and Luigi Federico Signorini (2009), 'Measuring the district effect', in G. Becattini, M. Bellandi and L. De Propris (2009a), pp. 381–93.
Dei Ottati, Gabi (2009), 'Semi-automatic and deliberate actions in the evolution of industrial districts', in G. Becattini, M. Bellandi and L. De Propris (2009a), pp. 204–15.
De Propris Lisa (2008), 'Trust and social capital in glo-cal networks', in P. Bianchi, M.D. Parrilli and R. Sugden (eds), *High Technology, Productivity and Networks: A Systemic Approach to SME Development*, Basingstoke: Palgrave Macmillan, pp. 155–74.
De Propris, Lisa and Olivier Crevoisier (2011), 'From regional anchors to anchoring', in B. Asheim, R. Boschma, P. Cooke and R. Martin (eds), *Handbook of Regional Innovation and Growth*, Cheltenham, UK and Northampton, MA, USA: Edward Elgar, pp. 167–77.
De Propris L., N. Driffield and S. Menghinello (2005), 'Local industrial systems and the location of FDI in Italy', *International Journal of the Economics of Business*, **12** (1), 105–21.

De Propris, L., S. Menghinello and R. Sugden (2008), 'The internationalization of local production systems: embeddedness, openness and governance', *Entrepreneurship and Regional Development*, **20** (6), 493–516.

Dietrich, Michael and Jackie Krafft (2008), 'Towards an historically relevant theory of the firm', in W. Elsner and H. Hanappi (eds), *Varieties of Capitalism and New Institutional Deals. Regulation, Welfare, and New Economy*, Cheltenham, UK and Northampton, MA, USA: Edward Elgar, pp. 103–21.

Garofoli, Gioacchino (2009), 'Industrial districts in Europe', in G. Becattini, M. Bellandi and L. De Propris (2009a), pp. 488–500.

Goodman, Edward and Julia Bamford (eds) (1989), *Small Firms and Industrial Districts in Italy*, London: Routledge.

Langlois, Richard N. (2007), 'The entrepreneurial theory of the firm and the theory of the entrepreneurial firm', *Journal of Management Studies*, **44** (7), 1107–24.

Lester, Richard K. and Michael J. Piore (2004), *Innovation. The Missing Dimension*, Cambridge, MA: Harvard University Press.

Maillat, Denis (1998), 'Interactions between urban systems and localized productive systems: an approach to endogenous regional development in terms of innovative milieu', *European Planning Studies*, **6** (2), 117–29.

Mwuara, Samuel, Lisa De Propris and Ajit Singh (2010), *Enterprise, Entrepreneurship and Economic Development Dynamics: A Modular Approach*, EUNIP 2010 Conference Proceedings.

Patton, Donald and Martin Kenney (2009), 'The university research-centric district in the United States', in G. Becattini, M. Bellandi and L. De Propris (eds), *A Handbook of Industrial Districts*, Cheltenham, UK and Northampton, MA, USA: Edward Elgar, pp. 549–64.

Penrose, Edith (1959), *The Theory of the Growth of the Firm*, Oxford: Basil Blackwell.

Piore, Michael J. and Charles F. Sabel (1984), *The Second Industrial Divide. Possibilities for Prosperity*, New York: Basic Books.

Porter, Michael and Christian Ketels (2009), 'Clusters and industrial districts: common roots, different perspectives', in G. Becattini, M. Bellandi and L. De Propris (2009a), pp. 172–83.

Posthuma, Anne Caroline (2009), 'The industrial district model: relevance for developing countries in the context of globalization', in G. Becattini, M. Bellandi and L. De Propris (2009a), pp. 570–84.

Pyke, Frank, Giacomo Becattini and Werner Sengenberger (eds) (1990), 'Industrial districts and inter-firm cooperation in Italy', Geneva: IILS, ILO.

Robertson, Paul L., David Jacobson and Richard N. Langlois (2009), 'Innovation processes and industrial districts', in G. Becattini, M. Bellandi and L. De Propris (2009a), pp. 269–80.

Sforzi, Fabio (2009), 'The empirical evidence of industrial districts in Italy', in G. Becattini, M. Bellandi and L. De Propris (2009a), pp. 327–42.

Steindl, Joseph (1945), *Small and Big Business. Economic Problems of the Size of Firms*, Oxford: Basil Blackwell.

Sylos Labini, Paolo (1962), *Oligopoly and Technical Progress*, Cambridge, MA: Harvard University Press.

Tani, P. (2009), 'Flow-fund model, decomposability of the production process and the structure of an industrial district', in G. Becattini, M. Bellandi and L. De Propris (2009a), pp. 158–71.

Tattara, Giuseppe (2009), 'The internationalization of production activities of Italian industrial districts', in G. Becattini, M. Bellandi and L. De Propris (2009a), pp. 682–93.

Williamson, O.E. (1991), 'Strategizing, economizing, and economic organization', *Strategic Management Journal*, **12** (Special Issue), 75–94.

PART VII

FIRM STRATEGIES

28 Mergers and acquisitions and firm performance
Myriam Cloodt and John Hagedoorn

28.1 INTRODUCTION

Over more than 30 years the performance of mergers and acquisitions (M&As) has been a topic of interest to researchers in a number of sub-disciplines within economics and business administration. This is no surprise as we have witnessed an enormous increase in the total number of M&As during the past decades. Even though M&As are widespread and a popular vehicle for firm growth, practice shows that most M&As fail to meet expectations. Various publications estimate failure rates of between 60 to 80 percent (see amongst others Puranam et al., 2003).

The explanation for this high failure rate in contrast with the popularity of M&As is still very much in need of both theoretical and empirical research. Although already much attention has been paid to the performance effects of M&As, research so far remains inconclusive and provides somewhat of a mixture of results, to say the least (King et al., 2004). For that reason we will focus our attention on the variation in M&A performance research and attempt to enhance our understanding of post-M&A economic performance and post-M&A innovative performance. The latter will be particularly comprehensively addressed since M&As are nowadays very prevalent in high-tech sectors and innovation has become an important motive for companies to undertake M&As (Prabhu et al., 2005; Cloodt et al., 2006).

This chapter is organized as follows. First, we present and explain the historical importance and magnitude of M&A activity. Thereafter we will discuss the most important motivations for firms to enter into an M&A. Next, we show the effect of M&As on post-M&A economic performance followed by the effect of M&As on post-M&A innovative performance. Finally, we illustrate the evolution of post-M&A innovative performance research and we end with some important conclusions.

28.2 HISTORICAL IMPORTANCE OF M&As

M&As have a long historical importance and magnitude, revealing several significant merger waves from the turn of the century up till now. The explanation for this seemingly cyclical movement is generally related to a number of important developments in the business environment, which 'trigger' companies to undertake M&As (Golbe and White, 1988). For example, the completion of the transnational railroads and the development of communications, which established the USA as the first large common market in the world, took place during the first merger wave and acted as a huge stimulation for firms to undertake M&As (Carlton and Perloff, 1990; Weston and Chung, 1990). More in particular, the establishment of a large common market triggered firms to undertake mainly horizontal M&As with the primary reason to achieve market domination (Weston et al.,

1990; Oster, 1999). This striving for market domination transformed regional firms into national firms and formed many large industrial concerns we still witness today (Carlton and Perloff, 1990; Weston et al., 1990; Oster, 1999).

A stimulating event that led to an increase in mainly vertical M&As and product-line extensions during the second merger wave (1920s) refers to the increasing role of the automobile as a means of transportation (Weston and Chung, 1990). This development enabled firms to extend their sales areas and to create more effective geographic sales and distribution systems (Weston et al., 1990; Weston and Chung, 1990), especially in industries such as food processing and chemicals (Weston et al., 1990).

The third merger wave (1960–73) represented an era of tougher antitrust policies in the USA and leading European nations, which led horizontal and vertical M&As to be replaced by unrelated M&As. The enforcement of antitrust restrictions turned out to be very effective, resulting in a clear decrease in the number of related M&As (horizontal and vertical) and a relatively large increase in the number of unrelated M&As. For example, for the period 1948–77 unrelated M&As represented 75 percent of the total assets acquired (Weston and Chung, 1990, p. 6). However, this takeover of mainly unrelated business activities had severe consequences for the survival of the merged firms, whereby almost half of the acquisitions were divested within several years after the original M&A (Katz et al., 1997).

A possible explanation for the increase in M&A activity during the fourth merger wave (1980s) was the globalization of markets and a changing antitrust environment (Weston and Chung, 1990), which led to an expansion of markets with increased international competitive pressures (Weston and Chung, 1990; World Investment Report, 2000). Speed became the main incentive for survival and M&As are often seen as the fastest means of potential inter-corporate arrangements. By merging or taking over an existing firm one can respond quickly to business opportunities and preferably before competitors do (World Investment Report, 2000). The increase in M&A activity, characterized by a large number of hostile acquisitions, ended with the collapse of the junk bond markets and the savings and loan crisis during the recession of 1990–91 (DuBoff and Herman, 2001; Gaughan, 2002).

The fifth merger wave (1994–2000) came with the emergence of the Internet, the growing importance of biotechnology, and a consolidation in industries such as agrochemicals, pharmaceuticals, and financial services. There were a large number of megadeals during this wave and the total transaction value of M&As increased within five years from 1 trillion US dollars in 1995 to over 4 trillion in 1999 (Duysters, 2001). In addition, nine of the ten largest deals in economic history all took place during this period (Lipton, 2006). This merger wave ended with the worldwide decline in stock prices in 1999/2000 (Moeller and Brady, 2007).

During the sixth merger wave (2003–present) we again witness an enormous growth in the number of M&As. Especially, the high-technology sector is one of the most prominent sectors in M&A activity. For instance, in 2004 this sector took 15.3 percent of the total global M&A market (Thomson Financial Statistics, 2004). Besides the increase in number of M&As, the high-tech sector is also characterized by large transactions, with the top ten deals representing 54 percent of the total deal value in 2003 (PricewaterhouseCoopers, 2004). In 2006, technological M&As were valued higher than any year since the dot.com crisis (Chiara di Guardo and Valentini, 2007). All of his indicates that M&As are increasingly used to absorb external technological knowledge whereby the role of innovation as a motive for M&As is of growing importance. Furthermore, during the current merger wave we witness an increased focus on strategic fit and the post-M&A integration process (Moeller and Brady, 2007).

28.3   MOTIVATIONS TO IMPROVE PERFORMANCE BY MEANS OF M&As

In light of the above-mentioned historical importance and magnitude of M&A activity, research started to focus on the antecedents of M&As, as scholars sought to uncover the motivation of firms to enter into such a large number of M&As. It should be noted that although we discuss the different motives in isolation, it is important to realize when analyzing M&A activity that several of the motives for undertaking M&As are at work simultaneously (Mueller, 1980; Scherer and Ross, 1990).

Traditionally, most M&As are motivated by market entry, market structure, and synergy-related considerations such as gaining access to foreign markets, gaining market power, enlarging the scale of operations, and searching for economies of scale and scope (King et al., 2004; Mukherjee et al., 2004). With respect to market entry, organizations possessing ownership-specific capabilities often prefer to exploit these capabilities by means of M&As in new cross-border locations and as such get quick access to knowledge about local market conditions (Cooke, 1988; World Investment Report, 2000). Moreover, given the saturation of their home market a lot of firms can only enlarge their scale of operations and internationally expand the firm's product range by acquiring other firms in overseas markets (Trautwein, 1990; Berkovitch and Narayanan, 1993; Chakrabarti et al., 1994; Hagedoorn and Sadowski, 1999). This growth motive can be of a defensive nature as the greater size of a company makes it more difficult to be taken over, or it can be undertaken in order to expand aggressively (Cooke, 1988).

The pursuit of market power is mainly an important incentive for firms operating in concentrated industries where existing rivals are few (Hay and Morris, 1991; Oster, 1999). Only in these instances can one eliminate one of the competitors in the industry by undertaking a horizontal M&A and influence price, quantity, or the nature of the product in the market place (Singh and Montgomery, 1987; Carlton and Perloff, 1990; Oster, 1999). We should note that only limited empirical evidence supports the idea of market power as an acquisition antecedent (Haleblian et al., 2009) and a large number of horizontal M&As are restricted by the enforcement of antitrust legislation.

With respect to synergy gains, a substantial part of the management literature expects that related M&As should show superior performance because of value created by economies of scale and scope that ought to generate more synergetic benefits than in the case of unrelated M&As that have no relationship other than being held together by an overarching system of corporate control (Porter, 1987; Singh and Montgomery, 1987; Shelton, 1988; Healy et al., 1992; Hoskisson and Johnson, 1992; Hoskisson and Hitt, 1994). Examples of synergy gains include, using each other's distribution networks, economies of scale in production leading to cost reductions, or exploiting the relationships among business segments (Hitt et al., 1997; World Investment Report, 2000).

This non-exhaustive overview of traditional motives to enter into M&As says nothing yet about the relative merits of M&As in terms of success. Hence, it is necessary to carefully review the empirical evidence on the effect of M&As on post-M&A performance.

28.4   THE EFFECT OF M&As ON ECONOMIC PERFORMANCE

Early research, analyzing the post-M&A economic performance, has attracted strong academic interest from the fields of industrial economics, financial economics, strategic management, and organizational behavior. We will briefly summarize the main findings of these early studies.

Industrial economists studied the effects of M&As on efficiency and profitability and focused on merger motives such as economies of scale and scope or market power. Following this tradition, research done by Caves (1989) shows that mergers may be profitable. However on average, empirical analyses show that improved post-M&A performance is either non-existent or very limited. Meeks (1977) demonstrates that in the year of the M&A the profitability improves slightly. All subsequent years report a decline from the pre-merger level. Studies done by Mueller (1986a, 1986b) and Ravenscraft and Scherer (1987, 1989) illustrate that in general mergers have a neutral or negative effect on profitability and growth (market share). Based on the above-mentioned literature it can be said that in most of the cases the hypothesis that M&As improve economic performance is not supported.

Financial economists analyzed acquisition performance typically by using stock market data to assess it. More in particular, they used the event study methodology to measure performance by examining changes in the (stock market) value of the acquiring and acquired companies. Most merger event studies conclude that the shareholders of the acquired firm experience positive returns while the returns for the shareholders of the acquiring firm are by and large small or insignificant. This means that on average mergers are value-enhancing (Jensen and Ruback, 1983; Jensen, 1984; Jarell et al., 1988; Healy et al., 1992).

Research in strategic management has focused on the role of strategic fit. Strategic fit refers to the degree to which the acquired firm augments or complements the acquiring firm's strategy and the degree to which additional value is created (Jemison and Sitkin, 1986). As such, strategic fit is often measured in terms of the relatedness of M&As. A substantial part of the management literature expects that compared with unrelated M&As, related M&As should show superior performance because of value created by economies of scale, economies of scope, or market power (i.e., Singh and Montgomery, 1987; Shelton, 1988). Others show that unrelated M&As do not do worse than horizontally related or vertical M&As (i.e., Lubatkin, 1987; Seth, 1990; Datta, 1991) leading to inconclusive evidence with respect to strategic fit. Besides strategic fit, several researchers emphasize that organizational fit has an important effect on the M&A performance (e.g., Buono and Bowditch, 1989; Datta, 1991). Organizational fit focuses on the match between administrative routines and company-specific characteristics such as form and size (Jemison and Sitkin, 1986; Datta, 1991). Although several studies emphasize the importance of organizational fit, a recently conducted meta-analysis of prior M&A

studies concludes that in general size relatedness has a negative effect on acquisition performance (Homberg et al., 2009).

Contributions to the organizational behavior literature argue that the post-M&A integration process is another important factor in the enhancement of a firm's performance (Jemison and Sitkin, 1986; Haspeslagh and Jemison, 1991). An effective integration process is defined by Olie (1996) as the combination of firms into a single entity in such a way that the goals of the new organization are fulfilled. However, integration is complex, time consuming, full of risks, and strongly influenced by the amount of fit between partner firms (Haspeslagh and Jemison, 1991; Chakrabarti et al., 1994; Capron and Mitchell, 2000). From the perspective of the fields of strategic management and organizational behavior, one can conclude that the success of a merger or acquisition depends first on the strategic fit and/or organizational fit of the partner firms and second on the effective (post-M&A) integration process.

28.5 THE EFFECT OF M&As ON INNOVATIVE PERFORMANCE

The conclusions of the various studies analyzing the post-M&A economic performance, present a mix of results and often predict a negative effect of M&As on performance. According to King et al. (2004) a major reason for this finding is the short-term focus of most post-M&A research and the fact that M&A activity is often undertaken by reasons other than the traditional motives mentioned in section 28.3. In contrast to the past, when acquisitions were used to achieve market entry, economies of scale and scope, or gains in market power, many M&As are currently pursued for innovative purposes (Inkpen et al., 2000; Sleuwaegen and Valentini, 2006). As a consequence, we witness a substantial increase in the number of M&As undertaken in high-technology industries and recent work has addressed the growing importance of innovation as a motive for companies to engage in M&As (Hitt et al., 1991; Chakrabarti et al., 1994; Gerpott, 1995; Ahuja and Katila, 2001; Hagedoorn and Duysters, 2002; Cloodt et al., 2006). Yet, despite the large number of publications about the impact of M&As on the economic performance of companies, only a few researchers have studied the effect of M&As on the innovative performance (De Man and Duysters, 2005).

When reviewing the limited research related to post-M&A innovative performance, we would like to emphasize that it is important to make a clear distinction between input and output measures of innovation. The rationality behind this distinction is based on the fact that M&As often lead to a unification of the acquirer and target firms' knowledge bases that enable the combined firm to avoid or reduce duplicate R&D efforts and provide a larger research base to finance costs (Hall, 1990; Cassiman et al., 2005). Hence, the positive effect of these efficiency gains can be wrongly interpreted as a decline in input measures (i.e., R&D expenditures) while in reality innovative performance may remain the same or even show improvement but at a lower cost. In other words, output measures (i.e., patents, patent citations or new product announcements) may be more accurate when measuring a firm's post-M&A innovative performance than input measures (De Man and Duysters, 2005).

28.5.1   The Effect of M&As on Input Measures of Innovative Performance

Despite the fact that output measures of post-M&A innovative performance are more accurate we will shortly highlight the key findings related to the input measures of innovative performance, which show a mixture of results. Several studies exemplify that M&As hurt the innovative performance of a firm. For example, Hitt et al. (1991, 1996) show that acquisitions have a *direct* negative effect on R&D investments. This effect is likely due to transaction costs, which are present during the takeover process (Williamson, 1975). Potential difficulties with respect to M&As are, for example, the complexity of the acquisition process, information asymmetry, and asset specificity that firms engaged in M&A negotiations face (Hitt et al., 1996; Vanhaverbeke et al., 2002). The complexity of the acquisition process and in particular the complexity of M&A negotiations are based on the multiple parties that are often involved, that is, bankers, lawyers, and executives (Hitt et al., 1996). The information asymmetry argument addresses the problem of valuing a potential candidate for a merger or acquisition, while asset specificity deals with the difficulties associated with separating needed assets from undesired assets (Duysters, 2001; Vanhaverbeke et al., 2002). To deal with these transaction difficulties, M&As require extensive managerial time and energy and the use of substantial resources, which postpones investments in R&D and complicates the realization of potential innovative returns (Barney, 1988; Hitt et al., 1996). In other words, investments in R&D are often substituted for investments in M&As (Hitt et al., 1991). In addition, Miller (1990) shows that, due to undertaking the M&A, an increase in financial leverage diminishes R&D for some time. However, as a result of data limitations very little can be said about the time period over which such effects may extend. So, it is difficult to discern whether these short-term R&D cutbacks will indeed harm the long-term effectiveness of the firm (ibid.).

Others provide a more positive picture. For example, Healy et al. (1992) show that the improved cash flow returns of the merged firms do not come at the expense of long-term performance as the merged firms maintain their R&D rates relative to their industries. Such a relative test approach can help to exclude the influences of other explanations, like business cycles for example (Ikeda and Doi, 1983). In a study carried out by Hitt et al. (1998) results show that two-thirds of the successfully merged firms maintain their investments in R&D after the M&A takes place. Bertrand (2009) finds that acquisitions have a positive effect on the in-house R&D expenditures of the acquired firm, thereby contradicting the idea that managers take short-term finance-driven decisions at the expense of long-term R&D investments (no substitution effect). When comparing the post-merger performance of the merging firms with their pre-merger performance, Ikeda and Doi (1983) also find that R&D expenses mostly increase. However, R&D intensity (R&D expenses divided by sales) increases only in about half of their sample cases. Within the context of market dominance, Cefis et al. (2007) confirm that M&A activity has a direct positive effect on innovation inputs such as R&D investments. Finally, Cefis (2009) argues that in-house R&D expenditures increase after an M&A takes place in order to enlarge the absorptive capacity of the acquiring firm and to consolidate and integrate the newly acquired knowledge.

Overall, the existing empirical studies show a mix of results, which could be explained by the fact that they measure the *direct* impact of M&As on performance and largely

gnore the *conditions* that guide the relationship between M&A activity and its consequent innovative performance (Veugelers, 2006). This suggestion warrants an alternative
approach to investigating M&A performance. For instance, Gerpott (1995) shows that
R&D integration success after an M&A is higher for those acquirers that have a better
product/technology or market/customer relatedness with the target firm. Cassiman et
al. (2005) advance this discussion by arguing that product market relatedness and technological relatedness are important conditions when analyzing the impact of M&As on
innovation. According to them, technological relatedness will have a direct effect on the
R&D process while product market relatedness will have an indirect effect. More in particular, they find that for partners that are active in complementary technological fields,
M&As will have a positive effect on R&D inputs. Relative to these firms, M&As will
have a negative effect on R&D inputs for partners that are active in the same technological fields. Cassiman et al. (2005) confirm that product market relatedness has a negative
indirect effect on R&D inputs. However, we have to note that their sample only consist
of horizontal M&As for which they make a distinction between rival firms and other
horizontal M&As.

28.5.2   The Effect of M&As on Output Measures of Innovative Performance

When reviewing the effect of M&As on output measures of innovative performance,
we start by discussing two studies that include both R&D inputs as well as R&D
outputs in their analysis (so the findings of these studies are partly discussed in this
section and partly in the previous section). First, Hitt et al. (1991) argue that M&As
not only have a negative effect on R&D inputs (as described above) but also have a
negative effect on R&D outputs (e.g., patent intensity). Again it is argued that M&As
need so much managerial time and attention that this leads to a lower commitment
to long-term investments such as innovation (Hitt et al., 1990, 1991). Second, Cefis
et al. (2007) find that in addition to a positive effect on R&D expenditures, M&A
activity also has a positive effect on the level of sales from products new to the firm.
However, M&A activity has no significant effect on the sales from products new to
the market.

Overall, both studies largely fail to prove a strong positive effect of M&As on innovative performance (with the exception of enhancing the level of sales from products
new to the firm), which can be explained by the fact that their sample consists of several
manufacturing industries ranging from low-tech to high-tech. Within such a broad
range of industries firms will enter M&As for multiple reasons and only a part of these
M&As are deliberately pursued for innovative purposes by obtaining new technological
knowledge that is essential to a firm's success (Sleuwaegen and Valentini, 2006). Given
that high-technology industries are classified as the most technologically oriented and
knowledge-driven industries (Link, 1988; OECD, 1997), it turns out that especially firms
operating in such a high-tech environment demonstrate an assertive acquisition behavior
and they use extensive knowledge recombination in order to improve their innovative
performance and survive in the long run (Bierly and Chakrabarti, 1996; Capron and
Mitchell, 2000). Not surprisingly, recent studies of post-M&A innovative performance
all focus on high-tech industries, where M&As have become a vital source of innovation.
Such a clear focus is very important since prior research confirms that the knowledge

intensity of the industry is indeed an important moderator of acquisition performanc and research results become different when this contingency is ignored (Homberg et al 2009).

We will now illustrate the results of several studies in high-tech industries that spe cifically focus on post-M&A innovative performance in terms of output measures However, before we do so we would like to emphasize that these studies clearly mov away from analyzing the direct effect of M&As on output measures towards under standing the conditions under which M&As in a high-tech environment might have positive effect on the post-M&A innovative performance. For example, Ernst and Vit (2000) show that a high degree of technological relatedness between the acquiring and acquired firm results in lower fluctuation rates of key inventors in the acquired company However, those key inventors who remained with the acquired company after the M&A was completed significantly reduced their innovative performance in terms of patenting activity and patenting performance. Lin and Jang (2009) conclude that there is a clear positive relationship between technological relatedness and the innovative performance of the acquiring firm (in terms of patenting).

Extending the number of conditions, Hagedoorn and Duysters (2002) argue that stra-tegic fit, in terms of product market relatedness, technological relatedness, and the leve of R&D intensity of partner companies, will have a direct positive effect on the innova-tive performance of the combined firms. An important contribution made is the clear distinction in different types of relatedness, as relatedness in product markets does not automatically entail relatedness in technological domains and the other way around (Cassiman et al., 2005; Makri et al., 2010). Moreover, they find a positive relationship between the organizational fit, in terms of the similarity in size of M&A partners, and the innovative performance of the combined firms.

Ahuja and Katila (2001) and Cloodt et al. (2006) extend previous studies by making a clear distinction between the effect of non-technological M&As and technological M&As on the post-M&A innovative performance. Although most of the reviewed studies are undertaken in high-tech industries, research shows that even in those indus-tries non-technological motives to acquire a target firm can be important (Cloodt, 2005). A possible reason is that firms operating in high-tech sectors are often rapidly growing, which creates a shortage of managerial and/or financial resources (McGowan, 1971). This motivates firms to acquire targets that can offer these resources, even if they cannot make a significant contribution to the existing knowledge base of the acquiring firm.

Results of the studies by Ahuja and Katila (2001) and Cloodt et al. (2006) show that non-technological M&As in high-tech industries have a negative effect on the post-M&A innovative performance of the acquiring firm. These M&As create a disruption of the established organizational routines, thereby consuming so much managerial time and energy that this leads to a lower managerial commitment to long-term investments in innovation (Hitt et al., 1996; Ahuja and Katila, 2001).

When analyzing the conditions under which technological M&As might have a posi-tive effect on innovative performance, both the technological unification of the partners in terms of size of the acquired knowledge bases (absolute and relative) and relatedness of the partners' knowledge bases play an important role (Ahuja and Katila, 2001; Cloodt et al., 2006). This focus on the knowledge bases of both partners is based on the idea that or firms operating in high-tech industries, knowledge will be the most important source f competitive advantage (Cloodt et al., 2006; Makri et al., 2010).

According to Ahuja and Katila (2001) the absolute size of the acquired knowledge ase has a positive effect on the post-M&A innovative performance of the acquiring rm. In contrast to Ahuja and Katila (2001), Cloodt et al.'s (2006) study shows that the cquisition of a large absolute knowledge base only contributes to improved innova- ive performance during the first couple of post-M&A years. Thereafter this kind of cquisition appears to have a negative influence. Results of both studies show that if he acquired firm's knowledge base is relatively large compared to the acquiring firm's :nowledge base, this can have serious consequences for the integration of the innovative ctivities of both M&A partners with a negative impact on the acquirer's innovative)erformance. Finally, to enhance the innovative performance through M&As compa- ies have to target firms with moderately related knowledge bases, avoiding targets with :nowledge bases that are either too closely related or too unrelated (Ahuja and Katila, ?001; Cloodt et al., 2006).

As illustrated in the above, the concept of knowledge becomes an important one and several studies argue that previous research analyzes technological relatedness or knowl- :dge relatedness too much in aggregate. When examining post-M&A innovative per- 'ormance, differences in the nature of knowledge have to be explored further by making a clear distinction between the different dimensions of knowledge (e.g., depth, breadth, and relatedness) or different types of knowledge (e.g., science and technology). Drawing on the knowledge-based view of the firm and the understanding of the relevance of the notion of absorptive capacity from organizational theory, Prabhu et al. (2005) analyze not only the relatedness of knowledge bases but also focus on the depth and breadth of the acquiring firm's technological knowledge base. They argue that firms with a higher depth of knowledge have a higher post-M&A innovative performance than firms with a lower depth of knowledge. The impact of M&As on innovative performance for firms with a higher breadth of knowledge compared to firms with a lower breadth of knowl- edge is insignificant. Comparable to Ahuja and Katila (2001) and Cloodt et al. (2006), Prabhu et al. (2005) also find that acquiring firms with knowledge bases that are mod- erately similar to that of their targets have a higher post-M&A innovative performance than acquirers with knowledge that is very similar to or very different from that of the targets.

Finally, Makri et al. (2010) differentiate the nature of knowledge by making a distinction between the effect of science (basic research) relatedness and technology (applied research) relatedness on the innovative success of high-technology acquisi- tions. In addition, it is interesting to note that the dependent variable innovative success is not only defined in terms of invention quantity (patent counts), but also in terms of invention quality (patent citations) and invention novelty (technological diversification). Their study shows that the combination of both science and technol- ogy complementarities leads to an increase of invention quality and novelty and a marginal increase in invention quantity as well. Knowledge similarity (in terms of science and technology) has a negative effect on novelty due to path dependencies that lead to a constrained search process, and no effect on invention quantity or invention quality (ibid.).

28.6   THE EVOLUTION OF POST-M&A INNOVATIVE PERFORMANCE RESEARCH

Focusing on the effect of M&As on input and output measures of innovative performance, the studies reviewed so far clearly show an evolution in research. First, over time we witness an apparent change in measuring the direct impact of M&As on input and output indicators of innovative performance (do M&As have a positive or a negative effect on innovation?) towards a more contingency-oriented approach (under which conditions does a merger or acquisition improve innovative performance?).

Second, in the later studies we see a much stronger focus on high-tech industries and within these industries on the division of technological M&As versus non-technological M&As. As mentioned earlier this addresses the growing importance of innovation as a motive for companies to engage in M&As.

Third, given that innovation is such an important motive we see that knowledge becomes a vital concept in the evaluation of the performance of high-technology M&As. Studies contributing to this research perspective are mainly embedded within the resource-based view and knowledge-based view of the firm, in combination with some related contributions that stress the importance of organizational learning (e.g., Levitt and March, 1988; Huber, 1991; Boisot, 1995; Grant, 1996). More in particular, in the context of post-M&A innovative performance, the resource-based view and the knowledge-based view have been presented as theoretical perspectives that support several major views on acquisitions by arguing that the resource profiles (or knowledge profiles) of acquiring and target firm can explain the variance in M&A performance (Hitt et al., 1998; King et al., 2008). The opportunities for organizational learning increase when a firm is exposed to new and diverse ideas based on differences in technological capabilities between the acquiring and the acquired firm (Goshal, 1987; Hitt et al., 1996). By making accurate use of the acquired knowledge base a firm can not only develop a strong and coherent technological profile but also access and monitor all the necessary technologies embedded in a broad range of unrelated technological areas, thereby increasing its flexibility (Grant, 1996).

As a consequence, not only product market relatedness but also technological relatedness and science relatedness are seen as important antecedents of post-M&A innovative performance in recent research. The same trend is observable for size. Not only is the size of the M&A partners imperative, the absolute and relative size of their knowledge bases also play an important role. Even more so, research shows that in a context in which innovation is an important strategic motive to undertake an M&A, knowledge relatedness has a higher significant impact on post-M&A innovative performance than product market relatedness or relative size of the firms (Prabhu et al., 2005). In addition, besides relatedness other characteristics of a firm's knowledge base (for example, depth and breadth) are characterized as significant antecedents of success.

Finally, it is argued that we should not only examine post-M&A innovative performance by analyzing the effect of acquisitions on the quantity of the acquiring (or combined) firm's knowledge base in terms of an increase in R&D expenditures, patents, patent citations or new products. Current research should be extended by also examining the effects of M&As on the nature of knowledge in terms of the *quality* of the acquiring (or combined) firm's knowledge base and its *novelty* (see Makri et al., 2010).

Despite this clear evolution in research we still fail to find many coherent results. The variance in results is, for example, illustrated by the effect of technological relatedness on the post-M&A innovative performance. While Hagedoorn and Duysters (2002) and Lin and Jang (2009) find a positive linear effect of technological relatedness on the post-M&A innovative performance, Makri et al. (2010) find no effect (with the exception of a negative effect on novelty), while Cassiman et al. (2005) find a negative effect. In addition, Ahuja and Katila (2001), Cloodt et al. (2006), and Prabhu et al. (2005) all find a curvilinear effect. Also the effect of product market relatedness leads to inconclusive results. Cassiman et al. (2005) conclude that product market relatedness has a negative indirect effect on innovative performance, while Hagedoorn and Duysters (2002) show that product market relatedness has a direct positive effect on innovative performance.

These examples clearly highlight the mixed bag of findings, although we would like to stress that we have to interpret such a direct comparison with caution. Differences between the studies in terms of coverage of industries (ranging from low-tech to high-tech), analysis of direct effects versus conditional effects, types of M&As (technological versus non-technological), definition of success (e.g., in terms of innovative benefits to the acquiring firm, the acquired firm or the combined firm) as well as to the measurement of innovative performance (input versus output measures and/or quantity versus quality/novelty) make a direct comparison somewhat difficult, to say the least.

28.7   CONCLUSIONS

Prior M&A performance research, showing on average deteriorating or stagnating post-M&A economic performance, is largely based on the traditional motives of market entry, market structure, and synergy-related considerations. Still, the evolution of M&A research shows that firms' motives for engaging in M&As evolves over the years, with innovation becoming an even more important rationale during the last merger wave.

Although innovation has become such an important motive, so far only a limited number of studies has analyzed the post-M&A innovative performance of companies. And while each of these studies substantially contributes to the understanding of performance variance, a mix of empirical results has emerged. In addition, there is no agreement in the current body of literature on the explanation for these widely varying results in the innovative performance of M&As.

We argue that the differences between the existing empirical studies or the 'myopia' of performance studies themselves could be an important explanation for the contradictory findings in M&A performance. While it is logical that research from a certain academic discipline develops along a specific line of specialization, insights are fragmented and build too much in isolation from each other. Even within the same academic discipline it is no surprise that there appears to be hardly any clear understanding of M&A performance given the variety in types of M&A, measurements of performance, samples, databases, industry settings and the inconsistency in definitions of M&A performance success.

Until now these differences have been largely overlooked by academics, which illustrates the necessity of an alternative research approach. As such, while it has been possible to discuss only a few of the relevant contributions, the aim of this review is to enhance our insight into the diversity of existing research. We hope that this will be a first step towards a satisfactory progress in M&A performance research and provides a starting base for future research by calling upon scholars to develop a much more holistic understanding of M&A performance.

REFERENCES

Ahuja, G. and R. Katila, 2001, Technological acquisitions and the innovation performance of acquiring firms: a longitudinal study, *Strategic Management Journal*, **22**(3), 197–220.

Barney, J.B., 1988, Returns to bidding firms in mergers and acquisitions: reconsidering the relatedness hypothesis, *Strategic Management Journal*, **9**(51), 71–8.

Berkovitch, E. and P. Narayanan, 1993, Motives for takeovers: an empirical investigation, *Journal of Financial and Quantitative Analysis*, **28**(3), 347–62.

Bertrand, O., 2009, Effects of foreign acquisitions on R&D activity: evidence from firm-level data for France, *Research Policy*, **38**(6), 1021–31.

Bierly, P. and A. Chakrabarti, 1996, Generic knowledge strategies in the U.S. pharmaceutical industry, *Strategic Management Journal*, **17**(Winter Special Issue), 123–35.

Boisot, M.H., 1995, Is your firm a creative destroyer? Competitive learning and knowledge flows in the technological strategies of firms, *Research Policy*, **24**(4), 489–506.

Buono, A.F. and J.L. Bowditch, 1989, *The human side of mergers and acquisitions*, Jossey-Bass, San Francisco.

Capron, L. and W. Mitchell, 2000, Internal versus external knowledge sourcing: evidence from telecom operators in Europe, Working Paper, INSEAD, France.

Carlton, D.W. and J.M. Perloff, 1990, *Modern industrial organization*, HarperCollins Publishers, New York, London.

Cassiman, B., M.G. Colombo, P. Garrone and R. Veugelers, 2005, The impact of M&A on the R&D process: an empirical analysis of the role of technological and market relatedness, *Research Policy*, **34**(2), 195–220.

Caves, R.E., 1989, Mergers, takeovers, and economic efficiency: foresight vs. hindsight, *International Journal of Industrial Organization*, **7**(1), 16–30.

Cefis, E., 2009, The impact of M&A on technology sourcing strategies, *Economics of Innovation and New Technology*, **19**(1), 27–51.

Cefis, E., A. Sabidussi and H. Schenk, 2007, Do mergers of potentially dominant firms foster innovation?, Tjalling C. Koopmans Research Institute, Discussion Paper Series No. 07-20, Utrecht School of Economics, Utrecht University, Utrecht.

Chakrabarti, A., J. Hauschildt and C. Sueverkruep, 1994, Does it pay to acquire technological firms?, *R&D Management*, **24**(1), 47–56.

Chiara di Guardo, M. and G. Valentini, 2007, Explaining the effect of M&A on technological performance, *Advances in Mergers and Acquisitions* series, **6**, pp. 107–25.

Cloodt, M., 2005, Mergers and acquisitions (M&As) in high-tech industries: measuring the post-M&A innovative performance of companies, PhD thesis Maastricht University, Maastricht.

Cloodt, M., J. Hagedoorn and H. van Kranenburg, 2006, Mergers and acquisitions: their effect on the innovative performance of companies in high-tech industries, *Research Policy*, **35**(5), 642–54.

Cooke, T.E., 1988, *International mergers and acquisitions*, Basil Blackwell, Oxford.

Datta, D.K., 1991, Organizational fit and acquisition performance: effects of post-acquisition integration, *Strategic Management Journal*, **12**(4), 281–97.

De Man, A-P. and G. Duysters, 2005, Collaboration and innovation: a review of the effects of mergers, acquisitions, and alliances on innovation, *Technovation*, **25**(12), 1377–87.

DuBoff, R.B. and E.S. Herman, 2001, Mergers, concentration, and the erosion of democracy, *Monthly Review*, **53**(1), 14–29.

Duysters, G., 2001, Partner or perish, surviving the network economy, inaugural lecture given on 22 June 2001, Eindhoven University of Technology, Eindhoven.

Ernst, H. and J. Vitt, 2000, The influence of corporate acquisitions on the behaviour of key inventors, *R&D Management*, **30**(2), 105–19.

Gaughan, P., 2002, What is the outlook for M&A in an uncertain market?, *The Journal of Corporate Accounting & Finance*, **13**(5), 51–3.

Gerpott, T.J., 1995, Successful integration of R&D functions after acquisition: an exploratory empirical study, *R&D Management*, **25**(2), 161–78.

Golbe, D.L. and L.J. White, 1988, Mergers and acquisition in the US economy: an aggregate and historical overview, in: A.J. Auerbach (ed.), *Mergers and acquisitions*, The University of Chicago Press, Chicago, pp. 25–47.

Joshal, S., 1987, Global strategy: an organizing framework, *Strategic Management Journal*, **8**(5), 425–40.

Grant, R.M., 1996, Toward a knowledge-based theory of the firm, *Strategic Management Journal*, **17**(Winter Special Issue), 109–22.

Hagedoorn, J. and G. Duysters, 2002, The effect of mergers and acquisitions on the technological performance of companies in a high-tech environment, *Technology Analysis & Strategic Management*, **14**(1), 67–85.

Hagedoorn, J. and B. Sadowski, 1999, The transition from strategic technology alliances to mergers and acquisitions: an exploratory study, *Journal of Management Studies*, **36**(1), 87–107.

Haleblian, J., C.E. Devers, G. McNamara, M.A. Carpenter and R.B. Davison, 2009, Taking stock of what we know about mergers and acquisitions: a review and research agenda, *Journal of Management*, **35**(3), 469–502.

Hall, B.H., 1990, The impact of corporate restructuring on industrial research and development, *Brookings Papers on Economic Activity*, **3**, 85–135.

Haspeslagh, P.C. and D.B. Jemison, 1991, *Managing acquisitions: creating value through corporate renewal*, The Free Press, New York.

Hay, D.A. and D.J. Morris, 1991, *Industrial economics and organization*, Oxford University Press, Oxford.

Healy, P.M., K.G. Palepu and R.S. Ruback, 1992, Does corporate performance improve after mergers?, *Journal of Financial Economics*, **31**(2), 135–75.

Hitt, M.A., R.E. Hoskisson and H. Kim, 1997, International diversification: effects on innovation and firm performance in product-diversified firms, *Academy of Management Journal*, **40**(4), 767–98.

Hitt, M.A., R.E. Hoskisson and R.D. Ireland, 1990, Mergers and acquisitions and managerial commitment to innovation in M-form firms, *Strategic Management Journal*, **11**(Special Issue), 29–47.

Hitt, M.A., J.S. Harrison, R.D. Ireland and A. Best, 1998, Attributes of successful and unsuccessful acquisitions of US firms, *British Journal of Management*, **9**(2), 91–114.

Hitt, M.A., R.E. Hoskisson, R.D. Ireland and J.S. Harrison, 1991, Effects of acquisitions on R&D inputs and outputs, *Academy of Management Journal*, **34**(3), 693–706.

Hitt, M.A., R.E. Hoskisson, R.A. Johnson and D.D. Moesel, 1996, The market for corporate control and firm innovation, *Academy of Management Journal*, **39**(5), 1084–119.

Homberg, F., K. Rost and M. Osterloh, 2009, Do synergies exist in related acquisitions? A meta-analysis of acquisition studies, *Review of Managerial Science*, **3**(2), 75–116.

Hoskisson, R.E. and M.A. Hitt, 1994, *Downscoping: how to tame the diversified firm*, Oxford University Press, Oxford.

Hoskisson, R.E. and R.A. Johnson, 1992, Corporate restructuring and strategic change: the effect on diversification strategy and R&D intensity, *Strategic Management Journal*, **13**(8), 625–34.

Huber, G.P., 1991, Organizational learning: the contributing processes and literatures, *Organization Science*, **2**(1), 71–87.

Ikeda, K. and N. Doi, 1983, The performance of merging firms in Japanese manufacturing industry: 1964–75, *The Journal of Industrial Economics*, **31**(3), 257–65.

Inkpen, A.C., A.K. Sundaran and K. Rockwood, 2000, Cross-border acquisitions of US technology assets, *California Management Review*, **42**(3), 50–71.

Jarell, G.A., J.A. Brickley and J.M. Netter, 1988, The market for corporate control: the empirical evidence since 1980, *Journal of Economic Perspectives*, **2**(1), 49–68.

Jemison, D.B. and S.B. Sitkin, 1986, Corporate acquisitions: a process perspective, *Academy of Management Review*, **11**(1), 145–63.

Jensen, M.C., 1984, Takeovers: folklore and science, *Harvard Business Review*, **62**(6), 109–21.

Jensen, M.C. and R.S. Ruback, 1983, The market for corporate control: scientific evidence, *Journal of Financial Economics*, **11**(1–4), 5–50.

Katz, J.P., A. Simanek and J.B. Townsend, 1997, Corporate mergers and acquisitions: one more wave to consider, *Business Horizons*, **40**(1), 32–40.

King, D.R., R.J. Slotegraaf and I. Kesner, 2008, Performance implications of firm resource interactions in the acquisition of R&D intensive firms, *Organization Science*, **19**(2), 327–40.

King, D.R., D.R. Dalton, C.M. Daily and J.G. Covin, 2004, Meta-analyses of post-acquisition performance: indications of unidentified moderators, *Strategic Management Journal*, **25**(2), 187–200.

Levitt, B. and J.G. March, 1988, Organizational learning, *Annual Review of Sociology*, **14**, 319–40.

Lin, C-H. and S-L. Jang, 2009, The impact of M&As on company innovation: evidence from the US medical device industry, *Scientometrics*, **84**(1), 119–31.

Link, A.N., 1988, Acquisitions as sources of technological innovation, *Mergers and Acquisitions*, **23**(3), 36–9.

Lipton, M., 2006, Merger waves in the 19th, 20th and 21st centuries, The Davies Lecture, Osgoode Hall Law School, York University.

Lubatkin, M., 1987, Merger strategies and stockholder value, *Strategic Management Journal*, **8**(1), 39–53.

Makri, M., M.A. Hitt and P.J. Lane, 2010, Complementary technologies, knowledge relatedness, and invention outcomes in high technology mergers and acquisitions, *Strategic Management Journal*, **31**(6), 602–28.

McGowan, J.J., 1971, International comparisons of merger activities, *Journal of Law and Economics*, **14**(1), 233–50.

Meeks, G., 1977, *Disappointing marriage: a study of the gains from merger*, Cambridge University Press, Cambridge.

Miller, R.R., 1990, Do mergers and acquisitions hurt R&D?, *Research Technology Management*, **33**(2), 11–15.

Moeller, S. and C. Brady, 2007, Intelligent M&A: navigating the mergers and acquisitions minefield, John Wiley & Sons Ltd., Chichester.

Mueller, D.C., 1980, *The determinants and effects of mergers, an international comparison*, Oelgeschlager, Gunn & Hain, Cambridge, MA.

Mueller, D.C., 1986a, *The modern corporation – profits, power, growth and performance*, Wheatsheaf Books, Brighton.

Mueller, D.C., 1986b, *Profits in the long run*, Cambridge University Press, Cambridge.

Mukherjee, T.K., H. Kiymaz and H.K. Baker, 2004, Merger motives and target valuation: a survey of evidence from CFOs, paper presented at the Financial Management Association annual meeting, JEL classification G34, October, New Orleans.

OECD, 1997, *Revision of high technology sector and product classification*, OECD, Paris.

Olie, R.L., 1996, *European transnational mergers*, Datawyse Maastricht, Maastricht.

Oster, S.M., 1999, *Modern competitive analysis*, Oxford University Press, New York.

Porter, M.E., 1987, From competitive advantage to corporate strategy, *Harvard Business Review*, **65**(3), May–June, 43–59.

Prabhu, J.C., R.K. Chandy and M.E. Ellis, 2005, The impact of acquisitions on innovation: poison pill, placebo or tonic, *Journal of Marketing*, **69**(1), 114–30.

PricewaterhouseCoopers, 2004, *Technology sector insights: analysis & opinions on merger & acquisition activity 2003*, PricewaterhouseCoopers, London.

Puranam, P., H. Singh and M. Zollo, 2003, A bird in the hand or two in the bush? Integration trade-offs in technology-grafting acquisitions, *European Management Journal*, **21**(2), 179–84.

Ravenscraft, D.J. and F.M. Scherer, 1987, Life after takeover, *Journal of Industrial Economics*, **36**(2), 147–57.

Ravenscraft, D.J. and F.M. Scherer, 1989, The profitability of mergers, *International Journal of Industrial Organization*, **7**(1), 101–17.

Scherer, F.M. and D. Ross, 1990, *Industrial market structure and economic performance*, Houghton Mifflin Company, Boston.

Seth, A., 1990, Value creation in acquisitions: a re-examination of performance issues, *Strategic Management Journal*, **11**(4), 99–115.

Shelton, L.M., 1988, Strategic business fits and corporate acquisition: empirical evidence, *Strategic Management Journal*, **9**(3), 279–87.

Singh, H. and C.A. Montgomery, 1987, Corporate strategies and economic performance, *Strategic Management Journal*, **8**(4), 377–86.

Sleuwaegen, L. and G. Valentini, 2006, Trends in mergers and acquisitions, in: B. Cassiman and M.G. Colombo (eds), *Mergers and acquisitions: the innovation impact*, Edward Elgar, Cheltenham, UK and Northampton, MA, USA, pp. 11–28.

Thomson Financial Statistics, 2004, Thomson financial worldwide M&A; mergers unleashed, www.thomson.com.

Trautwein, F., 1990, Merger motives and merger prescriptions, *Strategic Management Journal*, **11**(4), 283–95.

Vanhaverbeke, W., G. Duysters and N. Noorderhaven, 2002, A longitudinal analysis of the choice between technology based strategic alliances and acquisitions in high-tech industries: the case of the ASIC industry, *Organization Science*, **13**(6), 714–33.

Veugelers, R., 2006, Literature review, in: B. Cassiman and M.G. Colombo (eds), *Mergers and acquisitions: the innovation impact*, Edward Elgar, Cheltenham, UK and Northampton, MA, USA, pp. 37–62.

Weston, J.F. and K.S. Chung, 1990, Takeovers and corporate restructuring: an overview, *Business Economics*, **25**(2), 6–11.

Weston, J.F, K.S. Chung and S.E. Hoag, 1990, *Mergers, restructuring, and corporate control*, Prentice-Hall, Inc., New Jersey.

Williamson, O.E., 1975, *Markets and hierarchies, analysis and antitrust implications*, The Free Press, New York.

World Investment Report, 2000, *Cross-border mergers and acquisitions and development*, United Nations, New York and Geneva.

29 R&D and the firm
Pier Paolo Saviotti

29.1 INTRODUCTION

In this chapter we are going to discuss the relationship between R&D and the firm on the basis of three components. First, R&D is a new activity that emerged in the economic system towards the end of the nineteenth century. Since that time a growing number of firms, especially large ones, have adopted R&D as one of their internal functions. Second, starting from the Industrial Revolution the firm has been undergoing very profound transformations. Thus, the type of firms that use R&D and the uses they make of it have not been constant but have been changing in the course of time. Third, during the twentieth century and until the present the theories of the firm that economists have created underwent changes at least as important as the firms themselves. In this chapter the emergence of R&D as a new function and the evolution of the firm, including the internalization of R&D, are going to be discussed as a background to the analysis of the theories of the firm that economists have developed.

29.2 THE EMERGENCE OF R&D AS A NEW ECONOMIC ACTIVITY

29.2.1 Technology and the Firm

Organizations constituted by a group of people and operating to achieve objectives that were at least partly economic have existed for a very long time. Antecedents of such organizations can even be located in Roman times (Rosenberg and Birdzell, 1986). Important examples of such organizations are the medieval guilds and the chartered corporations, such as the East India Company. However, these organizations differed from the modern corporation in that they required special permission to operate, or sometimes a monopoly, issued by the state (ibid.). The concept of a corporation that could be formed by a group of individuals to trade or to manufacture and that could hold property rights, act as moral persons and accept liability only emerged in the second half of the nineteenth century, mostly in the UK and in the USA (ibid.). It is probably no coincidence that such joint stock corporations became a permissible legal form during the second part of the Industrial Revolution when they represented the most appropriate form to exploit the productive potential such revolution had unlocked.

The evolution of the modern firm is in many ways closely linked to technological evolution. Before the Industrial Revolution the scale of most manufacturing firms was small and essentially home based. For example, the textile industry was dominated by the so-called cottage industry. The large machines and the consequent capital requirements of the factory system started the growth of the manufacturing firms (see Marx in *Das Kapital*, 1867–94), growth that was to accelerate considerably towards the end of the nineteenth century (Chandler, 1962, 1977; Hannah, 1976). Such further spurt of growth in firm size was due to a combination of new technologies and of the resultant process of market expansion. The new technologies that contributed to the emergence of large corporations were of two types: first, there were the new technologies that led to the creation of new sectors, thus providing new productive opportunities. Examples of these could be found in the chemical and electrical industries. Second, other technologies were enabling in the sense that they allowed the transport and communication required for the geographical enlargement of markets. Examples of such technologies were railways, refrigeration and the telegraph. According to Chandler (1977, pp. 287–9) the modern corporation was created by the integration of mass production with mass distribution. Thus, technology has shaped and accompanied the evolution of the modern firm since the Industrial Revolution. However, the mechanisms whereby technology affected industry and the firm changed substantially with the institutionalization of R&D.

29.2.2   The Institutionalization of R&D

Today R&D is a common function of both modern economic systems and of most manufacturing firms, at least in developed countries and, even in developing and emerging countries a growing percentage of firms do some R&D. However, R&D as an independent economic function is little more than 100 years old. We could say that R&D is the result of an increasing division of labor, influenced partly by the growing utilization of science in industry during the nineteenth century and partly by the considerable enlargement of markets that such utilization of science indirectly contributed to. R&D is a result of an increasing division of labor in the sense that although both learning and knowledge had always been part of human activities, in previous times learning had generally been obtained as a joint product of production activities. Using modern terminology, before R&D activities existed learning had occurred by 'learning by doing'. The institutionalization of R&D gave rise to a separation of learning activities from production activities. We could say that R&D differed from learning by doing because it was *learning by not doing*. In this sense Freeman and Soete (1997) are right when they consider that the emergence of R&D was a true revolution, which fundamentally changed modern industry.

The word revolution implies that R&D was a complete break with respect to past trends. Of course, scientific activities had previously existed, but their volume was extremely low with respect to even R&D in the late nineteenth century. Furthermore, until the second half of the century the evolution of technology tended to be separate from that of science. Technologies themselves were called the industrial arts. During the nineteenth century, and even before large R&D laboratories were created, science started to exert a growing influence on technology. Historians differ as to the extent of such influence. For example, although most historians would probably agree that innovations in some industries (textiles, steam engines, railways, steel etc.) fundamentally contributed to the Industrial Revolution, there is still disagreement about the extent to which such innovations were affected by science (see Hobsbawm, 1968; Landes, 1969; Musson and Robinson, 1969; Mokyr, 1990, 2010; Lipsey et al., 2005). While it seems that science started having some effect on industry during the Industrial Revolution such effect could not be measured by R&D expenditures or by the citation of scientific work by patents. The institutionalization of R&D had to wait until the end of the nineteenth century.

Two very important events marked the beginning of the institutionalization of R&D. First, around the mid-nineteenth century the German, or von Humboldt university system for the first time systematically combined higher education and research. Second, during the second half of the nineteenth century some firms, mostly in Germany and the USA, started to create their own internal R&D laboratories (Mowery and Rosenberg, 1989; Freeman and Soete, 1997; Murmann, 2004). The German university system was later largely imitated and improved upon. The adoption of R&D by firms proceeded rapidly, but it is only after World War II that R&D became a systematic component of both the economic system and of firms in developed countries (Mowery and Rosenberg, 1989; Freeman and Soete, 1997).

Two questions can be raised at this point. First, why did the internalization of R&D occur at this particular moment? And second, why was R&D internalized in vertically integrated corporations rather than being produced in specialized research institutions? A tentative answer to the first question could be that at only this moment had science made enough progress to be applied systematically to industry. This answer is subject to many caveats. It is undoubtedly true that the progress of disciplines like chemistry and physics had been particularly fast in the period between the end of the nineteenth century and the beginning of the twentieth. However, it is clear that the relationship between science and technology had not been then and did not become subsequently one of passive application of science to technology. On the contrary, especially during the early part of the nineteenth century the role of science tended to be mainly concentrated on support activities like chemical analysis, or in general and often ex-post rationalization of processes that had been developed empirically. Important examples are the use of chemical analysis in the selection of iron ores in steel-making (Mowery and Rosenberg, 1989) and the development of thermodynamics following the progress of the steam engine. The contribution of academic research to development of the German chemical industry was probably an exceptional case, and it was largely due not only to the organization science but also to the co-evolution of scientific institutions, of intellectual property rights and of political institutions (Murmann, 2004). Furthermore, Layton (1974) and Vincenti (1990) have shown that technology creates knowledge in a form different from that of science.

The second question was related to the organization of industrial R&D. In principle, three modes of organization could have been expected to occur: first, industrial R&D could have been carried out in academic institutions; second, it could have been located in specialized firms or research organizations; third, it could have been undertaken in large, vertically integrated corporations. Although examples of all three types of organization existed, by far the most common form of internalization of industrial R&D was the internalization in large, vertically integrated corporations. In this sense the institutionalization of industrial R&D proceeded in parallel with the emergence of the large corporation.

The reasons for the dominance of this form of organization of industrial R&D can be found in the particular features of knowledge as a product of human activities. Knowledge is at least a partly public good in the sense that (1) a given piece of knowledge can be reused indefinitely without being consumed and that (2) it is difficult to prevent agents who have not paid for the creation of a given piece of knowledge from using it.

In this sense, internalization into large, vertically integrated corporations would have largely reduced the risk that knowledge created by a specialized organization external to the corporation could be equally available to its competitors. The internalization into large corporations was the dominant form of organizational industrial R&D from the end of the nineteenth century until the 1970s.

Starting from the 1970s a process of vertical disintegration, or externalization, of R&D began to be observed (Langlois, 2004). This process occurred in the form of inter-firm technological alliances, sometimes described as innovation networks (see for example, Hakansson, 1987; Mowery, 1989; Callon, 1991; Freeman, 1991; Saxenian, 1991; Hagedoorn, 1993, 1995; Powell et al., 1996). This phenomenon seemed to be a reversal of the previous trend and it is part of the evidence used by Langlois (2004) to argue that Chandler's visible hand was vanishing. This does not seem to be happening (Dosi et al., 2007). However, in a number of knowledge-intensive sectors high-tech start-ups and innovation networks have become a new form of industrial organization in addition to large, vertically integrated corporations. The precise reasons for this transition are related both to the dynamics of knowledge and to the evolution of industrial organization. The general evolution of the firm will be discussed in greater detail in the next section.

During the period 1950–90 there was a change described by Das Gupta and David (1994) as the transition between the old and the new economics of science. The old economics of science (Nelson, 1959; Arrow, 1962) insisted on the public character of science and in particular on its lack of appropriability. Such public good features would have resulted in the social organization of knowledge production. For example, in most circumstances highly risky fundamental research was likely to be carried out in public research organizations (PROs) while firms and private research organizations would focus on more applied and less risky research. Furthermore, intellectual property rights (IPRs) needed to be designed to protect the interests of the inventor by granting him or her a temporary monopoly as an inducement to innovate. Also, in these conditions the internalization of R&D in corporations seemed eminently sensible as a way of limiting the possible leakages of knowledge outside the boundaries of the firm.

The new economics of knowledge differed from the old one by stressing not only the influence of the properties of knowledge but also that of the social organization of knowledge production. Thus, amongst other differences, the new economics of science differed from the old one as to the cost of imitating a given piece of knowledge relative to that of creating it. The basis for the existence of patents is the need to compensate for the relative cheapness of imitation by awarding the inventor a temporary monopoly. However, as Cohen and Levinthal (1989) pointed out, imitation of a given technology requires carrying out R&D in the same technology in order to create the required absorption capacity. To the extent that the cost of creating the required absorption capacity becomes comparable to that of innovating, knowledge turns out to be much less public than was previously thought, thus substantially undermining the case for IPRs.

The recognition of the importance of spillovers was another important development that took place in the 1980s. Although the involuntary character of spillovers can be rather doubtful, the large amounts of knowledge above that internally created by a corporation can exert a powerful impact on the economic system at different levels of aggregation. At the macroeconomic level spillovers are the externalities resulting from

ncreasing returns to knowledge generation that can account for the long-run continu-
tion of growth (Romer, 1990). At the level of the firm spillovers pass from being an
xpression of waste in knowledge production to that of being a powerful resource that
nhances the collective performance of industries and economies.

Another change that is likely to have an important impact on the firm and on indus-
rial organization is the rate of knowledge production and utilization. According to
Agarwal and Gort (2001) the average delay between the creation of a new idea and its
ndustrial utilization fell from 39 years at the end of the nineteenth century to three years
at the end of the twentieth. This increased rate of utilization is likely to have stretched the
capabilities of incumbent large firms to learn, thus favoring the emergence of high-tech
start-ups and of innovation networks.

29.3   THE EVOLUTION OF THE FIRM

Until the Industrial Revolution most firms were small. Some large organizations existed
(for example, the East India Company) but they were the exception rather than the rule.
Furthermore, until the mid-nineteenth century the creation of an organization that could
carry out the type of functions that are nowadays carried out by corporations required
the permission of the state (Rosenberg and Birdzell, 1986). Only in the second half of
the nineteenth century did western countries start to confer the legal status of persons
on groups formed for economic purposes without requiring an act of legislature or other
political authority (ibid., p. 207). Thus, the modern firm owes its origin to a legal change.
However, it seems unlikely that this legal change occurred when it did just by chance. As
has already been pointed out, the emergence of railways, of the telegraph and of refrigeration technology enabled the creation of large corporations that could serve customers
in very distant and scattered markets. The legal change itself cannot be considered the
cause of the emergence of the large corporation but one of the factors that contributed to
it. The changes in technology that started occurring from the beginning of the Industrial
Revolution provided potential for the creation of new firms that could not have been
realized unless an adequate legal framework was established. Thus, neither legal changes
nor changes in technology can be interpreted as the cause of the emergence of large
corporations. Rather, these two factors have been co-evolving in the sense that changes
in technology induced the establishment of a new type of institution. In a more general
sense it is clear that the modern firm could not have emerged the way it did without the
changes in technology that took place since the Industrial Revolution.

Until the Industrial Revolution the organization of the textile industry, the first
modern industry, was described as a 'cottage industry', in which textile merchants would
take fibers (cotton, wool etc.) or cloth to the houses of the spinners or weavers and collect
the output later. This organizational form lasted until the early years of the Industrial
Revolution when it was gradually replaced by the factory system. Such a system consisted
of large purpose-built buildings containing not just workers but very large machines,
which greatly enhanced the efficiency of production. While not yet reaching the size of
today's industrial firms those of the factory system were systematically larger than those
that had preceded them. Thus, the first systematic enlargement of the firm and its distinction from handicraft production began during the Industrial Revolution in the UK. The

emergence of the factory system coincided with that of capitalism. As the new capita goods became larger and more powerful they required a much greater investment an gave rise to the capitalist class. The emergence of the capitalist economy was brilliantl analyzed by Marx in *Das Kapital* (1861–94). Thus, the first systematic enlargement o the firm was partly driven by changes in technology, the innovations of the Industria Revolution, accompanied by changes in legal and financial institutions that allowed th increased investment required during the Industrial Revolution to be made.

In spite of their increased size, the firms of the Industrial Revolution were still smal compared to today's. A further spurt of growth in firm size came from a combination o new technologies and of enlarged market sizes. The first example of this new period o firm growth began in the United States towards the end of the nineteenth century. The main technologies that contributed to this development were the railways, the telegrap and refrigeration technology (Chandler, 1962). Railways allowed goods to be transporte over very large distances covering even a country of the size of the USA. The telegrap allowed the different points of shipping and of arrival of the goods to be coordinated These technologies allowed the creation of large corporations to have many offices an factories scattered over very large geographical areas. Refrigeration technology allowe the transport of perishable goods, such as meat, over very long distances, thus increasin the number of sectors in which large corporations could be created. This developmen was not unique to the USA, but occurred, although more gradually, in other countries such as Britain and Germany. Large corporations similar to those existing today startec to be created then. Of course, not all the firms became large. Many small firms continued to exist and were numerically dominant but they were secondary characters in the corpo- rate economy. This type of industrial organization dominated most developed economic systems between the end of the nineteenth century and the 1970s.

As Alfred Chandler (1962, 1977), perhaps the greatest interpreter of the corporate economy, pointed out, increased firm size could not occur without adequate organiza- tional changes. The large corporation was not simply a larger version of previous firms but a large firm organized according to very different principles. In his early work (1962) Chandler used the concepts of *strategy* and *structure* to interpret the evolution of large corporations. He defined strategy as the set of broad objectives of the corporation and structure as the corporation's internal organization. According to Chandler the strategy defined the prevailing structure. The first type of corporation to emerge, the multifunc- tional or U-form, was characterized by having many divisions, each corresponding to a function, such as finance, production, sales and so on. In other words, the firm organiza- tion could not remain flat as its size increased by orders of magnitude. A form of division of labor had to be introduced not only at the individual level but also at the level of the corporation as a whole. Thus, there was a division of labor with different divisions corre- sponding to different functions, but also a hierarchical structure, at the top of which was the general office. The general office not only coordinated the activities of divisions of the firm but it carried out the new function of planning. In other words, the general office not only provided the coordination of existing activities, but tried to anticipate future evolutions and the possible adaptations or creation of new activities required. As the economy grew during the twentieth century and as standards of living improved markets for higher quality and more differentiated goods and services provided firms with new profit and opportunities. Both the strategy and the structure of the firm needed to change accordingly. This change in the economic environment induced the transition from the multifunctional to the multidivisional or M-form corporation. In this new structure each division was responsible for a different product or market. Thus, a change in the economic environment induced a change of strategy, which in turn entailed a change in structure. Of course, the concept of strategy is to be interpreted here in a very general way, such as pursuing market growth in a series of relatively homogenized markets or shifting to more highly differentiated markets.

The emergence of the corporate economy was held by Chandler (1977) to have substantially changed the mechanisms of the capitalist economy by replacing Adam Smith's invisible hand (*Theory of Moral Sentiments*, 1759) with the visible hand of the large corporation.

As we have previously seen, the largely increased size of the corporation and the consequent organizational changes were, at least in part, induced by new technology. It is to be observed that both in the USA (Chandler, 1962) and in the UK (Hannah, 1976) the multifunctional form was pioneered by the railways, probably the first industry to attain a very large firm size. However, not only the corporate economy shaped and was shaped in a co-evolutionary pattern by new technologies, but it also had a fundamental influence on the institutionalization of R&D. Given the considerable progress in science that occurred in the nineteenth century three options were in principle possible for the organization of R&D. First, R&D could have been carried out in universities or in research institutes; second, it could have been carried out in organizations specializing in R&D; third, it could have been internalized into large firms. Although all these forms were used to a certain extent the first and the third became dominant, but they were not carrying out the same type of research. Typically, universities and research institutes performed fundamental research while industrial firms performed applied research. A number of firms specializing in R&D existed at all times, but they declined as a percentage of total R&D activity in the course of the twentieth century (Mowery and Rosenberg, 1989).

A number of studies have been carried out on the firms that pioneered the R&D function. Du Pont, General Electric, Bayer and so on were amongst the first firms to establish internal R&D laboratories. In these firms the problems that would have been recurrent in R&D management started to present themselves. For example, the location and nature of research immediately became the subject of controversy. The temporal horizon of R&D projects as well as the degree of centralization of R&D labs kept changing within the history of firms (Reich, 1985; Hounshell and Smith, 1988). In summary, from the end of the nineteenth century to the 1970s the main organizational form of industrial R&D was its internalization within vertically integrated corporations. The coincidence of the institutionalization of industrial R&D and of the emergence of the corporate economy did not occur by chance. On the one hand to establish separate R&D laboratories could be easier in a large firm, especially in the presence of the general office, one of the functions of which was to define the firm strategy. On the other hand, the decision to internalize R&D rather than purchasing it from external suppliers depended on the nature of knowledge, which would have the result of external R&D being equally available to the firm purchasing it and to its competitors. During the whole period from 1900 to the 1970s R&D was predominantly carried out in universities and research institutes when it was fundamental or in large vertically integrated corporations when it was applied. This division of labor was later justified by the lack of appropriability, knowledge common to all, and to higher level of risk inherent in fundamental research (Nelson, 1959; Arrow 1962).

During the 1970s a growing trend towards vertical disintegration started to be observed (Langlois, 2004) with examples of large firms externalizing a growing number and percentage of their functions. This trend did not replace large corporations with small firms or with market relations (Dosi et al., 2007) but provided opportunities for the entry of a new type of firm, high-technology start-ups, and significantly changed inter-firm relations. Examples of these new organizational arrangements included the rise of firms like the ill-fated Enron or the emergence of what were alternatively called technological alliances or innovation networks (see for example, Hakansson, 1987; Mowery, 1989; Callon, 1991; Freeman, 1991; Saxenian, 1991; Hagedoorn, 1993, 1995; Powell et al., 1996). These were essentially two distinct phenomena, although they were in different ways related to the mechanisms whereby firms learn and use knowledge. Some forms of knowledge can be conveniently externalized when they become modular and when they do not involve core competencies (Prahalad and Hamel, 1990) of the firm. Other types of knowledge can be so new and disruptive for incumbent firms that internal learning is likely to be inferior to alliances with start-ups highly competent in these types of knowledge. The latter category is both very different from pre-existing types of inter-firm collaboration and highly dependent on the dynamics of knowledge. When they first emerged in the 1970s technological alliances were interpreted by many economists as a temporary phenomenon unlikely to last for a long time. At that time markets and large hierarchical corporations were considered the only two stable forms of industrial organization. However, in some sectors such as ICT and biotechnology, technological alliances continue to be an important form of industrial organization. This seems to indicate that they are not a temporary phenomenon but a new form of industrial organization. While in spite of a large amount of research the dynamics of technological alliances has not yet been fully understood, it has some clear implications for the theory of the firm. Inter-firm collaboration can provide a greater increase in performance than the sum of the individual efforts of isolated firms. The increase in the rate of creation of new knowledge and in its variety and the presence of knowledge discontinuity are amongst the possible causes of this phenomenon.

The collaboration of large diversified firms and of high-technology start-ups in technological alliances seems to be a combination of the two mechanisms by means of which Schumpeter (1934, 1942) thought innovations were introduced into the economic system. High-technology start-ups are typically entrepreneurial while large diversified firms represent the corporations that the late Schumpeter (Mark 2) thought would have replaced entrepreneurs as innovators and would have routinized the creation of innovations. Technological alliances are a proof that entrepreneurs have not disappeared and that innovation cannot be routinized. Both entrepreneurs and large diversified firms are required to innovate in the present economic system.

29.4   THE EVOLUTION OF THE THEORIES OF THE FIRM

The previous description gave evidence of what the firm is and helped to define what should be the main objectives of a theory of the firm. Greatly simplifying we could summarize these objectives under four categories:

. the firm as an organization;
. knowledge and the firm;
. the firm and its external environment;
. the evolution of the firm.

In what follows I will attempt to analyze the way in which the various theories of the firm that were proposed during the twentieth century attempted to clarify these issues or did not do so. For reasons of space the following part of the chapter will not be a complete analysis of theories of the firm. Only a selection of theories and authors will be discussed in order to focus attention on how each theory dealt with the above issues.

The standard neoclassical theory of the firm, which still occupies most of the space in economics textbooks, does not deal with the firm as an organization. In this theory the firm is treated as if it were an individual, or a firm 'point' (Coriat and Weinstein, 1995), which has only one dimension and no internal structure. In the same theory knowledge is assumed to be perfect. The main objective of this theory is to make it compatible with the theory of markets and equilibrium (ibid.; Ricketts, 1987). In a sense the standard neoclassical theory of the firm only takes into account category 3 above, the adaptation of the firm to its external environment. The external environment is here extremely simplified by making it constant. The firm's adaptation then occurs by profit maximization. Of course, no serious analysis of the evolution of the firm would be possible in this case. The firm can only adapt to changes in prices by moving along a production function. Any change in knowledge would be completely exogenous to the firm and the firm could instantaneously and at a zero cost adapt to it by moving to a new production function. Questions such as 'Is the firm large or small?', 'What is its productive specialization?', 'How do firms change in the course of time?' find no answer in this theory. Of course, today most economists would agree that this theory of the firm is far too limited. However, it is interesting that even in very widely used microeconomics textbooks of the 1990s (see, for example, Varian, 1992) the word firm was not present in the index.

29.4.1 Transaction Costs and Agency Theory

That the firm was an organization and that its role was not simply to complete the theory of markets and equilibrium became clearly established with the work of Coase first and of Williamson later. Coase (1937) started raising the basic question 'Why do firms exist?'. His answer was that there are costs involved in using the market and that, as a consequence, many transactions can be carried out at a lower cost within firms. The lower cost of such transactions is due to the fact that within the firm the costly contracts required to cope with market uncertainty are replaced by the less expensive transactions defined by the internal rules of a hierarchical organization. Coase did not specify the nature of the transactions but his undoubted merit was to have raised a question to which economists had been miraculously blind. In fact Marx's analysis of the capitalist firm (Marx in Putterman, 1986, pp. 44–60) provided ample evidence that it existed as an organization and that it had plenty of internal transactions.

The organization of the firm was further articulated by Williamson (1985). He combined Coase's point of departure with Simon's analysis of the limited rationality of human agents. Simon (1969, 1978) criticized the assumption that agents had perfect

knowledge and that they could optimize. Even if optimization had been possible in pri-
ciple the computational cost of it would have been so high as to make it impossible or n
convenient to achieve in most economic situations. As a consequence agents' rationali
could be of two types, *substantive* or *procedural*. The former coincided with the best sol
tion of a problem while the latter was the type of rationality that would determine th
choice of agents with limited computational ability and that depended on their presen
circumstances. In view of the above limitations, in most situations agents would choos
a course of action that was satisficing as opposed to the optimum. Williamson combine
Coase's objective of defining the firm as the locus of the transactions that could be carrie
out more effectively there than in the market with Simon's analysis of human rationality
In fact, for Williamson the limited rationality of human agents becomes the root cause c
the existence of organizations. As a consequence contracts are inevitably incomplete an
the incompleteness of contracts leads to opportunism. According to Williamson transac
tions have three dimensions (Williamson, 1985; Milgrom and Roberts, 1992; Coriat an
Weinstein, 1995):

- asset specificity;
- uncertainty;
- frequency.

An asset is specific when it is only used in very special applications. This completel
changes the nature of transactions with respect to those occurring in a market wher
standardized assets are exchanged between anonymous agents. The importance o
asset specificity in Williamson's work is not related to technological reasons, but t
its implications for behavior, when it is combined with limited rationality, opportun
ism, and uncertainty to induce a durable personal dependence between the partie
involved.

Uncertainty had been stressed by Knight (1921) as the fundamental cause of the exist
ence of the firm. Coase had accepted the important role played by uncertainty but di
not consider it the root cause of the existence of the firm. Williamson places uncertainty
in a very central position in his theory of transaction costs but clearly states that he
focuses mainly on one dimension of uncertainty. In particular, Williamson stresses that
the main type of uncertainty relevant for transaction costs theory is behavioral. By this
he means uncertainty of a strategic kind attributable to opportunism, arising from the
possibility that 'parties make strategic plans in relation to each other that are the source
of *ex-ante* uncertainty and *ex-post* surprises' (Williamson, 1985, pp. 57–8).

The frequency of a transaction is important because no firm is likely to internalize
transactions that occur very infrequently, especially if they require a specific investment.

There would have been potential links to innovation and knowledge in Williamson's
analysis of uncertainty but he did not exploit them. For example, both asset specificity
and uncertainty could be expected to vary during the lifetime of a technology, as in the
different phases of a dominant design (Abernathy and Utterback, 1975) or of a technological paradigm (Dosi, 1982). We will come back to these considerations later in this
chapter. Here it is worth noting that the lack of emphasis on knowledge and innovation was not an oversight but an explicit objective of Williamson's analysis. In fact
Williamson explains his lack of interest in technology as a compensation for the excessive

ttention previously paid to it, an opinion that would certainly have set him apart from volutionary economists.

An aspect in which Williamson's work went beyond Coase is the boundaries of the rm. While Coase (1937) only briefly dealt with the relationship between small and large rms, Williamson raises the question of the boundaries of the firm. These cannot be onsidered as fixed but we can expect them to shift in the course of time as the relative osts of transactions change. However, this more dynamic aspect of transaction costs vas never fully exploited by Williamson. Phenomena like technological alliances or utsourcing were definitely not of interest to him in the early part of his work. In more ecent work he made some gestures towards both acknowledging their existence and rguing that transaction costs theory could be modified to explain them (1985, p. 83). iven recognizing this belated interest in new organizational forms Williamson's work vas mainly conceived to explain the existence and the boundaries of firms in the corpo-ate economy when the market and firms large and small were the only stable forms of ndustrial organization. Extensions of transaction costs theory to technological alliances r to outsourcing are not too difficult to imagine, but they are unlikely to be developed vithout taking into account the nature of the knowledge created and used by firms.

Whatever its limitations transaction costs theory was important progress in the theory •f the firm, focusing on its behavioral and organizational aspects. However, although it ad a considerable following, transaction costs theory was never integrated within the heory of the firm accepted by the core of the economics profession. A number of aspects ould explain this reluctance to accept it, amongst which the opposition to the concept •f opportunism and the difficulties encountered in mapping and measuring transaction osts. However, the problem of the firm as an organization would not simply disappear. Other attempts to explain the existence of the firm and to deal with its organization nore in line with the assumptions of neoclassical theory were developed in the 1970s and 1980s.

In a general sense these theories of the firm can be grouped together for two reasons: irst, they are an attempt to generalize microeconomic theory to the study of economic nstitutions, preserving the essential foundations of neoclassical theory; second, they are largely relying on an analysis of property rights (Coriat and Weinstein, 1995, p. 78). The neoclassical assumptions and methods that are preserved are:

- stable preferences;
- perfectly rational behavior;
- an analysis of individual behavior and of the relationships between agents by means of the equilibrium method.

The progress these theories made with respect to standard microeconomics is based on the introduction of imperfect information, on the existence of information asymmetry amongst agents, and on the costs of exchange, or of transactions, that follow from such asymmetries (ibid., p. 79).

Alchian and Demsetz (1972) tried to explain the existence of the firm by representing it as a team. Why would we need to form teams to produce? Because it is difficult or impossible to measure the performance of individuals within teams. Given this difficulty the team can only be viable if someone is in charge of measuring and coordinating the activities of the members of the team. The person in charge of this would become the residual claimant, he or she who has the right to receive any net income that the firm produces. The net income would be what is left over after all revenues have been collected and all debts, expenses, and other contractual obligations have been paid (Milgrom and Roberts, 1992, p.291).

Alchian and Demsetz's analysis follows from the importance attached to property rights. Property rights play a fundamental role in economic activities because they induce individuals to create, conserve, and give value to assets. Assets themselves are heterogeneous and have different attributes. Thus, they are partitionable, separable, and alienable in the sense that different agents can have different rights on the same asset. The modern firm relies on this idea that property rights can be partitioned so that several agents can have rights on the same asset (Coriat and Weinstein, 1995, p.84). A firm can then be considered a set of contracts that establish a given structure of property rights (Ricketts, 1987). This concept of the firm underlies not only Alchian and Demsetz' approach but also the agency theory of the firm.

The name of the agency theory of the firm owes its origin to the observation of Berle and Means (1932) that there can be a conflict between the objectives of the owners and those of the managers of the firm. Such conflict does not in general arise from managers' laziness or incompetence but from the possibility that they can pursue goals other than maximizing the long-run value of the firm (Milgrom and Roberts, 1992, p.181). Jensen and Meckling (1976, p.307) define the agency relationship as 'a contract under which one or more persons (the principal(s)) engage another person (the agent) to perform some service on their behalf which involves delegating some decision making authority to the agent'. Jensen and Meckling maintain that the agency relationship is very general and occurs in many organizations, not just in firms. The principal can avoid divergences of the agent from his or her expected behavior by establishing appropriate incentives and by incurring monitoring costs. The agent, on the other hand, will need to expend resources either to make sure he or she does not harm the principal or protect him or herself from the principal's claims of wrong behavior (bonding costs). Furthermore, however perfect the arrangements devised to control and limit the divergence between the agent's decisions and those decisions that would maximize the welfare of the principal, some divergences will remain. This reduction in welfare experienced by the principal can be called a residual loss. Thus, the agency relationship gives rise to three types of costs:

- the monitoring expenditure by the principal;
- the bonding expenditure by the agent;
- the residual loss.

As a consequence of the above and in the presence of information that is both limited and asymmetrically distributed amongst agents, contracts are necessarily incomplete and the principal does not have the means to control the agent (Coriat and Weinstein, 1995, p.94). Any organization, and not just a firm, can then be defined as a nexus of contracts. In this sense Jensen and Meckling (1976) and Fama and Jensen (1983) claim that their theory is more general than that of Alchian and Demsetz (1972).

Within agency theory the firm as a nexus of contracts is a legal fiction. Jensen and Meckling (1976) stress that the firm is not an individual. Therefore, it does not make any sense to ask questions such as 'Who is the owner of the firm?' (Fama, 1980) or 'What are the firm's objectives?', 'Does the firm maximize?' and, if so 'What does it maximize?' (Putterman, 1986). In this theory all transactions are reduced to inter-individual contractual relationships between the owners of the factors of production and their customers. In this sense intra-firm relationships are reduced no different from market relationships. Both of them are ruled by the need to choose efficient contractual firms. Pertinent questions are the consequences of different types of contracts and the way in which exogenous changes, such as changes in technology, can affect contractual relationships.

Thus, the concept of the firm loses all its significance as an organization and no opposition can be found between the firm and the market. In this respect agency theory is strikingly different from Coase and Williamson.

Agency theory can have extensions to the explanation of the difference between small and large firms. According to Fama and Jensen (1983) the central problem in analyzing the organizational structure of a firm consists of identifying the main contracts that define the rules of the game, the rights of contractants and the evaluation systems. Two characteristics are particularly important in defining this organizational structure: (1) the attribution of residual claims, and (2) the attribution of decision power to agents.

Condition (2) leads to the separation between management and control functions of an organization. Depending on the nature of the organization the management and control functions can be combined in a small number of agents or attributed to a large number of them. An organization is called complex or non-complex if the information specific to the firm is owned by a large or by a small number of individuals respectively. In a non-complex organization it is more efficient to attribute both the management and control functions to the small number of agents owning the firm-specific information. Conversely, in a complex organization firm-specific information is distributed amongst a large number of agents. In this case it is more efficient to take advantage of specialization attributing decision powers to the agents who have the information, an arrangement that is likely to reduce costs.

The previous theories of the firm, starting from Coase and Williamson and ending with Alchian and Demsetz and agency theory, have in common a focus on explaining the firm as organization but differ in a number of ways. Coase and Williamson are perceived as having departed from at least some aspects of neoclassical microeconomic theory while Alchian and Demsetz and agency theory are attempts to reconstruct a theory of the firm strictly following the neoclassical assumptions. To put things in perspective we have to bear in mind that both Coase and Williamson intended to construct a theory of the firm under a series of constraints, including the difficulties that could arise in using the market due, for example, to opportunism and asset specificity. None of these difficulties are acceptable to Alchian and Demsetz and to agency theorists. Their objective is to show that no deviation from neoclassical principles of behavior can arise either in the market or in the firm. Although transactions are interpreted as if they were between individual contractants the very same concept of the firm loses most of its significance by becoming a legal fiction designed to make the behavior of the firm indistinguishable from that of the market as both of them are the outcome of a complex equilibrium process (Putterman, 1986, p. 216). In spite of these differences all these theories have in common the neglect of two fundamental aspects of a firm: power and knowledge. The former aspect will not be treated here, not because it is considered irrelevant but because the latter aspect is more closely aligned with the title of the chapter. The next section will deal with evolutionary theories and with the way they have dealt with the problem of the use of knowledge in the firm.

29.4.2   Evolutionary Theories

The period after World War II saw an unprecedented expansion of the R&D function, first in developed countries and later in emerging and less developed countries. The enormous increase in investment that this entailed could not have occurred without raising questions on the effectiveness of such investment. The resulting innovations started to be studied and soon a field called innovation studies arose with its new institutions. Innovation turned out to be a phenomenon very difficult to analyze by means of existing economic theories, which tended to assume perfect knowledge on the part of firms. A series of studies of innovation followed, which created what could be called a natural history of innovation. Soon this empirical approach led to the attempt to create new concepts and a new theoretical framework, later called evolutionary economics, which seemed more appropriate to interpreting the evolution of innovations. The new concepts that emerged were intended to represent patterns of evolution in technologies.

The concept of dominant design was proposed by Abernathy and Utterback (1975) to explain the evolution of automobile technology, but deemed to be in principle applicable to many industries. The underlying idea was that a technology would follow a life cycle starting with a multiplicity of product designs, most of which would become extinct and give way to a dominant design on which all products would subsequently converge. Nelson and Winter (1977) introduced the similar concept of technological regime, exemplified by the convergence of aircraft producers on a common design, the prototype of which was the Douglas DC3, and the related concept of natural trajectories. Dosi (1982; Dosi and Nelson, 2010) called a technological paradigm the common approach to production, which was expected to emerge in a given technology upon which all producers would converge. A technological paradigm would include both dominant designs and the common knowledge that engineers and designers would use after a paradigm was established. These new concepts had two important features: first, they established that the knowledge used to create innovations would not develop by random accumulation of new discoveries but would evolve according to specific patterns; second, they introduced the idea that there were *discontinuities* in the evolution of technology and of knowledge. All these concepts were not immediately related to the existence of the firm, but they had implications for the way in which firms were expected to behave. Thus, once a given technological paradigm had been established all firms using the corresponding technology were expected to converge upon it. This raised interesting questions about what would happen when an old technological paradigm would give way to a new one. To the extent that a knowledge discontinuity existed firms wanting to make the transition between the old and the new paradigm could be expected to introduce drastic changes in their competencies. This point was clearly stated by Tushman and Anderson (1986) who distinguished technological change in competence destroying and competence enhancing.

What is today called evolutionary theory arose from the combination of a number of research traditions. These include the work of Schumpeter (1934, 1942) and his emphasis on the role played by innovation in economic development, some concepts of biological origin, such as variation and selection, the conceptual approach to knowledge and rationality developed by Simon (1969, 1978), Cyert and March (1963), the work of Alchian (1950) and Penrose (1959). These different research traditions were for the first time combined in a book by Nelson and Winter (1982). See also Dosi and Nelson (2010).

We can now very briefly survey the main evolutionary concepts relevant for the analysis of R&D and the firm. Variation gives rise to changes in the attributes of the members of a given population (of firms, of products etc.) leading either to the internal differentiation of the population or to the emergence of new populations. Selection eliminates a number of the new entities created by variation. Heredity reproduces some relevant features of the members of a population across time.

Variation in economics is created by innovation, whether of the radical or of the incremental type. Selection occurs mostly by competition, although competition is conceptualized in evolutionary economics differently from neoclassical economics. In particular, one can contrast the static approach to competition in an equilibrium framework with the more dynamic one in evolutionary economics. In evolutionary economics selection processes can be expected to eliminate firms with lower than average fitness, but they do so in ways that depend on the selection environment present (Metcalfe, 1998).

Two concepts that are crucial in the representation of firms in evolutionary economics are those of *routines* and of *search activities* (Nelson and Winter, 1982). Firms are not expected to optimize or to have a perfect knowledge but to have a rational behavior in the presence of imperfect knowledge. Thus, firms construct repertoires of routines that they keep using as long as some threat or failure does not suggest that such routines are becoming inadequate. Routines play a number of roles in the firm. They are its memory, in the sense that the firm needs to keep practicing them to remember (ibid., pp. 99–107). Furthermore, routines can establish a truce in inter-organizational conflict (ibid., pp. 107–12). Thus, routines are not changed frequently but have a considerable persistence in the firm. In this sense the presence of routines indicates that the firm does not instantly adapt to changes in its external environment but does it infrequently and shows a degree of inertia. In principle, both events internal to the firm and external events, for example a change in technological paradigm, can induce a firm to change its routines. The ingredients required to change come from search activities, a term introduced by Nelson and Winter (1982) to represent a general analog of R&D. Search activities can be considered all the activities by means of which firms scan the external environment looking for new knowledge which could later be used to create new routines when required. Thus, search activities would be carried out all the time and their results would be used when needed.

Firms can be expected to be subject to common constraints, for example when they operate in the presence of a common technological paradigm, and to differ in their routines and search activities. Even in a very static external environment firms need to keep learning. Given that knowledge is cumulative for each firm, learning is likely to depend on past knowledge. Furthermore, the learning of each firm depends on its organizational capabilities. Routines are partly tacit and thus difficult to transfer. As a consequence the diversity of firms is likely to persist (Dosi et al., 1990). What differentiates a firm from another is its organizational capabilities. This point combines the emphasis of evolutionary economics on technology and on knowledge with a focus on the nature of the organization.

The concepts of competencies and capabilities occupy a central place in the evolutionary conception of the firm. Both concepts find their roots in the work of Penrose (1959). In a way, competencies and capabilities are concepts more specifically linked to the technologies a firm uses and to the products it produces than routines and search activities. Not only do firms need different competencies to make shoes or semiconductors, but such competencies need to be combined, or coordinated, within the firm. According to Teece et al. (1994) such coordination is more likely to be effective in a coherent firm than in a conglomerate. They obtained this result by measuring the coherence of a large sample of firms in the USA. Nesta and Saviotti (2005, 2006) and Nesta (2008) measured the coherence of the knowledge base of a sample of firms and showed that it affected the performance of those firms. The concept of coherence is very important in the evolutionary theory of the firm because it combines the organizational and technological aspects of the firm.

No treatment of evolutionary economics, however short, can neglect to mention the work of Schumpeter (1934, 1942) and his emphasis on the entrepreneur. In his early work Schumpeter (1934) considered the entrepreneur the character who introduced innovations into the economic system. However, in the later part of his work (1942), and particularly after he had emigrated to the United States, he shifted his emphasis to the large corporations that were then beginning to carry out R&D systematically. Schumpeter then predicted that such corporations would routinize the production of innovations, implicitly leading to the demise of the entrepreneur. If this prediction could have seemed almost right during the corporate economy of the period 1900–70, it seems increasingly inadequate after more than 30 years of technological alliances. These alliances combine large diversified firms with entrepreneurial high-technology start-ups.

The previous very brief notes have given an idea of how the main focus of evolutionary economics is on processes that allow firms to learn and to innovate. In this sense we could say that evolutionary economics has given rise to a cognitive theory of the firm. This theory is partly concentrated on internal firm processes, but also pays attention to the external environment of the firm by means of concepts such as innovation systems and the co-evolution of technologies and institutions. The influence of the external environment can be perceived in concepts such as technological paradigms and trajectories, which are common to many firms and reflect knowledge structures at a higher level of aggregation than the firm itself. However, the external environment is much more explicitly present in innovation systems and the co-evolution of technologies and institutions.

Innovation systems can be national, sectoral or regional (Freeman, 1987; Lundvall, 1992; Edquist, 1997; Malerba, 2004). They exist because firms and research organizations do not create innovations in an institutional vacuum but interact with many other firms and other types of institutions that affect the choices of projects and their development. The co-evolution of technologies and institutions (Nelson, 1994) occurs because no important technology likely to have a major impact on the economy can develop without appropriate institutions. Such institutions can then be said to be complementary to the technology.

In both of the above cases the evolution of the firm does not occur in an isolated way due only to internal resources but involves the interaction with many different institutions. Thus, the time path of the evolution of the firm can be fully understood only by taking into account the interactions with the innovation system of which they are a part and with the institutions and organizations with which they need to co-evolve. This is a subject that is still poorly understood and one of the frontiers of the theory of the firm.

29.5 SUMMARY AND CONCLUSIONS

In this chapter it has been shown that the existence of the modern firm could not have been conceived without the changes in technology that started with the Industrial Revolution. The increasing capital intensity, the emergence of R&D within the firm, the new products and services that it has been capable of supplying played a fundamental role in the evolution of the modern firm. This does not mean that science and technology were the only cause of the emergence of the firm. The enlargement of markets and institutional changes of various types heavily affected its evolution.

Any theory of the firm should explain why all these factors and conditions were combined to create the firm, how its organizational structure evolved and how the relationships with its external environment affected its evolution. This chapter could hardly do justice to the wealth of literature written about the theories of the firm that were very briefly surveyed. The limited evidence that could be presented here is intended to stress a fundamental point: all theories of the firm that have so far been created are partial, in the sense that each of them focuses on one or few of its aspects. The standard neoclassical approach to the firm was only concerned with making it compatible with a general theory of markets and equilibrium. Transaction costs theory, with the contributions of Coase and Williamson, focused on the existence of the firm as an organization and on its boundaries and stressed the difference between firms and markets. Alchian and Demsetz and agency theory tried to conceive firms as a 'nexus of contracts', but mostly, tried to conceive the firm as a legal fiction, the transactions and contracts of which were in principle not different from those in the market. These theories focused on the firm as an organization and diverged as to its difference with respect to the market and to the rationality that economic agents were endowed with. None of them paid any serious attention to technology, innovation, and knowledge. These aspects were instead central to evolutionary economics. It seems quite clear that this research tradition has contributed more to the analysis of R&D and the firm than any of the previous ones.

Whatever the merits of each of the theories of the firm briefly surveyed here, each of them focuses on different aspects. None of them can be called a comprehensive theory of the firm. The object 'firm', in spite of the frequency with which it occurs and of its recognized importance in the capitalist system, still eludes us in all its complexity. One can imagine trying to combine all these theories and the aspects of the firm they describe. Any such synthesis is likely to be exceedingly difficult given that these theories start from different and often contrasting assumptions.

Whatever their limitations all these theories amount to considerable progress in the analysis of the firm. An aspect about which all of them are virtually silent is the transformations that the firm underwent in the course of its history and their relationship with the external environment of the firm. The analysis of this aspect is likely to involve an approach based on the co-evolution of technologies, institutions, and organizational forms.

REFERENCES

Abernathy, W.J. and J.M. Utterback (1975), 'A dynamic model of process and product innovation', *Omega*, **3**(6), 639–56.

Agarwal, R. and M. Gort (2001), 'First mover advantage and the speed of competitive entry, 1887–1986', *Journal of Law and Economics*, **44**(1), 161–77.

Alchian, A. (1950), 'Uncertainty, evolution and economic theory', *Journal of Political Economy*, **58**(3), 211–21.

Alchian, A. and H. Demsetz (1972), 'Production, information costs and economic organization', *American Economic Review*, **62**(5), 777–95.

Arrow, K.J. (1962), 'Economic implications of learning by doing', *Review of Economic Studies*, **29**(3), 155–73.

Berle, A.A. and G.C. Means (1932), *The Modern Corporation and Private Property*, New York: Macmillan.

Callon, M. (1991), 'Réseaux technico-economiques et irréversibilités', in R. Boyer, B. Chavanne and O. Godard (eds), *Les Figures De L`Irréversibilité en Economie*, Paris: Editions de l'Ecole des Hautes Etudes en Sciences Sociales.

Chandler, A.D. (1962), *Strategy and Structure*, Cambridge, MA: MIT Press.

Chandler, A.D. (1977), *The Visible Hand*, Cambridge, MA: Harvard University Press.

Coase, A. (1937), 'The nature of the firm', *Economica*, **4**(16), 386–405.

Cohen, M. and D. Levinthal (1989), 'Innovating and learning: the two faces of R&D', *Economic Journal*, **99**(397), 569–96.

Coriat, B. and O. Weinstein (1995), *Les nouvelles théories de l`entreprise*, Paris: Librairie Générale Française.

Cyert, R.M. and J.G. March (1963), *A Behavioral Theory of the Firm*, Englewood Cliffs, NJ: Prentice Hall.

Das Gupta, P. and P. David (1994), 'Toward a new economics of science', *Research Policy*, **23**(5), 487–521.

Dosi, G. (1982), 'Technological paradigms and technological trajectories: a suggested interpretation of the determinants and directions of technical change', *Research Policy*, **11**(3), 147–62.

Dosi, G. and R.R. Nelson (2010), 'Technical change and industrial dynamics as evolutionary processes', in K.J. Arrow and M.D. Intriligator (eds), *Handbook of the Economics of Innovation*, Amsterdam: North Holland/Elsevier.

Dosi, G., D.J. Teece and S. Winter (1990), 'Les frontières des entreprises', *Revue d'Economie Industrielle*, **51**(1), 238–54.

Dosi, G., A. Gambardella, M. Grazzi and L. Orsenigo (2007), 'Technological revolutions and industrial structures: assessing the impact of new technologies on size, patterns of growth and boundaries of the firms', LEM working paper series, May.

Edquist, C. (1997), *Systems of Innovation: Technologies, Institutions and Organizations*, London: Pinter.

Fama, E. (1980), 'Agency problems and the theory of the firm', *Journal of Political Economy*, **88**(2), 288–307.

Fama, E. and M.C. Jensen (1983), 'Separation of ownership and control', *Journal of Law and Economics*, **26**(2), 301–25.

Freeman, C. (1987), *Technology Policy and Economic Performance*, London: Pinter.

Freeman, C. (1991), 'Networks of innovators: a synthesis of research issues', *Research Policy*, **20**(5), 499–514.

Freeman, C. and L. Soete (1997), *The Economics of Industrial Innovation*, 3rd edition, London: Pinter.

Hagedoorn, J. (1993), 'Understanding the rationale of strategic technology partnering: interorganizational modes of cooperation and sectoral differences', *Strategic Management Journal*, **14**, 371–85.

Hagedoorn, J. (1995), 'Strategic technology partnering during the 1980s: trends, networks and corporate patterns in non-core technologies', *Research Policy*, **24**(2), 207–31.

Hakansson, H. (1987), *Industrial Technological Development. A Network Approach*, London: Croom Helm Limited.

Hannah, L. (1976), *The Rise of the Corporate Economy*, London: Methuen.

Hobsbawm, E.J. (1968), *Industry and Empire*, Harmondsworth: Penguin Books.

Hounshell, D.A. and J.K. Smith (1988), *Science and Corporate Strategy: Du Pont R&D 1902–1980*, Cambridge: Cambridge University Press.

Jensen, M. and W. Meckling (1976), 'Theory of the firm: managerial behavior, agency costs and ownership structure', *The Journal of Financial Economics*, **3**(4), 305–60, reprinted in Putterman (1986).

Knight, F. (1921), *Risk, Uncertainty and Profit*, New York: Houghton Mifflin.

Landes, D. (1969), *The Unbound Prometheus*, Cambridge: Cambridge University Press.

Langlois, R.N. (2004), 'The vanishing hand: the changing dynamics of industrial capitalism', *Industrial and Corporate Change*, **12**(2), 351–85.

Layton, E.T. (1974), 'Technology as knowledge', *Technology and Culture*, **15**(1), 31–41.

Lipsey, R.G., K.I. Carlaw and C.T. Beckar (2005), *Economic Transformations*, Oxford: Oxford University Press.

Lundvall, B.A. (1992), *National Systems of Innovation*, London: Pinter.

Malerba, F. (2004), 'Sectoral systems, how and why innovation differs across sectors', in J. Fagerberg, D. Mowery, R.R. Nelson, *The Oxford Handbook of Innovation*, Oxford: Oxford University Press, pp. 380–406.

Metcalfe, J.S. (1998), *Evolutionary Economics and Creative Destruction*, London: Routledge.

Milgrom, P. and J. Roberts (1992), *Economics, Organization and Management*, Englewood Cliffs: Prentice Hall.

Mokyr, J. (1990), *The Lever of Riches: Technological Creativity and Economic Progress*, New York: Oxford University Press.

Mokyr, J. (2010), 'The contribution of economic history to the study of innovation and technical change: 1750–1914', in B.H. Hall and N. Rosenberg (eds), *Handbook of the Economics of Innovation*, Oxford: Elsevier.

Mowery, D. (1989), 'Collaborative ventures between US and foreign manufacturing firms', *Research Policy*, **18**(1), 19–33.

Mowery, D.C. and N. Rosenberg (1989), *Technology and the Pursuit of Economic Growth*, Cambridge: Cambridge University Press.

Murmann, J.P. (2004), *Knowledge and Competitive Advantage: The Co-evolution of Firms, Technologies and National Institutions*, Cambridge: Cambridge University Press.

Musson, A.E. and E. Robinson (1969), *Science and Technology in the Industrial Revolution*, Manchester: Manchester University Press.

Nelson, R. (1959), 'The simple economics of basic scientific research', *Journal of Political Economy*, **67**(3), 297–306.

Nelson, R.R. (1994), 'The co-evolution of technology, industrial structure, and supporting institutions', *Industrial and Corporate Change*, **3**(1), 47–63.

Nelson, R. and S. Winter (1977), 'In search of useful theory of innovation', *Research Policy*, **6**(1) 36–76.

Nelson, R. and S. Winter (1982), *An Evolutionary Theory of Economic Change*, Cambridge, MA: Harvard University Press.

Nesta, L. (2008), 'Knowledge and productivity in the world's largest manufacturing corporations', *Journal of Economic Behavior & Organization*, **67**(3–4), 886–902.

Nesta, L. and P.P. Saviotti (2005), 'Coherence of the knowledge base and the firm's innovative performance: evidence from the U.S. pharmaceutical industry', *Journal of Industrial Economics*, **53**(1), 123–42.

Nesta, L. and P.P. Saviotti (2006), 'Firm knowledge and market value in biotechnology', *Industrial and Corporate Change*, **15**(4), 625–52.

Penrose, E. (1959), *The Theory of the Growth of the Firm*, Oxford: Blackwell.

Powell, W., K.W. Koput and L. Smith-Doerr (1996), 'Inter-organizational collaboration and the locus of innovation: networks of learning in biotechnology', *Administrative Science Quarterly*, **41**(1), 116–45.

Prahalad, C.K. and G. Hamel (1990), 'The core competences of the corporation', *Harvard Business Review*, **68**(3), 79–90.

Putterman, L. (1986), *The Economic Nature of the Firm: A Reader*, Cambridge: Cambridge University Press.

Reich, L.S. (1985), *The Making of American Industrial Research*, Cambridge MA: MIT Press.

Ricketts, M. (1987), *The Economics of the Business Enterprise*, Brighton: Wheatsheaf.

Romer, P. (1990), 'Endogenous technical progress', *Journal of Political Economy*, **98**(1), 71–102.

Rosenberg, N. and L.E. Birdzell (1986), *How the West Grew Rich*, New York: Basic Books.

Saxenian, A. (1991), 'The origins and dynamics of production networks in Silicon Valley', *Research Policy*, **20**(5), 423–37.

Schumpeter, J. (1934, original edition 1912), *The Theory of Economic Development*, Cambridge, MA: Harvard University Press.

Schumpeter, J. (1942, 5th edition 1976), *Capitalism, Socialism and Democracy*, George Allen and Unwin.

Simon, H.A. (1969), 'Economic rationality, adaptive artifice', Ch 2 in *The Sciences of the Artificial*, 1st edition, Cambridge, MA: MIT Press.

Simon, H.A. (1978), 'Rationality as process and as product of thought', *American Economic Review*, **68**(2), 1–16.

Teece, D.J., R. Rumelt, G. Dosi and S. Winter (1994), 'Understanding corporate coherence: theory and evidence', *Journal of Economic Behavior & Organization*, **23**(1), 1–30.

Tushman, M.L. and P. Anderson (1986), 'Technological discontinuities and organizational environments', *Administrative Science Quarterly*, **31**(3) 439–65.

Varian, H.R. (1992), *Microeconomic Analysis*, New York: Norton.

Vincenti, W.G. (1990), *What Engineers Know and How They Know It*, Baltimore: Johns Hopkins University Press.

Williamson, O.E. (1985), *The Economic Institutions of Capitalism*, New York: The Free Press.

30 Creating novelty through vertical relationships between groups of complementary players
Martin Fransman

30.1 INTRODUCTION

This chapter deals with the creation of novelty through vertical symbiotic relationships between groups of complementary players. The chapter begins with a general discussion of the creation of novelty in economics by drawing on some of the work of Adam Smith (dealing with innovation in machinery) and Joseph Schumpeter (and his distinction between invention and innovation). The discussion goes on to examine the importance of what is called the value-creating conjecture, which plays a key role in the innovation process. A theory of open symbiotic innovation is then developed in order to elaborate on the journey taken by the value-creating conjecture, which may or may not end up being embodied in marketed new products, processes and technologies, forms of organization, and markets and ways of marketing. Finally, the approach is applied to the innovation process in the new ICT ecosystem.

30.2 NOVELTY

Socio-economic systems change primarily through the endogenous creation of novelty. This novelty comes essentially in the form of new knowledge. This new knowledge becomes part of the thinking of the players in the system and becomes embodied in the new products and services, new processes and technologies, new forms of organization and new markets and ways of marketing that they create. As their thinking changes and they innovate so novelty is injected endogenously into the system and ripples through it as other players are affected and respond.

It is the creation of new knowledge that differentiates human socio-economic systems from complex biological and physical systems. In the latter, change is primarily a random phenomenon while in socio-economic systems the creation of new knowledge is a purposeful, continual and essentially human process.

However, although new knowledge is the main driver of the dynamics of change in socio-economic systems very little attention, remarkably, is paid in economics to the process of new knowledge creation. Instead the assumption is usually made that the state of knowledge is given and held constant (even if it is unequally distributed amongst the players) and that the task of the players is to optimize the outcome from their point of view on the basis of this given knowledge. Knowledge that is changing in an ex ante uncertain way would throw a spanner into the optimization works, preventing a determinate outcome.

30.3   ECONOMICS AND THE CREATION OF NOVELTY

30.3.1   Adam Smith and the Creation of New Machinery

This has not always been the approach taken in economics. For example, Adam Smith's analysis of the process of specialization has changing knowledge at its heart. In his explanation of the increasing productivity that underlies the growing wealth of nations Smith emphasized the importance of improved machinery. These improvements, he explained, flow out of the division of labour as human attention is focused on aspects of the machine and the production process of which it is a part.

More specifically, Smith identifies three sources of improvement in machinery. The first is what, since the work of Eric von Hippel (1988) in the 1980s, has come to be called user-generated innovation, in Smith's (1910) words, 'the inventions of those who had occasion to use the machines'.[1] Smith noted that:

> A great part of the machines made use of in those manufactures in which labour is most subdivided, were originally the inventions of common workmen, who, being each of them employed in some very simple operation, naturally turned their thoughts towards finding out easier and readier methods of performing it.[2]

Or, as David Lane (2011) puts it, interactions in this 'agent-artefact space' lead to the generation of new ideas regarding the artefact.

The second source of improvement comes from the 'ingenuity of the makers of the machines, when to make them became the business of a peculiar trade'.[3] But, apart from the direct makers and users of machinery, there is also a third source of improvement that leads Smith on to discuss the implications of the division of labour for the development of science.

This third category of players refers to 'those who are called philosophers or men of speculation, whose trade it is not to do anything, but to observe everything'.[4] These agents of change, Smith notes, provide their contribution by making what Brian Loasby (2003) calls 'new connections' since as a result of their broader perspective they are, again in Smith's words, 'often capable of combining together the powers of the most distant and dissimilar objects'.[5] He points out that:

> In the progress of society, philosophy or speculation becomes, like every other employment, the principal or sole trade and occupation of a particular class of citizens . . . it is subdivided into a great number of different branches, each of which affords occupation to a peculiar tribe or class of philosophers. [In this way] the quantity of science is considerably increased.[6]

However, while the growth of knowledge is facilitated by the division of labour, the other side of the coin is the fragmentation of knowledge that follows. Different players have different sets of knowledge, thus creating what Hayek (1945) called *the* economic problem, namely the 'problem of the utilization of knowledge which is not given to anyone in its totality'.[7]

For Metcalfe (2009) the immediate solution to this problem of coordinating the use of knowledge lies in what he calls the correlation of knowledge across players. However, this solution, even when it can be successfully instituted, is only temporary. The reason is that correlated knowledge precludes the creation of new knowledge. New knowledge can only emerge in part of the socio-economic system. If it is found to be useful by other players it will begin to diffuse more widely. But the creation of new knowledge requires what Metcalfe calls the 'de-correlating' of existing knowledge. De-correlated knowledge rocks the systemic boat by requiring adjustments in order to establish new patterns of coordination. By making 'new connections' inventors and innovators de-correlate knowledge, thus contributing to the ongoing process of economic and social change.

The combined effect of the knowledge-creating efforts of the producers and users of machinery and of the scientists and R&D workers who apply their efforts to various kinds of machinery is a continual stream of improvements over time. But at any point in time future improvements, from an ex ante point of view, are uncertain. The process of knowledge creation renders future changes in knowledge unpredictable.

30.3.2   Joseph Schumpeter on the Inventor and the Innovator

But there are other problems that arise in Adam Smith's account of the process of novelty creation in the machinery industry. As we have seen, Smith identifies three categories of player who initiate the novelty. These players may, in the course of their activities, come up with new ideas for improvements using their creative imaginations. However, to create a new idea is one thing; to implement it and turn it into a new or improved machine available for purchase in the market by potential users is another. The weakness in Adam Smith's account is that he jumps from the creator of the new idea, paying little attention to how the idea gets transformed into a new marketed machine. It is this issue that Joseph Schumpeter focused on.

Schumpeter is famous, at least in part, for his analysis of the role of the entrepreneur in the dynamics of capitalist development. But what role precisely does the entrepreneur play in this analysis?

For Schumpeter the role of the entrepreneur is to 'carry out' new combinations (or innovations). As he puts it: 'The carrying out of new combinations we call "enterprise"; the individuals whose function it is to carry them out we call "entrepreneurs"' ([1934] 1961, p. 74).

But to carry out, or implement, new products, processes, forms of organization and so on implies that someone else apart from the entrepreneur has created these innovations in the first place. Clearly, it is not possible to carry out or implement a new product unless that product has already been created. However, this raises the question of who did the creating. From the point of view of the dynamics of the capitalist system as a whole this is a crucial question. The reason is that, as Schumpeter himself has stressed, it is new combinations that are the main engine of the capitalist system. 'The fundamental impulse that sets and keeps the capitalist engine in motion comes from the new consumers' goods, the new methods of production or transportation, the new markets, the new forms of industrial organization that capitalist enterprise creates' ([1942] 1966, p. 83). New combinations cause the motion and restlessness of the capitalist system through their disruptiveness, through their destruction of the old and its continual replacement by the new.

But, to return to the question, who creates the ideas for the new products, processes, forms of organization and so on before they are carried out and commercialized by the entrepreneur? Schumpeter, strangely, neither asks nor answers this question directly. However, indirectly he does refer to the issue through his distinction between the inventor and the innovator.

In all his major works Schumpeter insists on the importance of the distinction between the inventor and the entrepreneurial innovator. For example, in *Business Cycles* he points out that the new combinations that allow for "'doing things differently" in the realm of economic life' are 'instances of what we shall refer to by the term Innovation'. However, he goes on immediately to state that 'It should be noticed at once that that concept [i.e., innovation] is not synonymous with "invention"' (1939, p. 59). Invention, says Schumpeter, 'carries misleading associations' and he identifies two of them.

First, 'Although most innovations can be traced to some conquest in the realm of either theoretical or practical knowledge, there are many which cannot. Innovation is possible without. . .invention and invention does not necessarily induce innovation' (ibid.). Furthermore, Schumpeter argues, it is misleading to associate invention and innovation because they are two fundamentally different activities with different consequences for the economic system:

> Second, even where innovation consists in giving effect, by business action, to a particular invention which has either emerged autonomously or has been made specially in response to a given business situation, the making of the invention and the carrying out of the corresponding innovation are two entirely different things. (Ibid., p. 60)

He acknowledges that invention and innovation may be undertaken by the same person: 'They often have been performed by the same person; but this is merely a chance coincidence which does not affect the validity of the distinction' (ibid.). But he insists on their fundamental difference:

> Personal aptitudes – primarily intellectual in the case of the inventor, primarily volitional in the case of the businessman who turns the invention into an innovation – and the methods by which the one and the other work, belong to different spheres. The social process which produces inventions and the social process which produces innovations do not stand in any invariant relation to each other and such relation as they display is much more complex than appears at first sight. (1939, pp. 60–61)

If 'most innovations can be traced to some' invention, even if invention and innovation are fundamentally different processes, why does Schumpeter attach more weight, and pay more attention to, innovation? There seem to be two components to the answer to this important and under-addressed question. To begin with, Schumpeter appears to have believed that the capitalist system has little difficulty in creating an adequate supply of inventions. This is apparent in his statement in *The Theory of Economic Development* that 'New possibilities are continuously being offered by the surrounding world [i.e., the world surrounding the entrepreneur], in particular new discoveries are continuously being added to the existing store of knowledge' ([1934] 1961, p. 79). Furthermore, Schumpeter argued, *from an economic point of view* invention per se is irrelevant: 'As long as they are not carried into practice, inventions are economically irrelevant' (ibid., p. 88).

The real bottleneck, Schumpeter seems to be saying, lies not in the creation of inventions (no matter their source), but in the ability to attract resources away from their old occupation and put them to effective work in the new entrepreneurial venture. It is the latter set of activities that Schumpeter sees as constituting the rupture produced from within the capitalist system, its main dynamic:

> As soon as it is divorced from invention, innovation is readily seen to be a distinct *internal* factor of change. It is an *internal* factor because the turning of existing factors of production to new uses is a purely economic process and, in capitalist society, purely a matter of business behaviour. It is a *distinct* internal factor because it is not implied in, nor a mere consequence of, any other. (1939, p. 61; original emphasis)

30.3.3   Discussion on Schumpeter

But has Schumpeter not gone too far, albeit in making a valid and important distinction between the nature and function of invention and innovation? In driving this distinction as far as he has done has Schumpeter not split off two intimately interrelated parts of the process of creating novelty in the capitalist system? More concretely, does not Schumpeter's sharp distinction between invention and innovation risk obscuring the way in which firms – large and small, in all sectors of the economy – go about the process of creating new knowledge embodied in new products, processes and technologies, forms of organization and markets, and turning this knowledge into revenue and profit?

Indeed, critical questions such as these have been raised regarding the Schumpeterian schema. One critic is Ulrich Witt (2002) who argues that Schumpeter did not deal adequately with the process of knowledge creation relating to the innovation process. According to Witt:

> An explanation of how new knowledge is created, and what the feedback relationships between search, discovery, experimentation, and adoption of new possibilities look like, and the respective motivations – all this would be necessary in order to really be able to treat economic change as being endogenously caused. With [Schumpeter's] focus on entrepreneurial skills in *promoting* innovations, rather than conceiving them, attention is diverted from general human creativity and inventiveness and the motivations underlying it as crucial elements of evolutionary change.[8]

We conclude, therefore, that an understanding of the process of novelty creation requires an analysis of both the creation of the original ideas on which the innovation is based and the implementation of those ideas. In the following section these two parts of the process are integrated by introducing the notion of the value-creating conjecture.

30.4   THE VALUE-CREATING CONJECTURE, ITS CONTEXT AND ITS FORTUNES

All innovation (in the Schumpeterian sense of the word) can be traced back to what we will call a value-creating conjecture. This is a conjecture regarding how additional value might be created by the change envisaged. The conjecture emerges in a human mind through the exercising of imagination, imagining a future where the change envisaged brings about improvement.

But conjectures do not emerge out of nothing. They are influenced by context. The context includes material, social and economic influences. However, the context of a onjecture does not fully determine its content. Different human minds within the same ontext can and do come up with different conjectures. This is the source of the fundaiental uncertainty that characterizes the process of innovation knowledge creation, endering it unpredictable.

Not only does context influence the content of the value-creating conjecture, it also nfluences its fortunes, that is, what happens to it over time. For example, many things ieed to happen in a firm for a value-creating conjecture to make progress down the long oad that may, if all goes well, lead to the conjecture being turned into a commercially uccessful new product or service, process or technology, form of organization, or market or form of marketing. And as it travels down its road the conjecture itself will be transormed as it adapts to the circumstances that help and hinder its progress. As this account uggests, Schumpeterian invention and innovation become part of the same process.

The final hurdle that the conjecture faces in the private sector of a capitalist economy s the selection process determined by the market. But there are many earlier hurdles that iave to be crossed. Many (indeed most) conjectures make little progress down the road.

30.5   INNOVATION, THE FIRM AND THE WEB OF SYMBIOTIC RELATIONSHIPS

Firms are not a sufficient unit of analysis when the aim is an understanding of the process of novelty creation. The reason is, is that firms are not self-sufficient. In order to survive and perhaps thrive firms need to interact appropriately with other entities external to them.

Four such entities (groups of players) are particularly important: customer-users, suppliers, partners and competitors. In any sectoral setting firms have an intimate set of relationships with the particular customer-users, suppliers, partners and competitors with whom they regularly interact. These may be thought of, as in biological ecosystems, as a set of symbiotic relationships. Symbiosis comes from the Greek meaning living together. Given the extent of the interdependence these four relationships may be thought of as the firm's four primary knowledge-creating symbiotic relationships as shown in Figure 30.1.

30.5.1   Firms' Relationships with their Customer-users

In order to survive over time, pay their workers, suppliers and bond-holders, and earn a profit firms must generate revenue. This requires having customers. To have and retain customers firms must supply them with value. To do so firms must have knowledge of their customers.

Living with their customers will sooner or later require that firms improve the value that they offer. For example, customers could be persuaded to buy more, the wants of customers may change, or competitors may start offering preferable deals. This context may motivate individuals or groups in the firm to come up with value-creating conjectures. As discussed earlier, these conjectures, if they pass the hurdles, may ultimately turn into new products or services for customers.

But the novelty-creating story does not necessarily end there. Typically, firms specialize in production and distribution. However, their customers specialize in using firms'

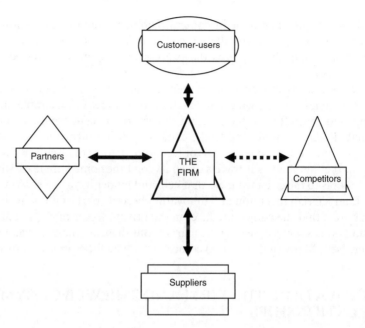

Figure 30.1   The primary novelty-creating symbiotic relationships: firms as part of a web of symbiotic knowledge interactions

products within their specific set of circumstances (which will differ across customers) By using the product the customer will get to know about its strengths and weaknesses. This knowledge may be put to work by the customer through the generation of value-creating conjectures. These conjectures may be fed back to the firm supplying the products or, as Eric von Hippel has shown, may be exploited by the customer-users themselves. (Indeed Franke et al., 2006 go one step further showing how frequently so-called lead users, who may not even be consumers of the product but who may have particular knowledge of the uses to which this kind of product may be put, play a key role in the innovation process.)

In turn, firms become the customer-users of the products of their own suppliers. In this role they may also facilitate the generation of value-adding conjectures by their suppliers or by themselves become user-innovators. The ever-growing process of specialization means that firms are forever tapping into new sources of supply, thus widening the possibilities for further conjectures.

The division of labour also multiplies the possibilities for partnerships through which firms can coordinate their complementary knowledge sets and in this way add value for customers. Innovation platforms that provide the foundation for complementary economic activity may facilitate such inter-firm cooperation.

Competitors, although actual or potential threats in the market, may also play a key role in stimulating the generation of value-creating conjectures. By observing or imitating their competitors or attempting to go one step better than them firms may come up with valuable conjectures. In this way firms may derive significant benefit by 'living with' their competitors.

.5.2 The Internet and the Knowledge Boundaries of the Four Primary Players

is worth noting that the Internet, as a radical infrastructural innovation, has transrmed the four primary knowledge-creating symbiotic relationships. It has done this y reducing significantly the transaction costs between the four groups of players and y making possible instant interactivity that would have been inconceivable in the pre-ternet age.

In turn this has shifted the knowledge boundaries of firms, their customer-users, supiers, partners and competitors. The latter four groups of players are now routinely corporated into firms' generation of value-creating conjectures. The result is that e distinction between 'internal' and 'external' knowledge is becoming increasingly lurred. From a novelty creation perspective, therefore, the firm is being replaced y the web of symbiotic relationships as the appropriate framing unit of analysis. owever, the firm continues to be the locus of ownership, legal responsibility and ecision-making.

0.6 INSTITUTIONS AND THE FOUR PRIMARY SYMBIOTIC INNOVATION RELATIONSHIPS

he four primary symbiotic innovation relationships are also subjected to other factors hat influence them. These factors provide an even wider context shaping the processes of he generation and implementation of value-creating conjectures. Some of these factors re shown in Figure 30.2.

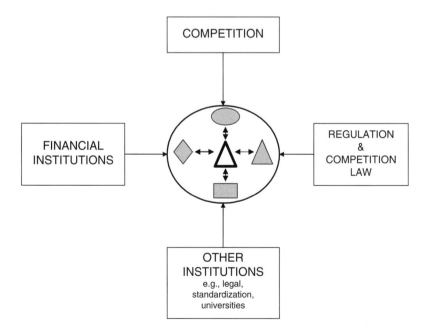

Figure 30.2 Wider contextual determinants of value-creating conjectures

Amongst the factors referred to in Figure 30.2 are institutions defined by Dougla North (1990) as the rules of the game, for example regulation and competition lav which will obviously influence the symbiotic relationships. But it is not only rule whether formal or informal, that will influence these relationships. Organizations suc as universities and financial institutions will also exert influence. In addition, structure such as modularized architectures and innovation platforms will also shape both th conjectures that are made as well as their content. All these factors, collectively an individually, will help and/or hinder the novelty-creating process.

30.7   AN APPLICATION OF SYMBIOTIC INNOVATION THEORY: THE NEW ICT ECOSYSTEM

The idea of an ecosystem, originating in biology, provides a rich metaphor in the contex of socio-economic systems. An ecosystem consists of a set of interdependent organism interacting in an environment. The interactions between the organisms together witl their interactions with their environment feed into processes of variety generation an selection that drive the co-evolution of the organisms and the ecosystem. The interac tions between players in a socio-economic system can be looked at in a similar way.

Who are the main creators and users of innovation-knowledge in the ICT ecosystem At a high level of aggregation there are four groups of players: equipment providers network operators, content and applications providers, and final consumers (the firs three groups being intermediate consumers who consume each other's output). Thes four players are organized into a hierarchically structured, modularized architecture a: is shown in Figure 30.3.[9]

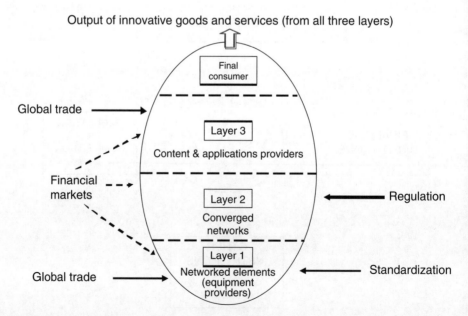

Figure 30.3   A simplified model of the new ICT ecosystem

The players in this ecosystem, it should be noted, may be involved in more than one layer. Furthermore, over time the boundaries between layers tend to shift (as indicated by the dotted boundary lines). What drives evolutionary change in the new ICT ecosystem, making it the restless system that it is? The answer to this question is that it is innovation that is the driver, innovation emerging largely from the symbiotic open innovation relationships between the four groups of players.

As Figure 30.3 shows, it is the equipment providers who provide the elements that go into networks and enable access to them (e.g., routers, servers, switches, transmission equipment, PCs and mobile phones). Network operators buy equipment from the equipment providers, string them together into networks, and provide network services. (They include telecoms, cable and satellite operators as well as broadcasters.) These two groups jointly provide general purpose innovation platforms that provide the foundation for the third group, content and applications providers. (These platforms include the PC and TV and, more recently, the mobile phone. The Internet might be thought of as a platform of platforms, including the increasingly networked PC, TV and mobile phone and facilitating a collection of further symbiotic relationships.) The fourth group consists of final customer-users who interact with the other three groups, using the knowledge that they create and adding to it.

30.8   THE SIX PRIMARY SYMBIOTIC RELATIONSHIPS IN THE ICT ECOSYSTEM

Each of the four groups interacts with the others, making a total of six symbiotic relationships as shown in Figure 30.4. Symbiotic relationship 1 includes the telecoms operator–equipment vendor relationship (studied in detail in Fransman, 2010), a classical example of provider–user creation of novelty. At first, during the monopoly era in telecommunications that came to an end in the mid-1980s as a result of policy and regulatory changes, most of the research relating to telecoms took place in the central R&D laboratories of the telecoms operators (such as Bell Labs, BT's Martlesham Laboratories, France Telecom's CNET and NTT's Electrical Communications Laboratories) with development being done by the telecoms equipment supplier.

Over time, however – as a result of specialization, learning and competition between equipment suppliers – the symbiotic relationship changed with most R&D moving to the equipment providers. Currently, the latter companies account for three-quarters of the total R&D expenditure of the ICT ecosystem. The main R&D engine of the ecosystem, therefore, is located in the group 1 players (although the software-based providers of content and applications – including the Internet content and applications providers such as Google, Yahoo, eBay, Amazon, Skype and so on included in group 3 are also relatively R&D-intensive). However, most of the investment in the ICT ecosystem is made by the capital-intensive high-fixed-cost network operators in group 2 who account for about 70 per cent of the total capital expenditure undertaken in the ecosystem.[10]

Symbiotic relationships 2 and 5 involve the provision by the equipment providers and the network operators of a general purpose innovation platform for the content and applications providers (including the Internet content and applications providers).[11]

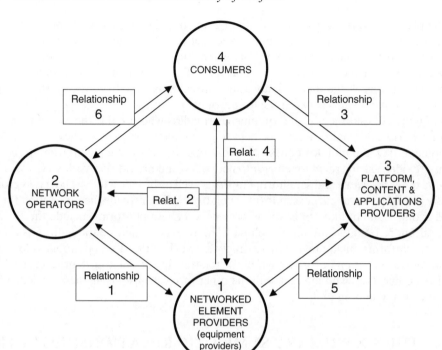

Figure 30.4   Six primary symbiotic relationships in the ICT ecosystem

While the symbiotic relationships in most ways are mutually beneficial there are also tensions[12] providing a reminder that symbiosis is not always mutually and equally beneficial.

Symbiotic relationship 3 involves the content and applications providers on the one hand and final customer-users on the other. This relationship has seen the emergence of so-called Web 2.0 interactions with final customer-users becoming both users and creators of innovation knowledge embodied in new content and applications. Social networking (the stock-in-trade of a new subset of players that include YouTube, MySpace, Facebook and others) has emerged from this symbiotic relationship.

Symbiotic relationship 4 includes the interactions between equipment providers and final customer-users. An example is the PC providers whose interactions with final customer-users has resulted in many fundamental and incremental hardware and software innovations over the years.

Finally, symbiotic relationship 6 deals with the interactions between network operators and final customer-users. Traditionally, this is the relationship between telephone company and phone customer. But this symbiotic relationship has been transformed by many factors including the changes in regulatory environment that introduced competition to the incumbent operators from new entrant operators and the advent of the Internet.

0.9 CONCLUSION

his is an all too brief account[13] of the process of novelty creation in the new ICT eco-
ystem based on an analysis of the evolution of value-creating conjectures that emerge
a and are shaped by the symbiotic relationships between the players in this ecosystem.
. is this process that, in Schumpeter's words, drives the restlessness of this ecosystem,
aking it the major contributor to economic and social development that it is.

NOTES

1. Smith (1910), p. 9.
2. Smith (1910), p. 9.
3. Smith (1910), p. 9.
4. Smith (1910), pp. 9–10.
5. Smith (1910), p. 10.
6. Smith (1910), p. 10.
7. Hayek (1945).
8. Witt (2002), p. 15; original emphasis.
9. Fransman (2010).
0. See Fransman (2010).
1. The importance of this platform is currently being researched by the present author.
2. An example of the tensions is the so-called network neutrality debate that has taken place mainly in the USA involving telecoms operators and Internet content and applications providers over the question of the right of the operators to charge differential prices to different groups of Internet users.
3. For further detail the reader is referred to the author's book, Fransman (2010).

BIBLIOGRAPHY

Bloch, H. and S. Metcalfe (2011), 'Complexity in the Theory of the Firm', in C. Antonelli (ed.) *Handbook on the Economic Complexity of Technological Change*, Edward Elgar, Cheltenham, UK and Northampton, MA, USA.
Franke, N., E. Von Hippel and M. Schreier (2006), 'Finding Commercially Attractive User Innovations: A Test of Lead User Theory', *Journal of Product Innovation Management*, **23**(4), 301–15.
Fransman, M. (2010), *The New ICT Ecosystem – Implications for Policy and Regulation*, Cambridge University Press, Cambridge.
Hayek, F.A. (1945), 'The Use of Knowledge in Society', *American Economic Review*, **35**(4), 519–30.
Lane, D. (2011), 'Complexity and Innovation Dynamics', in C. Antonelli, (ed.) *Handbook on the Economic Complexity of Technological Change*, Edward Elgar, Cheltenham, UK and Northampton, MA, USA.
Loasby, B. (2003), 'The Innovative Mind', paper presented at the DRUID Summer Conference 2003 on Creating, Sharing and Transferring Knowledge, Copenhagen, 12–14 June.
Metcalfe, S. (2009), 'University and Business Relations: Connecting the Knowledge Economy', University of Manchester and University of Cambridge, mimeo.
North, D.C. (1990), *Institutions, Institutional Change and Economic Performance*, Cambridge University Press, Cambridge.
Schumpeter, J.A. (1934), *The Theory of Economic Development*, Oxford University Press, New York, 1961 edition.
Schumpeter, J.A. (1939), *Business Cycles*, McGraw-Hill, New York.
Schumpeter, J.A. (1942), *Capitalism, Socialism and Democracy*, Harper and Brothers, New York, 1966 edition.
Smith, A. (1910), *An Inquiry into the Nature and Causes of the Wealth of Nations*, J.M. Dent, London.
Von Hippel, E. (1988), *The Sources of Innovation*, Oxford University Press, New York.
Witt, U. (2002), 'How Evolutionary is Schumpeter's Theory of Economic Development?', *Industry and Innovation*, **9**(1/2) 7–22.

31 Product innovation when consumers have switching costs
Evens Salies

31.1 INTRODUCTION

A primary weapon of a capitalist society is the development of new products that firm race to introduce before a competitor comes out with a model that consumers will lik much better (Baumol, 2006). Economists have long recognized, however, that in fre markets, incentives to innovate will be diluted unless some factors grant innovators a temporary monopoly (Tirole, 1988). Patenting is the most cited factor in the economi literature. This survey concentrates on another factor that confers innovators with first mover advantage over their competitors, namely consumer switching costs, whereby 'a consumer makes an investment specific to her current seller, that must be duplicated fo any new seller' (Klemperer, 2008, p.9). This concept that has been formally introduce in theoretical economics in the seminal journal articles of Von Weizsäcker (1984) an Klemperer (1987),[1] can be dated back to Schumpeter ([1942] 1962) who suggested a role of long-period contracts as devices for tying prospective customers to investing firms.

Unlike patenting or other price or non-price strategic instruments, temporary monopoly power can arise as a purely demand-side phenomenon when, for example, consumers want to avoid transaction costs (the cost of using the market in the sense of Coase, 1937) or learning how to use another firm's technology. The effect of consumer switching costs on innovation is controversial, however, and has been largely neglected in the economics of the firm literature, in which the focus on demand inertia is for the case of business-to-business relationships, where buyers are firms.[2] On the one hand, it is natural that consumers who have developed product usage skills on one innovative product will want these product-specific skills to be transferable across all functionally identical product classes. Thus, as asserted by Pae and Hyun (2006, p.22), many consumers who develop those skills will be unwilling to learn how to use a new product, which will give advantage to the incumbent technology, the provider of which may be able to charge a price above its competitive level to recoup innovation expenditures (Baumol, 2002, p.113).[3] There are also situations however, where consumer switching costs actually are an impediment to technological progress. The presence of high switching costs can be detrimental to innovation because it tends to 'buffer consumers from information about competing technologies and derives continuous commitment to incumbent technologies' (Pae and Hyun, 2006, p.25). This is not surprising as technology-driven markets are characterized by a high level of uncertainty; more particularly when technologies are quickly replaced and information relevant to consumers is temporarily absent.

This chapter provides a survey of the links between innovation strategies and consumer technology patronage via switching costs. The chapter will essentially focus on product innovation, regardless of whether it is incremental or radical.[4] Baumol (2002, pp. 154–5) defines product innovation as something that shifts the demand curve for the affected final product to the right.[5] Models where there is no patent protection will be discussed. Moreover, the effect of switching costs due to direct network externalities will not be addressed in this survey.[6] The survey does not totally ignore network industries, using examples from broadband Internet, computer software and banking. Finally, consumers here are buyers in the retail market.

Given the variety of components of consumer switching costs, it is worth emphasizing that 'consumer switching cost' is an all-inclusive term that may lead to some confusion, more particularly regarding the distinction between 'good' or 'bad' switching costs, perceived or paid switching costs, and between switching and search costs. Regarding the former distinction, our classification follows the literature by separating exogenous (they affect all firms similarly and are intrinsic to the product itself; Chen and Hitt, 2006) and endogenous switching costs (induced by a firm's marketing strategy) where only the latter are subject to specific manipulation by firms to render consumers 'captive'. Perceived and paid switching costs are identical, and search costs are part of switching costs. Distinguishing the former two costs is not important if non-switchers know perfectly what their switching cost would be, should they switch. The rationale for not disentangling search from switching costs is that for most individuals, running the risk to switch without entering a search process would be too hazardous a decision. To put it another way, switching always involves some degree of search.

Consumer switching cost theory has matured to the point that some classification of switching costs for both understanding innovative firm behaviour and building policy-oriented models is necessary. Several components of switching costs (lock-in factors) that are relevant concerning firms' innovation behaviour are thus listed in section 31.2. In section 31.3 we survey the existing literature on the effect of switching costs on innovating firms' behaviour and the way they compete for consumers. Section 31.4 raises important regulation and competition policy questions, using broadband Internet as the main example. Section 31.5 concludes.

31.2 DEFINITION OF RELEVANT CONSUMER SWITCHING COSTS FOR PRODUCT INNOVATION

'Consumer switching cost' is a catch-all term that includes all demand-side factors that affect consumer willingness to switch between products (see, for instance, Chen and Hitt, 2006, who offer an exhaustive list of types of consumer switching costs in the particular case of information technology markets).

Switching to a different technology requires specific investments in terms of how to use it (learning cost), because it involves different technical difficulties. For example, changing one's smart phone may require switching to more sophisticated functionalities or to a new operating system. Shy (2002, p. 4) also refers to training cost (see also Chen and Hitt, 2006). Therefore, a consumer already using one technology may consider an alternative as both functionally and qualitatively different, and thus perceive this as a cost for switching to this alternative technology. One interesting case is in broadband Internet where each ISP, by providing its own branded modem, makes it not redeployable in Williamson's sense[7] (for almost all users modems are not interchangeable between

Internet services). Similarly, new product releases in the computer software market can involve significant changes to the user interface. Consumers 'must [therefore] weigh the potential benefits of any new features against the time and effort involved in relearning the interface. They are prone to remain with their existing choice options. . . . [However], switching to an upgrade module imposes lower switching costs on consumers than shifting technologies entirely' (Pae and Hyun, 2006, p. 21). The effect of learning costs on customer migration are even stronger when 'bought-in' customers are misinformed about the technologies that are available, and how they work.

Consumers also have to pay transaction costs that include the costs to consumers of using the market, in Coase's sense (Coase, 1937). Consumers must find out alternative sellers, and which offers the best price for their needs (search costs). This expenditure on information is an investment (Von Weizsäcker, 1984). In subscription markets, consumers also have to pay transaction costs in closing an account with one's current supplier and opening another with a competitor. Note that search costs can be significantly lower in some industries, since free ranking services are available for many products on the web (see Chen and Hitt, 2006). But, as noted earlier by Coase, specialists who will supply this information will not eliminate the costs of searching for prices within the market.

Consumers may also have to overcome cognitive costs (or psychological costs; see Tirole, 1988; Klemperer, 1995, p. 518). Tirole (1988, p. 110) made the following point that consumers are not reluctant to buy a new product if the psychological cost of trying it is low and the prospect of many future purchases is high. The success of an innovative product is far from certain, which arises from the psychology of gains and losses as developed by psychologists (see Kahneman, 2011 for a survey). In innovative markets where product change often requires behavioural change, which entails costs, we think this bias is more particularly important and can easily be considered as part of consumer switching costs. Indeed, the adoption of an innovation almost always involves giving up things we currently have and getting other things we do not have (Gourville, 2004). The Prospect theory of Kahneman and Tversky (see Kahneman, 2011) and the endowment effect highlight that the benefit given up will loom larger than the benefits to be obtained. An innovation must thus be significantly better to overcome the biases consumers bring to their analysis. The concept of cognitive dissonance, which refers to people's desire to reduce the psychic 'cost' of exposure to information inconsistent with continuing to consume one's product offers a further explanation. For example, one would not search for alternative branded products to avoid the discomfort of learning that cheaper products with similar quality levels are available. When the new product is offered by an alternative seller, cognitive costs are likely to increase with brand reputation and experience with one's current supplier.

Transaction costs as defined above are real costs and exogenous. But, firms may also find it profitable to lock consumers in by creating endogenous switching costs (endogenous switching costs are also termed artificial). These lock-in devices designed by firms are not necessarily detrimental to consumers. As suggested by Klemperer and Padilla (1997) consumers may have psychological feelings of loyalty. The resulting loyalty cost (see Shy, 2002, p. 5) arises, for example, when switching technology results in losing some preferred customers' benefits (for example, frequent flyer programmes). In some cases, however, firms may want to behave against consumers' interests. For example, in network industries, consumers have to pay cancellation fees that may be relatively high.

This type of cost belongs to the set of monopolistic practices listed by Schumpeter ([1942] 1962). More explicitly, Schumpeter suggested the role of long-period contracts as devices for tying prospective customers to investing firms.

31.3 PRODUCT INNOVATION WHEN CONSUMERS HAVE SWITCHING COSTS

The consumer switching cost literature takes individual choice as a root of its models. All models on consumer switching costs rely on the following premise. If a consumer is initially indifferent between the goods of two competing sellers, the fact of using one of them will change his or her relative utilities for the products, meaning that he or she will perceive a cost in switching brands. Consequently, the consumer will tend to stick to his or her past/current product choice (Von Weizsäcker, 1984, p. 1089). These potential barriers to mobility introduce friction into markets akin to entry and exit barriers faced by firms. Although firms can develop devices to lock their consumers in, exogenous consumer switching cost is a very valuable resource because firms do not have to invest to create them. According to Morgan and Hunt (1999, p. 286), 'perhaps the most valuable resources are those that are the least mobile, such as consumer loyalty'.

It is noteworthy that in a static model with no repeated purchases, horizontal differentiation establishes clienteles, as is the case in models with consumer switching costs. In models with repeated purchases, horizontal differentiation and switching costs are not the same concepts as shown by Klemperer (1987), however. One rationale for this is that, as pointed out in Von Weizsäcker (1984, p. 1088), the information that consumers must gather about competing firms and their products is like an investment, the effect of which is necessarily of an intrinsically intertemporal nature. In models with consumer switching costs, firms are induced to introduce new products at low prices or with special offers to get people to try the product and develop the habit of buying it (Mueller, 1997, p. 836). They may be willing to even incur losses in the process, because they may charge higher prices over their existing consumers for repeated purchases.[8]

The effects of consumer switching costs on the decision by firms to sell differentiated products are well understood (see Farrell and Klemperer, 2007). These effects on innovative firms introducing a new product have received little attention, however, in the literature. Several results emerge from this literature. They are surveyed in the following sub-sections. Let use examine these results.

31.3.1 The Retention–Acquisition Trade-off

When a firm has a fraction of its consumers who are attached to it, this lack of consumer mobility can lower this firm's incentive to innovate unless one or more competitor comes out with a new product that consumers value significantly more. Innovative firms launching a new product face the retention–acquisition trade-off (often termed *harvesting vs investing*) pointed out in the early literature on consumer switching costs when firms do not innovate (see Klemperer, 1995 for a concise presentation of this issue, or the more recent survey of Farrell and Klemperer, 2007). The incumbent firm can temporarily elevate its price so as to recoup its innovation expenditure. But this strategy, known as harvesting, makes the firm more vulnerable to undercutting by one or more competitors offering a similar product. This strategy can also be outweighed by the firm's incentive to charge lower prices to acquire new customers who will be valuable repeat purchasers in the future (investing).

It is noteworthy that entrants do not face such trade-off in setting prices.[9] They do not necessarily price low. In his model of a durable good and a vertically differentiated entrant that may or not innovate, Gerlach (2004) indeed shows that switching costs affect pricing in an unexpected way.[10] For example, if the entrant introduces a drastic innovation, it tends to set its price at the monopoly level. The first reason for this can be attached to consumers' behaviour: '[b]uying the old technology in period 1 implies the risk of being locked in and not having the flexibility to later purchase a new technology' (ibid., p. 189). Consumers are more willing to buy at a high price in the second period because 'it is more likely that they will buy the new major technology anyway'. (ibid., p. 188). The second reason is that the incumbent firm chooses a price–quantity pair for the first period such that high willingness-to-pay consumers stay in the market in the second period (the fewer consumers served in the first period, the higher the price in the second period and the less consumers are willing to wait).

31.3.2   Product Innovation, Timing of Innovation

Once the firm has built a customer base:

> with incremental innovations it can enhance the salience of non-price criteria vis-à-vis price in buyers' choice decisions. Such a strategy will enable the firm to enhance its financial performance, provided the *marginal* cost associated with the incremental innovation is lower than the increase in price that the incrementally innovative product is able to command in the marketplace. (Varadarajan, 2009, p. 27)

For example:

> incremental innovations that manifest as added new features in a firm's current product offerings suggests that those added features provide positive differentiation by giving a product perceived advantages over competitors' products. Consumers seem to use added features in an instrumental-reasoning process that makes the brand with more features appear superior in a choice set. (Ibid.)

But, purchasing the presently available product implies lock-in and entails the risk of economic obsolescence from a future innovation (Gerlach, 2004, p. 184).

To our knowledge, Beggs (1989) is the first model to study the effect of consumer switching costs à la Klemperer on innovation. Assuming decreasing average costs and a sufficiently large switching cost, Beggs (1989) provides a theoretical foundation for the observation that the less efficient technology may be adopted by firms when consumers have switching costs. Consumers differ with respect to their valuation of the product/service they purchase but they are not attached differently to the different brands (identical and exogenous switching costs). It is nonetheless important that the switching cost be sufficiently large to rule out the possibility of subscribing to another seller in a later period. Note that the condition that consumers' preferences exhibit direct network externalities is not necessary for Beggs's result to hold. Switching costs and decreasing

verage costs together generate an indirect network externality, in that the greater the
opulation of consumers who buy a firm's product, the more likely it is to survive and
ie more attractive it is to other customers, regardless of whether this product performs
etter. As this firm's price would inevitably be low if it wanted to serve all customers,
ius, any consumer could expect a low price should he or she select that firm, provided
iat all other consumers select that firm too. Schematically, the utility of each firm *a*
ustomer, using technology 1, does not need to increase directly with an increase in the
otal number of consumers adopting technology 1. Beggs (1989) suggests that it is likely
o increase with an increase in the number of consumers subscribing to *a*. In the author's
vords (p. 437): 'the more consumers who buy a product the more likely it is to survive
nd the more attractive it is to other consumers'.

But the model does not capture essential features of several industries, which we believe
re brand differentiation and the perceived cost of learning how to use the different (albeit
ubstitutable) technologies. A competitor offering an alternative technology knows that
t may not be easy to attract the incumbent's customers as they would be obliged to learn
iow to use the new technology. Moreover, firms rarely enter the market simultaneously
ind there is a long-established incumbent competing with new and aggressive entrants.
Ghemawat's (1991) model goes a little farther than Beggs's by considering a three-stage
game (innovation decision, entry, then production) where consumers have a preference
or a second-generation product. This second-generation product is innovative enough
(drastic innovation) to obsolesce the incumbent's leadership. One rationale for this is
.hat unlike the entrant that has nothing to lose, the incumbent fears that introducing a
second-generation product will cannibalize its first-generation product. By using quite
general assumptions (e.g., multiple entry threats), his model provides useful insights on
the role played by consumer switching costs on technological inertia.

Finally, in their model of financial innovation when consumers have switching costs,
Bhattacharyya and Nanda (2000), find that when the cost of delayed adoption is small,
the amount a client can be charged for a new product is limited since he or she can always
wait until competition from rivals drives down the price. A consequence of this is that
once a large base of customers invests in one provider's technology (installed base; see
Shy, 2002, p. 5), that provider may have no incentive to design one or more of the alternative technologies already supplied by competitors (see Krafft and Salies, 2008 who
reached the same conclusion in the case of the French broadband Internet market). The
role of incumbent size is explored below.

31.3.3   Market Share, Firm Size

Switching costs grant firms with some degree of monopoly power which they may
want to exploit in order to maintain or increase their market shares. As pointed out by
Bhattacharyya and Nanda (2000), the possibility of a positive association between market
share and incentives to innovate was first raised by Schumpeter ([1942] 1962). It is outside
the scope of this chapter to review the innovation-size literature, but everyone agrees that
a larger market share allows firms to derive greater revenues from a given innovation and,
hence, gives it greater incentives to engage in innovative activity. As far as we know, the
interplay between consumer switching cost and the size of innovating firms has received
little attention. In Bhattacharyya and Nanda (2000) in the case of banking, small firms

have incentives to follow more aggressive introduction strategy (a more valuable innovation at a low price) than large firms in order to induce switching of clients from large
banks. As a consequence, the distribution of market shares across banks is important
to the financial innovation process and an asymmetric distribution of market share
supports a higher level of innovation activity (ibid.). A similar conclusion is reached by
Ghemawat (1991, p. 170) who asserts that 'privileged access to a large customer base can
shrink the incentives to develop and apply the next generation of know-how'.

31.3.4   Product Line Enhancing

Consumer switching costs also help explain the existence of product line extension,
simply because with a complete line of products a firm can more easily develop brand
loyalty (Tellis, 1986, p. 156). In an oligopoly market where one firm pays a sunk cost to
sell an additional product and consumers from competing firms have shopping costs
the innovator can also glue its consumers on the old product (Klemperer and Padilla
1997). By increasing its product line, economies of scope arise on the demand side
which increases the cost of switching to single-product alternative sellers (ibid., p. 473
and see Chen and Forman, 2006 for an application of this concept to the router and
switch market). As asserted by these authors, the 'firm that sells [the new product] is
a more attractive firm for consumers to buy [the old product] from' (Klemperer and
Padilla, 1997, p. 475). This result supports the existence of multiproduct firms when
consumers value variety (Klemperer, 1995, p. 533). It also suggests that brand extension
as it exploits consumer loyalty, puts firms that sell a single product only at a serious
disadvantage relative to full-line producers (ibid.).

31.3.5   Announcement, Entry and Reputation

Switching costs more often act as a barrier to new entrants by making consumers favour
incumbent technologies (Pae and Hyun, 2006, p. 22). Preannouncement of a new product
is thus an effective mechanism when consumers have switching costs: 'sending strong
signals of market commitment to potential consumers [is] associated with consumers'
expectations for relationship continuity with the incumbent product/technology' (Pae
and Hyun, 2006, p. 21). Several examples exist in the computer software market where
firms like Microsoft use preannouncement to help consumers avoid switching costs.
Gerlach (2004) asks whether announcement of a vertically differentiated product can
facilitate entry of an innovating firm when a fraction of consumers is locked in on the
old product. His main conclusion is perhaps that the size of consumer switching costs
not only affect pricing but also the decision to announce entry. Though the high levels
of switching costs may act as barriers to entry, announcements by an innovating new
entrant firm may facilitate its entry by lowering the search costs for consumers seeking
out new technologies.

  Regarding the interplay between switching costs and firms' reputation, Von Weizsäcker
(1984) developed the appealing idea that when firms have to invest in reputation, constant prices can be interpreted as resulting from the existence of consumers' switching
costs. By maintaining its price constant, a firm reduces the switching cost of its rivals'
customers, more particularly those due to uncertainty, because its pricing policy is more

ransparent. We are not aware of such a model, although evidence exists in several markets.[12] Pae and Hyun (2006, p. 21) used a similar argument in the computer software market: 'firms that divulge future product plans to consumers. . .are likely to forestall consumers moving from incumbent technology to other technologies, as consumers know when they can expect upgrades of existing technologies. As an example, Microsoft preannounced Windows NT to protect its customer base from the release of IBM OS/2.2'.

31.3.6   Patent Protection

The role of consumer switching costs should thus be importantly weakened when there is patenting because patenting prevents competitors from freely imitating a firm's innovation during several periods. A simple way to model non-patented innovation is, as in Bhattacharyya and Nanda (2000, p. 1102), to assume that the lack of patent protection leaves firms with only a single period to recover their innovation expenditures (see subsection 31.3.2).

31.4   REGULATION OF INNOVATIVE MARKETS WHEN CONSUMERS HAVE SWITCHING COSTS: APPLICATION TO BROADBAND INTERNET

As long as switching costs are voluntarily established by consumers (e.g., psychological feelings of loyalty), there is a minor role for competition policies. As we saw above, they can be useful devices for temporarily ensuring some degree of monopoly power that firms seek so as to recoup their innovation expenditures. But, consumer switching costs may be subject to manipulation by firms as we asserted in section 31.2. Given this dual nature of consumer switching costs, competition authorities may find it difficult to determine why and when switching costs are to be condemned or not.

Let us pursue this section with a concrete example from broadband Internet showing the difficulties faced by regulators and competition policies when they have to decide upon reducing the detrimental effect of consumer switching costs on innovation. Despite supporting entry of new ISPs, the French broadband Internet industry is undoubtedly characterized by important inertia phenomena in terms of choice of technologies, and in terms of providers. This is problematic since one of the expected consequences of the emergence of the innovation 'broadband Internet' in France (and in Europe as well) was the creation of real competition between technologies. What was intended, especially from the regulators' viewpoint, was a decisive contest between the incumbent's choice of technology (DSL) and alternative technologies (such as Cable or WiFi) supported by new entrants providing high-quality packages at cheaper prices. While broadband Internet can be provided by different technologies, the DSL-based technology largely dominates (in December 2005, Cable represented 4.5 per cent) with the incumbent, France Telecom, still having the lion's share of end consumers (48.6 per cent in December 2006).

Consequently, if regulation and competition policies ignore switching costs, then reluctance by consumers to switch suppliers can lead to a lower innovation rate (see Waterson, 2003 for evidence in several retail markets, including non-innovative ones).

Further measures to stimulate competition may not bring more innovation, affecting productive efficiency in the short run (exit of potentially efficient competitors), and dynamic efficiency in the longer run (elimination of higher-quality/cheaper-price emergent offers). Making technologies more transparent to consumers could be as important Product announcement by innovative entrants can serve this purpose, and as such truthful information about products is pro-competitive and should be encouraged by the regulator. But, this should not preclude information that adopting a new technology may involve sunk costs for most consumers. Firms may have to subsidize those costs to attract customers. Therefore, too low switching costs may discourage firms from subsidizing these costs since they cannot be certain that they will keep their consumer base. This might induce them to favour technologies that require less learning, and possibly involve lower levels of innovation. This is certainly the reason why in the early stage of the market development, firms mainly advertised their offers based on price and speed where the latter clearly is an element of vertical differentiation.[13]

Krafft and Salies (2009), from a policy perspective, emphasize that the existence of consumer switching costs in new industries reinforces the importance of competition and regulation policies co-existing while playing different roles. Regulation is needed ex ante and over time to assess and diffuse to consumers all information required to appreciate their switching costs whilst competition policy should act ex post if the switching costs remain high over time despite the switching expertise developed by the regulator. A rationale for this is that purely deregulated situations – even based on strong competition policy principles – led to inefficient outcomes when innovation and consumers' switching costs are involved. Besides, the increasing role for competition laws over regulation rules has not eliminated the existence of switching costs.

Finally, competition policies tend to apply uniformly to all sectors whereas the types and degree of consumer lock-in is industry-specific. For example, retailed electricity is a quite homogeneous product, at least from consumers' perception and in addition retail activities embody sunk costs of operation. This implies that pricing in the market is not particularly competitive (see Waterson, 2003, pp. 137–41, who addresses the issue of consumers' switching costs between electricity retailers). Therefore, there was not much to say about regulation and competition policies targeted at innovative entrants in retail electricity markets compared to broadband Internet where new entrants tended to offer products vertically differentiated in terms of speed of connection.

31.5   CONCLUSION

This survey leads us to conclude that, although switching costs create dependence and inertia in technology-driven markets, the introduction of new products is likely to remain one of the most common strategies for signalling current users to stick with incumbent technologies. More particularly because 'products become more complex, and services become more important' (Klemperer, 2008). Pae and Hyun (2006, p. 21) seem less optimistic, however, regarding the effect of consumer switching costs on new entrants launching incremental innovations into high-technology markets: 'where a dominant technology emerges, switching costs may make its position unassailable unless there is fundamental shift in the technology paradigm'. This suggests that consumer

vitching costs could be a driver of drastic innovation by new entrants in highly competi-
ve markets.

This survey also gave us an opportunity to explore several concrete examples, yet
mpirical/econometric analyses or well-investigated case studies on the role of con-
umer switching cost on innovative firms are largely lacking (see Klemperer, 2008, who
lso points out other limits of existing empirical studies). There exists a literature on the
ffects of switching costs on buyer choice of vendor and on new product adoption in
ne market for routers and switches in the USA (see, e.g., Chen and Forman, 2006 and
he references therein). In the software computer market, which is driven by quickly
hanging technologies, Pae and Hyun (2006) have shown that consumer switching
osts encourage technology commitments and technology commitments secure return
atronage of incumbent technology. Ghemawat (1991) analyses the effect of consumer
witching costs in the private branch exchange industry after noting that incumbents
ended to lag in both product innovation and imitation and that patent protection
vas unavailable. In the case of video game consoles, which are a consumer durable,
Gerlach (2004) examined the effect of announcement on entry and pre-emption when
onsumers have switching costs. His results should be relevant for our understanding
of barriers to innovative entrants in industries such as TV sets and other consumer
lurables (or more generally electric appliances). For example, the increasing interest
n smart meters, enabling technologies and consumption control devices in electricity
uggests the emergence of a non-price competition phase with environmentally friendly
products as a competitive weapon. Experiences from other industries witnessed in the
iterature suggest that incumbent firms who generally hold the majority of retail customers will have some advantage in introducing such products. This should accelerate
the diffusion of smart meters. But it might also happen that the less efficient technology
wins.

This chapter also provided examples of application to ISP innovation although, one
has to recognize, this industry is less innovative than it used to be. Measuring the per-
customer switching costs between ISPs offering broadband, it is possible complete the
supply-side analysis of the reasons for technological inertia. Supply-side inertia such as
the first-mover advantage is pointless here as an explanation as the incumbent entered
quasi-simultaneously with other firms. These authors concluded that consumer switching costs must have been high so that the dominant technology is that of the firm with
the largest number of customers. Assuming consumers have developed brand loyalty,
the incumbent had little effort to make to attract its fixed-line consumers on basic
DSL. Besides, by offering access to the Internet the firm showed itself as innovative.
Accordingly, low switching rates would be a cause not only of consumer inertia (high
switching costs) but also of technological inertia. Investigation of the role of consumer
switching costs in other innovative industries could help to answer the question of
whether this type of market imperfection actually is welfare-enhancing or not.

NOTES

1. Von Weiszäcker also suggested the term substitution cost, which is no longer used.
2. As far as we know, Nielson (1996) is the sole addressor of the issue of buyer switching cost in the case of

business-to-business marketing relationships. In that paper, the concepts of switching cost investment and transaction-specific assets à la Williamson (1979) are synonymous.

3.   This idea that innovative firms cannot survive if their pricing approach precludes recouping R&D investments dates back to Schumpeter ([1942] 1962).

4.   From a consumer perspective, radical innovations 'refer to innovations that are new to the. . .industry which incorporate a substantially different and new technology; and which provide substantially higher customer benefits relative to current products'. This is to be distinguished from incremental innovation that 'refer to improvements in a firm's existing product offerings that better satisfy the needs of its current and potential customers' (see Varadarajan, 2009, p.21).

5.   Basically, product innovations create new goods and services (Tirole, 1988, p. 389). If successful, product innovation will increase final-product output, but its general effects on price and welfare notably depends on the shape of demand parameters, and hence on consumer switching costs.

6.   Farrell and Klemperer (2007) provide an exhaustive survey on this issue.

7.   Reference to Williamson's (1979) concept of relationship-specific investments by customers was first provided in Farrell and Shapiro (1988), although there is no innovation in their model.

8.   This is termed as *bargain-then-rip-off* in the literature.

9.   This trade-off is more an issue when firms have to set a single price (Klemperer, 2008). To avoid it firms can set more sophisticated pricing policies over time. Firms practice third- (bargain-then-rip-off) or second- (non-linear pricing) degree price discrimination. This has the consequence that marginal cost pricing will generally not be viable for oligopoly firms undertaking innovation (Baumol, 2006).

10.   This author captures the effect of switching costs by assuming that a proportion of consumers are locked in to the old product in the second period provided they have purchased it in the first period from the incumbent (only switchers buy the new technology to the entrant in the second period). A distance parameter differentiates consumers with respect to their willingness to pay (Gerlach, 2004, p.186).

11.   The term 'shopping costs' is preferable here (see Klemperer, 2008). But, for the sake of consistency, we prefer to stick with that of 'consumer switching costs'.

12.   Von Weizsäcker (1984) assumed that firm price is constant over periods but firms do not innovate in his model. They are differentiated by some transportation cost à la Hotelling (1929) and consumers have to pay a cost to switch.

13.   The range of speeds provided by a firm warrants future research as an element of vertical differentiation common to all firms while they would be differentiated with respect to switching costs. This assumption remains speculative in the French context as no household survey is available regarding customers' choice of broadband ISPs.

REFERENCES

Baumol, W.J., 2002, *The Free-market Innovation Machine – Analyzing the Growth Miracle of Capitalism*, Princeton: Princeton University Press.

Baumol, J.W., 2006, Entrepreneurship and innovation: (micro)theory of price and profit, paper at the ISS Conference, Innovation, Competition and Growth: Schumpeterian Perspectives, Nice – Sophia Antipolis, 21–24 June.

Beggs, A., 1989, A note on switching costs and technology choice, *The Journal of Industrial Economics*, **37**(4) 437–40.

Bhattacharyya, S. and V. Nanda, 2000, Client discretion, switching costs, and financial innovation, *The Review of Financial Studies*, **13**(4), 1101–27.

Chen, P.-Yu and C. Forman, 2006, Can vendors influence switching costs and compatibility in an environment with open standards?, *MIS Quarterly*, **30**, Special Issue on Standard Making, 541–62.

Chen, P.-Yu and L.M. Hitt, 2006, Information technology and switching costs, in T. Hendershott (ed.), *Information Systems Outsourcing: Enduring Themes, Global Challenges, and Process Opportunities*, Amsterdam: Elsevier, pp.437–70.

Coase, R.H., 1937, The nature of the firm, *Economica*, **4**(16), 386–405.

Farrell, J. and P. Klemperer, 2007, Coordination and lock-in: competition with switching costs and network effects, in *Handbook of Industrial Organization*, Amsterdam: North-Holland, Chapter 31, pp.1968–2072.

Farrell, J. and C. Shapiro, 1988, Dynamic competition with switching costs, *Rand Journal of Economics*, **19**(1), 123–37.

Gerlach, H.A., 2004, Announcement, entry, and pre-emption when consumers have switching costs, *Rand Journal of Economics*, **35**(1), 184–202.

Ghemawat, P., 1991, Market incumbency and technological inertia, *Marketing Sciences*, **10**(3), 161–71.

ourville, J.T., 2004, Why consumers don't buy: the psychology of new-product adoption, *Harvard Business School Note*, April, No. 504-056.

otelling, H., 1929, Stability in competition, *The Economic Journal*, **39**(153), 41–57.

ahneman, D., 2011, *Thinking, Fast and Slow*, New York: Farrar, Straus and Giroux.

lemperer, P., 1987, The competitiveness of markets with switching costs, *Rand Journal of Economics*, **18**(1), 138–50.

lemperer, P., 1995, Competition when consumers have switching costs: an overview with applications to industrial organization, macroeconomics, and international trade, *Review of Economic Studies*, **62**(4), 515–39.

lemperer, P., 2008, Switching costs, in S.N. Durlauf and L.E. Blume (eds), *The New Palgrave Dictionary of Economics*, 2nd edition, London: Palgrave MacMillan.

lemperer, P. and J. Padilla, 1997, Do firms' product lines include too many varieties? *Rand Journal of Economics*, **28**(3), 472–88.

rafft, J. and E. Salies, 2008, The diffusion of ADSL and costs of switching Internet providers in the broadband industry: evidence from the French case, *Research Policy*, **37**(4), 706–19.

rafft, J. and E. Salies, 2009, Why and how should new industries with high consumer switching costs be regulated? The case of broadband Internet in France, in C. Ménard and M. Ghertman (eds), *Regulation, Deregulation, Reregulation: Institutional Perspectives*, Cheltenham, UK and Northampton, MA, USA: Edward Elgar.

lorgan, R.M. and S. Hunt, 1999, Relationship-based competitive advantage: the role of relationship marketing in marketing strategy, *Journal of Business Research*, **46**(3), 281–90.

lueller, D.C., 1997, First-mover advantage and path dependence, *International Journal of Industrial Organization*, **15**(6), 827–50.

lielson, C.C., 1996, An empirical examination of switching cost investment in business-to-business marketing relationships, *The Journal of Business & Industrial Marketing*, **11**(6), 38–60.

ae, J.H. and J.S. Hyun, 2006, Technology advancement strategy on patronage decisions: the role of switching costs in high-technology markets, *Omega*, **34**(1), 19–27.

chumpeter, J.A. [1942] 1962, Monopolistic practices, in *Capitalism, Socialism and Democracy*, Chapter 8, 3rd edition, New York: Harper Torchbooks.

hy, O., 2002, *The Economics of Network Industries*, 1st edition, New York: Cambridge University Press.

ellis, G.J., 1986, Beyond the many faces of price: an integration of pricing strategies, *The Journal of Marketing*, **50**(4), 146–60.

irole, J., 1988, *The Theory of Industrial Organization*, Cambridge, MA: The MIT Press.

aradarajan, R., 2009, Fortune at the bottom of the innovation pyramid: the strategic logic of incremental innovations, *Business Horizons*, **52**(1), 21–9.

on Weizsäcker, C.C., 1984, The cost of substitution, *Econometrica*, **52**(5), 1085–116.

Vaterson, M., 2003, The role of consumers in competition and competition policy, *International Journal of Industrial Organization*, **21**(2), 129–50.

Villiamson, O.E., 1979, Transaction-cost economics: the governance of contractual relations, *Journal of Law and Economics*, **22**(2), 233–61.

32 Modularity and its implications for the theory of the firm
Andreas Reinstaller

32.1 INTRODUCTION

Since the late 1980s an increasing number of researchers in the field of economics and strategic management have started to conceive technologies, firms and the economy in general as complex hierarchical systems (e.g., Anderson et al., 1988; Levinthal, 1997; Arthur, 1999). The concept of modularity refers to one set of principles related to the design and management of such systems. It is based on the seminal contributions by Herbert Simon (e.g., Simon, 1996) on human learning in complex environments and the design of complex adaptive systems. Research on modularity in economics and management has given rise to a large and still growing body of literature. This chapter gives a selective overview on important contributions to this field of research. It is organized as follows. In section 32.2 it will define the concept of modularity and examine how it is related to complex systems and near-decomposability. In section 32.3 it will discuss several aspects related to modularity as a strategy of human problem-solving. Section 32.4 then reviews recent contributions that have applied the concept of modularity to the theory of the firm and section 32.5 concludes.

32.2 COMPLEXITY, NEAR-DECOMPOSABILTIY AND MODULARITY: DEFINITIONS

According to Simon (1996, p. 195), a system is complex if it is 'made up of a large number of parts that interact in a nonsimple way', and where the 'whole is more than the sum of its parts' insofar as given the characteristics of the parts and the ways they interact it is 'not trivial to infer the properties of the whole'.[1] As a consequence it cannot be comprehended and controlled by a single person. Many publications rely on Kauffman's NK model (Kauffman, 1993) to illustrate and study complex systems in economics, organizational studies or management sciences. The NK model studies the performance of a system Π in dependence of two parameters, N, the number of components of the system, and K, the degree of interdependence of these components. The system is defined as a binary string of the N components corresponding to different system configurations and associated performance levels derived from them. The number of different configurations is then 2^N, and the performance π_i of each component T_i is a function of the component itself and the K other components impinging on it, $\pi_i = \pi_i(T_i; T_1, \ldots, T_k)$. The performance Π of the system is then given by the average over all component performances, $\Pi = 1/N \sum_i \pi_i(T_i; T_1, \ldots, T_k)$.

Figure 32.1 illustrates one possible configuration for a system with 12 components,

	T_1	T_2	T_3	T_4	T_5	T_6	T_7	T_8	T_9	T_{10}	T_{11}	T_{12}
T_1	0		X	X	X	X		X			X	
T_2		0	X	X	X	X			X			X
T_3	X	X	0	X	X		X			X		
T_4	X	X		0	X	X			X		X	
T_5		X	X	X	0		X		X	X		
T_6		X	X		X	0	X	X	X			
T_7	X	X	X	X			0				X	X
T_8			X	X	X	X	0	X				X
T_9	X			X		X		X	0	X	X	
T_{10}	X	X	X				X	X	0	X		
T_{11}			X	X			X	X	X	X	0	X
T_{12}			X				X	X	X	X	X	0

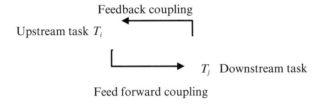

Feedback coupling

Upstream task T_i

T_j Downstream task

Feed forward coupling

Source: Illustration of feedbacks from Gomes and Joglekar (2008, p. 446).

Figure 32.1   NK model with N=12 and K=6 in a task structure matrix (TSM)

$N=12$, which are on average influenced by six other components, $K=6$, using a task structure matrix (cf. Ulrich and Eppinger, 2008). We may assume that the depicted complex system is a schematic representation of a production process that consists of 12 tasks, T_i, that are interdependent and have to be executed to produce some output at some cost and with a specific quality. Interdependencies are marked by an 'x'. The performance of any task is therefore determined by the number of entries in the related row. The entries in each column in turn indicate which other elements are actively influenced by a specific task. Elements in the lower off-diagonal part of the matrix represent feed forward linkages and therefore capture some inherent sequence or hierarchy between the tasks and the elements in the upper off-diagonal part of the matrix represent feedback linkages. They indicate that a change in a downstream task affects tasks upstream. The performance of task T_4, for instance, is affected by upstream tasks T_1 and T_2 and downstream tasks T_9 and T_{11}. A change in any of these tasks will affect its performance. On the other hand, task T_4 affects tasks, T_1, T_2, T_3, T_5, T_7, T_8, T_9, and T_{11}, such that any change in its performance will positively or negatively affect these other tasks. Any adjustment in the production process shown in Figure 32.1 is likely to be difficult especially if the effect of the linkages on the performance of any task is not additive.

Kauffman (1993) has shown that it becomes more difficult to improve the overall performance of a system like the one in Figure 32.1 if its elements are more tightly coupled. If $K=0$, that is, no linkages exist, then each single component of the system can be improved and contributes independently to its performance. Hence, a unique configuration of the system exists that is associated with the global optimum that can be reached by gradually improving each single component. If on the other hand, complexity is at its maximum, $K=N-1$, which implies that all components are linked to each other, then small changes in one component trigger adjustments in all other components. Higher interdependence therefore leads to less correlated outcomes for small changes in the elements of the system. The number of local optima increases in K, and this makes it very difficult to find the global optimum. Only a complete search of the state space will allow agents to identify a global optimum. However, exhaustive search explodes as the number of components N increases. For agents with limited time, memory and cognitive capacities the problem will quickly become intractable. Indeed, it is comparable to other NP-complete problems such as the travelling salesman problem (see Kauffman, 1993, pp. 63ff.). Hence, with increasing system size and interdependency the danger for a system to remain locked in in a local optimum increases, as does the difficulty to manage the system.

As will be discussed in detail in the next section of this chapter, a strategy to deal with this complexity is to decompose the original complex problem into manageable sub-problems, solve these and recompose the system. This process will transform the system into a composite one, 'constructed through the superposition of: (1) terms representing interactions of the variables within each subsystem; and (2) terms representing interactions among the subsystems' (Simon and Ando, 1961, p. 132). The subsystems are structurally independent but operate together to fulfil the primary purpose of the system. Such composite systems are referred to as near-decomposable systems. Near-decomposability and modularity are architectural features shared by most complex systems.

Figure 32.2 gives an example of a near-decomposable system. As compared to Figure 32.1 most feed forward and feedback loops between the 12 tasks, T_1. . .T_{12}, are now concentrated in four subsystems or modules, M_1. . .M_4, made up of three tasks each. Between these modules only a few linkages exist. Hence, the tasks within each subsystem are tightly coupled whereas across subsystems they are much more loosely coupled if compared to the system depicted in Figure 32.1. This reduction of linkages to tasks outside the own subsystem implies that each subsystem hides information insofar as other subsystems cannot access and modify this information. It acts as a black box that transforms some inputs into specific visible outputs for other modules or the system user.

Modularization is one heuristic through which a decomposition of a complex system into independent or quasi-independent modules can be achieved. In modular system designs the interaction between modules is typically organized according to a specific architecture and the interaction is mediated through standardized interfaces. The architecture establishes which modules are part of the system and which is their role. It also establishes a hierarchy between different modules, which results from the recursive decomposition of the subsystems and their functionality. Interfaces establish how the different modules interact. They define which information or output from a module is visible or passed on to other modules. The architecture and the interfaces define the overall design of a modular complex system. The modularity of a system is therefore defined through:

		M 1			M 2			M 3			M 4		
		T_1	T_2	T_3	T_4	T_5	T_6	T_7	T_8	T_9	T_{10}	T_{11}	T_{12}
M1	T_1	0	X	X								X	
	T_2	X	0	X				X		X			
	T_3	X	X	0			X					X	
M2	T_4	X			0	X	X						
	T_5			X	X	0	X		X			X	
	T_6		X		X	X	0			X			
M3	T_7	X			X			0	X	X		X	
	T_8		X			X		X	0	X			X
	T_9							X	X	0			
M4	T_{10}				X						0	X	X
	T_{11}			X					X		X	0	X
	T_{12}						X			X	X	X	0

Note: The blocks inside the matrix capture interdependencies of tasks inside a subsystem; 'x' off the main diagonal indicates either feed forward or feedback loops between tasks.

Source: Adapted from Baldwin and Clark (2000, p. 60).

Figure 32.2 Near-decomposable system consisting of 12 tasks, $T_1 \ldots T_{12}$, and four modules or subsystems, $M_1 .. M_4$, depicted in a task structure matrix (TSM)

- a primary purpose of the system requiring specific functions or service characteristics;
- mutually balanced modules or subsystems transforming inputs into visible outputs;
- an architecture organizing the modules in nested hierarchical relationships;
- interfaces connecting the modules and determining which information is hidden and which is visible across modules; and
- a complete description of all modules and interfaces such that the system is a bijective representation in the domain of possible system configurations.

Often the terms modular system and near-decomposable system or modularity and near-decomposability are used interchangeably. However, this is not correct. A modular system is one obtained through a process of modularization leading to specific *design rules*. These establish the architecture of the system as well as standards for the inter-action of modules through interfaces. They also determine which system parameters are hidden within modules and which are visible to other modules. These design rules ensure that 'plug-and-play' flexibility is achieved (see Baldwin and Clark, 2000, pp. 88ff.) if the interface standards are kept constant for some time. This means that in a fully modular system modules can be replaced by other modules operating on the same range of visible parameters and using the same interface standards without compromising the operation of the entire system. If such design rules exist and structure the interaction between subsystems then a near-decomposable system is also modular, else it is just near-decomposable. Figure 32.3 gives an example of a complex system modularized through specific design rules. In this example the design rules specify for which module interact with which, and which tasks in a module interact with other modules through standardized interfaces (implying standardized information formats and parameter ranges) Hence, as long as the design rules are observed 'plug-and-play' flexibility is achieved.

Typically a system will not be fully modular, but there will be certain degrees to which this is the case. The two extremes on the scale are 'fully modular' and completely 'integral' (cf. Ulrich, 1995). Modularization increases with the independence of components. Full modularity (Figure 32.3) implies a loose coupling between modules, perfect substitutability and complete standardization of modules and interfaces, whereas perfect integration (Figure 32.1) captures tight coupling, a very limited substitutability and the absence of standardization of modules and interfaces.

32.3   THE BEHAVIOURAL FOUNDATIONS OF NEAR-DECOMPOSABILITY AND MODULARITY

32.3.1   Problem-solving and the Emergence of Near-decomposable or Modular Designs

According to Simon (1976, p. 293), 'factoring the total system of decisions that need to be made into relatively independent subsystems, each one of which can be designed with only minimal concern for its interactions with the others' is the solution to manage complex systems such as firms. This behavioural strategy is typical for human problem-solving in the face of substantive and procedural uncertainty (Simon, 1978).[2] It requires a division of labour as well as a division of information and knowledge and a reorganization of tasks and decisions related to the management of the whole system. Marengo et al. (2000) show that through decomposition every complex problem can be transformed into one of minimal complexity. The difficulty of transforming a complex system into a near-decomposable one is, however, to identify and specify the subsystems or modules such that the need as well as the cost for problem-solving across subsystem boundaries is minimized.

If a system design has to be modular and not just near-decomposable the search for suitable partitions of the system will involve the specification of interfaces and modules prior to any other design and problem-solving activity. A designer called 'architect' (Baldwin and Clark, 2000, p. 68) establishes the central design parameters of the system a priori at four levels (see Ethiraj and Levinthal, 2004, p. 162): (1) the appropriate number of modules, (2) the link between service characteristics providing value to the users of a system and the internal structure of the system, that is, its technical characteristics (cf. Saviotti and Metcalfe, 1984), (3) the interaction of service and technical characteristics within each module, and (4) the interfaces defining the interaction between the modules and specifying what information remains hidden and which is available to other modules. In other words, an architect defines what a system will do, which parts of the system will do what, and how they will fit together, connect and communicate. He or she establishes *design rules* that are binding for any other agent working on the system. By defining crucial aspects of the system before starting any other problem-solving activity the architect restricts the search to specific parts of the space of possible designs.

Design rules

		Design rules				M_1			M_2			M_3			M_4		
		M_1	M_2	M_3	M_4	T_1	T_2	T_3	T_4	T_5	T_6	T_7	T_8	T_9	T_{10}	T_{11}	T_{12}
M_1	T_1				x	o	x	x									
	T_2			x		x	o	x									
	T_3		x		x	x	x	o									
M_2	T_4	x							o	x	x						
	T_5	x							x	o	x						
	T_6	x							x	x	o						
M_3	T_7	x	x									o	x	x			
	T_8	x	x									x	o	x			
	T_9				x							x	x	o			
M_4	T_{10}			x											o	x	x
	T_{11}		x	x											x	o	x
	T_{12}		x												x	x	o

Note: The matrix now contains a column specifying which module interacts with other modules and through which tasks this interaction is managed on the basis of a standardized interface.

Source: Author.

Figure 32.3 A modular system design. Interactions between modules are mediated standardized interfaces specified in design rules

453

It is much more difficult to design modular systems than comparable interconnected systems as the designers must possess considerable knowledge of the inner workings of the system and its elements (Baldwin and Clark, 1997, p. 86). As architects and system designers will usually construct design rules on the basis of previous knowledge their search for solutions is at first localized. To extend the breadth of their search process they can rely on a number of actions to change the given structure (or first guesses about the actual structure of a complex system) into a new structure. According to Baldwin and Clark (2000, Chapter 5), these actions are:

- splitting a system into two or more modules;
- substituting one module design for another;
- augmenting the system by adding a new module;
- excluding a module from the system;
- inverting the (hierarchical) relationship between modules to create new design rules;
- porting a module to another system.

Splitting is the typical decomposition operator that subdivides modules in order to disentangle their inner complexity. Through substitution existing modules are replaced by better ones. Substitution is therefore an action leading to a *modular innovation* in a system (cf. Langlois and Robertson, 1992; Sanchez and Mahoney, 1996). This type of innovation does not alter the structure or architecture of a given system. The next three actions, augmenting, excluding and inverting are instead operators leading to an *architectural innovation* (cf. Henderson and Clark, 1990) insofar as the structure and the design rules of a given system will change as a consequence of their application. Through augmentation new modules are added to a given system whereas through exclusion a module is left out. Through inversion, information previously hidden to other modules is moved up the design hierarchy so that it becomes visible to other modules (Baldwin and Clark, 2000, p. 138). In this way redundant information and related problem-solving tasks can be consolidated into one single module.

Finally, porting occurs when a module breaks loose from a particular system and is able to function with a number of different systems. For this to work it needs some functionalities translating information from different sources in such a way that it can be processed internally and the outcome transmitted back to other modules. Portable modules are essentially interface techniques that support *combinatorial innovation* in the sense that functionalities of different systems can be linked together to obtain a larger range of service characteristics to final users of the system, or by making specific services of one system available to another system. However, portability is not equivalent to another important aspect of learning and adaptation in complex environments – integration (or crossing over). This is a process where parts of two modules are combined into a new module to produce a new set of service characteristics (cf. Holland, 1992, pp. 97ff.). This operator is at the core of recombinant search. Only this operator will allow agents to explore the design space extensively and generate *any* design (cf. Fixson and Park, 2008, p. 1310). However, its application potentially reduces the degree of modularity in a system.

Baldwin and Clark (2000, p. 144), argue the listed operators are complete insofar as every conceivable modular design or system structure can be generated from them.

This implies that by scanning the design space broadly agents may be able to find a decomposition that effectively maximizes a given objective function. Schaefer (1999), however, has proven rigorously that finding an optimal modular design partition is an NP-complete problem. Hence, it is unlikely that agents will be able to find the decomposition of a system maximizing a given objective function in finite time. Designing a modular system that captures the 'real' underlying structure of a given design problem is therefore equally hard in terms of the computational burden as finding a global optimum in a complex system. Furthermore, the restriction of search induced by design rules may imply that those parts of the design space where an optimal decomposition can be found are excluded a priori from the search.

Generally the optimal partition of a complex system into manageable modules with respect to some objective function is not known. The decomposition therefore happens in a gradual recursive problem-solving process (cf. von Hippel, 1990). The search for new solutions is based on practices that experience has shown to be successful, and on forward-looking mental models that are developed to abstract self-contained functions of the system from the whole and identify related parts. The interaction of these two types of problem-solving ensures that the complexity of a problem can be successfully reduced. It allows agents to scan large parts of the space of possible designs (cf. Gavetti and Levinthal, 2000).

32.3.2   Benefits and Dangers of Near-decomposability and Modularity

A crucial advantage of near-decomposable or modular system architectures is that they allow different parts of the system to be worked on concurrently. They also cut down on the coordination burden between the people involved in the search for solutions to sub-problems. This shortens the time needed to improve or adapt the system vis-à-vis systems with a comparable degree of complexity that are not near-decomposable or modular. Furthermore, near-decomposability and modularity accommodate uncertainty related to both the operation of the system and its capability to adapt to changes in its environment that affect its capability to fulfil its purpose and hence its value in use. In an innovation context these two types of uncertainty may be viewed as technological uncertainty and market uncertainty. On the one hand, as it is possible to single out working functions, separate improvement, modification and testing lead to a better understanding of the causal relationships underlying the operation of the system. This narrows down the search space for solutions to problems and reduces uncertainty related to the system itself. On the other hand, near-decomposable systems are easier to reconfigure due to the low degree of interdependence between modules, which ensures that subsystems are easier to replace. This increases the domain of potential applications as a system can be more easily adapted to suit changing purposes. This reduces uncertainty related to the environment.

Complex systems that are near-decomposable or modular are also adaptive. Simon (1996) therefore conjectured that near-decomposable or modular systems will, on average, be better able to compete in environments subject to constant change and unanticipated external shocks than comparable complex systems that are not near-decomposable or modular due to their better rate of adaptation. This conjecture has been validated in simulation studies carried out by Frenken et al. (1999). They have demonstrated that the decomposition of the system into subsystems, even if it is only an approximate decomposition, allows agents to improve their performance in a very short time. Therefore, in evolutionary environments where constant and speedy adaptation is crucial for survival, strategies aiming at a high rate of improvement of a complex system outcompete optimizing strategies that aim at the maximum end result. However, near-decomposable or modular systems generally will not reach, or even approach, the global optimum in the state space. Their crucial advantage is their ability to adapt more quickly and therefore to improve their performance more rapidly vis-à-vis changes in the environment in which they operate. Indeed, a recent paper by Gomes and Joglekar (2008) shows that modularity increases the transactional efficiency and reduces task completion times.

There are, however, limitations to modularity that under some circumstances outweigh the benefits. Some authors point out that the development of modular system architectures may not pay off (cf. Langlois, 2002; Arthur, 2009). They involve high fixed costs that do not arise in the development of comparable integrated systems. As a consequence it pays to partition a system only if there is a sufficient volume of use for all modules such that the fixed costs of modular design decrease in the intensity of use of the system.

Another strand of literature points out that for modular systems there is a trade-off between the speed of search and the breadth of search (cf. Fleming and Sorenson, 2001; Brusoni et al., 2004; Ethiraj and Levinthal, 2004). Modular systems clearly offer the advantage of fast adaptation because they enable a greater number of possible system configurations to be tested in parallel and improve the system through the substitution of modules. However, as has been mentioned previously, modular system architectures also imply that the search for an adequate system configuration is more localized as design rules restrict the search in the space of possible designs. Integral systems instead enable a broader even though slower search. On the one hand, due to the interdependence of their parts, changes in the system reveal inconsistencies or problems more readily. Hence, integrated systems command a joint improvement of parts and therefore a broader search in the design space. On the other hand, some authors argue that modularity is negatively associated with technical problem-solving efforts (cf. Gomes and Joglekar, 2008).

One important argument in this context is that only the interplay of modularization and integration (i.e., recombinant search) leads to breakthrough innovations (cf. Fleming and Sorenson, 2001; Fleming, 2001; Sorenson, 2003; Arthur, 2009). Modularization without integration will quickly exhaust the potential to create new combinations. Exclusive reliance on modularization also blinds the designers for potentially important interactions at the level of modules. Indeed, modularization is an instrument for the incremental improvement of systems. Several studies therefore have suggested that designers should strive for the development of near-decomposable systems with an intermediate degree of interdependence across modules (cf. Fleming and Sorenson, 2001; Rivkin, 2001; Ethiraj and Levinthal, 2004; Rivkin and Siggelkow, 2006).

Competitive advantage typically not only depends on the speed with which systems can adapt to changes in the environment, but also on the sustainability of this advantage over time. In the presence of spillovers and imitation competitive advantages arising from the modularization of a system may erode rather quickly. Components and the system architecture are easier to imitate in modular systems as modularizaion also implies a high level of codification of knowledge. Hence, there is a trade-off. Modularization enables a fast improvement of a system and performance gains, but at the same time it also lays the basis for this competitive advantage to be eroded through imitation. A number of studies have shown that intermediate levels of interdependence in a system offer important benefits when the aim is to sustain a competitive advantage over time. Rivkin (2001), for instance, shows that the largest performance gaps between innovation leaders and imitators arise when innovation leaders design their systems with moderate interdependence. Ethiraj et al. (2008) instead provide evidence that performance differences between innovation leaders and imitators are persistent for integrated systems and systems with intermediate interconnection.

32.4 MODULARITY AND INDUSTRIAL ORGANIZATION

As technologies, firms or more generally organizations and the economy in general are best conceived as complex hierarchical systems fulfilling some purpose, the concepts of complexity, near-decomposability and modularity have been applied in the study of firms and their strategies in the areas of organization, innovation and product design. Numerous authors have contributed to this strand of research at the intersection between strategic management and the theory of the firm. This section will present some of the aspects that this rich body of literature has discussed.

32.4.1 The Mirroring Hypothesis of Problem-solving and System Structure

Most of the recent work on modularity in the area of strategic management and the theory of the firm can be traced back to the contributions by Henderson and Clark (1990), von Hippel (1990) and Langlois and Robertson (1992). These papers explored the relationship between product architecture and the knowledge and information processing structure of a firm, task partitioning in the innovation process, and the innovative potential of industries based on modular products respectively. These seminal contributions rely on the concepts of problem decomposition and near-decomposability as the basic toolkit in their analysis. A remarkable aspect is that these papers share what some authors call the 'mirroring' hypothesis (cf. Baldwin, 2008). This hypothesis links the knowledge and information processing structure that emerges from the process of problem decomposition to the internal structure of the system that is being designed (cf. Henderson and Clark, 1990, p. 27). More specifically, all these early studies link an organization's task structure to the actions undertaken to develop, make and sell products. This has implications for the theory of the firm.

Figure 32.4 gives a summary overview on the bottom line of the 'mirroring' hypothesis and on the implications it has had in subsequent studies on industrial organization, the theory of the firm or product development. In order to solve a complex problem tasks will be divided between different people. The way these people communicate, share information and knowledge reflects the hierarchical relationships and interdependencies among the components of the system and their technical characteristics (or design parameters). Hence, task structure and design structure are assumed to be isomorphic (cf. Baldwin and Clark, 2000, p. 47).

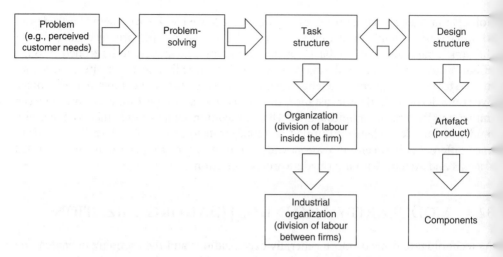

Figure 32.4   The hypothesis of fundamental isomorphism between task structure and design structure

The 'mirroring' hypothesis can be extended to organizations and products as particular task structures create specific patterns of knowledge in an organization. People exchange information and knowledge within workgroups that deal with closely related tasks. Exchanges across workgroups in contrast become less frequent. The organization therefore reflects problem-solving efforts related to the design and production of an artefact. If the task structure mirrors a rather integrated internal structure of the product it has designed an organization may become quite inflexible (Henderson and Clark, 1990). Sanchez and Mahoney (1996) suggest that modularity offers ways to preserve flexibility: if firms design modular products they will create modular organizations, which in turn will increase their strategic flexibility and as a consequence raise their economic performance. At the firm level the 'mirroring' hypothesis therefore links the architecture of the products of a firm to its performance through the transmission channel of strategic flexibility.[3]

Moving across the boundaries of the firm the 'mirroring' hypothesis implies that modular product and organizational architectures favour vertical and horizontal disintegration (cf. Langlois and Robertson, 1992). By limiting the interconnection between modules, by standardizing the information exchange, and by hiding information (and knowledge) inside specific components, modularization creates breakpoints where firms are able split up and outsource activities, or where new industries emerge as the modular design of a product with 'plug-and-play' offers opportunities to entrants with ideas on how to improve or extend its functionalities. Hence, the existence of complex modular products will lead to an increase of the specialization in an industry and intensify the division of labour in the economy as a whole (see also Baldwin and Clark, 2000).

Combined together the two main implications of the 'mirroring' hypothesis suggest that as modularity conveys important competitive benefits products are generally becoming more modular over time and this development is associated with changes in the organization of firms and in the structure of an industry. This will be discussed on the basis of a few important contributions in the remainder of the chapter.

32.4.2 Modularity and the Boundaries of Firms

32.4.2.1 Modular production networks as a new industrial paradigm?

Langlois and Robertson (1992) have examined industries producing modular systems such as high-fidelity and stereo sound reproduction systems or the microcomputer industry. These products are complex artefacts that offer a wide range of service characteristics to their users through different components that are produced by different firms. Common industry standards of compatibility link the firm in this industry producing the different components into a modular production network. According to Langlois and Robertson the division of labour between firms in these industries is essentially determined by the interplay of economies of scale of assembling the components and transaction costs to users of finding out about the different components. As both types of costs are low, firms have little incentive to supply more complex products integrating all components and users have the benefit of being able to maximize the utility from using these products by choosing and assembling the different components themselves. They can also be better tuned to user needs more rapidly because innovation takes place concurrently for each component. As modular production networks seem to offer superior benefits, Langlois and Robertson conclude that their importance will increase.

Arora et al. (1997) have explored the trade-off between economies of scale and transaction costs and its implications for inventive activities in modular production networks further. They argue that the production of standardized components or modules benefits from economies of scale. For this reason it is carried out by specialized firms. On the other hand, following Langlois and Robertson (1992), they argue that the combination of modules is more efficiently carried out by the users of the assembled product, or firms that are close to final demand. If now for technical reasons the production and combination of modules is not separable, producers will carry out both activities. The precondition is that the market is large enough. In this case the economies of scale will offset the transaction costs of acquiring and processing user-specific information. If on the other hand, production and combination of modules are separable, specialization between producers of standard modules and firms combining modules into complex artefacts will take place if the cost of transportation of the general modules is small if compared to the cost of interacting with local users. The implications for the innovation process are that in the former case the entire innovation process will be concentrated in a few larger markets, whereas in the latter case innovation activities will be more prominent in smaller markets where the combination of modules creates quasi-rents.

Sturgeon (2002) finally analyses the emergence of modular production networks and contract manufacturing in the US electronic industry. He goes so far as to argue that this may be viewed as the paradigmatic case of a 'New American Model' of industrial organization. Sturgeon characterizes the firms in this new industry structure as consisting of two types: (1) deverticalized lead firms, and (2) 'turn-key' suppliers. The lead firms focus on the design and the marketing of complex artefacts. The turn-key suppliers, that is, contract manufacturers, instead produce modules on the specifications provided by lead firms. Industry standards and the transmission of highly codified information lower the transaction costs in this interaction. Hence, lead firms provide new combina- tions, whereas turn-key suppliers exploit economies of scale as suggested by Arora et al. (1997). In such a network barriers to entry and exit are lower as the mutual interdepend- ence between single firms is lower as well. Hence, firms are more flexible to access and exploit location-specific factors and markets. The services of turn-key suppliers can also be shared by a variety of lead firms. An important competitive advantage of this New American Model is that it builds up external economies of scale (Sturgeon, 2002, p. 489).

Langlois (2002, 2003) has explored the location and form of transactions and hence the boundaries of the firm in such modular networks further. On this basis he advances a modularity theory of the firm. In essence he argues that the modularization of eco- nomic activities in an economy solves rights assignment and control problems leading to holdup by repartitioning and reintegrating property rights and critical knowledge across firms (Jensen and Meckling, 1992). Dynamic efficiency requires that firms seek to place all relevant knowledge and property rights related to specific technological processes under their control.[4] The aim thereby is to internalize externalities or tightly coupled activities subject to the cost of setting up and maintaining the control as well as other aspects such as the presence of economies of scale. In the extreme case each module can become the business of a single specialist firm that has complete control over all aspects of the module. Technical standards on the other hand permit the externalization of mechanisms of coordination to the market that were previously integrated into one large firm. Hierarchical coordination becomes increasingly unnecessary also because modular product and process architectures reduce transaction costs and decrease the minimum efficient scale of production as external economies of scale are built up. As a conse- quence, large vertically integrated corporations of the 'Chandlerian' type (Chandler, 1977) will disappear, and we should observe a modularization of economic organiza- tions.[5] The invisible hand of the market will become more important again.

Schilling and Steensma (2001) provide empirical evidence that integrated hierarchical organizations have been replaced by non-hierarchical, modular forms of organization in many industries. Using a large dataset for a number of US industries they show that het- erogeneity of industries' production processes in terms of inputs and demand drive this process. They are positively associated with greater use of modularity in the organization of production. Modularity seems to convey a higher level of flexibility to meet uncer- tainty in upstream and downstream markets. Rapid technological change in an industry increases the pressure for flexibility. Therefore it favours the adoption of modular forms. The use of industry standards on the other hand reduces the need for integration. They facilitate the use of modular forms when pressure for flexibility is high.

Other empirical work also documents that in several industries loosely coupled pro- duction systems have emerged where system integrators or innovation platforms take over the role to coordinate and exploit complementary and dispersed capabilities and skills among specialized organizational units (for an in-depth review see Patrucco, Chapter 26 in this volume). These are specific organizational arrangements that have the aim of sharing a number of core components and interfaces in complex products and production systems. They are set up in order to effectively adapt or create new complex products. Innovations are therefore created by keeping the core parts of an existing design largely unchanged and by modifying or adding non-core components. This implies that novelty is generated by reconfiguring products without redefining their ntire architecture. In this way firms are able to cut innovation costs. The presence of system integrators or innovation platforms significantly affects the competitive dynamics in an industry as the repartitioning and reintegrating property rights and critical knowledge across firms may change the balance of power between suppliers and assemblers. Independently of whether the 'mirroring hypothesis' is valid, the research reviewed in this section provides evidence in support of the rise of a new organizational paradigm in some industries related to the modularization of products and technologies. The evidence on innovation platforms also seems to indicate that even in the face of increasing modularity in production, some form of hierarchical coordination mechanism continues to exist. This will be discussed in the next section.

2.4.2.2   The 'mirroring' hypothesis revisited

More recent contributions have come to view the 'mirroring' hypothesis and other aspects of the 'modularity theory of the firm' as presented in the previous section with increasing scepticism. Hoetker (2006), for instance, has tested the assumption that increased product modularity is associated with increases in organizational modularity empirically. His analysis shows that product modularity is positively correlated with supplier turnover. Modular products therefore lead to more reconfigurable organizations and hence higher organizational flexibility. Nevertheless, he also shows that product modularity is not associated with the decision to outsource. He concludes that product modularity contributes less or not at all to. . .firms shifting activity out of hierarchy' (Hoetker, 2006, p. 514). Hence, there is no or little evidence that loosely coupled networks of firms supplant integrated hierarchies.

Hoetker's study suggests that the development of loosely coupled networks of firms and deverticalization of firms are separate phenomena that can exist one without the other (see also Benassi, 2009). Several other contributions reach similar conclusions. Hoetker (2005) himself points to the importance of internal supply relations. In environments that are characterized by high uncertainty the value of internal supply relations is highest to downstream firms. Past relationships with other suppliers as well as differences in technical capabilities between internal and external long-term suppliers are of little importance under these conditions. However, environments of high uncertainty are those for which most proponents of the 'mirroring' hypothesis postulate the highest advantage of modular production networks. Hence, firms may not be willing to outsource activities to specialized suppliers even if their products are modular.

Another important strand of criticism (cf. Brusoni and Prencipe, 2001; Brusoni et al., 2001; Brusoni, 2005; Hobday et al., 2005) highlights problems that derive from the assumption that knowledge and property rights in modular production networks are perfectly partitioned. These authors use case studies of aeronautical engineering and chemical industries to argue that the knowledge boundaries of the firm differ from the boundaries of the firm as defined by outsourcing decisions. The diffusion of modularity as a design strategy leads to an increasing division of labour across firms at the product level, 'but only once someone has made it so. And this "someone" is a firm that maintains a "higher-level understanding" necessary to be able to frame problems, and the division of labour around them, i.e. the system integrator' (Brusoni, 2005, p. 1900). System integrators are firms that 'guarantee the overall consistency of the product and. . .orchestrate the network of companies involved' (Brusoni and Prencipe, 2001,

p. 185). This, however, requires that these firms maintain knowledge that is wider tha~~n~~ their productive activities would suggest. They know more than they do.[6] These firms a~~re~~ necessary as modular product architectures in themselves do not provide all the info~~r~~mation such that the actions of different actors can be coordinated through the mark~~et~~ mechanism. Hence, hierarchical organization will take over this role and act as a visib~~le~~ hand in such modular production networks. In this sense system integrators are differe~~nt~~ from lead firms (Sturgeon, 2002) or firms that carry out combinations of modules (Aro~~ra~~ et al., 1997).

In line with our discussion on the limits of modularity other authors instead argu~~e~~ that in order to develop *new* and *better performing* designs firms will not only rely o~~n~~ modularizing products and organizations. They will change product architectures als~~o~~ by integrating and consolidating tasks (cf. Fixson and Park, 2008). This is an iterativ~~e~~ process of co-design in which firms will explore which and how activities can be decom~~-~~ posed and what types of interfaces are required to reintegrate the modules into comple~~x~~ artefacts (Sabel and Zeitlin, 2004). Such a process can change the nature of competitio~~n~~ in an industry as it can drive out firms that are specialized on a few modules and are n~~ot~~ capable of competing at the level of a more complex, integrated artefact. From this large~~r~~ complexity more hierarchical firms emerge. While this does not necessarily contradic~~t~~ the assumption that a modularization of industry is driven by the search for an efficien~~t~~ repartition and reintegration of property rights and knowledge, it shows that a modula~~r~~ division of labour may be just a transitory state in an industry. Its structure may we~~ll~~ fluctuate between stages in which its structure is more modular and stages where it i~~s~~ more integrated.

32.5   SUMMARY AND CONCLUSIONS

This chapter has reviewed the growing body of literature that has studied the implica-tions of modular system architectures for firm strategy and the division of labour across firms. Modularity is a concept used to characterize specific designs and design heuristics for complex systems. Modular systems have been shown to convey superior capability for adaptation and flexibility in uncertain environments. Many scholars have therefore explored the value of modular products or organizations for firms and concluded that firms will benefit from the use of this strategy. However, other research shows that the fixed structure as well as technical standards and interfaces predetermined in the design rules of a modular system restrict the search for solutions to well-defined areas in the domain of possible designs. Near-decomposable (but not modular) and integrated designs are better suited to generating novelty even though their capability of adaptation is inferior.

Other research has analysed the impact of the diffusion of modular design heuristics for the development of products and organizations on the division of labour across firms. The principal finding is that product modularity increases the division of labour across firms at the product level. Under well-defined conditions it will give rise to modular production networks that are conceived as loosely coupled networks of firms in an industry. Some authors argue that modular product designs and related industry standards lower different types of transaction costs and create external economies scale, thereby favouring indirect coordination of economic activities through ^e market. The hypothesis is therefore that the division of labour in an industry ^ill mirror the modular architecture of its products. It directly implies that modular-^y in production and organizations will lead to the demise of vertically integrated ^rms.

This hypothesis is rejected by a number of contributions. The chief reason for the ^jection is the argument that there is a divergence between the division of labour ^etween firms and the distribution of knowledge across firms in an industry. Standards ^nd semi-fixed module interfaces do not provide enough information for firms in a ^arket to perfectly coordinate their actions. Some firms must have the capability to ^ame the problems related to the production of a complex artefact. For this reason they ^ave to rely on broader knowledge bases and carry out coordination tasks. Hence, indi-^ct coordination in modular networks is unlikely to replace direct coordination through ^ierarchies. The research on modularity has enriched our understanding of problem-^olving processes in organizations, and it has helped to frame the question of what the ^ivision of labour looks like in the New Economy. However, more research is needed to ^nderstand why modularity does not supplant the visible hand of hierarchies as part of ^he literature claims it should.

NOTES

. The term 'system' used in this section is a template for concepts such as 'product', 'firm', 'organization' or 'technology'. The term 'problem' is instead a generalized way to say that every system has a purpose and that under some circumstances a system may not be able to fulfil this purpose adequately or that for a given purpose there is no adequate system yet.
. In cognitive psychology the phenomenon is referred to as 'chunking' (cf. Gobet et al., 2001).
. Strategic flexibility implies that firms are able to pursue parallel development efforts and adaptations across modules, by multiplying design options, and by achieving 'economies of substitution' (Garud and Kumaraswamy, 1995). Recent studies have found some mixed evidence for this hypothesis (cf. Worren et al., 2002; Todorova and Durisin, 2008) indicating that modularity increases are positively associated with firm performance but that firms often fail in their quest for flexibility.
. Langlois refers to this process as 'demodularization'.
. Reinstaller (2007) shows that such a development also depends on the institutional arrangements sur-rounding the firm. The repartition and reintegration of property rights and knowledge may be different in dependence of these arrangements. Hence, ceteris paribus we might observe differences in the degree of decomposition of the division of labour.
. Patrucco (Chapter 26 this volume) provides further evidence on different types of system integrators or innovation platforms.

REFERENCES

Anderson, P.W., K.J. Arrow and D. Pines, 1988. *The Economy as an Evolving Complex System.* Reading, MA: Addison-Wesley.
Arora, A., A. Gambardella and E. Rullani, 1997. Division of labour and the locus of inventive activity. *Journal of Management and Governance* 1(1), 123–40.
Arthur, B.W., 1999. Complexity and the economy. *Science* 284(5411), 107–9.
Arthur, B.W., 2009. *The Nature of Technology.* New York: Free Press.
Baldwin, C.Y., 2008. Modularity, transactions, and the boundaries of firms: a synthesis. *Industrial and Corporate Change* 17(1), 155–95.
Baldwin, C.Y. and K.B. Clark, 1997. Managing in an age of modularity. *Harvard Business Review* 75(5), 84–94.

Baldwin, C.Y. and K.B. Clark, 2000. *Design Rules. Vol. 1: The Power of Modularity*. Cambridge, MA: MI Press.

Benassi, M., 2009. Investigating modular organizations. *Journal of Management and Governance* 13(3), 163–9

Brusoni, S., 2005. The limits to specialization: problem solving and coordination in 'modular network: *Organization Studies* 26(12), 1885–907.

Brusoni, S. and A. Prencipe, 2001. Unpacking the black box of modularity: technologies, products and organ zations. *Industrial and Corporate Change* 10(1), 179–205.

Brusoni, S., A. Prencipe and K. Pavitt, 2001. Knowledge specialization, organizational coupling, and th boundaries of the firm. Why firms know more than they make? *Administrative Science Quarterly* 46(4 597–621.

Brusoni, S., L. Marengo, A. Prencipe and M. Valente, 2004. *The Value and Cost of Modularity: A Cogniti Perspective*. Working Paper No. 123. Brighton: SPRU Electronic Working Paper Series.

Chandler, A.D., 1977. *The Visible Hand: The Managerial Revolution in American Business*. Cambridge, M/ The Belknap Press.

Ethiraj, S.K. and D. Levinthal, 2004. Modularity and innovation in complex systems. *Management Scienc* 50(2), 159–73.

Ethiraj, S.K., D. Levinthal and R.R. Roy, 2008. The dual role of modularity: innovation and imitatio *Management Science* 54(5), 939–54.

Fixson, S.K. and J.-K. Park, 2008. The power of integrality: linkages between product architecture, innovatio and industry structure. *Research Policy* 37(8), 1296–316.

Fleming, L., 2001. Recombinant uncertainty in technological search. *Management Science* 47(1), 117–32.

Fleming, L. and O. Sorenson, 2001. Technology as a complex adaptive system: evidence from patent dat *Research Policy* 30(7), 1019–39.

Frenken, K., L. Marengo and M. Valente, 1999. Interdependencies, near-decomposability and adaption. In T Brenner (ed.), *Computational Techniques for Modeling Learning in Economics*. Boston: Kluwer, pp. 145–65.

Garud, R. and A. Kumaraswamy, 1995. Technological and organizational designs for realizing economies o substitution. *Strategic Management Journal* 16(S1), 93–109.

Gavetti, G. and D.A. Levinthal, 2000. Looking forward and looking backward: cognitive and experimenta search. *Administrative Science Quarterly* 45(1), 113–37.

Gobet, F., P.C.R. Lane, S. Croker, P.C.H. Cheng, G. Jones, I. Oliver and J.M. Pine, 2001. Chunking mecha nisms in human learning. *Trends in Cognitive Sciences* 5(6), 236–43.

Gomes, P.J. and N.R. Joglekar, 2008. Linking modularity with problem solving and coordination effort *Managerial and Decision Economics* 29(5), 443–57.

Henderson, R.M. and K.B. Clark, 1990. Architectural innovation: the reconfiguration of existing produc technologies and the failure of established firms. *Administrative Science Quarterly* 35(1), 9–30.

Hobday, M., A. Davies and A. Prencipe, 2005. Systems integration: a core capability of the modern corpora tion. *Industrial and Corporate Change* 14(6), 1109–43.

Hoetker, G. 2005. How much you know versus how well I know you: selecting a supplier for a technically innovative component. *Strategic Management Journal* 26(1), 75–96.

Hoetker, G., 2006. Do modular products lead to modular organizations? *Strategic Management Journal* 27(6) 501–18.

Holland, J.H, 1992. *Adaptation in Natural and Artificial Systems*. Cambridge, MA: MIT Press.

Jensen, M.C. and W.H. Meckling, 1992. Specific and general knowledge, and organizational structure. In L. Werin and H. Wijkander (eds) *Contract Economics*. Oxford: Basil Blackwell, pp. 251–74.

Kauffman, S.A., 1993. *The Origins of Order: Self-organization and Selection in Evolution*. Oxford, New York: Oxford University Press.

Langlois, R.N., 2002. Modularity in technology and organization. *Journal of Economic Behavior & Organization* 49(1), 19–37.

Langlois, R.N., 2003. The vanishing hand: the changing dynamics of industrial capitalism. *Industrial and Corporate Change* 12(2), 351–85.

Langlois, R.N. and P.L. Robertson, 1992. Networks and innovation in a modular system: lessons from the microcomputer and the stereo component industries. *Research Policy* 21(4), 297–313.

Levinthal, D.A., 1997. Adaption on rugged landscapes. *Management Science* 43(7), 934–50.

Marengo, L., G. Dosi, P. Legrenzi and C. Pasquali, 2000. The structure of problem solving knowledge and the structure of organizations. *Industrial and Corporate Change* 9(4), 757–88.

Reinstaller, A., 2007. The division of labour in the firm: agency, near-decomposability, and the Babbage prin ciple. *Journal of Institutional Economics* 3(3), 293–322.

Rivkin, J.W., 2001. Reproducing knowledge: replication without imitation at moderate complexity. *Organization Science* 12(3), 274–93.

Rivkin, J.W. and N. Siggelkow, 2006. Organizing to strategize in the face of interactions: preventing premature lock-in. *Long Range Planning* 39(6), 591–614.

Sabel, C.F. and J. Zeitlin, 2004. Neither modularity nor relational contracting: inter-firm collaboration in the New Economy. *Enterprise & Society* **5**(3), 388–403.

Sanchez, R. and J.T. Mahoney, 1996. Modularity, flexibility, and knowledge management in product and organization design. *Strategic Management Journal* **17**(Winter Special Issue), 63–76.

Saviotti, P.P. and J.S. Metcalfe, 1984. A theoretical approach to the construction of technological output indicators. *Research Policy* **13**(3), 141–51.

Schaefer, S., 1999. Product design partitions with complementary components. *Journal of Economic Behavior & Organization* **38**(3), 311–30.

Schilling, M.A. and H.K. Steensma, 2001. The use of modular organizational forms: an industry-level analysis. *Academy of Management Journal* **44**(6), 1149–68.

Simon, H.A., 1976. *Administrative Behavior: A Study of Decision-making Processes in Administrative Organization*. New York: Free Press, 3rd edition.

Simon, H.A., 1978. Rationality as a process and a product of thought. *American Economic Review* **68**(2), 1–16.

Simon, H.A., 1996. The architecture of complexity. Chapter 8 in *The Sciences of the Artificial*. Cambridge MA: MIT Press, pp. 183–216. Reprinted from the *Proceedings of the American Philosophical Society* **106**(6), 467–82.

Simon, H.A. and A. Ando, 1961. Aggregation of variables in dynamics systems. *Econometrica* **29**(2), S111–S138.

Sorenson, O., 2003. Interdependence and adaptability: organizational learning and the long-term effect of integration. *Management Science* **49**(4), 445–63.

Sturgeon, T.J., 2002. Modular production networks: a new American model of industrial organization. *Industrial and Corporate Change* **11**(3), 451–96.

Todorova, G. and B. Durisin, 2008. Mixing and matching modularity: a study of strategic flexibility. Mimeo.

Ulrich, K., 1995. The role of product architecture in the manufacturing firm. *Research Policy* **24**(3), 419–40.

Ulrich., K. and S.D. Eppinger, 2008. *Product Design and Development*. Boston: McGraw Hill, 4th edition.

Von Hippel, E., 1990. Task partitioning: an innovation process variable. *Research Policy* **19**(5), 407–18.

Worren, N., K. Moore and P. Cardona, 2002. Modularity, strategic flexibility, and firm performance: a study of the home appliance industry. *Strategic Management Journal* **23**(12), 1123–40.

33 Innovation networks
Tobias Buchmann and Andreas Pyka

33.1 INTRODUCTION

Notions like clusters of innovation, innovation systems and innovation networks have become very popular in innovation economics and policy today. Often these concepts are used synonymously to describe the phenomenon of non-market interactions in innovation processes between various actors, which might be geographically (e.g., regional innovation networks) or technologically (e.g., sectoral innovation networks) concentrated. Contrary to the systemic view of the innovation systems approaches, in the theory of innovation networks an actor-based dimension joins the aggregate network dimension. Therefore, the network-based theories can be characterized to share a closer affinity to economic reasoning compared to the systemic approaches that are successfully applied in sociologically motivated innovation research. The actor-based dimension also connects the economic theory of innovation networks to the topic of this handbook – the theory of the firm.

Innovation networks can be considered to blur firm boundaries and are pervasive. They ask for an encompassing framework in economic analysis. Agents are linked (1) intra-industrially in multilateral relationships with other agents in one industry as well as (2) inter-industrially with other agents from different industries either vertically or horizontally. Typical instances of intra-industrial linkages are mutual development of new products and services and various forms of knowledge exchange either framed by contractual agreements between the firms or informally organized among the scientists and engineers working for different companies. Typical instances of inter-industrial linkages are user–producer relationships between manufacturing companies and their suppliers or customers focusing on particular features of new technologies and services. It is also important to acknowledge that networks are continuously changing. New actors join the network and link to its participants. This leads to specific structures concerning the distribution of links in a network with severe consequences for the control of knowledge and information flows in the network. Successful networks may trigger entrepreneurial action and occasionally the dissolving of a network coincides with the emergence of a start-up jointly formed by previous network members. Networks in different knowledge areas may interlink and by bridging so far disconnected knowledge fields create the potential for cross-fertilization and new knowledge dynamics. Network dynamics are also connected to the dynamics of industry life cycles and show different features depending on the relative stage of technological maturity. For instance, in new technological areas higher entry rates in innovation networks are to be expected because of the explorative character of the network, whereas in mature industries the number of links in the network might grow, indicating an exploitative orientation of the innovation network. To cut a long story short, dealing with innovation networks means dealing with complex structure and dynamics.

Most basically, innovation networks consist of actors and linkages among these actors. The idea of actors is conceived very broadly and also encompasses besides firms, individuals, research institutes and university laboratories, venture capital firms or even standardization agencies. Links among the actors are used as channels for knowledge and information flows as well as financial flows in the case of venture capitalists. The links among actors can either be formal (R&D joint ventures, strategic alliances, research consortia etc.) or informal, based on personal contacts and recommendation. In essence, innovation networks provide the networking actors with knowledge that might be complementary to their own knowledge as well as with other resources necessary to run an enterprise and to survive in innovation competition. Accordingly, innovation networks are a means for the industrial organization of research and development, which are particularly relevant in knowledge-intensive industries with high requirements concerning the competences of involved actors, for example, fast development of new knowledge, design of interfaces between different (modular) technologies, combinatorial (complex) innovation and so on.

Due to their prominence today, meanwhile a rich literature on innovation networks has emerged tackling the phenomenon in a multifaceted way. The aim of this chapter is to give an overview on the most important strands of literature. For this purpose we begin in section 33.2 to outline the awareness and treatment of innovation networks in economic theory. Section 33.3 deals with the roles played by network participants, the strategic meaning of joining a network and the dynamics of innovation networks. In section 33.4 the major methods to tackle the complexity of innovation networks are discussed.

33.2   INNOVATION NETWORKS IN ECONOMICS – A LATE ENCOUNTER

In this section we briefly outline the emerging awareness of innovation networks in economics (for a detailed version see Pyka, 2002). Although the impact of technological change on economic development, progress and growth was always widely recognized in economics, no detailed study of the emergence and diffusion of innovation, not to mention innovation networks, was performed. Even an economist such as Schumpeter (1911), who puts innovation at the centre of his theory of economic development, in the first place attributed innovative success just to the specific feature of entrepreneurship of outstanding individuals in an economy. Thirty years later Schumpeter (1942), inspired by the development of US industries, identifies a significant change in the organization of R&D processes in the specialized R&D laboratories of large firms (*routinized innovation*). And another 40 years later, again a significant change had taken place in the organization of R&D. This change manifested in the interaction between these R&D labs and other innovative actors such as universities and public research institutes constituting innovation networks. Nevertheless, only since the end of the 1980s a certain interest in the theoretical explanation of this phenomenon started to arise in economics. An important reason for the late interest can be seen in the difficulties the theory of the firm poses for economists (see e.g., Holmström and Tirole, 1989). Here, the questions 'Why do firms exist?' and 'What are their boundaries?' are analysed and controversially discussed. Winter (1991, p. 179), reflecting on this problem, has to admit that the preser state of the art is characterized by incoherence and contradictions. In an econom without firms, a specific industrial sector would consist simply of isolated labour-sharin individuals connected by markets. Only the bundling and organization of several activ ties within a firm gives this branch its specific structure (e.g., small and medium-size firms, large enterprises etc.). However, not only firms themselves, but also on a highe level, their embeddedness in networks, are decisive features of the industrial patterns w are observing. In the theory of the firm three different approaches exist, which can als be used to explain networks, and to differing degrees to explain the observed structures In these approaches networks are considered either as a means to minimize R&D costs or as a means to minimize transaction costs, or as a means to create novelties.

In the first approach the firm is seen as a functional relationship between inputs an outputs of production. This production function approach constitutes the basis o mainstream neoclassical economics. Accordingly, the questions posed are those on the optimality in the allocation of resources and the respective incentives of firm behav iour. With respect to industrial innovation processes, since the early 1980s a brancl of literature (new industrial economics) also analyses the conditions and incentives of firms to engage in R&D cooperation by drawing on a game-theoretic framework (e.g. D'Aspremont and Jacquemin, 1988). In this literature cooperation can be beneficial ir cases when the appropriability conditions for R&D investments are weak, and thus the rate of knowledge spillovers among different actors is high. Consequently, it seems to be wise for companies to cooperate in order to benefit from other firms' knowledge and to compensate for the outflow of own knowledge.

The second approach can be traced back to Ronald Coase (1937) and no longer focuses on immediate production processes but on transaction costs of economic proc esses. For Coase and his followers the main reason for the existence of firms is costs that arise through the price mechanism of markets. Therefore, firms come into being because the costs of coordinating the transactions via markets are higher than the costs of a hierarchical organization within a firm; in other words, there are incentives for cost saving. These considerations were transferred to networks by Oliver Williamson (1975) and others. In this perspective, networks are an intermediate coordination form between the dichotomy of hierarchy and markets. With the introduction of uncertainty and spe cificity of assets in an environment of bounded rationality and opportunistic behaviour, networks are considered as a hybrid form between markets and hierarchy, balancing the costs for controlling an organization and the costs for acting on markets. In order to optimize the organizational structure, a firm has to take into account the frequency of transactions and the importance of asset specificity: for intermediate degrees of asset specificity and intermediate levels of uncertainty innovation networks are considered to be optimal.

These first two approaches to explaining the existence of innovation networks are increasingly criticized. The major critical issue is the focus on cost considerations only, that is, that among a portfolio of alternatives the less costly alternative is to be chosen. The creative potential of innovation networks, however, bringing together complementary knowledge and technologies, is not considered.

The third strand of literature, the knowledge-based approach, differs sharply from the incentive-based approaches. Early proponents of this theory are Alfred Marshall

1890) who recognizes knowledge as the decisive factor in production processes and Edith Penrose (1959) who identifies the knowledge base of a firm as its main asset. In the early 1980s this approach is taken up by neo-Schumpeterian economics. Here, the role of knowledge for economic development and the success of firms is explicitly recognized and constitutes the cornerstone of economic analysis. In the neo-Schumpeterian perspective networks are seen as a central determinant in the industrial creation of novelty, and are therefore a decisive coordination mechanism. In networks new technological opportunities are created via technological complementarities and synergies by bringing together different technological and economic competencies. Knowledge is no longer considered as a pure public good but as local, tacit, firm-specific and complex. These characteristics hamper technological knowledge from being easily exchanged on markets. Technological spillovers are no longer freely available as in the models of growth theory but have to be acquired actively by participating in innovation networks. Paul Geroski (1995, p. 85) stressed this point: 'In particular, what often appears to be an involuntary flow of knowledge between firms may be nothing more than a pair of draws from a narrow but common pool shared by a group of agents within a common set of problems'. In other words, firms may have to take positive actions to make their newly developed knowledge available to others (Nelson, 1988) in order to spur on the collective innovation process in which they participate. Technological spillovers are hardly conceivable without being embedded in innovation networks.

Concerning the positive actions, informal networks are considered of major importance. Chris Freeman (1991, p. 500) states 'Although rarely measured systematically, informal networks appeared to be most important. Multiple sources of information and pluralistic patterns of collaboration were the rule rather than the exception'. A particular form of informal networks is observed by von Hippel (1987) as informal knowledge exchange among scientists and engineers working for different companies. Informal know-how trading is the extensive exchange of proprietary know-how in informal networks of engineers in rival (and non-rival) firms. This exchange is based on trust and personal contacts that are systematically developed as a function of personal judgements of the usefulness and value of knowledge to be received or to be transferred. Under certain conditions informal exchange of know-how works better than formal R&D cooperation or licensing because of lower transaction costs. And even though the exchange does not undergo a formal evaluation process the decision of an individual engineer to trade know-how is reasonable. The quality of advice can be immediately tested by applying it, while the sender can test the quality of expertise of the receiver by evaluating the sophistication of the demand.

The knowledge-based neo-Schumpeterian approaches show that firms cannot be considered as atomistic entities in perfect markets, aiming to maximize their profits by internally optimizing their processes. In contrast, firms act in complex environments that consist of numerous interconnected actors trying to reach heterogeneous goals and to improve their imperfect knowledge bases. From this follows that the embedment in networks is a prerequisite for the survival of firms in the innovation-centred competition.

In the literature on innovation networks, network structures as well as the position of a firm within a network are considered to be important determinants of firm performance. The value of an innovation network for a firm is linked to the concept of *social capital*, which is related to the opportunities offered by network participation.

Social capital can be regarded as the portfolio of social interactions in a network. Social capital refers to aspects in the context of collective action such as trust and a system of values that determines the possible intensity of cooperation (e.g., Coleman, 1988, p. 95; Burt, 1995; Walker et al., 1997, pp. 109–25). The amount of social capital is given by the quantity of network resources invested by a network actor, which in turn influences the space of opportunities and therefore gains a strategic dimension (Vonortas, 2009, p. 30). The trading of these assets on markets is impossible (Gulati et al., 2000, pp. 203–15; Vonortas, 2009, p. 27) and the links within innovation networks are, as we have seen, not only based on formal contracts but also based on informal relationships (Pyka, 1997 and Vonortas, 2009, p. 28). Consequently in the recent literature a strong focus is put on the possibilities offered by network participation for strategic decision-making. To shed more light on the role of network structures and the different roles played by network actors the following section surveys this emerging literature.

33.3   INNOVATION NETWORKS FROM AN ACTOR'S PERSPECTIVE AND THEIR DYNAMICS

Why do firms participate in innovation networks? In the early 1980s the opinion prevailed that the core of the competitive advantage of firms is related to its knowledge base. From this perspective it was anything but clear why firms join collaborative innovation networks in which knowledge is shared among participants, which can even be horizontal competitors. In particular, firms that operate at the technological frontier and also endowed with strong commercial skills run the risk of losing valuable knowledge and of strengthening their competitors (Kitching and Blackburn, 1999). For them a go-it-alone strategy in innovation seems to be more plausible. At the other extreme, firms with rather poor technological competencies are considered not to be attractive to connect with in an innovation network (Ahuja, 2000). What then are the advantages of network participation on the firm level and why are innovation networks a frequently found form of industrial organization of R&D?

In economic literature (e.g., Gulati, 1998) two lines of reasoning concerning the benefits of firms participating in innovation networks can be found: (1) network members benefit from information and knowledge that outsiders do not get access to; and (2) network actors may influence information and knowledge flows, which gives them a certain degree of power and influence.

Following Burt (1995) informational and knowledge benefits are characterized by three distinct features: access, timing and referrals. The first feature is related to the provision of information and knowledge from partners in the network as well as from potential future partners. Because timing matters a lot in innovation processes, firms also benefit from an accelerated knowledge transfer that is possible in network structures. Finally, valuable knowledge and information required by a network actor might not be found in the intermediate neighbourhood, that is, from actors directly connected with it. Instead the respective knowledge might flow through the dispersed channels in the network stemming from more remote actors in the innovation network. In an increasingly faster and complex knowledge generation and diffusion process, therefore, participating in an innovation network supports learning and updating of knowledge bases of the actors that are members of the innovation network.

Hagedoorn (1993) reports a number of specific motives for network participation that empirically explain why firms benefit from cooperative structures in their R&D processes. In various industries three reasons are identified to be important: technology complementarities, shortening of the innovation time and market access, as well as influence on market structures. In a recent survey of the literature Pittaway et al. (2004) list a comprehensive number of key motives of network participation: (1) risk-sharing, (2) obtaining access to new markets and technologies, (3) speeding products to market, (4) pooling complementary skills, (5) safeguarding property rights when perfect contracts are not possible, and (6) acting as a key vehicle for obtaining access to external knowledge. Most of these motives are related to the reasons derived from the changes in innovation processes in knowledge-based industries: firms cooperate as a reaction to an increased complexity in knowledge generation and diffusion processes and to cope with technological uncertainty. Obviously the motives are also related to the relative position in an industry life cycle: in early phases of the life cycle learning motives dominate whereas in mature industries market-related motives like cost reductions, efficiency improvements and so on become increasingly important. We will return to this issue below when we discuss the dynamics characterizing innovation networks.

Besides allowing access to external knowledge, another aspect matters in innovation networks, which affects the ease of knowledge transfer and mutual learning. Reciprocal knowledge exchange and synergistic creativity in innovation networks will not work without trust among the network participants (Almeida and Kogut, 1999). This holds even more in informal innovation networks, which play a decisive role in speeding up the knowledge spillovers (Conway, 1995; Robertson et al., 1996; Pyka, 1997, 2000). From this follows a strategic dimension related to the reputation as a reliable networking partner: firms that follow an isolation strategy and do not actively seek to exchange knowledge in cooperative structures also limit their possibilities to get access to external knowledge in the future since they lose the competences to participate in network structures (Shaw, 1993). Network strategies are likewise important for start-up companies as an entry strategy. Innovation networks provide access to informational and knowledge resources that increase the chances of survival (Ostgaard and Birley, 1996). Entering established innovation networks opens up possibilities for young and small firms, which are rarely available outside the innovation network (Rothwell and Dodgson, 1991).

From the discussion of firm motives to join innovation networks it becomes clear that not only the decision to join a network matters but also that the actor's position in a network plays an important role and determines the access and absorption of external knowledge. Participants in innovation networks obviously benefit from their *relational embeddedness*, that is, direct linkages to other network participants. The relational embeddedness depends on the strength of the ties, which is a function of joint action in the network and of the development of mutual trust. Whereas strong ties allow for the exchange of complex information and tacit knowledge because of the possibilities of further inquiries, weak ties instead enable the network actors to access entirely new information and knowledge. Weak ties connect actors to remote subgroups in the innovation network where there is a higher probability that rather different knowledge can be found (Granovetter, 1973; Rowley et al., 2000). Furthermore, the indirect linkages via other participants also play a role, which is expressed by the so-called *structural embeddedness* that depends on the specific architecture of an innovation network and the position in a network of an individual actor. Structural embeddedness can be formally expressed by the density of a network (Burt, 1995). High network density is not advantageous per se, in cases where a firm seeks to access new knowledge: many close linkages make redundant knowledge and information very likely. Coleman (1988) suggests that a dense network enhances the creation of trust and shared social norms. Oliver (2001) shows that firms acting in densely connected networks develop similar expectations concerning the behaviour of other network participants, that is, a system of norms and mutual control is established. Rowley et al. (2000) find that this also allows for sanctioning actors who are not sticking to the commonly introduced rules.

However, to get access to new knowledge, which is the core function of an innovation network in order to substantially support novelty generation and diffusion, different knowledge becomes attractive. Distant knowledge can be reached only by linkages to actors in more remote technological areas, actors that can often be found in less well-connected subgroups of an innovation network or in thus far not connected knowledge areas. In network terminology this means to bridge so-called *structural holes* (Ahuja, 2000).

For this strategic decision of with whom to connect, the concepts of (1) *cognitive distance* and (2) *geographic distance* play an important role. In cases where knowledge is tacit, cognitive proximity in combination with strong ties is necessary. Knowledge that is sent from one actor to another is always subject to the interpretation of the receiver, that is, what is sent is never identical to what is received, which gives rise to misperception and misunderstanding. Consequently, with higher tacitness, in innovation networks knowledge transfer also becomes more difficult (Nooteboom, 1999). However, the right balance between cognitive distance and proximity has to be found in order to guarantee a significant degree of novelty of the external knowledge. On the one hand, cognitive closeness guarantees efficient communication, comprehensibility and thus the exchange of knowledge; on the other hand, larger cognitive distance increases the probability for getting access to substantially new knowledge with a higher impact on learning and innovation.

Besides the cognitive distance the geographic distance plays an important role for innovation networks and many innovation networks in reality show a regional dimension. Geographic proximity facilitates the exchange of knowledge among firms. Feldman (2000, p. 373) defines location in the context of knowledge creation 'as a geographic unit over which interaction and communication is facilitated, search intensity is increased, and task coordination is enhanced'. The extent to which firms tend to network with other firms in close geographic distance certainly depends on the degree of tacitness of the relevant knowledge. The transfer of codified knowledge via journals, books, and so on is independent from the geographical distance. However, the exchange of tacit knowledge requires personal contacts and trust, which is easier to develop in a regional context with close distances (Von Hippel, 1994). For example, Jaffe (1989) provides strong evidence for the effectiveness of spillovers by considering a regional parameter in his estimations. In his work, spillovers are restricted to the region where the knowledge originally stems from. To understand the mechanisms by which knowledge spills over from one actor to another, regional innovation networks play a decisive role. The regional dimension of innovation networks always matters when knowledge cannot be easily transferred and the amount of tacit knowledge in innovation processes is large.

Besides the cognitive and geographical distances that influence the emergence and shape of innovation networks, joining an innovation network will feed back on the behaviour of other network members. Social norms of behaviour are likely to emerge in densely connected innovation networks. With high network density a specific culture evolves framing the way actors think and act, which distinguishes insiders from outsiders. Additionally, the costs for membership in networks are linked to the degree of density. For insiders of dense networks costs can become low as the level of trust is expected to be high. Since the building of network linkages requires a considerable investment there is no interest for opportunistic behaviour and switching costs from one network to another are high.

This self-structuring process of a network is influenced by the specific characteristics of an industry and the knowledge dynamics to be observed. A strong link between network structure and behaviour of network participants makes innovation networks stable but also very likely reduces knowledge variety and the chance that new actors with different knowledge enter the network. In particular, mature innovation networks might show this rigidity. Consequently, the major advantage of an innovation network, namely knowledge creation from the variety of knowledge of network participants, might be sacrificed for the sake of specialization and a lock-in of well-specified technological trajectories (e.g., Kogut, 2000 and Vonortas, 2009, pp. 34–5).

Relatedly, Walker et al. (1997) find a trade-off between stability and variety in network structures. From this the question arises whether there is an optimal structure balancing the two diverging tendencies, stability and variety. On the one hand, links in an innovation network are established to connect formerly not connected knowledge areas, which give access to so far unexploited knowledge from cross-fertilizations, that is, bridging structural holes. Innovations networks of this kind aim at the exploration of the knowledge space. On the other hand, network links are established to exploit better the techno-economic opportunities of a well-defined knowledge area.

Whether a rather loose network with flexible structures or a more dense network with well-rehearsed routines is more advantageous, therefore depends on the actual problem that an innovation network is confronted with. Accordingly, the idea of an equilibrated network structure might be misleading as an innovation network is exposed to continuous network dynamics determined by the phases of the industry life cycle. Efficient exploitation is based on experienced practices while exploration is a routine-changing activity itself. In the literature so far no consensus exists and different relations between low and high density of linkages in innovation networks are discussed: Rowley et al. (2000) reckon that high density and strong ties are better conditions for exploitation while low density and weak ties ease exploration. Hagedoorn and Duysters (2002) do not share this opinion and claim that the propensity to search for more radical innovations and to learn by exchanging knowledge with network partners increases with network density. They argue that for boundedly rational actors acting in a permanently changing environment, connections between remote areas of the network are not of high relevance. Instead the promotion of openness, network density and tie redundancy is more effective. To complicate things even further, Nooteboom and Gilsing (2004) suggest that new knowledge can best be discovered in structures of loose ties whereas the transfer of

complex and tacit knowledge requires dense networks. For the transition from exploration to exploitation they assume mixed forms of structures with a combination of exploative and exploitative elements. For instance, a core group of actors doing exploitativ
work is also linked to surrounding networks for sourcing new ideas (Vonortas, 200
pp. 39–41). This approach clearly refers to Granovetter's (1973) concept of the *streng*
of weak ties where weak ties avoid redundancy in the network and enables easier acces
to novelties.

So far we have seen that there is no *one structure fits all network*, but network structure
are tailored to specific tasks. Take, for instance, the case where all partners are faced wit
similar new technological opportunities. In such a case redundant interlocking ties ar
beneficial since they allow for the establishment of a high level of trust (Almeida an
Kogut, 1999). Conversely, for a network that is more dependent on external informatio
or the brokerage of technology, loose but non-overlapping ties are more appropriat
(Arndt and Sternberg, 2000). Networks can be regarded as dynamic, constantly evolvin
and adapting structures steered by actors' desires and environmental frameworks (Kas
and Rycroft, 2002).

Innovation networks are of special importance for small companies. The exchang
of tacit knowledge involves high transaction costs as it demands close interaction
and synchronizations of knowledge bases. Small firms are particularly affected by th
problems that are related to the tacitness of knowledge. First, smaller firms often sel
very specialized products characterized by a high share of tacit knowledge for nich
markets. Second, procedures tend to be less formal and explicitly written down, whic
makes them more flexible and gives employees a higher degree of freedom, whic
increases their motivation. In these cases knowledge transfer has proven to be best ir
the form of labour mobility. As a firm grows, however, it will reach a point where th
formerly established procedures will not work sufficiently well anymore. New structures have to emerge and instructions must become more explicit so that they can be
transferred over larger distances and distributed to many co-workers (Nooteboom.
1999, pp. 13–16).

From the previous sections, it has become clear that firms systematically need to incorporate external knowledge that extends their own knowledge base and allows them to
operate at the cutting edge and to survive in innovation competition. However, the fact
that companies open their boundaries and join innovation networks for internalizing
external knowledge does not mean that internally created knowledge and internal capabilities become obsolete. The opposite is true: internal skills are a condition sine qua non
to detect, evaluate and integrate external knowledge. The effective exchange of knowledge requires a high level of so-called *absorptive capacity* (Cohen and Levinthal, 1990).
Previously acquired knowledge enables firms to understand what is going on outside its
boundaries. Thus, firms that conduct own R&D are more likely to absorb valuable external knowledge. A network is the tool to access knowledge that is available in the network
and to test own research in the community (Cohen and Levinthal, 1990). Giuliani and
Bell (2005) apply this approach on a cluster-level perspective, when they empirically
analyse how the absorptive capacity of individual firms affects the knowledge system
within an innovation network as well as the links to sources of knowledge outside the
network. This is in fact an innovative approach since it shows what influence individual
actors have on the system as a whole. They demonstrate that knowledge in networks is

ot evenly distributed but concentrated within a group of core firms that have significant above-average absorptive capacities.

The network absorptive capacity can be defined as 'the capacity of a [network] to absorb, diffuse and creatively exploit extra-[network] knowledge' (Giuliani, 2005, p. 280). Without a continuous integration of external knowledge, innovation networks might mutate to less innovative cliques as the knowledge of network members increasingly becomes similar by mutual knowledge exchanges. For this reason the possibilities of *refreshing* the innovation network's internal knowledge significantly matter. Findings indicate that firms with higher absorptive capacities are better connected to sources of knowledge located outside the network. This can be explained with the size of a firm's individual knowledge base that determines the probability of creating links with external actors. Firms with a high level of absorptive capacity are cognitively closer to external knowledge and play the role of an information gatekeeper that supports the diffusion of external knowledge inside the network. In other words, high absorptive capacities indicate that a firm's knowledge base allows for more interfaces with the knowledge bases outside the network, which enables knowledge transfers into the network. Inside the network, firms differ in terms of their centrality. While some firms are part of a dense intra-network others have more peripheral positions. The result is a network with a clear divided core–periphery structure. The firms that build the core group have higher absorptive capacities.

Empirical findings indicate that there is a significant relationship between different forms of centrality and the absorptive capacity. Firms with low absorptive capacities can become isolated in a network because their cognitive distance to other firms gets too large. Accordingly, once firms have reached a relatively high level of absorptive capacity they are more likely to have many links in the network, which, in turn, increases the production and overall firm performance. Also, within the network a clear division between a core group and a periphery group is detected with a concentration of knowledge transfer within the core group. On the basis of these findings three main roles of firms in innovation networks can be conceptualized:

1. *Technological gatekeepers.* These actors have a high degree of centrality in the network, that is, they are well connected within the network and they are also strongly connected with external sources of knowledge. Due to these characteristics these actors are a main knowledge source for other actors in the network and control for knowledge flows. Concerning the strategic position, the role of gatekeepers offers the highest possibilities for firms in an innovation network: bringing in new external knowledge might refresh the innovation activities in the network and re-focus the activities from exploitation towards exploration. Of course, being a gatekeeper asks for higher networking costs.
2. *Isolated firms.* These actors benefit only rudimentarily from the network as they have only weak links. From a strategic point of view this is not a desirable position as isolated firms might not exert a severe influence on the direction and intensity of innovation activities. However, in many cases more peripheral roles might also be attractive, for example, in some user–producer relationships where already the information on innovation activities of other actors might be beneficial and an intermediate influence on knowledge creation and mutual learning is not necessary.

3. *External stars.* Such actors possess strong linkages with external sources, but only weak connections inside the network. These intra-network connections are almost exclusively focused on knowledge absorption. The role of external stars is often played in innovation networks composed of firms characterized by very different sizes. For example, in biopharmaceutical industries the large pharmaceutical companies are typically connected with various small firm networks engaged in innovation in different areas of the knowledge space (Giuliani and Bell, 2005).

Accordingly only the technological gatekeepers have strong connections inside the network and can, thus, enrich the learning dynamics with fresh external knowledge. They constitute the central part of a network's absorptive capacity. Strong external links enable these companies to enlarge their own knowledge base and to improve their position in competition. Less connected actors become aware of this and tend to build up links to actors that are relatively stronger than themselves, a process that aggravates the link concentration. In the next section a similar mechanism, namely preferential attachment is introduced, which strongly shapes the dynamics of innovation networks.

Actors that want to play a gatekeeper's role and thereby strengthen the absorptive capacity of the whole network generally follow a process that consists of three steps: (1) they intend to access external network knowledge; (2) thereby, they create new knowledge that is also exchanged with other members of the innovation network; (3) by this they foster the intra-network knowledge diffusion process. The observed provision of new knowledge without necessarily expecting reciprocal transfers is notable. The reason for this behaviour is not altruism but the expectation of positive externalities, for example, an improvement in the reputation of the whole network, which is linked to the overall improvement in production technologies.

33.4   MODELLING AND MEASURING INNOVATION NETWORKS

In the above sections we introduced innovation networks as a complex phenomenon characterized by heterogeneous actors and dynamically shifting interrelations. Without doubt, modelling in traditional equilibrium-oriented settings quickly reaches its limits and hardly allows the depiction of the self-organizational features that are characteristic for innovation networks. Agent-based modelling (ABM) instead seems to be better suited to acknowledging the complexity of innovation networks (e.g., Pyka and Fagiolo, 2007). Additionally, social network analysis (SNA) is used as a tool to disentangle the complexity of networks, which also allows for the comparison of real networks and artificial networks created by ABM. The following will briefly introduce ABM and SNA as increasingly used methodologies in the analysis of innovation networks.

Capturing the real-world dynamics of innovation networks requires the application of methodologies that allow for the explicit consideration of the rich dynamics of actors' interactions and learning processes. In the recent literature, the agent-based modelling approach has proven to be a powerful toolkit to analyse evolutionary processes in networks (e.g., Beckenbach et al., 2009; Ahrweiler et al., 2011). Agent-based models allow for a consideration of heterogeneous knowledge bases of actors in an innovation etwork and the exchange of knowledge and the related learning processes of actors. In this framework complex network phenomena such as path dependencies, dynamic returns, emergence of structures and manifold interactions among innovation network participants encompassing market transactions as well as mutual knowledge generation and learning can be analysed. In particular, agent-based models of innovation networks focus on the interaction of agents, their changing relationships and the co-evolutionary processes of knowledge creation and network evolution. In addition, the computational framework of agent-based models can be used as kind of an economic laboratory in which one can simulate the influence of different institutional settings on development paths. In this sense, ABM simulators allow for policy experiments to evaluate the effect of different instruments on the emergence and evolution of innovation networks.

The starting point of ABM is the individual actor characterized by imperfect knowledge and the aim to improve its knowledge base (i.e., learning) and confronted with *Knightian uncertainty* vis-à-vis the environment and technological developments. Knowledge imperfections and uncertainties are targeted with the help of cooperation partners. Also, in ABM, knowledge dynamics on the firm and the network level are taken into account. Firms can improve their innovation performance by increasing the size and quality of their knowledge base through learning from others. By these mutual exploration and exploitation activities, the actors create new knowledge areas and/or are confronted with decreasing technological opportunities due to imitation and so on. The agents furthermore have to balance the loss of competitive edge by sharing proprietary knowledge with other network participants and gaining access to external knowledge.

In ABM it is shown that innovation networks are a persistent form of organization of innovation processes in knowledge-based industries and that different firm populations can co-exist in the networks (Pyka and Saviotti, 2005). Moreover, typical characteristics of real-world networks such as scale-free distribution and small-world structures can be reproduced in a simulation model (e.g., Pyka et al., 2009). Scale-free networks emerge as the result of preferential attachment, which describes the fact that newcomers in a network preferably connect to established actors that are already well connected. By this positive feedback effect, these actors become hubs with a high degree of network centrality (Albert and Barabasi, 1999, p. 510; Barabasi and Albert, 2002, p. 70). This is formally expressed by stating that there is no random degree distribution in such networks but the proportion of nodes with degree k varies as a function of $1/k^\alpha$. This implies an inverse power law $P(k) \sim 1/k^\alpha$, with alpha as the power coefficient (Price, 1976, pp. 294–5).

Besides the dynamic aspects of scale-free networks, another feature describing the architecture of networks becomes increasingly en vogue (Baum et al., 2003). A network is considered a *small-world* if its clustering coefficient is significantly higher than the one of a random network and if the average path length is small. Innovation networks with a small-world architecture combine two advantages: (1) the prerequisites for a fast knowledge diffusion and (2) provision of new knowledge to all network participants. In large networks with high levels of clustering, it is often sufficient to establish some links between remote actors in order to fulfil the prerequisites of a small-world network (Watts and Strogatz, 1998, p. 440). The small-world feature characterizes many empirically observed innovation networks and can be reproduced in agent-based models of innovation networks, highlighting the plausibility of the behavioural rules applied (Pyka et al., 2009).

Figure 33.1   Part of an innovation network in biopharmaceutical industries in 1993 (own data)

Complementary to agent-based modelling, social network analysis (SNA) is applied to disentangle the complexity of the architecture and dynamics of innovation networks. Figure 33.1 displays a part of an innovation network in biopharmaceuticals in the mid-1990s as an example. It can immediately be seen that the individual actors are connected in different ways to each other with varying intensities: some have many linkages, others have only a few. The description of the complex architecture is a non-trivial task, which becomes even more difficult in cases where different networks are to be compared and/or their dynamics are to be described. Figure 33.2 displays the largest component of an artificial innovation network from an agent-based model (Scholz et al., 2010). An immediate comparison of the structure as well as of the underlying dynamics of these two networks is hardly possible. This is where SNA enters the scene: in SNA indicators are developed that allow for a description of networks, their structures as well as their evolution. Only with the help of SNA indicators do inter-network comparisons become possible, which are increasingly also applied on innovation networks. In the remainder of this section we will give a few examples and briefly outline some of the most important indicators (for more details see Pyka and Scharnhorst, 2009).

For firms that are involved in network structures it is important to understand the functioning and evolutionary dynamics of the whole network and the specific roles of

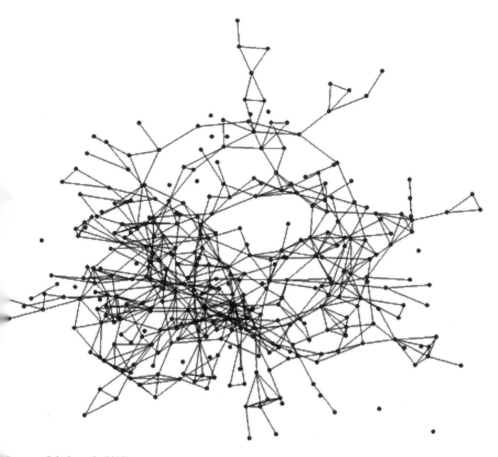

Source: Scholz et al. (2010).

Figure 33.2   Largest component of a simulated innovation network

single actors. Social network analysis offers a toolkit that helps to gain deeper insights into the functioning of collective innovation. Relations are built of linkages between actors called nodes (e.g., Knoke and Yang, 2008). Nodes can be persons but also larger structures such as firms, research institutes and university laboratories as well as venture capital firms or even standardization agencies. The linkages connecting nodes are directed or undirected. In the former case knowledge flows go from node A to B but not in reverse, whereas in the latter case there is a reciprocal exchange of knowledge. Since not all actors are connected with each other, the links are dichotomous, that is, present or absent. Also, links can be strong or rather weak, which is expressed by attributing weights to the links. What makes the SNA approach especially attractive is its dynamic view. Dynamics of networks are represented by the evolution of the network structure, which is determined by the establishment of new links and breaking-up of existing links. The challenge for research in this field is to identify the driving forces behind a specific network structure.

A few examples of the indicators used in network analysis might help to illustrate their explanatory power for the analysis of innovation networks. One of the most frequentl applied indicators from SNA is the *density* of a network. It describes the realized links i proportion to all possible linkages. As a proportional figure it varies between zero an one. Comparisons between network densities are nevertheless difficult, as the numbe of nodes is negatively related to network density. A high network density signifies tha knowledge can easily spread within the network (Scott, 2006, pp. 74–5). Not all firms ar embedded in a network and linked to other actors to the same extent. While some ar central others are more located at the peripheries. The *degree centrality* is a measure of th connectedness of a company to all other companies in the network. A high number ind cates that a company is highly visible. Actors with high centrality exert power in the sens that they can control and broker information in the network (Knoke and Yang, 200€ pp. 63–4). From a strategic point of view not only the number of links with other firms i relevant but also the distance to other firms. The *closeness centrality* indicator capture the distance of an actor to all the other actors in a network. It gives an idea of how eas and quickly an actor can get in touch with other actors in the network directly or via onl few actors in between (ibid., pp. 65–6). If an actor has a central position in the sense tha he or she controls information flows between other actors in the network then *between ness centrality* is high. That is, the more often an actor is located on the shortest patl between other actors, the higher is the potential to control or moderate flows of informa tion and resources. Such an actor plays the role of a broker or gatekeeper (ibid., pp. 67–8)

33.5   SUMMARY AND CONCLUSIONS

The aim of this chapter has been to give an overview of the development of theoreti cal concepts in economics to investigate innovation networks. Drawing as a starting point on the theory of the firm, it is obvious that the analysis of innovation networks is confronted with the same obstacles as economic innovation theory in general. The difficulties can mainly be traced back to the incentive-based perspective of traditiona approaches. Both the production function approach of neoclassical economics as well as transaction costs analysis view innovation networks from a too-narrow incentive-based perspective. Because of neglecting basic features of innovation processes and focus ing on a cost perspective only, these approaches do not catch the essential features of present-day innovation networks. Without drawing on the knowledge-based perspective of evolutionary economics, the crucial characteristics of innovation networks, that is, inter-firm learning, the exploitation of complementarities and the creation of synergies, cannot be captured. This knowledge-based perspective is supported by the motives of the firms participating in innovation networks – here, firms regularly state synergistic partnering as the reason for their engagement in cooperation. To underline the strategic importance of innovation networks for survival of firms in innovation competition, the impact of firms on the structures of innovation networks as well as the possibilities of strategic positioning in innovation networks is discussed. Finally, the main concepts that modern economic innovation theory draws upon in the analysis of innovation networks, namely agent-based modelling and social network analysis were introduced. These very recent and promising directions of research are opened up by network analysis coming from theoretical physics and networks studies in sociology. The brief discussion of these new methodologies should illustrate their analytical power and invite an application in a field from which extremely exciting results are to be expected.

REFERENCES

Ahrweiler, P., A. Pyka and N. Gilbert (2011), A new model for university–industry links in knowledge-based economies. *Journal of Product Innovation Management* **28** (2): 218–35.

Ahuja, G. (2000), The duality of collaboration: inducements and opportunities in the formation of interfirm linkages. *Strategic Management Journal* **21** (3): 317–43.

Albert, R. and A.L. Barabasi (1999), Emergence of scaling in random networks. *Science* **286** (5439): 509–12.

Almeida, P. and B. Kogut (1999), Localization of knowledge and the mobility of engineers in regional networks. *Management Science* **45** (7): 905–17.

Arndt, O. and R. Sternberg (2000), Do manufacturing firms profit from intraregional innovation linkages? An empirical based answer. *European Planning Studies* **8** (4): 465–85.

Barabasi, A.L. and R. Albert (2002), Statistical mechanics of complex networks. *Reviews of Modern Physics* **74** (1): 47–97.

Baum, J.A.C., A.V. Shilpilov and T.J. Rowley (2003), Where do small worlds come from? *Industrial and Corporate Change* **12** (4): 697–725.

Beckenbach, F., R. Briegel and M. Daskalakis (2009), Evolution and dynamic of networks in regional innovation systems. In: A. Pyka and A. Scharnhorst (eds), *Innovation Networks – New Approaches in Modeling and Analyzing.* Heidelberg/Berlin: Springer.

Burt, R.S. (1995), *Structural Holes: The Social Structure of Competition.* Cambridge, MA: Belknap Press.

Coase, R.H. (1937), The nature of the firm. *Economica* **4** (16): 386–405.

Cohen, W.M. and D.A. Levinthal (1990), Absorptive capacity: a new perspective on learning and innovation. *Administrative Science Quarterly* **35** (1): 128–52.

Coleman, J.S. (1988), Social capital in the creation of human capital. *American Journal of Sociology* **94** (S1): 95.

Conway, S. (1995), Informal boundary-spanning communication in the innovation process: an empirical study. *Technology Analysis & Strategic Management* **7** (3): 327–42.

D'Aspremont, C. and A. Jacquemin (1988), Cooperative and noncooperative R&D in duopoly with spillovers. *The American Economic Review* **78** (5): 1133–7.

Feldman, M.P. (2000), Location and innovation: the new economic geography of innovation, spillovers, and agglomeration. In: G.L. Clark, M.P. Feldman and M.S. Gertler (eds), *The Oxford Handbook of Economic Geography*, pp. 373–94.

Freeman, C. (1991), Networks of innovators, a synthesis of research issues. *Research Policy* **20** (5): 499–514.

Geroski, P. (1995), Do spillovers undermine the incentives to invent? In: S. Dowrick (ed.), *Economic Approaches to Innovation.* Cheltenham, UK and Northampton, MA, USA: Edward Elgar.

Giuliani, E. (2005), Cluster absorptive capacity: why do some clusters forge ahead and others lag behind? *European Urban and Regional Studies* **12** (3): 269–88.

Giuliani, E. and M. Bell (2005), The micro-determinants of meso-level learning and innovation: evidence from a Chilean wine cluster. *Research Policy* **34** (1): 47–68.

Granovetter, M.S. (1973), The strength of weak ties. *American Journal of Sociology* **78** (6): 1360.

Gulati, R. (1998), Alliances and networks. *Strategic Management Journal* **19** (4): 293–317.

Gulati, R., N. Nohria and A. Zaheer (2000), Strategic networks. *Strategic Management Journal* **21** (3): 203–15.

Hagedoorn, J. (1993), Understanding the rationale of strategic technology partnering: interorganizational modes of cooperation and sectional differences. *Strategic Management Journal* **14** (5): 371–85.

Hagedoorn, J. and G. Duysters (2002), Learning in dynamic inter-firm networks – the efficacy of multiple contacts. *Organization Studies* **23** (4): 525–48.

Holmström, B. and J. Tirole (1989), The theory of the firm. In: R. Schmalensee and D. Willig (eds), *Handbook of Industrial Organization*, Vol. 1. Amsterdam: North-Holland, pp. 63–133.

Jaffe, A.B. (1989), Real effects of academic research. *The American Economic Review* **79** (5): 957–70.

Kash, D.E. and R. Rycroft (2002), Emerging patterns of complex technological innovation. *Technological Forecasting and Social Change* **69** (6): 581–606.

Kitching, J. and R. Blackburn (1999), Management training and networking in small and medium-sized enterprises in three European regions: implications for business support. *Environment and Planning C: Government and Policy* **17** (5): 621–35.

Knoke, D. and Song Yang (2008), *Social Network Analysis.* Quantitative Applications in the Social Sciences Series Vol. 154. Los Angeles: Sage.

Kogut, B. (2000), The network as knowledge: generative rules and the emergence of structure. *Strategic Management Journal* **21** (3): 405–25.

Marshall, A. (1890), *Principles of Economics*. London: Macmillan.

Nelson, R.R. (1988), *Understanding Technical Change as an Evolutionary Process*. Amsterdam: Elsevier.

Nooteboom, B. (1999), *Inter-firm Alliances: Analysis and Design*. London: Routledge.

Nooteboom, B. and V.A. Gilsing (2004), Density and strength of ties in innovation networks: a competence and governance view. Working Paper.

Oliver, A.L. (2001), Strategic alliances and the learning life-cycle of biotechnology firms. *Organization Studies* **22** (3): 467.

Ostgaard, T.A. and S. Birley (1996), New venture growth and personal networks. *Journal of Business Research* **36** (1): 37–50.

Penrose, E.T. (1959), *The Theory of the Growth of the Firm*. New York: John Wiley.

Pittaway, L., M. Robertson, K. Munir, D. Denyer and A. Neely (2004), Networking and innovation: a systematic review of the evidence. *International Journal of Management Reviews* **5** (3–4): 137–68.

Price, D.S. (1976), A general theory of bibliometric and other cumulative advantage processes. *Journal of the American Society for Information Science* **27** (5): 292–306.

Pyka, A. (1997), Informal networking. *Technovation* **17** (4), 207–20.

Pyka, A. (2000), Informal networking and industrial life cycles. *Technovation*, **20** (1): 25–35.

Pyka, A. (2002), Innovation networks in economics: from the incentive-based to the knowledge-based approaches. *European Journal of Innovation Management* **5** (3): 152–63.

Pyka, A. and G. Fagiolo (2007), Agent-based modelling: a methodology for neo-Schumpeterian economics. In: H. Hanusch and A. Pyka (eds), *Elgar Companion to Neo-Schumpeterian Economics*. Cheltenham, UK and Northampton, MA, USA: Edward Elgar.

Pyka, A. and P.P. Saviotti (2005), The evolution of R&D networking in the biotechnology-based industries. *International Journal of Entrepreneurship and Innovation Management* **5** (1–2), 49–68.

Pyka, A. and A. Scharnhorst (2009) (eds), *Innovation Networks – New Approaches in Modeling and Analyzing*. Heidelberg, Berlin: Springer.

Pyka, A., N. Gilbert and P. Ahrweiler (2009), Agent-based modeling of innovation networks – the fairytale of spillovers. In: Andreas Pyka and A. Scharnhorst (eds), *Innovation Networks: New Approaches in Modeling and Analyzing*. Berlin, Heidelberg: Springer, pp. 101–26.

Robertson, M., J. Swan and S. Newell (1996), The role of networks in the diffusion of technological innovation. *Journal of Management Studies* **33** (3): 333–60.

Rothwell, R. and M. Dodgson (1991), External linkages and innovation in small and medium-sized enterprises. *R&D Management* **21** (2): 125–37.

Rowley, T., D. Behrens and D. Krackhardt (2000), Redundant governance structures: an analysis of structural and relational embeddedness in the steel and semiconductor industries. *Strategic Management Journal* **21** (3): 369–86.

Scholz, R., T. Nokkala, P. Ahrweiler, A. Pyka and N. Gilbert (2010), The agent-based Nemo Model. In: P. Ahrweiler (ed.), *Innovation in Complex Social Systems*. London: Routledge.

Schumpeter, J.A. (1911), *Theorie der wirtschaftlichen Entwicklung*. Munich and Leipzig: Duncker & Humblot.

Schumpeter, J.A. (1942), *Capitalism, Socialism and Democracy*. New York: Harper.

Scott, J. (2006), *Social Network Analysis: A Handbook*. London and Beverly Hills: Sage.

Shaw, B. (1993), Formal and informal networks in the UK medical equipment industry. *Technovation* **13** (6): 349–65.

Von Hippel, E. (1987), Cooperation between rivals: informal know-how trading. *Research Policy* **16** (6): 291–302.

Von Hippel, E. (1994), 'Sticky information' and the locus of problem solving: implications for innovation. *Management Science* **40** (4): 429–39.

Vonortas, N.S. (2009), Innovation networks in industry. In: F. Malerba and N.S. Vonortas (eds), *Innovation Networks in Industries*. Cheltenham, UK and Northampton, MA, USA: Edward Elgar, pp. 27–44.

Walker, G., B. Kogut and W. Shan (1997), Social capital, structural holes and the formation of an industry network. *Organization Science* **8** (2): 109–25.

Watts, D.J. and S.H. Strogatz (1998), Collective dynamics of 'small-world' networks. *Nature* **393** (6684): 440–42.

Williamson, O.E. (1975), *Markets and Hierarchies: Analysis and Antitrust Implications; A Study in the Economics of Internal Organization*. New York: The Free Press.

Winter, S.G. (1991), On Coase, competence and the cooperation. In: O. Williamson and S.G. Winter (eds), *The Nature of the Firm: Origins, Evolution and Development*. Oxford: Oxford University Press, pp. 179–95.

PART VIII

ECONOMIC POLICY AND THE FIRM

34 Cartel and monopoly policy
Hugues Bouthinon-Dumas and Frédéric Marty

34.1 INTRODUCTION

Firm strategies cannot be analysed without taking into consideration the legal frame-work that governs the relationships between economic agents, especially competition law. As a consequence, firms have to manoeuvre through a complex universe, taking account of both the rules of the economic game and the legal ones.

Our purpose is to analyse the legal treatment of anticompetitive practices (agreements and concerted practices that restrict competition and abuse of a dominant position), which are at the heart of modern competition law (in the American context generally referred to as 'antitrust law' and in the European one as 'competition law'). However, we must keep in mind that competition law also covers the control of vertical practices, merger policy (cf. Chapter 28 in this volume), control of state aids and, in some countries, the prohibition of unfair competition. Considering competition goals is essential for understanding enforcement of competition law.

Even if the wording of the general competition rules seems to be fairly similar, the consequences of competition law may vary considerably among countries (and across time periods), revealing differences in their underlying principles and purposes. Therefore, it is essential to identify the intentions of the law-makers and the priorities of competition authorities. Competition policies and decisional practices are closely dependent on various and sometimes conflicting views related to what competition should be and how firms should develop and interact. This chapter is focused on the examples of the United States of America and the European Union and points to their divergences and convergences. At a high level of abstraction, we may consider that competition law aims at ensuring a well-functioning market by punishing free trading and competition system infringements. However, such a general definition is highly imprecise and the implementation of such principles remains uncertain for firms. How can they be sure that their market practices are always compliant with the competition law?

Indeed the concepts of 'competition', 'market' and 'free trading' cover a wide array of meanings. To provide economic agents with appropriate rules of conduct, we need to outline the specific substance of those concepts. There are as many monopoly and cartel policies as there are economic theories. If one of the most salient characteristics of competition policy is its strong connection to economic analysis, this one is everything but univocal.

Also, the dependence of competition law on economics means that antitrust, in various ways, constitutes an 'economic law'. The subject of the law is economic since it deals with the behaviour of economic agents and it is aimed at certain economic goals that are considered desirable. The law is also economic in its method. Indeed, the enforcement of rules implies an understanding of reality through concepts that originally are economic (such as market or dominant position). Additionally, its enforcement by competition authorities requires the implementation of an economic reasoning (e.g., evaluation of a practice through an assessment of the costs and benefits linked to that practice) (see Sibony, 2012).

Competition policy also often incorporates objectives that cannot be exclusively deduced from competition, whatever it may mean. Competition law enforcement integrates other goals of economic policy, even though the legitimacy of such non-competitive goals within competition policy remains controversial. Competition law can be used for achieving political purposes (for instance, European integration), economic ones (promoting of innovation), or social ones (ensuring an open access to essential services). Let us consider the European case more precisely at this point. One of the main (and the more specific) purposes of European competition law is the achievement of an integrated (or 'common', 'single' or 'internal') European market. The idea that was mooted in the early 1950s was that the fight against monopolies and even more against cartels, was aimed at preventing (or at remedying) the segmentation of the European market. Segmentation initiated by firms would substitute for trade barriers between member-states, something that the Treaty of Rome sought to abolish.

Since we admit that competition is not necessarily being pursued for itself, but rather for the economic incentives it creates, we have to consider competition policy as a vehicle of a wide range of economic goals. For instance, innovation or competitiveness should be taken into account when assessing potentially anticompetitive structures or behaviours. Competition law enforcement also has to balance the opposite effects of some practices or even of some rights. If, intellectual property rights that protect innovation are receiving greater acknowledgment, they are simultaneously more and more challenged by competition policy since they exert the same kind of effects as legal monopolies but on a smaller scale. Indeed, they can both stimulate or restrict competition depending on the circumstances. The more complex the economic effects of such rights, the more sophisticated the implementation of competition law.

Such an approach, based upon the ultimate goals of competition law, paves the way to an integration of industrial policy purposes within the framework of competition policy. This connection might seem unnatural to those who link a market economy to the laissez-faire principle, however, in practice, concerns for the promotion of efficient and competitive firms are far from being external to competition policy. The pursuit of critical size by domestic firms can be a justification for a greater degree of tolerance towards national champions when firms have to vie with foreign competitors. Consideration of international competition by the authorities explains why competition policy might be tinged with public interventionism that favours national champions or protects 'strategic' activities.

Due to the multiplicity of their objectives, monopoly and cartel policies would seem to be rather unpredictable and are seen as imposing major limitations on the freedom of action for firms. They may be seen as a source of risk because some firm behaviours or choices are likely to be challenged and even punished if the competition authorities consider that the firms are liable to harm the competition process. However, the temptation is great for firms to escape from competition, insofar as cartels and monopolies are generally efficient means for reaching higher profit levels and enjoying of a 'quiet life' based on a better control over their environment.

34.2 HISTORICAL AND THEORETICAL BACKGROUND TO CARTEL AND MONOPOLY POLICY

Competition policy appeared in the late nineteenth century mainly as a reaction to the concentration of economic power induced by the second Industrial Revolution.

34.2.1 Background to US Cartel and Monopoly Policy

The Sherman Act promulgated in the USA in 1890 was the first competition law enacted (Kovacic and Shapiro, 1999). In a context of political debates induced by the huge growth of trusts in the US economy, concerns grew about the risks of a US market foreclosure aggravated by the unfair practices of the 'robber barons'. A strong social consensus led to a political pressure for preventing and sanctioning market practices that were likely to impede competition and, eventually, to compromise economic freedom.

The relative vagueness of the concepts introduced by the Sherman Act and the new antitrust legislation enforcement in the judicial courts made its implementation very difficult despite some very memorable cases such as the dismantling of the Rockefeller Standard Oil trust in 1911. As a result, the US competition policy framework was completed in 1914 with two acts. The first one was the Clayton Act, which, amongst other things, allows private antitrust law suits. If the US Department of Justice (DoJ) is reluctant to engage in law suits against firms this could be bypassed by the agents harmed by the anticompetitive practices. The incentives to take legal action were also increased by the possibility of obtaining treble damages. The second one was the Federal Trade Commission (FTC) Act. As a consequence, since 1914, the enforcement of competition law is no longer the sole responsibility of the Antitrust Division of the US DoJ, but is shared with an independent regulation authority. If the sharing of responsibilities between these two bodies was often complex, economic history reveals that the FTC, in some cases, is able to compensate for what appeared to be an antitrust enforcement cycle, particularly observable in the Antitrust Division.

Until the end of the 1970s, US competition policy was influenced by the Harvard School, which was very concerned with market structures. Antitrust law suits appeared necessary to prevent – even to correct – unreasonable concentration of market power. This meant that the courts became highly suspicious of dominant firms and could enjoin them to reduce their market power through asset divestitures or even dismantling. Nevertheless, the AT&T case in 1982 was the last and a very late manifestation of this view (*United States* v. *AT&T*, 552 F. Supp. 131 [D.D.C. 1982]).

In the 1960s, the Harvard approach received harsh criticism from the Chicago School, which redeemed several market practices by considering their effective impact on consumer welfare (Easterbrook, 1984). In other words, the main issue was no longer market dominance as such, in that incentive structure was now seen as the main determinant of competition. Even a hugely dominant company has no incentive to behave monopolistically since its market position is 'contestable', in the sense of an absence of barriers to entry or exit. Consequently, US competition policy shifted towards a more lenient treatment of dominant firms. According to the US Supreme Court, extracting the rent induced by a dominant company's market power does not constitute an antitrust law infringement, as long as the market power results from its past investments, business acumen or even historic accident. Only monopolization strictly defined would constitute infringement of Section 2 of the Sherman Act.

The rise of the Post-Chicago Synthesis in Antitrust economics since the 1980s leads to moderation of some of the Chicago School's normative position. Scholars now recognize that some strategies that could impair the rivals to compete could be detrimental to consumers. A case-by-case analysis is necessary to compare the potential damage to competition, resulting from a business practice with the efficiency gains it would induce. This makes cartel and monopoly policies more economics-oriented.

34.2.2 Background to European Cartel and Monopoly Policy

European competition policy also shows shifts from a rules-based approach to more economic appraisal of competition concerns (Petit, 2009). However, both its history and its practice are very specific compared to those in the USA (Gerber, 1998). European competition law should not be considered as a legal transplant of the US antitrust laws operating after World War II and following the Marshall Plan. European competition policy has its roots in some Austrian government bills submitted before World War I, and in feedback from the first German competition law promulgated in 1923 and implemented –unsuccessfully – during the Weimar Republic. This experience was the object of in-depth analysis by a group of lawyers and economists at Freiburg University in the 1930s and 1940s. They developed – mainly in secret – a theoretical analysis of what would become the Ordoliberal School.

Ordoliberals consider that competition by itself is auto-destructive because it leads to the concentration of economic power. This concentration is an issue per se because it creates potential coercive power on new entrants to the market. But since economic freedom is considered a prerequisite of political freedom, it is necessary to help the market process to realize its function of dispersion of economic power. Therefore, government intervention is essential to prevent its natural and irreversible exhaustion. Intervention is necessary to prevent the exercise of economic power against other market participants. Ordoliberal scholars advocated that dominant firms should behave as if they were deprived of any market power. Otherwise some asset divestitures had to be imposed as structural remedies. It should be noted, however, that if government intervention is required to protect the market process against itself, then it is necessary also to prevent discretionary intervention. Therefore, interventions must be based on rules. Competition policy, in this sense, is an essential component of the economic constitution.

The ordoliberals exercised a significant influence on the economic policy of West Germany after the war and, to some extent, shaped German competition law promulgated in 1957. They also had inspired German negotiators of the Treaty of Rome although it would be excessive to maintain that the treaty provisions relative to competition policy were shaped in an ordoliberal way and that their influence alone explains the specificities of European case law (Akman, 2009).

Indeed, Article 102 as it was written in 1957 does not explain by itself the specificity of EU treatment of dominant firms. We have to acknowledge that law is characterized by its open texture. The sense of a legal text becomes manifest through its implementation and through its interpretation by the courts. Concerning the abuse of dominant position, he ordoliberal theory was influential through the decisional practice of the European Court of Justice (ECJ). As Giocoli (2009, p. 779, fn. 90) considered: '[Gerber, 1998 states hat] the Court made teleology the cornerstone of its interpretative strategy... The Court nterpreted the Treaty's competition law provisions according to its own conceptions of what was necessary to achieve the integrationary goals'. In other words, the Court nterpreted the treaty provisions relative to competition law not just as a sanction of anticompetitive practices, but also as a tool to build an internal competitive market.

The role of the European Court of Justice illustrates a second difference with the US case. This difference relies on the institutional framework of competition policy implementation. In the USA, the Antitrust Division has to bring cases before the courts. In the European case, the Commission makes the enquiries, prepares the case for judgement and makes a decision. In other words, the Commission brings together investigative and adjudicatory functions. Nevertheless, the European situation is very specific in terms of the nature and practice of the judicial review of the decisions of the Commission. This control is realized by the Court of Justice (and also at a first stage by the General Court – the former Court of First Instance). Géradin and Petit's (2010) exhaustive analysis of Court of Justice competitive case law establishes that such control is exercised differently for merger and acquisition decisions and cartel judgements on the one hand, and for unilateral practices on the other hand. They demonstrate that no sanctioned firm has ever successfully challenged a Commission decision on the basis of Article 102 before the Court of Justice. In addition, even when the Commission adopts a more economic approach to its decisions, it would appear that the Court maintains a form-based (or per se) attitude and in its jurisprudence follows cases where interpretation of the span of Article 102 was extensive.

34.3   LEGAL FRAMEWORK OF CARTEL AND MONOPOLY POLICY

The fundamental rules that prohibit anticompetitive practices lie in the European treaties for European law, and in the Sherman Act and the Clayton Act for American law. These provisions are supplemented by additional statutes, regulations, case law and guidelines issued by the competition authorities.

European and American competition laws are framed in general and fairly similar terms. While the implementation of these sets of rules may differ and even diverge, the general concepts of competition law (such as 'relevant market' or 'market foreclosure') are shared by European and American and even other countries' policy-makers.

We present the main rules of antitrust law under two headings: the types of firms or groups of firms targeted by antitrust law, and the kind of behaviour that constitutes anticompetitive practice.

34.3.1   Firms

The types of firms that might undermine competition include monopolies and businesses more generally that are in dominant positions, and firms involved in cartels and other restrictive practices.

Any attempt by a firm to monopolize a particular market is prohibited under both American and European law (through the concept of abuse of dominant position). For instance, the Sherman Act Section 2 targets 'every person who shall monopolize, or attempt to monopolize, or combine or conspire with any other person or persons, to monopolize any part of the trade or commerce among several States, or with foreign nations'. Article 102 of the Treaty on the Functioning of the European Union (TFEU) (formerly Articles 86 then 82 of the previous European treaties) states that 'Any abuse by one or more undertakings of a dominant position within the common market or in a substantial part of it shall be prohibited as incompatible with the common market'.

Dominant position is not an autonomous concept: it depends on the market in which the firm is selling its products or services, namely the 'relevant market'. Dominant position refers to substantial market power. In the *Hoffmann-La Roche* case, the ECJ gives the following definition of dominant position: 'the dominant position. . .relates to a position of economic strength enjoyed by an undertaking which enables it to prevent effective competition being maintained on the relevant market by affording it the power to behave to an appreciable extent independently of its competitors, its customers and ultimately of the consumers' (Case 85/76, 13 February 1979, *Hoffmann-La Roche* v. *Commission of the European Communities*).

Market share is the first, but not the only criterion used to determine whether a particular firm occupies a dominant position in the market. It also depends on market structure, that is to say the relative market shares of the actual competitors, the potential competition (the likelihood of potential new competitors entering the market) and firm performance (large profits may be evidence of market dominance). However, as is often the case in antitrust matters, it may be difficult to decide whether a firm makes huge profits because it is inherently superior and outperforms its competitors, or because it indulges in illegal anticompetitive practices. In the first hypothesis, any intervention by the competition authorities may distort and severely damage the competition process rather than restore competition.

We can draw a parallel between Article 101 and Article 102 in the TFEU, and Sections 1 and 2 of the Sherman Act, to consider the distinction between coordinated and unilateral practices. However, we still find a significant difference in the treatment of market practices of dominant firms. While the Sherman Act Section 2 does punish monopolization practices, Article 102 in the TFEU sanctions abuses of dominant position. Thus, the acquisition of a dominant position, understood as a monopoly position, is not directly forbidden by EU competition law. On the contrary, US law considers such a situation as a violation of Section 2 if it is not based on merits. In both cases, a dominant position is not sanctioned on its own: the crucial point is to define what constitutes an abuse of this market position. We will see that one of the main sources of divergence between US and EU law derives from this point.

Agreements and concerted practices, including cartels, which restrict free trading and competition among businesses, are the second category of anticompetitive practices prohibited by antitrust law. Thus, the Sherman Act Section 1 states that: 'Every contract, combination in the form of trust or otherwise, or conspiracy, in restraint of trade or commerce among the several States, or with foreign nations, is declared to be illegal', while European law states that: 'The following shall be prohibited as incompatible with the common market: all agreements between undertakings, decisions by associations of undertakings and concerted practices which may affect trade between Member States and which have as their object or effect the prevention, restriction or distortion of competition within the common market' (Article 101, TFEU, formerly Articles 85 and 81 of previous European treaties).

A wide range of coordinated actions falls within the scope of these provisions: from formal anticompetitive agreements to concerted parallelism and even to tacit acquiescence to a conduct that disrupts the market. As long as firms are independent economic entities, they are supposed to compete and not cooperate with each other, unless this collaboration is mandated or tolerated by government (for instance, cooperations in research and development may benefit from antitrust immunity because of the efficiency gains it can generate). Unlike the case of dominant position, restrictive agreements involve at least two firms, but they can be located at different stages in the production/ distribution process. Both horizontal agreements, involving firms at the same level of production, as in the case of many cartels, and vertical arrangements or joint ventures, might raise competition issues.

34.3.2 Behaviours

The particular position of a firm – such as market dominance – is usually not sufficient to incur sanctions from the competition authorities, especially in Europe, where antitrust has never been used to dismantle monopolies as such. It is only specific collusion and abuse of dominant position that are subject to scrutiny as anticompetitive practices. Also, some cartels and restrictive agreements may be cleared under the rule of reason standard or may benefit from individual or group exemptions.

Cartels and other collusive arrangements are prohibited as far as their objective or effect is to prevent, restrict or distort market competition. European and American law describes the main anticompetitive practices as price-fixing, market-sharing, collective boycott and concerted limitation of production. Some practices are prohibited per se – price-fixing based on horizontal agreements, for instance. In the case of others there is some ambivalence. If, vertical restraints limit the freedom of resellers, they can also improve the economic process and even enhance the competition among several distribution networks and brands. In this case, the practice deserves careful analysis to determine whether the restriction should be permitted, or not, because it does not actually result in a restraint on trade and competition.

In relation to monopolies and dominant position, attention must be paid to the concept of 'abuse' in itself. Again, the law-makers, judges and competition authorities provide examples of abusive behaviours: predatory pricing, strategic deterrence, foreclosure of adjacent markets, refusal to supply an essential facility to a competitor, and so on. The Clayton Act contains specific provisions on discrimination. For example, it is not allowed to apply dissimilar conditions to equivalent transactions with other trading counterparts, thereby placing them at a competitive disadvantage. The distinction between illegal abuses and firms' acceptable legal strategies within the economic environment may be very subtle.

For practices not judged illegal per se, the necessary assessment may adopt different methods and procedures. There is currently a mix of self-assessment based on guidelines and detailed regulations, and ex-ante or ex-post evaluation provided by the competition authorities and the courts. In EU law, the so-called 'block exemption' regulations exclude the application of competition law to certain agreements. This approach can improve the legal certainty for firms by providing them with a clear dividing line between legal and illegal practices. The alternative and complementary system based on individual exemptions gives the competition authority flexibility that goes far beyond the application of clear-cut established competition rules. Given the sensitivity of competition matters, the law allows a significant margin of appreciation, which has a major influence on the nature of competition policy.

34.4   A COMPARISON OF CARTEL AND MONOPOLY POLICY IMPLEMENTATION

The areas where US and EU enforcement of competition law diverge are related mainly to unilateral practices. In the case of coordinated practices, there are similar tendencies towards increasing severity in the sanctions on collusive agreements.

34.4.1   Concerted Practices

Fines imposed for anticompetitive concerted practices have increased sharply in Europe and in the United States. However, during the Republican administration from 2000 to 2008, when no antitrust cases related to monopolization were brought before the court by the US DoJ, there was something of a deadlock in the public enforcement of Section 2 (but not Section 1) of the Sherman Act. Both the US and EU authorities are engaged in devising policies to increase fines in order to deter collusive practices. The fines imposed in successive individual cases illustrate this tendency. For example, in a decision in the European court in December 2010 relative to price collusion in the LCD panel market, the fines imposed on the six firms involved totalled €649 million (Commission decision of 8 December 2010, Case COMP/39.309 – LCD). The highest sanction so far for a cartel agreement was in the car glass decision where the cumulated fines were €1.38 billion (Commission decision of 12 November 2008, Case COMP/39.125 – Car Glass). Although the severity of the anti-cartel clause enforcement has decreased since the financial crisis, cumulated fines in 2010 reached €3.06 billion, very close to the 2007 record of €3.38 billion.

Cartel deterrence is also increased by leniency programmes' impact on the intrinsic instability of such agreements by allowing a firm that denounces the agreement to benefit from immunity and the threats constituted by follow-on suits for damages and, especially in the US case, by criminal sanctions. These cover both individual fines imposed on the executives concerned, and also imprisonment, which is applied effectively in the USA. The deterrence effect is significantly increased and this risk helps to align individuals' and firms' incentives.

The severity of the sanctions on cartel agreements is common to both systems, which is no surprise since coordinated practices are the most harmful anticompetitive practices.

34.4.2   Unilateral Practices

In the context of unilateral anticompetitive practices the situation is more complex. US and European practices show some divergences that can be explained by differences

etween Section 2 of the Sherman Act and Article 102 of the TFEU, but also by two very
ifferent conceptions of competition.

In the US case, the Sherman Act aims at punishing monopolization strategies. That is
) say, the market practices used by the firm to acquire, maintain or extend (to another
1arket) a monopoly position, based on unfair practices. If such a position is obtained on
1erit there is no reason to contest it. The market process is driven by the search for such
position, which gives market power, for example the ability to raise prices above the
1ure and perfect competition equilibrium level. Deterring such behaviour by forbidding
1he firm to benefit from this market power would thwart the competition process and
1onsequently harm consumers. So, the Sherman Act does not forbid a dominant firm
1rom extracting the rents resulting from its market power. In other words, a monopoly
an – and also must – charge monopoly prices. This behaviour is desirable just because
1 produces incentives for firms to invest in order to get this position. Therefore, only
1onopolization is sanctioned and not what the European courts term 'exploitative
1buses'.

In the European case, excessive pricing is an abuse in itself. In an ordoliberal sense,
1harging monopoly prices does not respect the *as if* condition. It should be borne in
1ind that ordoliberal thinkers advocate that firms with market power must behave
1s if they were price-takers not price-makers. If exploitative abuses are considered as
1oming under the scope of Article 102, very few decisions target excessive pricing.
[n fact, exclusionary abuses quickly become predominant in EU competition law
1nforcement. The European Commission guidance on exclusionary abuses by domi-
1ant undertakings, published in February 2009, testifies to this pivotal position in
1European competition policy. Some of the Commission's decisions related to such
1market strategies are striking examples of the differences with the USA, and help to
1define more precisely the specificities of the European competition policy applied to
1dominant firms.

A key point to understanding European law is to consider the concept of the special
1responsibility of the dominant firm not to impair by its market practices, genuine undis-
1torted competition in the common market. A dominant firm cannot adopt strategies that
1might be lawful if they were being performed by a firm deprived of market power, if the
1effects of these strategies could jeopardize the durability of the market structure enabling
an effective competition. This not only induces asymmetric regulation of competition,
but also can lead to the dominant firm being unable to implement any strategy that might
lead to the market exit of a competitor. Competition is construed as rivalry between
the competing firms. However, the protection of competition could easily shift to the
protection of competitors. Although undertakings are incentivized to acquire market
power and the natural result of the competition process could induce the exclusion of less
efficient firms, European competition policy leads to the imposition of sanctions against
the dominant operator if its conduct is at the origins of this exclusion. In ordoliberal
thinking, any competitor exclusion is likely to harm the consumer because it limits the
span of its potential choices and, at the same time, reduces the competitive pressure on
the dominant firm. In the USA, competitor exclusion would be sanctioned only if it is the
consequence of unfair practices that led to an equally efficient firm being ousted from the
market. If the firm achieves a monopoly position on its own merits, this does not constitute a violation of the antitrust laws. If a less efficient firm is excluded from the market,

it does not harm consumers, since the criterion is maximization of consumer welfare an does not take into account freedom of choice.

There are similar divergences related to several unilateral market practices. Her we provide three examples: predatory pricing, loyalty rebates and refusal to deal. Th criteria used to characterize predatory strategies in European and US case law are ver different. The economic literature establishes that a firm engages in these strategies b accepting losses (or forgoing profits) in the short term, in order to foreclose the market c to discipline actual or potential competitors, in a bid to acquire or to strengthen marke power at a later stage. In other words, predation is nothing but an investment in marke power.

For the European Commission, predatory pricing occurs as soon as an undertakin sets its prices below the average avoidable cost, or when its price levels are betwee this cost and the average total cost and it is possible to demonstrate that it is par of a predation plan. According to US case law, a firm cannot violate Section 2 b accepting losses if it does not have a reasonable chance to recoup its investment in th second period. In other words, if the practice does not result in an increase in marke power – for example, because of new or potential entries – this strategy does not harn consumer (on the contrary). So the *Brooke* decision of the US Supreme Court in 199 (*Brooke Group Ltd* v. *Brown and Williamson Tobacco Corp.*, 509 US 209) establishe that two conditions need to be met to characterize anticompetitive behaviour. First the firm must establish a price below cost and second it must have a real chance tc recoup its initial loss. The standard of proof is higher than for European practic (for an example, see the *Wanadoo* decision of the Court of Justice, *France Télécom* v *Commission*, 2 April 2009, C-202/07P) and the burden of proof is on the plaintiff, no the defender.

A second example is the case of loyalty rebates. For the European Commission some conditional rebates given by a dominant undertaking could exclude an equally efficient competitor. The *Intel* decision by the Commission in May 2009 (13 May 2009. Case COMP/C-3/37.990 – Intel) is a recent example of such a treatment of marke practices of dominant undertakings by the European competition authority. If a dominant firm proposes to its consumers a retroactive rebate if its purchases exceed a given threshold over a defined period of reference, it can choose a threshold that induces the eviction of an equally efficient competitor as soon as it becomes unable to compete for the whole demand. For example, if the competitor faces capacity constraints, the dominant firm can use the 'non-contestable' part of the demand to leverage its dominant position on the 'contestable' one. If the threshold is set sufficiently high, even competitors become more efficient, but the consumer might prefer to choose the dominant firm if the price difference does not compensate the loss of the rebate on the 'non-contestable' part.

The issue here is that such analysis must not lead to the prohibition per se of loyalty rebates for dominant undertakings. They may be welfare enhancing and be justifiable on an objective basis (e.g., anticipating economies of scale). However, EU case law does not require the Commission to demonstrate that the practices of the dominant firm have an effective exclusionary effect on the market (*Wanadoo*, General Court, 2007, Case T-340/3, *France Télécom* v. *Commission*). There is a great contrast between such an analysis, which, amongst other things, led to a fine of €1.06 billion, and the attitude of e US DoJ, which did not bring a lawsuit against Intel. But, we should also note that a ocedure was finally launched in the USA by the FTC on these exclusionary practices. July 2010, Intel and the FTC reached a settlement on this case.

The last example of such transatlantic differences deal with the treatment of refusals deal (Korah, 2007; Mateus and Moreira, 2010). According to US case law, a firm, en a monopoly, remains free to contract or to refuse to contract with other firms and choose the contractual terms. The price, in principle, is set through bilateral bargain-g regardless of whether the price is a monopoly price. An integrated firm, in particular, not deterred from supplying an input to one of its competitors in the downstream arket, since it is possible to capture all the rents produced through this price. As a nsequence, there are no incentives (if some very restrictive hypotheses are verified) to gage in exclusionary strategies against competitors. This reasoning can be applied to argin-squeezing claims.

In the European case, refusal to supply can constitute an exclusionary abuse. In some rcumstances, a refusal to deal with a competitor in a downstream market could lead eviction from the market. This issue is embodied in the essential facility doctrine. efusal to contract constitutes an abuse of dominant position if this refusal relates to a roduct that is objectively necessary for the second firm to compete effectively in a down-tream market, if it is likely to lead to the elimination of effective competition within the nal market, if it is not based on an objective justification and if it is likely to harm the onsumer.

The essential facility doctrine, in fact, stems from US case law, especially from he *Terminal Railroad* decision of the Supreme Court (*United States* v. *Terminal Railroad Ass'n*, 224 US 383, 1912). However, since the 1990s, US courts and scholars ave been more and more reluctant to apply this doctrine (Areeda and Hovenkamp, 2002). The main reason for this is the risk of strategic lawsuits and the consequences or the incentives to invest and to innovate for both the dominant firm and its com-etitors. In addition, deterrence effects on investment levels might be more important han the access price set by a poorly informed third party, that is, the court. As a onsequence, the US Supreme Court has rejected this doctrine with its *Trinko* deci-ion (*Verizon Communications Inc.* v. *Law offices of John Curtis Trinko*, 540 US 398, 2004).

At the same time, the essential facility doctrine is used increasingly in the European ase for both tangible (e.g., network industries) and intangible assets. The latter covers ntellectual property rights. Some compulsory licensing decisions have resulted in severe ontroversies, for example, the *Microsoft* decision relating to the interoperability proto-col with the Windows operating system (*Commission* v. *Microsoft Corp.*, Case COMP/C-3/37.792, 2004). The European Commission has introduced two additional criteria to apply the essential facility doctrine to intangible assets. The first is the new product criterion, the second is the balance of incentives. These two additional tests should avoid mandating an access that ultimately harms consumers.

The new product condition is supposed to help to prevent parasitism by competitors. A licence is required if it relates to satisfaction of potential demand. It appears that this requirement for a licence is significantly weakened by European case law. From *Magill* (Case C-241/91, *RTE and ITP* v. *Commission*, 1995) to *IMS* (*IMS Health* v. *NDC Health*, Case C-418/01, 2004) and *Microsoft* (op cit., 2004), the new product has become a potential or hypothetical product. Consequently, access no longer deals with only the downstream market but with the same market. Although this decision helps to create level playing field for competing firms, it also implies a kind of asymmetric regulation of competition to the detriment of the dominant firm. The consequences in terms of incentives should be taken into account.

Court decisions should seek to balance the incentives for radical and incremental innovations. In other words, we should observe an implicit trade-off between radical and incremental innovation. Implementing the essential facility doctrine demonstrates that the market is not seen as sufficiently turbulent to make a dominant position contestable, but, in every case, granting compulsory licences or deciding on mandatory access always induces a trade-off between short-term and allocative efficiency and long-term and productive efficiency.

It also implies some hypothesis concerning intellectual property rights. First, granting compulsory licences would make sense if we consider that competition policy has to counter possible excesses regarding the practices of patent offices. For example, if patents are too broad, they can be (mis)used as foreclosing tools. In this case, the decisions of competition authorities could restore collective optimality. However, the question remains whether the judge is the best suited in terms of the information structure to perform this kind of task. Second, compulsory licences could induce a shift in intellectual property rights from the right to exclude a third party to a right to obtain financial compensation.

34.5   CONCLUSION

To conclude this chapter, we should underline that the differences between US and European competition policy do not derive from statute law, but from the historical procedural and institutional dimensions and even more from the decisional practice of the authorities that have to interpret the legislative acts.

Competition law is undoubtedly case-based. Both its interpretation and its dynamic derive from decisional practices. It induces legal uncertainty for firms since the decision criteria are not always clear ex ante and the outcomes of trials are difficult to predict. Such uncertainty might be especially harmful to dominant firms. This kind of legal risk could compromise the fundamental purpose of competition policy, that is to say the promotion of economic efficiency. Dominant firms could renounce the use of certain market strategies that might benefit consumers.

Consequently, even if cartel and monopoly policy is an essential requirement to ensure the functioning of the market process and to guarantee economic (and perhaps political) freedom, we should bear in mind that this policy could also carry some legal risks for firms. These risks might be due to the difficulties to anticipate court decisions and to the risk of inconsistent decisions between different jurisdictions, induced, for example, by the specificities of the US and the European systems.

Improving the efficiency of cartel and monopoly policies should make court decision criteria clearer and advance the process of international harmonization (Gerber, 2010).

REFERENCES

Akman, P. (2009), 'Searching for the Long-lost Soul of Article 82EC', *Oxford Journal of Legal Studies*, **29**(2), 267–303.

Areeda, P. and H. Hovenkamp (2002), *Antitrust Law*, 2nd edition, New York: Little, Brown and Company.

Easterbrook, F. (1984), 'The Limits of Antitrust', *Texas Law Review*, **63**(1).

Géradin, D. and N. Petit (2010), 'Judicial Review in European Union Competition Law: A Quantitative and Qualitative Assessment', Tilburg Law School Research Paper No. 01/2011.

Gerber, D. (1998), *Law and Competition in the Twentieth Century: Protecting Prometheus*, Oxford: Clarendon Press.

Gerber, D. (2010), *Global Competition: Law, Markets and Globalization*, Oxford: Oxford University Press.

Giocoli, N. (2009), 'Competition vs Property Rights: American Antitrust Law, the Freiburg School and the Early Years of European Competition Policy', *Journal of Competition Law and Economics*, **5**(4), 747–86.

Korah, V. (2007), *An Introductory Guide to EC Competition Law and Practice*, Oxford: Hart Publishing.

Kovacic, W.E. and C. Shapiro (1999), 'Antitrust Policy: A Century of Economic and Legal Thinking', University of Berkeley, Center for Competition Policy Working Paper, No. CPC99-09.

Mateus, A.M. and T. Moreira (eds) (2010), *Competition Law and Economics. Advances in Competition Policy Enforcement in the EU and North America*, Cheltenham, UK and Northampton, MA, USA: Edward Elgar.

Petit, N. (2009), 'From Formalism to Effects: The Commission's Communication on Enforcement Priorities in Applying Article 82EC', *World Competition*, **32**(4), 481–500.

Sibony, A.-L. (2012), 'Limits Imported From Economics', in I. Lianos and D. Sokol (eds), *The Limits of Competition Law*, Stanford, CA: Stanford University Press.

35 R&D and industrial policy: policies to coordinate investments in research under radical uncertainty
Jean-Luc Gaffard, Sarah Guillou and Lionel Nesta

35.1 INTRODUCTION

In the past decades, industrial policy has had to address fundamental issues like de-industrialization, growth of high-technology industries, export promotion, and inter alia, creation of national champions to go and compete on international markets (Maystadt, 2006). Industrial policy may be defined as a policy that aims at altering the existing allocation of resources between firms. Admittedly, this definition is extremely broad, and is likely to embody a large range of government objectives and policy tools. Subsidies, tax credit (e.g., conditioned on the level of research activities), public support to specific industries (e.g., support to the car industry in 2008–09 in most developed economies) are all examples of industrial policies. It is convenient to classify them as being either vertical, that is, dedicated to the support of specific industries, or horizontal, that is, supporting specific activities, which are transversal to all industries (e.g., exports). Clearly, research and innovation are transversal to all industries, so that policies supporting R&D activities are classified as horizontal industrial policy.[1]

R&D investments have had an ever increasing role in the performance of firms, industries and countries. We now commonly admit that competition is knowledge based, that is, science and technology as an additional production factor outplay the more conventional role of homogeneous labour and capital. For example, since the early 1980s, the number of (public or private) researchers per (1000) labour force has increased impressively in the top world economies. This number has more than doubled in France and has increased by 50 per cent in Germany, Italy, Japan, UK and the USA (OECD ANBERD database). Hence both firms and governments devote substantial resources to the advancement of knowledge, to the development of new production processes and to the introduction of new products into the market. In fact, innovation by firms is the key element affecting economic growth. It is the source of transformation within industries, by selecting out less performing firms to the benefit of the most profitable ones, and also between industries, by reallocating resources between expanding, mature and declining industries. All in all, research activities are a key ingredient to moulding industry structures.

In essence, innovative activities are radically uncertain (Knight, 1921). Faster technical change increases technological uncertainty, and decisions by firms as to which technology to adopt, when and how to acquire it, which partners to collaborate with, now determine the efficiency of R&D investments. Therefore, not only are the results of innovative efforts highly uncertain but also the very implementation of the innovation process is itself likely to be hard to organize. Beyond invention, innovation necessarily implies conjectures by firms about demand factors (e.g., consumer preferences, budget onstraints), about complementary investments by upstream and downstream partners nd about investments by rival firms – what Richardson (1960) calls respectively comple- nentary and competitive investments. We call the latter triptych (demand, partners and ompetitors) market uncertainty. Hence all firms cope with both technological uncer- ainty and market uncertainty, and their ability to cope with both forms of uncertainty ill determine their growth.

We argue that industrial policy should aim at providing firms with both technical nformation and market information (Richardson, 1960), so as to reduce technologi- al and market uncertainty. Following Rodrik (2004), a key argument of this chapter s that 'industrial policy is as much about eliciting information from the private sector n significant externalities and their remedies as it is about implementing. . .collabora- ions between the *public and/or private actors* with the aim of uncovering where the most ignificant obstacles to restructuring lies' (p. 3, adapted by the authors where italicized). As research activities – the outcome of which is generally impossible to predict – are par- icularly subject to problems of radical uncertainty and coordination, we also argue that nonitoring research, promoting inter-organizational R&D collaborations, encouraging he diffusion of knowledge, are all crucial aspects of defining R&D policy as a process of sharing information. In other words, research activities exemplify the need to think of industrial policy not only in terms of expected policy outcomes but also in terms of a policy process.

This chapter focuses on innovation policies, that is, policies that support both the very activity of invention and the introduction of new products into the market. Originally, innovation policies were concerned principally with the organization of research. These research policies were following a neat division of labour where public laboratories supplied private parties with fundamental knowledge. Firms were responsible for the development of new products and processes, that is, the production of applied knowl- edge. In this setting, public authorities had to address the issue of positive knowledge externalities, regarded as leading to systematic underinvestment in R&D. Over time, increased complexity in products and processes and in the organization of industries has challenged this simplistic view, so that nowadays, policies supporting innovation have to address a wider spectrum of phenomena, ranging from providing incentives for R&D investment to encouraging partnership between private parties, developing ties between public and private research centres and stimulating the sharing of information with policy-makers, stakeholders and research organizations.

This chapter is structured as follows. Section 35.2 presents how our economies are becoming more engaged in high-technology sectors, to stress the role of knowledge- based activities across all sectors, more so than the mere R&D investments. Such struc- tural change forces policy-makers to rethink at once both industrial and R&D policies. Section 35.3 presents a rapid overview of how both types of policies, while initially independent from one another, have actually converged. The current commitment of our economies to innovation activities has blurred the frontier between industrial and R&D policies. Section 35.4 presents the normative implications resulting from this ongoing process, arguing that competition is not so much a state of affairs, but is a process by which actors must gather economic, technical and organizational information in order for them to base their investment decisions, including the R&D investments, in an environment of great uncertainty.

35.2   EMPIRICAL EVIDENCE ON STRUCTURAL CHANGE AND KNOWLEDGE-BASED COMPETITION

Structural change in industrialized countries has led to a higher human capital an technology content in production and exports. This was enabled by a larger R&D effor moving the comparative advantage of industrialized countries more strongly towarc high-technology goods. Still, this overall achievement cannot conceal the followin issues: (1) the existence of clear differences between countries and notably betwee Europe and others; (2) the ongoing challenge that technological improvements must b made permanent; (3) the new competition from emerging economies.

Structural change in industrialized countries can be measured through the increasin share of high-tech industries in the total value-added of manufacturing observed in th last 30 years. Figure 35.1 shows the evolution of the share in value-added of manufactui ing industries grouped by technological intensity (defined by the OECD STAN database since 1980. At first glance, Figure 35.1 reveals the increase in the share of production tha stems from high-tech industries. Apart from Italy, all countries experience a rise in th share of productions that embody high-tech products.

Figure 35.1 also shows the technological profile of countries. Germany stands ou by its remarkable specialization in middle high-tech industries. This reflects the spe cialization of Germany in machine tools (machinery and electrical equipments) and the automobile industries. Low-tech industries have the biggest share in most countries reflecting the idea that modern economies still rely on traditional industries. High-tech industries are more and more present but are still a minor share of manufacturing production. Hence, analysing the share of high-tech industries is only part of the story about structural change. The issue is much more the share of R&D in every industry and the share of information and communication technology imbedded in production, and, what concerns these shares show, is that the European countries, except Germany, display some weaknesses relative to the United States, as can be seen in Table 35.1.

In Europe, worries about the productivity gap between the Old Continent and the United States soon emerged. In March 2000, European governments launched the Lisbon Agenda set out by the European Council in Lisbon. The Agenda claimed to make the EU 'the most competitive and dynamic knowledge-based economy in the world capable of sustainable economic growth with more and better jobs and greater social cohesion' by 2010. One of the main objectives of this Agenda was to increase the amount of private R&D spending in percentage of GDP to at least 3 per cent. This objective was built on the common views that (1) all industries should imbed more R&D in order to multiply innovation opportunities and (2) R&D intensity is a key element of countries' competitiveness.

A primary observation of R&D and market share indicators supports this last hypothesis. Table 35.1 shows a clear correlation between R&D indicators and macroeconomic performance in terms of market shares. Country ranks are similar whether one considers R&D indicators, production and export. The triad composed of the United States, Japan and Germany (not Europe) dominates all performance measures. These countries invest more in R&D, patent more, and have both a larger share of world manufacturing production and world manufacturing exports. The trade market shares in middle high-tech and high-tech industries are obviously correlated with R&D intensity.

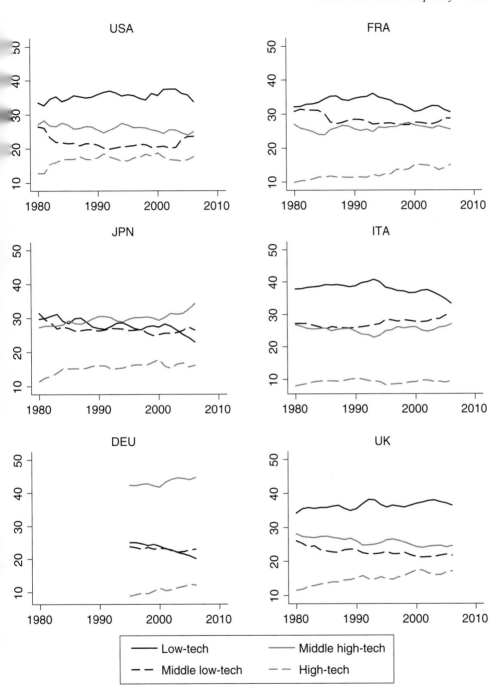

Source: Structural Analysis Database (STAN), OECD, 2008 edition.

Figure 35.1 *Composition of OECD economies by technological sectors (in percentage of GDP)*

Table 35.1   R&D, patents and international market shares

	R&D/ GDP[a]	Manuf. R&D[b]	Country R&D Share[c]	Patents[d]	Y_{2006}^{e} ΔY_{96-06}	X_{2007}^{f} ΔX_{97-07}	X_{MHT}^{g} $\Delta X_{MHT, 97-07}$	X_{HT}^{h} $\Delta X_{HT, 97-07}$
France	2.04	86.3	6.7	433.37	3.4 (−3.2)	4.4 (−2.1)	5.0 (−2.2)	4.3 (−1.8)
Germany	2.53	90.9	11.9	805.40	6.2 (−4.7)	10.5 (−0.7)	15.2 (0.1)	7.9 (1.7)
Italy	1.18	73.8	2.0	467.15	3.6 (−2)	4 (−0.3)	4.7 (−1.1)	1.8 (−0.5)
Japan	3.44	88.9	24.5	818.28	9.6 (−9.4)	6.3 (−3.3)	10.1 (−2.2)	6.1 (−6.5)
UK	1.81	77.0	5.5	441.84	4.2 (0.3)	3.3 (−1.9)	3.7 (−3.5)	3.6 (−5.6)
USA	2.66	63.3	42.1	858.91	21.4 (−0.3)	8.9 (−1.4)	10.0 (−3.8)	12.3 (−4.7)

Notes:
a.   R&D/GDP: R&D relative to GDP (2007).
b.   Manuf. R&D: share of private R&D performed by manufacturing industries.
c.   Country R&D share: country share of manufacturing R&D of major OECD countries (CAN, DAN, DEU, ESP, FIN, FRA, GBR, IRL, ITA, JPN, SWE, USA).
d.   Patents: EPO and USPTO patent applications (per billion of R&D dollars).
e. Y_{2006}: share of manufacturing production in world manufacturing production (ΔY_{96-06}: compound annual growth rate from 1996 to 2006).
f. X_{2007}: share of manufacturing exports in world manufacturing export.
g. X_{MHT}: share of manufacturing middle high-tech exports in world manufacturing middle high-tech export.
h. X_{HT}: share of manufacturing high-tech exports in world manufacturing high-tech export.

Sources: OECD, Main Science and Technology Indicators, 2008; and CEPII, BACI database 1997–2007, calculus from authors.

It is worth pointing out that Europe as a whole differs clearly from other industrialized countries: high-technology industries accounted for only about 20 per cent of total EU manufacturing exports in 2003, compared with some 29 per cent in the United States and 27 per cent in Japan (European Commission, 2005). Nevertheless, all old industrialized countries are strongly challenged by the growth of Chinese manufacturing production. China is quickly gaining a larger share of world manufacturing production (9.4 per cent in 2006) and of world manufacturing exports (nearly 12 per cent in 2007). With the exception of Germany, all countries have suffered substantial losses in their market shares to the benefit of China in the last decade. In the current globalized manufacturing markets where emerging markets are gaining more and more market shares, the comparative advantage of old industrialized countries should undoubtedly rest on high value-added products. Unfortunately for Europe, the 3 per cent objective of the Lisbon Agenda is far from having been reached, and this failure, already stated in 2004 (Kok, 2004) has definitely disqualified the countable objective. The need to discuss the focus on R&D level and R&D content is now pressing.

Today, competition by the so-called low-wage countries is not restricted to low-technology sectors. It is reasonable to expect emerging economies to move gradually

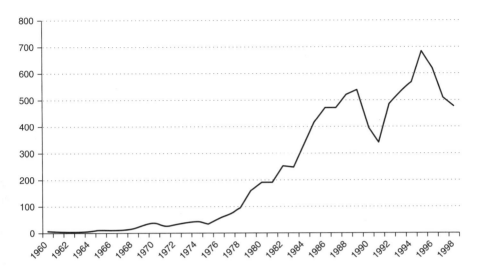

Source: Hagedoorn (2002).

Figure 35.2 *The growth of newly established R&D partnerships (1960–98)*

towards producing and exporting goods with ever higher human capital and technology intensity. Inevitably, this will increase competitive pressure in markets where European producers have their current comparative advantage, that is, markets for products based on high-skilled labour and high technology. Empirical evidence suggests that high-tech industries too are being challenged by emerging countries. Product innovation by low-wage countries is very likely to challenge the current dominance of modern economies in the future. More must be done to foster innovation in all industries, and it is the role of modern industrial policy to ensure that R&D efforts diffuse pervasively across all sectors. To focus invention policies on high-technology sectors alone will therefore prove very wrong.

The linear model of innovation (Stephan, 1996), which views technological advances as a series of sequential steps starting with idea formalization and moving through basic research, applied research, development, commercialization and diffusion into the economy, is no longer accurate. The policy consisting of supporting R&D investments is simply insufficient. Many innovations require neither basic nor applied research but, are incremental improvements on existing products or processes, using various stimuli from customers, suppliers, competitors and partners. Therefore, more than R&D activities per se, appropriate innovation policy should be concerned with all types of knowledge-based activities and should understand their complex organization connecting public and private actors, domestic and foreign agents, customers and suppliers.

Today, more than ever before, firms must establish relationships with various actors so as to keep track of the latest technological developments. Figure 35.2 exhibits the long-term trend of inter-firm R&D partnership from 1960 to 1998 (Hagedoorn, 2002), which is only one particular aspect of the different types of ties that can be established by any two organizations. The sharp increase from the 1980s onwards reflects various aspects ranging from increased scientific complexity of products, faster technical change and fiercer technological uncertainty to larger R&D costs and shortened innovation cycles. This rise conceals a significant increase in geographical scope of collaboration and is pervasive across all sectors, although preferably in high-technology sectors. The overall pattern suggests that firms are not islands of production (Richardson, 1972). Instead firms establish ties to exploit latent economies of scale and scope, to overcome increased R&D costs and to access relevant technology and market information not otherwise available.

The development of inter-organizational collaborations should lead to a reconsideration of the theory of the firm, that is, the theory of the nature and the boundaries of the firm originally developed in Coase (1937). Beyond the vision of the firm through the exclusive lens of the production function framework,[2] transaction cost theory of the firm has gained momentum in the past three decades by focusing on make or buy decisions. The resource or competence-based perspective also offers an insightful complement to the theory of the firm by providing a comprehensive account of why and how firms differ (Nelson, 1991). One of the major characteristics of this line of inquiry lies in its persistent efforts to isolate the sources of heterogeneity amongst firms,[3] one of which is their intangible assets together with the network of collaborations that firms establish over time. However, the focus on knowledge and competencies has downplayed the role of information in shaping firm decisions about strategic investments. Besides heterogeneous scientific knowledge and technical competences, information and access to it are key to firm growth. What is really at stake is the capacity of firms to share relevant market information and this draws upon what Richardson (1960) calls market connections (see also Metcalfe, 1998).

The development of these new theoretical advances suggests that policy-makers must address the issues of collaborations and of knowledge and information exchange in their policy design. Although quantitative targets must remain a strong policy objective, R&D investments cannot play the only role in a fully-fledged innovation policy. In what follows, we argue that innovation policy should focus on the concretization of R&D efforts into innovation across all sectors. Relative to emerging economies, old industrialized countries do have a comparative advantage in terms of human capital and institutions in favour of innovations. Education, property rights, infrastructures, the legal environment, and financial systems are all key elements of an environment in favour of innovation. This can be achieved with a good understanding of the challenges faced by firms: diffused R&D efforts, modular production processes and feedback from downstream customers. At the core lies the idea that it is the quality of these interactions, that is, the information shared by several actors, that dictates the success of innovation efforts.

35.3 THE CONVERGENCE BETWEEN R&D POLICY AND INDUSTRIAL POLICY

Both have undergone tremendous changes in the past 60 years, reflecting the increased role of scientific knowledge and innovation in modern economies. If innovation is at the core of competition, then the capacity of industries to restructure and adapt to abrupt modifications of production processes and the sudden introduction of new products comes an essential ingredient of economic growth. In turn, the success of both R&D and industrial policies lies not so much in the definition of appropriate policy goals and tools, but more in the capacity of the policy itself to adapt both its objectives and its means.

5.3.1 A Historical Appraisal of Industrial Policy

Industrial policy alone is probably one of the least understood areas of government intervention. All economic textbooks include recommendations regarding budgetary, monetary and/or employment policies. Targets may leave room for discussion, but tools are identified and, in general, well accepted amongst scholars and policy-makers. Conversely, policy-makers will hardly find any clear-cut recommendations on industrial policies as such. Ready-to-use guidelines corresponding to specific industrial difficulties simply do not exist. The reason is that the set of possible configurations is virtually infinite, for they depend on a host of factors that cannot be defined a priori. The nature of the technologies involved, the appropriation regime for intellectual property, the set of destination markets, and so on, are all ingredients that impede the definition of pervasive policy recommendations.

Yet industrial policies do exist. Markets may in some circumstances malfunction, and the very presence of market failures calls for some form of state intervention, either to support industries in downturns or to internalize externalities and restore the proper role of markets. In its broadest sense, industrial policies are viewed as those supporting specific industries or activities. From a historical viewpoint, industrial policies of a traditional tone are vertical, supporting the development of specific industries. Examples of this type abound all over the world. Asian countries have favoured the development 'from scratch' of, inter alia, the electronic and car industries, which nowadays operate at the quality frontier. In France, the settlement of 'national champions' was substantially backed by government subsidies and support for downstream demand.

Over time, vertical industrial policies gave way to the rise of horizontal policies. Such policies support activities considered as strategic to all sectors – mainly innovation, exports and more recently activities that somehow affect the environment. This was in line with the growing view in the 1980s that government support should not distort competition, and that national support to specific industries would be considered as infringement to competition. State intervention should be limited to the realm of market failures. Yet in the 1990s, both types of government interventions have been subject to heavy criticism. Perhaps the most substantial objection to state intervention is simply that governments do not have more information than private actors do, so that their interference will inevitably lead to government failures. In the end, why would governments pick winners any better than markets do? Why would government failures be preferable to market failures?

Rodrik has addressed this issue in a series of contributions (2004, 2006, 2007). His main message is that industrial policies should not be viewed exclusively as tools by which given objectives can be defined and achieved once and for all. Rather, such industrial policies should be designed to be able to adapt tools and objectives to changes in the environment: 'effective industrial policy is predicated less on the ability to pick winners than on the ability to cut losses short once mistakes have been made. In fact, makir mistakes is part. . .of good industrial policy when cost discovery is at issue' (Rodri 2004, p. 34). Hence the convincing argument opposes industrial policies focusing c policy outcomes and industrial policies interested in getting the policy process righ This argument is extremely relevant when innovation and changes in market conditior become more and more pervasive across economic activities. What is important is nc so much to restore well-behaved markets – however one defines them – than to ensur that public and private actors engage in strategic cooperation and accumulate relevar market information.

35.3.2   The Old Economics of Science and its Discontents

Research policies have followed a somewhat different path. First of all, research policie have always had, and still have, a high vertical content. Large programmes in scientifi areas of high strategic content have been persistent over the years: nuclear programmes space programmes, electronics, biotechnology, nanotechnology. All exemplify the objec tives of government to develop areas of national excellence. Over time however, the design of these programmes has changed dramatically. This design is related to how one conceptualizes knowledge, either as a fully public good or as a semi-public good, witl some form of excludability.

In the 1960s, scientific knowledge was considered a public good, available to all actors immediately and at no costs. Positive knowledge externalities prevented firms from per forming basic research, the benefits of which were readily available to competing firms To the extent that private R&D investments generate positive externalities that accrue to other firms, the incentive for private parties to invest in R&D is socially too low. In consequence, the standard analysis of R&D initially focused on the existence of the gap between social and private returns to R&D, which arises because the individual profit-maximizing firm ignores the effect that its actions have on the welfare of consumers and on the profit of other firms. Public policies, which may consist in R&D subsidies (or taxes), stronger intellectual property rights or encouragement to research joint ventures, are aimed at compensating the effects of market failures.

Following the writings of Nelson (1959) and Arrow (1962), private research was viewed as the locus of applied research, where developments could be protected via intellectual property. Public research, in turn, had to concentrate on the diffusion of basic research, precisely where there would be underinvestment by firms. Knowledge as a public good has therefore led scholars to design a neat division of labour – where public research organizations perform fundamental research and private firms carry out applied research. This view has been coined the old economics of science (Dasgupta and David, 1994).

This view also has serious shortcomings. Subsidies policies are subject to moral hazard. Stronger intellectual property rights may reduce the effective sharing of R&D. More generally, it should be clear:

> that market failure as a technology policy framework leaves much to be desired. The logical underpinning it provides tells us nothing about the design of policy instruments, nor their appropriate method of implementation, nor the areas which are most appropriately in need of support in their attempts to innovate. (Metcalfe, 1998 p. 113)

ocusing on Pareto optimality fails to grasp that competition is a process of discovery, ot a particular state of the economy. Firms compete by creating new and specific goods, ot to allocate resources in a Pareto-efficient way. The latter cannot be a criterion for erformance, since 'imperfections identified in the market failure approach. . .can be iewed. . .as necessary aspects of the production and the dissemination of knowledge in market economy' (ibid., p. 114).

5.3.3 The New Economics of Science

The fundamental objection came with the writings of Cohen and Levinthal (1989, 1990). n their two papers, they show that to view scientific knowledge as a public good is not obust to empirical evidence. Firm-level evidence suggests that private and public R&D nvestments are complements (in statistical terms, their partial correlation is positive), so hat fields where public research is significant corresponds to areas of substantial R&D nvestments by private parties. The reason for this is the following: if knowledge is a semi-public good, then to assimilate and initially exploit external knowledge is a costly process. In order to benefit from external knowledge, firms themselves must invest in knowledge so as to boost their absorptive capacity. To view private and public research as two independent spheres was simply proven wrong. Instead, both public and private research could benefit from one another, which opened the path to the new economics of science (Dasgupta and David, 1994).

In the early 1990s, research policies started to promote interactions between different types of actors. Public research laboratories are now expected to intervene in down-stream research with private firms; universities are encouraged to increase their revenues from downstream applications, beyond and above their secular missions of teaching and doing research. Support to private research is often conditional on the explicit collabora-tion of public laboratories. Building on the idea that knowledge transfer and absorption is more efficient with direct interactions, the designs of specific research programmes are all based on boosting public and private collaborations.

Initially concerned with restoring well-behaved scientific and technical knowledge markets by limiting positive knowledge externalities, research policies have been extended to take full account of the growing role of knowledge in economic activities. Today, firms must also perform basic research in order to benefit from new products and processes developed outside their boundaries. Boosting interactions both between firms and with public sector research has now become a key policy objective. But beyond mere R&D investments by firms – which are more than necessary in knowledge-based competition – research policies insist on the whole process of innovation, involving a variety of actors, insisting on knowledge transfer mechanisms. A deep comprehension of the mode of innovation pertaining to specific industries, as is proposed in Pavitt's taxonomy (1984), becomes a central element to design innovation policies.

Let us recall Patel and Pavitt's statement that firms rarely choose the 'wrong' technol-ogies: 'if you want to design and make automobiles, you must know about mechanics; if you want to design and make aeroplanes, you must know about aeronautics; if you want to design and make all manner of complex products, you must know about computer applications' (1997, p. 155). Hence the question for firms is not so much which technol-ogy to acquire, but how fast and effectively to assimilate and exploit new technologies.

In other words, the problem is not only one of knowledge transfer, it is also a problem c coordination of partners and information about market conditions, about complemen tary investments by suppliers and by downstream distributors and about competitiv investments by rival firms (Richardson, 1960). Below we argue that another – perhap more important – role of innovation policies is precisely to motivate the sharing o information amongst partners so as to facilitate investments in research activities and ultimately, innovation. By doing so, innovation policies become in essence policies fo industrial development.

35.4   R&D AND INDUSTRIAL POLICY FOR THE TWENTY-FIRST CENTURY[4]

In a world of rational expectations, there would be no room for R&D cooperative agreements: any firm with profitable R&D projects will obtain the required financia resources as sunk costs will be necessarily recovered when time has elapsed. The amount of these costs cannot matter. In such a world, the only room for R&D policies is the one that fills the gap between private expenditures and a so-called social optimum. Conversely, when individual firms have neither complete nor perfect information, potential lenders cannot accurately assess the credibility of claims made by firms: 'To some degree this puts large firms at an advantage in that they can pool the risks from a portfolio of projects and helps us to understand the pressures towards more collaborative work in R&D and towards mergers and acquisitions between technology based companies' (Metcalfe, 1998 p. 112). In what follows, we argue that policies supporting innovation are also about overcoming technical and market uncertainty by promoting the exchange of information regarding promising technologies and future market conditions.

35.4.1   Uncertainty and the Coordination of Investments

R&D policies are becoming elements of a wider policy that concern the whole innovation process. This process is not only long and uncertain but also complex, combining the research phases with the development phase and the ultimate industrial phase. In this perspective, industry performance depends on the selection process of projects and firms, that is, on the way the market converges to a stabilized structure. Entry and exit of firms, reallocation of the market shares and in-house learning are all key elements of this process.

For a process of growth to take place, investments must be implemented, so that a phase of construction will result in a new productive capacity to be matched with a corresponding demand for final output. As Richardson put it (1960), the profitability of a firm's investment, and hence its growth rate, will depend on how the firm will obtain sufficient information on which to base its investment decision. A specific coordination problem is then involved, due to the existence of these two delays – the delay of gestation of investment and the delay of transmission of market information. On the one hand, investment represents a firm commitment, and this commitment will give rise to an additional output only after a certain interval of time has elapsed. On the other hand, ntrepreneurs will learn about the commitments of others and also about the needs of customers only after a certain period of time.

Imperfect information and imperfect mobility of resources are at the heart of competition. Fundamentally, competition is a coordination mechanism, which is relevant especially in an environment characterized by imperfect information and imperfect mobility of resources. However, coordination through market transactions is only possible by virtue of existence of circumstances that set bounds to what happens, in particular to investment behaviours. These enabling circumstances exist naturally (such as differential capabilities) or may be contrived through collective action. All represent deviations from pure competition: in order to take investment decisions, firms need a certain degree of stability in their environment.

This is provided by what Richardson calls natural or contrived restraints, which permit industries to converge towards a state of dynamic equilibrium. Contrived restraints correspond to agreements that exist in a great variety of forms. Among them, R&D agreements play an essential role. Of course, they allow firms to share heavy costs of development, but, more fundamentally, they allow firms to share market information, which is made available, only step by step, with the effect of avoiding an excess of competitive investment. The nature of these restraints should orientate both instruments and objectives of policies aimed at sustaining firm growth and innovation, which implies both the promotion of cooperation between firms and the adaptation of competition policies to foster innovation.

35.4.2 The Non-monotonicity of the Competition–Innovation Relationship

Current literature on the relation between competition and innovation mainly focuses on the existence of barriers to entry. Thus they miss the point, neglecting the barriers to growth. An alternative analysis, instead of considering competition as a state, focuses on the market process. Then, it focuses both on rivalry and cooperation between firms, and tries explaining why and how innovation processes can be efficient and viable. This orientates objectives and means of innovation policy.

Competition is consensually viewed as a process that raises firms' efficiency, increases the consumer surplus and thus enhances growth. By putting firms in a battle for market shares, competition appears as a natural incentive for firms to innovate in order to gain new customers. But at the same time, in a Schumpeterian perspective, monopoly rents (current and/or expected) would be necessary in order to motivate and afford firms to innovate. The dominant firms would be the vector of the future growth. Hence, there is a real dilemma for the social planner having to know the influence of market structures on innovation. Actually both theoretical models and empirical studies are really at odds.

An interesting piece of evidence is from Aghion et al. (2003). Using data on UK firms, they show that the relation between competition (measured by the opposite of the Lerner index) and the innovative output (measured by the citation-weighted patent count) is an inverted U shape. They also show that, at any level of competition, firms facing a higher debt pressure innovate more.

Aghion and Griffith (2005), taking advantage of several papers (Aghion et al., 2003, 2004, 2005), propose an interpretation of these empirical results that focuses on the role that the distance to the technology frontier plays in the firms' behaviour. According to their model increased competition has opposite effects depending on whether firms are the technology frontier or not. When near the technology frontier, firms are incentivize to innovate because innovation offers a means to 'escape' competition. In neck-and-nec industries where numerous firms locate near the technology frontier, tighter competitic increases the incentive to innovate by exerting a down pressure on current profits befor innovation. Firms have to innovate to restore their rents. Conversely if firms are far fron the frontier, their incentive to innovate decreases with competition. These firms are on able to imitate. An increase in competition will reduce their incentive to innovate.

The effect of competition on innovation depends on the position of firms relative to th technology frontier. Competition increases the growth of productivity in industry wher firms are all near the technology frontier, whereas it decreases the growth of productiv ity in industry where firms are more dispersed. The aggregate industry growth depend on the productivity and product distribution of firms. In turn, the effect on the whol economy depends on the relative size of each kind of industry, size that also depends o the level of competition. Indeed, if the competition is weakening in dispersed industry the incentive to innovate by imitation will increase and thus enhance the number of firm near the technology frontier. Then, in this new configuration competition could becom a great incentive to innovate.

Due to this endogenous effect, the whole result of a competition policy on innovatio is hard to predict. It depends on the relative size of each type of industry and on th pace at which firms come nearer the technology frontier facing the competition policy Hence the contrasted effect of competition on innovation leads to a curvilinear, inverted U-shape, relationship.

Recent theoretical models and empirical findings strongly support the fact that the relationship between competition and innovation is non-linear, implying a mix of effect: that may go in opposite directions. However, such research cannot suffice to delineate a proper competition policy that would be – so to speak – optimal. Chances are that thi: level of competition that would be optimal for innovation is hard to depict. Lastly, one runs the risk of focusing on a relatively minor issue. Recall Nickell's warning (1996, that we may be barking up the wrong tree. More than the effect of market *structures* on firm's R&D incentives, it is market selection that boosts economic growth by promoting successful firms at the expense of less efficient firms. More than within-firm growth, it is industry churning that accounts for economic growth.

35.4.3 Overcoming Barriers to Firm Growth

The observed patterns of firm demographics and survival in several modern economies provide meaningful insights. Entrepreneurship and industry churning is rather high in most OECD countries. Empirical evidence suggests that the market selection mechanism is working properly in almost all developed countries (Bartelsman et al., 2005), with the exception of Japan during its recession of the 1990s (Nishimura et al., 2005). There are no large differences in firm turnover across countries, once account is taken of differences in the sector composition of the economy, and there are no large differences in firm rate of survival a few years after birth. But the rate of post-entry growth of survivors is het-erogeneous across countries, leaving room for factors that may impede or support firm growth. As a matter of fact, the main problem lies not so much in the existence of barers to entry, but in the existence of barriers to the growth of small – generally younger firms (Bellone et al., 2008).

Barriers to growth cannot be assimilated with barriers to entry. Firms are not only concerned with incentive issues in industries characterized by a full coordination on a good or a bad equilibrium, they also have to face coordination failures, in fact market imbalances and financial constraints that hamper their ability to grow. While the main discussions in industrial organization consist of determining the outcomes, which correspond to different information structures, the real issue is to identify how firms may have access to the relevant technology and market information. In this context, cooperation is a means by which firms share market information and make decisions to engage irreversible R&D and capacity investments.

However, high costs in R&D investments are more easily funded by a group of firms than by a single firm. Examples abound of policies providing incentives for firms to engage in research collaborations with other public or private entities. One objective is obviously to share the costs of R&D, which has increased tremendously over past decades. Incentives to develop innovations jointly with other firms will depend on the degree of substitution and/or complementarity between any two R&D projects. When firms develop innovations that are substitutes, they will be reluctant to share technical knowledge. Yet in most of the innovative sectors, products are evolving, and improvements are heterogeneous and gradual. Anticipating that what may be substituted one period may become complementary the next period, firms will have incentives to enter into R&D collaborations. From a social viewpoint, coordination among innovative firms helps not only to internalize externalities and but also to increase the incentives to invest.

Here it is worth mentioning the role of US competition legislation. Under the provisions of the National Cooperative Research Act of 1984 (NCRA), firms that notify their intent to enter into a joint R&D agreement can reduce their exposure in private antitrust litigation. More importantly, the National Cooperative Research and Productive Act of 1993 follows the principles embodied in the NCRA but extends the protection to the joint production, manufacture and marketing of any product, process, or services that are the outcome of cooperative R&D (see on this point Katz and Ordover, 1990 and Mowery, 2009). Clearly, competition law does not prevent agreements aimed at accessing market information required by each firm for investing in new technologies or new products.

What is at stake is not only cost sharing, but also the sharing of technical and market information. These pieces of legislation reveal that what is at stake are not R&D incentives alone, but the coordination of the series of complementary investments that characterize any innovation process. Hence to equate the role of such policies to the support of cost sharing exclusively would be simply wrong. Government support for collaborative R&D agreements also has to do with the dissemination of technology. In this case, such policies are also about overcoming the technological uncertainty that may limit the scope of firms to venture in given technological trajectories.

As pointed out by Baumol (2002), the dissemination of technology not only matters for the efficiency of the economy's growth process, but it is also 'a part of the regular portion of the firm's voluntary activities' (p.75). There are several reasons that lead firms to engage in dissemination of their own proprietary technology. Perhaps the most important one is that being a member of a technology-sharing agreement offers benefits.

More exactly, markets may impose penalties upon any firm that remains outside such a agreement and does not share its technical knowledge with others:

> That isolated firm will be able to offer products and use processes that are improved only by i own research efforts, whereas its rivals will each benefit from their combined innovative activ ties; thus, exchange of technology (in contrast to pure licensing), rather than increasing th vulnerability of the participating firms to successful 'enemy attack', provides them with a degre of protection. (Baumol, 2002, p. 79)

In other words, it enhances the firm's growth process.

35.5   CONCLUSION: THE PILLARS OF INNOVATION POLICY

Industrial policies should be horizontal. But instead of replicating or re-establishing th conditions of full (perfect) competition, they should aim at validating restraints tha allow firms to acquire market information. This implies privileging subsidies to suppor cooperation between the various actors of the innovation process through large publi programmes.

As innovation is an activity in which inter-firm coordination, even among horizonta competitors, can bring substantial benefits, the willingness of antitrust authorities tc tolerate research joint ventures and technology licensing is, in this context, fully justi fied. However, policy-makers cope with a real dilemma, one that brings us back to the very roots of political economy. While contrived arrangements help firms to invest and innovate, these arrangements may also shelter inefficiency and extract undue profits. The dilemma faced by antitrust authorities is that market imperfections are, on the one hand, necessary to convince firms to launch innovative investment and, as such, they are not something to be systematically condemned. On the other hand, these imperfec tions reveal real market failures as they hamper the viability of the innovation process. Further research is needed to understand how given policies may be preferable to others, so as to offer policy-makers some practical guidance by specifying the circumstances in which these practices may or may not be justified.

R&D and innovation policy should undoubtedly be at the core of any industrial policy for two reasons. First in the current process of globalization and accelerated techni cal change, R&D investments and innovation are obviously the means by which the growth of firms and industries will be determined. Second, for the innovation process to succeed, firms have to deal with coordination issues concerning investment decisions: their amount, their timing, their coherence with complementary investments by partners, their degree of substitution with investments by rivals.

All this information is far from being public, and industrial policy should support the diffusion of such market information. In fact, the transformation of R&D efforts into actual innovation is strongly dependent on how firms envisage their future competitive environment, that is, on how they proceed with their investments under substantial uncertainty about future market conditions (demand, complementary investments by partners and competitive investments). Success in R&D investments is therefore heavily reliant on the availability of market information, more so than on technological information. Industrial policy is the basis for a sound innovation policy.

Industrial policy must aim at favouring the emergence of market information. One way to do so is to promote coordination between agents and various types of R&D cooperation. This would provide firms with a better understanding of the different strategies of public and private agents for the future. Instead of replicating or re-establishing the conditions of full (perfect) competition, industrial policy should aim at helping firms to acquire market information. This implies privileging subsidies to support cooperation between the various actors involved in the innovation process through large public programmes. Lastly, care should be taken to define an *appropriate* geographic level, that is, a level that would avoid destructive competition among regions or countries.

NOTES

1. This taxonomy should be taken with care, given that support to a specific industry translates into indirect support to other industries (via the Leontief coefficients), and that supporting specific activities is likely to affect only those industries that are heavily engaged in these activities.
2. For an extensive review of the literature, see Garrouste and Saussier (2005).
3. Studies of individual firms have thus greatly contributed to our better understanding of intra-firm mechanisms yielding heterogeneous performances. The work of Chandler (1992), Teece and Pisano (1994) and Loasby (1998) all specify the organizational, or collective, nature of the firm. Firms are different because they adopt unique organizational arrangements, distinctive technological combinations and incentive devices.
4. This section title is inspired from Rodrik's working paper (2004) entitled 'Industrial Policy for the Twenty-first Century'.

REFERENCES

Aghion, P. and R. Griffith (2005): *Competition and Growth*, Cambridge MA: MIT Press.
Aghion, P., N. Bloom, R. Blundell, R. Griffith and P. Howitt (2003): 'Competition and Innovation: An Inverted U Relationship', NBER Working Paper No. 9269.
Aghion, P., N. Bloom, R. Blundell, R. Griffith and P. Howitt (2005): 'Competition and Innovation: An Inverted-U Relationship', *The Quarterly Journal of Economics* **120**(2): 701–28.
Aghion, P., R. Blundell, R. Griffith, P. Howitt and S. Prantl (2004): 'Entry and Productivity Growth: Evidence from Microlevel Panel Data', *Journal of the European Economic Association* **2**(2–3): 265–76.
Arrow, J.K. (1962): 'Economic Welfare and the Allocation of Resources for Invention', in R.R. Nelson (ed.), *The Rate and Direction of Inventive Activity*, Princeton, NJ: Princeton University Press/NBER.
Bartelsman, E., S. Scarpetta and F. Schivardi (2005): 'Comparative Analysis of Firm Demographics and Survival: Evidence from Micro-level Sources in OECD Countries', *Industrial and Corporate Change* **14**(3): 365–91.
Baumol, W.J. (2002): *The Free Market Innovation Machine*, Princeton: Princeton University Press.
Bellone, F., P. Musso, L. Nesta and M. Quéré (2008): 'Market Selection along the Firm Life Cycle', *Industrial and Corporate Change* **17**(4): 753–77.
Chandler, A. (1992): 'Organizational Capabilities and the Economic History of the Industrial Enterprise', *Journal of Economic Perspectives* **6**(3): 79–100.
Coase, R.H. (1937): 'The Nature of the Firm', *Economica* **4**(16): 386–405.
Cohen, W.M. and D.A. Levinthal (1989): 'Innovation and Learning: The Two Faces of R&D', *Economic Journal* **99**(397): 569–96.
Cohen, W.M. and D.A. Levinthal (1990): 'Absorptive Capacity, a New Perspective of Learning and Innovation', *Administrative Science Quarterly* **35**(1): 128–52.
Dasgupta, P. and P. David (1994): 'Toward a New Economics of Science', *Research Policy* **23**(5): 487–522.
European Commission (2005), *Implementing the Community Lisbon Programme: A Policy Framework to Strengthen EU Manufacturing – Towards a More Integrated Approach for Industrial Policy*, COM(2005) 474 final.
Garrouste, P. and S. Saussier (2005), 'Looking for a Theory of the Firm: Future Challenges', *Journal of Economic Behavior & Organization* **58**(2): 178–99.

Hagedoorn, J. (2002): 'Inter-firm R&D Partnerships: An Overview of Major Trends and Patterns Since 1960' *Research Policy* **31**(4): 477–92.

Katz, M.L. and J.A. Ordover (1990): 'R&D, Cooperation and Competition', *Brookings Papers on Economi Activity – Microeconomics*: 137–203.

Knight, F. (1921): *Risk, Uncertainty and Profit*, Boston and New York: Houghton Mifflin Company.

Kok, W. (2004): *Facing the Challenge, The Lisbon Strategy for Growth and Employment*, Report from the Hig Level Group, November, Office for Official Publications of the European Communities.

Loasby, B. (1998): 'The Organization of Capabilities', *Journal of Economic Behavior & Organization* **35**(2) 139–60.

Maystadt, P. (2006): '"Preface", An Industrial Policy in Europe: Context and Concepts', *European Investmen Bank Papers* **11**(1).

Metcalfe, J.S. (1998): *Evolutionary Economics and Creative Destruction*, London: Routledge.

Mowery, D.C. (2009): 'Plus ça Change: Industrial R&D in the Third Industrial Revolution', *Industrial and Corporate Change* **18**(1): 1–50.

Nelson, R. (1959): 'The Simple Economics of Basic Scientific Research', *Journal of Political Economy* **67**(3) 297–306.

Nelson, R. (1991): 'Why Do Firms Differ and How Does it Matter?' *Strategic Management Journal* **12**(S2) 61–74.

Nickell, S.J. (1996), 'Competition and Corporate Performance', *Journal of Political Economy* **104**(4): 724–46.

Nishimura, K.G., T. Nakajima and K. Kiyota (2005): 'Does the Natural Selection Mechanism Still Work in Severe Recessions? Examination of the Japanese Economy in the 1990s', *Journal of Economic Behavior & Organization* **58**(1): 53–78.

Patel, P. and K. Pavitt (1997): 'Technological Competencies of the World's Largest Firms: Complex and Path-dependent, But Not Much Variety', *Research Policy* **26**(2): 141–56.

Pavitt, K. (1984): 'Sectoral Patterns of Technological Change: Towards a Taxonomy and a Theory', *Research Policy* **13**(6): 343–73.

Richardson, G.B. (1960): *Information and Investment*, Oxford: Clarendon Press.

Richardson, G.B. (1972). 'The Organization of Industry', *Economic Journal* **82**(327): 883–96.

Rodrik, D. (2004): 'Industrial Policy for the Twenty-first Century', J.F.K. School of Government, Harvard University, mimeo.

Rodrik, D. (2006): 'Industrial Development: Stylized Facts and Policies', J.F.K. School of Government, Harvard University, mimeo.

Rodrik, D. (2007): 'Normalizing Industrial Policy', J.F.K. School of Government, Harvard University, mimeo.

Stephan, P. (1996), 'The Economics of Science', *Journal of Economic Literature* **34**(September), 1199–235.

Teece, D.J. and G. Pisano (1994): 'The Dynamic Capabilities of Firms: An Introduction', *Industrial and Corporate Change* **3**(3): 537–56.

36 Public policy in an entrepreneurial society
Zoltan J. Acs

36.1 INTRODUCTION

In exogenous entry, the firms exist exogenously as well as the product. Firms compete in the market on price and quantity. With endogenous entry, influenced by the work on endogenous technical change, competition is for the market, where entry can replace the incumbent. This distinction between competition *in* the market and *for* the market is a novel way of bringing insights from new growth theory to industrial organization.

Industrial organization has four models of competition. The first typology goes back to the early analysis of Augustin Cournot, whose equilibrium concept corresponds to the one that today we associate with John Nash: each firm independently chooses its strategy to maximize profit given the strategy for each of the other firms. The second typology extends these models to endogenous entry. This Marshallian equilibrium can be thought of as Nash equilibrium with free entry. The third typology of competition was introduced by Heinrich von Stackelberg where a firm has a leadership over others, that is, first mover advantage. Under Stackelberg competition, a leader can exploit its first mover advantage taking into account the reaction of its rivals. The final typology of competition completes the taxonomy of the basic market interactions combining the analysis of leadership and endogenous entry. The development of such a framework is the focus of this chapter whose whole theoretical contribution is the characterization of the Stackelberg equilibrium with endogenous entry.

The main theoretical contribution of the model is that under endogenous entry, the Stackelberg framework generates a crucial result where the leader always invests in R&D and more so than any other firm. The Stackelberg assumption with endogenous entry delivers a new rationale for the persistence of monopoly, and leads to the relevant applications of the new growth theory in the new economy.

First, markets in the 'new economy' work radically differently from markets in the 'old economy'. The point is that markets in the old economy were characterized as competition *in* the market, while in the new economy competition can be characterized as competition *for* the market. This is consistent with the accelerated use of knowledge in an economy of ideas and bits of information. This subtle point is useful because, in fact, traditional oligopoly markets in steel, autos, and tires were indeed characterized as competition in the market, at least in theoretical models. The second point is that the behavior of firms that are leaders in the new economy like Microsoft can be better understood through the concept of Stackelberg competition with endogenous entry. With endogenous entry, the incumbent firm will invest in R&D to improve quality and introduce new products.

This chapter addresses the most fundamental and important links between entrepreneurship and public policy, and identifies key salient implications for an entrepreneurial society, from the perspective of American exceptionalism. The chapter first focuses on the link between entrepreneurship and public policy in the USA and then addresses the relationship between entrepreneurship and economic development in the global economy. This chapter concludes that there is no such thing as 'entrepre neurship policy' per se, only public policy in an entrepreneurial society (Stough et al. 2002).

36.2   THE ENTREPRENEURIAL SOCIETY

The entrepreneurial society has been decades in the making. It is characterized by dramatic innovation and productivity growth. The USA – with its strong anti-statist traditions – maintained substantial control of the economy by the state until the 1970s. However, growing international competition forced the USA to rethink its position in the global marketplace (Audretsch et al., 2007). Economists regularly demonstrated how regulated systems actually create higher, not lower, costs for consumers. Thus, the USA began an economic era of reform and deregulation, which has led to the emergence of the present state: the entrepreneurial society (Acs and Audretsch, 2002)

In *The Changing Structure of the U.S. Economy* (1984), Acs first articulated that markets, new technology and entrepreneurship are at the heart of the transition from a managerial economy to an entrepreneurial society. The full flowering of this process has recently been described by David Audretsch in *The Entrepreneurial Society* (2007), and Carl Schramm in *The Entrepreneurial Imperative* (2006a). These three books push against the same thing: the managed economy.

Audretsch and Schramm describe in detail this economy of the 1950s, carefully documenting the interaction between labor, big business and government. In their chapters 'Our Lazarus Moment' and 'The Deluge', Schramm and Audretsch, respectively, describe the moment of the tipping point for the years of transition in the United States. In a remarkable way, both of these books come to similar conclusions about the nature of the new American society. However, they do not see its future in the same way. Audretsch believes that the rest of the world learned from the American model, thereby threatening its own comparative advantage. He notes:

> America had in ten years transformed itself from a self-doubting society to one of self-celebration. America had it, and the rest of the world did not. . . . Having spent considerable time in Europe and Asia observing recent efforts to create their versions of an entrepreneurial society, 'I wondered, What will the United States do when the rest of the world catches up?' (Audretsch, 2007, p. 192)

Carl Schramm has an answer for Audretsch: far from fearing an entrepreneurial trans-formation around the globe, the future of the American experiment actually depends on the rest of the world emulating it!

> For the United States to continue its global leadership, it must help the world see clearly the breadth and depth of our economic evolution. . . It is in American's interest to see our system replicated all over the world. We must believe that in flourishing entrepreneurial economies the widening distribution of wealth and the creation of new jobs will naturally help lead to the spread of democracy. . . . *It is imperative that we – everyone everywhere – go into this entrepreneurial future together.* (Schramm, 2006a, p. 176; emphasis added)

Before we go further, we should first understand what this increasingly entrepreneurial society looks like. Five distinct features are noteworthy:

- *Markets and individual firms are replacing bureaucracies.* The implicit compact between 'big labor, big business and big government' (Galbraith, 1967) that once existed in the managed economy has disappeared. Labor's share of the workforce has fallen dramatically, big business is in flux[1] and government functions across sectors are increasingly being contracted to the private sector.
- *Knowledge is more important.* Knowledge and the universities that produce new knowledge play a far more important role than in the early twentieth century. Today, the university is an integral part of the institutional infrastructure of the entrepreneurial society, where knowledge has replaced brawn as the most important input into production. As suggested by *The Economist*, The 'Knowledge Factory' has become the most important institution in generating knowledge to fuel the entrepreneurial society (*The Economist*, 1997).
- *Firm structure is more dynamic.* After World War II, large firms dominated the US economy, often in oligopolies. Turnover among these firms was minimal and new firms played a minor role. This has changed dramatically in the last several decades. New firms offering new products and services (in IT, biotechnology, and retail) and foreign entrants into traditional industries (such as automobiles and steel) have been major drivers, if not *the* main driver, of economic growth. A hallmark of entrepreneurial firms is relatively flat management structures with rapid responsiveness to market demands, whereas large firms host more bureaucratic, hierarchical management and thus, decision-making takes longer.
- *The nature and process of innovation is very different.* Led by risk-taking entrepreneurs, new firms are disproportionately responsible for 'radical' or 'breakthrough' technologies, although larger managerial firms are typically needed to refine, mass-produce and market these technologies (Baumol, 1993). The innovations that now characterize modern life – the automobile, telephone, airplane, air conditioning, personal computer, most software and Internet search engines – were all developed and commercialized by entrepreneurs. Radical innovations tend to generate faster overall growth than incremental improvements. For example, the IT revolution, which was ignited largely by entrepreneurial companies, has statistically accounted for the significant acceleration in US productivity growth over the last decade (Acs and Audretsch, 1989).
- *Equal opportunity for all.* In the managed economy, government closed the model. In other words, government was the recipient of residual income through income and inheritance taxes. In an entrepreneurial society, the final arbiter of wealth reconstitution is the third sector, or philanthropy. This uniquely American mechanism allows society to sustain itself without institutionalizing existing class structures (Acs and Phillips, 2002).

The entrepreneurial society has enjoyed remarkable economic success during the past decade, as indicated by the most important economic statistic: rate of productivity growth. Over the long run, this determines the rate of improvement in average living standards. After surging to 2.6 percent annually from 1950 to 1973, productivity growth dropped to 1.4 percent in the period from 1973 through 1995. Although this decline may seem trivial, it has enormous consequences over time: living standards double every 28 years at the earlier rate of 2.6 percent, whereas this doubling would take more than 50 years at the rate of 1.4 percent. But between 1995 and 2002, it recovered to 2.8 percent per year and through 2005 advanced at an even higher rate of a little more than 3 percent. What accounts for this good fortune so far? Conventional economic wisdom has converged on the opinion that the IT revolution – especially rapidly falling prices of computer chips and dependent products – has been critical. When measured by conventional statistics, there seems to be much truth in this (Oliner and Sichel, 2002).

This decades-long structural transition, from a managed economy to an entrepreneurial society, seems to have played an important role in the acceleration of economic growth (Acs and Armington, 2006; Audretsch et al., 2006; Baumol et al., 2007).

36.3   AMERICAN EXCEPTIONALISM

Why did this transformation occur? First, the USA has always been an entrepreneurial society, with a brief exception between the presidencies of Roosevelt and Reagan. Much of the early understanding of American exceptionalism is derived from the 'foreign traveler' literature, most notably *Democracy in America* by Alexis de Tocqueville (2000). The use of the descriptor 'American exceptionalism' refers not to the embodiment of a superior domestic culture, but to the idea that the USA is fundamentally 'qualitatively different'. Most other countries, the Soviet Union being the exception, define themselves via a common history or birthright (Lipset, 1996, pp. 18–19).

The United States is exceptional because it started from a revolutionary event, as the 'first new nation', and the first colony other than Iceland, to become independent. It has defined its raison d'être ideologically: 'It has been our fate as a nation not to have ideologies, but to be one' (Lipset, 1996). The American creed can be described in five terms: liberty, egalitarianism, individualism, populism and laissez-faire. A modern translation can be summarized in terms of action and behavior, as entrepreneurship, philanthropy, and the creation of opportunity. In other words, the goal is not to reproduce the class structure but to prevent this from happening.

In this context, egalitarianism implies equality of opportunity but not equality of outcomes. This grew from the absence of feudal structures – as such, class structures and hierarchy were less important than in more aristocratic societies. Religious participation has been voluntary, and it has been reinforced by sociopolitical individualism and not the state. According to John Hancock, a party to the Declaration of Independence: 'The more people who own little businesses of their own, the safer our country will be, for the people who have a stake in their country and their community are its best citizens'.

Americans have traditionally eschewed statism; in fact, the USA Constitution does not provide positive rights, in stark contrast to many other democracies (Lipset, 1996, p. 22). To some extent, American exceptionalism is 'the absence of significant socialist movement', as evidenced by less union participation than in other countries (ibid., p. 23).

The focus on individualism and a weak state sets American public policy apart from the polities of other developed countries. Exceptional American societal aspects are class structure and religious system. In the former, an insistence on meritocracy results in a more productive climate. Coupled with a continued emphasis on equality of opportunity, the USA has provided strong motivation for individual success and mobility (ibid., p. 54):

> Americans have never accepted the idea of rigid hereditary classes. . . Hard work, ambition, education, and ability have been regarded as more important for succeeding in life than social background. Recent opinion poll results indicate that almost three quarters of Americans believe they have a good chance of improving their standard of living, while only two fifths of Europeans display this level of optimism.

The religious system is that of the Protestant sect – the 'Protestants of Protestantism, the Dissenters of Dissent' – the epitome of bourgeois values (ibid., p. 60). 'Americans are utopian moralists who press hard to institutionalize virtue, to destroy evil people, and eliminate wicked institutions and practices' (ibid., p. 63). The Protestant sense of personal responsibility has led the intensely committed to follow their consciences, as reflected by those who have supported and opposed wars. Further, the underlying support for private social coping mechanisms, such as philanthropy, is rooted in individualistic philosophy and suspicion of government (ibid., p. 68).

The New Deal significantly altered one fundamental aspect of the American creed. The rise in state power during the postwar period realigned the American system closer to European values, pushing the country towards regulation rather than a market economy. This had consequences far beyond those intended, or expected, and it led to a revolution in the 1960s.

36.4   BACK TO THE FUTURE

Why did this change come about? The 1960s in the USA was a period of social transformation and a return to roots: liberty, egalitarianism, individualism, populism and laissez-faire. Although this decade is often viewed as a mixed blessing by those that lived it, one thing is certain: the rules had changed! Perhaps the main contribution of the 1960s' generation was the tearing down of many institutions that were the cornerstone of the managed economy, thus freeing the way for entrepreneurs – who would ultimately save the American economy in the 1990s. Opportunities at the end of the decade were far more vast and numerous than at its start. Blacks and whites could attend the same school, sit on the same bus and eat at the same restaurant. It became possible for women to pursue education and careers in nearly all professions. If this period did not completely undo the New Deal, it altered its direction over the next two decades.

The generation of the 1960s seemed to have had consistent difficulties adjusting and adapting to everything that came after. This generation knew what it did not want, but was far less certain about what it wanted. According to Audretsch (2007, pp. 15–16):

> If the 1950s produced the organization man, the 1960s produced the young men and women who were the organization man's antitheses. Young people certainly did not feel compelled to conform or fit in – at least not with the norms, modes, and rules inherited from the 1950s. While it was not the end of the organization man, it was the beginning of something else, something more important. . . . Americans were liberated and freed from the constraining rigidities that had enabled the 1950s managed economy to thrive in the first place. By tearing down a

number of rules, regulations, habits and traditions – the values and institutions of the managed economy – the 1960s opened up the possibility for the next generation to not only deviate from norms but to deviate in such a way as to create new values, create new products and ultimately generate entire new industries like software, biotechnology. The sameness of the managed economy – the conformity, monotony, rigidity, and homogeneity – had been replaced by non-conformity, autonomy, creativity, and self-reliance.

In other words, a return to American exceptionalism!

In *The Vantage Point* (1971), the late President Johnson outlines the legislative accomplishments of his service with respect to civil rights, poverty, healthcare, and global challenges. Following the rewriting of social rules, changes in institutions of the managed economy were paramount. Several federal policy initiatives during Democratic and Republican administrations over the past three decades have supported these changes. They have allowed the transition from a managerial economy to the entrepreneurial society so that Americans could invent the future. These included among others (Le, 2008):

- *Reducing institutional barriers to entry.* The removal of legal barriers to entry and price controls in key industries – specifically transportation and communications.
- *Awareness and action against excessive regulation.* Successive executive orders required executive branch agencies to at least study the costs and benefits of introducing new regulations prior to adoption. Agencies were also required to tailor regulations to the 'size and the resources of the affected business', with special flexibility for small businesses seeking to raise capital.
- *Tax system enhancements.* Various reforms had the effect of enhancing rewards from entrepreneurship, including cuts in the capital gains tax rate (from 49 percent prior to 1977 to a current rate of 15 percent) and reductions in the top individual marginal tax rate (from 70 percent prior to 1981 to a current rate of approximately 38 percent).
- *Financial market reforms.* Legal changes have allowed pension funds to finance the formation and growth of new firms, by investing in venture capital partnerships.
- *Improving access to knowledge and innovation.* Federal legislation targeted accelerating the commercialization of innovations in universities and in small business. In universities, this was done through the Bayh-Dole Act of 1980, which granted exclusive control over federally funded inventions; in small business, this was done through the Small Business Innovation Development Act of 1982, which earmarked 1.25 percent of federal R&D funds for these companies.

By the mid-1980s, the entrepreneurial spirit would rise once more, to challenge bureaucratic hegemony, thereby catalyzing the end of the managed economy. Kirchhoff (1994) demonstrates that entry is a necessary condition for economic development, if long-run market concentration and declining innovation rates are to be avoided. The re-emergence of entrepreneurship in the United States during the 1980s – and the positive channeling of it – are a triumph of the system. Michael Milken made much of the financial investment in American information infrastructure during the 1980s. According to the *Wall Street Journal* (2 March, 1993) he was one of the supreme investors in the history of finance, and invested $21 billion in the information industry. His largest conributions were to MCI, Tele-Communications Inc., McGraw Cellular Communications nc., Turner Broadcasting, Time Warner Inc. and Metromedia Broadcasting. These ompanies could likely never have raised comparable amounts from other sources of inance, as they were virtually devoid of conventional collateral. The original investment of $10 billion in these companies had a market value of $62 billion in 1993. This web of glass and light is now an essential resource in the information economy, and a key comparative advantage of the American economy. A second wave of entrepreneurial companies, financed in part by venture capital, is in the process of completing the infrastructure for the information age: America Online, Cisco Systems, Amazon.com, Netscape, and Yahoo.

36.5   PUBLIC POLICY IN THE ENTREPRENEURIAL SOCIETY

This introduction is written from the perspective of the US economy, which is generally accepted as the leading entrepreneurial society in the world. This provides an excellent background against which we may evaluate policy in other countries, both developed and developing. We are able to take an integrated approach to understanding how other countries fit into this framework (Kauffman Foundation, 2006), across multiple levels of analysis ranging from the individual to the macroeconomy.

36.5.1   Policies Relating to the Global Economy

It has become a cliché to make reference to a global economy, but it is true nonetheless. As a result, entrepreneurs that ignore the global market do so at their peril when designing and implementing business plans. Likewise, the implication for policy-makers is clear: in order to promote entrepreneurship, they must think globally rather than locally or even nationally (Schramm, 2004). This manifests in at least the following major policy arenas: trade, immigration, and technology:

- *Trade policy*. Capitalist economies rest on a fundamental principle: the freedom of exchange. This allows individuals and firms to contract with one another, thereby allowing economies to realize benefits from specialization, economies of scale and comparative advantage. Together, this maximizes economic welfare – and when exchange moves across countries, benefits are maximized. In essence, this is the classic case for free trade. Entrepreneurs and established firms alike cannot succeed in a global environment without the ability to move quickly and contract for the lowest-cost and highest-quality inputs, wherever they may be found. They also need to sell to purchasers, wherever they may be located. This cannot be possible if governments maintain artificial barriers to restrict the movement of goods, services, capital, and ideas across borders (Brainard et al., 2005).
- *Immigration policy*. In the wake of 9/11, legal immigration in the USA has been tightened in the name of national security. More recently, Congressional proposals to criminalize and deport millions of illegal immigrants have generated vigorous debate and mass protests throughout the nation. An entrepreneurial perspective implies several policy approaches with respect to immigration. The implication for

legal immigration policy is clear: emphasize educational background of potential immigrants, but maintain deference to the needs of national security (i.e., prevent the entry of individuals with criminal backgrounds or associations and activities that pose a real threat). Future advances require the commercialization of continued improvements in technology. In the past, immigrants have made huge contributions and can continue to do so, if policies permit.

- *Access to foreign technology*. One of the worst economic mistakes any business or country can make is to adopt the 'not invented here' syndrome: refusal to embrace something developed and used elsewhere. Certainly, this is not the case for many countries that have licensed or used American technology – and in the process, also improved economic welfare. In some cases, this has occurred at a faster pace, though from a lower starting level, than in the USA. Likewise, the USA has benefited from investment by foreign companies – especially in manufacturing – that have enabled technology transfer and introduced new products in the domestic market. For example, where would the American manufacturing sector be without 'just-in-time' production systems or 'quality circles' pioneered in Japan? The USA, and its entrepreneurs, could do even better if government took an active role in facilitating awareness of foreign technologies (Brezneitz, 2007).

36.5.2   Taking Entrepreneurship into Account in Setting National Policies

Policy-makers constantly confront questions of importance to the national economy, and many factors affect how decisions are made. Given a presumptive causal link between long-term economic growth and entrepreneurial activity, it behooves policy-makers to consider the impact of their decisions on entrepreneurship. There are several essential points in this regard: education policy, science and technology policy, health policy and litigation and regulation:

- *Education policy*. Although not a guarantee of success, a strong educational system (primary, secondary, tertiary, and above) is a clear prerequisite for continued economic growth. Assuming that the right incentives are in place to reward innovation: the greater the proportion of highly educated people, the more likely it is that some will generate and commercialize breakthroughs. These will then generate growth in incomes and living standards for all residents, and for many around the world as well. Even innovations by a relative few require many skilled workers to refine, produce, market, and distribute their resulting products and services. The USA owes much of its economic success to its enviable record in providing universal primary and secondary education to citizens. It is possible that in the two models of a managed economy versus an entrepreneurial society, the optimal educational systems may differ in structure, character, and content.
- *Science and technology policy*. Productivity improvements come from technical change, which requires both the discovery of new ideas and commercialization by entrepreneurs and existing firms. In turn, new ideas result from research and development, which span the range from basic research (such as the discovery of new scientific laws or improvements in understanding basic science) to development activities (the embodiment of new ideas in products, services or production

techniques). It is now well understood that because the benefits of basic research cannot be fully captured by those who pursue it, that society is better off if government funds it and either pursues it directly, or contracts it to universities and private sector research organizations.

- *Health policy.* Regardless of the mechanism of healthcare provision, health policy in an entrepreneurial society should be directed at improving individual health in order to free people to pursue their interests professionally. It cannot create 'job-lock' or prohibitive selection for small, entrepreneurial ventures. Instead, it must provide optimal choice for consumers (i.e., entrepreneurs), to ensure adequate protection at reasonable cost and be supremely flexible.
- *Litigation and regulation.* It is important not only for government to facilitate the formation of new businesses but also to encourage their growth and expansion. At the very least, this should not be penalized. In this respect, government across levels should be committed to analyzing the costs and benefits of new regulations before adopting them. Where possible, there should be allowances for streamlining procedures for new businesses. Particular attention should be paid to regulations that ultimately deter entry by new businesses, as they typically do not have the resources or capability for compliance as do more mature firms. At the same time, existing regulatory regimes bear examination and some may need modification (the Sarbanes-Oxley Act is a prime example). Litigation can have the same effect as regulation, resulting in verdicts that set norms for behavior by firms and individuals in specific industries or across many, or all, sectors of the economy. This allows for precedent to be established in a specific context and place, but to apply across the board elsewhere.

36.5.3   Regional Policies to Promote Entrepreneurship

As Thomas P. O'Neill Sr. noted to his son and budding politico (O'Neill and Novak, 1987): 'All politics is local'. So, too, all entrepreneurship is local. If successful, individuals expand into other locations. Still, all new firms must start somewhere, even if business is conducted largely or exclusively on the Internet. Policy-makers likewise are increasingly recognizing entrepreneurship as the key to building and sustaining economic growth. Policy has historically focused on attracting existing firms *from somewhere else*, either to relocate or build new facilities in a particular area. Such 'smokestack chasing' has degenerated into what is essentially a zero-sum game for the national economy. When one city or state successfully attracts firms away from other locations through tax breaks or other inducements, an alternate city or state loses that activity. However, zero-sum arguments assume away an alternate condition: the actual decision to establish a new firm or plant. Simply put, a zero-sum game only exists *after* the decision to establish has been made. In an entrepreneurial society, policy considers that this alternative hypothesis is not a foregone conclusion – thus, the idea of economic development centered around entrepreneurship is a fundamentally different approach. The formation and growth of new firms, regardless of location, is clearly a positive-sum game for the locality and more importantly, for the nation as a whole.

A brief look at various 'high-tech' clusters around the country – from Silicon Valley, to Austin, Research Triangle Park (North Carolina), San Diego, Boise, Denver, Madison,

Route 128 around Boston, Northern Virginia, to name just a few – demonstrates the overall positive effects of development around entrepreneurship. The United State economy has benefited, as a whole, from the innovative products and services that have emerged from these clusters. The same is true for other countries. High-tech and high-growth clusters in India, China, Taiwan, Ireland, and Israel, for example, are powering economic growth far beyond these countries (Brezneitz, 2007). Some clusters host firms that have become essential within worldwide supply chains. Others are becoming leaders in new product and services development. Still others are doing both (Karlsson et al. 2005).

36.5.4   Policies that Primarily Affect Entrepreneurs

Any society interested in encouraging entrepreneurship must make it relatively easy to transition from the drawing board to the marketplace, and rewarding enough so success results in repetition. Entrepreneurs that repeat the process make multiple contributions to the market, thereby increasing consumer welfare. For the most part, the USA has developed institutions over time to allow this: the legal system protects contracts and property (including intellectual property), state and local registration systems facilitate business formation, the tax system has evolved towards lower marginal tax rates and the financial system generally favors the formation and growth of new ventures (Wennekers et al., 2005).

There are policies directed at entrepreneurs themselves within any entrepreneurial framework. These affect individual decisions to 'take a job or make a job' – that is, to work for someone else or make the riskier but potentially more profitable choice and launch an enterprise. These policies include: easing business formation, easier access to finance, protection of intellectual property and tax policy:

- *Easing business formation.* Entrepreneurs cannot be expected to 'take the plunge' unless it is easy and inexpensive to do so. The US government has done this well at all levels, a judgment confirmed by the World Bank (2007). Still, there is room for improvement, particularly at the state and local levels, where businesses actually register and must acquire various permits. For example, it is possible to make it easier for new and existing firms to obtain and submit forms on the Internet. This is likely to be cheaper and more quickly accomplished than building new (or retrofitting existing) physical facilities, such as 'one-stop shops'. Some cities have already done this, and other cities and states may wish to consider this in conjunction with an active web-based initiative (Klapper et al., 2006).
- *Ensuring access to finance.* Virtually all-new ventures require some initial amount of capital and often more as they grow. The USA has created a financial system conducive to business formation and growth. The 'democratization' of credit markets, whether through credit card or mortgage lending, has supported many entrepreneurs without access to social networks of wealth (Blanchflower et al., 2003). In the past several decades, a vibrant venture capital industry has developed to fund the relatively small but vital number of technologically sophisticated or capital-intensive start-ups. In recent years, 'angel investors' – wealthy individuals or groups of such individuals – have become an increasingly important source of

early-stage equity capital as well. By some accounts, angel investors may now be more important than venture capital, especially after the 'Internet stock bubble' burst of 2000. As for debt finance, banks and finance companies have been the traditional sources of funds. However, both types of lenders face increasingly stiff competition from securities markets, which are financing a growing share of debt from larger entrepreneurial firms that have gone public.

- *Appropriate protection of intellectual property.* One of the ways entrepreneurial economies motivate people to become entrepreneurs is by promising legal protection for their ideas. This is accomplished with intellectual property laws such as patents, copyrights, and trademarks. There is a complicated tradeoff involved when providing exclusive protection to inventors or creators (Merrill et al., 2004). If protection is granted for too long or is excessively easy to obtain, then government essentially permits monopolies and public returns are limited. On the other hand, if protection of intellectual property is too weak, or if legal protections can be easily circumvented through technological means, then inventors and creators may have insufficient incentives to bring their ideas to market.
- *Tax policy.* Rewards for entrepreneurial activity, as for any other economic activity, are reduced by taxes on earnings. At the same time, tax revenues fund public goods, such as physical and legal infrastructure, education, defense and crime detection, punishment and prevention. Without public goods, entrepreneurs (and all citizens) would be unable to pursue their endeavors. A central challenge for policy across levels of government is to undertake measures whose benefits outweigh costs, and to implement and fund them to least distort economic activity (Gentry and Hubbard, 2004). Taxes are – and should be – determined with more than just entrepreneurship in mind. Considerations of revenue adequacy, simplicity, and fairness play an important role.

36.5.5 Policies that Primarily Affect Society

The final facet of public policy is the issues of social equity and justice. It is well known that these issues are at the heart of survival for any society (Desai and Acs, 2008). The equity issue has two sides. One is equal opportunity participation in the entrepreneurial process: women, minorities, the elderly and so on. The second element is equity of outcome with respect to wealth creation. This is the core of legitimacy. The fundamental issue here is the sustainability of an entrepreneurial society, which by nature does not reward citizens equally, and the eventual feedback of wealth into society. Both aspects of equality – equality of access and equality of outcome – can be addressed through philanthropy, the process by which people and institutions give both their wealth and time freely (Schramm, 2006b).

At the heart of American exceptionalism is the idea that rigid social classes should be avoided. One way to achieve this is to ensure the reconstitution of wealth: 'Philanthropy has been one of the major aspects of, and keys to, American social and cultural development' (Curti, 1957, p. 353). To this we add that philanthropy has also been crucial in economic development. Entrepreneurship and philanthropy together are a potent force that explains the continued dominance of the US economy. In an entrepreneurial society, much new wealth created is given back to the community to build institutions that have a positive feedback on future economic development. This has sustained American capitalism over three centuries (Acs and Phillips, 2002). Rather then constraining the rich through taxes, we should allow the rich to campaign for social change through the creation of opportunity. If we stifle opportunities for wealthy individuals to give back their wealth we will impede the future creation of wealth, which has far greater consequence for an entrepreneurial society (*The Economist*, 23 July, 2006).

36.6　MOVING TO AN ENTREPRENEURIAL SOCIETY

An entrepreneurial society is different from the managed economy because of the way entrepreneurs facilitate knowledge spillovers (Acs et al., 2009). In the managed economy, organizations existed permanently and engaged knowledge creation through investment in research and development. However, as Arrow (1962) pointed out, investment in knowledge creation is not straightforward. Organizational inertia may result in new ideas not being commercialized by the incumbent firm. This organizational rigidity serves as a knowledge filter preventing the commercialization of knowledge. The knowledge filter serves to impede the spillover and commercialization of knowledge.

Entrepreneurship can contribute to economic growth by serving as a mechanism to penetrate the knowledge filter. It is a virtual consensus that entrepreneurship revolves around the recognition of opportunities along with a cognitive decision to exploit them by starting a new firm. Thus, according to the knowledge spillover theory of entrepreneurship, entrepreneurship permeates the knowledge filter by serving as a conduit for knowledge spillovers (Braunerhjelm et al., 2010). Entrepreneurship is the missing link for economic growth because it allows for the commercialization of ideas that would otherwise remain untapped, thereby improving the welfare of consumers.

This leads to the question: what is good public policy in an entrepreneurial society? An emerging policy approach focuses on enabling the creation and commercialization of knowledge. This differs from small business policy that tried to alleviate the cost disadvantage of small firms due to scale economies. Public policy in the entrepreneurial society has a much broader focus, and comprises measures intended to directly influence the level of entrepreneurial activity in a country or region, and the consequences of that action for society. A string of initiatives in the 1990s started to place attention on individuals instead of firms. However, many of these approaches treated 'SME policy' and 'entrepreneurship policy' as one and same. They are essentially different, as SME policy focuses on bringing disadvantaged individuals into the economic mainstream (Storey, 2003). Entrepreneurship instead leverages the 'best and the brightest'.

In fact, policy approaches have been so misaligned that they have, thus far, missed the essential point: that there is no such thing as 'entrepreneurship policy' per se. There is only public *policy in an entrepreneurial society*. Acs and Armington (2006, Chapter 7) lay out, for the first time, a policy formulation for an entrepreneurial society and the chapters in this book deconstruct multiple applications and levels of analysis. The key question is: how can policy-makers maintain and ideally accelerate the continued transition toward a more entrepreneurial society? What policies affect firm formation?

atter (2008) constructed a simulation model where various policies were grouped into our categories: tendency to effect entrepreneurial action, effect on quality of human apital, effect on availability of financial capital, and effect on stream of innovations or ew routines. Policies that promote firm formation are the quality of human capital and novations.

What about developing countries? Traditional development strategies of import ubstitution and export promotion have been largely unsuccessful in lesser-developed ountries, primarily because they leave no room for the entrepreneur (Virgill, 2008). Development theory and strategy has led to misguided and often failed attempts. This terature on import substitution and export promotion offers no evidence on the relvance of the entrepreneur. Roger Stough (2008) provides a perspective on why entrereneurship has gained importance in developing countries in recent years. He offers nsight into why entrepreneurship policy and programs have become popular development tools, both in developed and developing economies. This growing emphasis brings with it the basic strategic question of how entrepreneurship can be applied as a tool to romote growth and development at the regional level, within a development framevork. Further, he recognizes the dramatic relevance of entrepreneurship in social, political, and economic realms. This is supported by the enormous growth of scholarly and ntellectual interest in entrepreneurship

ACKNOWLEDGMENTS

We wish to thank Scott Jackson for valuable research assistance and Sameeksha Desai for editorial assistance at various stages of this manuscript. We would also like to thank our students in the Entrepreneurship and Public Policy Seminar at George Mason University.

NOTE

1. The rankings of leading firms in the United States are constantly changing.

REFERENCES

Acs, Z.J. (1984), *The Changing Structure of the U.S. Economy*, New York: Praeger.
Acs, Z.J. and C. Armington (2006), *Entrepreneurship, Geography and American Economic Growth*, Cambridge: Cambridge University Press.
Acs, Z.J. and D.B. Audretsch (1989), 'Innovation in Large and Small Firms: An Empirical Analysis', *The American Economic Review* **78**(4), 678–89.
Acs, Z.J. and D.B. Audretsch (2002), 'The Emergence of the Entrepreneurial Society', Stockholm: Swedish Foundation for Small Business Research.
Acs, Z.J. and R.J. Phillips (2002), 'Entrepreneurship and Philanthropy in American Capitalism', *Small Business Economics* **19**(3), 189–204.
Acs, Z.J., D.B. Audretsch, P. Braunerhjelm and B. Carlsson (2009), 'The Knowledge Spillover Theory of Entrepreneurship', *Small Business Economics* **32**(1), 15–30.
Arrow, K. (1962), 'Economic Welfare and the Allocation of Resources for Invention', in R.R. Nelson (ed.), *The Rate and Direction of Inventive Activity*, Princeton, NJ: Princeton University Press, pp. 609–26.

Audretsch, D.B. (2007), *The Entrepreneurial Society*, Oxford: Oxford University Press.
Audretsch, D.B., I. Grilo and R.A. Thurik (2007), *Handbook of Research on Entrepreneurship Polic* Cheltenham, UK and Northampton, MA, USA: Edward Elgar.
Audretsch, D.B., M.C. Keilbach and E.E. Lehmann (2006), *Entrepreneurship and Economic Growth*, Ne York: Oxford University Press.
Baumol, W.J. (1993), *The Free Market Innovation Machine*, Princeton, NJ: Princeton University Press.
Baumol, W.J., R.E. Litan and C.J. Schramm (2007), *Good Capitalism, Bad Capitalism*, New Haven, CT: Ya University Press.
Blanchflower, D., P. Levine and D. Zimmerman (2003), 'Discrimination in the Small Business Credit Market *Review of Economics and Statistics* **85**(4), 930–43.
Brainard, L., R.E. Litan and N. Warren (2005), 'Insuring America's Workers in a New Era of Off Shoring *Policy Brief No. 143*, Washington, DC: The Brookings Institution.
Braunerhjelm, P., Z.J. Acs, D.B. Audretsch and B. Carlsson (2010), 'The Missing Link: The Knowledge Filte and Entrepreneurship in Endogenous Growth', *Small Business Economics* **34**(2), 105–25.
Brezneitz, D. (2007), *Innovation and the State*, New Haven, CT: Yale University Press.
Curti, M. (1957), 'The History of American Philanthropy as a Field of Research', *The American Historica Review* **62**(2), 352–63.
Desai, S. and Z. Acs (2008), 'Democratic Capitalism and Philanthropy in a Global Economy', Chapter 11 i Z.J. Acs and R.R. Stough, *Public Policy in an Entrepreneurial Economy*, New York: Springer.
De Tocqueville, A. (2000), *Democracy in America*, Chicago: University of Chicago Press.
Galbraith, J.K. (1967), *The New Industrial State*, New York: New American Library.
Gentry, W.M. and R.G. Hubbard (2004), 'Success Taxes, Entrepreneurial Activity and Innovation', NBEI Working Paper No. 10551, Cambridge, MA: National Bureau of Economic Research.
Johnson, Lyndon, Bains (1971), *The Vantage Point: Perspectives of the Presidency 1963–1969*, New York Holt, Rinehart and Winston.
Karlsson, C., B. Johansson and R.R. Stough (eds) (2005), *Industrial Clusters and Interfirm Networks* Cheltenham, UK and Northampton, MA, USA: Edward Elgar.
Kauffman Foundation (2006), 'On the Road to an Entrepreneurial Economy: A Research and Policy Guide' Kansas City, MO: Kauffman Foundation.
Kirchhoff, B. (1994), *Entrepreneurship and Dynamic Capitalism*, New York: Praeger.
Klapper, L, L. Laeven and R. Rajan (2006), 'Entry Regulation as a Barrier to Entrepreneurship', *Journal o Financial Economics* **82**(3), 591–62.
Le, L. (2008), 'Entrepreneurship and Small Business Policies Under the Presidential Administrations o Presidents Carter, Regan, Bush and Clinton', Chapter 2 in Z.J. Acs and R.R. Stough, *Public Polic) in an Entrepreneurial Economy: Creating the Conditions for Business Growth* (International Studies ir Entrepreneurship), New York: Springer.
Lipset, S.M. (1996), *American Exceptionalism: A Double-edged Sword*, New York: W.W. Norton and Company.
Merrill, S.A., R.C. Levin and M.M. Meyers (eds) (2004), *A Patent System for the 21st Century*, Washington, DC: The National Academies Press.
Oliner, S.D. and D.E. Sichel (2002), 'Information Technology and Productivity: Where Are We Now and Where Are We Going?' *Federal Reserve Bank of Atlanta Economic Review* **Q3**: 15–44.
O'Neill, T.P. and W. Novak (1987), *Man of the House: The Life and Political Memoirs of Speaker Tip O'Neill*, New York: Random House.
Schramm, C.J. (2004), 'Building Entrepreneurial Economies', *Foreign Affairs* **83**(4): 104–15.
Schramm, C.J. (2006a), *The Entrepreneurial Imperative*, New York: Collins.
Schramm, C.J. (2006b), 'Law Outside the Market: The Social Utility of the Private Foundation', *Harvard Journal of Law & Public Policy* **30**(1), 356–415.
Storey, D.J. (2003), 'Entrepreneurship, Small and Medium Sized Enterprises and Public Policies', in D.B. Audretsch and Z.J. Acs (eds), *Handbook of Entrepreneurship Research*, Boston/Dordrecht: Kluwer Academic Publishers, pp. 476–511.
Stough, R. (2008), 'The Entrepreneurship and Development Nexus', Chapter 10 in Z.J. Acs and R.R. Stough, *Public Policy in an Entrepreneurial Economy: Creating the Conditions for Business Growth* (International Studies in Entrepreneurship), New York: Springer.
Stough, R.R., R. Kulkarni and J. Paelinck (2002), 'ICT and Knowledge Challenges for Entrepreneurs in Regional Economic Development', in Z.J. Acs, H.L.F. De Groot and P. Nijkamp (eds), *The Emergence of the Knowledge Economy: A Regional Perspective*, Heidelberg: Springer.
Sutter, R. (2008), 'Simulating the Impact of Policy on Entrepreneurship', Chapter 7 in Z.J. Acs and R.R. Stough, *Public Policy in an Entrepreneurial Economy: Creating the Conditions for Business Growth* (International Studies in Entrepreneurship), New York: Springer.
The Economist (1997), 'The Knowledge Factory', 4 October, 1–22.

The Economist (2006), 'The Business of Giving', 23 July, 1–16.

Virgill, N. (2008), 'Putting the Entrepreneur Back into Development and Foreign Policy', Chapter 8 in Z.J. Acs and R.R. Stough, *Public Policy in an Entrepreneurial Economy: Creating the Conditions for Business Growth* (International Studies in Entrepreneurship), New York: Springer.

Wennekers, A.R.M., A.J. van Stel, A.R. Thurik and P.D. Reynolds (2005), 'Nascent Entrepreneurship and the Level of Economic Development', *Small Business Economics* **24**(3), 293–309.

World Bank (2007), *Doing Business 2007 – How to Reform*, Washington, DC: The World Bank.

37 The regulated firm in liberalized network industries

Aad Correljé, John Groenewegen and Jan Jaap Bouma

37.1 LIBERALIZATION, PRIVATIZATION AND (DE)REGULATION

In this chapter we discuss the firm as a 'public utility': firms operating in sectors like telecoms, electricity and public transport that have a specific function to fulfil. Firms in such network industries are controlled by the state, because public values are involved. Over the past decades, many countries liberalized network industries like telecoms, energy, public transport and drinking water. The services in these sectors were traditionally provided by vertically integrated public utilities taking care of the production, transmission, distribution and selling in one hierarchical organization. In Europe, Asia and Latin America, these public utilities were publicly owned and controlled. Elsewhere, like in the USA, they were privately owned but regulated and controlled by specific commissions or governmental agencies. Next to reasons of market failure, the argument of public values is also important to understand the control of government over network industries. Those values involve issues of safety, security of supply, acceptable prices for specific types of users, objectives of local and sectoral development, the supply of jobs, and – more recently – sustainability and environmental protection. The provision of drinking water is sometimes considered as being part of human rights.

Many of the network industries have been liberalized, deregulated, and firms are often privatized. Liberalization means that the sector is opened up to new entrants, which can compete with the incumbent firm and each other. The idea behind liberalization is to create a competitive market to provide 'high-power' incentives to the firms to minimize production and transaction costs, as well as stimulate firms to invest in innovations. Consumers can choose between a number of suppliers and the one with the best price and quality will survive. In network-based industries liberalization often implied unbundling: a separation of the potentially competitive parts of the industry from the natural monopoly networks.

Privatization has a similar efficiency objective in transferring the ownership from public to private shareholders, to force management to improve on efficiency and if the market is functioning well, the benefits will be transferred to the consumers. Indicators of increased short-term efficiency include, for example, the lowering of consumer prices, whereas innovations would show long-term efficiency (Megginson and Netter, 2001).

Deregulation is often discussed in relation to liberalization and privatization. It aims at a reduction of laws, rules and regulations that constrain consumers and producers in their behaviour while increasing the costs of economic transactions. The idea is that deregulation liberalizes the actors from bureaucratic constraints and consequently stimulates innovative competitive behaviour. However, when the goods and services are

onsidered to provide 'public value', government agencies regulate the firms, monitor
he performance and intervene when the societal objectives are not met. So, one cannot
xpect that deregulation automatically emerges as a by-product of liberalization. On
he contrary, other types of regulation are needed that can be very strict and that can
ecome rather complicated and costly for all actors involved. In section 37.2 we present
our options for governments to liberalize, privatize and deregulate network industries.
n section 37.3 we discuss some regulatory instruments with special attention to the issue
f unbundling, that is, the policy of governments to separate the natural monopoly part
f the firms from the competitive parts.

In the literature, the relationship between the regulator and the regulated firm is often
characterized as a principal–agent relationship. When the principal and agent have dif-
erent objectives and an information asymmetry exists, it can be expected that parties
want to safeguard themselves against opportunistic behaviour of governments and of
so-called third parties including firms (Spiller, 2009). The fourth section is devoted to the
issue of regulatory risk and regulatory capture.

We will analyse the regulated firm being embedded in an institutional setting of informal and formal institutions. The firm is constrained and enabled by the informal values
and norms of the society in which it operates. A network firm embedded in an individualistic value system like that of the USA (Hofstede, 2001) receives very different incentives
from its environment than a firm in a collectivistic value system like that of the so-called
Rhineland countries in Europe (Albert, 1992). The formal institutions of property rights,
competition laws and specific directives and regulations reflect the informal institutions
(North, 1990; Williamson, 1998).

In our system approach firms are not only constrained and enabled by institutions,
they are able to influence and manipulate the institutions as well. The degree to which
this is possible depends on the nature of the institutions, as informal ones are less flexible
than the formal ones. It also depends on the 'discretionary power' of the firms, which is
associated with the market structure and more generally with their bargaining power.

37.2   HOW TO LIBERALIZE

Throughout the 1990s, the contours of a framework emerged for the restructuring of
network industries in different types of utility sectors, in which liberalization, privatization and regulation were connected. On the basis of a number of sector-specific
characteristics, the framework provides options for restructuring and suggests adequate
forms of regulation. During 'the age of privatization', it had appeared that simply
turning public monopolies into private ones did not solve much (Armstrong et al., 1999;
Newberry, 1999).[1] The main issue became the introduction of competition to discipline
the industry, supported by an adequate regulatory regime. Regarding privatization, the
issue became the right way to attract private capital into the industry and to determine
under what conditions private actors could play an effective and efficient role (Baldwin
and Cave, 1999).

This framework gained a fair degree of acceptance in the USA (Kahn, 1998; Joskow,
2007), in the World Bank and IMF (Klein, 1998, 1999), in the UK (Armstrong et al.,
1999) and later on in the EU and its member-states (Coen and Doyle, 2000; Coen and

Héritier, 2005), as well as elsewhere in the world (Dinar, 2000; Crew and Kleindorfer 2002; Crew and Parker, 2005). The framework proposes four options to introduce competition in network industries: (1) competition between different network systems providing substitute utility services; (2) competition over the existing network system by a number of suppliers; (3) competition for the market, through competitive bidding; and (4) corporatization and benchmarking of public enterprises, in markets that cannot be liberalized.

The relevant option to introduce competition should be selected through an evaluation of the economic characteristics of the market, like the size, the maturity and the speed of innovation, as well as the technical features of the supply system (Klein, 1998, 1999; Joskow, 2007). The nature of the networks is particularly important, involving the presence of assets with large sunk costs and network externalities, as well as the presence of significant economies of scale and scope. Moreover, notions of public values and social acceptability are involved. These notions may concern the universal service provision, the protection of vulnerable customers, security and quality of supply, and environmental, safety and health issues. A further important aspect is the expected effectiveness and costs of implementing the ex ante restructuring and of overseeing, monitoring and controlling the market behaviour ex post. A final, but crucial, consideration is the willingness of private actors to contract with and to invest in a 'liberalized' utility sector, which could be a problem when there is too much uncertainty about (future) government regulation.

37.2.1   Option 1: Competition Between Different Network Systems

This option is relevant for restructuring in the case that the services provided by different networks are (near) substitutes and no natural monopoly characteristics and substantial sunk costs characterize the industries. Moreover, the size of the market should provide sufficient room for a number of competing systems, without a significant loss of scale efficiency. Examples are in freight transport on the road as well as in shipping, in non-urban long-distance bus lines, in segments of the postal market and in garbage collection and processing. Also in the telecoms sector a variety of competing firms provide fixed and mobile telephony and Internet and cable connections as substitute services.

In such industries, the preferable option is to allow competition for the retail consumers between different independent suppliers of similar utility services, making use of their own networks and supply systems. This implies that the former franchise monopoly of the incumbent has to be ended; its retail clients should be free to choose their supplier. To facilitate the entry of new providers into the market, it will be necessary to remove licensing restrictions, to reduce switching costs for customers and to provide access to essential inputs. Depending on the number of new entrants, the incumbent firm can be allowed to continue to provide its service, or it can for the sake of competition be horizontally split up into a number of firms. These 'descendants' may be either privatized, or not. In the latter case it is considered more efficient (lower transaction costs) to safeguard specific public values when the firms are in the hands of public owners. So, eventually, the retail customer of the service is able to choose between a number of alternative suppliers, on the basis of their performance in terms of tariffs, quality and conditions of service.

The feasibility of this approach not only depends on the availability of substitutes provided by different industries, but also on technological development and innovation, allowing for new competing substitutes for traditional services. 'Skype', for example, is an alternative to telephony, created such cost reductions that duplication is possible.

A related issue refers to the differentiation of the services: instead of one stringent universal standard the regulation should allow for a differentiation in several 'classes' of supply, appealing to the differing preferences of consumers, while enabling the competing firms to focus on particular sub-markets. An example is the postal service, where several firms have carved up the traditional market into international deliveries, bulk deliveries from door-to-door and specifically addressed bulk mail from large senders.

Public interest and social acceptability issues remain important to services provided by network industries. Hence, standards for universal service provision, the protection of vulnerable customers, security and quality of supply, and environmental and health issues, are to be dealt with by the forces of competition complemented by a regulating public agency. In principle the consumers should be able to choose and pay for products that have special characteristics in terms of, for instance, the protection of the environment, but when such voluntary market principles do not result in outcomes desired from a societal point of view, then government should guide consumers in the right direction (creating awareness and using financial incentives).

It can be concluded that the monitoring and regulatory demands of this first option are relatively small, particularly when public interest aspects are reduced to minimum standards. Private customers and suppliers will enter into voluntary contracts on a competitive market, supported by the general legal framework to prevent or settle conflicts. Professional and branch associations may be created by the private actors themselves as providers of information and standards.

37.2.2 Option 2: Competition Over the Existing Network System

The provision of services like the supply of electricity, natural gas and rail transport are fully dependent on access to (inter)national transport systems or rail tracks and local distribution networks; the so-called essential facilities. Often, the network components in these industries constitute a natural monopoly, involving high sunk costs, extensive network externalities and strong economies of scale and scope in the construction and operation of these systems. This may impede the entry of competing suppliers with their own network into the market. Duplication of the network is not efficient and involves high risks for the newcomers, as they will be a relatively easy target for the incumbent providers with their large and powerful networks. The solution is that government guarantees new entrants access to the incumbents' network(s) enabling competition over the existing infrastructures.

37.2.2.1 A single buyer and independent producers

The simplest option to introduce some degree of competition is to maintain the former public supply system and to allow new independent suppliers of, for instance, power, gas and water access to this system. Such liberalization is often chosen when the market is small, like on an island, or immature, like in developing countries and emerging economies. Generally, the main objective is to attract new private capital to expand the supply capacity. New independent producers sell their products mostly under long-term contracts to the incumbent state-owned monopolist. Often, this so-called single buyer continues to produce these services itself as well, while taking care of the transport, the distribution and the supply to the final customers. This structure allows the incumbent to continue the economic coordination of the system. This includes the control over retail prices and supply conditions to specific categories of consumers, like large industries, agriculture or vulnerable groups of consumers. The public provider also retains control over the further extension of the supply system into new service areas, such as low-income suburbs or new industrial locations.

The main economic advantage of allowing new providers in the industry is that they finance the expansion of the system, instead of having to rely on public sector funding. Moreover, the new independent providers may set benchmarks through which the performance of the incumbent can be better evaluated by the government. Yet, due to economies of scale and the long life cycle of key production assets, this option is not likely to lead to a level playing field for competition. To introduce 'real' competition, it may be necessary to break up the incumbent into a number of smaller private supply companies or to force the incumbent to sell some of its assets to new parties.

The construction of one monopolistic buyer and a number of independent suppliers requires a relatively light monitoring framework, while allowing a continuation of public oversight over the public interest issues, like the expansion of the system, pricing and connection issues. However, an essential aspect of the governance under this approach concerns the stability of the relationship between the public incumbent, as the single buyer, and the private investors. Actually, when the investment is made ex ante, the 'independent' producers are dependent on the state-owned incumbent in honouring the supply contract and vice versa. This introduces the classical possibility for opportunistic behaviour on both sides and the well-known problems of renegotiating contracts ex post. Also, the reputation of the state involved, including the credibility of the legal framework and the judiciary, is a crucial condition in providing ex ante sufficient certainty to the independent investors. This includes the ability of public authorities to withstand or manage interest group pressures on utility pricing and supply conditions. In section 37.3 we will discuss this issue in more detail related to the dangers of regulatory risk and regulatory capture.

37.2.2.2   A wholesale market
When the market is large enough to sustain sufficient producers to create competition and when improving the efficiency of the existing system and stimulating innovation are primary objectives, the more ambitious option is to create a competitive wholesale market, by removing the single buyer. Under this approach, a number of producers compete for the supply of large customers and distribution companies. These distribution companies continue to operate their own local networks to supply the small customers; the so-called retail franchise, with regulated prices and supply conditions.

This approach requires that all producers, or providers, wherever located, should be able to acquire so-called third party access rights to the essential facility, the main transmission network, to sell their goods and services in competition in the wholesale market. In the electricity and the gas market, a main role for the network operator is to facilitate a safe operation of the system by dispatching the supply of power and gas into the system, dealing with congestion, and by instantaneous balancing supply with the amounts of power and gas consumed at the different locations. This implies that the system operator is in need of full oversight of the activities of all producers and customers in the system. Yet, in addition to that, in a liberalized competitive system the supply of power and gas has to be organized on a market basis, selecting the most efficient, low-cost suppliers first. Depending on the type of the services, different forms of access are suggested. In the natural gas and the electricity industry and in rail transport as well as in electronic communications systems, generally, the incumbent supplier is required to provide third party access to its network, at non-discriminatory tariffs and conditions.

This approach raises a number of issues. First of all, the owner of the network should be kept from abusing its monopolistic position in controlling the essential facility by over-charging the third party users of the system. This requires regulatory oversight of the tariffs for transport and other services provided by the network operator, like storage, balancing and quality management. Second, when the owner of the network is also engaged in production and supply activities, regulatory oversight should prevent third parties from being discriminated against via the access conditions imposed by the network owner to enhance its own competitive position. Networks may, for example, set the minimum volume in transport contracts at a size such that small new entrants are barred from using the network. Third, in order to enhance the efficiency of the monopolistic networks, incentive regulation[2] may be applied to reduce the level of transport costs as a component of overall supply cost.[3] A fourth aspect, which was initially not really taken into consideration, is the fact that the essential networks also have to respond adequately to spatial and quantitative shifts in supply and demand and to invest in new infrastructures according to such changes. Therefore, the tariffs have to allow for the financing of such investments.

The fundamental solution to these issues is the unbundling of the monopolistic and the potentially competitive activities of the incumbent. An unbundled network company provides access at regulated tariffs and conditions. There is no incentive anymore to favour his supplier above its competitors, while the possibilities to cross-subsidize are removed. It also provides the regulator with relatively transparent insights into the costs of the network operation as these are separated from the other activities.

Unbundling may take a variety of forms, varying from administrative unbundling, such as accounting unbundling and functional unbundling of the network from the other activities of the incumbent, to legal unbundling by the establishment of separate subsidiaries and even to full ownership unbundling of the network activities. In practice we observe that administrative unbundling evolves towards the more rigorous solutions of ownership unbundling in order to avoid abuse and to facilitate an independent role of the network operator of the wholesale market.

The most advanced stage of introducing competition in gas and power supply provides the retail customers with the freedom to select their supplier and, thus, the emergence of consumer-oriented retail companies, instead of the retail franchise utilities. This implies that there is competition between producers/suppliers, between wholesale traders and between retail traders (Hunt and Shuttleworth, 1996; Juris, 1998). In other systems, like airlines, railways and electronic communications, similar unbundled systems have been created, in which independent suppliers of services use the monopoly networks of the former incumbents. The main difference with power and gas is that the service provided is not homogeneous, as specific cargos or passengers travel between particular points on the network and telecoms users require specific connections at a specific time. This implies that transport companies have to offer rather customized services and that the operator of the system has to allocate specific rights to use parts of the system at a certain moment to these companies. This requires smart systems of auctioning, in which the providers bid for particular slots and tracks in the system.

It is evident that the introduction of extended degrees of competition in these industries requires an increasingly complex set of institutions to coordinate a growing number of transactions between an expanding number of actors in the system. In section 37.5 we will further elaborate on the consequences for opportunistic behaviour and the efficiency of the network.

37.2.3   Option 3: Competition for the Market

Many services are operated on a stand-alone basis or only involve a local network, like drinking water supply and sanitation and sewerage services, garbage collection and urban transport service likes buses, metro and trams. In these systems, it is technically impossible or economically inefficient to separate the components of the system. When it is not feasible to have competing producers and suppliers of a service or good, using one transport system, it can be concluded that it is structurally impossible to replace the monopolistic nature of a service (Gal, 2003). In such a situation a concessionary system can be introduced: competition for the market (Demsetz, 1968). The public authorities then allow independent parties to bid in competition with others for a contract to operate the supply system. On the basis of a list of normative qualitative and economic requirements, the winning operator is selected. After a fixed period, the (private) operator returns the concession and a new contest is organized (Kerf et al., 1998).

A crucial requirement for effective competitive franchise bidding is that there are sufficient, independent ex ante competitors with access to productive resources and information. If the service involves mobile assets from one community to another and when the attributes of the service are relatively simple, potential suppliers can offer their services, based on a series of short-term contracts and competitive bidding. Yet, if the service requires substantial long-lived sunk costs and involves information asymmetry, uncertainty, shifts in input prices, and changing technologies and consumer preferences, then contracts will be notoriously incomplete (Williamson, 1976). Long-term contracts will prove inefficient, whereas short-term franchise contracts in the presence of sunk costs and asymmetric information will invite opportunistic behaviour by one or both parties.

The implication is that institutional mechanisms to adjudicate contractual disputes become crucially important. These mechanisms, either a court or a (higher-level) government agency, should be able to monitor contractual performance, to negotiate adjustments to the franchise contract over time and to resolve disputes with the franchisee. Actually, such an agency becomes the regulator of the single incumbent in enforcing and temporarily adjusting the terms of its contract (Goldberg, 1976). Obviously, this requires a credible and committed government.

Similarly to the single buyer option, discussed above, the essential aspect of governance under the concessionary contract also concerns the stability of the relationship between the public authority and the private investors. Concessionary systems, by nature, include the classical possibility for opportunistic behaviour on both sides and the

ell-known problems of renegotiating ex post. The reputation of the state, including the
redibility of the legal framework and the judiciary, are crucial conditions to provide ex
nte sufficient certainty to investors.

7.2.4   Option 4: Corporatization and Benchmarking

ometimes, it is decided that for reasons of public interest, liberalization is not an option.
'or example, the water supply companies in many countries, with exception of the UK
nd France, are not privatized or awarded under concessions. Sometimes, water supply
ystems stand alone, with only one or two sources from which they take their water.
'his reduces the potential for up-stream competition. Moreover, often water supply is
onsidered too important for health and other reasons of public interests to be left to
he private initiative. An ultimate resort in restructuring publicly owned industries then
s their corporatization. Public enterprises normally operate in a principal–agent rela-
ionship under the responsibility and control of a particular governmental body, often
vith 'soft' budget constraints. Placing the enterprise at arm's length, while imposing a
ard budget constraint, is a first step towards enhancing the efficiency of the firms in the
ector, while making it also less responsive to political and interest group capture. In this
context benchmarking with other, similar companies is then an option, particularly when
t is combined with the publication of the different results of the companies involved
'naming and shaming').

37.3   REGULATORY INSTRUMENTS

In the section above, we have shown that the liberalization of utility services requires
some form of oversight to secure the public interests involved. Depending on the sector
involved, this oversight may be exercised on a local, provincial, national or even supranational level. It may be sector specific, or not. Depending on the way a market is liberalized, the nature of this oversight may range from a relatively light control over quality of
the service and security standards, to a much more pervasive regulatory role.

The essential task of a regulator should be 'to protect the consumers from exploitation
and to provide investors with the confidence to maintain the infrastructure needed to
provide the service' (Baldwin and Cave, 1999, p. 224). The allocative and dynamic efficiency of the sector depends on the role of the regulator and its position among the regulated firms, in the policy-making arena and vis-à-vis interest groups. In this section, we
will explain the main instruments for the behavioural regulation of network industries:
rate of return regulation, price cap regulation, revenue cap regulation and benchmarking
or yardstick regulation.

Rate of return regulation is the simplest form of economic regulation. Under this
approach, the regulated firm is allowed to earn enough income on its sales to cover its
variable costs and to generate a sufficient rate of return on the capital invested. This
allows the firm to replace and expand the network and other assets involved in a timely
manner. Generally, operators ask the regulator for a price review, if they find that their
revenues fall short in providing an acceptable rate of return. Sometimes third parties,
customers, may require such a review, if they feel that they are overcharged. Regulators

may also establish periodical price reviews. In the review, the regulator estimates the 'used and useful' asset base of the firm and establishes an acceptable rate of return as compared to similar investments. This is compared with the turnover of the firm, as a function of sales and prices. If a discrepancy emerges, the prices are adjusted up or downward.

This form of regulation is also called cost-plus regulation and was already applied in utility regulation in the pre-liberalization period. It is considered less efficient, however, as it does not give the firm any incentive to operate more efficiently to guarantee the coverage of the costs incurred. Moreover, it will stimulate firms to invest excessively in capital, if the regulatory allowed rate of return is higher than the required rate of return, that is, the real cost of capital the firm is facing. Hence firms will overcapitalize, a phenomenon called 'gold plating' or the Averch Johnson effect. Alternatively, the allowed rate of return may be too low to allow the firm to invest. Essentially, this problem arises from the asymmetry of information between the regulated firm and the regulator; the latter being unable to observe the real use and productivity of the assets and the cost of capital (Baldwin and Cave, 1999, p. 225).

In order to reduce the asymmetry of information, Littlechild (1983) proposed a new form of incentive regulation: the so-called price cap regulation or RPI-X regulation. RPI is the retail price index as a measure for inflation. In essence, the regulator sets a price cap for a 'basket' of products or services the firm sells on the market, which is annually adjusted according to the rate of inflation. Within that basket, the firm is free to vary the prices for the individual services it supplies. The X factor represents a measure capturing an increase in the productivity in the industry, which the regulator considers realistic. The regulated firm is faced with a reduction in its prices with the factor RPI-X and in order to maintain its profitability it has to improve its productivity accordingly. The level of prices is set, generally, on a four- to five-year interval, annually adjusted for inflation. This implies that when the firm improves its profitability more than the required RPI-X early on in the period, it is able to reap considerable benefits. So, there will be an incentive to reduce its cost. Yet, for the regulator, this will reveal the potential for further cost and price reduction in the following period and form the basis for the new X. Obviously, the regulated firms will anticipate such adjustments and strategically apply cost reductions and performance-enhancing measures. If the firms are confronted with specific circumstances that bring about the need for new investments, like mandatory environmental requirements, the X factor may of course signal an increase in prices.

Nevertheless, in many network firms, or service providers, the overall operational costs do not vary with the sales, as they incur a relatively large amount of fixed capital costs on their network investments. If this is the case, revenue cap regulation may be applied, in which the regulator establishes a revenue cap over a basket of services, allowing the operator to vary the tariffs for these services, as long as the total revenues remain below the cap. Sometimes, for the same firm, price caps are used for services that involve a high degree of variable cost, while services that mainly involve a fixed cost are capped on the basis of revenues. In essence, this approach transfers the risk of underutilization to the users of the system.

An alternative to price cap incentive regulation is benchmarking, under which the performance of firms is compared to similar firms. The regulator than establishes a specific rice for a service at about the average performance level of all firms. This provides an incentive to all firms to enhance their performance in such a way that they end up among the most efficient firms in order to make extra profits. Sometimes, by publishing the outcomes of the benchmarks, regulatory agencies press the firms to improve their relative performance. Often benchmarking is used in the process of price cap regulation to determine the X factor. In setting the tariffs, regulators do have to take into account that some cost push factors may be beyond the control of the operators, like the density of networks, the environment and climate in which the systems operate and historical path dependencies.

An important issue is how the results of improved performance are shared among the regulated firms and their customers. Essential elements are the degree to which the additional profits or losses are shared and the timing thereof, the so-called regulatory lag. Under so-called high-power incentive schemes, in which the operator faces all risk, the firm has to face all profits and losses arising from the difference between its performance and the regulatory cap, until a new cap is established. Under a low-power incentive scheme, only a portion of positive or negative revenues are incurred by the operator, while the remainder comes to the account of the customers through lower, or higher, prices.

The regulatory lag determines the timing in adjusting the price or revenue caps. In a way it balances the 'power' of the incentive schemes. Under a high-power scheme a regular adjustment of the cap reduces the probability that an operator will be either collecting extra profits for a long time, or that that they will face too low revenues. Hence, some of the risk is shifted back from the firms to the customers. In situations of a stable economy with high levels of trust between the industry and the regulator, high-power incentives go together with long regulatory lags.

Under low-power regimes, customers are confronted with substantial shifts in the costs in the market via regular reviews, but longer periods of adjustment will enhance the impact of structural changes and input price shocks in markets, not being accounted for in the prices. So, a low confidence of the parties involved, an unstable economy and low-power incentives require regular adjustments.

In the context of what follows below, it is important to realize that price and cost reviews by regulators provide substantial opportunities for third parties to become involved in the regulatory process, to provide information and to lobby for their interests (so-called third party opportunism).

37.4   REGULATORY RISK AND REGULATORY CAPTURE

In the so-called optimistic public interest approach, the designers of the regulations assume that the regulators may not be as well informed as the regulated, but that they are always well intended (Savedoff and Spiller, 1999; Spiller, 2009). In the more realistic, or for some the more cynical view, the point of departure in designing regulations is the emergence of regulatory risk and the risk of the regulators being captured by interest groups.

Regulatory risk involves the unexpected, opportunistic, adjustment of regulatory rules at the expense of the regulated firm. In the case of privatization, property rights are

transferred to private actors who then have incentives to use the property in a lucrativ
way. What a property right means in terms of decision rights about the control over th
property and the benefits depends on other laws and regulations. Above we discusse
how the regulated firm is embedded in a setting of (in)formal institutions. These inst
tutions reduce the uncertainty for all actors in the system, by constraining behaviou
setting expectations and stabilizing the environment, so that firms are able to make plan
for the future and decide about their investments.

   Yet, institutional structures can also become too rigid and hinder adaptations t
new technologies or changing preferences. Government should also adapt the law
and regulatory instruments when new circumstances arise, as was also noted above
We talk about regulatory risk, however, when government adapts the regulation fo
opportunistic reasons. Then the adaptations are geared towards the interests of th
politicians and bureaucrats, thus weakening the trust the firms should have in th
stability of the regulatory system. When governments have a reputation for oppor
tunistically changing the 'rules of the game', or even expropriating assets or expectec
revenues, private actors will take that into account when investing and maintaininɡ
their properties.

37.4.1   Regulatory Capture

The notion of regulatory capture can be found in the work of Marx and institutionaɩ
economists like Galbraith (1967) and Munkirs (1985), who in great detail show how biɡ
business successfully controls formal institutions like laws and regulations. Economist˜
refer in this context to the rent-seeking behaviour of interest groups, of which corrup-
tion would be the extreme case. Stigler (1971), applying Olson's (1965) theory of collective action, argues that small effective groups in society can capture regulatory agents.
Pelzman (1976) elaborated on Stigler's insights and pointed to the role of consumer
groups in altering distributional aspects. More recently, Laffont and Tirole (1991, 1993)
also showed that in complex transactions with large information asymmetries interest
groups may strongly influence the outcomes of the regulatory process to their advantage
and at the expense of the regulated firms and/or society at large. Fundamental in the
capturing of the regulatory process is the manipulation of information to pervert the
public interest. To understand the captive behaviour of interest groups institutional
economists like Estache and Martimort (1999), Spiller (2009) and Spiller and Tommasi
(2005) have drawn attention to the role of the institutional and political environment,
in which the relationship between the regulated industry and the public regulatory
authorities evolves.

37.4.2   Public Contracting

To understand the specificities of the relationship between the regulator and the regulated firm, the concept of public contracting, involving the state as contracting partner, is
insightful (Spiller, 2009). Generally, private contracting is geared towards completing the
contract in a transaction-cost-minimizing manner, in which governance structures safeguard against opportunism (Williamson, 1975, 1979; see also Collins, 2002). Public contracting is different from private contracting because the state as a contract partner can

nilaterally alter the rules of the game. In addition to the hazards arising from 'standard opportunistic behaviour' in any transaction, however, public contracting introduces two additional sources of hazard: first, governmental opportunism and, second, third party opportunism.

Governmental opportunism essentially involves decisions by national, regional and local governments and their agencies, to unilaterally change the nature and obligations of contracts after the investments have been made by the (foreign) companies (see also Stevens, 2008). Taxes and licences are examples of instruments governments can use in an opportunistic way, causing regulatory risks for the actors in the system. Governmental opportunism may affect private firms as much as publicly owned enterprises.

Spiller (2009) argues that the potential for governmental opportunism depends on the institutional environment and the political structure of a country. More centralized countries in which the power is concentrated in the hands of a few provide less checks and balances against governmental opportunism. An independent judiciary, in turn, reduces such opportunism. In general, faced with potential governmental opportunism, private firms will require stronger safeguards in their contracts, or will make the contract more complete and consequently more rigid. Private firms can also try to deal with regulatory risk through the inclusion of the public partner in specific assets, or by demanding larger up-front revenues, allowing for a fast recovery of the investment 'at risk'. The private firm also can decide, in the case of unilateral changes of rules, to reduce its costs, for example by reducing the expenditures for the maintenance of the network. If, after all, transaction costs turn out to be excessively high and no contract with a private firm seems possible, government may be forced to provide the service to the customers through a state-owned enterprise (see Spiller and Tommasi, 2005).

The notion of third party opportunism arises from introducing a more complex playing field, which involves not only the state and its several layers and departments. It is the specific interaction of the regulated firms, the regulatory agency, the governmental agencies, but also the general public and interest groups as active players. Sure, in democratic societies interest groups can play a very effective and efficient role in monitoring the politicians, the bureaucrats and regulators. Interest groups invest in monitoring public agents, in making their behaviour transparent (so-called 'fire alarms') and in correcting governmental opportunism. But that is only one side of the coin. Interest groups will also try to realize their specific objectives without delivering productive output in exchange (rent-seeking). This implies that earlier regulatory decisions of a public agent can be politically challenged by interest groups. The higher the information asymmetries between the actors, the easier it is to challenge such a decision. Such challenges may take place via lobbying and 'informing' the politicians, via putting pressure on the (outcomes of the) regulatory process and via the courts (Spiller and Liao, 2006). The larger the asymmetry of information, the higher the risk of conflict between political agents and the higher the probability of third party opportunism.

It is argued that, in this situation, the public agent will prefer a low-power incentive contract, which means that the revenues are not directly related to the performance. Under a high-power incentive contract, the political competitor and the public at large would have more insights into the performance of the public agent as a contractor and an opportunity to challenge their role. Moreover, the private and public contracting parties will prefer a high degree of contract specificity, to limit the discretion to the public agent and to increase procedural rigidity. Rigidity and complexity, in turn, increase t potential for conflicts. Relational contracting, which could make adaptations possible low transaction cost, is then not feasible in the public contracting sphere. 'Government and third party opportunism interact and increase the specificity and rigidity of pub contracts causing difficulties in adapting to shocks and leading to low power incentive (Spiller, 2009, p. 56).

37.5   THE GOVERNANCE OF LIBERALIZED SYSTEMS; SOME CONCLUDING REMARKS

It is evident that the introduction of extended degrees of competition in the former publ utility industries is stimulated by the unbundling of potentially competitive activitie from the inherently natural monopoly parts. This is requiring an increasingly comple set of institutions and regulations to coordinate the transactions between the expanc ing set of actors in the system. Indeed, the number of transactions between producer transporters, wholesale traders, distributors, retail traders and their subcontractors, t provide an end use service to a customer has grown tremendously. We could speak c 'fragmented network industries with splintered transactions', in which a whole rang of public and private operators and monitoring agencies are involved and are (partly responsible in delivering the service (Hancher et al., 2008).

In this new type of regulated network industries the firms are confronted with on th one hand a regulated environment, with standards and universal pricing rules, whil the firms on the other hand operate in a highly competitive and unpredictable enviror ment. These two worlds have a different impact on the possibilities of the opportunisti behaviour of the different actors in the network industries. In other words: currently, i: their day to day operations, the producers, the traders, the retail suppliers and the systen operators are confronted with, on the one hand, regulated tariffs and conditions that ar established and known beforehand, while on the other, they face prices that are estab lished by relative scarcity on the commodity markets. These two worlds form the basi for the investment decisions they make and eventually determine the performance, eithe as producer, as trader and as a network operator.

The new situation in the regulated network industries also has an impact on th potential for governmental and third party opportunism. An interesting question i: the light of the central argument in this chapter is about the relation between the nev regulatory framework, the potential opportunism of government and third parties anc the consequences for the performance of the industry. If we consider the evolution o: the regulation of the unbundled supply systems, involving a large number of contractinε firms and agencies in a tightly regulated market context, what then are the implication: for opportunism and consequently for the allocational and dynamic efficiency of the system?

It is clear that in studies where the abstract view of the benevolent regulator is replaceď by a more realistic perspective on regulation, issues of regulatory risk and capture anc the related opportunism become apparent. This opens up a wider and richer perspective on the different modes of public contracting and regulation, the context in which they are applied and the related consequences for their effectiveness and efficiency.

NOTES

The influential critique by Vickers and Yarrow (1988) showed that privatization had not promoted economic efficiency. Above all, economic efficiency implied tough regulation. Otherwise, a public monopoly might simply give way to a private monopoly. If a government aims to increase economic efficiency, privatization as such is irrelevant; what matters is the opening of industry to competition. See Section 37.4 below.

The overall cost to the end-user, the retail price, comprises the cost of the good itself, often called 'the commodity' provided in the competitive market, plus the several categories of cost of (bulk) transmission and local distribution, provided by the regulated network monopolies.

REFERENCES

Albert, Michel (1992) *Capitalism Against Capitalism*, London: Wiley-Blackwell.

Armstrong, Mark, Simon Cowan and John Vickers (1999) *Regulatory Reform: Economic Analysis and British Experience*, Cambridge, MA: The MIT Press.

Baldwin, Robert and Martin Cave (1999) *Understanding Regulation: Theory, Strategy, and Practice*, Oxford: Oxford University Press.

Coen, David and Chris Doyle (2000) 'Liberalisation of Utilities and Evolving European Regulation', *Economic Outlook*, **24** (3), 18–26.

Coen, D. and A. Héritier (2005) *Refining Regulatory Regimes. Utilities in Europe*, Cheltenham, UK and Northampton, MA, USA: Edward Elgar.

Collins, H. (2002) *Regulating Contracts*, Oxford: Oxford University Press.

Crew, Michael A. and Paul R. Kleindorfer (2002) 'Regulatory Economics: Twenty Years of Progress?' *Journal of Regulatory Economics*, **21** (1), 5–22.

Crew, M. and D. Parker (2005) 'Development in the Theory and Practice of Regulatory Economics', in M. Crew and D. Parker (eds) *International Handbook on Economic Regulation*, Cheltenham, UK and Northampton, MA, USA: Edward Elgar.

Demsetz, H. (1968) 'Why Regulate Utilities?' *Journal of Law and Economics*, **11** (1), 55–65.

Dinar, A. (2000) *The Political Economy of Water Pricing Reforms*, Oxford: Oxford University Press for the World Bank.

Estache, Antonio and David Martimort (1999) 'Politics, Transaction Costs, and the Design of Regulatory Institutions', World Bank Policy Research Working Paper No. 2073.

Gal, Michal S. (2003) *Competition Policy for Small Market Economies*, Cambridge, MA: Harvard University Press.

Galbraith, John K. ([1967] 2007) *The New Industrial State*, Princeton, NJ: Princeton University Press.

Goldberg, V. (1976) 'Regulation and Administered Contracts', *Bell Journal of Economics*, **7** (2), 426–52.

Hancher, L., W.M. Dicke, T. van den Brink, A.F. Correlje, G. Arts and N. Feitsma (2008) *Infrastructures, Time to Invest*, The Hague/Amsterdam: WRR/Amsterdam University Press.

Hofstede, Geert (2001) *Culture's Consequences; Comparing Values, Behavior, Institutions and Organizations across Nations*, London/New Delhi/Thousand Oaks: Sage Publications.

Hunt, S. and G. Shuttleworth (1996) *Competition and Choice in Electricity*, Chichester: John Wiley and Sons Ltd.

Joskow, P.L. (2007) 'Regulation of Natural Monopolies', in A. Mitchell Polinsky and Steven Shavell (eds) *Handbook of Law and Economics*, Dordrecht: Elsevier Science.

Juris, Andrej (1998) 'Competition in the Natural Gas Industry: The Emergence of Spot, Financial, and Pipeline Capacity Markets', Note No. 137 in *Public Policy for the Private Sector*, Washington, DC: World Bank Group.

Kahn, Alfred (1998) *The Economics of Regulation: Principles and Institutions*, Cambridge, MA: MIT Press.

Kerf, Michael et al. (1998) *Concessions for Infrastructure: A Guide to Their Design and Award Finance*, Public Sector, and Infrastructure Network, WTP 399, Washington, DC: World Bank.

Klein, M. (1998) 'Network Industries', in D. Helm and T. Jenkinson (eds) *Competition in Regulated Industries*, Oxford: Oxford University Press, pp. 40–76.

Klein, M. (1999) 'Competition in Network Industries', World Bank Policy Research Working Paper No. 1591.

Laffont, J.J. and J. Tirole (1991) 'The Politics of Government Decision Making: A Theory of Regulatory Capture', *Quarterly Journal of Economics*, **106** (4), 1089–127.

Laffont, J.J. and J. Tirole (1993) *A Theory of Incentives in Procurement and Regulation*, Cambridge, MA: MIT Press.

Littlechild, S.C. (1983) *Regulation of British Telecommunications' Profitability*, London: Department of Tra∎ and Industry.

Megginson, W. and J.M. Netter (2001) 'From State to Market: A Survey of Empirical Studies on Privatizatior *Journal of Economic Literature*, **39** (2), 321–89.

Munkirs, John R. (1985) *The Transformation of American Capitalism: From Competitive Market Structures Centralized Private Sector Planning*, Armonk, New York/London: M.E. Sharpe Inc.

Newbery, David M. (1999) *Privatization, Restructuring, and Regulation of Network Industries*, Cambridg∎ MA: MIT Press.

North, Douglass C. (1990) *Institutions, Institutional Change and Economic Performance*, Cambridge, UK Cambridge University Press.

Olson, M. (1965) *The Logic of Collective Action: A Theory of Interest Groups in Public Goods*, Cambridge, M∕ Harvard University Press.

Pelzman, S. (1976) 'Toward a More General Theory of Regulation', *Journal of Law and Economics*, **19** (2 211–40.

Savedoff, William and Pablo Spiller (1999) 'Government Opportunism and the Provision of Water', in Willia∎ Savedoff and Pablo Spiller (eds) *Spilled Water: Institutional Commitment in the Provision of Water Service* Washington, DC: Inter-American Development Bank, pp. 1–34.

Spiller, Pablo T. (2009) 'An Institutional Theory of Public Contracts: Regulatory Implications', in C. Ménar and M. Ghertman (eds) *Regulation, Deregulation and Reregulation*, Cheltenham, UK and Northampto∎ MA, USA: Edward Elgar, Chapter 3.

Spiller, P.T. and S. Liao (2006) 'Buy, Lobby or Sue: Interest Groups' Participation in Policy Making: ∕ Selective Survey', National Bureau of Economic Research Working Paper No. 12209, Cambridge, MA.

Spiller, P. and M. Tommasi (2005) 'The Institutions of Regulation', in C. Ménard and M.M. Shirley (eds *Handbook of New Institutional Economics*, Dordrecht: Springer.

Stevens, Paul (2008) 'National Oil Companies and International Oil Companies in the Middle East: Under th∎ Shadow of Government and the Resource Nationalism Cycle', *The Journal of World Energy Law & Business* **1** (1), 5–30.

Stigler, G. (1971) 'The Theory of Economic Regulation', *Bell Journal of Economics*, **2** (1), 3–21.

Vickers, John and George Yarrow (1988) *Privatization: An Economic Analysis*, Cambridge, MA: MIT Press.

Williamson, Oliver E. (1975) *Markets and Hierachies*, New York: Free Press.

Williamson, Oliver E. (1976) 'Franchise Bidding for Natural Monopolies – in General and with Respect t∎ CATV', *The Bell Journal of Economics*, **7** (1), 73–104.

Williamson, Oliver E. (1979) 'Transaction-cost Economics: The Governance of Contractual Relations' *Journal of Law and Economics*, **22** (2) 233–61.

Williamson, Oliver E. (1998) 'Transaction Cost Economics: How it Works; Where it is Headed', *De Economist* **146** (January), 23–58.

38 From the corporation to venture capitalism: new surrogate markets for knowledge and innovation-led economic growth
Cristiano Antonelli and Morris Teubal

38.1 INTRODUCTION

The corporation has been able for a large part of the twentieth century to fulfil the pivotal role of intermediary between finance and innovation. Yet the discontinuities brought about by the ICT revolution have progressively undermined its efficiency. The span of competence of incumbents was unable to match the new radical technologies: a case of lock-in competence could be observed. Venture capitalism seems more and more likely to emerge as the third major institutional set-up able to manage the complex interplay between finance and innovation when radical changes take place (Lamoreaux and Sokoloff, 2007).

The information and communication technological revolution has led to a new set of private (venture capital) and public (epitomized by NASDAQ) capital markets for 'technology companies' including high-tech start-ups (SUs), which, by supporting such companies and enabling the anticipation of returns, have for the first time in history, promoted the creation in advanced economies of a specialized segment of 'inventor' companies.[1] These markets, which emerged in the USA during the 1970s, specialize in knowledge-intensive assets or knowledge-intensive property rights (KIPRs). For this reason they have been termed 'surrogate knowledge markets'. Their emergence parallels the demise of the Chandlerian corporation and can be considered as a major institutional innovation (Antonelli and Teubal, 2010).

38.2 FROM THE CORPORATION TO VENTURE CAPITALISM

The relationship between finance and innovation is crucial. Radical uncertainty and hence major knowledge and information asymmetries shape the interaction between prospective funders and prospective innovators. Different institutional solutions have been elaborated through time. Emerging venture capitalism seems to mark a third phase. The 'innovative banker' and the 'corporation' have preceded venture capitalism. Schumpeter was able to identify these two phases.

In his *Theory of Economic Development* (1934) Schumpeter stresses the central role of the provision of appropriate financial resources to entrepreneurs. The natural interface of the entrepreneur, as a matter of fact, is the innovative banker. The banker is innovative when he or she is able to spot new opportunities and select among the myriads of business proposals that are daily submitted, those that have higher chances to get through the system. With a given quantity of financial resources the innovative banker should be able to reduce the flow of funds towards traditional activities and switch them towards the new firms. Actually the innovative banker should be able to identify the obsolete incumbents that are going to be forced to exit by the creative destruction that follows the entry of successful innovators.

The level of competence and expertise necessary for a banker to fulfil such a role is clearly impressive. As Schumpeter himself realized, this model, although practised with some success in Germany in the last decades of the nineteenth century suffered from a number of limitations.

Schumpeter not only realized the limits of the first model but clearly understood the asymmetry between debt and equity in the provision of funds for innovative undertakings, an insight further developed by Stiglitz and associates. In their 1981 and 1985 articles (Stiglitz and Weiss, 1981; Stiglitz, 1985) they have shown that equity finance has an important advantage over debt in the provision of funds to innovative undertakings because it can participate in the bottom tail of the highly skewed distribution of positive returns stemming from the generation of new knowledge and the introduction of new technologies (Hall, 2002). Schumpeter's insight into and analysis of the corporation as the institutional alternative to the 'innovative banker' has been laid down in *Capitalism, Socialism and Democracy* (1942). Here Schumpeter identifies the large corporation as the driving institution for the introduction of innovations. His analysis of the corporation as an innovative institutional approach to improving the relationship between finance and innovation has received less attention than other facets (King and Levine, 1993). Yet Schumpeter is very clear in stressing its role as an internal market where the resources extracted by extra profits can better match the competences of skilled managers and the vision of potential entrepreneurs. Moreover, the corporation can act as an intermediary between the credit markets and the provision of funds, for new innovative undertakings. Schumpeter praises the large corporation as the institutional device that makes it possible to increase both the incentives and the efficiency of the innovation process. The internal markets of the Schumpeterian corporation substitute external financial markets in the key role of the effective provision and correct allocation of funds, combining financial resources and entrepreneurial vision within competent hierarchies (Chandler, 1962, 1977, 1990).

The new financial markets are becoming a key component of an innovation-driven novel institutional setting and subsystem termed 'venture capitalism', which is key for a new model of 'knowledge-based' growth potentially relevant not only for information and communication technologies (ICTs) but also (with adaptations) for biotechnologies and new technologies at large.

Venture capitalism is a major institutional innovation based upon the identification of economies of scope in the transactions of technological knowledge bundled with managerial competence, reputation, screening procedures and equity. It has paved the way for the emergence of new surrogate markets for knowledge, that is, financial markets specialized in the trade of knowledge-intensive property rights (KIPRs) with important benefits in terms of economics of size in portfolio management and hence profitability of investments in high-tech start-ups. The emergence of venture capitalism has important effects in national systems of innovation of advanced countries, and it is a powerful mechanism for the production, dissemination and integration of knowledge in advanced capitalistic economies, and thereby a main driver of a 'knowledge-based' growth.

This chapter explores the new market-mediating mechanisms linking SU invention on the one hand and economic growth on the other. Two such mechanisms come to mind under venture capitalism (of which venture capitalism is *directly* involved only in the first): (1) a *systemic* rather than haphazard link between radical inventions and the emergence of new product markets; and (2) a link between new product markets (including post-emergence market growth that would include diffusion of technology to other user groups and/or markets) on the one hand and invention and unbundled technology markets on the other. The first highlights not only the volatility and precariousness of the R&D companies that operated prior to venture capitalism, but also, and related to this, the weak links that existed then between radical invention and the emergence of new markets. There are two aspects of (2) above: (2a) derived demand for improvements in the product and process technology underlying a market (and industry); and (2b) a demand for a substitute, disruptive technology that could replace the existing one. In both cases market size signals the 'benefits' to be derived from improving or substituting the underlying technology.

The above themes will be implemented by suggesting an evolutionary theory of the emergence of new markets (based on what markets are as social institutions). Moreover, our attempt to begin to unravel the above dynamic will suggest ways to assess the dynamic efficiency of venture capitalism. Thus, if venture capitalism enhances the rate of new market (and industry) creation, then venture capitalism could indeed be a dynamically efficient form of modern capitalism.

38.3   THE EMERGENCE OF NASDAQ AND VENTURE CAPITALISM

The core of venture capitalism is the triplet SU segment, venture capital and NASDAQ where the latter represents 'global (public) capital markets for technology companies'. Venture capitalism as a system arose during the 1960s and 1970s in the USA in response to the early phases of the ICT revolution (integrated circuits, minicomputers and microprocessors) that enhanced the relative advantage of SUs vis-à-vis incumbents. Most inventive activity prior to venture capitalism took place in-house within incumbent companies that were also involved in production and/or marketing of goods. With a background of a continued process of creation of new technological opportunities the central process can be visualized as comprising four phases:

1.   bundling in the VC investment market and facilitating KIPR asset creation (in SUs);
2.   trading KIPRs in VC markets;
3.   creation/emergence of NASDAQ as a public capital market focused on IPOs;
4.   transformation/expansion of NASDAQ into a public capital market for KIPRs.

A dynamic, phase analysis leading to emergence of a VC market/industry in Israel can be found in Avnimelech and Teubal (2006) (for a dynamic comparison with VC in the USA see Avnimelech et al., 2005). We therefore focus below on the emergence of NASDAQ.

Phase I: bundling in the VC investment market and facilitating KIPR creation (in SUs)   As mentioned, since the early days of VC the financial product offered was equity finance as distinct from loans that were the prevailing product offered by existing financial institutions (banks). Equity finance was offered to SUs bundled together with added-value, which included business services and management advice, management services, certification and networking functions as well. This was exchanged for SU shares and other rights concerning the management of the company. The bundling aspect is, for a (new) VC market, an additional dimension of what has been termed the dominant (product) design, which lies at the origin of what will become a new market. In this early phase of the VC market, venture capital stimulates and co-evolves with the organizations specializing in creating KIPR – high-tech start-up companies (SUs).

Phase II: trading KIPRs in private VC exit markets   The company shares received were transformed through the passage of time into bundles of knowledge, managerial competence, innovation capabilities, and so on (KIPRs) particularly so when the original VC investment took place at the seed or early phase of SU operations where R&D is the main activity (in practice this is defined as the period between SU foundation and early, non-routinary sales, say during the first five to six years of operation). This was the result of the financial and other added-value received by SUs, which, together with the experience accumulated, underpinned the inventive activity of such companies.

Till approximately the mid-1970s when NASDAQ as a fully public market did not yet exist, VC exits took place principally through the sale of SUs (or M&As) or so-called trade sales, that is, sales of SU shares to individuals or organizations. These were private transactions, an increase in the volume of which might eventually have triggered a private VC exit market. During the first half of the 1970s we also observe over-the-counter (OTC) initial offerings of shares of SUs undertaken under the aegis of the recently formed new institution – NASDAQ. At the time these were yet another form of private VC exits through sales to specific individuals or organizations rather than to the public at large.

Phase III: creation/emergence of NASDAQ (public capital market for IPOs)   Eventually NASDAQ became a new market for selling KIPRs to the public at large rather than only to private individuals or organizations. Our hypothesis is that *initially* NASDAQ was an initial public offering market both for VC-backed SUs (a new public exit option for VCs) and for non-VC-backed SUs.

Phase IV: expansion/transformation of NASDAQ into a public market for KIPRs   Emergence of NASDAQ with its focus on IPOs gave an enormous boost to both VCs and SUs and the number of IPOs increases dramatically (see comments at the end of this section). This in turn enabled exploitation of significant economies of scale and scope and a momentum for further expansion (dynamic economies or cumulative processes with positive feedback). NASDAQ thereby eventually became the market for KIPR transactions in general. Beyond initial public offerings that involved SUs directly, we find various classes of KIPR transactions involving other agents without SUs participating (i.e., between existing holders of KIPRs and other participants). These include transactions involving specialized investors or demanders/suppliers of KIPRs only, transactions involving the public at large as both demanders and suppliers; and other transactions involving both the public on the one hand and specialized agents (e.g., financial investors and specialized demanders/suppliers of KIPRs) on the other. NASDAQ in effect became a 'supermarket' for products generating income streams for the general public.

The transition from SU invention to emergence of a new product market may take many forms, depending on numerous factors including SU strategy and its success in accessing the required complementary assets to transform the invention/new technology into an innovation (Teece, 1986) and in some cases into a new industry/market. In some industries, SUs became the driver of a creation of a new market; in others incumbent companies in existing markets accessed the new technology and became the dynamic factor leading to the new market/industry.

Gans and Stern (2003) have undertaken a systematic theoretical analysis of the strategies of SUs with radical inventions. They follow and extend the analysis of Teece (1986) by considering a number of additional strategic options opened up by venture capitalism (only marginally considered by Teece) particularly concerning SU 'cooperation' with incumbent companies in the relevant market. 'Cooperation' in their analysis is an 'aggregate category' essentially linked to licensing knowledge/technology (in their terminology, the market for ideas) and to related SU-incumbent mergers, strategic partnerships or incumbent acquisition of the SU. The licensing and strategic partnership option played a relatively minor role in Teece since his emphasis lies in profiting from innovation through accessing complementary assets either through vertical integration or through market contracts with external suppliers of inputs, for example, marketing services or 'standard production' services.

38.4   A DYNAMIC PERSPECTIVE TO MARKETS AND MARKET BUILDING

An effort to understand the institutional characteristics of markets in a general context seems necessary in order to grasp properly all the implications of the creation of the new financial markets associated with venture capitalism. Markets are social institutions that perform a variety of functions and exhibit different forms, organizations and characteristics. Moreover, markets are a dynamical construct. Hence markets are being created, emerge, occasionally their performances and functions improve and possibly decline. In other words, markets evolve.

What is missing in the literature is a theory of markets as social institutions, which includes markets' role not only in the allocation of resources but also in promoting 'knowledge-based growth'. This theory should also make a distinction between simple markets and multilayer supermarkets such as NASDAQ that enable participants to relate to a number of markets simultaneously, thereby better coordinating their needs to the capabilities offered.

There are two well-established notions of 'market' in the literature: (1) a textbook, abstract notion where it is self-evident that markets exist so that any transaction presupposes existence of an underlying market; (2) markets as devices for reducing transactions costs and thereby facilitating exchange (Coase, 1988).

A major contribution to the discussion of markets comes from Coase, whose work clarifies both (1) and (2) above: 'In mainstream economic theory the firm and the market are for the most part assumed to exist and *are not themselves the subject of investigation*' (Coase, 1988, Chapter 1, p. 5; our italics). By mainstream economic theory Coase means economic theory without transactions costs. Transactions costs are the costs of market transactions that include 'search and information costs, bargaining and decision costs, and policing and enforcement costs' (Dahlman, 1979, quoted by Coase), which of course, includes the costs of contracting. In Coase's theory, transactions costs exist and can be important; and they explain the existence of the firm: 'Markets are institutions that exist to facilitate exchange, that is they exist in order to reduce the cost of carrying out exchange transactions. In Economic Theory which assumes that transaction costs are non-existent markets have no function to perform' (Coase, op cit., p. 7).

There is a third notion of 'market' originally proposed by Adam Smith (1776), namely a device that promotes division of labour, learning/innovation, and economic growth. This is the notion we would like to futher develop here. Our position is that it is not possible to uncover the distinctive characteristics and functions of such a dynamic view of markets exclusively by making reference to Coase's facilitation of exchange and reduction of transactions costs. This could be one of the outcomes of a market. However, if rather than spontaneously making their appearance markets emerge or are built, then the required pre-conditions for emergence became central. In this other factors are in play, for example, asymmetric information, regulatory changes, a critical mass of producers and consumers (since there is an important element of collective interaction and of collective transacting that must precede actual market emergence), and other factors. Box 38.1 lists the defining characteristics of markets following the above-mentioned dynamic perspective; and Table 38.1 shows how these relate to market functions.

A new market may emerge when a set of previously isolated precursor transactions sparks an emergence process. For this to happen a number of conditions may be required (see below) and these may depend on area and specific context. Frequently these will include pre-emergence processes of interaction and information flow among agents together with experimentation and learning concerning product characteristics and user/producer organization and strategy. In some cases like venture capital in the USA and in Israel (Avnimelech et al., 2005; Avnimelech and Teubal, 2006) these led to a new, effective intermediation form, a qualitative dimension that largely precedes the actual emergence process. Emergence may also require a critical mass of precursor transactions both to underpin the above-mentioned interaction, learning and experimental process and to enhance the expected 'benefits' derived from creating a new market. Moreover, when a new market *place* is also required, the successful emergence of a new market may depend critically on the appearance of an 'entrepreneur' or a consortium of agents in charge of undertaking the required planning, coordination and investments. The analysis that follows largely ignores this issue. Table 38.2 summarizes the phases of emergence of a new market according to our perspective.

The table is part of a market life cycle perspective that parallels the extended industry life cycle perspective with background and pre-emergence phases (Phases 1 and 2 respectively). m_1 is a critical mass of precursor (Phase 1) transactions required to trigger, for example, through variation, a more systematic and focused search and experimentation process leading to selection in Phase 2 of a product class and dominant design/product

---

BOX 38.1   DEFINING CHARACTERISTICS OF MARKETS

A well-defined product/service category
A dominant design and product standards
A market place ('space', organization or information highway)
A critical mass of supply and demand agents
A critical mass of transactions volume
A measure of stability of supply and demand

Agent interaction
A measure of reputation
Transparency of transactions

Saves transactions costs compared to an equivalent but disconnected set of transactions
Institutions and rules underpinnings, e.g., in relation to: product quality and standardization, certification of agents, contracts, transactions' transparency, etc.
Emergence involves a momentum leading to further growth (diffusion of the product category)

Other characteristics
Thickness, frequency and recurrence of transactions
Density of agents
Formal institutions

Table 38.1   Functions of a market

Basic Function	Links To Defining Characteristics (and to Specific Functions)
Stability of supply	Critical mass of agents and transactions volume
Agent coordination	Agent interactions, transactions transparency
Promoting static efficiency	Save transactions costs, incentives to producers, selection, coordination, management of risks
Promoting dynamic efficiency	Specific functions
	Signaling extent of need, inducing division of labour and learning/specialization, drivers of improvement and disruptive technology/invention, integration mechanisms, converting uncertainty into risk and institutions reducing path dependence (market demise/substitution by another market)

standard with high value to user/demand agents (Abernathy and Utterback, 1978). Appropriate product/services' bundling and, depending on case, selection of a new intermediation form, that is, the mutual adaptation of the organization and strategy of supply and demand agents (and of both to the institutional environment) may be critical

Table 38.2   Phases in market building

Phase 1: Background Condition – Variation	Phase 2: Pre-emergence Conditions – Selection	Phase 3: Emergence – Development
Appearance of a 'precursor' set of transactions; and of a critical mass of such transactions (m_1)	I. Focused business experiments leads to the identification and adoption/ selection of (i) product class, dominant design and product bundling; (ii) supply/demand agent types; and (iii) regulatory environment/institutions II. Appearance of a critical mass of transactions (m_2) with the above characteristics III. In some cases, new mechanisms of interaction	m_2 (and possibly policy) sparks a self-sustained cumulative process of growth; this leads to a new market with emergent properties

(see Petit and Quéré, 2006 and Avnimelech and Teubal, 2008). Thus in the history of emergence of a venture capital market and industry in the USA (Gompers and Lerner, 1999, 2001, 2004), the supply agents (VC organizations) eventually adopted a limited partnership form of organization, while the demand agents (high-tech start-up companies) had to accept dilution of ownership and other changes. Meanwhile there were significant adaptations of the institutional environment, for example, modifications of the ERISA (Employment Retirement Income Security Act) including the 1979 amendment to the 'prudent man' rule governing pension fund investments in the USA (Gompers and Lerner, 2004, pp. 8, 9).

Sparking or triggering emergence frequently requires a critical mass of transactions involving the selected product class, dominant design and intermediation form (m_2). As mentioned these should provide a new value proposition to users. Moreover, whenever a new market *place* involving coordination and heavy investments is required, the existence of such a level of demand may be critical for the appearance of a 'new market entrepreneur or consortium' in charge of planning and building such a market place.

The above framework suggests that failed market emergence could be the result of two general causes. One is failed selection processes in Phase 2 resulting from too little search/ experimentation and/or inappropriate selection mechanisms, for example, due to institutional rigidity. The other is failure to spark or sustain an evolutionary cumulative emergence process (e.g., due to system failures that policy has not addressed). Not all radical inventions, even those leading to innovations and having potential, will automatically lead to new product markets.

A related issue is the post-emergence growth of new markets, with NASDAQ's Phase 4 being the major and probably paradigmatic example of a multi- or supermarket. This will be termed 'post-emergence market growth'. In previous work and in relation to new industries it was pointed out that the momentum leading to emergence also continues beyond this state (Avnimelech and Teubal, 2006). Here and in relation to markets we would like to emphasize the following sources of such expansion: (1) the market place that serves the initial product market may, through economies of scope and scale, carry new, related categories of products (Antonelli and Teubal, 2010); (2) diffusion of the underlying product technology to new applications (see the analysis of the machine tool sector and market by Rosenberg (1963) and in general purpose technologies more generally speaking); and, related to the previous point, (3) diversification and niche development by the leading firms who developed and co-evolved with the new market (this, which is frequent in many new ICT areas, e.g., the cases of Nokia and Google, could include both new applications and developing specialized products and solutions for different market segments). The last two point to a link between new product markets and new (including 'unbundled') technology markets.

38.5   NEW MARKET-MEDIATED INNOVATION-BASED GROWTH

The new financial markets of venture capitalism supported the fledging specialized inventor SU segment. SUs are a new institution with, in many areas, potentially strong advantages over incumbent companies as far as invention and beginning of commercial exploitation of the new ICTs are concerned. These and their impact on economic growth through new market building are summarized below in terms of a number of interlinked relationships (Modules A, B and C). Module A links venture capitalism (and the ICT revolution) to an acceleration of radical inventions; Module B links these inventions and related improvements and innovations to the accelerated emergence of new product markets; and Module C focuses on the reverse process, namely, how new product markets stimulate new invention (both radical and incremental) and possibly the emergence of unbundled technology markets. We can already see that under this perspective, a *push* of radical invention (Module A) will lead to a new market-mediated subsequent *pull*, that is, dynamic economies of scale in invention at the overall system level.

Module A

Venture Capitalists

(1) ICT Revolution ↔ (2) SU Segment ↔ (3) Accelerated Radical Invention

NASDAQ

The links among the three elements of venture capitalism (see above) are co-evolutionary. We should also be aware (not shown in the above sequence) that accelerated invention not only 'inputs' Modules B and C but feeds back into (1) the new set of ICT opportunities.

The central issue is: what are the implications of accelerated invention for the rate and direction of market-building processes (element 5 in Module B)? Radical inventions plus improvements may, through innovation and diffusion, stimulate the creation of new product markets (Module B) as well as Module C's post-emergence market growth (and indirectly, creation of unbundled markets for 'technology/invention'). There are both direct and indirect effects because the link between inventions/innovations and creation of new markets is a two-way, possibly co-evolutionary, relationship with the mix between radical and improvement inventions (and innovations) being a critical dimension. Thus, as indicated in Module C the opposite is also true, namely that existing product markets can induce new invention, both improvements in the technology underpinning existing markets and radical, disruptive inventions (see 9 in Module C) that reinforce the ICT revolution's *push*. Needless to say and following the enormous literature on these matters (e.g., Gans and Stern op cit.) SU-incumbent interactions are critical to analysing the pattern of emergence both of new products and of unbundled technology markets.

Module B

> (3) Enhanced Radical Inventions/Improvements → (4) SU ↔ Incumbent Links →
> (5) Enhanced Rate of Emergence of New Product Markets

Module C

> (6) Post-emergence Market Growth + (7) [Growth of New Incumbents & Links with
> SU]→ (8) Improvement Inventions + Some New Unbundled Technology Market +
> (9) New Radical Inventions

As with Module A the above processes are non-linear; rather they involve numerous feedback loops and co-evolutionary processes, for example, between invention/improvement and product markets; and between both and knowledge markets. As mentioned above, invention spurs emergence of new product markets; and new product markets and their size will induce both (8) improvement inventions (and potential emergence of unbundled knowledge/technology markets for improvement innovations) and (9) new radical inventions. Moreover, these Module C effects feed back into Module A, thus initiating a new invention→market emergence→invention cycle.

SU-incumbent links are crucial both for new market emergence (Module B) and for the subsequent link between post-emergence market growth and subsequent invention, technology transactions and emergence of unbundled technology markets. Thus, an important pattern underlying Module B's acceleration of new market emergence is the transformation, either through 'cooperation' with incumbents or through a strategy of 'head on competition', of SU invention first into 'innovation' (Gans and Stern, op cit.) and then and in a subset of cases, into the building of new markets. In contrast, in Module C SU-incumbent links are intertwined both with the growth of leading incumbents (which co-evolve with the new markets and their subsequent expansion, see 5 and 6) and with subsequent invention particularly of the improvement type (see 8). These links are related to incumbents' attempts at growing after emergence and during 'maturity' of their main market. Since their possibility of exploring all options is limited, by necessity they develop new links with SUs as part of stimulating an appropriate ecosystem for post-emergence growth and search for new value for existing users. Major differences seem to exist between the SU-incumbent links of Module A (especially in the 'early' rounds of the A↔C cycle) and those of Module C (especially beyond the early rounds of the cycle). This happens because in the former the influence of new markets and associated 'mature' incumbents is not strong enough relative to the latter case. The strong and varied SU-incumbent links of Module C are connected both to the process of diffusion of the new technology underpinning incumbents' main market and to the process of searching for new value for existing users. In these processes, incumbent companies tend to 'cooperate' (through an extended network) with new SUs.

38.6   A DISGRESSION ON MARKETS AND THE VISIBLE HAND

What is the role of markets and the 'visible hand' in the new venture capitalism system described in this chapter? In a number of papers Richard Langlois raises a number of issues that are relevant for our understanding both of venture capitalism as a new innovation subsystem of modern capitalist economies and of the nature and characteristics of SUs.

In his 2003 paper (Langlois, 2003) and in a long 2002 draft (Langlois, 2002) Langlois focuses on these issues by contrasting the systems of innovation and nature of firms towards the end of the nineteenth century up to and including venture capitalism at the end of the twentieth century. Both are 'revolutions' induced by increases in population, income and technology; and in the sense that radical changes have occurred in the relative roles of firms and markets in coordinating economic activity.

Following Chandler in *The Visible Hand* (Chandler, 1977) and subsequent works like *Scale and Scope* (Chandler, 1990), Langlois emphasizes that by the end of the nineteenth century we observe the appearance of the large, integrated corporation, which replaced a previously existent fragmented and localized structure of production and distribution. The outcome was the appearance of the visible hand of managerial coordination, one that replaced Adam Smith's (1776) invisible hand of the market. In contrast, by the end of the twentieth century Langlois states that Smithian Forces may be replacing Chandlerian ones in what he has termed the vanishing hand hypothesis. This latter hypothesis accepts the idea that population and income growth together with the accompanying technological changes (including improved coordination technology) has led to enhanced division of labour, specialization by function and coordination by markets.

Still it is not clear from Langlois' analysis whether the visible hand has itself disappeared, being replaced by a market-based invisible hand like in Smith,[2] or whether – with respect to venture capitalism and the role of SUs – a hybrid mechanism involving both an enhanced role of markets (or market transactions) and a measure of visible hand could co-exist at end of twentieth-century capitalism. For example, a visible hand may be important when a firm embedded in a network or network of firms wants to undertake complex knowledge-economy-type transactions, where pre-existing links and trust are critical, for example, in connection with SUs or inventors accessing specialized or co-specialized complementary assets à la Teece (Teece, 1986). These considerations apply also to other complex transactions involving SU companies under venture capitalism, for example, R&D licensing whether or not part of a broader 'strategic partnership' with a larger 'incumbent' company; acquisition by or merger with another company, and so on. They also apply to networks of innovators involving the cooperation of large, diversified, incumbent companies and specialized SUs (e.g., in drugs, certain ICT areas and other areas involving complex transactions and 'asymmetrical information'), a phenomenon expected as long as 'there is a high rate of creation of novelty'.

Thus we conclude that while markets are or have indeed been 'taking over', it does no follow that the invisible hand is returning, since, as mentioned, firms must have links network embeddedness, and mutual trust (and sometimes, reputation) in order to effec tively make use of markets.

The changing nature of many markets and the existence of a 'visible hand component in venture capitalism also have implications for SU (and VC) organization and strategy As mentioned in this chapter and by other authors, in order for SU companies to adapt themselves both to VC and to NASDAQ, they had to adopt a 'born global strategy' and their commercialization strategy should consider not only the market for goods, but also capital markets (for IPOs and for M&As) and markets for knowledge. Also owners and founders should be willing to dilute their ownership. This is a completely different inventor company, even when compared to the specialized R&D or small inventor companies considered by Freeman in his 1974 book and even to some extent those considered by Teece in his 1986 article (who operated prior to full-fledged venture capitalism and the new options for such companies opened up by the new financial markets).

Grebel et al. also suggest that a modified industry life cycle model should be constructed, one more attuned to the post-1970 reality of industries involving both incumbents and knowledge-intensive start-ups, with market forces (but not necessarily to the invisible hand) playing a greater role than in the prevailing model. This view is further reinforced once we recognize that many transactions related to new technologies in very dynamic areas are, almost by definition, not undertaken under the umbrella of markets (although, following the analysis of section 38.3, some of these may lead to new markets). This fact would further enhance the role of 'managerial coordination' and 'management capabilities' and would enhance the importance for the firm to build and be embedded in networks.

This chapter's model of venture capitalism is a preliminary attempt to integrate some of these issues at a higher level of analysis than that of an industry life cycle. It could provide insights about the relevant ecosystem and the framework of analysis of individual industry life cycles in this new phase of high-tech, global capitalism.

38.7   CONCLUSIONS AND IMPLICATIONS OF THE ANALYSIS

In previous work we (and others) have analysed the *nature* of venture capitalism understood as the subsystem comprising a segment of independent inventor companies (SUs) *and* a new private and a new public financial market supporting it by trading in what has been termed knowledge-intensive property rights (KIPRs; Antonelli and Teubal, 2008). KIPRs bundle knowledge/technology with other assets, for example, innovation capability, knowledge competence and so on. The new financial markets, by virtue of trading in KIPRs and therefore constituting surrogate knowledge markets (together with the fact that SUs create and offer KIPRs), have helped to overcome the two central problems with knowledge creation and business sector R&D in market economies: the incentives problem facing inventors and inventor companies (related to externalities on the one hand and to Arrow's disclosure paradox (1962) and the related non-existence or strong imperfection of knowledge markets on the other); and the invention/R&D finance problem (summarized in Gompers and Lerner, 1999). An additional albeit related conusion concerning markets versus managerial coordination and the role of the visible and is that while markets are or have indeed been 'increasing their scope', it does not ollow that the invisible hand is returning, since, as mentioned, firms must have links, etwork embeddedness, and mutual trust (and sometimes, reputation) in order to effectively make use of markets.

The present chapter extends the analysis to consider the economic impact of venture apitalism for what increasingly is being defined as innovation-based economic growth. Central to our approach is the view that economic growth requires structural change, which first and foremost is new markets and industries (in this chapter they go together since we are assuming a closed economy); and this defines our 'market-mediated' link between invention/innovation and economic growth. The core of our analysis is three sequential and linked modules involving the same number of sets of variables. Module A represents the link (largely co-evolutionary) between the ICT revolution and associated new technological opportunities on the one hand and (1) venture capitalism (as defined above) and (2) accelerated invention/innovation (particularly by SUs) on the other. Module B links the enhanced invention/innovation generated by venture capitalism to the creation or emergence of new product markets; and Module C an almost reverse link, namely that between post-emergence market (or mature market) growth and new invention and innovation.

A critical aspect of the process throughout is SU-incumbent company links. This is particularly so in Module C where the new incumbent companies that grew with the new markets (think of Nokia, Cisko and Google nowadays) require, in order to sustain growth despite the onset of maturity in their original product class, a strategy of building the required ecosystem both to diversify and to generate specific solutions to particular user segments. At least some of the SU-incumbent links that emerge from this process are part of Gans and Stern's cooperation strategy followed by start-up innovation companies (Gans and Stern, 2003). That strategy includes SU licensing of technology to incumbents; acquisition of the SU; strategic partnerships and mergers. It is noteworthy to mention that the new technology induced by large and relatively mature markets is both improvement inventions and radical inventions. The former, which relates to the licensing SU-incumbent link mentioned above, may lead to the emergence of unbundled knowledge/technology markets (as a derived demand from the new product markets and based on an extended Schmookler-type framework of analysis; see Schmookler, 1966). The latter radical inventions, which are signalled by (large) markets, may or may not be disruptive of existing markets. They constitute a major feedback link between what can be considered the first round of traversing Modules A→C and the second round.

The outcomes of the above dynamic relationships will be further enhancement both of the SU segment and of the new, ICT-related, capital markets serving them (Module A). The Module C stimulus of radical inventions and new SUs represent a 'demand pull' effect that complements the 'supply push' impact of continued new ICT-related opportunities (which revolution is propelled by other factors both exogenous and endogenous). The open architecture of NASDAQ and dynamic scale/scope economies explain why these new SU companies and more and more related companies, for example, providing additional services, will be active in and increasingly be listed in NASDAQ (this process may explain both the enormous increase in SUs in many countries, and the shift from Phase 3 in the evolution of NASDAQ to Phase 4.

Through this process NASDAQ evolves to become a multi-supermarket with stror dynamic efficiency implications. While a regular market for a specific good, for exampl a food item or for shares of a specific company (or group of companies operating in particular technological area) quoted in NASDAQ coordinates the supply and deman of that good, a multi-market coordinates a generic need (e.g., 'nutrition' or incon streams from KIPRs' assets) to capabilities, which could be considered as the 'prim tives' of standard demand and supply. While the link in such markets to a need categor is clear this is less so in relation to the 'capabilities' variable. There are two componen to the latter: creation of capabilities (where the private VC market plays the critic role through its stimulation of SUs) and their actual coordination with needs (wher NASDAQ plays the central role). Needs–capabilities coordination means not onl coordination among agents operating in a specific 'product market' but coordination c agents operating in a large set of related markets. It follows that venture capitalism a a system will stimulate invention and, through multi-agent and cross-market coordina tion, will also promote innovation-based growth.

Prior to venture capitalism, radical inventor SUs (the so-called 'R&D companies'; se Freeman, 1974) faced difficulties in creating a new market. This takes place because th SU inventor frequently faced many obstacles either to access the complementary asset directly and profit from the invention (Teece, 1986) or to sell the technology. Relativel speaking, prior to venture capitalism, radical inventions by specialized inventor compa nies only very occasionally led to new product markets.

It is possible to summarize the main reasons why the process of transformation o radical inventions into new product markets will become more certain, frequent anc routinized under venture capitalism: (1) increased numbers of new SUs with radica inventions; (2) new systemic and generic mechanisms of direct or indirect transformatior of such inventions into new product markets; (3) the effect of new markets and more rapic market growth on invention including radical (both disruptive and non-disruptive) inven tions; (4) the possible emergence of unbundled markets for technological improvements.

The combination of continued generation of new opportunities and the mechanism for 'unlocking' the system from potential, strong path dependence, assures that venture capitalism could become a feature of sustainable innovation-based growth economic systems able to complement if not substitute the corporation as the leading institutiona mechanism for the generation and exploitation of technological knowledge.

AKNOWLEDGEMENTS

Thanks to Jackie Krafft for useful comments and suggestions on a previous draft.

NOTES

1. There are numerous advantages as far as economic impact is concerned of having an independent, special-
    ized 'inventor' segment of companies (relative to having inventions being developed and commercialized
    within existing incumbent companies), for example, motivation, flexibility, learning, avoidance of disec-
    onomies of scope and inherent interest in continuing to commercialize existing products among others.
    Throughout the chapter the term NASDAQ expresses not only the leading public global capital market

for technology companies but the concept itself of '*public* market for technology companies'. While transactions involving equity of 'technology companies', both SUs and well-established high-tech companies ('incumbent companies'), are undertaken in NASDAQ, the venture capital market involves *private* equity transactions of high-tech SUs only (SUs are young 'inventor' companies whose initial and main activity is R&D). For the definitions of venture capital and of private equity (PE) see Lerner (1999) and Avnimelech and Teubal (2006).

See Grebel et al. (2006).

REFERENCES

Abernathy, W.J. and J.M. Utterback (1978), Patterns of industrial innovation, *Technology Review* **80**(7), 40–47.

Antonelli, C. and M. Teubal (2008), Knowledge intensive property rights and the evolution of venture capitalism, *Journal of institutional Economics* **4**(2), 163–82.

Antonelli, C. and M. Teubal (2010), Venture capital as a mechanism for knowledge governance: new markets and innovation-led economic, in R. Viale and H. Etzkowitz (eds) *The Capitalization of Knowledge: A Triple Helix of University–Industry–Government*, Cheltenham, UK and Northampton, MA, USA: Edward Elgar.

Arrow, K. (1962), Economic welfare and the allocation of resources to invention, in R.R. Nelson (ed.), *The Rate and Direction of Inventive Activity*, Chicago: University of Chicago Press for the National Bureau of Economic Research.

Avnimelech, G. and M. Teubal (2006), Creating venture capital industries that co-evolve with high tech: insights from an extended industry life cycle perspective of the Israeli experience, *Research Policy* **35**(10), 1477–98.

Avnimelech, G. and M. Teubal (2008), Evolutionary targeting, *Journal of Evolutionary Economics* **12**, 233–57.

Avnimelech, G., M. Kenney and M. Teubal (2005), A life cycle model for the creation of venture capital industries: comparing the US and Israeli experiences, in E. Giulani, R. Rabellotti and M.P. van Dijk (eds) *Clusters Facing Competition: The Importance of External Linkages*, London: Ashgate.

Chandler, A.D. (1962), *Strategy and Structure: Chapters in the History of the Industrial Enterprise*, Cambridge, MA: The MIT Press.

Chandler, A.D. (1977), *The Visible Hand: The Managerial Revolution in American Business*, Cambridge, MA: The Belknap Press of Harvard University Press.

Chandler, A.D. (1990), *Scale and Scope: The Dynamics of Industrial Capitalism*, Cambridge, MA: The Belknap Press of Harvard University Press.

Coase, R. (1988), *The Firm, the Market and the Law*, Chicago: The University of Chicago Press.

Dahlman, C.J. (1979), The problem of externality, *Journal of Law and Economics* **22**(1), 141–62.

Freeman, C. (1974), *The Economics of Industrial Innovation*, Harmondsworth: Penguin Books.

Gans, J. and S. Stern (2003), When does funding research by smaller firms bear fruit? Evidence from the SBIR program, *Economics of Innovation and New Technology* **12**(4), 361–84.

Gompers, P. and J. Lerner (1999), *The Venture Capital Cycle*, Cambridge, MA: The MIT Press.

Gompers, P. and J. Lerner (2001), The venture capital revolution, *Journal of Economic Perspectives* **15**(2), 145–68.

Gompers, P. and J. Lerner (2004), *The Venture Capital Cycle*, Cambridge, MA: The MIT Press, 2nd edition.

Grebel, T., J. Krafft and P.P. Saviotti (2006), On the cycle of knowledge intensive sectors, *Revue de l'OFCE*, No. 97.

Hall, B.H. (2002), The financing of research and development, *Oxford Review of Economic Policy* **18**(1), 35–51.

King, R.G. and R. Levine (1993), Finance and growth: Schumpeter might be right, *Quarterly Journal of Economics* **108**(3), 717–37.

Lamoreaux, N.R. and K.L. Sokoloff (eds) (2007), *Financing Innovation in the United States: 1870 to the Present*, Cambridge, MA: MIT Press.

Langlois, R.N. (2002), The vanishing hand: the changing dynamics of industrial capitalism, typescript.

Langlois, R.N. (2003), The vanishing hand: the changing dynamics of industrial capitalism, *Industrial and Corporate Change* **12**(2), 351–85.

Lerner, J. (1999), *Venture Capital, Private Equity: A Case Book*, New York: John Wiley and Sons Inc.

Petit, P. and M. Quéré (2006), The 'industrialisation' of venture capital: new challenges for intermediation issues, *International Journal of Technology Management* **34**(2), 126–45.

Rosenberg, N. (1963), Technological change in the machine tool industry, 1840–1910, *Journal of Economic History* **23**(4), 414–43.

Schmookler, J. (1966), *Invention and Economic Growth*, Cambridge, MA: Harvard University Press.

Schumpeter, J.A. (1934), *The Theory of Economic Development*, Cambridge, MA: Harvard University Press.
Schumpeter, J.A. (1942), *Capitalism, Socialism and Democracy*, New York: Harper and Brothers.
Smith, A. (1776), *An Inquiry into the Nature and Causes of the Wealth of Nations*, London: W. Strahan and T. Cadell.
Stiglitz, J.E. (1985), Credit markets and capital control, *Journal of Money Credit and Banking* **17**(2), 133–52.
Stiglitz, J.E. and A. Weiss (1981), Credit rationing in markets with imperfect information, *American Economic Review* **71**(3), 912–27.
Teece, D. (1986), Profiting from technological innovation: implications for integration, collaboration, licensing and public policy, *Research Policy* **15**(6), 285–305.

ndex